CONTEMPORARY MANAGEMENT

Issues and Viewpoints

JOSEPH W. MCGUIRE, Editor
University of California

PRENTICE-HALL, INC., Englewood Cliffs, New Jersey

Library of Congress Cataloging in Publication Data

McGuire, Joseph William.
Contemporary management: issues and viewpoints.

Includes bibliographical references.
1. Management—Addresses, essays, lectures.
I. Title.
HD31.M23 658.4 73-4706
ISBN 0-13-170159-2

10 9 8 7 6 5 4 3 2

Prentice-Hall International, Inc., London
Prentice-Hall of Australia, Pty. Ltd., Sydney
Prentice-Hall of Canada, Ltd., Toronto
Prentice-Hall of India Private Limited, New Delhi
Prentice-Hall of Japan, Inc., Tokyo

Contents

Preface

This book has its origin in a suggestion I made a few years ago to the Executive Committee of the Academy of Management. At that time I believed that the field of management was in considerable danger of splintering apart completely into small, diffuse, and diverse areas, and into a multitude of special interest groups, isolated societies, and weak associations. Consequently, I believed that some sort of "regrouping" and "culling" of the approaches, concepts, and methods was desperately needed to give the field a solid base of promising developments and ideas from which fresh and fruitful advances might be made in the future. I believe more strongly today that the establishment of such a base is necessary for management. This belief has led to this book on contemporary management.

In the very early stages of this project, it became evident that I had neither the time nor the expertise to survey the entire field of management. From this awareness came the not-too-novel idea of asking well-known experts in each area to write about their subjects. More novel, perhaps, I then asked two additional experts in the area to add their comments to each chapter. As a result, the reader obtains three independent views of each of the major areas of interest in contemporary management. And, finally and most novel, I asked each author to write with clarity and simplicity so that this book could be used as a text by the management student and the practicing manager. It is not intended that this book be a handbook or an encyclopedia. It is meant to be a book that can be used profitably in the classroom by students in beginning courses in management.

One of the major problems confronting an editor of a book like this is the establishment of style and quality criteria. At one extreme, style standards may be established, as, say, on *Time* magazine, wherein every section reads as though it was written by the same adjective-loving author. Or, at the other extreme, the editor can permit each chapter to be written in individual style, with no attempts at uniformity. The style choice in this volume was made deliberately to fall between these extremes, with instructions given to the authors and with considerable editorial work on the chapters. Nevertheless, it was believed that the book would be more interesting, and the students would obtain the "flavor" of the areas more satisfactorily, if the style of the authors was permitted to be individualistic. Thus, footnote forms vary in the different chapters, and there is a considerable variance in style. I, for one, find these style differences attractive rather than distracting, for after all this book is written by many persons.

Quality criteria are more difficult to establish than criteria for style. For the most part, quality was enhanced by the knowledge that each principal contributor possessed—that his contribution was going to be reviewed in print by two critics. Probably not all of the contributions will be at the same level of interest for every reader, but each and every contributor possesses the capability of "striking the fancy" of any given reader. Each contribution, finally, is worthy of study and analysis, and the careful reader should be rewarded by learning a great deal about a variety of areas that compose the contemporary field of management.

For their helpful comments and suggestions I wish to thank the following: Prof. W. Jack Duncan, University of Alabama; Prof. Richard N. Farmer, Indiana University; Prof. Claude S. George, The University of North Carolina; Prof. Joseph L. Massie, University of Kentucky; and Prof. Martin K. Starr, Columbia University.

I wish to express my thanks to Kevin, who helped with the index and other things.

1

Management and Method

Joseph W. McGuire

Vice President—Planning,
University of California, Berkeley

People who don't manage are either too young, too old, or are found in institutions for the incompetent. And, indeed, the universality of managerial practice is part of the problem in developing a field of management. For in a world in which most persons quickly learn to manage their own affairs with varying degrees of success, the voice of the executive or the management professor frequently sounds irrelevant, redundant, trite, truistic, and common sensical. This condition has sometimes been aggravated by the experts' inability to present managerial concepts or to transmit managerial skills except as platitudinous generalities or as descriptions of specific techniques through which past success was attained in specific instances in specific organizations.

Yet despite the current difficulties in developing the field of management, despite the apathy and occasional disdain of the audience and the ineptness of some experts, it is impossible to avoid the inescapable conclusion that management is important; that the field must have significant content; that managerial skills are transferable; and that persons can learn both about management and how to be better managers. This conclusion is reached, of course, on the basis of empirical evidence. We see, everyday, the evidence of giant and complex organizations, many of which are managed with considerable élan and skill. We also observe that managers are selected, often from a field of contenders, to fill essential posts in business, government, and other fields. Certainly, unless we believe in some sort of mysterious, mystical, clockwork-like mechanical system of the universe, or in chance, we must assume that the persons who direct organizations have something to do with their successes and failures. And unless we believe only in the cult of personality, or politics, or conspiracy, we must assume that very often the persons selected from the crowd to manage have attributes or traits that others believe will lead them to manage successfully—and very often those so selected do remarkably well. Finally, unless we believe that certain people are born to manage or that management skills are acquired by a strange, osmosis-like process, we may assume that managers somehow learn to manage.

All of this, of course, leads the interested student of management to suspect that the fault lies not with his eagerness to learn nor with management itself, but rather with the inability of executives and management professors to communicate the concepts and skills of proper management clearly and appropriately. And as we look at the field of management, it does appear to be in considerable confusion. This disarray emerges, it seems, partly because of differences in approaches, partly because of differences in objectives, partly because of differences in interest, and partly because of the inherent analytical difficulties in the field itself.

This book has been written in an effort to resolve some of these difficulties—to take an honest look at the current state-of-the-art in management; to survey the field and to point out the contemporary problems and present trends; to indicate future directions. This book has as its objectives:

1. To evaluate, and contribute to, the present state of knowledge in the field of management.
2. To bring some order to a field that is in need of scholarly guidance and codification.
3. To present students, laymen, and managers with discussions by the leading experts in specific fields within the broad area encompassed by contemporary management studies.

This book, therefore, is not intended to be a reference work or a handbook. It is meant primarily to be a teaching instrument—a text.

The format of this book, with the exception of this chapter and the last chapter, is basically the same. A leading expert on a specific topic has written his chapter as clearly and succinctly as he can. His contribution is followed by critiques by two other expert scholars. The principal contributor to each topic was requested to avoid jargon, and to make a forthright and careful statement on the most significant developments he perceives in his area. In each chapter the major author was either to survey the literature or to make a judicious selection of important aspects of his subject, and where possible to report on the significance of past trends and future directions. Each contributor, too, was asked to devote some part of his chapter to a discussion of the past, present, and future utility of the concepts he presents to the study of management, although in some instances it was evident that the author might be able to address himself only to unresolved and unanswered questions. The critiques following each chapter were to point out the areas where the critics disagreed or agreed, or where they believed that the chapter contributors had omitted to mention, or to emphasize, important material.

CONTEMPORARY MANAGEMENT—AN APPRAISAL

The field of modern management does present a portrait of confusion to the student who approaches it. Not only are there different styles—Rembrandt mixed with Picasso with Wyeth with traces of Warhol and Van Gogh among others—but one is never certain that the artists are even painting the same picture. Certainly, as one will discover from reading this volume, it is not clear that Frederick Taylor's emphasis on "the best way to increase output" has anything in common with the modern behavioralists who desire "to increase the satisfactions of organizational participants." Harold Koontz, in a famous article, pointed out this confusion in the following passage:

> The noteworthy absence of academic writing and research in the formative years of modern management is now more than atoned for by a deluge of research and writing pouring from academic halls. What is interesting (but perhaps nothing more than a sign of the unsophisticated adolescence of management theory) is how the current flood has brought with it waves of differences and confusion. This welling of interest from every corner should not upset anyone concerned with seeing the frontiers of knowledge pushed back and the intellectual base of practice broadened. But what *is* upsetting to practicing managers, and, in fact, to all who see great potential social good emanating from improved management, is that the varied approaches to management theory have led to a kind of confused and destructive jungle warfare.[1]

In this section the reasons for the "management jungle" will, at least in part, be explored.

Confusions of Objectives

Perhaps one of the most basic difficulties afflicting management in academe today is the confusion in faculty objectives. What is it, the more perceptive faculty members ask, that management professors should try to accomplish? Should they—as the students hope and initially expect—attempt to teach students to become managers? Or, in the case of persons who are already executives, to teach them to become better managers? Or should the professors simply teach *about* management, describing, analyzing, and probing in scholarly fashion into the elements of the field itself? Or is this dichotomy both spurious and extreme, and may not in fact the best preparation for a management career be, happily, the academic investigations into the field itself?

In only a handful of collegiate schools of business or administration does the faculty systematically, overtly, and deliberately attempt to *train* students to become managers or, as the modern euphemism puts it, "to prepare them for a career in management." Unlike many faculty members in medicine, nursing, dentistry, or law, the contemporary management professor often finds the vocational connotations of "training" or "career preparation" to be distasteful to his academic value system. Among the few schools where the objective is to prepare students for a managerial career directly and without circumvention or subterfuge, the faculties have encountered grave problems of content and approach. We shall comment on these later in this chapter, but for our purposes here it should suffice to mention that some management professors do indeed have as their objective the preparation of students for careers in management.

At the other extreme are collegiate schools of business or administra-

[1] Harold Koontz, *Toward a Unified Theory of Management* (New York: McGraw-Hill Book Company, 1964), p. 2.

tion in which the purpose of the management professor seems to be the *pure* study of management. If the graduates of such programs do become good or bad managers, or even if they become teachers or firemen, it is of little consequence to this group of professors. It is their objective to teach *about* management, just as a professor of history would teach his subject with little expectation that his students would all want to become professional historians. This objective, of course, makes management professors more academically respectable within the university. It also, on the other hand, makes them appear somewhat irrelevant to their pragmatic students. Finally, this objective readily leads many of these management professors into academic esoteria—into the realms of abstract model building and theory construction common to their fashionable modern colleagues in the social and behavioral sciences.

The objectives of most collegiate schools of business or administration fall between these extremes . . . and the range is too wide to cover comprehensively here. For illustrative purposes we shall explore the situation wherein faculty members attempt to prepare students for managerial careers by focusing on those tools and concepts that they believe will be helpful in the future to managers. In other words, this group endeavors to pursue the goal of professionalism through indirection. The emphasis is on what the professors believe the students will need to know in their careers; to concentrate on those areas that, hopefully, will be useful to managers. The objective of this faculty is to prepare students for a career in management, but these professors believe that this objective can best be accomplished by ensuring that the students know something about economics, about organizational arrangements, about group and individual behavior, about the environment in which the manager and his organization exists, and about the techniques managers utilize and the functions they perform. This book conforms largely to the objectives of this group.

Confusion of Approaches to the Teaching of Management

The differences in objectives rather naturally leads to a multiplicity of approaches to the teaching of management. Let us examine some of these briefly in this section.

Preparing students for a career in management might, perhaps, best be conducted in a clinical setting, much as medical students learn by following their professors through a teaching hospital. There is little doubt that a student could learn a great deal under the tutelage of skilled executives. Unfortunately, management is not like medicine, and the former would be most difficult to learn comprehensively through observation alone. A student, watching a modern manager in action, would probably find that he sat and wrote reports, sat and talked on the telephone, sat and consulted with many people, sat in meetings and conferences, and sat in planes and in automobiles. The student might, if he were especially bright, soon discover that management was a function of the mind; but if he were not so thoughtful he might conclude that the prime requisite for management is to be found at the other end of the spine. Actually the clinical approach to management has not often been employed in collegiate business education, largely because of the time and expense involved, but also because of the suspicion that it would not be very useful to have the student learn only one managerial style in only one organization. On the other hand, the clinical approach is frequently used within the corporation or other large organization, precisely because this is the managerial style that the student should learn and because this is the organization in which he will perform.

> A next and long controversial element of quality construction in business courses is the use of the case method. As should be expected, the extent to which the case method is used in business education is much less important than the manner in which it is used. Quantitative and behavioral analysis, as well as communicating skill, can be developed within case study as well as outside such study. They can, however, be ignored in case study and such has too often been the case. It is increasingly clear that slavish dedication to case method is passing from the scene even in those schools which once demanded its total use as a matter of faith if not logic.[2]

The case method indeed has been losing ground throughout the academic world in recent years. However, it is not quite so easily dismissed as the above quotation suggests. For those professors who want to teach students to be managers, the case method still represents the closest approximation to the clinical approach. Cases, to some students, may give the illusion of reality. To most students, and at most schools, they do not. Cases do, however, even in their poorest presentation, expose the student to organizational situations and confront him with decision problems. At their most successful stage, cases may actually serve to indoctrinate the student with an administrative viewpoint, and give him an understanding of, and approach to, how decisions are made, which is at the core of all management.

Closely allied to the efforts to introduce reality into the management curriculum is the occasional employment of executives or ex-executives as professors in collegiate schools of business or administration. When these individuals are successful they truly contribute to the students' understanding of management. Unfortunately, most often the results are unsatisfactory. Successful managers are not necessarily successful professors. For one thing, they are affected (naturally) by their past experiences, and frequently do not understand that they must distill from these experiences the elements that will be useful to managers in the future. Their propensity to reminisce about the time that the president of the company said to them . . . is infectuous and interesting, but their ability to draw pertinent generalizations from these episodes is too often inadequate.

Another approach to the teaching of management is through the use of simulation or gaming. Management games, which perhaps enjoyed greater popularity in the 1960's than now, are designed to create an organizational environment in which students make decisions to attain organizational goals. Most often a class is divided into companies or "teams," each with a president and other officers, and the environment is competitive. The rules of the game are established externally by the professor, and each company makes decisions by which it attempts to make greater profits than

[2]William T. White, "The Business School Today: Its Challenge and Essential Characteristics," *AACSB Bulletin*, Vol. 6, No. 1 (October, 1969), p. 21.

its competitors. In order to approximate reality more accurately management games have become ever more complex and elaborate computer exercises and—unfortunately—more expensive.

All the approaches to management to this point are designed to teach students to be managers. This is accomplished in most of these approaches by trying to place the student in a managerial situation. None of these approaches is entirely satisfactory, however, because some of the crucial essentials of management, such as the tension, the rewards of success, and the penalties of failure, cannot be replicated in the classroom.

The difficulties of the approaches that emphasize management directly have led many faculty members to indirect approaches. The most popular of these has, in recent years, stemmed from professors ruminating over ideas similar to those expressed in the following passage:

> The students now in school should have a useful, productive management career that will extend for, possibly, forty years into the future. We know that this future is most uncertain. Consequently, it seems presumptuous of us to try to prepare these students for what we now think might be the future world when we cannot really predict what this world will be like with any confidence. Also, we really don't know what sort of a managerial career these students will have ... whether they will work as executives in business, in government, in education, or in some other broad segment of society. We don't know what managerial level they will reach, or in what specialty they will find themselves. Nor do we know whether they will work in giant-sized, large, or small organizations. Now, given all of these things that we don't know, how can we best prepare them for their managerial career in this dimly-perceived future? We do know, of course, that we only have part of four years—or perhaps only two—to get students started properly on their organizational adventure.

It is this sort of reasoning that has almost destroyed the world of management education, for when faculty members begin to ask themselves these types of questions they broaden their horizons beyond the confines of what was once called the field of management.

For example, several contemporary professors of management believe that their students will find many concepts and methods inherent to the field of economics to be very useful in their future careers. It would, for instance, be wonderful if all management students were inculcated with a cost-benefit approach to decisions—an approach that is now sometimes injected into economics courses. In this approach the benefits from all decisions are weighed against the costs, and action is taken only if net benefits are positive. Thus, when a fine arts major wants to get married, his thoughts might appropriately linger on beauty, sex, and moon and June. The management student, on the other hand, appropriately should weigh the benefits of marriage against the costs before he takes his final step into connubial bliss. In fact, an approach to all decisions in a cost-benefit fashion would stand every student of management in good stead regardless of the nature or size of his organization or his executive level. This is the type of result, then, that many management professors would like to produce through their curriculum, so that they could indeed be of maximum use to the student and future manager. This is the type of conclusion, too, that has broadened the field of management to include the social and behavioral sciences, mathematics and computers, so much so that it has become unrecognizable to those familiar with academic management curricula in the 1950's. It is as a result of asking these types of questions that this volume has been written. The question: What can we do now that will prepare the manager of the future for the future?—forms the nucleus around which the following chapters are built.

Confusion of Conceptual Approaches

Contemporary management is presented by faculty members using a variety of conceptual approaches. Of these, the "functional" or (as it is sometimes called) the "process" approach is the oldest and probably the most widespread. In recent years, however, the behavioral approach to management has gained considerable popularity, and the quantitative approach has for the last decade appeared to be on the verge of gaining more advocates. Quantitative approaches, however, have been slow in forthcoming, largely because of the paucity of management professors who have had adequate training in mathematics. And, finally, the so-called "systems" approach to management has been gaining ground somewhat in the last few years. Since this book is eclectic, it does not follow rigidly any of these conceptual approaches to the subject of management.

The functional approach focuses on the broad classes of activities in which all management is involved, such as planning, coordinating, budgeting, organizing, directing, staffing, controlling, and the like. This classification (or taxonomy) was developed in the 1920's and 1930's, and has continued to be used widely in the classroom ever since. One reason for its success and durability, certainly, is the evident completeness of the taxonomy—it appears possible to dissect management into rather neat and orderly separate boxes that encompass the entire spectrum of managerial activities. Furthermore, the functional approach does seem to answer nicely such student questions as: "What do managers do?" and "What do I have to learn about in order to become a manager?" And, finally, the functional approach does appear to be based on empirical evidence; managers indeed do plan, organize, and all the rest.

The dissatisfaction with the functional approach, on the other hand, comes mainly from those students who find that the neat taxonomy is filled largely with empty boxes, and who subsequently become quickly disenchanted with attempts to fill these boxes. The rational cataloguing of functions, so appealing at first, unfortunately has led mainly to description rather than to analysis and understanding. Some of the boxes contain management "principles" of dubious value, but most are filled either with vague generalities that appear to be true or with descriptions of how planning is, or was, carried out. To a younger generation of professors, furthermore, the functional approach has lacked rigor, depth, and scholarly content. As a result, although functionalism remains strong, it has been losing ground in recent years.

During the 1960's the behavioral approach to management gained considerable attention. This approach is based on the premise that, after all, management is mainly (some would say entirely) applied behavioral science. The manager is most commonly defined as "a person who gets things done through other people," and consequently an executive should understand how to motivate, lead, and direct people. He should understand interpersonal relationships, the operations of groups and organizations, politics, influence, communications, and the concept of authority. In other words, the behavioralist insists that the budding manager should be well prepared in psychology, sociology, political science, and other "behavioral" subjects.

Almost every management course today contains some discussion of behavioral topics, stressing those, in particular, that indicate how managers can get their subordinates to *want* to act in the interests of the organization. Such concepts, for example, as the hygienic needs and satisficers of Herzberg, theory *X* and theory *Y* of McGregor, and the hierarchy of needs advocated by Maslow are part of most management repertoires.

Nevertheless, as Leonard Sayles recently pointed out:

> What do all of these behavioral science studies have in common? *First,* they all involve a "go-for-broke" technique; the emphasis is on almost unbelievable results. Everything gets better—efficiency, satisfaction, profitability. *Second,* they represent simplistic models often dressed up with a profound caption. There is little concern with the whole array of variables that realistically confront and need to be administered by the executive: structure, controls, symbols, and a great deal of his own behavior aside from direct supervisory skills. *Third,* many have been roundly criticized for ignoring variables that are relevant to the observed effects or including some that are inaccurate.[3]

The behavioral approach to management, it would seem, is not codified firmly as yet . . . and perhaps never will be. Nevertheless, the central premise —that managers must know how to deal with people—is basically attractive and would appear to be sensible. At present, however, there is considerable ferment among advocates of behavioral approaches to management, and theories and methods run rampant with little agreement about the propriety of any particular theory, method, or approach.

The quantitative approach to management, as the name would suggest, is oriented toward methodology. Mathematical techniques can be of value in assisting management in making decisions. Mathematics always requires that problems, parameters, and variables be defined precisely. The quantitative approach also necessitates a clear understanding of values and outcomes. It forces rigor, care, and thought. Mathematical approaches have a long history, going back at least to the nineteenth century. However, the modern school of quantitative management did not really begin to expand until the 1940's and 1950's with the advent of operations research, management science, managerial economics, probability analysis, and the computer.

Today mathematics helps management to solve all types of problems—but not all problems. Unfortunately, many of the variables that managers must consider in many decision situations are simply not quantifiable. The quantitative approach, therefore, cannot provide a complete answer for all management problems. However, it is an invaluable tool for managers, and all modern executives should be conversant with computers and a wide range of mathematical techniques, and also be aware of their uses and limitations.

[3]Leonard Sayles, "Whatever Happened to Management?—or Why the Dull Stepchild?" *Business Horizons,* Vol. XIII, No. 2 (April, 1970), p. 30.

The modern systems approach to management is perhaps too new to evaluate fairly. Frankly, however, its usefulness is somewhat questionable, largely because it appears to be tending toward description rather than analysis, prediction, or career preparation. A passage in a recent book by Kast and Rosenzweig illustrates this propensity:

> There are several key characteristics of organizational systems. They are not natural, like physical or biological systems, but are *contrived*. There are *boundaries* which separate the organization from its environment. In general, a system is composed of subsystems of a lower order and is also part of a supersystem; there is a *hierarchy* of systems. In open biological or social systems, entropy can be arrested and may even be transformed to *negative entropy*—a process of more complete organization. The concept of *steady state* is closely related to that of negative entropy. The organization is able to adapt to changes in its environment and to maintain a continual dynamic equilibrium.
>
> ...Through the process of feedback, it (a system) continually receives information from its environment which helps it to adjust. A system must have both *adaptive and maintenance* mechanisms.... Finally, open systems have the characteristic of *equifinality*—objectives may be achieved with varying inputs and in different ways.
>
> There are three levels in the managerial system of complex organizations: technical, organizational, and institutional. The *technical* level is involved with actual task performance. The *organizational* level integrates the technical and institutional levels. The *institutional* level relates the activities of the organization to its environment. The view of the organization as a sociotechnical system creates a different role for the manager. He must integrate and balance the various subsystems and their activities in the environmental setting.[4]

Whether the systems approach to management will eventually produce fresh insights as well as new jargon remains to be seen. There are some scholars who believe that it offers great promise as a novel catalyst within which the behavioral and mathematical approaches to management can be fruitfully explored. Others feel that the systems approach is simply a throwback to the description of functionalism–reworked and reworded. Only time will tell.

Max Wortman recently wrote:

> In the next twenty years, the approaches to the field of management will evolve even more rapidly than they have in the past. We must begin to pick up the strands of the behavioral sciences, quantitative management sciences, and systems approaches quickly so that we will be able to integrate these and the process approach for the new and better eclectic approaches which we do not yet see on the horizon.[5]

And, indeed, this is what this book attempts to accomplish. It is wedded to no single approach to management. Rather it is an effort to summarize where we are now in the field of management, and through its eclecticism to bring that horizon a little more clearly into view.

[4]Fremont E. Kast and James E. Rosenzweig, *Organization and Management: A Systems Approach* (New York: McGraw-Hill Book Company, 1970), pp. 135–136.

[5]Max S. Wortman, Jr., "Shifts in the Conceptual Approaches Which Underlie Principles of Management," *Academy of Management Journal*, Vol. 13, No. 4 (December, 1970), p. 448.

THE ORGANIZATION OF THIS BOOK

The preceding pages of this chapter have set forth some of the areas in which confusion currently exists in the field of management. In the following chapters the authors attempt to dispel this confusion wherever they possibly can. However, their primary purpose is to discuss the developments, trends, and significant concepts in the areas of their expertise in order to give the reader a good idea of the state-of-the-art in contemporary management.

There are three broad sections that form the framework within which most of the chapters conveniently fit. These are (1) The disciplinary foundations of management; (2) The environment—both organizational and external—within which managers operate; and (3) The management "core."

It is generally recognized today that contemporary management is heavily dependent on, and related to, the theories, methods, and empirical developments that have emerged in the disciplines of economics and mathematics, and in the behavioral sciences. It is also probable that contemporary management results in part from the investigations and explorations into management by scholars and practitioners in the past. In the first section of this book, therefore, there are chapters on each of these foundations. In each of these chapters the author attempts to relate the discipline to contemporary management, selecting those features from the area that he believes should be emphasized. Given the scope and breadth of these areas, and the impossibility of covering the entire area in one chapter, the selection of topics to be included or emphasized was a major problem for each of the authors. The quality of their choices, and the treatment of the subjects included, is noted by the two critics of each chapter. Although typically the critics are gentle with the principal author of the chapter, in most cases their differences in approach, in selection of topics, and in treatment come through this collegial facade.

The environment within which the manager operates can be compartmentalized into the organization (the "internal" environment) and the external world—the environment that exists externally to the organization. In the second major portion of this book both of these environments are explored, although four of the six chapters are oriented toward the internal organizational setting. The bias toward the organization reflects, in itself, the state of contemporary management. Investigations into the characteristics of the organization and its problems have a longer history, and have probed more frequently and deeply, than have explorations into the external environment. Thus, there are chapters on organizational theory, organizational objectives, and how these coincide with or conflict with the objectives of organizational members, communication and information systems, and organizational change. All of these chapters relate to the subject of management within the organization, although they are not necessarily confined exclusively to this focus and indeed do at times extend beyond this boundary. The remaining two chapters deal with organizations and the external environment and with the special problems of international management. The subject of international management, although somewhat unique in its problems, is included largely because of its development in somewhat isolated form in the 1960's and because of the interest in this field both by students and practitioners. Most importantly, however, it is included in this section because the international scene is an important part of the managerial environment, and one that will probably become more important in the future.

The final major segment of this book has been labeled the management "core." "Core" means those topics that constitute the heart of contemporary management as taught in many (most?) beginning management courses. "Core" also means those activities that all managers perform in common, and those qualities and attitudes that good managers should possess. Since the topics covered in this section form the nucleus around which most modern courses in management seem to revolve, they encompass many of the elements that historically have constituted the field of management itself. Thus, there are chapters on (1) planning and strategy, (2) leadership, (3) authority, influence, and power, (4) decision-making, (5) control, (6) motivation, (7) development, and (8) the social attitudes of managers. Some of these topics have been taught since the early days of managerial studies; others do not have such a long tradition. Whether new or old, however, each author has concentrated on the present, so that all chapters (and their reviews) reflect the contemporary views of the topics included. This set of chapters fits well into the environmental framework earlier established.

The final chapter of this book attempts to look at the future of management and to draw some observations from the earlier chapters relevant to this future.

The field of management currently is in considerable flux and confusion. Several of the areas of confusion have been discussed in this chapter. The remainder of this book attempts to clear up some of this confusion and to give the reader a firmer grasp of the nature of contemporary management, the issues that engage its attention and energies, and the problems that confront it.

DISCUSSION QUESTIONS

1. What do you expect from this course in management?
2. What objectives do you believe your professor should have in this course? Comment on the three objectives given.
3. Is there, or should there be, a difference between professional education and undergraduate or graduate education in the liberal arts or sciences?
4. What is the functional approach? the behavioral approach? the systems approach? Which one do you prefer? Why?
5. Many contemporary scholars believe it is "healthy" to have such a profusion and confusion of theories and approaches to management. Why do you think they hold this position? Do you agree with them?

PART ONE

THE DISCIPLINARY FOUNDATIONS OF MANAGEMENT

2

Behavioral Sciences for Management

Edgar H. Schein

Professor,
Alfred P. Sloan School of Management,
Massachusetts Institute of Technology

The assessment of the relevance of the behavioral sciences to management confronts us with an immediate paradox. Organizations are composed of people producing things for other people; hence, any science of people would appear to be totally relevant to what happens in organizations. Yet the behavioral sciences are relatively little utilized by managers if one considers that full potential of their applicability. If the behavioral sciences are so relevant to managerial problems, why are they not more fully utilized? The answer is complex and multifaceted.

First of all, every manager by virtue of his own experience as a person, believes himself to be something of an expert and authority on people. He would be the first to acknowledge that the managerial job involves all kinds of "people problems," but he might also argue that he knows from his own experience how to deal with most of those problems. For the manager to accept the input of the behavioral scientist requires some admission that he is not as expert in handling people problems as he might like to believe.

Second, the behavioral sciences have accumulated a body of knowledge but have done a poor job of communicating this knowledge. They have played the science game, which involves the erroneous assumption that once some findings are published in a technical journal, it is someone else's responsibility to figure out how to use the knowledge. Until recently, behavioral scientists have not been willing to take their knowledge and know-how out into the organizational world, translate what they know into language that the manager can understand, and help the manager to utilize the knowledge in solving managerial problems.

Third, behavioral scientists have tended to study problems that *they* thought were important, rather than those that managers who had to deal with "people problems" thought were important. To a considerable extent this approach was a necessary and legitimate one in developing the field. Behavioral scientists had to work within the context of theories and methods they could handle. Managerial problems often were too difficult and complex to encompass, and so were not studied. Managers rightly complained that much of the knowledge accumulated was trivial and irrelevant, or, at least, they could not see the relevance; the behavioral scientist was too busy with his next piece of research to show the manager where the relevance lay.

Fourth, in those cases in which behavioral scientists have been called in to help with organizational and managerial problems, it has been very difficult to evaluate the results of their efforts. Just as it has been difficult to evaluate the effects of any kind of procedural changes without the luxury of a control group, so it has been difficult to determine whether the efforts of psychologists to improve the quality of managerial decisions were actually paying off. The person being helped might feel the help was well worth it, but the skeptic could easily sit at the sidelines and argue that there was no solid evidence. In fact, he could make the valid argument that if a manager had committed himself to using some new approach, he was usually psychologically biased toward seeing good results, since it was his own decision to try the new approach. Much effort has gone into testing behavior knowledge against hard criteria, but as yet we have not solved the problem of how to carry out good evaluation research in a setting in which it is not possible to control all the other factors affecting the situation..

While the behavioral sciences have evolved, managerial attitudes have also changed. Traditionally the psychologist was expected to get involved in little more than aiding decisions on whom to hire, how to train people, and how to set up work measurement, do job descriptions, and study worker productivity. Contributions in these areas have been plentiful and many of the approaches initially introduced by psychologists and sociologists have become standard practices in organizations. In the last several decades, the psychologist and sociologist have been given opportunities to observe and help with *higher-level* management problems, such as how to design the organization structure, how to improve communications among top echelons of managers, how to solve problems of inter-group or inter-divisional conflict, and how to help to create a climate in which the employees and the organization could effectively grow and develop. The contact with higher levels of management has been a tremendous stimulus both to the behavioral scientist and to the manager, leading to more productive research and consulting at the level of the company president and his immediate team. Once the role of the behavioral scientist was legitimized at this level in organizations, it was easier for him to gain acceptance at other levels and easier to see the impact of his efforts (Schein, 1969, 1970).

AREAS OF APPLICATION

In what areas are the behavioral sciences relevant to management? The answer is—in all areas—but this answer is not very helpful without some categorization of what these areas are. We can conceive of the manager's job as being concerned with the processing of three kinds of basic resources: (1) money or financial resources; (2) people or human resources; (3) information of various kinds. The managerial job is to utilize information, money, and people in the service of some task or goal. Most of the decisions that the manager makes involve putting together the right mix of human, financial, and informational resources to transform some kinds of raw materials into useful products and/or services. The behavioral sciences have a potential relevance to the utilization of all three of these resource areas, although traditionally they have been linked only with the utilization of human resources. Let us explore each of the areas in turn. As we will see, one of the chief contributions of the behavioral sciences has been to show how financial, production, marketing, and personnel decisions are closely linked and interwoven.

Area I: Utilization of Human Resources

Behavioral scientists have worked on human problems in organizations since the turn of the century. But the nature of the problems studied has evolved from individually oriented industrial psychology focused on problems of recruitment, selection, and testing, to organizational psychology and sociology focused on managerial style, how groups and teams work, intergroup collaboration and competition, and total systems analyses of organizational and managerial effectiveness.

Problems of Recruitment, Selection, Training, and Management Development. One of the major early impacts of the behavioral sciences was in aiding organizations to make better selection decisions. By World War I the field of interviewing, testing, and statistics had developed to a point where it was possible to improve selection decisions substantially over what the individual manager could do using only his experience and intuitive judgment. However, such improvement only resulted if the position for which a person was selected could be reasonably well described and if there was a clearly specifiable set of skills that led to success or failure in the job. So, for example, in World War II the selection of pilots was greatly aided by the development of a battery of tests, partly because the skills needed in passing flight training could be fairly well defined. On the other hand, after several decades of effort, we are still very unsuccessful in selecting potential managers, largely because of the difficulty in specifying what blend of skills, aptitudes, and attitudes are needed in the successful manager, and the difficulty of specifying what is success across a wide variety of organizations.[1]

There are enough clearly specifiable jobs in industry to warrant a constant exploration of how the selection and testing approach of the industrial psychologist might enhance the quality of the selection decisions. However, one must also consider the impact that the whole approach has on entrants into the organization. That is, if the selection/testing approach makes people feel demeaned and makes them feel that their employer is seeing them as an impersonal resource, they may develop attitudes toward work and the employer that later will undermine their growth and commitment. There is increasing evidence that the motivation of employees is directly influenced by their early experiences in the organization; hence, the impact of those early experiences must be carefully assessed (Berlew and Hall, 1966; Schein, 1964, 1968).

One of the most obvious areas of relevance for the psychologist in or-

[1]Recent efforts by large companies to use Assessment Centers are beginning to pay off in better prediction of long-range managerial effectiveness.

ganizations was the area of training and development. As work became more complex, training became more important, and the role of the psychologist in setting up training situations that reflected what was known about how people learn became more important. Two basic approaches developed, both valid up to a point and both with some inherent problems. One approach built on the improvements in selecting and classifying people and attempted to fit people to jobs by a combination of selection and training. The other approach attempted to assess from the outset what the human potentials and limitations were, to design jobs and equipment to take those into account, and to train the man-machine system to function effectively. We see the former approach exemplified in our efforts to train the disadvantaged members of our society to be able to fill certain jobs that already exist. We see the latter approach in the space program, wherein the design of the equipment has to be carefully calibrated to human limitations, and a person has to be trained as part of the man-machine system but machine redesign would continue until the whole system functioned effectively.

The function of industrial engineering, focusing on job analysis, work measurement, and time and motion studies, is gradually being enlarged to encompass the interaction between the worker and his job, the worker and other workers, and the worker with society. Much of this enlargement has resulted from studies carried out by industrial sociologists, which showed that the initial assumptions underlying much of industrial psychology were not tenable. Early approaches toward job "simplification" have been replaced by efforts to elicit worker involvement and creativity (Lesieur, 1958).

Problems of Work Organization and Worker Relations. Early approaches to work and worker motivation were built on the individualistic model of economic man. If the industrial engineer could design the job properly and if management could think of the right individual incentive, productivity should be maximized. The industrial psychologist aided this approach by his individualistically oriented philosophy of selection and training. Both management theorists and psychologists worked together to develop a "scientific management" approach that would permit one to specify not only how to lay out work and motivate workers, but also stated all kinds of "principles" of organization pertaining to a manager's "span of control," "unity of command" (that every man should have only one boss), clear separation of staff and line functions, and authority must equal responsibilty. These various principles (Koontz and O'Donnell, 1964) have been labeled "classical management theory."

It was with the Hawthorne studies of the 1920's, when industrial sociologists first began a serious inquiry into the nature of work and worker relations, that the individualistic, economic man assumptions began to be seriously challenge (Roethlisberger and Dickson, 1939). The sociologists moved into the plant and used observational techniques to gather their data. They discovered among other things that workers tended to form close ties to other workers and these group relations influenced the work in important ways. For example, the production workers in the Hawthorne plant of the Western Electric Co. formed their informal groupings first around the geographical layout of the room (Homans, 1950). Once the groups had been formed, they developed various norms, some of which were in direct violation of company procedures. Different classes of workers were forbidden to trade jobs because industrial engineering had designed the jobs to match the skills of the particular workers; yet the men routinely traded jobs to reduce their monotony and were clearly able to do one another's work. The company paid on the basis of a regular output of units from the group, and the records showed a "straight-line output" of so many units per day; the observer noted that the workers would overproduce on one day and store part of their output and add it to their work on another day when for one or another reason they underproduced. The supervisor of the group was required to report irregularities and enforce company policy; the workers had a norm that any supervisor who was "officious" was not part of the gang and found ways to make his life so unpleasant that the officious ones left until someone who would let the workers do it their own way ended up with the group.

Worker output was assumed by the company to reflect individual ability and the pay structure; the observer noted that the group had a norm of "a fair day's work for a fair day's pay" and that individual worker output related more closely to group membership than individual ability. That is, there were two sub-groups in the total group, one of which saw itself as higher status than the other. All of its members produced at or near the norm. The other sub-group, in reaction to their lower status, deliberately underproduced in order to get back at the others. Those workers who were markedly overproductive or underproductive, relative to the norm, turned out to be social isolates, to belong to neither group.

The company had an inspector in each group to control quality. If the inspector challenged any of the group's norms or threatened to report its activities, the group found ways to sabotage the equipment in such a way that it would pass inspection but break down later, thus forcing the inspector to cooperate. All this was going on in a group that was performing quite adequately by management standards. Productivity was reasonably good, there was excellent morale, partly because the group felt it was allowed to do things its own way, and quality reached acceptable standards. But clearly, any resemblance between the economic man model of the early industrial psychologist and these workers was purely coincidental.

Subsequent studies of worker behavior in industry repeatedly confirmed the findings of the Hawthorne studies and led to a different set of assumptions about "human nature" and launched the human relations approach to managing people (Mayo, 1945). Both psychologists and sociologists began to attack the dehumanizing aspects of bureaucratic forms of organization and the scientific management approach. There was a flurry of programs to teach foremen how to understand their people better, how to accept groups among workers and to facilitate informal organization rather than trying to break it up as the assembly line had done in many instances, how to involve workers in decision-making on those aspects of their job that were under their control, how to be their subordinate's friend and champion rather than merely his boss.

With the aid of the behavioral scientists the pendulum swung completely from a very depersonalized view of man to an overpersonalized one. Industrial psychologists (Likert, 1961; Fleishman, 1953) developed concepts that focused on concern for people rather than the job or production, and it was assumed that if such concern strengthened people's morale, it surely would pay off in greater productivity. Some companies set up counseling programs that would allow workers to air their frustrations to a supportive neutral person in an effort to humanize the industrial environment even more.

This "human relations movement," which held sway in the 1930's and 1940's, has left a strong residue of important concepts, research findings, and values about the role of the individual in the large organizations. Much of its philosophy and value system was embodied in the writings of Likert, McGregor, Argyris, and others, who saw the need for a theory that put some faith in human capacities and potentials. McGregor put it most clearly in his classic *The Human Side of Enterprise,* published in book form in 1960, although the ideas had developed during the preceding decade. He pointed out that any given manager could build his approach on one of two basic sets of assumptions: theory *X,* an essentially cynical negative view of man, and theory *Y,* an essentially idealistic positive view of man.

According to theory *X,* man is lazy, self-seeking, can only be motivated by economic incentives, and must be controlled by management because he would not voluntarily work toward organizational goals. According to theory *Y,* man is capable of self-direction and self-control, will integrate his efforts with those of the organization's if his inner needs for a sense of meaning and worth in his job are met, and if his basic needs for physical and economic security are satisfied. McGregor's key argument was that if a manager held a theory *X* set of assumptions, he would tend to develop a managerial style not unlike that of the scientific management school, involving a tightly structured job situation and controls, and that if he managed subordinates in this manner they would learn to behave according to the theory *X* assumptions. That is, they would feel that the manager had a cynical view of them and would therefore respond with an anti-management attitude. For many workers such an attitude would be supported by their union and by their previous history or the attitudes of their parents, who might have been involved for several generations in labor-management disputes. In other words, McGregor acknowledged that much of worker behavior fitted theory *X* assumptions, but that such behavior was *learned* behavior not inherent "human nature." If one looked at the accumulated research findings of the behavioral scientists, one would find that human nature is much more consistent with theory *Y,* and one could find evidence of this point in studies that attempted to involve workers more and found very positive responses to such attempts (Lesieur, 1958; Likert, 1961; Whyte, 1955).

One of the real weaknesses of the human relations approach was its tendency to forget the task that people were working on and the organization structure and technology that related to this task. Sociologists like George Homans, William Whyte, and Conrad Arensberg in this country, and Eric Trist and Kenneth Rice in England, began a series of studies that led to the concept of "socio-technical systems," a concept that tries to acknowledge explicitly that the nature of the task and the nature of the human relations among workers performing that task are integrally related. In other words, human relations occur within an environment that is itself determined by technology, culture, organization structure, and specific work settings. Even in the Hawthorne studies it was evident that the groups that emerged reflected the layout of the room and the nature of the jobs. Eric Trist's work on the conversion from short-wall to long-wall coal mining methods, facilitated by the invention of long-wall mining machinery, is a landmark comparable to the Hawthorne studies (Trist *et al.*, 1963).

Trist showed that the technology of short wall mining required a vertically integrated effort among the men who cut, loaded, and carried the coal away in tubs (Trist and Banforth, 1951). These groups developed very close relations, which carried over into their life off the job and met important needs, such as reducing the anxiety of working underground. The long-wall method involved a larger group of men under a supervisor working on a machine that did most of the cutting. The men were spread out, which made social contact difficult and thus undermined the close relations that the short-wall method had fostered. It was then discovered that the men did not like the disruption of those close relationships and that the greater tension of working in the mine could not be worked through as well in the larger groups as it had been in the smaller ones. The work lost much of its meaning and the miners became less committed, which showed up in lower productivity, greater carelessness, and less maintenance of the equipment. Thus, the new technology did not in fact produce more coal because of the disruption of the social structure of the workers. Only when this factor had been recognized and a new kind of training program set up to deal with the social factors could the technology begin to prove itself superior. Subsequent studies in other industries again confirmed these kinds of findings in a variety of settings and emphasized the need to think both about task (technology) and human factors. Consideration of either one alone failed to solve the productivity problem, and also failed to solve the morale problem.

Just as economic man as a model of the individual person in the organization proved to be an oversimplification, so social man also proved to be an oversimplification. Increasingly the emphasis of the behavioral scientist shifted to the nature of the work itself, and the degree to which there was potential in the work for the fulfillment of man's basic need to use his skills, abilities, and talents. Man's needs for contact with other workers was only part of the story; man also needed work that was inherently meaningful and contributory. (Maslow, 1961; McGregor, 1960; Argyris, 1964; Herzberg *et al.*, 1957).

Many of the studies that had argued for participation on the part of workers could be interpreted to mean that participation did not so much fulfill the worker's *social* needs as it fulfilled his needs to be *meaningfully involved* in his work. Workers in highly automated industries could still be meaningfully involved if they had a high degree of responsibility, such as the operator in an automated oil refinery; but if the worker was on an assembly line attaching one small part to a complex product all day long, he would gradually lose his sense of involvement and begin to feel that if work was that meaningless, he might at least seek more economic rewards and get meaning in off-the-job leisure-time activities (Blauner, 1964).

The human relations movement now shifted to a concern for job enrichment, job enlargement, and more worker involvement in planning the work (Herzberg *et al.*, 1959, 1966). Human relations training is still a popular activity, but the content of the programs has shifted away from training managers simply to be more concerned about people to helping managers to diagnose what the task and human requirements are in the socio-technical systems of their organization, and how to change not only their management style but also the organization structure, the reward system, and the culture of the organization toward more effective total utilization of human resources. This more broad approach has led to what is currently called organization development (see below for a more detailed discussion).

Group and Inter-group Problems. As technology has become more complex, organizations have found themselves having to divide the labor among more and more different specialists and then having to coordinate and integrate the work of those specialists. In a simple technology, the hierarchy of authority could adequately handle the integration problem—i.e., the manager one or two levels up could collect information from production, engineering, and marketing and make reasonably good product and/or marketing decisions. However, as technology became more complex, the manager could not comprehend all the issues and could not process all the information needed to make a decision. To some extent the resulting greater information processing need has been dealt with by more effective computer-supported information and control systems. But the problem of how to make a good decision involving technical specialties which the manager could not himself totally comprehend could not be solved by this means. Increasingly, therefore, organizations have had to rely on decision mechanisms that involved bringing together the representatives of several specialities and conducting group meetings to acquire all the information and cover all the issues. The manager of the group might then choose one of a number of decision-making styles—just listening and then deciding, making tentative decisions for the group to react to; giving alternatives among which the group might choose; or giving the group complete decision-making power—but in one way or another he had to use a group in support of the decision process (Galbraith, 1973; Tannenbaum and Schmidt, 1958).

For the manager who was brought up in the traditional management approach, the use of meetings and groups was often awkward and uncomfortable. If the group did not work well, the manager often blamed the group decision method, failing to recognize that it was his approach to the group that might have caused the problem. The behavioral scientists, particularly those who were expert in group dynamics (Schein and Bennis, 1965; Miles, 1969; Schein, 1967), found themselves developing methods that would aid managers to learn how to be effective members and leaders of groups, and how to make group decision processes more effective. The great popularity of *T*-groups throughout the 1950's and 1960's resulted in part from the need of managers in organizations to learn more about groups and how to work in them.

Whereas earlier studies of groups among workers treated them as part of the informal system to be tolerated because it met some interpersonal needs of workers, the emphasis now shifted to groups as formal organizational mechanisms for solving problems and making decisions. The group became a management tool rather than a worker phenomenon, and behavioral scientists focused more of their attention on the role of management groups in increasing organization effectiveness. This trend has continued unabated and will continue as organizations become more and more complex.

With the recognition of groups as essential elements of organization structure has come the additional recognition that groups within organizations could either work in support of one another or actually get in one another's way. It has always been recognized that problems arise in the flow of work from engineering to production to sales and back to engineering via new marketing information. Each functional grouping tends to develop a particular approach to problems based on the background of the people in it and the kind of environment in which they work (Lawrence and Lorsch, 1967). If the reward system of the total organization is such that each function does its best as it sees it, there are strong pressures set up for groupings in the organization to compete with one another. If they compete there are then strong tendencies set up to hide information, to try to blame errors on other groups (throw the dead cat in the neighbor's yard), and to fail to perceive how a decision that is good within a given function might be bad for the total organization. Thus engineering designs elegant products that can't be built, production subverts quality requirements or elegance in order to get out large numbers within the schedule and at the cost prescribed for them, sales blames production if delivery times slow down, production blames sales for making unrealistic commitments to customers on delivery times or special alterations, and so on.

As the competition among functional groups has become recognized, management has invented compensatory devices such as integrating departments like production engineering, or product teams, which embrace representatives from all the functions under a product manager. At a higher level of integration, organizations have invented project management or divisionalization to integrate whatever specialities are needed, even if that meant breaking up the functional departments. In each of these cases new groups are created that must learn to work together effectively, often requiring the aid of behavioral scientists in training the members of the group as a whole.

Where such new groupings are not possible or where new levels of competition arise that the total organization considers destructive, behavioral scientists have adapted conflict resolution methods to the study and amelioration of inter-group conflicts (Blake and Mouton, 1962). Special kinds of workshops, meetings, or training activities have been developed to help groups that have problems with one another to explore those problems historically, to set new and integrative goals, and to develop methods for achieving more collaboration in achieving the goals. Such methods have also been applied in reducing headquarters/field problems, in facilitating mergers, and in introducing new management teams into organizations.

Organization Structure and Design Problems. The traditional role of the behavioral scientist working in organizations was to work on individual or group problems that were identified by higher levels of management. Often the behavioral scientist helped to identify such problems by working with these higher levels, but only rarely did he get involved in top-level corporate issues and problems of organizational strategy and tactics. The main reason, I suspect, is that he had relatively little to contribute to this area up until the last ten or twenty years when his theories and research methods developed to the point where they could encompass organizations as total systems and begin to help the top manager to think through total organizational problems. If the organization had problems about how to set goals, how to structure itself, or how to adapt to changing environmental conditions, it typically turned to planners or management consultants who might or might not have been exposed to any psychology, sociology, or anthropology. As the business schools introduced more of the behavioral sciences, more research was done on organizational problems, and more links were developed with top management.

Much of the theorizing about organization structure and design has come from the studies of socio-technical systems already referred to. A number of empirical studies were done of effective and ineffective companies in different kinds of industries, and it was found that effective structures varied as a function of the type of task and type of environment in which the company existed. Highly stable and predictable tasks in fairly stable environments were most effectively dealt with by companies that had tightly structured formal hierarchies—i.e., that were coordinated from power centers at the very top of the organization; complex tasks in fairly turbulent or less predictable environments were most effectively handled by companies that had fairly decentralized structures with a high degree of diffusion of decision-making power and a greater use of lateral coordinating structures such as project teams or integrated divisions rather than functionally organized departments (Dalton, Lorsch, and Lawrence, 1970; Galbraith, 1972). The significance of these studies has been that an area that had traditionally been considered to be far too complicated to be studied empirically and had been relegated to men of wisdom and experience, has increasingly come to be clarified by theorists and researchers.

The essence of most of the theories is that one must view the organization as a total system in interaction with its environment (Schein, 1970; Likert, 1967), and must apply criteria of effectiveness that apply to systems as a whole—i.e., the ability to survive and grow in the face of environmental change through better sensing of what change occurs, better ingestion and digestion of relevant information, better ability to make internal changes to adapt to new information, and better ability to obtain valid feedback on changes made. Profits, return on investment, turnover, etc., are all still critical measures of performance, but they are increasingly to be viewed only as *symptoms* of organizational health, that must be supplemented by other basic criteria. Behavioral scientists have not only developed theoretical and research tools for studying organizational structure and design, but have also developed methods for improving organizational performance by helping organizations intervene effectively in their human and informational processes. This area has come to be known as organization development and will be discussed next.

Problems of Organization Improvement Through Organization Development. The field of organization development (O.D.) is recent and as yet not well defined. It is distinguished by the fact that it is heavily based on behavioral science concepts and methods, heavily committed to viewing the organization as a total system, and heavily committed to improving the long-range effectiveness of organizations through constructive interventions in organizational processes and structures (Bennis, 1969; Beckhard, 1969; Schein, 1969). There are some variations in the approaches of different O.D. practitioners; hence, a particular methodology that is associated with the field cannot as yet be defined. But some of the different methods that have been developed and that are used in varying combinations depending on the kind of organizational problems that are being worked on and the style of the consultant can be outlined. Incidentally, most organization development work is being carried out by consultants who function from inside the organization (they may be members of a corporate staff group or a separate O.D. department) and/or who are brought in from outside the organization directly by line management or by the internal consultant. Usually the inside and outside man will form a team to carry out the project.

The essential elements underlying any organization development effort are that it be long-range in its orientation, that it involve efforts to improve the overall effectiveness of the total organization, that it concern itself with the total system not only part of it, even though a given activity may occur in only one part of the organization, and that the diagnostic and intervention steps be shared by both the line managers and the consultants. In other words, one cannot come in as an outsider and do organization development work, but one can help line managers improve their organization by working closely with them in helping them to diagnose their problems and helping them to invent appropriate interventions or changes.

Most of the actual activities of organization development projects derive from what Kurt Lewin called "action research." The basic idea is that one cannot study a system like an organization without changing it by the very act of studying it, but that this should not be seen as a disadvantage so much as an opportunity. In other words, one can learn the most about an organization in the process of trying to change it. Interventions to produce change and diagnosis of what changes are needed are thus completely intertwined with each other, even though most O.D. practitioners talk as if diagnosis preceded intervention. With this background comment we can look at some of the specific techniques used:

1. *Survey feedback methods*—some portion of the organization is interviewed and/or given questionnaires dealing with various aspects of organizational process, morale, the reward system, management style, etc., and the data are fed back to one level at a time in a series of meetings that involve (a) an analysis of the results, and (b) planning of remedial measures by every level of the organization. It is this last step that differentiates the use of these methods in O.D. programs from the more traditional attitude surveys carried on in industry.

2. *Team building and team training methods*—most of these methods are coordinated with individual management development activities and are distinguished by the fact that the group being trained is selected on the basis that they will have to work together in the organization. Thus, if the organization is planning to go to a form of project management, it becomes highly relevant to give team training to the members and leader of that team as an aid to making it effective. One version of such methods that has achieved considerable prominence is the use of the "managerial grid" in team training programs (Blake and Mouton, 1964).

3. *Job enrichment and job enlargement*—a number of O.D. practi-

tioners are putting their primary focus on training programs that facilitate redesigning the work itself toward jobs that are more interesting and involving to the people in the organization. Where such work would traditionally have been done by industrial engineers aiming at work simplification, these programs put more emphasis on involving the organization as a whole in redesigning its own work (Herzberg, 1966).

4. *Sensitivity training*—the use of T-groups, encounter groups, and sensitivity groups antedates organization development by ten to fifteen years (Schein and Bennis, 1965). The real growth of such groups was supported by their key role in individual management development programs, although the use of the method in a number of companies in combination with team training produced major impacts on the organization as a whole. Such groups are often used as part of an overall effort and are combined with other techniques mentioned above, but they are by themselves rarely sufficient to produce major organizational change. They have their biggest impact in unfreezing some of the attitudes of managers and making them more amenable to other kinds of interventions.

5. *Process consultation*—this concept cuts across many of the others in that it is more of an approach to *how* to work with the organization in whatever specific method one uses (Schein, 1969). The basic idea is that the consultant should not really function as an expert on what the organization is trying to do, but should help the organization to improve whatever human and informational processes it is using in accomplishing its goals. If the goals or decision processes are themselves not clear, the consultant can help line managers to clarify issues by focusing on how they are working together. The consultant's expertness lies in his ability to help the organization to help itself.

There are many other specific kinds of techniques that have acquired labels and become part of the kit-bag of the organization development consultant, but most of them are closely related to one of the five categories just outlined. It should be said in concluding this section that, although the behavioral scientist functioning as an inside or outside consultant plays a key role in facilitating organization development, it must be the line managers who take the initiative and manage the project if real organization improvement is to result.

Area 2: Utilization of Financial Resources

Budgeting Most managers are involved, as part of their job, in developing budgets and administering those budgets through a system of financial controls. The budgets are typically built on the basis of information that is supplied by subordinates and checked by the manager. Once the budget is made, the manager is typically involved in selling that budget to a higher level in the organization. Both the building and selling of the budget involves multiple interaction among many people, creating multiple opportunities for psychological distortions, misinformation, overselling, and inter-group competition for scarce resources (Argyris, 1953).

The behavioral scientist is not really needed to convince the manager that these things occur; if he has any experience in organizations he has witnessed them with dismay. Where the behavioral scientist often can contribute, however, is in helping the manager to understand *why* people behave in these situations the way they do, and how the manager might set up a situation that would reduce distortion, misinformation, and destructive competition. For example, most managers are well aware that if they do not spend all the money that they asked for in their budget, their boss will assume that they padded the budget and will cut the next year's budget by a certain amount. They will tell their own subordinates to find ways of using up the resources or concealing them by investing them in "kitties" to be used later. Yet they will expect those same subordinates to give them accurate information when the subordinates are submitting their own budgets.

The behavioral scientist can bring to bear the knowledge that people will adapt very efficiently to how the organization's reward system or norms work, and that if the subordinate's behavior is to be made more "rational," the boss's own behavior will have to set a climate in which such rational behavior is rewarded. Sometimes this means that the norms or climate emanating from the very top of the organization have to be reexamined and rebuilt. I have seen organizations spend literally months developing presentations to accompany budgets and business plans, where the sole purpose was to get top management to agree, while top management tried to figure out as best they could how the different groups competing for resources were trying to fool them. Yet those top managers did not see any connection between their own management style and the behavior of their subordinates.

Financial Controls When we examine the area of financial controls a similar picture emerges. The organization designs an information system that will provide accurate figures on costs, on schedules, on inventory, and the like, and then typically assumes that it can accurately measure the progress of different departments against these figures (Argyris, 1971). Let us look at how the process often works. In most organizations the control functions are given to a special staff unit like the accounting department, which collects and centralizes information across a number of operating departments. A higher level of management typically scans the information and raises questions about those departments that show irregularities. The questions come back down the chain of command until the responsible worker or manager is confronted by his boss with a question concerning the irregularity (McGregor, 1967).

Such a system has several psychological consequences that have been observed by behavioral scientists, but are less visible to the managers: (1) Workers and lower level managers become highly dependent on the system and cease to monitor their own areas as closely as they should; they develop the attitude that if they are not doing their job the control system will let them know soon enough, hence why worry about it; (2) Workers and lower-level managers become resentful that they are called on the carpet by their boss for things that they may already have known about and fixed, or that they feel they should have been told about in order to fix without involving higher levels of management; (3) Workers and lower-level managers treat the accountants and representatives of other control functions as an enemy to be beaten rather than as an ally in getting a job done better; often they hide information or falsify it to make their operation look better than it is in order to avoid being penalized. These responses are normal, given the system as it is set up. The behavioral scientist can help the higher-level manager analyze the system, its impact on people, and how to change it if the impact is undesirable (Likert and Seashore, 1963).

Budgeting and control processes involve financial operations within the firm. Another aspect of financial management has to do with investments, cash flow, and the like wherein a person or small group has to make sound decisions given the company's particular needs and situation. A number of studies have been undertaken in recent years attempting to understand how individuals make investment decisions and how such decisions can be improved. Such studies have typically combined the talents of the econometrician the information systems expert, and the behaviorally oriented psychologist. Sophisticated techniques involving simulation of the decision-making process have been undertaken with as yet limited but promising results. Within the next decade we should see the development of decision support systems that will help the individual decision-maker analyze his own problem-solving process, will reveal his biases, and help him to correct errors and generally improve decision quality.

Although the role of the behavioral scientists in helping the manager deal with his financial management is not as yet well accepted, there is an increasing need for managers to recognize the interaction between people and systems. No matter how rational the design of a budget, control system, or investment plan, as long as people are involved in carrying it out and in contributing the raw data with which the system operates, there will be a need to examine how people feel about and use the system in order to examine its utility to the organization. The behavioral scientist will play a key role in helping the manager to make such an assessment.

Area 3: Utilization of Information

The manager makes his basic decisions on the basis of information that he acquires directly from his own experience, is given by subordinates, peers, and supervisors, and digs out of financial, marketing, and other analyses made available to him. The quality of his decisions cannot be better than the quality of his information; hence real attention must be given to the process by which the manager acquires, evaluates, and digests information. Behavioral scientists have played two roles in this process: (1) they have aided in the acquisition of information; and (2) they have aided the process of information digestion, interpretation, and utilization in the decision-making process.

Information Acquisition One of the major research tools of psychologists has been the use of interviews and questionnaires to obtain information on beliefs, attitudes, values, and behavior patterns. This type of information is of prime relevance to the marketing man; hence the field of market research has developed around advances in survey design, statistics, and more subtle methods of obtaining information about consumer behavior, such as motivation research. Most market research departments in organizations and most advertising agencies employ behavioral scientists to obtain information about consumers and to utilize this information in designing advertising and marketing strategies (Green and Tull, 1970).

Behavioral scientists are also used to gather data about the morale of employees, and, in connection with organization development efforts, about their attitudes toward various organizational and managerial issues. Usually such information is gathered by an outside consulting agency, but many large corporations maintain a full-time in-house staff to do continuous attitude and morale surveys of their employees.

Information Processing and Decision-Making The way in which the manager acquires, processes, and utilizes information in making decisions has only come under scrutiny by behavioral scientists in the last decade or so, but it is one of the most promising and fruitful areas for future study and application. Several approaches have been used. Psychologists interested in learning, thinking, and problem-solving have attempted to apply some of their theories and research methods to understanding and simulating how managers make their decisions. Herbert Simon's work stands out as classic in this area in providing, among other insights, the crucial one that managerial decision-making is characterized by "satisficing" rather than maximizing (March and Simon, 1958). In other words, the manager typically operates with imperfect and incomplete information under time pressure and tends, therefore, to seek a solution that will suffice, which will get the job done, rather than a solution that will be the best possible one under the circumstances. Simulation of managerial decision-making has so far limited itself to manageable areas like investment decisions, but in these areas considerable understanding has been acquired of how the manager obtains and digests information, what kinds of assumptions or premises he holds, and how these enter into his decisions (Clarkson, 1962; Wilcox, 1970).

Another approach has been to take problem-solving models that either an individual person or group can use and build a training program around them to improve individual and group decision-making. The Kepner-Tregoe program is perhaps the best known of these, although sensitivity training programs also typically devote some percentage of their time to improving decision processes. Process consultation is heavily involved in observing how groups process information and make decisions, and in helping managers to improve this process by learning to observe their own processes, and to improve them (Kepner and Tregoe, 1965; Schein, 1969). The use of business games and complex business simulations can be put into this same category. Usually, behavioral scientists are involved in the initial design and construction of the game, in the way in which it is used as an educational aid, and in helping individuals or groups learn from their experience in playing the game.

A third approach, which is perhaps the most exciting one, is for the behavioral scientist to collaborate directly with information system design experts in building better information and decision support systems. This whole area has been revolutionized by the computer and its true potential is only now beginning to be understood. For example, in its early history the glib assumption was made that the more information the manager had about everything and the quicker he could get it, the better off he would be. Problems of information overload and of seducing the manager into looking at interesting but irrelevant information are only now beginning to be recognized. For example, a computerized information system can give a division manager detailed performance information on each of his operating departments of which there may be a great many three or four levels below him, e.g., a president of a super-market chain getting information on each of several hundred stores. From the point of view of the system designer such access to information may be a virtue of the system. From the point of view of the analyst of managerial decision-making, such access may be a disaster, in that it would seduce the president into preoccupations that should be the responsibility of subordinates.

More sophisticated information system designers working with behavioral scientists are beginning to ask questions about what kind of information and what quantity of information the manager should have to optimize his decision processes. Maybe each level should get detailed information only about the level below it, with everything below that aggregated to prevent managers from getting lost in irrelevant detail and from getting involved in levels too far below them. The kinds of control system problems that were outlined in the preceding section often derive from an information system that makes detailed information about lower levels available at too high a level.

The behavioral science view has also entered information design thinking in terms of the interaction between the form in which the information is displayed and the kind of decision-making grouping that is needed. For example, if the task requires intensive effort from an individual manager using multiple information sources, he may be able to work successfully with well-designed computer printouts, written summaries, and other materials that he can read at his leisure. If the task required team effort in interpreting complex information and in reaching a decision, it may be more appropriate to design visual displays that can be viewed simultaneously by a number of managers. In one study of the installation of such a system it was found that the visual display terminal encouraged a group of managers to get together and begin to work as a team in a situation in which it was initially unlikely that they would have gotten together, even though the task they were working on required it (Scott-Morton, 1971).

CONCLUSION

As the behavioral sciences have matured and as behavioral scientists have been accepted by higher levels of management, it has been possible to study the *central* processes in organizations and to contribute in areas other than "people problems." It is in these new areas that we will probably see the greatest payoff in the next decade, because they will encourage all of us to think in a more integrated way about the utilization of financial, informational, and human resources.

SUGGESTIONS FOR FUTURE READING

ARGYRIS, C. *Integrating the Individual and the Organization* (New York: John Wiley & Sons, 1964).

ARGYRIS, C. "Human Problems With Budgets," *Harvard Business Review,* Vol. 31 (January, 1953), pp. 97–110.

ARGYRIS, C. "Management Information Systems: the Challenge to Rationality and Emotionality, *Management Science,* Vol. 6 (1971), pp. 275–292.

BECKHARD, R. *Organization Development: Strategies and Models* (Reading, Mass.: Addison-Wesley, 1969).

BENNIS, W.G. *Organization Development: Its Nature, Origins, and Prospects* (Reading, Mass.: Addison-Wesley, 1969).

BERLEW, D.E., AND D.T. HALL. "The Socialization of Managers: Effects of Expectations on Performance, *Administrative Science Quarterly,* Vol. 11 (1966), pp. 207–223.

BLAKE, R.R., AND JANE S. MOUTON. "Headquarters Field Team Training for Organization Improvements," *Journal of the American Society of Training Directors* (1962), p. 16.

BLAKE, R.R., AND JANE S. MOUTON. *The Managerial Grid* (Houston: Gulf Publishing Co., 1964).

BLAUNER, R. *Alienation and Freedom* (Chicago: University of Chicago Press, 1964).

CLARKSON, G. *Portfolio Selection: A Simulation of Trust Investment* (Englewood, Cliffs, N.J.: Prentice-Hall, 1962).

DALTON, G.W., P.R. LAWRENCE AND J.W. LORSCH, *Organization Structure and Design* (Homewood, Ill.: Irwin-Dorsey, 1970).

FLEISHMAN, E.A. "Leadership Climate, Human Relations Training, and Supervisory Behavior, *Personnel Psychology,* Vol. 6 (1953), pp. 205–222.

GALBRAITH, J. *Organization Design* (Reading, Mass.: Addison-Wesley, 1973).

GREEN, P., AND D. TULL. *Research for Marketing Decisions,* 2nd Ed. (Englewood Cliffs, N.J.: Prentice-Hall, 1970).

HERZBERG, F., B. MAUSNER, AND B. SNYDERMAN. *The Motivation to Work* (New York: John Wiley & Sons, 1959).

HERZBERG, F. *Work and the Nature of Man* (New York: World Publishing, 1966).

HOMANS, G. *The Human Group* (New York: Harcourt-Brace, 1950).

KEPNER, C.H., AND B.B. TREGOE. *The Rational Manager* (New York: McGraw-Hill Book Company, 1965).

KOONTZ, H., AND C. O'DONNELL. *Principles of Management.* 3rd Ed. (New York: McGraw-Hill Book Company, 1964).

LESIEUR, F. *The Scalon Plan* (New York: John Wiley & Sons, 1958).

LAWRENCE, P.R., AND J.W. LORSCH. *Organization and Environment: Managing Differentiation and Integration* (Cambridge, Mass.: Harvard University Press, 1967).

LIKERT, R. *The Human Organization: Its Management and Values* (New York: McGraw-Hill Book Company, 1967).

LIKERT, R. *New Patterns of Management* (New York: McGraw-Hill Book Company, 1961).

LIKERT R., AND S.E. SEASHORE. "Making Cost Control Work," *Harvard Business Review,* Vol. 41 (November, 1963), pp. 96–108.

MARCH, J.G., AND H. SIMON. *Organizations* (New York: John Wiley & Sons, 1958).

MASLOW, A. *Motivation and Personality* (New York: Harper, 1964).

MAYO, E. *The Social Problems of an Industrial Civilization* (Cambridge, Mass.: Harvard University Press, 1945).

MCGREGOR, D.M. *The Human Side of Enterprise* (New York: McGraw-Hill Book Company, 1960).

McGregor, D.M. *The Professional Manager* (New York: McGraw-Hill Book Company, 1967).

Miles, M. *Learning to Work in Groups* (New York: Columbia University Press, 1959).

Roethlisberger, F.J., and W.J. Dickson. *Management and the Worker* (Cambridge, Mass.: Harvard University Press, 1930).

Schein, E.H. "How to Break in the College Graduate," *Harvard Business Review*, Vol. 42 (November, 1964), pp. 68–76.

Schein, E.H. "The First Job Dilemma," *Psychology Today* (March, 1968), pp. 22–37.

Schein, E.H. *Process Consultation: Its Role in Organization Development* (Reading Mass.: Addison-Wesley, 1969).

Schein, E.H. *Organizational Psychology*, 2nd Ed. (Englewood Cliffs, N.J.: Prentice-Hall, 1970).

Schein, E.H., and W.G. Bennis. *Personal and Organizational Change Through Group Methods: The Laboratory Approach* (New York: John Wiley & Sons, 1965).

Scott-Morton, M. *Management Decision Systems: Computer-Based Support for Decision Making* (Cambridge, Mass.: Division of Research, Harvard Business School, 1971).

Tannenbaum, R., and W.H. Schmidt. "How to Choose a Leadership Pattern," *Harvard Business Review*, Vol. 36 (March, 1958), pp. 95–101.

Trist, E.L., and K.W. Bamforth. "Some Social and Psychological Consequences of the Longwall Method of Coal-getting," *Human Relations*, Vol. 4 (February, 1951), pp. 1–38.

Trist, E.L., G. Higgin, H. Murray, and A. Pollock. *Organizational Choice* (London: Tavistock, 1963).

Wilcox, J. *A Methodology for Decision Assumption Measurement* (Cambridge, Mass.: Alfred P. Sloan School of Management Working Paper, December, 1970).

Whyte, W.F. *Money and Motivation: An Analysis of Incentives in Industry* (New York: Harper, 1955).

Behavioral Science Is More

Blair J. Kolasa

Dean
School of Business and Administration
Duquesne University

"Please, sir, I want some more."
Dickens, *Oliver Twist*

On finishing the preceding essay one might readily guess, if one did not already know of Schein, that the piece was written by a keen analyst of behavior in organizations. The author covers well the area of most direct interest to managers, an understandable emphasis because it is usually the one containing the most immediate inputs with which managers have to contend daily in the office environment.

The only complaint with this delineation of the area is that it paints a narrower picture for the reader than must be given and is, therefore, like a little bit of learning, dangerous. There is much more to behavioral science than organizational behavior. A chapter like this must serve as an introduction to the area and hence ought not jump into a sketching of one aspect in greater depth and ignore the other areas that would show breadth of the field (and define it by doing so). By such a restriction the manager's awareness of the greater number of concepts and skills present in the discipline and available for application in a variety of situations in the external as well as internal environment is reduced significantly.

It might be thought that by this time no definition of behavioral science, either in words or by describing its breadth of applications, is needed. There is plenty of evidence that this is not so. One recent work in a well-known series, for instance, defined behavioral science by asking corporation executives what it is. The subsequent collection of narrow stereotypes or half-truths is misleading, to put it mildly. Limiting an essay on behavioral science in management to organizational behavior, no matter how well written or accurate (as Schein's certainly is) is not nearly that misleading but still is deficient.

What is behavioral science? The definition can be given verbally but then must be repeated through applications to everyday events to make it more meaningful. Behavioral science is the systematic study of behavior—what "is" rather than what "ought to be." It is, therefore, empirical and not speculative. Instead of relying on what individual notions of behavior might be, the behavioral scientist gathers data to find out what is so or not. This "hard-nosed" empiricism is often missed by many who believe that one can stop after reading about McGregor, Maslow, Herzberg, or others. As a result of limiting themselves to a few more popular points, readers misjudge the main thrust of the discipline and call it qualitative, normative, value oriented, or even one focusing solely on participative approaches to group functioning. That it is *not.* Behavioral science entails rigorous research design, unbiased data collection, organization of results, and analytical attempts at ordering the data in order to add to the cumulative reservoir of knowledge that makes for human progress. Even the "humanistic" among the behavioral scientists did not reach the results they did "off the tops of their heads." A reader often has to go beyond the more popular, colloquial writings to recognize the scientific base and process that contributed to the conclusions.

The additional common feeling that behavioral science is not in the same league as the "hard" sciences is related to the stereotypes stemming from the symbols associated with physical science laboratories. Lab coats and test tubes do not a scientist make nor does one have to possess such apparatus to be a scientist.[1] It may be, and often is, much more difficult to gather good data in the complex area of human behavior than in other settings. Behavioral scientists often wish they had the opportunity to regulate and vary circumstances as readily as physical scientists can control impersonal physical and chemical conditions. Behavioral researchers just have to try harder.

Behavioral science is just that, a science, because it shares certain characteristics with other sciences. Using the scientific method involves:

1. being *systematic*
2. in gathering *data*
3. that can be *ordered*
4. for *analysis*
5. and *communicated*
6. to add to the *cumulative* fund of knowledge.

It relies on basic *premises* and then develops *hypotheses*, or educated guesses, that must be checked to determine whether the results call for an acceptance or rejection of the statement of relationships in the data. A more general *theory* can develop and give rise to further hypotheses to be tested. The word "theory" may cause many managers to "tune out" since it has long carried the connotation of impracticality. Yet each of us is constantly a theorist to one extent or another (the manager often without realizing it) in that we do construct shorthand explanations for relationships among events and on this basis try to predict results. Things would not make much sense otherwise. As Kurt Lewin was once said to have remarked "there is nothing as practical as a good theory." Behavioral science may not have enough good theory yet, but the work proceeds.

Perhaps, quite simply, behavioral science may be viewed as a frame of mind or as an approach to problem-solving. The precise and painstaking study of a situation to develop a framework to avoid easy opinion-giving is what it's all about.

Now to the specifics, of which there are many, too many. Just as Schein could use the argument that there is very little space in which to cram in all that must be covered, so it is even more the case here. Trade-offs can be attempted, however. A good place to make room would be to reduce the discussion of theory *X* and theory *Y*. If there is one thing that managers these days have heard about behavioral science it's *X* and *Y*. Start instead with the *a*, *b*, and *c* and go all the way to *z*. The same tendency, incidentally, exists in academic publications and in college classrooms. An instructor-researcher teaching or writing on "behavioral science" has a tendency to focus on his narrow area of interest and send the student away with the feeling that this little bit was all there was to behavioral science.

The elements of individual behavior are often glossed over. Students and managers discuss organizations without a clear knowledge of the fundamentals of human behavior. People who should know better make statements like "managers must motivate," which miss the entire point about how internal a factor motivation is. "Communicate" stimulates much discussion in management without a clear knowledge of what communication really is. Not one in ten in the target group is likely to know the first thing about semantics or other basic bits of knowledge.

More important, there is probably little understanding, even in sophisticated managerial circles, of the specific

[1] J. Chaplin, and T. Krawiec, *Systems and Theories of Psychology* (New York: Holt, Rinehart and Winston, 1960).

nature of human abilities through the age span. What are men and women of specific ages capable of, physically and mentally? Decisions are made every day in corporations based not on factual knowledge, in most cases, but on perpetuated stereotypes.

Although the in-house group applications of behavioral science have been covered quite well by Schein, what is bothering more and more managers these days is the challenge from forces external to the corporation. The social issues in the larger environment often tax and perplex the executive more than the usual and familiar problems he is used to facing within the organization. This is unknown territory and there has been little management training or development along these lines. It may be that corporations have failed to respond to the challenges of a changing environment because they have not yet recognized public values as part of their own; they still see society as composed of independent sub-systems rather than as a larger, unified system.[2] The interrelatedness of all activity of the corporation and its environment necessitates an awareness of the dynamics of social forces on the part of the executive.

Discussions of social patterns presuppose, however, the prior understanding of the interrelatedness of individual and group behavior. Culture, for instance, is a concept based on aggregates, but the transmission of culture through interpersonal channels or as the result of geographic mobility can be grasped well only if one understands individual development and the differences that can result from it. The broad and basic pattern of social life that we call culture, with all its attitudes and material possessions, is not passed on unchanged. The mediation by intermediate transmitters in the environment or by the family is critical. Can one really understand the Protestant Ethic, Black attitudes, reactions to welfare programs, women's lib, or any other contemporary social factor without some pre-awareness of the dynamics of culture and its transmission (a knowledge established on the basis of empirical data and not on biases, fictions, or stereotypes)?

Social structure and process are easily seen in ongoing events. Someone with middle-class values who puts a high premium on education and achievement, for instance, may find it difficult to comprehend actions that arise from other values. To make it even more complex recently, sons and daughters of the establishment or newer managers in the corporation have been questioning the goals and values of the system into which they were born or moved into. Mobility, both geographic and generational, puts further stresses on familiar ties (ask today's manager about transfers within the company). Broader questions of population movements and the changing composition of the populace concern the average thinking citizen, but these matters interest the organizational planner, personnel administrator, and the marketer even more. What are people like in terms of age, sex, education, or occupation are only the beginning questions.

The processes of social change are even more pertinent for the administrator. The manager has often been called a change agent and this function of organizational behavior has been termed the most important aspect of management. The internal requirements for change may rest approximately on individual and small-group dynamics, but they are reflections of broader patterns of social change. Discordant consequences of change in society manifest themselves in conflict and disintegration in individuals and groups. Whether it takes place as industrial strife in various kinds of industries or in other moves toward power, a manager feels the impact keenly.

Behavioral science contributions to an understanding of politics and law range from establishing a basic framework of concepts to recognizing applications in specific situations. Managers do

[2]D. Votaw and P. Sethi, "Do We Need a New Corporate Response to a Changing Environment?" *California Management Review*, Vol. 12, No. 1 (Fall, 1969), Part I, pp. 3–16; Part II, pp. 17–31.

not need to be told, perhaps, about the impact of law and politics in the functioning of their organizations. What does need telling is something like the relationship between personality and politics, attitudes or other characteristics of political agents, variables in participation, voter preference patterns, and other specific aspects of politics. In the law, an understanding of the behavioral basis of the legal process should be gained before (or instead of) substantive rules of law are memorized. What is the purpose of law? What are concepts of control and how it is achieved? What is basic to the functioning of an ordered society? Does punishment deter? Can law induce social change or is it the other way around? How do agents of public government and private government (corporations, colleges, etc.) relate to one another? What are the consequences of attempting to balance concerns for the consumer and the development of the economy?

We can come full circle now to the prior discussion of organizational behavior and add an interface with the environment that is part of the everyday functioning of virtually every corporation—the market. What makes the consumer tick and how does the message get across to him? The fundamental influence process in marketing and advertising involves all aspects, from mass communication at one end of the spectrum to a one-to-one personal relationship at the other. It can be the knowledge that is most crucial to the continuing existence of the organization and the manager's job.

All the above may really be leading up to the fundamental questions faced in viewing the role of the person in an organization and in society. Addressing oneself to the problem of quality of life on an individual basis or in the broader environment is often cast, for business, in terms of social responsibility. The critical questions lie, however, in determining the behavioral elements of identity, equality, privacy, security, and other primary or secondary needs. All this is part of the job of the behavioral scientist and may even be his most important task in the long run.

The Underutilization of Behavioral Science By Management

Edwin B. Flippo

Professor
College of Business and Public Administration
Department of Management
University of Arizona

The extensive and impressive itemization of behavioral science contributions to management theory and practice by Edgar Schein adds to the enigma of managerial neglect and underutilization of such contributions. Certainly, the four reasons cited for this lack of utilization are valid, but two others might be added. In the first place, there is a considerable lack of unanimity among behavioral theorists about normative prescriptions for management. Harold

Koontz pointed out long ago that there exists a "management theory jungle" with multiple and often conflicting proposals from practicing managers, functionalists, behaviorists, mathematicians, and decision theorists.[1] Among behavioral scientists there are the psychologists, who have a more individualistic approach and often set forth normative prescriptions, and the sociologists, who attempt to explain how organizations and groups form and adapt, frequently without making specific recommendations. Within these two broad groups, different emphases are advocated some say that the important factor is the design of the job whereas others say that power and politics should constitute the focal point of analysis and action.[2] Thus, a fifth possible reason for the limited use of behavioral science contributions to management is the confusion among practicing managers about which behaviorist to believe.

One final suggestion can be made concerning the puzzle of nonuse. Had I been asked to prepare the original statement, contributions of behavioral science for managers, I would have substantially duplicated Edgar Schein's material, but my orientation would have been slightly different. My perspective would have advocated the position, attitude, and problems of the *manager*. Utilizing the contributions of early management theorists, the statement that a manager must (1) plan, (2) organize, (3) direct, and (4) control the work of others provides some insight into the nature and demands of his task. Thus, the question could be asked of the behaviorists, "How can you help me perform these tasks?" In general, as Schein's statement shows, the behaviorists have been most helpful in the "people-oriented" functions of *organizing* and *directing*. In *organizing*, we are concerned with establishing conditions necessary for effective accomplishment of goals. This would encompass designing jobs, obtaining personnel, differentiating structure, and developing effective interpersonal and intergroup relations. As Schein points out, the early behaviorists were industrial psychologists who provided direct assistance in selecting personnel to fit predetermined jobs. This approach has since been enlarged to include study and recommendations in such areas as job enrichment, socio-technical systems, and organization development. In similar fashion, the behaviorists have made substantial contributions with respect to the directing function. *Direction* can be defined broadly as the process of initiating action, and is sometimes termed "motivation." It is readily apparent that this is a subject of vital concern to behaviorists and perhaps does not receive the space in Schein's statement that it deserves. McGregor's theory was appropriately emphasized, but it, in turn, rests partially on the underpinning of Maslow's hierarchy of needs, showing a sequential development of human needs that the manager can utilize in motivating employees. To motivation can be added expectancy theory. The actual effect of a manager's attempt to motivate another person comes from that person's assessment of (1) the anticipated *value* of the perceived outcome of the behavior wanted by the manager, and (2) the strength of the *expectancy* that the act will actually result in a realization of the outcome.[3] The Maslow hierarchy may well explain that a particular person is currently interested in monetary rewards. But if that person does not believe that the higher output desired by the manager will actually bring about an appropriate increase in his compensation, it is not likely that he will be motivated. Thus, the behaviorist has aided the manager in assessing current employee needs, analyzing incentive schemes to ascertain how they

[1]Harold Koontz, "The Management Theory Jungle," *The Journal of the Academy of Management*, Vol. 4, No. 3 (December, 1961), pp. 174–188.

[2]Frederick Herzberg, *Work and the Nature of Man* (Cleveland: The World Publishing Company, 1966); and Melville Dalton, *Men Who Manage* (New York: John Wiley & Sons, Inc., 1959).

[3]Victor H. Vroom, *Work and Motivation* (New York: John Wiley & Sons, Inc., 1964), Chap. 2.

fit these needs, and developing educational and action programs that will demonstrate to the employee that the reward is effectively connected to the behavior desired.

Although Schein did devote a portion of his paper to information and financial control, most of it was concerned with detailing the contribution in the human resources area. Thus, most of the work has been in relation to the organizing and directing functions of management. The behaviorists have not been of equal help in the planning and control functions. To many managers who are concerned with immediate results, the effective execution of the planning and controlling functions will make a far greater contribution to success than those dealing with establishing and maintaining the human organization that carries out the necessary work. What *is* the necessary work? What should be the goal of the organization? Should a company manufacture this product and compete in that market? What technology should be used, and what should be developed in the future? And after undertaking operations, is the system under control? Is enough of the right information coming through soon enough to avoid disaster if not mediocrity?

Managers are all too willing to discuss the human elements of organization and deliver speeches about human values to civic groups, but many feel that the essentials to success lie elsewhere. In a survey of over 1,000 business managers, George England attempted to determine the goals that they deemed *important* as well as those regarded as *essential* to the success of an enterprise.[4] With respect to the goals of efficiency, productivity, profit, growth, and stability, from 60 to 80 per cent felt that these were *both* important and essential. With respect to the goal of employee welfare, 65 per cent felt it to be important, but only 20 per cent deemed it essential. There seems to be a kind of credibility gap between behaviorists and practicing managers. Despite the research that "proves" a cause-and-effect relationship between behaviorally recommended practices and managerially valued results such as productivity, managers tend to give only lip service to the findings of behavioral scientists. The cynical observer would conclude that behavioral practices that are pushed by labor unions or demanded by government laws or edicts will constitute the majority of behavioral contributions actually placed into practice.

This writer joins Edgar Schein in contending that the body of knowledge in the behavioral sciences has not been well marketed. Certainly the organization and direction of all types of institutions could be improved by a greater utilization of the behavioral sciences. There is a considerable overlap between the interests of the manager in productivity and efficiency, and the interests of individuals and groups in satisfaction and self-actualization. However, this writer is not among those who believe that there is a *complete* overlap, that what is best for the organization is best for the individual, or that a maximum concern for output can always be aligned with a maximum concern for people. But the overlap is far greater than many practicing managers believe. And it is up to the behaviorists to prove its existence through research, and to convince the manager of this fact through an appropriate marketing job. In the areas outside the overlap, if certain behavioral recommendations are to be implemented, it will require the external forces of unions and government, or perhaps the internal force of conscience and personal codes of ethics. And similarly, in other areas outside the overlap, if certain managerial demands are to be implemented, disciplinary action or the politics of compromise or purchase will be required.

In dealing with the human resources area, Schein emphasized developing an effective organization. Although Schein's itemization of behavioral con-

[4]George W. England, "Organizational Goals and Expected Behavior of American Managers," *The Journal of the Academy of Management*, Vol. 10, No. 2 (June, 1967), pp. 107–117.

tributions was comprehensive, it is important to recognize a philosophical difference between certain organization psychologists and organization sociologists. This difference was briefly referred to in the early paragraphs of this critique. The organization psychologists are perhaps better known to managers because of their consulting activities and their publication of articles in periodicals oriented toward business management. If one studies the theories of McGregor, Argyris, Likert, Herzberg, and Blake and Mouton, a common thread seems to emerge. As Schein stated, McGregor argued that basic human nature is much more consistent with theory *Y*.[5] Management should therefore structure the firm in a more participatory, trusting, and open manner. Specific suggestions would include abandoning time clocks, self-evaluation in merit rating, joint determination of job goals, and substituting consultative relationships for surveillance relationships between line and staff. Argyris, in his well-known maturation theory, recommended that organizations be restructured to reduce the clash of interests between mature personalities and traditionally managed institutions.[6] Specific recommendations included design of jobs that permit closure and self-actualization and increased subordinate participation in management decisions. Likert approached the problem by delineating alternative leadership styles ranging through coercive autocracy, benevolent autocracy, and consultative management, to the participative group.[7] The last style, he suggested, was most effective because it ensured the greatest degree of subordinate involvement. Similarly, in Blake and Mouton's Management Grid, the single style most recommended is the 9, 9 type wherein the manager exhibits a maximum concern for output simultaneously with a maximum concern for people.[8] The Herzberg motivator-hygiene theory contends that job content variables tend to elicit greater motivation than environmental factors.[9] Specific recommendations to the manager would include redesign of jobs to permit closure and self-determination of methods, pace, and quality. It should be readily apparent that these recommendations are entirely compatible with McGregor's theory *Y*, Argyris's maturation concept, Likert's participative group and supportive style, and the 9,9 position of Blake and Mouton. Visualize the type of organization that would be created—one that is open, honest, trusting, participative, problem-solving, supportive, self-controlling, and collegial.

The efforts in the field of organization development as described by Schein are in line with the above theories. The survey feedback method provides data concerning morale and management style with the implication that the manager alter his approach in the direction of the values of McGregor, Argyris, and the others. Team building, team training, job enlargement, job enrichment, and sensitivity training are similarly oriented toward recognition and development of theory *Y* personnel and relationships. Thus, the theories and implementations of this well-known group of organization psychologists are heavily normative in the direction of a more participative type of management. There seems to be only limited recognition of different types of personnel available and state of technology utilized.

On the other hand, a second group of behaviorists, who might be termed "organization sociologists," appear to be less normative and more tolerant of varying management approaches. Outstanding within this group would be James D. Thompson, Charles

[5]Douglas McGregor, *The Human Side of Enterprise* (New York: McGraw-Hill Book Company, Inc., 1960).

[6]Chris Argyris, *Personality and Organization* (New York: Harper & Row, Inc., 1957).

[7]Rensis Likert, *The Human Organization* (New York: McGraw-Hill Book Company, Inc., 1967).

[8]Robert R. Blake and Jane S. Mouton, *The Managerial Grid* (Houston: Gulf Publishing Company, 1964).

[9]Herzberg, *op. cit.*

Perrow, and Joan Woodward. Central to the approach of this group is an analysis of varying types of technology that are utilized to accomplish organization objectives. In considering the variety of activities and the degree of uncertainty regarding cause-and-effect relations in the performance of such activities, Perrow establishes two extreme types of technology—routine and nonroutine[10] and two hybrid, intermediate types—craft and engineering. The manager's task, according to Thompson, is the "Co-alignment of technology and task environment with a viable domain, and of organization design and structure appropriate to that domain."[11] Thus, the implication is that routine technology will demand more centralized and autocratic management approaches, whereas the nonroutine will call for the type of organizational action envisioned by the McGregor, Likert, Argyris group. The normative prescription of *this* group of behaviorists is to *co-align* the technology, structure, and decision strategies. Certainly, if one attempted to manage a research and development unit in an autocratic fashion, there would be little co-alignment. And in this the organization psychologists would agree. But if one attempted to manage an automobile assembly line in a participative fashion, there would *also* be little co-alignment. But here the organization psychologists perhaps would *not* agree. Although many behaviorists have criticized early classical management theorists for proposing the determination and enforcement of the "one best way" of operating, perhaps some of them are similarly vulnerable for proposing the one best management style or the one best type of interpersonal or inter-group relationship. In Woodward's famous study of business firms in England, she could make sense of her findings only when she correlated managerial practices with the various types of technology utilized.[12]

Again, one possible reason for the underutilization of the contributions of the behavioral sciences is the multiple and sometimes conflicting prescriptions for the practicing manager. Perhaps the implication is that management is still heavily an art, rather than a science, resting on multiple disciplines and fields of knowledge.

As the final point in this critique, this writer is in full agreement that the significant future contributions of the behavioral sciences should lie in the information and control areas of management. As suggested above, many managers view these aspects of their jobs as more connected to immediate success. But even in this regard, the behavioral contribution might be regarded as peripheral and only supplementary by the manager. For example, Schein suggests that the behaviorist approach can be used in establishing better information and decision support systems. He points out specifically that behavioral data should be collected to supplement the usual economic and technical data, and that too much technical and economic data might make higher levels of management become too centralized and autocratic toward lower levels. Although this behavioral attitude should assist in the creation of a more comprehensive and balanced system, the same credibility gap between manager and behaviorists still is likely to persist. The behavioral model implied in this case is a decentralized, participatory one.

Similarly, in the control area, the behaviorists point out the numerous negative consequences of particular control systems that are unbalanced, excessively tight, and enforced through overt or covert threats. Again, this is a valued and legitimate contribution, but its role is supplementary to the task of establishing the content and level of control standards to be administered by the

[10]Charles Perrow, *Organizational Analysis: A Sociological View* (Belmont, California: Wadsworth Publishing Company, Inc., 1970).

[11]James D. Thompson, *Organizations In Action* (New York: McGraw-Hill Book Company, Inc., 1967), p. 147.

[12]Joan Woodward, *Industrial Organization; Theory and Practice* (London: Oxford University Press, 1965).

manager. When we get to the actual process of how managers *utilize information* in making decisions of all types, whether behaviorally, classically, or otherwise oriented, this writer fully agrees that this "is one of the most promising and fruitful areas for future study and application."

DISCUSSION QUESTIONS

1. Why aren't behavioral science research findings used more fully by managers?
2. What sorts of assumptions about human nature are inherent in the scientific management, industrial sociologists', and industrial psychologists' conclusions about worker behavior?
3. Explain and discuss theory *X* and theory *Y*.
4. Trace the human relations movement from the early 1930's through the late 1960's. What should managers learn from this movement?
5. What is O.D.? How may it help management?
6. How can behavioral scientists help management in such practical activities as budgeting, financial control, information acquisition, and information processing?
7. How does Kolasa's idea of the behavioral sciences differ from Schein's?
8. Can many of the theories presented by Schein be categorized simply as directing and organizing, as Flippo suggests, so that behavioral approaches simply entail filling in the "empty" boxes of functionalism?
9. How important should employee "happiness" be? Give some reasons to support your answer.

3

The Contributions of Economics to Management

Lee E. Preston

Melvin H. Baker Professor of American Enterprise
School of Management
State University of New York at Buffalo

INTRODUCTION

The economy is always and everywhere an integral and important part of the environment of management. And the process of economizing is an equally central and critical part of management practice. Yet, practicing managers and students of management alike are often hard put to express precisely, even to themselves, their notions of the economy and of economizing, or to describe the elements of economic analysis that they are utilizing in routine operations and long-range plans. This chapter presents some key concepts of economic analysis and explains both their use and their usefulness in the practice of management. It may well happen that the reader—student or manager—will discover that he knew it all along; that is, that he has been ordinarily thinking and working with fundamental economic concepts. This should come as no surprise. Joseph Schumpeter, one of the most distinguished economists of this century, once described his discipline as a "body of refined commonsense."

Economics is sometimes defined as the study of the allocation of scarce means among competing ends. It is also the study of the economy—its components and structure, the way it works, and the way it changes over time. These two definitions are different, but quite consistent. The components of the economy are the means and ends themselves—resources, industries, products, users, and uses—and the economy works and changes by the continuous adjustment of means to ends and ends to means. Yet, to examine the key concepts of economics used in the study and practice of management, a useful distinction can be made among economic processes that take place *within* individual managerial units, processes that involve the *interaction* of several units, and processes that involve economic *aggregates* or concepts of the economy as a whole.

Following this distinction, our discussion of the contributions of economics to management will focus on three key concepts:

1. The concept of *economizing*, with the associated concepts of optimization and marginal analysis. Economizing takes place within an individual

managerial unit, which may be as small as a single individual or as large as an entire economy, if that economy is being "managed."

2. The concept of the *market mechanism,* the interaction among managerial units and private persons that generates forces of supply and demand for individual goods and services, and hence determines their prices and sales volumes in particular markets.
3. The concept of the *macro-economy,* the structure and operation of the total system within which individual economizing units and markets exist and operate. (The Greek word *macro* means "large"; hence, the term macro-economy refers to the economic system as a whole and to its aggregate parts.)

Economics and Management

Before developing each of the concepts in more detail, it may be well to point out the connection between economic analysis and other disciplines and techniques used in management. Economics provides neither a complete theory of human behavior nor a comprehensive guide to the practice of management. On the contrary, just as the sales of products and services depend on both (1) the customers' ability to pay (economic factors) and (2) their wants, tastes and cultural patterns (social and psychological factors), so the operation of individual managerial units and of society as a whole involves the interaction of economic and non-economic elements. Few managerial problems are entirely economic; equally few lack entirely an economic aspect. Furthermore, every managerial unit searches for efficient ways to accomplish its tasks, seeks to understand and control its relationships with other units in markets, and tries to anticipate and adapt to changes in the larger economy within which it exists, grows, or declines.

In spite of their intimate concern with economic problems, practicing managers and students of management are often put off by the abstractness, the over-simplification, the lack of specificity—and, hence, the apparent irrelevance—of economic analysis. These characteristics (except the irrelevance!) are in the nature of the discipline itself, not simply the results of faulty understanding or poor presentation. The fundamental concepts of economics were developed for analyzing general relationships, typical patterns, trends and directions of change, not for studying particular relationships, specific patterns, and the precise timing and amount of change. Hence, the student or manager concerned with a specific problem will usually have to go beyond elementary economic concepts in search of a solution. However, he will go *through* and beyond these concepts, not off in some other direction. Precise and particular solutions to specific economic problems are obtained by developing detailed models and relevant data within the framework of basic ideas and tools of analysis. The detailed optimization techniques and models of management science are essentially aids to applying the basic concept of economizing. They make it possible to apply the general and simple notion of "getting the most for your money" to complex and concrete problems that cannot be solved by intuition or general reasoning. Similarly, specific analyses of trends and forecasts of industrial, regional, or national economic activity are built on a framework of general concepts and analytical techniques relating to the market mechanism and the macro-economy. The practicing manager conducts routine operations, makes plans and decisions, on the basis of specific decision rules, precise models, and detailed forecasts appropriate to his own tasks and problems. However, if he wishes to understand how these particular tools and guides have come into being and why they are useful—and particularly if he wishes to choose among different techniques or pieces of information, to select the right model or the critical piece of data—then he will find himself turning back to fundamental economic concepts for understanding and insight.

ECONOMIZING

The term "economizing" is used in common speech to convey the idea of "getting the most for your money." This is also the essence of its meaning in economic analysis, and in both usages two significant ideas are involved. One is that the benefit obtained from a given expenditure of money or effort is "worth it"—i.e., that what is gained is preferred to what is given up. The second idea is that the cost incurred is the *least* that can be incurred to obtain this particular benefit; or, alternatively, that the benefit is the *greatest* that can be obtained for the given cost. Concepts and techniques for comparing costs with cost (to find the *minimum*), benefits with benefits (to find the *maximum*), and costs with benefits (to find the *optimum*, or "best," combination of the two) constitute the core of managerial economics. The development of detailed models for applying these concepts to specific and complex problems of planning and production is a principal activity in management science. In this chapter we focus on the basic and elementary notion of economizing, which reappears in complex and sophisticated forms in other parts of this volume.

Marginal Analysis

The key to the concept of economizing—and hence to the associated concepts of maximization, minimization and optimization—is the *marginal analysis*. An example will illustrate this simple but fundamental idea. Imagine that there is a person (we refer to him as a "manager," although he has little to manage at the moment) with a small amount of money (his "capital") who wishes to preserve or increase his capital over time. Imagine that he is offered one and only one means of employing his capital: He can purchase units of X at $2 each and sell them at $1 each, in unlimited quantities for an unlimited period. Will he choose to do this? Evidently not, since it would exhaust his capital, and his goal was to preserve or increase it. (Notice that the goal *and* the alternatives determine the decision; if his goal were to decrease his capital, then the decision would be reversed.) Now, what if the manager were given the opportunity to purchase units of X at $1 each and resell them at $2 each, again in unlimited quantities for an unlimited period? Evidently, since, by assumption, no other opportunities are available to him, he would willingly start buying and reselling and, indeed, would be expected to buy and resell as many units as possible, turning over his capital as rapidly as possible, so long as the game is allowed to continue or until he acquired all the capital in the world.

Obviously, neither of these imaginary situations is typical of managerial decision-making; yet, there are elements of both in most management problems. On the one hand, there are possible activities in which the benefits—in this case, sales revenues—will exceed the costs; on the other hand, the difference between revenue and cost is not the same in all possible activities, nor is it necessarily constant in any one activity regardless of the scale of operation or the length of time over which it is conducted. The function of marginal analysis is to discriminate between profitable and unprofitable activities, and between more profitable and less profitable ones.

Imagine now that our manager has chosen the second activity—buying for $1 and selling for $2—but finds that, in fact, he cannot purchase and resell units of *X* at these prices in unlimited quantities. It may be that the first units may be bought at $1, but as his purchases increase he has to pay higher prices—$1.25, $1.50, and so on. Or, it may be that only a few units can be sold at $2, and to sell more he must accept $1.75, $1.50, or less. Or, finally, he finds that buying prices rise and sales prices fall at the same time. Whichever of these conditions prevails, the manager can pursue his goal (maintaining or increasing his capital) by following the same rule he used to reject the alternative of buying for $2 and selling for $1, and to choose to buy for $1 and sell for $2, in the first place. That is, he can determine whether each additional transaction, purchase and resale, maintains or increases his capital. So long as it does, and assuming no alternative activities are available, then he should continue to buy and resell. When the situation is reversed, so that an additional transaction will leave him with less capital than he had before, then he should stop the activity altogether.

Optimization

Our manager's behavior presents a simple example of the application of marginal analysis. The additional cost involved in each transaction—that is, the price of each additional unit of *X* bought for resale—is referred to as *marginal cost*. The additional revenues obtained from each successive sale are referred to as *marginal revenue*. In both cases the term *"marginal"* indicates a change in an aggregate (i.e., in *total* cost or *total* revenue) resulting from a particular transaction or decision. Notice that since our manager is buying and selling additional units of *X* at specific prices—not paying a higher price for *all* units in order to obtain larger quantities, or asking a lower price for *all* units in order to sell more—the marginal cost of an additional unit is simply the price paid for it, and the marginal revenue is the resulting price received. What our manager discovered is that he will achieve the greatest possible increase in his capital (i.e., maximize profits) by making all transactions for which marginal revenue exceeds marginal cost. This is the marginal decision rule: *To maximize profits, or minimize losses, operate at the point at which (rising) marginal cost equals (declining) marginal revenue.*

Stated in this form, the marginal decision rule is always and forever true; there are no exceptions. The rule does not, however, assure the manager that costs and revenues have been appropriately identified and measured. Nor does it tell him that he should attempt to maximize profit, rather than aim at some other goal; nor that the profit available in this particular activity is greater than that available from some other venture that he might undertake. It does tell him, however, that when cost and revenue are appropriately specified in relation to incremental decisions about some ongoing activity, then equality between the marginal changes in costs and revenues will result in the greatest difference (profits) between total costs and revenues for the activity as a whole.

Marginal analysis is usually taught in elementary economics as we have illustrated it—in terms of the costs and revenues of an entire managerial unit, a "firm" in the usual terminology. However, actual applications of marginal analysis in management usually involve only small segments of a large and complex operation. In these applications, there are two common pitfalls. One is the difficulty of identifying precisely the costs and revenues (or "benefits," which may take the form of cost-reductions) associated with a particular marginal change in operations. The other is the problem of sub-optimization, the possibility that the optimal solutions to each individual problem in a complex activity will, taken together, constitute a less than optimal solution for the activity as a whole. This latter problem is a principal concern of the systems analysis branch of management science. Identifying appropriate cost and revenue elements for applying the marginal analysis has, however, long been a major factor in economics.

Cost Analysis

With respect to costs, the critical distinction is between the costs that change and the costs that do not change as a result of the particular marginal decision under consideration. Thus, if one is considering expanding an ongoing activity, achieving a higher rate of operation with the same facilities and equipment, then only the direct costs of the added production—labor, materials, and the like—may be *marginal* to the decision at hand. However, if the increased rate of operations wears out equipment faster, causing shortages and breakdowns or additional costs for non-productive work and services, then these costs are also *marginal* to this decision. Finally, if additional equipment or facilities or additional working capital is required, then these costs also must be included in the marginal cost of the expansion.

These distinctions among relevant types of costs are often discussed in economics in relation to time. In the "short run," some costs are *fixed* and others are *variable*; hence, marginal adjustments in operations in the "short run" can give rise *only* to changes in *variable* costs. An additional distinction is sometimes made between *direct* and *indirect* costs, the former being "directly" associated with the rate of operation of the activity, whereas the latter continue at about the same level regardless of fluctuations in operating rates (production wages may be direct costs and administrative salaries indirect costs, for example). Each of these distinctions—and their many variations and refinements—is valid for some specific purposes. The danger, however, is that cost categories established to serve one purpose will be used uncritically to serve another, so that the true marginal costs associated with a particular decision will not be taken into consideration. The critical question to raise is: Which costs will be affected, and in what way, by the decision to be made. All the costs that will be affected are *marginal* for purposes of that decision, however "fixed" or "variable," "direct" or "indirect" they may be for some other accounting or analytical purposes.

Revenue Analysis

Similar problems arise with respect to identifying revenues or benefits associated with a particular marginal decision. Again, in elementary economics the concept of marginal revenue is usually presented in relation to the sales price of the single product of a managerial unit or "firm." This mode of presentation illustrates an even more general point: Obtaining additional revenues (or reducing costs) from some marginal adjustment within an activity may also involve the loss of some revenues (or increase in some costs) that might otherwise have been obtained. It is the net change in total revenue (or cost)—taking both the gain and the loss into account—that constitutes the true marginal revenue (or cost). The usual illustration of this proposition is as follows: Imagine that our manager now operates under conditions such that all units of X he offers for sale must be offered at the *same* price. Suppose that he can sell two units of X for \$2 each, but an additional unit at only \$1.50. If he sells only the first two units, the marginal revenue gained from the second is \$2, since no corresponding loss is involved. However, if he wishes to sell three units, he must offer *all three* at a price of \$1.50 each. The marginal revenue of the third unit is therefore its own sales price, \$1.50, *minus* the fifty cents he has lost on each of the other units by reducing their prices. Hence, marginal revenue for the third unit is \$1.50 — \$1.00 = \$.50. Evidently, if he is purchasing units of X for \$1, he will be less well off by selling three units than by selling only two, even though the sales price of the third unit is greater than its own direct cost. (His total profits are \$2.00 and \$1.50, respectively.)

The general relationship between sales price and marginal revenue is usually illustrated in a diagram such as Figure 1A, in which the various total numbers of units that might be sold at various prices (but the *same* price for all units sold, in each case) are shown by the line D (demand), and the associated marginal revenue by the line MR. If marginal costs (MC) are constant at a level indicated by the vertical distance OC, then profits are maximized when a price indicated by the vertical distance OP is charged for a quantity indicated by the horizontal distance OQ—the quantity at which $MR = MC$. The same set of relationships is shown in total terms in Figure 1B, drawn to a vertical scale one-tenth that of Figure 1A (compare the vertical distance OC on the two diagrams). Here an amount of fixed cost, $O'F$, is also shown; these costs affect the *amount* of total profit, but not the price and quantity at which profit is maximized. (Costs that effect the MR/MC relationship are not truly fixed!) Total costs, which equal the fixed cost ($O'F$) plus the marginal cost of each unit (OC), and total revenue are also shown. The difference between them, total profit, is clearly greatest at quantity $O'Q$ ($= OQ$), where there is a profit indicated by the vertical

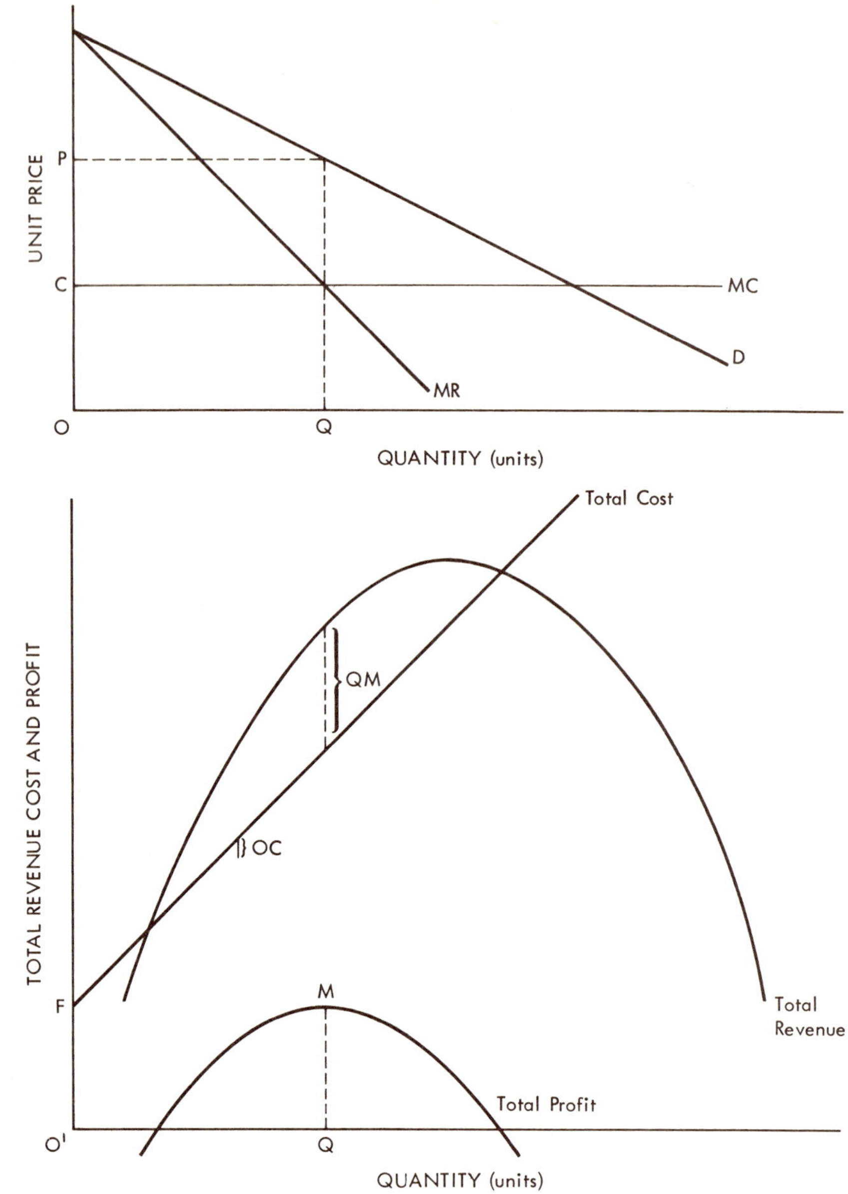

FIGURE 1. Marginal Analysis of Revenue, Cost and Profit

distance *QM*. The diagram also clearly shows that the profit-maximizing price and output have no connection with the point of maximum revenue (the peak of the total revenue curve), the point of minimum cost (which would be zero output), nor the minimum levels of marginal or average unit cost. (Marginal cost is the same for all units in this example. Average unit cost—total cost divided by the number of units produced—is not shown, but would decline continuously as output increased, since the fixed costs would be spread over larger and larger numbers of units and there are no offsetting increases in variable costs.)

Opportunity Cost

One final notion requiring attention in connection with the idea of economizing is *opportunity cost,* or the *trade-off* among alternatives. Imagine that our manager has, instead of a stock of money capital, a stock of raw material, *M,* which he can turn into either of two products, *X* or *Y,* both of which he can subsequently sell. Some of the material is better for making *X* and some is better for making *Y*; but all of it can be turned into either, and various combinations of both *X* and *Y* could be produced. Imagine that his complete range of alternatives—the different combinations of *X* and of *Y* that can be produced from the given stock, *M,* of raw material—are shown in Figure 2. How shall he decide what to produce?

The answer comes, again, from the marginal analysis. The critical balance is between the marginal trade-off between *X* and *Y* in production, on the one hand, and the trade-off (or exchange rate) between them in the market—i.e., the ratio between their prices—on the other. Thus, if our man-

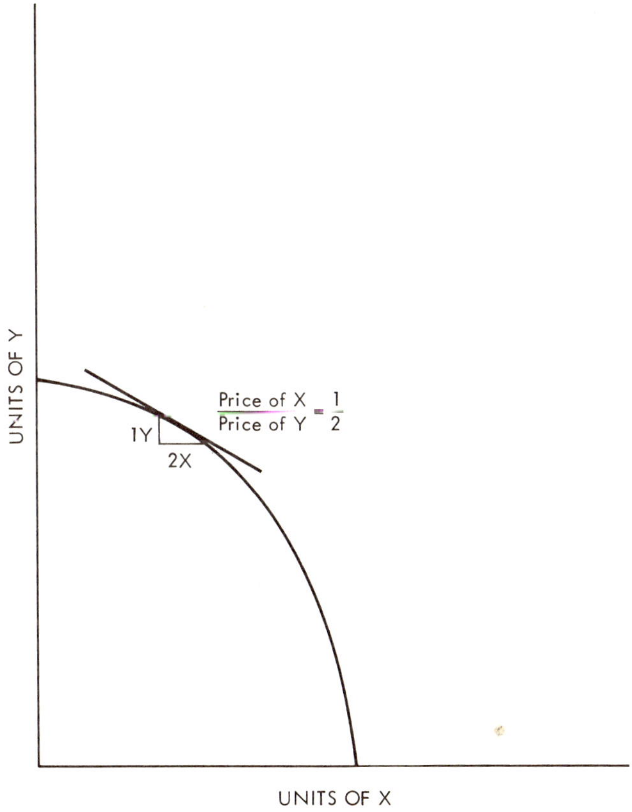

FIGURE 2. Marginal Analysis of Opportunity Costs

ager can produce two units of X or one unit of Y out of a particular batch of raw material, it will pay him to produce X if the price of X is one-half or more of the price of Y, and it will pay him to produce Y if the price of Y is twice or more the price of X. When the trade-off between X and Y in production is the same as in the market—the "opportunity costs" or "marginal rates of substitution" are equal—then the optimal combination of X and Y has been determined. Producing this combination of X and Y and selling them in the market will yield the greatest possible profit for the manager from his given stock of raw material.

Economizing Goals

One final word about economizing. The practice is so commonplace, the terminology so ingrained, the decision rules and their implications so timeworn and familiar, that one scarcely thinks to question them. Yet it cannot escape notice that the principal implication of the most familiar economizing decision rules is that the returns to money capital (i.e., profits) should be maximized. The logic of this is that money capital is a fundamentally scarce and flexible resource, which can be turned into other productive factors—labor, facilities, materials, or whatever—through market transactions. Yet the occasional appearance of some other resource-economizing decision rule—such as the rules aimed at optimizing revenue per unit of selling space in retailing, or per unit of raw material in extractive industries—suggests that the principles involved might be applied to many other managerial variables. The quantification of costs and benefits—at least to the extent of "more" and "less," "better" and "worse"—will still be required, but the traditional economizing rules can be adapted to many purposes other than profit maximization within the hypothetical "firm." Indeed, the whole Planning-Programming-Budgeting-System (PPBS) that has revolutionized the reporting and decision-making process within the federal government and many states during the past decade can be seen as a vast application of the basic economizing principle, and the problem of economizing the natural environment itself may provide the next extension of this simple but useful idea.

THE MARKET MECHANISM

In any large and complex economy, some means must be found to coordinate the activities of the various specialized managerial units among themselves and in relation to the wants and needs of private persons and households. Diverse activities under a single management can be coordinated administratively—indeed, the reporting procedures and decision rules of complex organizations are designed specifically to achieve this coordination—but activities that are separately owned and managed can be coordinated only by political compulsion or through the market mechanism. The market mechanism is, in fact, such an efficient and comprehensive means of adapting resources to uses and sacrifices to rewards that many internal administrative procedures are designed to simulate, within a single organization, the results that would be obtained in perfectly functioning markets.

A market is a system of information and interaction between supply and demand—between cost and scarcity, on one hand, and usefulness, preference, and ability to pay, on the other. The market mechanism is the adjustment process through which potential sellers communicate their willingness to sell, potential buyers their willingness to purchase, and—from the interaction of sellers with sellers, buyers with buyers, and sellers and buyers with one another—market prices and transactions quantities are determined.

Supply and Demand

The usual presentation of this idea assumes the existence of a group of potential buyers who are willing to purchase various amounts of a particular product (*X*) at various prices. If the number of buyers, their incomes and tastes, and the prices of other products all remain constant during the period of analysis, then it is usually assumed that the buyers will, in the aggregate, purchase larger quantities of *X* at lower prices than at higher prices. These assumptions give rise to the "demand curve," labeled *D* in Figure 3. We also assume the existence of a group of potential sellers who are willing to make available the product (*X*) in various quantities at various prices. If they are willing to supply larger quantities at higher prices

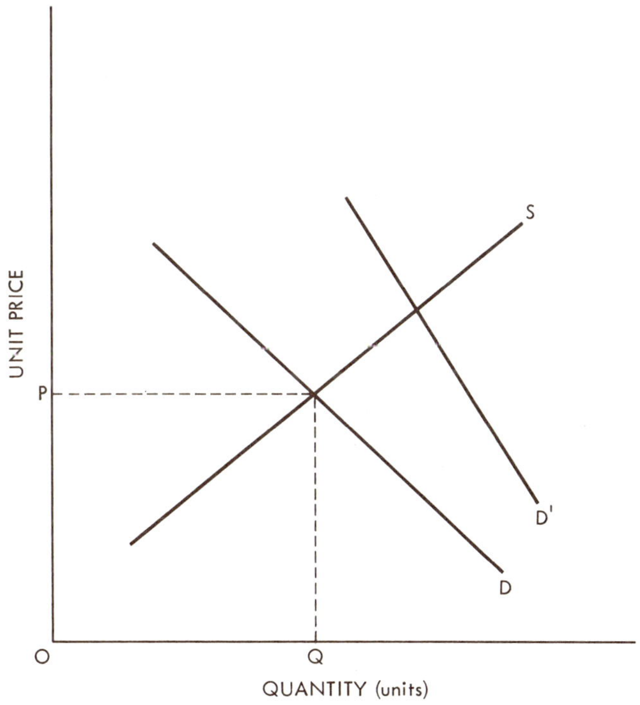

FIGURE 3. The Market Mechanism: Supply and Demand

than at lower ones (either because costs increase or because the higher price is more profitable, so that they shift out of other activities and into the production of X—recall the previous discussion of "opportunity cost"), then we obtain the rising supply curve labeled S in Figure 3.

A glance at Figure 3 suggests at once that the intersection of the supply and demand curves must determine the selling price (OP) and trading quantity (OQ) in the market. Since everything that is bought must be sold, and vice-versa, the quantity sold and the quantity purchased must be the same. Furthermore, since the quantity OQ would not be made available by suppliers at any price less than OP, nor would this quantity be purchased by the demanders at any price greater than OP, OP itself must be the price at which both demanders and suppliers are willing to trade (buy and sell) the quantity OQ. If the price were higher, suppliers would wish to sell more than demanders would be willing to buy; if lower, then the reverse. This analysis assumes, of course, that all sellers sell and all buyers buy at the *same* price; there are not different prices for different transactions. This is not a far-fetched assumption if there is open communication and information in the market; why should any buyer pay more, or any seller take less, than the lowest (highest) price available for the standard product? Of course, if the products are not standardized—if different varieties are available and different user needs are to be served—then there may be an array of related prices (and related supply and demand curves) reflecting these differences. Notice that there are potential sellers and potential buyers who are excluded from making transactions by the market mechanism; their selling prices are too high or their purchase prices are too low.

This simple model of the market mechanism deals with a single period, in which supply and demand forces come into being and interact in order to yield a specific trading quantity and a market-clearing price. In fact, of course, most actual market relationships persist over time, and the process of action and reaction between demand and supply—and among potential demanders and potential suppliers, separately—occurs continuously rather than in discrete time intervals. Market equilibrium, as depicted here, is observed only briefly, if at all. Instead, in actual markets we observe a series of continuing adjustments of supply and demand to each other—and continuous change in the underlying determinants of supply and demand themselves—so that *changes* in prices and sales quantities over time are more common than stability. This does not invalidate the concept of the market mechanism as an analytical device, but rather strengthens its importance as a tool for anticipating the direction and amount of change in price and quantity that can be expected as a result of changing circumstances.

An understanding of the market mechanism and of the underlying factors determining supply and demand is useful for management, not because it provides the basis for routine internal decision rules (which it does not), but because it provides a basis for understanding what is happening—and what is likely to happen—in the many different market environments within which each individual managerial unit operates. In order to illustrate these applications, we consider three aspects of market analysis: (1)

demand determinants and the concept of elasticity; (2) the relationship between costs and prices in competitive markets; and (3) the effect of differences in market structure and practices on the operation of the market mechanism.

Demand Determinants and Elasticity

The determinants of market demand for a particular product or service are usually analyzed under four headings: (1) the number of potential customers (individuals, families, firms, etc.), including their characteristics, locations, and organizational structures; (2) the ability of potential customers to purchase, as determined by their incomes, assets, and expectations; (3) their needs, wants, tastes and preferences; and (4) the quality and variety of alternative products and services that these potential customers might purchase, and their respective prices. *Given* all of these factors—none of which is under the direct control of a managerial unit operating in the particular market—the willingness of potential customers to buy various quantities of merchandise under various conditions of price, advertising, quality, packaging, or whatever, constitutes the "market demand" for the product or service in question.

The significant managerial question—and the subject of all serious market research—is: How responsive is demand, both in total and with respect to individual items or brands, *either* to changes in the underlying demand determinants that are beyond managerial control *or* to changes in managerial variables such as price and promotional activity? The responsiveness of demand to changes in discrete and qualitative variables—such as the expansion of a geographic market because of transportation developments or the introduction of a new advertising campaign—is analysed in terms of *shifts* in the entire demand curve. We ask: How much more or less will be purchased, at every possible price, under the new conditions than under the old? The curve D' in Figure 3 illustrates a *shift* in demand. (A shift in demand may also involve a change in the shape of the demand curve, of course.)

The responsiveness of demand to changes in continuous quantative variables—such as price, promotional expenditures, and the incomes of potential customers—is analysed in terms of the concept of *elasticity*. *Elasticity* refers to the relative responsiveness of sales and purchase volume (either in quantity units or in monetary value) to changes in demand-determining variables. Thus, we speak of the elasticity of demand with respect to price, with respect to income (of customers), with respect to advertising expenditures, and so forth. (The concept of elasticity may also be applied to supply conditions and other variables of interest in managerial analysis.) The elasticity of demand with respect to price is formally defined as:

$$\text{elasticity} = \frac{\text{relative change in quantity purchased (sold)}}{\text{relative change in price}}$$

If a reduction of, say, 10 per cent in price leads to an expansion of more than 10 per cent in sales, so that the value of the ratio is greater than 1, then we speak of demand as being "elastic"—i.e., highly responsive—with respect to price; if the respective changes are such that the value of the ratio is less than 1, then demand is said to be "inelastic"—i.e., unresponsive. The same type of analysis can be made with respect to customer income, marketing expenditures, and other variables. It is not uncommon for demand for a particular product to be inelastic with respect to price but elastic with respect to income (this is generally thought to be true of the demand for automobiles, for example); or for total *market* demand to be price-inelastic, but *brand* demand to be price-elastic (as in the case of gasoline, for example). The concept of elasticity is thus useful for describing a broad and complex set of demand characteristics and for distinguishing among the demand-responsiveness of various products and services to changes in demand-determining variables.

Cost and Price

The operation of the market mechanism under conditions of competition carries with it the implication that the costs necessary to provide products and services in the market will determine their prices, and, conversely, that prices in the market will determine the costs that are incurred. The costs that determine prices are, of course, all the costs that are required to maintain the flow of products and services into the market over time. Total revenues obtained from sales (that is, prices multiplied by sales quantities) must recompense suppliers for all these costs, including the cost of their own time, effort, risk-taking, and so on, or else they will shift out of this market and into some other line of activity. At the same time, the prevalence of a certain price level in a market in effect "justifies" incurring an equivalent level of costs. If price were substantially above costs, we should expect supply to increase and costs to rise (as, for example, by increased expenditures for advertising) until (1) the price fell to some lower level and/or (2) the price-cost difference was eliminated by cost increases. These latter costs may be said to be price-determined rather than price-determining.

These general relationships between price and cost under competitive conditions do not, however, imply any necessary relationship between price and cost in particular transactions or at particular points of time. On the contrary, unusually well-situated sellers may regularly obtain abnormally large profits, whereas others barely break even or, incurring losses, are forced to abandon the market altogether. Some buyers may pay much less than the maximum they would be willing to pay for products and services, whereas others may have to pay almost exactly what the products and services are "worth" to them. And both groups of buyers (or sellers) may pay (receive) the same *monetary* price, of course. Competition in markets does not assure that everyone will be equally well off, nor that the array of products and services obtained will be the largest or best that could be produced under the circumstances. It simply assures that all buyers and sellers will have the opportunity to participate in the market if they choose to do so, and that the market results—the prices established and quantities traded—will reflect their mutual willingness to engage in this activity rather than some other one.

Market Structure and Practices

The stress laid on the role of competition in analyzing the market mechanism immediately suggests a question: What if competition does not prevail? The opposite of competition is "monopoly," a market situation in which a single supplier confronts a unique segment of demand, which no other supplier can satisfy. Complete monopolies of any importance are relatively rare in the U.S. economy, and are generally subject to government regulation when they are allowed to exist at all (as in the case of telephone service, for example). At the same time, there are monopoly elements present in many markets. Most sellers deal with at least a few customers who have a particularly strong demand for their products, whether for reasons of taste, location, or whatever. With respect to those customers, the particular supplier may be something of a monopolist. Similarly, some customers may have a clearly preferred position vis-à-vis their suppliers—because, for example, of the large volume or continuity of their purchases—so that they are, to some extent, monopoly-buyers (technically, "monopsonists"). Furthermore, the granting of patents, the advertising of brand names, and special advantages of location or experience may create partial monopoly (or monopsony) positions for many firms and managerial units in particular situations.

The presence of monopoly eliminates the essential connection between cost and price that is established by the market mechanism under competition. Instead, the monopolist—to the extent that his monopoly position permits—may establish whatever relationship between cost and price that best suits his own goals. He may maximize profits in the short run, in terms of a "given" set of demand conditions; or he may place primary emphasis on long-run demand expansion, technological change, or even the quiet life. The point is that the monopolist has a wider range of discretion both in setting goals and in choosing means to attain them than the firm operating under conditions of keen competition. The competitive firm cannot choose to price above the market, no matter how much it might wish to do so, because it will make no sales at such a price; nor can it choose to incur additional costs—unless it possesses some special offsetting advantages or all of its competitors also incur them—because such costs cannot be recovered out of market revenues.

It is important to draw a distinction between the presence of certain marketing practices, such as branding and price-posting, from the presence of monopoly. Although both the ability to distinguish the seller's own product from those of others and the ability to "name" the price are necessary conditions for monopoly, they are also quite consistent with competition. Indeed, in a market served by many sellers, their "naming" of price—each for his own product—serves to increase the amount of information available to potential buyers and thus to heighten the competition among the sellers themselves. Under such circumstances, market price levels are determined not simply by the sellers' price-postings but also by the response of the buyers to the alternatives available. Furthermore, competitive product differentiation—which requires brand or firm identification—can be a source of increased satisfaction to purchasers, providing greater adaptation to individual needs and the pleasure of variety and choice itself, as well as the basis of monopoly advantages or competitive waste.

THE MACRO-ECONOMY

The macro-economy is an abstraction. Everyone has had experience with the commonsense aspects of economizing, and has been at least an unwitting participant in the operation of markets, but no one has ever encountered the macro-economy directly. It exists only in the mind. The myriad firms, households, governments, and institutions whose buying and selling, hiring and firing, and saving and spending activities account for the flow of activity in the macro-economy are real enough. But the separate activities of all of these cannot be simply "added up" in order to obtain a useful view of the complete system. On the contrary, the gross grand total of all the individual activities occurring within an economy is a rather irrelevant statistic. For example, if *A* produces (from scratch) ten units of *X* and sells them to *B*, we might say that the output of the economy in which *A* and *B* are operating is increased by ten units of *X*. However, if *B* resells the same units to *C*, the output of the economy is either the same as it was before, or greater, at most, by the amount of service and value that *B* contributed by holding the units of *X* and making the resale. In no sense has total output increased by twenty units, although two participants in the economy have made sales of ten units each. The whole—the macro-economy—is not precisely the sum of its parts.

The concept of the macro-economy as an operating system with component elements—elements that are different from the individual persons and firms, products and transactions, that account for actual economic activity—is a relatively new idea. It was foreshadowed by Adam Smith in the famous dictum: "The annual labour of every nation is the fund which originally supplies it with all the necessaries and conveniences of life. . . ." This, the opening sentence of the *Wealth of Nations*, was the grave maker for the mercantilist idea that national wealth was measured by the accumulation of precious metals in the treasury. However, Smith's insight did not carry him all the way to a conception of the macro-economy as something other than the sum of individual activities, and the nineteenth-century economists fell back to the study of these separate activities themselves—the analysis of prices and markets. The role of money in the economy, and the study of the overall price level, also commanded attention, but lack of requisite data and statistical techniques prevented the development of a coherent analysis.

Modern macro-economic policy—the attempt to "manage" the macro-economy—had its formal beginnings in this country even before the modern concept of macro-economy itself was fully developed. It was well recognized in the nineteenth century that the availability of money and credit through the banking system played an obvious role in the level of activity throughout the economy, although precise concepts and measures of that level were not yet available. The reactions of banking institutions to business failures, falling prices, and defaulted loans were known to spread the effects of economic disturbances from the affected industry and region to other parts of the economy. Awareness of these relationships reached a peak during the financial panic of 1909, and the attempt to reduce the destabilizing impact of adjustments within the banking system on the economy as a whole led to the establishment of the Federal Reserve System in 1913. Unfortunately, neither the understanding of the macro-economy nor the powers of the Federal Reserve were sufficient to accomplish the purpose at that time. Further conceptual development occurred under the pressure of events—the mounting European economic problems of the 1920's and the worldwide depression of the 1930's. During these years, the British economist John Maynard Keynes and his chief American disciple, Professor Alvin Hansen, began the development of a new framework of analysis that underlies the modern conception of the macro-economy.

The Keynesian Model

The Keynesian conception was that the total output of the economy, which we now think of in statistical terms as the "gross national product" (GNP), was determined by the interaction of aggregate demand and aggregate supply. Aggregate demand in the economy was said to consist of four principal elements: Consumption expenditures (C); investment expenditures (I); government expenditures (G); and the net export-import balance (X-M). Aggregate supply was analyzed in terms of the disposition of income by suppliers (including suppliers of labor, capital, and facilities, of course, as well as of goods and services). Their total income was either consumed (C), saved (S), or paid in taxes (T). Hence, since for a single time period aggregate supply had to equal aggregate demand, the following equality held:

$$C + I + G = \text{GNP} = C + S + T$$

aggregate demand = total output of the economy = aggregate supply.

According to the Keynesian analysis, instability developed within an economy whenever the independent decisions and actions of individuals, firms, and governments failed to generate consistent levels of aggregate supply and aggregate demand. If total demand was greater than the total supply—as determined by suppliers' own intentions to consume, save, and pay taxes—then there would be pressure for the level of economic activity and employment to increase in order to meet the excess demand. If the economy were already at a state of "full employment," so that no further increases in output were possible without overtime and shortages, then prices (i.e., the overall price level) would rise. If the excess of demand over supply persisted continuously over time, then chronic inflation would ensue.

Similarly, if aggregate demand were less than the total suppliers had intended to supply, then in the short run they would be forced to "save" (i.e., to hold resources rather than send them on to final uses—the direct analogy is unintended inventory accumulation). Suppliers would react to this development by reducing production and employment—and hence reducing both their own demand for goods and services and eliminating the demand that would have been generated by the wages and salaries they would have otherwise paid—until the intended level of supply was the same as the level of demand. However, since supply reductions lead to demand reductions, and demand reductions to supply reductions, the downward adjustment process could continue until a very low level of economic activity, a high level of unemployment, and a deep depression were reached. In these terms, the Keynesian concepts appeared to explain the economic conditions prevailing during the 1930's better than any analysis that had previously been available.

Figure 4 is a conventional diagram of the Keynesian model of the macro-economy. Aggregate supply is shown on the horizontal axis and aggregate demand on the vertical. The aggregate supply function is shown as a 45° line (reflecting the assumption that supply adapts to demand) up to the level of full employment (*OY′*) beyond which it is vertical. Aggregate demand is shown as the sum of *C*, *I*, and *G*. (The foreign trade elements are neglected here.) An equilibrium level of GNP is indicated by the distance (vertical or horizontal) *OY*. Possible discrepancies between the levels of aggregate supply and demand that might be generated by the independent actions of individuals and firms within the economy are shown by the two

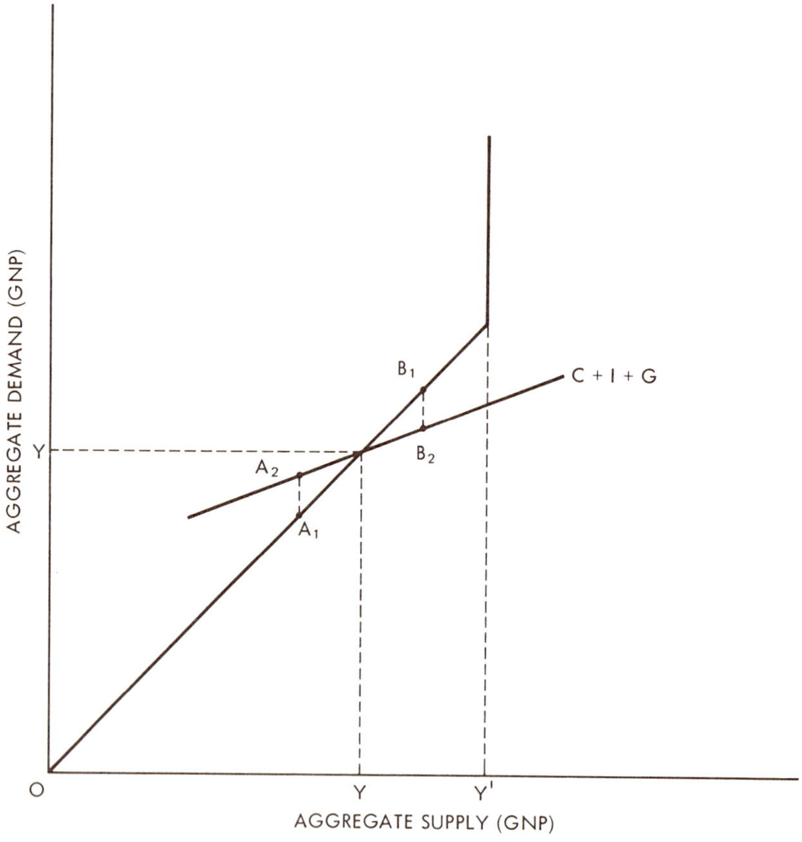

FIGURE 4. The Macro-Economy

"gaps" labeled $A_1 - A_2$ and $B_1 - B_2$. The discrepancy between A_1 and A_2 is usually referred to as an "inflationary" or "expansionary" gap. If aggregate demand (A_2) is greater than aggregate supply (A_1), then there will be a tendency for output and employment—and perhaps prices—to rise. Conversely, the discrepancy between B_1 and B_2 is termed a "deflationary" or "recessionary" gap, because if aggregate supply (B_1) exceeds aggregate demand (B_2), there will be a tendency for output and employment—and perhaps prices—to fall. Any attempt to increase total output beyond OY', the full employment level, will, of course, result only in price increases.

The level of employment and total output in the economy as a whole play the same role in the Keynesian analysis as the level of price and output in the analysis of market supply and demand. That is, employment and output adjust to differences or changes in the levels of aggregate supply and demand, just as market prices and output adjust to differences or changes in market supply and demand. And the contrast between the two models is equally clear. In the model of the market mechanism, adjustments of price and output are of equal importance in bringing about equilibrium. By contrast, in the macro-economic model, price adjustments take on a clearly secondary role. If aggregate demand exceeds aggregate supply, as long as the economy is short of full employment, price adjustments should occur only to the extent necessary to "signal" the existence of unsatisfied demand, and in specific "bottleneck" situations; the principal response should be increased output. At the full employment level, no additional output can be forthcoming; hence, if demand is still excessive, the price level will rise. However, this is only a numerical adjustment; the real economy remains as before.

Complications

Three decades of experience with policy-making and analysis have produced a number of qualifications and extensions of the elementary macroeconomic model outlined here. One of these has to do with the dual role of investment as a source of both immediate increases in demand (the principal Keynesian emphasis) and permanent increases in potential supply. Continuous increments of investment, which often also include technological change, expand the productive capacity of the economy. Hence, an economy in which a high rate of output expansion is desired *must* carry on a high rate of investment (and a correspondingly lower rate of consumption). At the same time, an economy in which high levels of investment occur as a result of independent decisions by various individuals and firms *must* also achieve a high level of demand expansion if chronic under-capacity operations and compensating long-term declines in investment and total demand are to be avoided.

A second qualification to the Keynesian analysis focuses on the role of the interest rate and the money supply. Without getting into highly technical definitions, it is sufficient to say that the money supply includes currency and bank deposits subject to ready access. The Keynesian macroeconomic model is cast in terms of "real" goods and services, which are valued in money terms only for convenience. It was thought that the total money supply would adjust itself to the level required to meet the various monetary needs of the economy—transactions, risk-protection, etc. The interest rate—being the "price" of money—played a correspondingly minor role in the analysis. Critics of this viewpoint—most notably, Professor Milton Friedman—have stressed the importance of the money supply as an independent variable, causing inflation when it increases too rapidly and recession when it expands too slowly, and the power of changes in interest rates to influence the level of investment.

Wage and Price Adjustments

A more general qualification to the role of the Keynesian model as the basis for analysis of the modern U.S. economy has to do with the speed and uniformity of output, employment, and price and wage adjustments throughout the system. The minor role of price changes in the Keynesian system was, as mentioned, based on the assumption that only slight price increases would be required to "signal" an excess of demand over supply, and thus to bring about output responses. Experience during the long period of economic expansion since World War II has revealed that price and wage increases follow a logic of their own, and that "bottlenecks"—situations in which supply does *not* respond rapidly to demand—are perhaps more characteristic of the modern economy than had earlier been realized. Hence, price changes generated, as expected, by temporary shortages or capacity limitations, may lead only slowly to increased investment and output, but very rapidly to "sympathetic" wage and price changes both in the affected sector of the economy and in others, and hence to "waves" of price and wage changes even while the economy as a whole is operating well below full employment levels. Furthermore, if there are also "bottlenecks" on the employment side—either in the form of limited access to jobs (because, for example, of unionization) or lack of necessary skills—then even very considerable increases in demand and wages may be insufficient to draw significantly greater numbers of people into steady and remunerative work.

Macro-Economic Policy

One reason why implications and deficiencies in the simple Keynesian model have become clear is that it has been for a quarter-century the basis of official national economic policy in the U.S., and to some extent in other countries as well. During World War II there was considerable concern that the U.S., and with it the non-Communist world, would lapse back into the economic stagnation and unemployment of the Great Depression as soon as hostilities ceased. The policy implication of the Keynesian analysis—that full employment and prosperity could be achieved if aggregate demand were maintained at high levels—had been generally confirmed by experience with large government expenditures during wartime. A political concensus was reached that, at a minimum, the analysis of the overall state of the economy and the consideration of policies designed to improve or maintain it should be made a matter of formal national policy. Hence, Congress passed the Employment Act of 1946, which declared explicitly that the objective of national economic policy was "to promote maximum employment, production, and purchasing power." The Act also directed the President to conduct analyses and present reports related to this objective. A new agency—the Council of Economic Advisors—was established to assist the President in this task; and the Joint Economic Committee of the Congress was set up to receive the reports and respond to them. Although the political and institutional aspects of this legislation need not concern us further, it cannot be overstressed that no such statement of national objectives could have been made, no subject identified for the Council to study and the President to report on, and no conception of modern economic policy attained without the prior development of the abstract conception, the model of the macro-economy.

An understanding of macro-economic concepts and elements of macro-economic policy is important for several reasons. In the first place, these concepts have entered the language of modern management. One cannot examine any significant management periodical, or even the daily newspaper, without encountering material cast in fairly sophisticated macro-economic terms. More important, each individual managerial unit exists and operates within the context of the larger economy. Past experience requires interpretation against the background of the general economic setting. (Were more customers attracted last year because of successful product development and merchandising efforts, or simply because the economy as a whole was somewhat more prosperous?) And anticipations and forecasts of future developments for industries, areas, and individual managerial units depend heavily on the developments projected for the larger economy. (We predict that market share for this year will be about the same as last, but how big will the total market be?) Finally, a quarter-century of experience has produced not only analytical refinements in the macro-economic model but also refinements in economic policy devices as well. Thus, the focus of policy-making has expanded from primary emphasis on the total amounts and levels of government expenditures and tax collections, the money supply and the rate of interest, to include a greater emphasis on their composition and structure. Hence, when tax collections are altered for macro-economic policy purposes, it is not likely that all taxes will change in equal amounts or proportions. On the contrary, sophisticated policy-making takes account of the differential effects of various tax rates and levels, so that tax reductions, for example, might be restricted solely to areas in which short-run expenditure increases were likely, or to sectors of the economy within which other social goals (such as reduction of hard-core unemployment, pollution control, etc.) might be achieved. Additional government expenditures for macro-economic policy purposes might also be channeled in such directions; or, conversely, desired reductions in the total level of government spending might be accomplished in selective ways. Hence, the impact of macro-economic policy developments is not likely to be the same among all industries, areas, and managerial units, and an understanding of the nature and importance of macro-economic policy actions and alternatives is a critical aspect of micro-unit management within a partially "managed" macro-economy.

CONCLUSION

The suggestion that the entire economy might be in some sense "managed"—that is, viewed as a whole in relation to a particular set of objectives, and total resources "economized" in relation to them—provides an appropriate basis for drawing together the three themes of this brief chapter. More extensive efforts are now being made to comprehend the working of our large and complex economy and to guide its direction of development than at any time in the past. At the same time, the primary focus of macroeconomic analysis and policy is on the development of limits and incentives that will serve to guide the independent actions of individual managerial units and private persons, not to control diverse and complex activities by central direction or political compulsion. Indeed, the experience of the centrally planned economies of the world—and even of very large administrative units (private firms as well as governments) within decentralized economies—has served to vindicate the market mechanism as a means of communication and coordination in complex systems. Large and diverse management systems—such as multiple-activity, divisionalized firms—rely increasingly on control techniques and decision rules that simulate the pressures and opportunities that would arise in efficient markets. And the growth in the size and complexity of individual managerial units throughout our society increases, rather than decreases, the importance of "economizing" rules and techniques as guides to effective management. Without straining too hard for a paradox, we may say that the extremes are, to some extent, coming together: As large managerial units increasingly approach the diversity and complexity that characterize markets and the macroeconomy itself, and as many individual markets and the entire macroeconomy come to be increasingly "managed" for purposes of public policy, the analysis of the market mechanism and the application of economizing decision rules become increasingly powerful and important elements in managerial planning and practice.

SUGGESTIONS FOR FUTURE READING

Managerial Economics and the Market Mechanism

The publication that first identified the field of managerial economics for serious study, and one that remains a useful and readable volume down to the present, is Joel Dean, *Managerial Economics* (Englewood Cliffs, N.J.: Prentice-Hall, 1951).

Two recent brief introductions to this range of topics are Robert Dorfman, *The Price System* (Englewood Cliffs, N.J.: Prentice-Hall, 1964), and Donald E. Farrar and John R. Meyer, *Managerial Economics* (Englewood Cliffs, N.J.: Prentice-Hall, 1970).

A more advanced treatment of the basic concepts is presented by William J. Baumol, *Economic Theory and Operations Analysis* (Englewood Cliffs, N.J.: Prentice-Hall, 1961), especially Chapter Three, "Marginal Analysis," and Chapter 11, "Market Structure, Pricing, and Output."

Macro-economics

A readable introduction to macro-economics is Charles L. Schultze, *National Income Analysis* (Englewood Cliffs, N.J.: Prentice-Hall, 1963). A more advanced presentation is Thomas F. Dernberg and Duncan M. McDougal, *Macro-economics,* 4th ed. (New York, N.Y.: McGraw-Hill Book Company, 1972).

An extremely readable and comprehensive discussion of macro-economic policy formation is presented in G. L. Bach, *Making Monetary and Fiscal Policy* (Washington, D.C.: The Brookings Institution, 1971).

For an interesting current analysis of the application of the economizing principle to problems of government and the macro-economy as a whole, see Charles L. Schultze and others, *Setting National Priorities: The 1972 Budget* (Washington, D.C.: The Brookings Institution, 1971).

The Virtues of Net Benefit Analysis

Oliver E. Williamson

Professor
Wharton School of Finance and Commerce
Department of Economics
University of Pennsylvania

Joseph McGuire has asked that I organize my remarks around the following standard: give the reader some idea of what you would have presented had you written the chapter. Lee Preston's survey of the contributions of economics to management is different from the one I would have written in several respects. First, it is a much more comprehensive and balanced presentation than I would have attempted. Second, the audience to whom he addresses his remarks is different from the one that I would have chosen. Third, it gives the reader much more of an idea of where economics has been than where it might be expected to go. I will elaborate in each of these three respects.

The scope of Professor Preston's survey is surely impressive. It pulls together in a compact and lucid fashion much of micro-economics and parts of macro-economics as well. Although the reader who is wholly unfamiliar with economics may find the going a bit rough, anyone who has had (and understood) a good economic principles course will find the language and concepts generally familiar. Professor Preston has performed a valuable service in synthesizing so much material so well. The reader whose prior familiarity with economics is roughly at the principles course level will find himself greatly in the author's debt.

This, however, brings us to the second question; namely, at what level "ought" the chapter to have been written? This depends presumably on the intended audience of this volume. I regard Professor Preston's chapter to be ideal as, say, an introduction to a course in economics being offered to first-year M.B.A. candidates. It surveys the terrain and raises many of the issues that subsequent lectures presumably will address in more detail. (Whether one wants to introduce total, average, and marginal cost diagrams for such an audience is perhaps debatable. Employing transformation curves for the purpose of illustrating opportunity costs, which of course is a core economic concept, is even more dubious. These are mere quibbles, however.) If indeed this is representative of the type of purpose to which the volume generally aspires, the Preston chapter is right on target.

My own feeling is that a survey of the contributions of economics to management could more usefully be pitched at a somewhat higher level and should consider some of the potential as well as the familiar applications of economic analysis. Also, to remain within space limitations, a choice between a micro-economic and a macro-economic orientation might have to be made. My preference would be to emphasize the applications of micro-economics to management. Although some gaps would develop in the process, I am not sure that these are greatly to be regretted. ("Simple Keynesian analysis," even with the precautionary statements that Professor Preston is careful to introduce, often gives rise to misconceptions—sometimes to an egregious degree. As any net benefit addict would agree, gap-filling that incurs opportunity costs (by preempting valuable space) has dubious impact, and is better avoided.

The audiences that I would aspire to address are M.B.A. graduates and their equivalents—whether they be in business or government. The objective that I would set would be to show how applied micro-theory can be made to address a wide variety of lively topics that managers in business and government regularly confront, or can be expected to confront. Partly this would entail the development and systematic application of net benefit analysis. This is all reasonably straightforward if not entirely familiar. Partly it would involve an introduction to the rudiments of what might be referred to as "transactional analysis,"—which requires an examination of more micro-analytic phenomena than economists have typically studied in the past.

The study of net benefit analysis would begin with the statement of the general net benefit expression $G(X) = B(X) - C(X)$, where G denotes net benefits, B is gross benefits, C is cost, and X is the decision variable. Assuming that both total and second-order conditions are satisfied, this expression is maximized when marginal benefits and marginal costs are equal. Generalization to several variables and maximization subject to constraint are easily handled as extensions to the basic model. Applications then come fairly easily. Profit maximization is obtained by substituting π for G and R for B, where π and R are net profit and gross revenue respectively, and C is interpreted as private costs. Monopoly distortions (of a partial equilibrium sort) can be assessed by comparing the solution that obtains when B is given by the sub of $R + S$ (where S is consumers' surplus) with that which results from profit maximization. Environmental problems can be investigated by noting that social costs properly include spillover costs as well as private costs, and by augmenting the cost expression accordingly. Bureaucratic phenomena can be studied by recasting the bureaucrat's objectives appropriately—which is to say that the operative bureaucratic benefits and costs need to be specified.[1]

[1]See in this connection William A. Niskanen, Jr., *Bureaucracy and Representative Government* (Chicago: Aldine-Atherton, 1971).

What is involved throughout is the recurrent application of the same basic net benefit maximizing apparatus. Matters that sometimes appear to the student (manager) to be disconnected problems are all seen to be amenable to analysis using the same common economic approach to issues.

Lest uncritical application of the basic paradigm be encouraged, some of the limits of economics for the study of complex organizational and social issues ought to be exposed. That economics is especially useful for studying efficiency attributes but is less well suited to deal with matters for which (in Etzioni's terms) "moral" rather than "calculative" involvements[2] are characteristic to the parties ought to be admitted and the implications assessed.

To some extent, however, some of the apparent limitations of economics can be overcome by shifting to what I have referred to as transactional analysis, especially if a comparative-institutional attitude is adopted. (Whether indeed the elements of such an approach can be described satisfactorily in a single chapter, much less in a comment such as this, is perhaps doubtful. I will attempt, nevertheless, to give a flavor of the approach that I have in mind.)

Starting from a basic economizing attitude, the effort would be made to extend the conventional paradigm in two respects. First, I would emphasize that the way transactions are organized—whether they are performed entirely within firms, take place across markets, involve government bureaus, etc.—is a matter for which the economic calculus can systematically be brought to bear. This would emphasize that organizations and the relations among them are amenable to rational design. The firm thus is regarded as one of several instruments that the manager has access to for purposes of economizing on the costs of completing transactions, rather than (as most economists tend to treat it) as an analytically convenient device by which to characterize optimum price and output, given pre-specified demand and cost functions.

The analysis here would focus on the costs of writing and enforcing both formal and informal types of contracts. Problems of adapting efficiently to unanticipated changes in the environment in the presence of bounded rationality need to be faced. Put briefly, the issues often reduce to when is an employment (internal) contract to be preferred to a sales (market) contract, and for what reasons?[3]

Second, and relatedly, I would urge that a comparative-institutional test be posed whenever a claim is advanced that a particular institutional unit (firm, internal operating division, government bureau, private non-profit organization, etc.) is "defective." The critical test is not whether the institution in question is defective relative to some hypothetical "ideal" for which assumptions of frictionlessness are (implicitly) employed. Rather, the policy-relevant issue is whether the condition in question is remediable, in the sense of realizing net gains, by implementing some feasible institutional reform.

An appreciation for the powers and limits of alternative forms of organizing transactions is essential to such an undertaking. Economics, for the most part, has not addressed this set of issues in a systematic way. The problem is that no other social science has the apparatus with which to do this job, but it is essential that it be done if reliably informed choices are to be made. Transforming management from an art to a science will be facilitated by developing an economics of organizational analysis that focuses on transactional relationships of a more micro-analytic variety than economists have previously been disposed to employ.

[2]Amitai Etzioni, *A Comparative Analysis of Complex Organizations* (New York: Free Press, 1961).

[3]This approach is illustrated, in a rudimentary way, in O. E. Williamson, "The Vertical Integration of Production: Market Failure Considerations," *American Economic Reviews*, Vol. 61 (May, 1971), pp. 112–123.

A Second Look at the Contributions of Economic Analysis to Management

Thomas H. Naylor

Professor, Director of
Social System Simulation Program
Department of Economics
Duke University

INTRODUCTION

The ostensible purpose of Preston's chapter was to "present some key concepts of economic analysis and explain both their use and their usefulness in the practice of management." Although I have no quarrel with Preston's stated objectives, I shall attempt to show that there exists a serious information gap between what Professor Preston describes as "key concepts of economic analysis" and the present state of the art of economic analysis and its relevance to management.

What Preston has in fact achieved in his piece is a reasonable representation of the contributions of economic analysis as it existed about twenty years ago to the practice of management. He has also provided the reader with a fairly accurate reflection of the applicability to management of the types of economic analysis that appears in most contemporary textbooks on "Principles of Economics." Unfortunately, Preston has totally ignored most of the major developments in managerial economics that have taken place during the past twenty years. Indeed, he has not even acknowledged their existence. Furthermore, he has blindly attempted to apply economic principles to management in a number of cases wherein extremely difficult practical and methodological problems arise when one attempts to apply conventional economic analysis to the operational decisions of "real world" managers. Although no one will deny the usefulness of the "Principles of Economics" as an initial way of analyzing a given problem situation, in all too many cases the "Principles of Economics" turn out to be totally non-operational as practical decision-making tools for managers.

MANAGERIAL GOALS

Most of Preston's analysis rests on the assumption that managers are attempting to optimize some specific objective function. He assumes that the manager is either trying to maximize profit or output or perhaps minimize cost. But it is well known that managers of business firms may have at least three different types of goals, including: (1) profit maximization, (2) functional goals, and (3) personal goals. That managers have goals other than profit maximization has been a well-established fact in the economics literature for over twenty years and the arguments need not be reproduced here. In addition to profit maximization, many managers also have functional goals, including production, inventory, sales, and market-sharing. Finally, there would be few who would deny that managers also have personal goals, including a concern for salary, security, status, power, prestige, social service, and professional excellence, to mention only a few. In other words, if one wants to provide managers of business firms with tools that are useful in making decisions, he cannot overlook the fact that most managers operate in a multiple-objective environment. Analytical tools that are restricted to single-objective situations are not likely to be very useful to managers. Although there are some economists who would contend that what managers are really trying to do is to maximize their own utility functions, no one has come forward with an operational way of defining and estimating the parameters of utility functions of managers. It is one thing to develop theories of the firm that assume known utility functions for managers, it is quite another thing to estimate empirically the utility function of a manager. Furthermore, even if such analytical tools did exist in the first place, it is unlikely that many managers would be willing to provide analysts with the necessary information required to estimate an individual's utility function.

Therefore, if one wants to glean from economic analysis those concepts that would be truly useful to managers, he is going to have to adjust to the fact that managers operate in a multiple-response environment and that naïve assumptions about profit maximization are not likely to be particularly useful to managers.

PRODUCTION PROCESS

Implicit in all of Preston's analysis is the existence of some type of production process or production function. That is, the firm is assumed to possess one or more production transformation processes that enable it to convert some finite number of inputs (factors of production) into a finite number of different outputs (products). The particular concept of the production function utilized by Preston is based on the assumptions of marginal analysis. Marginal analysis is primarily concerned with the process of making choices among alternative factor-product combinations, considering infinitesimal changes in factor-product combinations. To apply marginal analysis to managerial problems of the firm it is necessary to reduce the problem of the firm to one of finding the optimal values of some objective function subject to a set of production constraints. The objective function and the constraints must be continuous and of the proper shape with non-zero, first- and second-order partial derivatives. Preston seems to have completely overlooked the fact that there exist a number of important alternatives to the marginal analysis approach to the analysis of the firm's production process, in particular, linear programming.

Under the assumptions of conventional marginal analysis, the firm's production function is said to be a function of the quantities of fixed and variable factors that are used in the firm's production process. For any given factor quantities, the dependent variable represented by the function is usually defined as the maximum quantity of the particular product that can be produced, in a given state of technology, from the specified factor quantities.

The marginal analysis production function implies that a physical maximization of output for given levels of input has already been achieved. In essence this implies that the profit-maximization problem of the firm is a two-stage problem. The first stage consists of deriving a method of achieving the physical maximization presupposed in the definition of the production function. That is, stage 1 is equivalent to determining the technology for the firm. The second stage is merely the problem of maximizing total profit subject to the conditions imposed by the production function.

It should be pointed out that the first of the firm's two decision problems can be solved independently of the second, but the second problem must either be solved simultaneously with the first problem or after the first problem has been solved.

The distinction among the types of problems for which conventional marginal analysis and linear programming are best suited may be clarified by further examining the nature of the two different types of productive decisions made by the firm. The firm is assumed to have certain fixed factors at its disposal and access to variable factors through the open market.

The first decision is usually considered to be technical. That is, the firm must decide on the technology to be applied in the production of the set of product possibilities available to it. This involves determining the maximum quantity of output for each product variable attainable from specified factor quantities along with other specified product quantities.

Once technology is determined or fixed, the second decision is concerned with which products should be produced, and in what quantities, so as to maximize total profit. It should be remembered that at this point a decision to produce a particular set of products at a particular output level automatically determines the level of factor usage for the firm; for the production function prescribes the exact proportions for each level of output for all possible product combinations.

The marginal analysis model of the firm is concerned only with the second type of decision problem; for it assumes that the firm's technological problem has already been solved. Dorfman has summarized some of the difficulties involved in attempting to solve the second of the firm's two decision problems by marginal analysis.

> ..... Machinery, and especially the more advanced types, is likely to be inflexible with regard to the factors which must be combined with it and with regard to the rate and character of its output. Thus, when it has been determined to use a certain number of units of a specific machine, several of the other variables in the production function have been determined at the same time. It will not then be possible to move freely from point to point on the production surface except in an indirect manner. The type of decision which faces a firm using industrial processes is therefore essentially different from the decisions contemplated by marginal analysis. The firm may decide the extent to which to use each of the types of equipment it owns at any time. In that case any variation in the use of equipment implies simultaneous variation in the use of factors complementary to that equipment. The firm may choose among a number (generally finite) of ways of applying its equipment. Or it may select among a number of types of equipment offered for its purchase. All of these decisions differ in two respects from the kind of decisions treated by marginal analysis. First, they affect the quantities of a group of distinct inputs and outputs simultaneously. Second, the range of choice does not lie along a continuous scale, but involves selection among discrete alternatives. The effects of such decisions are therefore not adequately expressed by the theoretical operation of partial differentiation with respect to the quantities of separate inputs and outputs.[1]

In other words, the difficulty in solving the firm's second decision problem (profit maximization subject to the constraints imposed by the production function) stems from the fact that the solution of the firm's technological problem may yield a production function that does not possess such properties as continuity, concavity, and non-zero first- and second-order partial derivatives. Marginal analysis may not be at all appropriate for solving the second type of decision problem in industrial environments similar to those outlined by Dorfman. Linear programming was devised specifically to circumvent the difficulties described by Dorfman in solving the firm's second-stage decision problem.

Furthermore, linear programming can handle both decision problems simultaneously. That is, linear programming determines both the quantities of the products to be produced and the optimal technological arrangement of productive activities.

In the final analysis the principal difference between the assumptions

[1]Robert Dorfman, *Application of Linear Programming to the Theory of the Firm* (Berkeley, California: University of California Press, 1951), p. 10.

underlying marginal analysis models and linear programming models of the firm lies in the definition of an "activity." The salient differences have been summarized by Dorfman as follows:

> .... The (activity) of linear programming is a more specifically defined concept than the production function of marginal analysis. Indeed, a production function is a family of (activities) which use the same factors and turn out the same products. If we compare any two points on a production surface, if the internal ratios of the inputs and outputs at the two points are the same they will represent different levels of the same (activity); otherwise they will represent different (activities). The production function thus is a tool for exhibiting and comparing different but related (activities). What it fails to present adequately is the consequence of using several (activities) in parallel, and such combinations of (activities) are characteristic of modern industry.[2]

Although we do not wish to belabor the subject of linear programming, we think Preston's failure to mention it is indeed a serious omission.

INFORMATION

The type of economic analysis described by Preston implies that the decision-makers of the firm make two different types of decisions—factor input decisions and product output decisions. These decisions are made on the basis of three different types of information: product demand information, factor supply information, and production technology information. The economic analysis described by Preston assumes away any possible changes in the firm's demand, factor supply, and production functions. Furthermore, it assumes the absence of risk and uncertainty in terms of any of the information available to the firm's decision-makers. Yet we know in the real world that information is constantly changing and risk and uncertainty are omnipresent. The literature abounds with examples of dynamic models of the firm and the application of the concepts of risk and uncertainty to managerial economics. The book by Naylor and Vernon[3] entitled *Microeconomics and Decision Models of the Firm* treats these topics in some degree of detail.

OTHER ECONOMIC TOOLS

Within the past twenty years there have been a number of methodological advances in the body of knowledge known as the "Economic Theory of the Firm" that are directly applicable to management in general and managerial economics, in particular. These methodological advances include mathematical programming, dynamic programming, calculus of variations, computer simulation, investment theory, game theory, and behavioral theories of the firm. Yet Preston has not chosen to mention any of these recent developments in economics or their possible applicability to management.[4]

CORPORATE SIMULATION MODELS

We believe that one of the most promising tools of economic analysis in terms of its potential usefulness to managers is the relatively new concept of the corporate simulation model. Although the term "simulation" may mean many different things to different people, we use it to refer to an experiment conducted with a mathematical model of an

[2] *Ibid.*, p. 15.

[3] Thomas H. Naylor and John M. Vernon, *Microeconomics and Decision Models of the Firm* (New York: Harcourt, Brace and World, 1969).

[4] *Ibid.*

economic system on a digital computer over extended periods of time. The methodology of computer simulation and its applicability to management are described in the book entitled *Computer Simulation Experiments with Models of Economic Systems* by the author. Although economists have been advocating the use of simulation in managerial economics and the economic theory of the firm for over fifteen years, it has only been in recent years that a number of major corporations in the United States have been experimenting with simulation models of total corporate behavior. These companies include Xerox, IBM, Standard Oil of New Jersey, Anheuser-Busch and Pillsbury, to mention only a few. Interestingly enough, the development of corporate simulation models has proceeded almost independently of the development of contemporary micro-economic theory.

In our opinion, corporate simulation models may ultimately become the single most valuable tool of economic analysis available to corporate managers. With corporate simulation models it is possible for managers to perform a series of "What-if?" experiments to evaluate the effect of alternative policies on the long-range behavior of the firm. These policies might include production, marketing, financial, and accounting policies. With corporate simulation models, the manager can examine the response of a multiplicity of output variables and not simply the firm's profit index. Corporate simulation models overcome the sticky problems of multiple outputs already described in this piece. Unfortunately the evolution of corporate simulation models has taken place without the existence of a well-defined theory of corporate simulation models. This is a serious deficiency but one that is likely to be overcome in the near future. Corporate simulation models also require substantial amounts of data and in general necessitate an interdisciplinary approach to managerial economics. However, in spite of its limitations and the difficulties involved in building large-scale corporate simulation models, we believe that corporate simulation model building represents the most promising tool of economic analysis presently available to managers of large corporations. It seems likely that both managers and economists will be hearing a lot more about corporate simulation models in the near future.

SUMMARY

In summary, my criticisms of Preston's paper are not so much with what has been said but with what has been omitted. Many of the modern tools of economic analysis that have evolved out of the fields of operations research and management science simply have not been mentioned by Preston in his chapter. I feel that this represents a serious oversight and I have, therefore, attempted to shed some light on some of the options that are currently available to managers as decision-making tools.

SUGGESTIONS FOR FUTURE READING

Boulding, Kenneth E., and W. Allen Spivey (Eds.). *Linear Programming and the Theory of the Firm* (New York: The Macmillan Co., 1960).

Cohen, Kalman J., and Richard M. Cyert. *Theory of the Firm: Resource Allocation in a Market Economy* (Englewood Cliffs, N.J.: Prentice-Hall, 1965).

Cyert, Richard M., and James G. March. *A Behavioral Theory of the Firm* (Englewood Cliffs, N.J.: Prentice-Hall, 1963).

Dorfman, Robert. *Application of Linear Programming to the Theory of the Firm.* (Berkeley: University of California Press, 1951).

DORFMAN, ROBERT, PAUL A. SAMUELSON, AND ROBERT M. SOLOW. *Linear Programming and Economic Analysis* (New York: McGraw-Hill Book Company, 1958).

NAYLOR, THOMAS H. *Computer Simulation Experiments with Models of Economic Systems* (New York: John Wiley & Sons, 1971).

NAYLOR, THOMAS H., AND JOHN VERNON. *Microeconomics and Decision Models of the Firm* (New York: Harcourt, Brace and World, 1969).

DISCUSSION QUESTIONS

1. What is "economizing"? Why is it important that managers understand it? What is marginal analysis and how is it the "key" to economizing? Is marginal analysis "operational" for managers?
2. What is the marginal decision rule? Is it *always* true? Why?
3. How does an understanding of the market mechanism provide a basis for management to understand what is likely to happen in his market environments?
4. What does the elasticity of demand really mean? Isn't it stretching it a little to say that this concept is useful to managers? Why?
5. Why isn't the macro-economy the sum of its parts? What is the relationship between micro-economic units and the macro-economy?
6. What is net benefit analysis?
7. "Naive assumptions about profit maximization are not likely to be particularly useful to managers." Do you agree? Why?

4

Management Science and Management

Martin K. Starr

Professor
Graduate School of Business
Columbia University

Management is fundamentally an art, not a science. We should point out, however, that medicine also is considered an art. Times change, and the mixture of art and science involved in both medicine and managing has shifted. There is today more science in both areas because the simple economic rule prevails that resource allocations will be made by whatever methods promise greater marginal returns. For example, factories can be automated only if a wide variety of managerial functions can be mechanized. Control functions have been applied to those managerial levels in the organizational hierarchy wherein decision-making can be pre-programmed. Increasingly, the process of managing (even at high levels) is amenable to scientific treatment.

INTRODUCTION TO MANAGEMENT SCIENCE

Although an exact definition for management science cannot be given, some of the essential elements of management science can be set forth.

Science, as a concept, is not simple to define. There have been innumerable debates among physical scientists concerning who's science was better (for example, rationalists versus empiricists). Management science has not been exempt from such internal disagreement. A spectrum of opinions exists concerning the potential contributions of the hard sciences as compared to the soft sciences. (We refer to analytic and axiomatic mathematics as hard science; heuristic,* descriptive, and experimental methodology as soft science.)

The hard science school claims that fuzzy models of problems (which their colleagues develop using softer methodologies) are non-operational, sometimes even mystical. The soft methodologists assert that those who employ an elaborate mathematical approach often cannot find real systems that properly lend themselves to rigorous, hard descriptions.

*Heuristics are (in essence) rules of thumb.

Model-Building Focus

At the core of such management science discussions is the *model.* Its size and scope, the way the model is built, and the way to implement its results are controversial issues that can be resolved only in terms of how the manager *perceives* a specific system's attributes.

A model is a *representation* of reality. It can be constructed as a physical entity (e.g., an airplane flown in a wind tunnel) or it can be abstract, developed mathematically, then programmed for computer computations. Models of managerial systems often include mixtures of physical and abstract representations. Abstract verbal models, such as rules of thumb for dividing advertising and promotion budgets, are best described as soft, especially when contrasted with hard mathematical inventory and production scheduling models.

The philosophy of modeling remains intact, no matter what form of model is used. This philosophy recognizes that although the model is a simplified version of the real thing, it can be studied intensively with respect to certain specific problems. In all cases, the exact specification of the problem is essential as a statement of purpose. The solution obtained from the model should provide operational opportunities to effect purposeful changes in the real system.

Thus, management science provides a unique approach that augments the intuitive (principled) basis for achieving objectives that management has used traditionally. Management scientists (including organization theorists) always build explicit models, whether of the hard or soft variety.

Behavioral scientists are model builders. There is a distinction, however, between their approach and that of management scientists. Behavioral scientists attempt to discover how individuals, groups, and societies function. Behavioral scientists search for explanations of given behaviors. The management scientist makes use of such information, when possible, to provide organizational guidance concerning the probable implications of given actions and, therefore, to help determine what should be done.

Physicists and chemists, also model builders, strive to explain the behavior of physical aspects of the universe. As scientists, they are no more concerned with the economic performance of the systems they investigate than are behavioral scientists. Micro-economists come closest to modeling the same situations that interest management scientists, but as a rule, the micro conceptions of economists are relatively macro as compared to the problems considered by management scientists.

The Management Science Role

The management scientist is either a decision maker himself or else is responsible to one or more decision makers. The manager's problem is to determine how to make the best possible commitments. He has to choose among alternatives. Even to defer a decision is equivalent to choosing "no change." In this broad sense, the manager's organizational performance is always evaluated as a sequence of commitments.

The manager may be assisted by anyone who can evaluate the utility of new approaches or who can provide evidence that supports the status quo. In complex situations, the management scientist often does no more than provide the manager with descriptive models that evaluate the performance of various alternatives that management is considering. Descriptive models present relevant information to the manager who can *then* proceed to choose the best strategy to follow. (The normative decision criterion, specifying exactly what *ought* to be done, is not built into the descriptive model.) In different situations, the management scientist can build a normative decision model that supplies a final judgment. Often managers balk when confronted with normative conclusions. Most managers have learned how to circumvent normative instructions that run counter to their intuitive conclusions. It is reasonable to wonder, however, whether resistance to change, as a human foible, is an overriding factor when managers reject normative *procedures*.[1]

Although management science cannot be easily defined, certain characteristic properties of its approach are recognizably different from those of other supportive managerial functions. Management science proceeds in essentially three different ways. The *first* approach is to study the *properties* of certain models that have proved to possess interesting theoretical properties vis-à-vis managerial objectives. Mathematical programming, for example, has advanced from simple linear programming of resource allocation problems to non-linear forms of stochastic programming. Mathematical programming is a particularly important aspect of management science because of the connections between programming methodology and the economic behavior of the firm.

The *second* approach has been to study characteristic managerial *problems*. Each problem area brings to mind several existing models that might be applied to parts of the problem and the need for some new models as well. Questions arise concerning how to modify well-known models reported in the literature, how to assemble interacting groups of such models, and how to invent new models that might provide a basis for solving problems of larger systems.

Recently, pressure for utilizing (normative) management science conclusions for large-scale problems has arisen from outside the organization. Citizen, consumer, and stockholder groups have become aware that managerial intuition in government and industry can provide counter-intuitive results when applied to the behavior of large organizational systems. The counter-intuitive problem studied by Jay Forrester is that first- and second-order system's interactions may be converted at third- and fourth-order interrelations into reverse results.[2] Thus, an action can produce short-term beneficial results that in the long run may be disadvantageous.

The *third* approach is to analyze the *decision maker's* situation. Since a problem exists within a larger situational framework than specified by the

[1]See Donald A. Schon, *Technology and Change* (New York: Delacorte Press, 1967). The author describes and illustrates a management propensity to reject new technology that would alter the familiar and introduce uncertainty, albeit as a companion to opportunity.

[2]See Jay W. Forrester, "Counterintuitive Behavior of Social Systems," *Technology Review*, Vol. 73, No. 3 (January, 1971), pp. 52–68.

variables and relationships of the decision model, pre-decision and post-decision considerations are required.[3]

Pre-decisions determine the allocation of investment funds in the decision study—for example, whether to spend a greater part of the study budget on strategy creation or on forecasting. Post-decisions are required to determine how best to implement a solution and can lead to the conclusion that a different solution is needed.

Non-situational conclusions seldom reflect competition between managers, conflicts between personal and company objectives, and a host of other post-decision factors. In this area, hard methodology holds little promise for management science whereas soft methodology innovations have been used increasingly. Thus, the viewpoints of a political scientist are of benefit to the manager. The political advisor role of management science, although relatively new, is of growing importance to management.[4]

ACCOMPLISHMENTS OF MANAGEMENT SCIENCE

The history of management science reveals that all three approaches have significant precedents. Management science followed operations research, shifting the focus from military to industrial situations. The major impetus for operations research arose during the World War II. Logistics problems had become so severe that the British government set up *operational research* groups of multi-discipinary scientists who could examine complex situations with new tools and techniques. Radar, for example, represented a massive amount of information transfer that was new by any prior standards. There were no systems capable of processing this information and no past military experience to provide a background for handling these situations. The fact that a scientific approach was helpful in resolving complex problems led the military to include the capacity for such analyses within their own organizations. The approach was extended to supply and inventory problems for substantial troop movements and to the development of optimal convoy procedures. First Britain, and then the U.S. began to employ *operations research* analysts in each of its armed forces.

In the early 1950's, recognizing that most operations research work was militarily oriented and visualizing broader applications for the logic and direction of model building, a group of ardent practitioners formed The Institute of Management Sciences. Their concept was to carry model-building notions to managerial areas in industry and institutions. The result was successful. Management accepted the contributions of management scientists and incorporated them, where feasible, in their organizations. As computer systems grew, it became evident that management scientists were in an excellent position to deal with these large-scale generators of information.

Problems formed the first basis for interest in complex model building, but it soon became evident that certain major model classifications existed.

[3]Martin K. Starr, *Management: A Modern Approach* (New York: Harcourt Brace Jovanovich, Inc., 1971), pp. 199–241.

[4]Martin K. Starr, "The Politics of Management Science," *Interfaces*, Vol. 1, No. 4 (June, 1971), pp. 31–37.

Work could, therefore, proceed on models without requiring a specific problem base. The character of model differences attracted attention and a major distinction was drawn between normative and descriptive models. Normative models could be studied fruitfully apart from problems. Scientists proceeded to develop optimization models without particular applications in mind.

At the same time, industrial and other institutions rewarded solutions that improved their performance, with little regard to their mathematical generality. Results counted, not the elegance of the model. Gradually there developed a flow and interchange, back and forth, between modeling theory and model application. Overall, it led to management support of management science.

The journal *Management Science* began publishing two separate sections (Theory and Application) to foster the understanding of this relationship. Not everyone agreed that it was desirable to emphasize this distinction, a debate that still goes on. A specific piece of work cannot always be clearly categorized. Often, a problem requires model modification that accents theory; and, as often, theoretical developments lead to the recognition of specific applications that can be tested. There are both advantages and disadvantages in thinking about management science in these dichotomous terms.

The importance of budgetary pre-decisions and political post-decisions was first emphasized during the 1960's. Under the guidance of the McNamara philosophy, the U.S. Department of Defense engaged in complex system evaluations and developed powerful budgetary controls. Thus, cost effectiveness and cost/benefit studies were introduced. At the same time, conjectural methodologies for assessing the potential effects of political and social phenomena appeared. The management scientist who developed contingency plans based on alternative scenarios of what might occur did not act as a politician but rather as a political scientist advising the manager. By the early 1970's these advisory roles had been expanded in industry, government, and the military. Large-scale system studies began to include many (soft) behavioral and social variables that represented an awareness of political factors.[5]

The Nature of Hard Models

As could have been expected, the first positive contributions of management science to managing were related to well-defined situations. Once started, a surprisingly large repertory of hard models emerged that were based on network theory, mathematical programming, and mathematical optimization methods (with and without probabilistic dependencies).

With respect to network theory, *assignment* methods were developed wherein the objective was to reduce a rich combinatorial system to a unique set of one-for-one assignments having maximum value (or minimum cost). Distribution problems, assuming conditions of certainty (often as an approximation), led to resolution of the *transportation* problem. Here, assignments may be split between sources and destinations. As another variant of

[5]See footnotes 80 and 81.

network methods, projects were transformed into an assigned sequence of jobs. Time estimates were developed for accomplishing each job. The longest time path of consecutive jobs, called the critical path, determines the earliest possible date of project completion. Sometimes, resource trade-offs between branches of the project network can improve the project completion date. Management found realistic help in all of these solution methods.

The heart of hard-model building is mathematical programming. Linear programming (LP), being the simplest to resolve, has received a lion's share of management's attention. The linear assumption, although an approximation, was one that management found applicable to many real cases. As a result, LP was used to solve product-mix, diet-mix, and blending problems. For example, various grades of petroleum crudes can be blended to produce an optimal mixture of fuels. At one time, blending was considered a high-level managerial problem and, accordingly, it received a significant portion of operating costs. By investing in the development of a formal blending model, management reduced the substantial drain on its operating budget, shifting the expense to the investment-overhead area. Total costs were reduced in this way (even after discounting) and more accurate solutions were obtained Management welcomed the release from daily crises involving blending decisions. Adequate computer programs were developed for LP models. The blending problem was relegated to the automatic control sector of managerial responsibility.

Many other problem areas lent themselves to LP formats. Thus, LP could be used for aggregate scheduling with linear costs (as an approximation), shop loading, paper-cutting trim problems, cattle-feed diet problems, and media-mix problems. LP solutions were found to be superior in a variety of ways to traditional rule-of-thumb (heuristic) solutions.[6]

Other hard models are widely used. Optimization methods of calculus yield solid solutions to inventory-type problems. Methods of probability theory furnish rich descriptions of waiting-line (queuing) phenomena wherein arrivals and service intervals are statistically distributed in some specific way that can lead to idle equipment, and, at other times, to queues or waiting lines.

Managers accept hard-model solutions in much the same way that they accept technological changes. This is appropriate because the problems that can be treated by hard models are not puzzling. Combinatorial richness poses the real problem—i.e., too much information for strictly implicit solutions. Normative results, when they can be trusted (if appropriate data and sufficient analytic models exist), require no judgment. For management by exception (MBE) to work, such a state of affairs is essential.

A Shift from Hard to Soft Models

The hard models, however, rapidly encountered barriers that reflected the real difficulties of actual systems. Thus, management science tackled questions such as how to construct optimal stock portfolios, how to manage

[6]To solve programming problems, matrix mathematics is used; for network solutions, reduction theorems are employed. Most problems could be set up in either way, but some are easier to solve in one way than another.

new product decisions, how to design livable cities, and how to allocate medical funds. Such systems are affected by too many interrelated variables to be understood and successfully treated by the hard methods of management science. Various soft models began to appear, and managers indicated definite interest in their results.

Models turned softer as a higher percentage of effects were attributed to behavioral factors. Bayesian decision methods allowed managerial participation in achieving solutions. The manager's estimates became an accepted (soft) involvement in normative decision methods. Heuristic methods began to dominate soft models. Only with heuristics could complex interactive phenomena be simulated. Computer capabilities supported interesting innovations along that line of descriptive modeling.

NEW DIRECTIONS FOR MANAGEMENT SCIENCE ACHIEVEMENTS

Management science is a dynamic field. Significant changes have continued to occur in attitudes and perspective, not just in technical features. First, focus shifted from military to industrial problems. Now major shifts relate to the size of system's problems that are studied and to the parallel adjustments required as we move from hard to soft models.

The ability to control small systems has been established. Variants of mathematical programming, queuing theory, inventory models, sequencing and shop loading models, and many others have been developed to a fine point. Although many problem details remain unsolved, the specific difficulties are formal and technical (especially, of too much variety) rather than informal and intuitive (such as inability to understand the system's behavior). Some problems have been reclassified, from hard to soft, because the available formal solutions are too attentuated.[7] In general, dissatisfaction with strictly hard-modeling terms for organizational aspects of problems has increased. Thus, softer models that embody hypotheses of behavioral characteristics are attractive.

Another way of describing the changes that are taking place in the management science field is to point out the shift from deductive to inductive reasoning that is occurring. Induction assumes no catalog of prior techniques representative of existing theory. Instead, based on available facts, new models are developed. Inductive reasoning signals a time of theory development. Deductive methods work from postulated laws to specific instances of those laws. For hard models, the laws relate to small, stable, and well-regulated systems. There is no comparable information for large, unstable, and unregulated systems. Here, deductions may prove to be counterintuitive. In other words, simple, first-order deductions do not work for higher-order systems. Therefore, emphasis shifts to the inductive procedures of soft-modeling.

Inductive reasoning, applied to large systems, does not result in recommendations to use mathematical programming, queuing models, and the like. Rather, it calls for new forms of models. Optimality considerations appear as absurdities in the complex networks of large systems. The creative

[7]For example, portfolio- and media-mix models.

ability of the model builder is less mathematical and more architectural. Thus, for large systems, we have entered an era that appreciates the relevance of fuzzy, wicked, and even mystical problems.

A Unified Theory Based on Information Management

Within the organization, the control of large systems has been recognized and related to information flows. In the mid 1960's, the state of computer development led to the notion that a critical aspect of management was the Managerial *use* of Information Systems (MIS). Neither management scientists nor managers knew precisely what MIS involved. All agreed that it was (somehow) relevant. Now, it has become clear that information provides a common unit and specific dimensions (emphasizing *time*) to serve as an interface for qualitative (soft) considerations, quantitative (hard) modeling, and (inductive) computer operations. Thus, information is like a form of common currency that integrates behavioral science knowledge with the (accountable) activities of the firm. Accordingly, accountancy has enlarged its perspectives. Ultimately, the major function of accounting will be to supply relevant management information; tax considerations will become an auxiliary occupation.

Management science has begun to come to grips with the fact that the economics of many large systems with which it deals need not be related solely to monetary systems. Thus, in the management of a hospital, library, or government agency other utility factors than money have to be treated in an economically rational way. An understanding of utilities is central to a manager's activities, and utility theory has intrigued many social scientists who have attempted to examine its character by means of hard modeling. But the attenuated results yielded by hard models have led many managers to turn away from what seem like scientists' esoteric interests in their affairs. In general, management scientists agree with managers. Utility considerations require soft modeling.

Conveniently, the study of cybernetics[8] had advanced the understanding of information systems to a point at which their relationship to the utility concepts of behavioral science was not hard to grasp. Measures of order and variety based on entropy and redundancy have now begun to appear. The entropy and redundancy measures describe the degree of managerial uncertainty that exists because of the character of the system as it is translated by the manager's *perception* of the system's complexity. Thus, these measures can capture such utility notions as information privileges, the benefits of memory, the penalties of aging information, the value of surprise, the likelihood of information crises, the negative effects of noise in the information system, and the net benefits of auditing information systems. Each of these considerations are instances of operational forms of utility theory.

Many systems are complex because they can be described only vaguely. Cybernetic measures may permit otherwise fuzzy situations to be described clearly. By managerial induction, a relevant classification of the system's

[8]W. Ross Ashby, *An Introduction to Cybernetics* (New York: John Wiley & Sons, Inc.), 1956.

behavior is derived. This classification represents a theory that can be examined in entropic terms to determine the character of the *perceived* system.[9]

Behavioral scientists have begun to show an interest in using such structural measures to examine individual, group, and organizational patterns.[10] Thus, bridges are being built that can help management science span the abyss between the formal simplicity of hard-utility models (which force the executive to measure the consistency of his logic) and reality (which deals with the performance of profit centers). In such terms, management science can be an economic and political advisor to management.

Complex Objectives

Demands on management science have outstripped its abilities to provide hard-model solutions. Increased information flows produce larger systems that consistently thwart exact treatment in modeling terms. In particular, large systems must be taken into account because more kinds of interactive information reach more people over longer periods of time. For lack of anything better, management uses an intuitive approach to resolve problems.

Pre-decisions (concerning *what* problems to study, and *how* to study the selected problems) follow from tracking the system's past and present performance and from extrapolated predictions of future performance. The performance measures are derived in terms of the manager's conscious list of multiple objectives for himself and the system. Only some of these objectives are monetary. The problem of maximizing societal, enterprise, and individual utilities represents a major decision-making undertaking. Post-decision questions of *how* to achieve implementation are crucial. Although the total, pre-present, and post approach to decision-making may never be resolved, it is reasonable to believe that persistent efforts will secure improvements.

In the last decade, many non-monetary terms that relate to a company's long-run profitability have emerged. As these additional performance concepts have appeared, there have been new opportunities for those who seek to obtain a greater share of organizational power. Specifically, those who control decisions relating to monetary profit have a traditional form of power. If other measures of corporate performance (e.g., in the social sector) are acknowledged, then different opportunities for guiding the company's destiny (and thereby acquiring power) exist.

Enlarging the power base means that today management influences the quality of life in at least three areas: the economic, environmental, and societal.[11] Under present circumstances, the long-term survival of the enter-

[9]Entropy measures reflect the degree of organization of a system in terms of the size of the system, the detail perceived within the system, and the persistence of systems events (as frequencies of occurrence). The system's components and events may be fuzzy and ill-defined, but if they are recognizable, then entropic measures can be applied.

[10]Starr, *Management: A Modern Approach*, pp. 619–622.

[11]The Institute for the Quality of Life, Inc., was formed in 1971 to pursue just such a development—blending descriptive forecasts by experts on technical and cultural developments and inter-actions with the measures value systems of our culture and sub-

prise depends on this triumvirate of performance factors. But management is unable, at present, to measure its contribution to the quality of life in any but economic terms. Even in economic terms, the higher-order contributions to standard of living and GNP are relatively unknown.

Larger and larger institutional reality spheres are developing. Methodology is being developed for urban planning, national planning, and most recently, for world planning.[12] By utilizing innovative, heuristic techniques of management science in conjunction with computer capabilities, we now have real hope of putting together reasonable solutions to large, complex, and often counter-intuitive problems.[13]

As the manager's list of objectives has become more complex, the management scientist has been forced to study larger systems that are related to the manager's interests. A reasonable observation is that some managers perceive more complex, interactive systems than do others. In part, the differences among managers are related to personality and talent differentials. But such personal characteristics are highly correlated with the kinds of system involvements that managers choose for their jobs (and for which they are chosen). In essence, therefore, the nature of the system interacting with the type of manager becomes a single, fundamental consideration for management science. The question: What type of system *should* be perceived by the manager? represents a new, critical, normative consideration.

Complex Systems

To characterize a system, its relevant factors must be perceived. The list is analyzed and a classification of variables is derived by induction. This system, as it is *perceived*, is studied to determine its recurrent properties. The

cultures. Their QOL Index tracks and forecasts the quality of life for government and industry planning and investment purposes (QOL Index is the property of The Institute For the Quality of Life, Inc.); from "Marketing-Production Interaction" by William T. Moran in Martin K. Starr, *Production Management: Systems and Synthesis*, 2nd ed. (Englewood Cliffs, N.J.: Prentice-Hall, Inc., 1972).

[12]See, for example, R. L. Meir, and R. D. Duke, "Gaming Simulation for Urban Planning," *Journal American Institute of Planners*, No. 32 (January, 1966), pp. 3–16. Also, Jay W. Forrester, *Urban Dynamics* (Cambridge, Massachusetts: MIT Press, 1969). For national planning, note E. P. Holland and R. W. Gillespie, *Experiments on a Simulated Underdeveloped Economy* (Cambridge, Massachusetts: MIT Press, 1963). Some aspects of world planning are reflected by Buckminster Fuller, *The World Game Report* (New York: The New York Studio School of Painting and Sculpture, 1969); Jay W. Forrester, *World Dynamics* (Cambridge, Massachusetts: Wright-Allen Press, Inc., 1971); the January 14, 1972, report: "Project on the Predicament of Mankind" by Dennis L. Meadows; and D. H. Meadows *et al.*, *The Limits to Growth* (New York: Universe Books, 1972).

[13]Some relevant examples include: an entropic equilibrium theory of the marketplace, "Fundamental Laws of Consumer Dynamics," Chapter I, 1970, and Chapter II, 1971 by David H. Butler and B. F. Butler, Center for Research in Marketing Strategy, The Hendry Corporation, Scenic Drive, Croton-on-Hudson, N.Y., 10520; an ARF research project devoted to the study of complex consumer behavior predicated on entropy laws (Minutes of the Working Group on Theory and Models re "Consumenoid I"), Advertising Research Foundation, N.Y., 1972; a quality of life simulator that operates first on a micro basis, and then aggregates individual actions into large-group behaviors. The last mentioned is the author's present research project at Columbia University. After many trials with this simulator, it is apparent that counter-intuitive results appear with high frequencies in the behavior of the aggregations.

importance of *recurrence* for classifying systems must be fully understood by managers.

Two major classes of systems (policy and planning) have to be considered.[14]

Figure 5 maps out various systems configurations that can occur, but the major difference is between policy and planning systems. Policy systems are repetitive (or recurrent) in either the ergodic or the periodic sense. If they are ergodic, then, *at any time,* what has happened before can occur again. Periodic systems are constrained to repeat themselves, at specific instances, i.e., in cycles. For both ergodic and periodic types of recurrent systems, an investment in policy formulation and requisite control systems is likely to be warranted. On the contrary, since planning systems embody non-recurrent or transient properties, policy control investment is unlikely to be reasonable.

A system is ergodic when all of its randomly occurring environmental situations are certain to be repeated within a finite and non-cyclical period of time. On the other hand, if the probability that a state of nature (i.e., an environmental situation) will ever be repeated is less than one, the system is called transient. Thus, by definition, a transient system cannot be ergodic and it cannot be periodic. As an example of a periodic system, consider the use of historical forecasts wherein demand estimates change according to the progress of monthly calendar time (from one January to the next January). In contrast, a brand-switching matrix usually implies an ergodic sys-

[14]It is worth repeating that there is good reason to believe that managers tend to seek contact with types of systems according to personal predispositions.

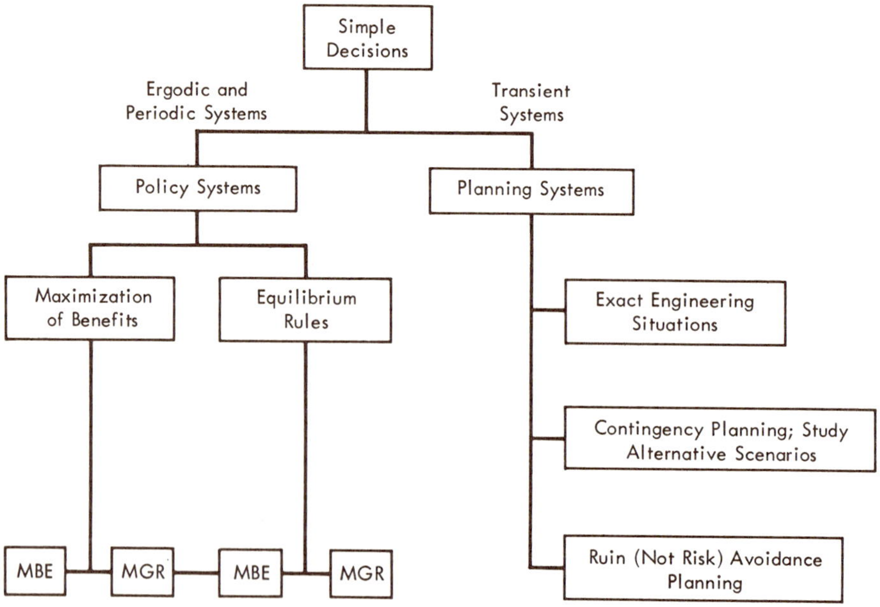

FIGURE 5. The Two Major Classes of Systems

tem—i.e., consumers can either repurchase the brand last bought or switch to another brand. If such freedom of choice doesn't exist (say once a consumer uses X she will never use Y again), then the system is not ergodic but transient. In general, the introduction of a new product requires the management of a transient phenomenon.

It is important to mention that the way a system is defined affects the way it is studied and the results that can be achieved. Monthly demand may not be repetitive in the periodic sense, but stable in terms of trend and the age of the system. A repetitive pattern such as controlled growth is required in order to treat a system in ergodic policy/control terms. Ergodicity must be present in a system before an economical controller can be developed that will respond appropriately to each repetitive environment. It is, therefore, of great importance to management.

Simple decisions apply only to static situations. When time is added to the manager's frame of reference, for large systems, it is generally unreasonable to assume that each decision in a sequence of decisions will be independent. Then, the two fundamental configurations of the system must be considered.

The *policy* frame is based on the belief that a system is stable and that comparable decision situations (composed of the same variables and relations) arise repeatedly. Effective control systems can be designed for such repetitive (ergodic) systems. Because of its recurrent properties, an investment in policy and control can be amortized over the stable life of the system. Although generally more complex, the same can be said for cyclical or periodic phenomena that are special forms of ergodic behavior.

Given the policy framework, two quite different managerial approaches are apparent. One of these attempts to establish optimal decision rules, as for inventory management. The second utilizes rules as constraints to eliminate the occurrence of unwanted results and to establish behavioral equilibriums (for example, the order to punch a time clock). There will be distinct anomalies between managers who prefer maximization policies and those who prefer equilibrium ones. Highly analytic managerial attitudes are attracted to maximization potentialities whereas the equilibrium approach to policy requires political abilities and such charismatic behavior as is associated with leadership. Thus, although policy-oriented managers prefer to deal with recurrent system properties, their approach to such systems can be evidenced in two distinctly different ways.

Planning factors attract entirely different managerial abilities and interests than do policy properties. Yet, in both areas basically different orientations exist. We have shown three types of planning systems in Figure 5. The first is essentially technological planning, which can be compared to engineering development work. Such project systems (associated with PERT and critical path analyses) are treated as deterministic. The second kind of planning recognizes that situational uncertainties can produce serious penalties. You plan for A and B happens. To avoid the penalty of misjudging, contingency plans are developed. They are based on predictive scripts of what could occur, . . . if such and such happened, . . . and what might be done about that, with what effect. The third planning variant occurs when a substantial percentage of the organization's assets are at stake and might be lost because of a mistake. If such a loss could result in organizational (or personal) failure, then ruin-avoidance planning is used. In this case, the prime objective is to minimize the probability of ruin. All other objectives concerning dollar volume, profit, share of market, net benefit, and so on, are treated as constraints.

MANAGERIAL AWARENESS

The decision about whether a system should be classified as planning or policy is seldom clear cut and is affected by the manager's perceptions. Tradition and training play a large part in conditioning the manager's classification of complex system's variables (i.e., organizing the list of variables, a step that precedes his policy/planning classification of the system).

The manager sets down a list of variables pertinent to his complex objectives. Say that he is aware of N such variables. When this list of variables and the relationships among them constitute a large system, the manager attempts to reduce the amount of information with which he must cope. He can choose to partition the large system, N, into mutually exclusive smaller ones, as shown in the left-hand section of Figure 6. Each subsystem, n_j, is studied, improved, and then reincorporated into the larger system with whatever changes have been made. Deterministic forms of planning and maximization forms of policy often use such partitioning.

Another partitioning approach allows overlapping subsystems (i.e., the right-hand section of Figure 6). Some of the variables and their relations appear, at the same time, in more than one subsystem's study. Here, normative contradictions in performance can occur. Nevertheless, overlapping partitions may stabilize policy and is inherent in contingency planning.

Whatever the form of partitioning, the result is to produce a new classification (of subsystems) with fewer factors to deal with. Such reductions, known as homomorphisms, represent a very important classification technique in management science. Faced with increased amounts and rates of information flow, and high-order interactions as well, (an aware) manager and (an astute) management scientist must coordinate their activities as never before. The effectiveness of the partition is directly a function of managerial awareness. One manager's partition may be ergodic whereas another manager may regard the same system as being transient.

$$\sum_i n_i = N \qquad\qquad \sum_i n_i > N$$

FIGURE 6. Breaking a Large System into Smaller Subsystems (Left) and Overlapping Subsystems (Right).

Problems of Organized Complexity

When various micro-phenomena can also be studied as a complex aggregate, then a problem of *organized complexity* exists. The management scientist analyzes the composite system to determine whether policy or planning considerations should be used. He can then further classify the situation.

In Figure 7, inputs (*I*) are transformed by a process (*T*) into selected outputs (*O*). If policy conditions exist, the performance of (*O*) is monitored by (*M*) and reported to the controller (*C*) so that the process (*T*) can be modified. If planning conditions exist, then the construction of such a feedback loop controller is unwarranted.

Given a transient system (*T′*), a major purpose of planning is to create an ergodic-type of system (*T*). Furthermore, when an ergodic process (*T*) is achieved, it is a primary management science function to design a controller (*C*) that matches the character of the process (*T*).

In the past, managers have planned recurrent systems and then designed appropriate monitors and policy controls for them without utilizing management science concepts. In fact, these steps are explicit (although partial) definitions of what managing is all about. Since management science is well suited to guide the manager in these areas, it is sensible that managers employ such counsel.

But only recently, after management science began to accept softer models as relevant, has management science come to believe in its own ability to handle large-system problems. Its past record in rationalizing simple, small-system problems and in treating complex, disordered problems with statistical tools (that simplified these problems), has been good. Now management science has been drawn into the large-system problem arena. The category (in problem taxonomy) is that of organized complexity. These obviously are the hardest problems to treat.[15]

Long before World War II, the Spanish philosopher José Ortega y Gasset faulted science for its inability to improve the society of man.[16]

[15]See Warren Weaver as described in D. B. Hertz, *The Theory and Practice of Industrial Research* (New York: McGraw-Hill Book Company, 1950), p. 28. Note the character of simple and disorganized complexity.

[16]José Ortega y Gasset, *History as a System* (New York: W. W. Norton & Co., Inc., 1941), pp. 165–233.

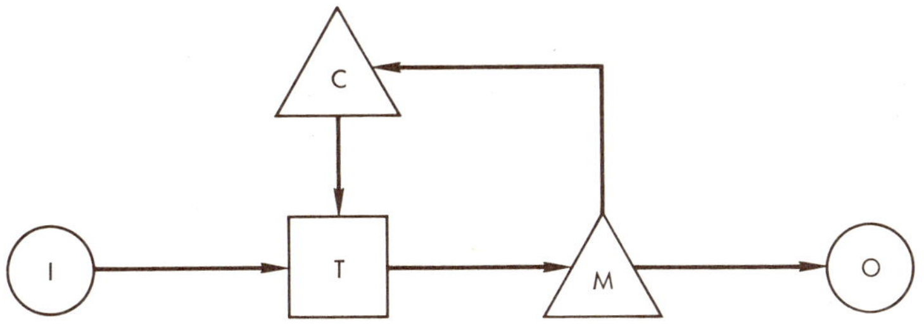

FIGURE 7. Classifying an Organized Complexity Problem

Since then, no branch of science has emerged to accept this burden; that is, until management science appeared in the 1950's.[17] Still, it has taken approximately 20 years for management science to recognize that management is *the* system responsible for the condition of society; that bureaucracy is only one (equilibrium policy) form of management; that management science in a bureaucratic system tends to explore hard models exclusively; and that management science in a situation sensitized to quality of life concepts can use softer models. Thus, over time management science has become less similar to physical science roles and more similar to social science. Gradually, it has dawned that the soft behavioral and hard physical, quantitative aspects of a problem are not only relatable but non-separable. This is the essence of organized complexity.

The Manager is a Decision Valve

Previously, we have described how management's systems participation can be viewed in explicit terms. No matter what the specific nature of the organization, in terms of its complex objectives, management:

1. identifies relevant variables and their functional interrelations;
2. classifies subsystems that then can be associated with specific system recurrence properties;
3. attempts to convert transient systems to ergodic ones;
4. designs control systems having adequate variety to manage the variety of ergodic systems.[18]

Now let us examine such issues in greater detail.

A special case of the ergodic system is the *stationary* process.[19] The forecast of event probabilities remains constant over time when the system is stationary. This is a more constrained situation than is required by the general recurrence conditions of ergodic systems—i.e., an initial system's state will repeat itself in the (finite) future. When a system is stationary, the manager acts as a simple decision valve. The stationary case is equivalent to a believable forecast. Thus, the manager, compelled to use the expected value criterion, is behaving as nothing more than an averaging mechanism, a simple valve that simply passes the best expected value.

A less rigid situation occurs when the forecast is not believable but must be tested against alternative forecasts. In Figure 8, the manager functions like a go/no go valve, accepting or rejecting the solution. Under certain circumstances, the manager passes the solution on to the system and implements it. At other times, the manager does not accept the solution but rejects it (perhaps returns it for further modeling work).

What aspect of testing accounts for the manager's decision to accept

[17]Scientific management, set forth by F. W. Taylor in the early 1900's, was actually recognition of the technological aspects of the management problem. It should have been called technological aspects of management.

[18]See Starr, *Management: A Modern Approach*, pp. 512–514.

[19]That is, the ergodic process is operating at *its* equilibrium or steady state.

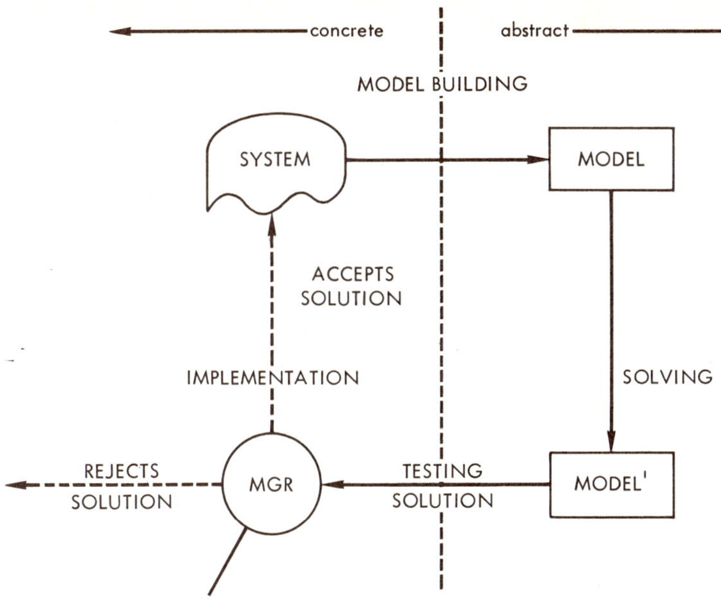

FIGURE 8. Testing Against Alternative Forecasts

a solution or to reject it? The manager can make two different kinds of errors. Type I error: he can reject a good solution; Type II error: he can accept a poor solution. These two error types always coexist when a non-stationary ergodic system prevails. The decision to accept or reject a solution is a fundamental policy consideration. Managers who are dealing with non-stationary systems (for example, marketing and personnel managers) prefer to minimize Type II errors, at the expense of increasing Type I errors.

All policy rules represent some kind of balance between the potentials to commit Type I and Type II errors. As one type of error increases, the other kind decreases. Managers dealing with systems that are close to being stationary tend to prefer small Type I errors and large Type II errors. Thus, the production manager requires strong evidence that his system is going out of control before he will take action. On the other hand, the marketing manager seldom trusts the stability of his forecasts, and, accordingly, he protects himself against accepting false solutions that provide visible evidence of his errors.[20] As another example of a relatively unstable system, consider the behavior of a stock market investor who feels less unhappy about stocks he did not buy that go up (Type I error) than when stocks he did buy go down (Type II error). The stock market (in the short term, at least) is hardly a good example of an ergodic system. But the stock market investor acts on special information and perceived patterns. The investor's personality is a positive determinant of his perceptions and Type I/Type II behavior.

[20]New product failures can be avoided by having no new products and minimized by using only sure-fire entries.

The Manager as a System's Transducer[21]

When a stationary system exists, the manager (as a decision valve) uses the expected value criterion. But he can also try to override the use of that criterion by creating an early warning control system composed of a monitor and a controller. If the manager embodies both of these functions, he acts as a transducer. Then, instead of selecting an action based on maximum expected value, he waits for advance notice concerning which system's state will prevail. Accordingly, he chooses that action that will optimize his system's performance. This manager, acting as a transducer, will achieve as good or better results than the manager acting as a decision valve. Usually, the results are better, but the cost of the transducer usually greatly exceeds the cost of the decision valve. Because his actions are readily understood, he can substitute mechanisms for his personal involvement and thereby achieve the release afforded by management by exception (MBE) systems.[22]

If a non-stationary ergodic system exists, the manager can still attempt to set up an early warning system. If he succeeds, there will be no difference, in a system sense, between the stationary and non-stationary cases. Here, the extra cost of the transducer may be more easily justified than in the situation we just described. However, it must be determined whether the net reward with a transducer is likely to be great enough to prompt the manager to override the non-stationary ergodic process with a control system.

As a transducer, the manager receives specific time-series information (i.e., all data are time-tagged), and he acts on the information sequence according to pre-designed policy rules. The response sensitivity of the control system decreases when cross-sectional data are used as its input. The character of cross-sectional data is that specific data sequence is lost and instead a compressed description of (say) a month's activities is reported. Many management information systems are designed in cross-sectional term—e.g., the balance sheet, quarterly report, annual P and L, and the like.

It is usually far too costly to use the manager as a transducer when the system is not ergodic. The transducer (under transient state conditions) will not possess sufficient instructions. The monitor may not be able to recognize evolving conditions, and the controller will not know what to do about early warnings for which it cannot be programmed.

The behavior of a transducer is represented by the diagram and matrix in Figure 9. Assume that the desired state is indicated by an asterisk. The system's states *A, B, C, D, . . .* are reported sufficiently in advance to permit a new strategy to be chosen. Our transducer design can succeed in maintaining the desired state $O(*)$ no matter what environmental situation occurs. Thus, if the system moves from *B* to *D* to *C* to *A*, the transducer's action alternatives shift from S_1 to S_2 to S_3.

Requisite response variety is essential (i.e., an asterisk must exist in

[21]Transducers are monitor-control units. They receive input information (monitor to controller) to which they respond according to their (policy) design. A transducer can be used to read outside environmental conditions and convert these data into instructions for maintaining a comfortable inside cabin system.

[22]Mechanical valves are usually less costly than mechanical transducers.

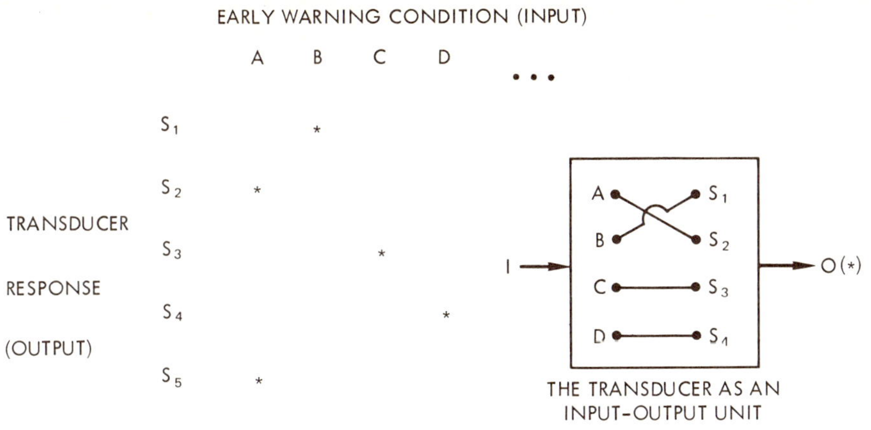

FIGURE 9. The Behavior of a Transducer

each column). If it did not, then for that column a new strategy would have to be found that could maintain control by assuring the $O(*)$ outcome. In this case, since S_2 and S_5 are equivalent, one or the other need not be maintained.

According to the law of requisite variety, at least one strategy must be able to provide the desired outcome state $O(*)$ for each different condition ($A, B, C, D, \ldots$) that can occur. No more than one asterisk-producing strategy need exist for each condition. Otherwise, the transducer's design is inefficient. The ergodic state assures that one of the conditions ($A, B, C, D, \ldots$) will occur, and that no condition will appear that is not part of the ergodic set. Because of this last assurance, it is more likely to be economical to design a transducer for a policy system than for a planning system.

A planning transducer for determinate situations is based on the prediction that one particular condition (such as $A, B, C, D, \ldots$) will occur. A contingency planning transducer is designed for the eventuality that more than one condition (say A or C) can occur. But in all planning circumstances, the predicted states might never materialize. This is in keeping with the definition of transient systems.

When a transducer can be designed to stand in for the manager, the important condition of management by exception (MBE) has been achieved. Although we ordinarily associate MBE with policy-type recurrence properties, it can also be applied to planning situations that are deterministic—i.e., to PERT-type projects. The fact is that deterministic planning conditions are convertible to ergodic systems by simple transformations of terms. Transducers work effectively in these cases. As we have already mentioned, a major purpose of planning is to convert non-ergodic systems to ergodic ones. We shall discuss now some ways in which such a system's effects are achieved.

The Manager as an Ergodic Converter

An important distinction can be drawn between upper-, middle-, and lower-management levels in terms of their types of effect on the system.

Upper management functions as an ergodic converter by creating new conditions that render planning situations ergodic.

Lower management operates as a policy/control transducer that could be mechanized or automated, but only at a greater cost than the managers' salaries. Policies are not designed at the lower-managerial levels; they are simply carried out there. Most of these policies are possible because of the activities of upper-management ergodic converters.

Middle management builds and installs transducers at lower levels, carrying out plans received from the upper levels. Thus, middle management implements top-management policy, assigning appropriate jobs to lower management and assuming authority for the way they are done. In this capacity, middle management serves as a decision valve. When, because of an exception, direct managerial action is called for, middle management wrestles with Type I and Type II decision errors. In fact, policy exceptions that require on-line management (i.e., the basis for MBE) are a major source of Type I versus Type II error decisions.

The above classification can be faulted on many levels, but it is important as a generalization of the managerial hierarchy.

Upper-management talents are very rare. It takes unusual special abilities to convert non-ergodic systems to ergodic ones. In our present-day social milieu, most of these skills are far removed from technical or methodological training. Primarily, these skills are derived from abilities to develop and direct systems and from leadership talents that utilize psychological and sociological factors. Sometimes, by redefining a situation, a consensus can be obtained acknowledging its accuracy. Behavioral systems often can be converted to ergodicity in this way. In other words, the participating individuals agree to accept specific standards of behavior. These standards, if properly designed, create an equilibrium-type of policy system. The basis of agreement about the standards can range from autocratic to intensely individual and highly motivated personal behaviors.

By rejecting new trends that threaten the status quo, existing ergodic conditions often can be maintained. Top management's drive to convert planning systems to ergodic conditions is reinforced by middle management's predilection against Type II errors. Donald Schon, observing that management is adroit at such maneuvers, has furnished evidence of these effects.[23] Specifically, managers can create the impression that stationary ergodic systems exist by assuming that certainty is a good approximation of the actual conditions. If the assumption is effective, the system will take on the assumed characteristics. A management failure occurs when the state of the system remains independent of the assumptions.

At a more complex level, a stationary condition is established when the manager accepts a forecast as being accurate so that the expected value criterion can be employed. It is in this complex, interactive sense that false assumptions will be penalized. By the time the discrepancies appear, however, it may be impossible to find out who was responsible for them.

Within all organizations, the difference between optimal individual and optimal organizational behavior should be considered and reconciled. Similarly, interactions between the organization and society must be evaluated on the basis of a sufficiently long planning horizon.

[23]Schon, *op. cit.*

The length of the planning horizon that is used affects the correctness of the assumption that recurrent conditions exist. One week is a reasonable time in which to assume that a stationary situation exists. Ergodicity may be an acceptable condition for one month. In this case, for periods longer than one month only transient conditions may be said to exist.

When the manager employs policy by shortening his planning horizon, he is seeking the economic benefits of policy and control. Nevertheless, in net, he may penalize his organization as the result of temporal suboptimization. In other words, when the result of many short-term decisions are viewed over the long run, the organization may be performing significantly below its capabilities. The use of shorter planning horizons, and the use of policy instead of planning, can produce good day to day results, but the energy of the firm may be subverted to these short-term goals. Characteristic of Type I errors, such effects will seldom be detected.

The appropriate length of the planning horizon is a complex question. It does have a theoretically obtainable normative solution based on the relations:

1. The SUM [of n optimal subsystems of interval T] $\leqq$ The optimal [SUM of n subsystems of interval T]
2. The value of using (formal) policy controls $\geqq$ The value of using planning methods (in the short run)
3. The cost of planning methods $\leqq$ The cost of control systems.

By using contingency planning, the manager acts as though he knows which of several possible future conditions will occur. The assumption that ergodic conditions will persist over the contingency planning horizon is always some degree of a gamble. Therefore, managers often spend much effort trying to guarantee that at least one of the contingencies for which they have prepared will occur.

It is evident why top managers will reject opportunities that make the future uncertain for alternatives that ensure secure situations. That is why much planning effort is predicated on the removal of uncertain paths rather than on the assumption that it is good to "progress" into new, uncharted situations. For this reason, planning the future can frequently be equated with maintaining the present. But the brilliant manager is the one who ventures ahead because of his ability to create new ergodic conditions from old ones, not just once, but continually.

CONCLUSIONS AND OPENINGS

Management recognizes that with increasingly larger systems, the old approaches for maintaining ergodic systems are in adequate. Until the 1960's, the main threat to ergodic conversion was market competition. Since that time, social forces have arisen that disturb the organization's division of hierarchical responsibilities.

Consumer behavior has changed in such a way that ergodic considerations apply for ever-shortening planning horizons. Social forces have deteriorated the stability of systems. Such problems force management to rely less on intuition and more on rational methods. It is difficult to be a great architect when the land is shifting and impossible to be a great leader when that very concept is anathema to increasing numbers of the population. The rational approach of management science (being fully aware of political ramifications) is far too attractive for management to ignore. The eventual result of unexpected perturbations and continual surprise will be a new definition of management that must affect the future of all organizations.

SUGGESTIONS FOR FUTURE READING

BECKETT, JOHN A., *Management Dynamics, The New Synthesis* (New York: McGraw-Hill Book Co., Inc., 1971).

BEER, STAFFORD, *Decision and Control* (New York: John Wiley & Sons, Inc., 1967).

EMERY, F.E., *Systems Thinking* (London: Penguin Books, Ltd., 1970).

FORRESTER, JAY W., *Industrial Dynamics* (New York: John Wiley & Sons, Inc., 1961).

HARE, VAN COURT, JR., *Systems Analysis: A Diagnostic Approach* (New York: Harcourt Brace Jovanovich, Inc., 1967).

HOPEMAN, RICHARD J., *Systems Analysis and Operations Management* (Columbus, Ohio: Charles E. Merrill Publishing Co., 1969).

JOHNSON, RICHARD A., FREMONT E. KAST, AND JAMES E. ROSENZWEIG, *The Theory and Management of Systems*, 2nd ed. (New York: McGraw-Hill Book Co., Inc., 1967).

MCKEAN, ROLAND N., *Efficiency in Government Through Systems Analysis* (New York: John Wiley & Sons, Inc., 1958).

MCMILLAN, CLAUDE, AND RICHARD F. GONZALEZ, *Systems Analysis*, rev. ed. (Homewood, Illinois: Richard D. Irwin, 1968).

MILLER, DAVID W., AND MARTIN K. STARR, *Executive Decisions and Operations Research*, 2nd ed. (Englewood Cliffs, N.J.: Prentice-Hall, Inc., 1969).

QUADE, E.S., AND W.I. BOUCHER (Eds.), *Systems Analysis and Policy Planning* (New York: American Elsevier Publishing Co., 1968).

STARR, MARTIN K. (Ed.), *Management of Production* (London: Penguin Books, Ltd., 1970).

STARR, MARTIN K., *Management: A Modern Approach* (New York: Harcourt Brace Jovanovich, Inc., 1971).

STARR, MARTIN K., *Production Management: Systems and Synthesis*, 2nd ed. (Englewood-Cliffs, N.J.: Prentice-Hall, Inc., 1972).

STARR, MARTIN K., *Systems Management of Operations* (Englewood Cliffs, N.J.: Prentice-Hall, Inc., 1971).

A Philosophical Comment on Management Science

C. West Churchman

Professor
School of Business Administration
University of California, Berkeley

It seems to me that the most helpful thing I can do in making comments on Professor Starr's paper is to attempt to perform the philosopher's task by trying to portray its message in a larger setting.

To begin with, management science is itself a set of systems, each system attempting to reflect and interpret some aspect of the managerial system. Since management science is a system, it also has a management and a set of policies that it hopes to follow. Management science is an "inquiring system" and faces much the same set of problems as does the manager of an enterprise.

Now, one of the most difficult problems of every manager of a business firm or a government agency is to understand the realities of his organization. This task is especially difficult since in most organizations there are many competing notions about this reality, the real objectives, the real environment, the real policies, and so on. Furthermore, it serves the purposes of certain individuals within the organization to attempt to convince the manager of a particular viewpoint with respect to these realities. The accountant will try to agree that the real issues are concerned with how resources are spent and how revenue is to be received and recognized. The sales manager tends to see the main reality of the organization as its relationship to its consumers. The bureaucrat will mainly see the organization as a set of structured communications and power links.

If we turn this fairly obvious piece of common sense back to the management scientist as a system, we can see that the issue here is the reality of the management science system. What is it really trying to accomplish, and how is it really organized to do what it sets out to do?

One response comes almost immediately to mind—namely, that the management scientist is essentially a disciplinarian; he has been trained to think of pieces of reality in the light of a particular discipline. Thus, the economist sees society and its managers as "essentially" individuals who are trying to cope with economic problems concerning allocation of resources, and the like. The psychologist sees society and the manager as "essentially" dealing with the psychological forces of the world. And of course the engineer will try to look at society in his "more precise fashion," as an extremely complicated type of machine.

Furthermore, if the management scientist can find evidence that supports his viewpoint, then his conviction about the reality of the system that he is observing, based on his disciplinary background, becomes even stronger.

I can illustrate this phenomenon by one example that Professor Starr himself uses in his article. When we decided to set up a journal for The Institute of Management Sciences that would be more responsive to managers and their needs, we hoped that the journal would contain articles by managers as well as scientists, so that the managers could in some sense teach the scientists as well as the scientists teach the managers. This hope has never been realized, and I think one explanation is that the managers never see themselves in the perspective of the management scientist. Very few managers, for example, would regard themselves as "transducers," and very few would see themselves as having anything to do with an ergodic process.

One rather famous management scientist is quoted as having said that most people in society (and I imagine he includes managers) cannot understand the realities of society because society is "by its very nature" a non-linear feedback system. One might go on to add that most managers don't even know how blind they really are in this regard, since most of them don't even conceive of looking at the world as this particular management scientist has done.

Lest these remarks seem to portray a rather negative criticism of Professor Starr's contribution, let me hasten to point out that one of the really serious needs of our society is for us collectively to acquire different perspectives of what we are really like, and to respect these perspectives, not as representing *the* reality, but as one of the many ways of looking at reality. From the philosopher's viewpoint, the multiplicity of ways of looking at reality is about as close as the human intellect can come to the *representation* of reality.

It is of course interesting for a sociologist or historian of science to see how each of the disciplines tries to put itself into a "fundamental" position. I am a philosopher and therefore I might argue with Professor Starr that the philosopher has the ultimate perspective, because the philosopher is primarily interested in the real meaning of Professor Starr's "improvement." The philosopher, for example, would want to know why Professor Starr seems so confident that the efforts of the management scientist will improve society. The philosopher also will wonder whether describing the manager as a transducer is nearly as important as describing the manager as a moral individual. Surely the "good" manager is not a good transducer; a good manager is one who strives for worthy goals or whose managerial practices are moral.

But then, you see, Professor Starr could reply that all of the above is a good example itself of a management process whereby the philosopher is trying to cope with a certain set of managerial problems, and this coping can be described in terms of an ergodic process. But there is a more important problem that lies outside our interdisciplinary quarrel. One of the deepest mysteries to those of us who have been trained in the disciplines is to try to understand how the managers perceive themselves and their realities. The frustrations involved in getting the managers to explain themselves in clear and precise disciplinarian language have led many management scientists to suspect that the managers have no such perspective. Alternatively, we might come to suspect that the question of perspectives is not one that even enters into managerial thinking. And yet managers certainly seem to distinguish between what they call facts and abstractions, and to regard what they call facts to be the realities, and abstractions to be irritating, unnecessary, costly activities.

But I'm an optimist. I hope that attempts like Professor Starr's to explain to managers how *he* perceives management will be intelligible to managers and read by them, and that their responses in turn may help Professor Starr and myself to begin to understand more clearly how the manager perceives reality, so that the communication between the scientist and the manager will become far richer than it has hitherto.

The Changing Field of Management Science

David B. Hertz

McKinsey and Company, Inc., New York

In attempting to describe the field of management science and its relationship to management, Professor Starr quite properly focuses on model building as the key element differentiating management science from other means of analyzing, understanding, and developing approaches to solving problems inherent in organizing and directing human endeavors. He appropriately emphasizes the relationship of management science to decision-making. Managers, through the ages, have looked for help in making decisions to achieve organizational and personal objectives. The effective tools of societal decision-making in any epoch are part and parcel of the managerial equipment of the time. In the last several decades, science, as exemplified by the development of logically consistent representations of decision situations, has increasingly found a place in the executive suite. These developments—systems engineering in the telephone industry in the 1920s, statistical quality control in the 1930s, operational research in World War II, among others—have come to be known as management science. It is basically an "action" science that attempts to explain the world around the manager in ways that provide better means for answering questions that seem significant.

In a sense, Professor Starr's sharp distinction between hard and soft models in the management sciences is misplaced. Models are mechanisms not only for describing the world around us but (*if* they are "managerial" in nature) also permit the manager to examine in some realistic way the consequences that may ensue from a decision taken from some set of alternative courses of action. In the long run, such models of necessity may be "soft," in Professor Starr's own terms. The question he leaves unanswered is whether our knowledge and understanding of social behavior is sufficient to suggest that better decisions will be made as a result of the use of effective models; that is, models that are logically consistent and have an inductive fit with the physical and social world around us. In other words, we are dealing with human behavior in organizing, coordinating, and directing the use of resources and the application of skills in providing for economic and social needs.

Thus we can say that the tools we have developed are appropriate to our abilities and therefore our needs, and that much has been done to apply them to a wide variety of problems. As Professor Starr suggests, management science has drawn on many threads of theoretical understanding in the behavioral and physical sciences. He bases much of his description of "a unified theory of management based on management information" on ideas and developments from the science of control mechanisms. There is no doubt that this area, as exemplified by Beer's work in cybernetics that Starr cites, influences the way in which models are built and the way in which social organizations may be described. On the other hand, it probably is pushing the state of our knowledge too far to suggest that we can do much more than improve to a small degree the kinds and quality of information on which managers base their choices, or that any of the cybernetic models do much more than suggest the direction that a theoretical framework for a "science of managerial choice" must take.

From a purely pragmatic viewpoint, the manager must find ways of choosing among alternatives for allocating his resources, for sequencing activities that he and others will carry out, and for acquiring new and different people and physical resources. To do this, he must rely on some reasonable descriptions of the character and stability of the environment in which the consequences of such decisions will unfold, both in the short- and the long-term future. He must face up to the patterns of uncertainty in these environments that are both inevitable and unpredictable. Professor Starr says that the manager generally wishes to avoid "unpleasant" consequences, but this is only one kind of value system or description of individual utility preference that is possible. Such value systems also depend very significantly on what an individual manager views as "unpleasant." To some managers the unexpected may be terribly unpleasant; to others the very fact of a high degree of risk and uncertainty and unexpectedness in the future may be exhilarating and challenging.

Thus, risk has its price and the decision maker does provide margins of safety to guard against universal uncertainty; but margins of safety are expensive and the management sciences provide measures of the cost and stabilizing effects of margins in terms of inventory stock levels, or the number of check-out counters, or airport runways, and the like. Programming methodologies that provide cost and benefit relationships, allocation questions such as scheduling and blending crude oil in a refinery, also turn out to be limited by uncertainty in virtually every activity being programmed—changes in the price of crude oil, delays in ship arrivals, equipment breakdowns, among a host of other unanticipated events. For these reasons the systems approach, which attempts to get beyond a single technique or methodology for a specific logical description, is the way management must deal with its decision problems.

Management science has shifted toward the systems approach as exemplified by Churchman.[1] The systems approach involves building goal-oriented models in a decision-making situation and attempts to account for as wide a set of circumstances and consequences (including the influence of the model builder and model) that will permit effective continuing management towards some chosen objectives. It also must permit trade-offs to be evaluated in terms of alternative choices of action, and is oriented as much toward the evaluation of means as toward the attainment of ends.

The question of how to combine individual utility preferences in some reasonably stable way remains unanswered and for the moment almost unanswerable. What the management sciences permit under such circumstances is an evaluation of organizational utilities based on argumentation and adversary-type proceedings; that is, the management scientist may produce a model suggesting various kinds of consequences that may arise from alternative resource allocation or sequencing decisions. If the model is realistic, it will take into account the effect on the outcomes of various forms of uncertainty and, in essence, portray and array the risks that are inherent in particular situations. Even in the examples that Professor Starr gives of the "hardest" models—say linear programming applied to a transportation network—the degree of uncertainty must be such that either the decisions will be almost trivial or that different risk-avoidance feelings on the part of individuals would yield different choices.

So, what happens in the management sciences when an effective model is built is that the managers are given the opportunity to agree on compromise criteria that ultimately yield a decision that in some sense represents the strength of the risk-taking positions assumed by various members of the group.

Systems analysis in production, marketing, and financial decision-taking has led to the development of models that include as variables a number of significant elements of these activities. These kinds of models provide business,

[1]C. West Churchman, *The Systems Approach* (New York: Dell Publishing Co., 1968).

institutional, and government planners with the opportunity to test alternative strategies or combinations of different courses of action taken in different sequences. Furthermore, they allow for rapid testing of useful shifts in strategies as one or more assumptions on which they are based are demonstrated to be false. In fact, the consequences of an assumption being subsequently found false may be identified in advance. This important step allows planners to develop and test contingency plans, and even contingency models based on different assumptions, and have them ready when needed. Such contributions by the management scientists and systems analysts have greatly strengthened the effectiveness of planners in non-military institutions and suggests that the organizational roles of planner, analysts, and decision takers be closely integrated. Only when this is done can the potential contribution of systems analysis and management science be translated into effective and realistic results.[2]

Professor Starr neglects the importance of the systems approach in favor of a control system description of the manager. Although there is nothing inherently wrong with this description, it is limited in that it really addresses itself only to the abstract statement of a manager's role in an organization in terms of what Starr calls an ergodic conversion. Perhaps it is a generalization about managerial hierarchies but it does not really tell us very much about the way in which management science adds to the decision-making capability of the wide variety of individuals who find themselves in managerial situations.

We have come a long way. We have increased dramatically the technical apparatus aimed toward the development of more scientific management. We know how to produce models that bear some reasonable resemblance to the real world today. When a manager is faced with a problem, the scientist usually can say with some assurance whether or not he can begin to build a practical model. Management science helps address the "what if" questions. Its kit bag of tools is rather full. One can describe in great depth the logical structure of inventory problems, job shop sequencing problems, and some simple resource allocation problems. (On the other hand, allocation of resources in, say, the national sphere has yet to be described effectively by decision-making models.)

The understanding of information systems on which management decisions are going to be based has been clarified. It has become increasingly clear that the network of information inputs that enable a social organization to operate with reasonable stability includes: (1) transaction systems describing the basic material or data flows; (2) decision systems oriented around the transactions, such as inventory control systems; (3) decision systems that require interrelated data from a multitude of activities, such as production scheduling or activity sequencing; (4) score card systems that measure the current state or level of the variables in an organization; (5) model structures describing the future as it may result from alternative actions taken internally and externally.

This network, when implemented effectively, permits the assumptions that underlie the predictions of consequences based on specific models to be continually checked and, as Starr points out, permits the manager to take continuing action (as he sees any assumption being falsified) to adjust the decisions and future actions to revised sets of such assumptions.

As the manager has been educated to the usefulness of the management science approach, so the management scientist has been getting educated to the realities of management. He finds that managers understand, perhaps more deeply than they have been given credit for, the difficulties of solving problems in their particular areas of uncertainty. And even if the manager puzzles about how to solve a problem, he realizes certainly how hard it is. And the good management scientist puts himself in the shoes of the manager and understands

[2]See, for example, Russell Ackoff, *The Concept of Corporate Planning* (New York: Wiley-Interscience, 1970).

that societal problem-solving has to be a cooperative effort.

As I have said elsewhere, in a volatile and mercurial world in which decisions are made in the face of complexity and uncertainty, it is an exciting experience to find the hidden parameters that enable the searcher to measure variation, remove assignable causes, and establish control; to determine how and why decision makers can supplement their intuition and judgment with adequate and effective quantitative support. This is what the action in the action science of management is all about.[3]

DISCUSSION QUESTIONS

1. What is a model? Why should managers be interested in models? What can models do for management?
2. What is management science? Isn't it true that there really isn't such a thing, that management is actually an art?
3. What is a "hard" model? Are there "soft" models? If so, what are they?
4. What is an "ergodic" system? How does it differ from a periodic system? A transient system?
5. Management science, unlike other sciences, exists to improve the society of man. Comment.
6. What is the difference between Type I and II errors?
7. Is the manager a "transducer"? And if so, so what?
8. Should managers sacrifice opportunities that create uncertain futures in return for secure situations?
9. Will (or must) better decisions result from the use of models?

[3]David B. Hertz, "Has Management Science Reached a Dead End?" *Innovation*, Vol. 25 (1971).

5

The Usefulness of "Management Thought" for Management

Richard G. Brandenburg

Dean and Professor
School of Management
State University of New York at Buffalo

This chapter is neither a comprehensive history nor a detailed explanation of the various schools of thought in management. Rather, the focus is on usefulness. What is management thought good for? What are its limitations? How are the major schools of thought used, and by whom?

Consideration of whether management thought is or is not useful has frustrating "now you see it, now you don't" characteristics. First, it is difficult to isolate any particular set of principles (scientific management, management process, human relations) in "pure" form from various adaptations, modifications, and efforts to translate the principles into practice or use them in research. Second, particular principles of management thought get mixed in with other methods, systems, practices, and styles involved concurrently in managing or in studying and doing research on management. Third, any evidence of a cause-effect relationship between following a particular school of thought and achieving a desired organizational performance result is at best documented only in isolated cases, frequently presented without attention to other significant factors that characterize the situation, and invariably evaluated without reference to how much better or worse some other alternative approach would have been.

Certain disciples and critics of management thought have added to the confusion. Depending on what conclusion they desire, some students of management thought have selectively emphasized certain points and suppressed others, asserted that the leading proponents really meant something more or different than they said, and have imputed relative importance among various ideas when there was no objective basis for doing so. Some experts have set up categories and classification schemes to place diverse elements of management thought into conceptual frameworks. Then they have attributed more substance to the categories per se than to the ideas subjected to categorization in the first place. The ambiguity inherent in who thought what, and what is or is not a legitimate part of an identifiable school of thought, requires an attitude of flexibility at the outset in judging the usefulness of managerial thought.

CRITERIA FOR ASSESSING SCHOOLS OF THOUGHT

An underlying issue basic to any discussion of the merits of management thought is that of criteria for judging its uses and limits. Criteria for whether and how management thought is useful are derived from several perspectives:

1. Putting available knowledge to work—practicing managers.
2. Introducing, and translating knowledge into forms intended to change and improve what managers do and how they do it—consultants to managers.
3. Transferring and interpreting knowledge to increase the capabilities of individuals to practice or do research on management—students and teachers of management.
4. Adding to the state of knowledge of concepts, facts, theories, and techniques related to management—researchers of management.

This discussion, therefore, rests on the premise that the meaning and merits of management thought can be approached in terms of its uses and limits in generating, transferring, disseminating, and applying information about management. To organize this approach, five criterion-oriented questions are specified, implications of each question are discussed, and several general conclusions are drawn. The basic questions are:

1. How well have schools of management thought helped to provide a vocabulary useful in defining, describing, and explaining the nature of management?
2. Has management thought helped contribute to the development of a cumulative, adaptive body of knowledge and practice that builds on and/or corrects the deficiencies of past experience and helps predict significant future trends?
3. Has management thought facilitated the generalization and transferability of notions about management from particular, individual situations to broader classes of situations, thereby suggesting common, generic characteristics and patterns among problems and processes of management?
4. How much does management thought help in translating broad concepts and principles into specific guidelines and operational tools tailored to particular management problems? Are there bases for evaluating the match between management technology on the one hand and specific organizational problems requiring the use of such methods on the other?
5. Does management thought indicate procedures for designing management processes and systems, including how desired system performance is related to design variables, and what steps should be followed in the design process? What indicators are available for determining if any one approach to managerial problem-solving is better than any other in a given situation, and if so, how much better?

BOUNDARY CONDITIONS FOR INTERPRETING AND APPLYING THE CRITERIA

The originators and developers of managerial thought (scientific management, human relations, management process) no doubt had particular purposes for their work in the first place. They often left unstated important assumptions about what they were trying to encompass or accomplish in their work and writing. However, criticizing them for failure to take into account innumerable other factors that the critic may wish to suggest degenerates into intellectual nitpicking. Such criticisms lead nowhere in making improvements. By focusing only on what a school of thought does not do, such critics avoid interpreting the significance of ideas or propositions under circumstances in which they should be relevant.

The usefulness of any principle of management thought for understanding, describing, predicting, or improving management behavior must be tested with awareness of the diversity of problem-solving techniques and problem-generating situations encountered in management. Illustrating the variety of decision analysis techniques, Ansoff asserts:

> Both managers and analysts can be observed to employ a variety of partially structured approaches to their problems [in addition to unstructured and fully structured methods].[1]

He identifies eight categories of management problem-solving methodologies, from "unstructured" to "algorithmic." Each is different with respect to how variables, models to operate on the variables, payoff functions, generation of solution alternatives, and solution selection are treated.

The diversity in the sources and types of problems that managers must solve is suggested by Newman.[2] He begins by sorting out characteristics of the technology by which organizations convert raw materials into finished products or services. He argues that the most appropriate features of formal organization structure and relationships, leadership styles, nature of plans and planning, and nature of controls should depend on the technological character of the work involved in converting human, physical, financial, and information resources into output products or services.

The Ansoff and Newman frameworks suggest the highly varied nature of different management problems, processes, and methods of analysis. It is simplistic to assume that any particular part of management thought can refer to more than a limited part of this total territory. The problem is that it is difficult to infer what the originator of any particular principle or concept assumed about boundaries of relevance and applicability. A further difficulty is judging if any recent progress toward pinning down boundaries on uses and limits of a concept has resulted from insights building on earlier

[1] H. I. Ansoff, "Managerial Problem Solving," *Journal of Business Policy* (Autumn, 1971), p. 18.

[2] W. H. Newman, "Strategy and Management Structure," *Journal of Business Policy* (Autumn, 1971), pp. 56–66.

stages in the evolution of management thought. Has there been any self-correcting trend toward defining more realistic limits on what management thought is and is not supposed to be good for?

In the discussion that follows, management thought is considered with respect to each of the five broad criteria listed previously. The diversity of processes and problems of management is a necessary underlying perspective that cuts across all five categories. In some cases recognition of this diversity enhances the value of a particular part of management thought, whereas in others it adds further justification to the view that traditional notions of management thought have little or no current utility.

MANAGEMENT THOUGHT AS A LANGUAGE TO DEFINE, DESCRIBE, AND EXPLAIN MANAGEMENT

Managerial thought has contributed terminology that has paved the way to understanding what managers do, has opened avenues of management, and has developed a management science.

Well known terminology for classifying the tasks managers perform is Fayol's ("planning, organization, command, coordination, and control." Fayol categorized industrial operations along functional lines: technical, commercial, financial, security, administration, and accounting. Furthermore, he stated fourteen principles of administration that blended technological and structural with behavioral and motivational concerns, based on his personal observations and experience. These terms and principles were intended to be a comprehensive "theory," combining both description of the current practice and guidelines for managerial effectiveness.

Other parts of the language of management, spelled out in Fayol's management thought, included the notion that his terms and principles were applicable not only to business management, but to management of all purposive organizations. In this respect, Cooke wrote about university management and city management in 1910 and 1919, respectively. Sheldon added still another dimension to the glossary of explanatory concepts by identifying social/community responsibility issues as concerns of business, as well as issues of internal operations. He also listed certain factors external to the firm as influencing business decision-making processes—government actions, public attitudes, foreign trade, education, finance, labor, and science/technology. Mayo and Follett were prominent among those who introduced notions of individual motivation, human relations, and leadership to a beginning vocabulary of modern management.

The above is illustrative of how management thought contributed to building up a set of terms to help label what goes on in managing. A second class of explanatory terms refers to management as a dynamic process. Follett, for instance, characterized management activity as undergoing continuous evolution and development, particular methods of which must be adapted to the changing situations managers encounter. Thus, recognition is given to the significant managerial skill of matching problems as they occur in ongoing organizations to preferred techniques and principles for effecting a solution.

A third type of terminological contribution by management thought is a vocabulary to describe how organizations work. Chester Barnard characterized an organization as a system of cooperative human activities having as its purpose the creation, transformation, and exchange of utilities. He laid the groundwork for explaining organizational behavior in terms of inducements and contributions for satisfying the motives of various individual organizational participants in ways that are sufficient and efficient in accomplishing the purposes of the organization as a whole.

Following from Barnard's viewpoint is Simon's highly significant work on organizational equilibrium, the meaning of organizational efficiency, the characteristics of organizations in terms of how decision-making functions are distributed, and the influences that shape premises on which individual managers make decisions.

In summary, therefore, management thought has laid the foundation for a language of management, encompassing terminology for:

1. Elements internal to the process of managing.
2. Pervasiveness of management as a societal function (not just a business function).
3. Scope of managerial concerns, covering factors both internal and external to the organization being managed.
4. Elements of the job of managing.
5. Organizational behavior as consisting of phenomena amenable to systematic description and understanding.

Managerial thought also introduced notions relevant to the beginning of an applied science of management. The most important of these concepts originate from the scientific management school and Frederick Taylor. Taylor's position was that management problems can be subjected to systematic data gathering, experimentation, and analysis to understand what mechanisms are at work, and thereby to obtain a basis for designing improvements in management processes.

Others before Taylor, such as Coulomb, Babbidge, and Gerstner, tried to measure and analyze how activities involving workers and machines should be carried out. But Taylor asserted that management activities, not just the tasks or technology to be managed, can be subjected to systematic research and study. He thereby recognized both the differences and interrelationships between theory and practice essential to the evolution of management toward the status of a discipline and profession.

However, Herbert Simon's specification of the limits of an administrative science is both consistent with the Taylor philosophy and suggestive of why most of the notions from the traditional schools of thought were far from scientific:

> Procedures are termed "good" when they are conducive to the attainment of specified objectives and "bad" when they are not conducive to such attainment.

That they are or are not so conducive is purely a matter of fact, and it is this factual element which makes up the real substance of an administrative science.[3]

Clearly, management thought as a source of working vocabulary and explanatory concepts has not been adequate in and of itself for the needs of practicing managers, consultants, assisting managers, teachers, students, or researchers. Although different terms are used, few underlying substantive concepts are available as guides to the practice of management. The language of management thought has been deficient as a stimulus for formulating hypotheses about management problems and processes that researchers can test. Issues such as how managers recognize and select which problem to work on, how solution alternatives are invented, how to choose a preferred course of action subject to organizational constraints on information availability, and attitudes and values of key individuals involved in decision implementation are hardly treated at all. Many labels lead nowhere—among them such terms as "decision-making," "management," and administration," because they are neither tied to any context nor related to any explicit statement of the purposes for which they are intended. Other terms take on unduly precise meanings because they are given false empirical characteristics when in fact they are abstract constructs.

Yet the language of management thought certainly has not hindered, and probably has helped to advance, the sophistication and operational usefulness of current terminology (however inadequate present ways of organizing our thinking about management might be). Terminological contributions of management thought take three forms:

1. facilitating the transfer of notions about management from teachers to students
2. illustrating the need for multiple perspectives and disciplines to be brought to bear in seeking an orderly understanding of what management is all about
3. identifying by the unanswered questions they raise the gaps in the state of knowledge as stimuli to further research.

MANAGEMENT THOUGHT AS A CUMULATIVE, ADAPTIVE BODY OF KNOWLEDGE

Most of the pioneers of management thought no doubt intended it to be a cumulative body of knowledge. Only in limited cases does it appear to have turned out that way. Later writers have indeed referred to or been influenced by the work of early contributors. But measures of any cumulative progress—previous gaps closed, deficiencies corrected, or systematic expansion of new concepts and findings that relate to and complement existing ideas—are lacking.

On the one hand is the assertion that ". . . many classical propositions have stimulated students to develop their own thinking related to manage-

[3]H. A. Simon, *Administrative Behavior* (New York: The Macmillan Co., 1947), p. 249.

ment and have helped operating executives perform their managerial functions."[4] On the other is the view that: "Confusion, by any other name, is progress to which we have not yet become accustomed."[5]

The hopes of pioneers in management thought that a body of knowledge should develop were apparent at an early stage. In the 1880's Towne urged that journals be published and professional associations be established to facilitate transfer of knowledge about the theory and practice of management. Wharton gave the University of Pennsylvania a grant to found the school that bears his name. Fayol argued that, because of their widespread values and applicability, management concepts should be taught in universities.

Certain schools of thought, especially scientific management and human relations, attracted critics who have filled many journal pages with discussions of deficiencies. Various areas of management thought also encouraged synthesis and integration such as Urwick's *Elements of Administration,* written in 1943 as a comprehensive consolidation and comparison of notions from Fayol, Follet, Mooney, and Taylor.

Taylor stated that the manager's role of planning methods of work should be carried out by evolutionary steps—planning, observing actions taken to comply with plans, replanning on the basis of new experience gained. Hence, from Taylor's perspective, the *practice* of management should be cumulative and adaptive over time, and changes in systems of management should follow an evolutionary pattern. It is less clear whether, in fact, the introduction of changes into the body of management thought have followed such a pattern.

Some efforts were made to make management thought a cumulative, systematically expanding body of knowledge. For example, a sampling orientation to the study of executive behavior was introduced by Holden, Fish, and Smith who interviewed managers in thirty-one companies in carrying out a research investigation.[6] Later attempts to relate concepts of management thought to empirical findings from other disciplines, and to apply comparative approaches, also should be noted. The question is whether these methodological changes were related to or independent of the then existing state of knowledge about how to study management.

It would appear that some parts of management thought were developed as reactions to other parts. Notions of efficiency, human rationality, economic motivation of workers, top-down coordination and authority, specialization of tasks, formal delineation of work plans, and instructions to workers are "classical" principles. Notions of designing and maintaining work situations in which the individual worker finds personal worth, an environment that supports his value systems, and arrangements tailored to his individual background and expectations are "human relations" principles, reflecting totally different underlying assumptions about how to manage an organization efficiently. However, both views suffer from the same limitations. They focus narrowly on only a few of the types of problems

[4] J. L. Massie in J. G. March (Ed.), *Handbook of Organizations* (Chicago: Rand McNally, 1965), p. 403.

[5] H. A. Simon in H. Koontz (Ed.), *Toward a Unified Theory of Management* (New York: McGraw-Hill Book Co., Inc., 1964), p. 82.

[6] P. E. Holden, L. S. Fish, and H. L. Smith, *Top Management Organizational Control* (New York: McGraw-Hill Book Co., Inc., 1941).

managers must solve. They fail to identify assumptions about the environment outside the organization, the technology inside it, or the nature of organizational objectives. They give no basis for estimating how much better one approach would be compared to any other with respect to performance results attained.

Barnard's elaboration of the importance of informal organizations within larger formal organizations has been an important influence on subsequent research work. Barnard drew attention to behavioral variables that influence the processes of decision-making as central to understanding organizational behavior. Simon, in turn, underscored the importance of formulating propositions about those variables and subjecting them to empirical testing in building toward a science of administrative behavior.

Modern management sciences have drawn heavily on methodologies from applied mathematics, economics, behavioral sciences, and statistics. More recently, however, there have been indications of the reverse—developments related to management, especially in the fields of computers and information processes, have stimulated further work in the traditionally more "basic" disciplines. This development is perhaps the most significant indication that a systematically expanding, cumulative body of knowledge is emerging as a foundation for a discipline of management. At issue is the extent to which managerial thought, per se, was the forerunner of and stimulus to the modern management sciences, thereby providing a historical link and thread of continuity in the changing state of knowledge relevant to management.

Another question fundamental to whether or not management thought is an adaptive body of knowledge is the nature of relationships between theory and practice. No doubt, various principles and concepts have influenced the activities of practicing managers. However, there is little evidence that application experience has been put to work in changing or improving theory and concepts. Furthermore, one is hard pressed to build a case that management practice has developed *because* of "theoretical" developments in schools of thought in management.

A different test of the cumulative character of management thought is whether different viewpoints in fact paralleled broad trends in the practice of management. Waldo argues this parallel.[7] Scientific management emerged in response to increasing pressures to obtain efficiency from man-machine configurations as a means of raising profits. This was followed by a "personnel movement" in which merit and training were substituted for loyalty and seniority, and organizational ends were thought to be best attained by effective management of human resources. Certainly, criticisms that managerial thought does not add up to a cumulative body of knowledge should be qualified by considerations of the context in which the thoughts of various management "schools" were stated. Information is inadequate, however, to make a strong case that the sequence in which elements of managerial thought were developed mirrored the historical sequence of fundamental problems in management practice.

The evidence about managerial thought as a cumulative, systematically expanding, and changing body of knowledge is "mixed-to-negative." There is indeed a history to be taught and learned. That there is a pattern, a sense

[7]D. Waldo, *The Administrative State* (New York: Ronald Press, 1948).

of direction and continuity that leads somewhere in terms of new methodologies for management research, new ways of introducing basic changes in management methods into organizations, and new tools for management practice in the future is highly doubtful.

TRANSFERABILITY OF MANAGEMENT THOUGHT

A third criterion for judging the usefulness of management thought is the degree to which principles and ideas can be generalized to cover diverse situations. Does management thought help in making comparisons, observing repeatable effects and behaviors, and discerning similarities among varied phenomena?

There are a few illustrations of problem-solving approaches, rather than particular rules or principles of action, relevant to the question of the transferability of management thought. For instance, Taylor's use of experimental methodology and an empirical attitude are presumably transferable from one operating problem to another. Similarly, Follett's approach to observing, recording, and relating management experiences to the total situation imply a transferable method for introducing organizational changes and improvements.

Both the scientific management and the human relations schools made distinct assumptions about how to do the work of an organization, which presumably were transferable from one organizational setting to another. Scientific management assumed that methods studies could identify the best way to do a job, that incentive systems could motivate workers to carry out the job at a desirable pace, using the best method, and that functional foremen could maintain conditions necessary for workers to do their jobs in the prescribed way. Human relations advocates assumed that maximizing employee participation, disseminating information throughout the organization, applying a uniform leadership style regardless of supervisor-subordinate relationships, and seeking a particular organizational climate regardless of the characteristics of the external environment were the best approaches. But, as pointed out, both philosophies failed to demonstrate their generality because of the wide disparity between hypotheses and empirical evidence.

Fayol asserted that certain principles of management could be used to make major improvements in the profit performance of any business. The techniques he prescribed included a program of action based on a 5-year to 10-year forecast of relevant factors, a survey of present/past business position, organization charts, and principles of command, coordination, and control. In all likelihood, Fayol's success resulted less from transferability of his principles than from his personal experience and skill as an executive in adapting general guidelines to suit the particular circumstances of the firms he directed. Fayol not only advocated the transferabiity of his management principles among different organizations but also made the case for transferability in another sense–teaching management to practioners. He stated that "Years of laborious effort are necessary to improve the technical knowledge of all personnel; to improve administrative competence, to introduce and make general among subordinates the use of sound methods (of administration) requires only months."[8] Why and how knowledge transfer about operational principles of management could be transferred so relatively easily and rapidly was not explained.

In summary, management thought is deficient on the transferability criterion for three reasons:

1. Generalizations, intended to describe and explain management and organization behavior, were not supported by systematically obtained observations of different situations.
2. Generalizations intended to prescribe improvements in organizational performance excluded other key variables characterizing the state of the organization in which the prescription was to be used, overlooked actions required to adapt the prescription to the peculiarities of particular situations, and gave no basis for comparing the costs with the benefits of implementing prescribed changes in management practices.
3. Generalizations tended to be too broad, thereby collapsing into tautologies or totally non-operational concepts.

Teachers, students, researchers, consultants, and practitioners can find little if any guidance on *how* to transfer principles of management thought among management problems beyond asserting that such transferability is desirable and somehow should be possible.

TRANSLATION OF GENERAL PRINCIPLES OF MANAGEMENT THOUGHT TO PARTICULAR PROBLEMS

Complementing the concern for transferability is the criterion of how useful management thought is in focusing or tailoring broad general concepts to fit specific, individual situations. This criterion of translation applies both to precise descriptive understanding of what is going on and to prescriptive application of an appropriate technique to assist a manager in solving problems.

Simon pointed out the deficiencies of management thought when certain general principles are evaluated on the basis of their capability for translation.[9] He stated that, for example, the specialization concept does not include guidelines about how to specialize so as to achieve greater efficiency in a particular situation. Neither are there guidelines for resolving conflicts among principles, such as specialization vs. unity of command, to indicate which principles should dominate, or how multiple conflicting principles should be blended to handle a given management requirement.

It can be argued, however, that although notions of managerial thought are limited in their ability to be directly and precisely translated into action guidelines, they do serve as diagnostic tools. Concepts can be useful in helping managers and researchers sense the existence of a problem and in serving as short-cut rules of thumb for identifying problems.

[8]Henri Fayol, "The Importance of the Administrative Function," translated by E. Dale, and in E. Dale (Ed.), *Readings in Management* (New York: McGraw-Hill Book Co., Inc., 1970), p. 149.

[9]Simon, *Administrative Behavior*, Chapter 2.

Several reasons why the translation capacity of management thought is limited include:

1. Failure to recognize that because organizations face different management problems at different stages in their development or as a result of differences in their external environments, appropriate adjustments in management styles and processes are required.
2. Failure to take into account those internal organizational characteristics that shape which problems are selected for attention, what comprises a satisfactory solution, and what determines the feasibility of implementing a chosen course of action. In this respect, processes by which managers make and evaluate estimates, deal with objectives other than profit maximization, "satisfice," search for problems and opportunities requiring follow-up, and accommodate key individuals in designing and implementing a decision are generally unaccounted for in statements about applying management thought.
3. Failure to develop an adequate typology of management problems against which to map the advantages and limitations of various elements of managerial thought. No guidance is given on how to start with the symptoms of a problem requiring a management response and select an appropriate concept from management thought to fit the problem characteristics, taking into account costs of problem analysis and solution implementation versus the payoffs achieved from the resulting solution.

Fayol, as in so many other aspects of management thought, explicitly recognized the translation problem:

> . . . there is nothing rigid or absolute about management affairs; it is all a question of proportions. Seldom do we have to apply the same principle twice in identical conditions; allowance must be made for different changing circumstances, for men just as different and changing, and for many other variable elements. Therefore, principles are flexible and capable of adaptation to every need; it is a matter of knowing how to make use of them, which is a difficult art requiring experience, decision, and proportion.[10]

Unfortunately, neither Fayol nor his fellow contributors to the foundations of management thought articulated the nature of this art, or recorded examples of how it should be practiced in translating generalizations into specific applications to specific problems.

MANAGEMENT THOUGHT AND THE DESIGN OF MANAGEMENT PROCESSES

A fifth criterion for judging the usefulness of management thought is how the principles and concepts assist in designing systems for management. Can management thought help in setting up a sequence of logical steps that will indicate a need for management action, steps that will aid in analyzing

[10]H. Fayol, *General and Industrial Management*, translation from the French edition (London: Isaac Pitman and Sons, 1949), p. 19.

the need, inventing alternative courses of action, evaluating each alternative, choosing a preferred action, implementing that choice, and monitoring the results accomplished? Does management thought provide assistance in organizing human, informational, and financial resources to carry out such a logic sequence?

In general, management thought has contributed more to identifying certain design variables and parameters, included in the vocabulary discussed earlier, than to methods for operating on and interrelating those variables and parameters. The contributions that have been made focus more on issues of logistics process design than on management process design.

For example, contributors to the so-called administrative management school, such as Urwick and Gulick, were concerned with how to configure various activities required to convert input raw materials or resources into output products and services. By implication, they treated this problem under the assumption that the objectives and purposes of the organization, and the technological content of each of the unit activities involved in resource conversion, were given. Then they proposed various types of administrative groupings of the necessary activities (by purpose, place, customer, or process). Advantages and disadvantages of each type were discussed and rules such as using only one method of grouping at each organizational level were stated. A trade-off between benefits of process specialization and costs of administrative-supervisory coordination was recognized.

Furthermore, classical management thought set forth the principle that the desirable sequence was, first, to specify the structure of tasks or jobs, and second, to staff-match people to the task structure. These notions were stimulated by Taylor's concepts of specifying output standards, defining work flow, assigning personnel by matching workers' abilities to jobs, using functional or technically specialized supervisors, and applying formal wage incentives to raise output.

The importance of this approach to the design of work processes cannot be overlooked. For example, Drucker asserted: "Altogether, it may well be the most powerful as well as the most lasting contribution America has made to Western thought since the Federalist Papers. As long as industrial society endures, we shall never lose again the insight that human work can be studied systematically, can be analyzed, can be improved by work on its elementary parts."[11]

What management thought has to say about design of *management processes* as distinct from logistic or resource conversion operations is more limited. In the 1880's, H. R. Towne pointed out that wage incentive systems could serve as an alternative to direct supervision in the face of the trend toward more widely dispersed, larger, business organizations. Without trying to overstate the case, this is an example of consciously substituting an information system for a "person-to-person" system in guiding the performance of an organization, wherein characteristics of the organization suggest that it is desirable to do so.

As indicated in the earlier discussions on terminology, Fayol stated key distinctions between problems of designing management processes versus

[11]P. Drucker, *The Practice of Management* (New York: Harper and Brothers, 1954), p. 280.

resource conversion processes. His concepts of different management functions (technical, commercial, financial, security, accounting, and administrative) and elements of administrative activities (forecasting, planning, organizing, coordinating, commanding, and controlling) were intended to be useful in designing management systems. He did not, however, indicate *how* to design a management organization that would incorporate appropriate proportions of the various management concepts consistent with business needs and characteristics. Nor did he suggest *how to configure processes* to plan, organize, or control.

Follet recognized, in a descriptive sense, the adaptive, continuous nature of management processes by pointing out that using a particular method to solve one coordination problem may result in another problem, which in turn will require a new method for its solution, and so on. How to set up and operate a management problem-solving system such that the costs of implementing the solutions it prescribes do not exceed the benefits of solving the problem was not discussed. Hence, again the needs for management design were stated, but procedures for doing the designing were not.

Barnard provided greater sophistication in characterizing factors relevant to the design of management processes by distinguishing between what general managers versus functional and staff managers do. Barnard's conception of the job of the general manager includes planning and structuring the organization's communication system, acquiring the resources needed to operate that system, and formulating organizational objectives. To this extent, Barnard's notions are forerunners of the modern conception that general managers are managers of systems that guide and control the work of other managers.

Barnard did not include criteria for comparing the relative merits of alternative designs or yardsticks for evaluating the performance of a management system. Sheldon identified social and community service concerns as a major area that business managers should be concerned about, thereby implying the multidimensional character of business objectives encompassing both economic and non-economic conditions.[12] The multidimensional criterion function concept is relevant to the problem of how to choose among alternative management systems. Alfred P. Sloan elaborated the idea of the profit center as a method of delimiting authority-responsibility relationships and as a basis for measuring performance. Simon's formulation of satisficing versus maximizing behavior, as descriptive of how certain management decisions actually are made, certainly applies in cases wherein alternatives must be compared on multiple dimensions. However, it would be an extreme exaggeration to argue that Sloan's or Simon's notions were derived in any systematic and significant way from the work of earlier contributors to management thought.

The contributions of management thought to the processes of management system design must be judged as minimal. Therein lies a significant deficiency of management thought for current teaching and for applications that would lead to changes and improvements in the management of modern organizations.

[12] O. Sheldon, *The Philosophy of Management* (London: Isaac Pitman and Sons, 1923).

CONCLUSIONS

The five criteria set forth in this chapter for testing usefulness suggest that management thought has contributed to a working vocabulary and has supplied a historical perspective on the evolution of management. However, management thought has contributed little to establishing a transferable set of concepts, methods of translating principles to specific practical applications, or guides for designing management systems. Students and teachers of management have benefited from both the content and the criticisms of the various schools of thought. No doubt, researchers have been led by perceived deficiencies in the body of traditional management thought to pursue lines of investigation leading to the modern management and behavioral sciences. Managers and consultants may have adapted certain concepts as starting points for diagnosing problems, constructing management processes, and formulating individual styles values that influence how they do their work.

Management thought has provided a base for modern managers and management scientists to learn how to avoid repeating past mistakes in the practice and theory of management. As a result, it is possible today to appreciate more objectively the complexity of management activities and to discriminate more sharply among relatively well-established versus underdeveloped or undeveloped areas of basic knowledge relevant to management. There is greater realism in evaluating the uses and limits of various methodologies currently available for management research.

The fundamental question implicit in any assessment of the usefulness of management thought is whether it has been part of a trend from approximate, limited, and shallow understanding toward rigorous, comprehensive, and intensive insights into what management is and how improvements can be made in managing. A fair assessment of management thought is that it has been a positive factor affecting the rate and direction of this progress, however modest may be the present state of development of management as a profession and discipline.

SUGGESTIONS FOR FUTURE READING

Extensive bibliographies of the works of major contributors to management thought and commentaries on management thought are included in:

C.S. George, *The History of Management Thought* (Englewood, Cliffs, N.J.: Prentice-Hall, Inc., 1968).

J.L. Massie, "Management Theory" in J.G. March (Ed.), *Handbook of Organizations* (Chicago: Rand McNally, 1965), pp. 387–422.

A representative sample of writings from the scientific management school, human relations school, and Fayol is contained in:

E. DALE (Ed.), *Readings in Management, Landmarks and New Frontiers* (New York: McGraw-Hill Book Co., Inc., 1970), pp. 107–149.

Other interpretations of the meaning of management thought are presented in:

H. KOONTZ (Ed.), *Toward a Unified Theory of Management* (New York: McGraw-Hill Book Co., Inc., 1964).

D.A. WOOLF, "The Management Theory Jungle Revisited," *Advanced Management Journal,* Vol. 30, No. 4 (October, 1965) pp. 6–15.

The Meaning of Management Thought

William B. Wolf

Professor
New York State School of Industrial and Labor Relations
Cornell University

As a critic I am unable to add much to Brandenburg's paper. I agree with the ambiguity, the difficulty in determining cause-and-effect relations, and the difficulty in segregating the so called "schools" of management thought. In fact, a critical review of the literature reveals a lack of distinctive schools. When I compare what various "authorities" said, it is amazing how few the original concepts, how great the overlap of ideas, and how diverse the vocabulary.

To evaluate the meaning of "management thought" we have to specify what management thought is and in whose eyes or by what standards we are evaluating its meaning. First, I find it difficult to separate "management thought" from the broader literature dealing with man in society. I think it relevant that those who dominate the literature that is labeled "management thought" frequently claim that their intellectual heritage is outside of management literature. For example, Chester I. Barnard felt he learned mainly from experience, but he listed five works that "as a whole seem to give a general background of scientific thought that leads ultimately to a sense of organization in general harmony [with his concepts]." They were:[1]

1. Eugen Ehrlich, *The Fundamental Principles of Sociology of Law,* translated by W. L. Moll (New York: Russell & Russell, 1936).
2. Vilfredo Pareto, *Mind and Society* (New York: Harcourt Brace & Co., 1935).
3. John R. Commons, *Institutional Economics* (New York: The Macmillan Co., 1934).

[1]William B. Wolf, *How to Understand Management: An Introduction to Chester I. Barnard* (Los Angeles: Lucas Bros. Publishers, 1968).

4. J. F. Brown, *Psychology and the Social Order* (New York: McGraw-Hill Book Co., Inc., 1936).
5. K. Koffka, *Principles of Gestalt Psychology* (New York: Harcourt Brace & Co., 1935).

Certainly, Barnard found little use for the contemporary management literature of his time. He quoted few "management writers" and those he did, such as Mary Parker Follett, found their stimulation in the broader areas of social science. For example, Follett tends to quote a wide variety of scientists such as the biologist, B. J. Haldane, the philosopher, Alfred North Whitehead, the psychologist, John Dewey, and the entomologist, William Morton Wheeler, as well as Albert Einstein. Similarly, Peter Drucker, who today is probably the most popular management writer, states "Books that have had an impact upon me have almost never been the books in the field; the greatest impacts upon me have probably been by assorted philosophers, assorted poets, and assorted historians."[2]

Similarly, Herbert Simon, who wrote one of the classic management texts, *Administrative Behavior*,[3] and collaborated on another, *Organizations*,[4] traces his intellectual heritage to such sources as a textbook on systems of ethics by F. C. Sharp, a graduate course in mathematical economics under Professor Schultz at the University of Chicago, and John Maynard Keynes' *Treatise on Probabilities*.[5]

In summary, those who are recognized as major contributors to management thought evidence little use of the literature of the field to which they contributed.[6]

If one talks to practitioners, it is soon evident that there is often a gap between theory and practice. Management thought has an impact but it is difficult to measure. As Chester I. Barnard observed about the influence of his book, *The Functions of the Executive:*

> Something that is quoted all of the time, especially after its survival 20 odd years, is having some influence, but you can't put your finger on it.

Barnard went on to say that despite its wide circulation, he felt there had been no follow-up on his book.[7]

At a technical level there is ample evidence that "management thought" has not been in vain. Frederick W. Taylor gave his paper on "A Piece-Rate System" in 1895.[8] It was a manual on conducting time study. There is no doubt that time study and its variations (i.e., synthetic time standards and standard data) are very much used by practioners. Similarly, H. L. Gantt's charts are probably one of the most used scheduling aids ever developed. Similarly, James O. McKinsey's book, *Budgeting Control*,[9] had a significant impact on practitioners. Moreover, management thinkers such as McKinsey, Drucker, and Barnard have carried their concepts into practice as consultants and/or practitioners.

My conclusion is that one shouldn't generalize on the impact of management thought. Rather, we should speak of the impact of a specific thinker on a specific audience. In such a framework

[2]Interview with William B. Wolf, March 16, 1966.

[3]New York: The Macmillan Co., 1947.

[4]James G. March and Herbert A. Simon, New York: John Wiley & Sons, Inc., 1958.

[5]Letter of March 3, 1969, to William B. Wolf.

[6]The exception is Col. Lyndall Urwick who was stimulated by a host of management writers such as Frederick W. Taylor, Henry Dennison, Mary Parker Follett, James Mooney, Henri Fayol, and others. But Urwick sees himself as an interpreter and popularizer rather than an innovator (Interview with William B. Wolf, 1964).

[7]William B. Wolf, *An Introduction to Chester I. Barnard and His Concepts of Organization and Management*, unpublished manuscript, II–31.

[8]F. W. Taylor, "A Piece-Rate System," *Transactions of the American Society of Mechanical Engineers*, XVI (1895), pp. 856–903.

[9]New York: Ronald Press, 1922.

Barnard, Simon, Lawrence, and others have influenced numerous academics. They have stimulated research, they are frequently quoted, and their works are "must" reading for graduate students. Others have contributed to debate and polemics but have had less influence. Similarly J. Forrester (Industrial Dynamics), Frederick Taylor (Time Study), Frank Gilbreth (Motion Study), Louis Davis (Job Design), and others have had a direct impact on practitioners.

The problem with which this chapter is concerned is in itself confusing. Management thought covers too broad a spectrum—ultimately analysis of it becomes a metaphysical consideration.

Before ending this critique I should like to turn to a few pet peeves of my own. First, I do not see management thought as developing a useful vocabulary. The semantics of management are horrible. Terms are used in different senses without precise definition–e.g., *organization* can be a noun synonymous with firm, or company, or it can be a process of management such as organizing the management of work. *Management* may refer to the processes of organization, direction, and control or to those carrying out these processes—i.e., managers. Most authors in the area are ignorant of or impervious to the definitions used by their colleagues. Hence, each contributes to the field by adding his own definitions, which are seldom integrated with what went before.

Second, I do not believe that the field grows in an orderly fashion. True, observations and experiments are conducted over time and books communicate across the years. But advancements often appear to wait until the times are ready. There is something in the environment that causes certain concepts to flourish. There is a *zeitgeist*—a climate of opinion—which admits new conceptualizations. Thus in Taylor's time we see a mechanistic approach to management; in Barnard's we see the start of an open-systems approach. Today the computer and advances related to the mathematical theory of communications have created a new climate. It is built on new concepts, a new vocabulary, and a new mathematics; it has not evolved from earlier management thought. In short, I do not believe it is relevant to look back at management thought to see if it has contributed to a cumulative and adaptive body of knowledge.

One looks back to get a feel of the field, to learn what has been done, to pose problems for future study and to check hypotheses. But this is not to say that knowledge of management or of any other field of science develops in an additive, sequential fashion. The great insights come sporadically. They are accepted when the *zeitgeist* provides a favorable climate.

BIBLIOGRAPHY

BARNARD, CHESTER I., *The Functions of the Executive* (Cambridge, Massachusetts: Harvard University Press, 1938).

DAVIS, LOUIS E., "The Design of Jobs," *Industrial Relations* Vol. 6 (October, 1966), pp. 21–45.

FORRESTER, JAY W., *Industrial Dynamics* (Cambridge, Massachusetts: M.I.T. Press, 1961).

GANTT, HENRY L., *Work, Wages, and Profits* (New York: The Engineering Magazine Co., 1910).

GILBRETH, FRANK B., AND LILLIAN M. GILBRETH, *Applied Motion Study* (New York: Sturgis and Walton Co., 1917).

MOONEY, J.D., AND A.C. REILEY, *The Principles of Organization* (New York: Harper and Brothers, 1939).

TAYLOR, FREDERICK W., *Shop Management* (New York: Harper and Bros., 1903).

SIMON, HERBERT A., *Administrative Behavior* (New York: The Macmillan Co., 1947).

SHANNON, CLAUDE E., AND WARREN WEAVER, *The Mathematical Theory of Communication* (Urbana: University of Illinois Press, 1949).

URWICK, L., *The Elements of Administration* (New York: Harper and Bros., 1944).

From Precedent Through Philosophy with Management Thought

Stanley C. Vance

H. T. Miner Professor of Business Administration
College of Business Administration
University of Oregon

Brandenburg's focus on management from taxonomic, technological, and teleological angles brings this elusive concept into better perspective. Ever since the Greek philosophers speculated on the meaning of life, scholars have ceaselessly tried to pigeonhole all things, thoughts, and actions into neat logical models. Millions of man-years have been squandered on the vain attempt at defining the philosophical absolutes, among which Good and Evil are still rather ephemeral. There is, of course, the absolute—Beauty—which poets after several milleniums of vain searching now despairingly say is solely in the eye of the beholder. And Truth, which is defined as conformity to fact, so often depends on who selects the facts.

Just as the philosophical absolutes prove to be on closer inspection far less absolute than we would like them to be, so too, as is evident in the preceding chapter, management can mean many things to many men. This seeming managerial Babel, however, does not mean chaos and futility. Management "languages" with specific refinements in word meaning, syntax, and even in prose and poetic expression, are in rapid evolutionary development. Brandenburg does point to Follett's reference to management as a process wherein continuous evolution and development shape this concept.

Keep in mind that stripped of frills and fancy phrases *management is simply getting things done through the efforts of others.* Yet, there are infinite things to be done in a near-infinite number of ways, by innumerable combinations of resources, and for countless reasons. Whenever we attempt to use logic, even as Chester Barnard did, to classify and to explain, we run the risk of stepping into a semantics muddle, or even worse, into a management morass.

One of the contributions of this

chapter is its stress on the multiplicity and mutability of management. There is no *one management* just as there is no one universally accepted deity, or sovereignty, or way of life. Nor does any one sector of society, such as business or government, have an exclusive claim on management.

Any management model, if it is to be useful, must be molded to current needs and circumstances. For example, consider the rapid acceptance of management practices in what too frequently are viewed as non-business endeavors: social agencies, health care, minority advancement, outer-space probings, big-league baseball, symphony orchestras, universities, and temples of worship. Each of these areas is expanding and intensifying its interface with business, and imperatively so. The evolutionary force is so evident in some areas that we already talk about agribusiness, the application of business methods and philosophies to farming. There are even references to the agricorporation, the big-business version of farming.

It is only a matter of months before we will be referring to health and hospital care as medicabusiness, or truncated, to medibusiness. We already have accepted terms such as medicare and medicaid. This terminological interfacing, however, is not the important point. Farming and health care, when referred to as agribusiness or medibusiness, have implicitly adapted their functions and thinking to evolving management, so recently localized in the business sector. And, as the evolutionary invasion of management principles and practices goes beyond business, farming, and health care, we will have, by analogy, disciplines of educabusiness, episcobusiness, militarbusiness, and even politicabusiness (the application of sound management to the running of political campaigns).

As managerial thinking and practice become more intensively applied in a growing number of areas, it becomes ludicrous to expect identity in all management terms, theories, and practices. Individual needs and specific circumstances must, of necessity, affect the several evolutionary developments. Just as Latin has been transformed into Italian, French, Spanish, Portugese, and Roumanian by adapting to different peoples and geographies, so too, despite some management theorists dreams of conceptual and terminological absolutes, we are destined to have more rather than less managerial dialects.

For instance, although there are and will be many financial and accounting similarities between buying a farm tractor (agribusiness) and buying a hospital renal dialysis unit (medibusiness), we can expect some differences. The tractor's performance will be reflected in a profit and loss statement; the renal dialysis unit will at best be the subject of a cost-benefit analysis. An even more ephemeral evaluation can be expected if, in episcobusiness, the manager-clergyman or manager-bishop should try to determine efficiency in the saving-of-souls business.

It is an equally futile exercise in semantics or sophistry to try to squeeze all management, past and present, into some supposedly singular, absolute, and optimal management model. Using a final and fine arts analogy, consider Johannes Brahms' "Variation on a Theme by Haydn," a classical work blending the styles of two musical masters. Brahms' masterpiece is properly called a variation; it never was intended as an authentic or even a duplicate Haydn. Therefore, as management evolves and as it expands into new areas, we will find variations, with increasing multiplicity of nuances in pitch, intensity or tempo, and subtleties in timbre caused by the blending of the fundamental tone with harmonics or overtones. Any attempt at computerized rigidity will yield only cacaphony.

The preceding commentary supports Brandenburg in his statement that "there is indeed a history to be taught and learned." However, his inference that it is highly doubtful that there is any pattern that "leads somewhere in terms of new methodologies for management research and new methods" seems to be unduly negative. As previously mentioned, managerial terminology, thought, techniques, and tactics are now being adapted to most areas in which human beings need to cooperate to get things done. The spiraling multiplicity of textbooks and articles on the subject of management testifies to innovation and progress rather than to status quo. For example, Frederick W. Taylor's contribution, although most significant, certainly cannot be considered as the last word and final discovery in scientific management. Taylor himself never thought of his contributions as being unique and definitive. In fact, he considered himself a synthesizer, an interpreter, an enunciator rather than a discoverer. His pig-iron and shoveling experiments, in particular, were illustrative rather than innovative. Taylor's indignant reply to criticism from a House of Representatives Special Committee investigating the potential of scientific management illustrates this point.

> Scientific Management is not an efficiency device, nor is it any bunch or group of efficiency devices; it is not a new system of figuring costs; it is not holding a stop-watch on a man, and writing things down about him; it is not time study; it is not motion study; it is not the printing and ruling and unloading of a ton or two of blanks by a set of men saying "Here's your system, go to it"; it is not divided foremanship, or functional foremanship; it is not any of the devices which the average man calls to mind when Scientific Management is spoken of. Now, in its essence, Scientific Management involves a complete mental revolution on the part of the working man engaged in any industry, and it involves an equally complete revolution on the part of those on the management's side—the foreman, the superintendent, the owner, the board of directors, and without this complete mental revolution on both sides Scientific Management does not exist.[1]

The stress, then, is more on the mental and the philosophical and less on techniques and the mechanical. A philosophy of management is what Taylor seemed to be aiming at, and a philosophy by definition is the love, study, or pursuit of wisdom and knowledge of things and their causes, both theoretical and practical. Perhaps inadvertently too many theorists, and most practitioners, get tired or sidetracked as they make their way up the scalar progression of management performance levels.

For example, a currently popular technique, such as project management, would actually rank rather low in the hierarchical sequencing. Even a loftier term, management by objective, stripped of its veneer, would have only a comparable ranking. More global approaches, sometimes referred to as schools, such as the behavioral scientists or the quantitative analysts, for the most part come to rest at the "procedure" level in the scalar progression.

What is imperatively needed in order to better understand management is better comprehension of peoples'

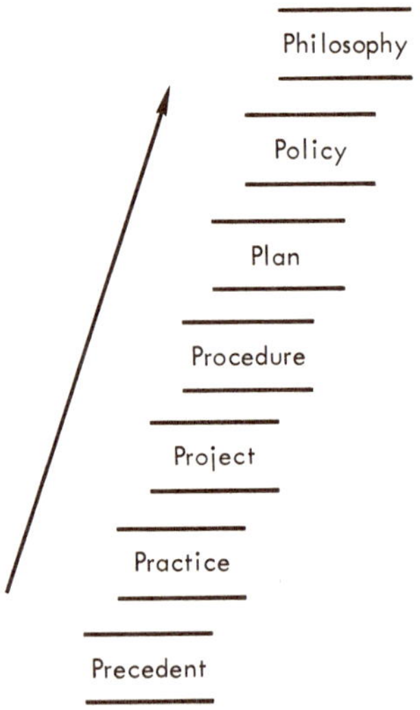

FIGURE 10. Scalar Progression of Performance Standards

[1]Testimony before the Special Committee of the U.S. House of Representatives, 1912, F. W. Taylor, *The Principles of Scientific Management* (New York: Harper and Bros., 1947).

value systems. Only then can we know why some individuals, the managers, strive to "get things done through the efforts of others" and why others, the workers, are willing to join up with the managers and provide the essential efforts. Focusing on value systems also can help us better to comprehend the meaning of organization: the juncturing of efforts by a group of people in a common endeavor toward a purposeful goal. A greater stress on the philosophical and on value systems can also provide both managers and the managed with improved insight concerning policy-making and planning. In simple terms: policies are statements about the action to be taken relative to the basic tenets of the organization's philosophy, and plans are the detailed courses of action by means of which the policies are activated and implemented. Unfortunately, when policies and plans, and to a lesser degree procedures and practices, are not seen as part of a specific value system or philosophy, the din in the management Babel becomes louder and more irritating.

Brandenburg does point to the significant weakness in the management chain when he stresses that many labels such as decision-making lead nowhere "because they are neither tied to any context, nor related to any explicit statement of the purposes for which they are intended." It is this myopic management that intensifies the confusion. Equally significant is his observation that some managerial terms convey a false impression of empirical exactitude when in fact they are abstractions and subjective appraisals.

The pessimism echoed in Brandenburg's observation that "Teachers, students, researchers, consultants, and practitioners can find little if any guidance on *how* to transfer principles of management thought among management problems, beyond assertions that such transferability is desirable and somehow should be possible" is understandable. It is as equally frustrating when the medical researcher fails to transplant certain vital organs among humans, or fails to build transplantable organs out of plastics and other synthetics. Present inability, however, does not mean future impossibility.

CONCLUSION

Brandenburg does a service in stressing the pluralistic character of management. His five criteria for testing management usefulness provide a base for discussion and analysis. Similarly, his reasons why the translation capacity of management thought is limited puts the problem into better perspective. In particular, his pointing to different management problems in the context of time and organization development is significant. By inference, a student of government must recognize that democracy in today's context is not Jeffersonian or George Washingtonian democracy. In the sphere of religion, neither are the Vatican's views or those of the Council of Churches identical with the theology and ethics of St. Augustine or St. Thomas Aquinas.

On variance in management arising from differences in internal organization, consider the near-infinite variety in value systems, and the fluidity even in this multiplicity.

Finally, on our failure to develop an adequate typology of management problems, perhaps Brandenburg is gazing too far into the hazy horizon. We might even raise the question, Is a rigid typology useful or necessary? Consider the field of sports. The Olympic games, initiated in 776 B.C., were originally foot races; then long runs were added, the pentathlon, boxing, wrestling, and even chariot racing. Greek women not only were forbidden to participate but even to watch. Today (27 centuries later) the Olympic games bear little resemblance to the original and during the interim 4 years Olympic games have been superceded everywhere by new and varied national sports. Yet, the basic ideal of contending and winning in a physical contest remains and becomes even keener. So, too, in the sphere of management there are many different ball games, played in different ball parks, and by different sets of rules.

DISCUSSION QUESTIONS

1. Would you agree with Dean Brandenburg's criteria for appraising the schools of management thought?
2. How has management thought laid the foundation for a language of management? Does it really matter? Why?
3. Do you think that management thought has developed cumulatively?
4. Vance seems to believe that the present state of management thought—although not ideal—is to be expected and is satisfactory. Do you agree that Vance holds this belief? Do you agree with it? Why?
5. Do you agree that the environment (*zeitgeist*, as Wolf calls it) is more important than the man in advancing new management concepts?

PART TWO

The Environment of Management: Internal and External

6

The Current State of Organization Theory

William H. Starbuck

International Institute of Management
Berlin, Germany

YESTERDAY

The actual date varied radically from one location to another, but about 6,000 years ago most people gave up trying to support themselves by hunting and fishing and resigned themselves to tilling the earth with hoes and herding pigs, cattle, and sheep. Evidently this transition to food production greatly reduced the time devoted to acquiring food and greatly increased the time available for leisure, because archeological evidence suggests that it was promptly followed by a population explosion. In addition, people found time to start polishing their chipped-stone tools, establishing small permanent communities, and inventing things. The next 2,000 years or so brought the inventions of ploughs, ships, wheels, and the appearance of skilled craftsmen, wars, kings, money, and social classes. And even though there is no sound archeological evidence for it, the development of food production must also have stimulated the invention of organization theorists, for how could society create chiefs and kings and mining and manufacturing without also creating people who stand at the side and advise, "This is how it should be done"?

Nevertheless, organization theorists did not really come into their own until the revolutionary period that Gordon Childe (1951) called the transition from barbarism to civilization. Rather suddenly, some communities grew into small cities, the number of full-time specialist occupations exploded, inter-community trade was organized on a regular basis, and writing was invented. Although social theorists have generally said little about why this revolution started at all or why it involved the particular components it did, the fundamental motive force seems obvious: organization theorists. The first written documents were organizational records and assignments of responsibility (George, 1968). Some familiar invisible hands must have had fingers in systematizing trade and in designing specialized occupations. And although writing has facilitated the work of scientists, academics, and communication in general, it would be hard to find a group that takes more pleasure in writing than organization theorists do. Indeed, around 2700 B.C. a shrewd Egyptian named Ptah-hotep wrote a book of management principles that is a strong contender for the best-selling textbook of all time—revised editions were still getting course adoptions 1,200 years later.

Since the birth of civilization, the history of organization theory has been studded by one success after another. Ptah-hotep's Egyptian students developed the ramifications of nepotistic hierarchies headed by omniscient and omnipotent chief executives. Chinese organization theorists established an elaborate governmental bureaucracy that proved that 2,000 miles of masonry facilitates environmental stability and that bureaucratic rigidities can stifle social change for thousands of years. Greek organization theorists conducted a series of experiments demonstrating the wide variety of feasible organizational forms and suggesting that differences in structure inhibit inter-organizational cooperation. Roman organization theorists explored the effects of diverse ideological and inducement systems on organizational loyalty and efficiency and exhibited the divisive consequences of geographic dispersion and intra-organizational status differentials. Medieval organization theorists integrated the findings of their Greek and Roman colleagues and then brilliantly showed the partial independence of organizational integration from organizational differentiation by simultaneously maximizing both. And throughout history, organization theorists have contributed greatly to industrial development, employment, urban renewal, and population control by focusing their innovative efforts on the design of military and governmental organizations (George, 1968; Price, 1971).

However, these and other achievements did little to foster organization theory's development as an integrated, full-time profession, because the theorists were trying to operate too close to the firing line. Their scientifically sound strategy of testing organizational designs to destruction tended to elicit hostility among their less scientific clients and to decrease the utility of one theorist cooperating with another. China fell to the warlords; the Greeks to the Romans; the Romans to the European barbarians; the European nobility to the bourgeoisie; and organization theorists to their clients or their clients' enemies. It was just not an environment that encouraged organization theorists to convert their preoccupation into a full-time occupation, or even to associate openly with their professional colleagues.

All of this changed with the industrial revolution. Manufacturing organizations grew large enough to pose interesting design problems, suddenly multiplying the number of potential experimental situations. Military and governmental organizations achieved sizes and degrees of complexity never before dreamed of. Successes in physics, geology, and chemistry were so impressive that anyone who could plausibly characterize himself as a scientist immediately acquired credibility. Affluence soared so high that some people could devote themselves to pure research that not only lacked a practical purpose but also decreased organizational efficiency. Funds poured into colleges and universities when working and middle-class parents discovered that degrees were keys to upward social mobility. Most important, schools of management were established within universities: these persuaded managers that methods of organization and decision-making were at least as important as the consequences; they dignified management teaching by eliciting the involvement of social philosophers, mathematicians, and similar otherworldly intelligentsia; and they provided stable full-time employment for organization theorists. Fertile ground indeed for the growth of an academic occupation.

One might even say that the new occupational specialty was propelled into being. Within economics and political science, the study of individual firms and government agencies and of their processes has consistently been a marginal pastime that added logical footnotes to the core of economic or political theory, but did so at the cost of raising conceptually messy problems that neither conformed to the existing theoretical frameworks nor yielded to conventional analytic methods. In addition, some of the economists and political scientists who have taken an interest in organizational behavior revealed their incomprehension of traditional theories by claiming that they were inconsistent with the way things really were. In psychology, the students of intra-organizational behavior tended to be counter-revolutionaries to the behaviorist revolution. They persisted in studying human beings and in using non-observable concepts like desire and satisfaction. They often conducted experiments outside laboratory settings or tried to analyze uncontrolled, real-life behavior. And some rejected the idea that psychology should be an ethically neutral, objective science: they embraced value-laden beliefs about the proper realtions between superiors and subordinates and about the proper role of work in man's life, and then they sought to implement their beliefs by changing the ways actual organizations operated. Anthropological organization theorists took a debased interest in large, accessible, overdeveloped societies, in some cases including societies in which the anthropologist himself was already socialized. Although this had the advantage of keeping one or two faculty around to meet classes and to talk with students, it betrayed a restricted view of culture, cast doubt on the objectivity of their research, and retarded their linguistic and dietary development. Max Weber got organizational sociology off to a bad start by persuasively arguing that bureaucracy was an absolutely rational problem-solving system that ought to be ranked among mankind's supreme achievements. Although Weber's analysis was consistent with his contemporaries' utopian perception of social processes and their tendency to act as apologists for the existing social system, Weber's followers found themselves increasingly lonely optimists in a world being progressively disillusioned by economic depressions, hot and cold wars, and growing awareness of the social system's failures and inequities.

Moreover, the organization theorists who moved into or grew up in schools of management found that they had erected a barrier between themselves and the mainstreams of social science. As all academia knows, anyone who investigates applied problems must be less intelligent and interesting than he who pursues learning for its own sake. If someone could work on abstract theory he would, and the rejection of conceptually clean and logically taut theories as being simplistic or irrelevant is only a mask for one's inability to comprehend them. Schools of management also paid higher salaries than most other departments, and everyone knows that one does not get money for nothing. The higher salaries compensate one for having a low commitment to his mother discipline, for wasting his time on dull, trivial problems, and for helping rich people become richer or bureaucrats become more powerful. Of course, many management-school faculty have attempted to counteract these criticisms by avoiding applied problems, by devoting their efforts to the development of simple, abstract theories, by describing their difficulties in getting cooperation from practicing executives and access to real-world data, or by pointing out that very few wealthy businessmen support business schools or departments of industrial engineering and that government administrators contribute little to schools of public administration. But such efforts have not succeeded, and still today organization theorists must choose between exiling themselves in schools of management or clinging to the fringes of social science departments where their perversions are displayed for all to see.

TODAY

Sociology is the only academically respectable social science that currently accepts organization theory as an important and central part of its domain. The accommodation began during the early 1950's when a few young sociologists tore loose from their teachers' rapture over Weber's logical brilliance and began observing the systems properties of actual organizations. They discovered that bureaucracies sometimes failed to carry out their designers' intentions. This penetrating insight embodied just enough cynicism to resurrect organizational behavior as a legitimate topic for study and initiated a wave of empirical investigations by sociologists who wanted to understand and improve the contemporary social system rather than throw it away and start all over. However, being scarred by some of the eccentricities that mar organization theory itself, sociology probably lacks full status as a respectable social science, and its welcome to organization theory may be wearing thin.

The basic problem is that anyone who looks closely at what happens inside organizations is prone to one or the other of two mental aberrations. One reaction pattern involves withdrawal into progressively less realistic theories about idealistic relations among aggregate, composite concepts. Really extreme cases reject all personal identification with their own theories: they attempt to define theoretical concepts by using mechanistic statistical techniques such as factor analysis and cluster analysis, and then deny the presence of analyzable causal relations among these invented concepts. In the other reaction pattern, the organization theorist slides deeper and deeper into a funk of outrage and demoralization and ultimately either refuses to undertake further organizational research or oscillates schizophrenically between embittered vituperation and hopeful proposals for change.

Of course, both reaction syndromes have been occupational hazards throughout recorded history, but their frequency and intensity spiraled under the impact of such recent events as the handling of student revolts during the late 1960's, the administrative struggles against racial equality, and the publication of the Pentagon Papers. And sociologists have been considerably more susceptible than their management school colleagues—probably because sociologists are confronted more sharply by the fact that they themselves chose to specialize in organization theory and have no one else to blame. Consequently, more and more organizational sociologists are beginning to suspect that they are deviates. Not only are other sociologists looking at them with bewilderment and pity, but the research of other organization theorists seems increasingly incomprehensible and purposeless.

Now and again over the past 20 years there have been diagnoses and predictions to the effect that organization theory is a new academic discipline in the process of being born. Certainly, there are several thousand academicians who publicly admit that they find organizations interesting, and several hundred of these are primarily interested in organizations. There are also several hundred academic departments that use "organization theorist," or some variant thereof, as a formal job description. Against the scale of human history, these are new phenomena. But it is doubtful that this amorphous crew of people ought to be considered a discipline. They are a pretty undisciplined lot who do not even recognize one another as being members of a common community (Leavitt and Bass, 1964; Price, 1968; Starbuck, 1968).

Studies of new academic disciplines (Ben-David and Zloczower, 1962; Clark, 1968; Hagstrom, 1965) indicate that ostracized academicians behave much like homosexuals, concentration camp prisoners, and similar social rejects. Being mutually evicted from some social group is not only insufficient to induce the rejects to band together, it inhibits cooperation between them. Each ostracized person knows he was rejected by mistake, but he suspects that there must be something really wrong with most of the others, and so he must not become too closely associated with them if he is ever to prove his innocence and be readmitted to his original group. Indeed, by criticizing the others and showing that he understands why they have been rejected, one may be able to ingratiate himself and hasten his reacceptance.

Such forces are difficult to overcome. But deviants can eventually surmount their suspicions of one another and form a cohesive subculture if the surrounding society is willing to accept them, if they develop effective intercommunication, if they can agree on a collective ideology, and if forceful leaders appear. The lack of cohesion among organization theorists demonstrates that they have not yet met these conditions, and besides being unsuccessful social scientists, they have some way to go before they succeed as deviates.

Environmental Acceptance and Rejection

One problem is that organization theorists represent a spectrum of deviance and rejection. A substantial minority work in respectable social science departments and are regarded by their departmental colleagues with attitudes varying from formalized tolerance to bemused affection. A few are even lionized. And many of the organization theorists who work in schools of management have maintained ties to their mother social sciences, ranging from personal friends who are willing to meet them quietly in out-of-the-way places to blatant and public appearances at professional conventions. In fact, a few of the management school organization theorists have been given professional honors and awards—although not, of course, for their contributions to organization theory.

The integration of organization theorists within the social science establishment can be quantitatively measured by memberships in academic societies in which admission is controlled by traditionally respectable persons. The Social Science Research Council includes 8 organization theorists among its 160 members, and the National Academy of Sciences includes 2 organization theorists among 69 social science members.

Another problem is that although schools of management might appear at first to offer a framework within which organization theorists could find social acceptance, most management school organization theorists are deviates from that environment too. For one thing, their ties to the basic social sciences create suspicion about their loyalties to the management schools themselves, because everyone knows that the pure and applied sciences have mutually inconsistent needs and that university budgeting is a competitive game in which one department's gain is another's loss. But beyond this, management-school faculties often hear their organization theorist colleagues voicing strange attitudes. The organization theorists do not fully understand how maximizing long-run profit can be an adequate criterion for business performance. They sometimes question the wisdom of senior executives, owners, or important politicians. They have even been known to argue that clients, suppliers, and ordinary workers should have as much say about organizational policies as the managers do—an attitude that the management schools' students especially find outrageous. On the whole, organization theorists are rather soft-headed about the importance of monetary incentives and criteria, preferring to talk instead about fuzzy concepts such as participative leadership, intrinsic job satisfactions, organizational loyalty, or conformity to work-group norms. They have never really become sophisticated enough in mathematical modeling to understand why algebraically convenient assumptions take precedence over conceptually realistic ones, and consequently they place more faith in obviously oversimplified and artificial laboratory experiments than they do in, say, intellectually elegant algorithms for decomposing quadratic programming problems.

Furthermore, although organization theorists in general can hardly be classified as wild-eyed radicals, the behavioral scientists in management schools are more likely than their colleagues to express liberal attitudes toward student rights and to harbor in their subculture the kinds of faculty who irritate the establishment. For example, one organization theorist proposed that his school should allow every masters student to include in the twenty courses taken for his degree one course that the student himself had chosen without obtaining a faculty adviser's approval. Naturally enough, a majority of the faculty rejected this dilution of their wisdom and authority, and the voting pattern reinforced the dichotomy between behavioral scientists and others.

Communication

In the words of Warren Hagstrom (1965, p. 210), "Communication precedes community, and community precedes self-identification. Scientific publications devoted to a special field precede the emergence of the field as a discipline, and the emergence of the discipline precedes the identification of scientists with it. . . . Only when a periodical is established that is devoted to a field with its own distinct goals and standards will it be possible for him to conceive of himself as a new kind of specialist; only then will it be possible for a self-conscious community of specialists to arise."

Organization theorists have such a journal, *Administrative Science Quarterly*. It began publication in 1956 and has gradually increased its circulation and prestige ever since. By now, in fact, *ASQ* does quite well in comparison to its competition—a majority of the organization theoretic articles published by other journals have been previously evaluated by the *ASQ* editors. But that may say more about the competition than about *ASQ* itself; social support for the journal is weak and its financial condition tenuous.

Some of the most famous organization theorists never publish in *ASQ*, or publish there only occasionally, because they seek recognition by larger, less specialized, and more prestigious audiences or by smaller, more specialized, and more prestigious audiences. There are several competing journals that concentrate on specific facets of organizational behavior, several more that regularly publish organizational studies as one component of larger topical domains, and many more that publish several pertinent articles each year. Forty-five of the most relevant journals are mapped in Figure 11, but someone who sought conscientiously to read every organizational study would have to survey well over 100 journals (Dill, 1964).

There are also organization theorists who feel that it is beneath their

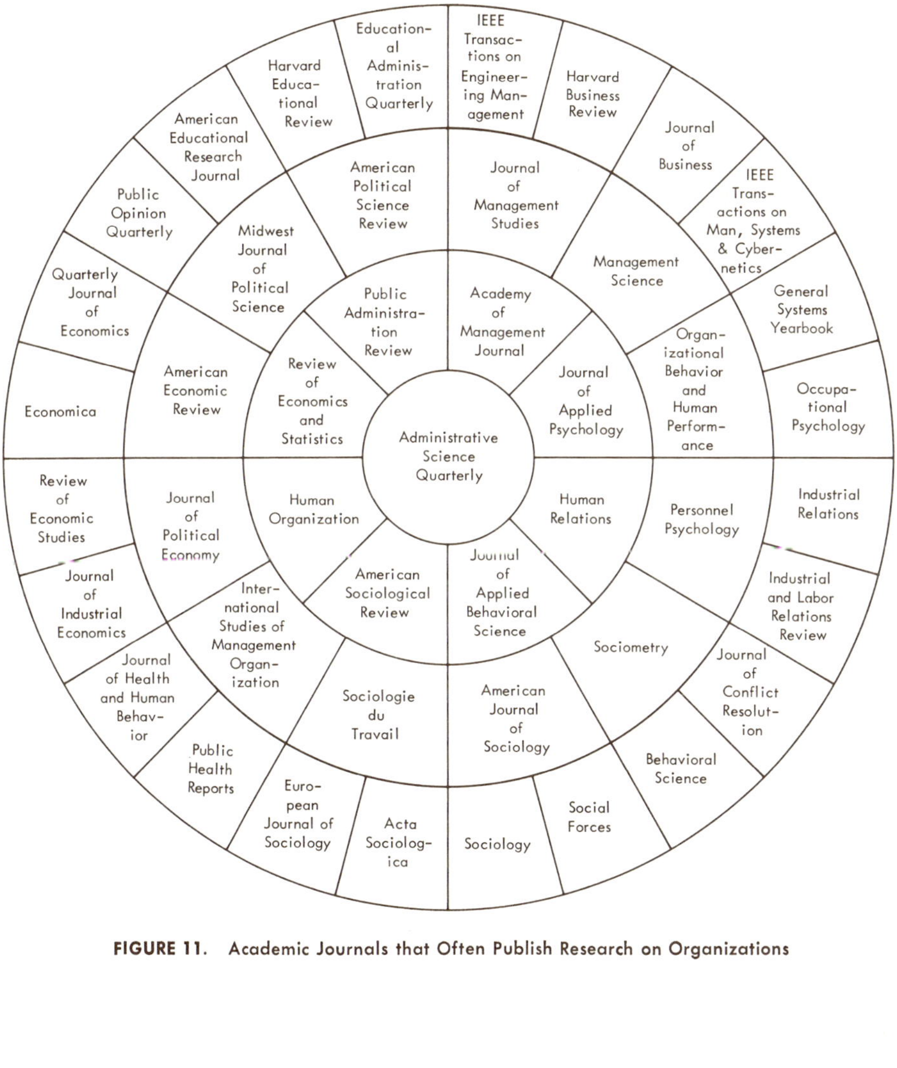

FIGURE 11. Academic Journals that Often Publish Research on Organizations

status to have to submit their writing to finicky evaluation and criticism by journal editors, or who believe that their ideas would suffer by compression into journal articles and deserve the thorough development (and royalties) of book-length treatment. Book publishers, university libraries, and even readers are happy to accommodate them—with the result that only 39 per cent of the bibliographic citations in *ASQ* refer to journal articles whereas 57 per cent refer to books. A survey of articles in the physical and biological sciences reveals 79 per cent references to journal articles and 13 per cent to books.

Leadership

One reason why there are no meetings of organization theorists is that there is no one to call them. Because the occupation offers little status and prestige, many potential recruits avoid it, and basically just two types of people become organization theorists.

One type starts out intending to become a rich and admired consultant to large, powerful organizations, suddenly illuminating board-of-directors' meetings with casually dropped bits of brilliant insight, smoothly turning antagonists into friends by inventing mutually advantageous schemes for resolving conflicts, and fabricating tailor-made organizational designs that solve intricate and elusive problems. Unfortunately, Savile Row contains only a handful of shops; most customers choose ready-to-wear solutions from mass producers like McKinsey and Booz-Allen; and even $500-a-day consultants spend nearly all their time letting out waistlines. The ideal soon palls, and the would-be oracles either develop an interest in research for its own sake or take up plumbing, carpentry, or some other well-paid occupation.

The other type—possibly because they have been bewildered by their encounters with organizations' behaviors, possibly because they are challenged by the difficulty of disentangling complex, interdependent systems, or possibly because they are the kind of people who start tidying up whenever they see a mess—is attracted by the idea of doing research on organizations. They are likely to begin with a disdainful attitude toward the quality of organizational knowledge and research, fully aware that existing theories say little or miss the point, and fully confident that things will shortly be set right once they themselves set to work with their newer, stronger research techniques and their fresher insights. So gradually that they are unaware of it, this objective self-confidence fades and is supplanted by a dawning suspicion that the puzzles really are unsolvable, the research tools inadequate, and platitudes more easily formulated than insightful analyses. By the time this suspicion crystalizes into conscious awareness, it is too late. The victim is caught, like a man staring into the eyes of a cobra, in a hypnotic trance that melds horror over the specter of his future with fascination over the impossibility of letting the problems go.

Clearly, neither type is inclined to hurl himself altruistically into negotiations with hotels, the conduct of elections, the planning of conference schedules, or committees debating bylaws. The consultants are reluctant to give free advice and, in any case, can only meet in airport lobbies between flights. The researchers are more than happy to give advice to anyone any time, for free or otherwise, but they are too absorbed in their own projects to actually take the time to implement solutions. Both types, having extensive acquaintance with leaders and leadership patterns, lack the ambition to build empires themselves.

Moreover, because organization theorists tend to have multidisciplinary orientations, the occupation is prey to periodic raiding by scientific bodies that need small numbers of comparatively objective social scientists. For instance, the U.S. President's Council of Scientific Advisors includes two social scientists, one of whom is clearly an organization theorist and the other of whom might be so classified. The National Science Foundation includes an organization theorist among the two social scientists on its main policy committee. Such raiding deprives the occupation of its more charismatic members and prevents a discipline from growing up around a coalition of strong, magnetic personalities.

Ideology

Just as the propensity for publishing books instead of journal articles is endemic to the social sciences as a whole, so is ideological discord. Thomas Kuhn (1962) observed that the natural sciences experience abrupt ideological revolutions in which one conceptual paradigm is suddenly rejected and another adopted. Such fickle instability is not characteristic of the social sciences (Bronfenbrenner, 1971). An old theory is not discarded solely because someone comes up with a better alternative; it is cherished and preserved by devout adherents until its day of resurrection and ultimate triumph, meanwhile being made more irrefutable, generally applicable, and ambiguous with every passing year. Having to build their disciplines without much precedent to guide them, the natural sciences created societies in which truth is believed to be demonstrable and every man is constantly in danger of having his wisdom and expertise destroyed by technological change. The social sciences have not allowed themselves to fall into the same error; they all include minorities who disagree with the majority about what topics comprise the discipline's legitimate domain, what utopias would be worth achieving, what conceptual frameworks are effective and believable, and what research methods are most revealing.

Because it alloys people from throughout the social sciences, however, organization theory may actually be pushing heterogeneity to a ridiculous extreme. True, there is no poverty of conceptual paradigms. The paradigms include, for example, the nineteenth-century utilitarians' notion that people seek maximum satisfaction, Herbert Simon's notion that people are content with adequate satisfaction, Kurt Lewin's proposition that attitude change must be preceded by an unfreezing of old attitudes and followed by a freezing of new attitudes, Max Weber's contention that bureaucracies are capable of greater performances than the people in them, Chris Argyris' contention that organizations prevent their members from developing into mature human beings, Abraham Maslow's conception that human needs are hierarchically nested with physiological ones at the base and self-fulfillment at the crown, Robert Dahl's definition that "*A* has power over *B* to the extent that he can get *B* to do something that *B* would not otherwise do," and Herbert Kaufman's observation that "voluntary conformity" induces subordinates to behave as their superiors wish without the superiors having to ask.

The supply of paradigms is so large that an organization theorist should never be left without intellectual resources. If in doubt, he can always refer to the 1,247-page *Handbook of Organizations.* In fact, a casual census discloses 6.7 paradigms per organization theorist, the average paradigm being only 1.009 times different from the adjacent ones. Unfortunately, many organization theorists must not know what paradigms exist: 13 per cent say they believe only two paradigms; 56 per cent only one; and 27 per cent believe none at all. Apparently they have some difficulty understanding one another's work, a conjecture that is supported by the findings of William Dill (1964) and James March (1965) that there is negligible overlap between the bibliographic citations of different authors.

Moreover, organization theorists have especially tenacious loyalties to old paradigms. Consider, for instance, the treatment one might accord Max Weber's proposition that bureaucracies are rational problem-solving structures. One could empirically test this proposition by developing operational definitions of bureaucracy and rationality based on Weber's descriptions of these properties, and then correlating the degrees of bureaucracy and rationality observed in various real organizations. If the observed correlation were only 0.3 or 0.4, indicating that the assumed relationship accounts for at most 15 per cent of the variance in these properties, one might well decide to transfer his attention to a more fruitful topic.

No self-respecting organization theorist would make such a mistake. For one thing, a correlation of 0.3 might be statistically significant, and thus eligible for acceptance as demonstrated truth. If not, it can be made statistically significant by increasing the number of organizations surveyed. For another thing, the first survey can become the basis for more effective definitions of bureaucracy and rationality. One can hold the definition of bureaucracy constant and search statistically for a definition of rationality that correlates highly with bureaucracy, then invert the process and improve the definition of bureaucracy. Or one can perform a factor analysis and experiment with factors until he creates two that can plausibly be labeled bureaucracy and rationality. In either case, the end result can be presented as an improvement over a famous classic, a characterization more marketable than the invention of two more new concepts, because it simultaneously enhances one's own achievement and reminds one's readers of organization theory's profound historical roots (Hoagland, 1964).

The supreme and ultimate achievement is an absolutely irrefutable paradigm—say, a definition of rationality as that property of organizations that is maximized by bureaucracy. However, systematic, large-scale research on organizations is too new and the financial resources too small to have enabled such accomplishments. Even the proposition that effective leadership requires both consideration for one's subordinates and structuring of task requirements is still subject to petty bickering about what constitutes consideration and what kinds of structuring are essential. So, except for a few generally applicable paradigms imported from the basic disciplines, such as the proposition that people behave so as to maximize subjectively expected utility, organization theorists must still content themselves with the assurance that the ideal is attainable and the future stretches limitlessly ahead.

TOMORROW

The Revolutionary Birth of Organizational Behavior

Late in 1969, Derek Pugh observed that organization theory was changing its name to organizational behavior and was sharply delimiting itself to "the structure and functioning of organizations and the behaviour of groups and individuals within them." He also reviewed the main trends determining organizational behavior's future: a reduced ideological commitment to managerial philosophy; a preference for research promising scientific yields instead of managerial yields; a deemphasis of discoveries about the dynamic processes occurring in single organizations; an emphasis on static generalizations obtained by comparing the properties of many organizations; an equalized concern for non-industrial organizations as well as industrial ones; and a general acceptance of the systems-theoretic view that "organizations have to be studied as environments for group and individual behaviour" because "the organization is a self-maintaining 'organism' rather than a 'mechanism' which can be designed and redesigned to achieve given ends."

It is easy to see why Pugh concluded that organizational behavior had become an emerging discipline. The trends add up to precisely the orientation that organization theory needs to convert it into an independent and respectable academic field. There is a burgeoning consensus about both what subjects comprise the discipline's domain and what research strategies are most worthwhile. Crass, applied values are being discarded in favor of pristine, theoretical ones. Concern for managerial values—already minimal, according to some managers—is being reduced further still. Allegiances to mother disciplines are breaking down as organizational researchers begin to collaborate with one another. And, although leadership group has not yet taken control, it is foreshadowed in the ideological convergence; as Pugh reported:

> The systems theory approach has great potential for organizational behaviour. ... A concept which can be used by mathematicians, biologists, physiologists, engineers, economists, experimental psychologists, social psychologists, sociologists, managers, and operational researchers ... must command respect by that very fact. ... It already has considerable achievements to its credit both conceptually and empirically. ... The main empirical achievements of the systems approach has been through the work of Trist & Emery and their colleagues at the Tavistock Institute. From a study of the changeover from the shortwall to the longwall method of coal mining . . . , Trist & Bamforth (1951) developed the conception of the working group as being neither a social system ... nor a technical system ... but an interdependent 'sociotechnical' system. ... This version of the systems approach has been developed in a large number of detailed studies, which have given considerable support to the utility of the 'sociotechnical' concept (Emery & Trist, 1960; Miller, 1959).

The new discipline's emergence is remarkable in part because of the field's disorganized and untidy past, but especially because of the abruptness with which it began. That it involved a revolution of impressive magnitude and suddenness seems undeniable. Only 18 months or so before Pugh's report was published, the National Academy of Sciences and the Social Science Research Council (1969) surveyed American universities and found no evidence of organizational behavior's promise as a distinct new discipline. Pugh himself had reviewed the ideological and substantive themes shaping organization theory up to 1966, and had labeled it an interdisciplinary, quasi-independent subdiscipline of, primarily, sociology and psychology. And at a 1962 conference, William Dill (1964) began a survey of the field by saying, "The dominant feature of contemporary research on organizations is its diversity. No brief survey can describe all that is being done. No theory of organization is comprehensive enough to subsume and order all that we have studied, and none is yet sacred enough to restrain or limit new kinds of research activity."

Like Pugh, Dill reported that organizational research was increasingly devoted to non-industrial organizations; he observed more and more collaboration among organization theorists from different backgrounds; he acknowledged the inadequacy of trying to explain intra-organizational behaviors as either purely social or purely technological phenomena; and he said organization theorists should devote more attention to establishing the generality of their findings, through replications and elaborations of existing studies and through comparative studies of organizations in different countries. However, Dill also thought he discerned increasing collaboration between organization theorists and specialists in such organizational functions as marketing, personnel management, and industrial relations. In this he had to be mistaken, for Pugh did not consider external collaboration a major trend in 1966, and the centrifugal force of extensive external collaboration should have prevented the new discipline from coalescing. Most strikingly, Dill expressed some value preferences that must have gone out-of-date before 1969, since they were rejected from the crystallization of organizational behavior. There should be, he said, more dynamic theories stated as computer programs and based on observations over long time spans, and there should be less segregation between descriptive (positive) studies and normative (prescriptive) ones, because "a great deal of the normative research on organizations does not rest on very valid assumptions about how the world works or about the extent to which the world will welcome new suggestions for organizing" and because "a great deal of our descriptive research is going to be wasted unless it takes better account of the directions in which the world is moving."

The Pro-Prescriptive Reactionaries

Being victims of antique values, people like Dill should not be personally blamed, but they do constitute a hopelessly reactionary rear-guard in organizational behavior's forward march.

For one thing, they do not fully appreciate the power and magnificence of modern statistical methods, and they are inclined to interpret the totally inexplicable randomness inherent in all behavior as being explicable curvilinearity. One does not, after all, need computer simulation to describe phenomena that can be analyzed perfectly well with straight lines and bell-shaped statistical distributions; and since the only truly interesting phenomena are the ones that are identical in all organizations, observations over time can be replaced by multiorganizational surveys.

A few extremist reactionaries argue that a scientist should not claim his theory is adequate until he has successfully used it to predict future events, and that organizational researchers should undertake design projects in order to test and improve their theories (Quinn and Kahn, 1967). This must be a rationalization masking unsavory pecuniary motives. The overwhelming majority of social science theories have gained acceptance solely through their consistency with past events. Theories that account for less than a third of the variance in behavior cannot predict the outcomes of unique changes in single organizations—unanticipated occurrences may produce events consistent with an invalid theory or inconsistent with a valid theory. Organizations tend to change faster than researchers can study them. And the managers of manipulated organizations only accept designs satisfying their own nonscientific criteria, and then interfere in the experiments as soon as undesirable consequences appear. How can one learn anything from situations like that? Science should never be polluted with the pragmatic compromises doctors and engineers accept.

True scientists maintain absolute objectivity toward the phenomena they observe, whereas the pro-prescriptive reactionaries get themselves all mixed up in issues of values, ethics, and goodness. They might look, for example, at the development of corporations with $14 billion in assets and 700,000 employees concentrated in 16 countries, and start asking whether these ought to be operated for the primary benefit of absentee owners by a managerial hierarchy that is subject to negligible external inspection, or whether such corporations have not grown so large and powerful that they ought to be classed with the nation states and governed democratically. No one can predict what a person who raises such issues might do next. He obviously thinks a scientist should try to use his knowledge to create a "better" world, not just impartially report the facts and leave the decisions to the decision makers. This upsets financial sources no end, casts doubt on the reliability of his own reporting, and disrupts the stability of processes other people are trying to study. He also wants to achieve ephemeral short-run results at the cost of sound, dependable long-run progress, and his ill-considered attempts to leap forward are more likely to disrupt than to contribute to the patient accumulation of knowledge increments by the corporate society of scientists. What a waste that a person should end his career without a single footnote in a required textbook, saying only that he had once contributed a small improvement in the welfare of a few million people.

A somewhat different group of reactionaries base their resistance on their desire to maximize the rate of scientific progress. They point to various studies of scientific research (Ben-David, 1960; Ben-David and Zloczower, 1962; Gordon and Marquis, 1966; Kuhn, 1962; Pelz and Andrews, 1966; Price, 1961 and 1963; Smith, 1971) which show that social processes within the scientific establishment discourage skepticism about accepted theories and penalize deviants who attempt to innovate, and that the pressures to conform are especially strong among homogeneous colleague groups in the respectable, non-applied departments of high-status universities. Gordon and Marquis (1966), for example, found that medical sociologists working in properly managed, academically marginal settings (health agencies, hospitals, or medical schools) were three times as likely as their higher status university colleagues to produce extremely innovative studies. Apparently reeling with shock, Gordon and Marquis made an iconoclastic inference:

> Given a research environment that allows freedom of choice, many scientists choose safe rather than dangerous but original research paths. If the resistances to innovation are not overcome, the effect of facilitating conditions such as freedom obviously is reduced....
>
> We believe that the visibility of research consequences, in addition to aiding in the location of relevant problems, is one of the more important factors in overcoming the resistance to innovation. For instance, in an organizational setting where the owner of an organization or his representative can accurately evaluate the findings of a project in terms of organizational goals, he can encourage the researcher who shows high probability of solving such problems. Also he can reward the researcher in relation to the extent to which the researcher aids in problem solution. As a consequence, the researcher is motivated to seek solutions to difficult but "relevant problems" in preference to less relevant but easier problems. In seeking a solution to the difficult problems the researcher at times must abandon traditional methods and thinking. This would appear to be as true for the academic as for the non-academic researcher. Kuhn, for instance, has observed that "the novel theory seems a direct response to crises."
>
> On the other hand, where it is difficult for an administrator to relate the results of research to the attainment of organizational goals, the difference between the competent and the better solution becomes blurred.... As a consequence, the constraint toward seeking the best solution is reduced, and extra impetus to go beyond competent but traditional research methods is lacking.
>
> Marginal institutions, such as the medical school, hospital, and health agency, allow for more visibility of consequences than the university because they are in closer contact with the population served by the research.

This sort of research leads some masochistic souls to say that organizational research should continue to be performed by heterogeneous collections of researchers working in low-status departments and displaying strong interests in engineering applications, because such people are more likely to gamble on new ideas and untried methods and thereby to make maximum progress. The argument obviously assumes that organizational behavior is a never-never land in which wishing makes things true, rather than a real-life occupation in which the reputations of real people are at stake (Dubin, 1969). There is a right way and a wrong way to do research, and since no one can forecast what direction the future will take, how research is done is much more important than the results it produces. Good grief, if everyone just charged around trying out eccentric ideas and being rewarded on the basis of whether their ideas worked, people's reputations would oscillate up and down like goldmining stocks, and many of the people who are distinctly brighter, more learned, and harder working than the rest would be failures. Moreover, even doctoral students might lose the incentive to study existing theories—on the ground that correlations of 0.8 or 0.7 or less have low predictive value—and teaching would become a never-ending challenge to the professor's superiority.

Onward and Upward with Organizational Behavior

The reactionary ranks are swelled by a few other eccentrics as well, such as Popper's (1959) followers who hold that a theory, like a politician, can only satisfy everyone by saying nothing (e.g., Gregg and Simon, 1967). But then, there are always conservatives who cling to the past and deplore progress. Organizational research has embarked on the brave new world of tomorrow, and already one can visualize the phalanxes of confident and enthusiastic organizational behaviorists who will fill the new discipline's ranks.

Armed with Biomed control cards and Organizational Climate Description Questionnaires, they will turn their backs on self-serving individualism and quietly, collectively push back the frontiers of ignorance. No contingencies will be left unexplored, no conceptualizations undebated, as new results are painstakingly fitted into appropriate crevices in the stockpile of knowledge, and then are checked and rechecked for reliability, stability, and generality. Research tools will be honed to the sharpness of a razor through such imaginative innovations as folded-J, semi-interval scales, cubic causal structure analysis, and computer programs that can compute significance levels to eight decimal places. Theories will glow with burnished logic and axiomatic simplicity, brilliant monuments to the intricate implications of fundamental truths.

Indeed, theoretical perfection will unite with the accumulation of massive data banks to reduce empiricism to a disposable avocation. Scientists will no longer have to waste their time eliciting cooperation from real organizations, conducting interviews and digging through historical records, or pursuing false leads created by inconsistent data sources and heterogeneous measurement techniques. To the extent that data are still needed, they will be obtained instantaneously by inquiry to a real-time computer terminal; and since newly extracted data will always be consistent with those previously obtained, theoretical development will be greatly accelerated. Organizational researchers will be able, for the first time, to replicate their studies without doubting that the organizations they originally observed are still the same. Of course, more perfect theories will gradually make even inquiries to the data bank redundant. More and more time will be devoted to exploring the logical implications of existing theories, to carefully weighing the contributions of different theorists, and to elaborating the discipline's social structure. Invisible colleges will spring up about the discipline's leaders; annual meetings in Miami, San Francisco, or Barcelona will be supplemented by invitation-only conferences at small New England colleges; fellows and association officers will be elected and medals awarded; committees will debate the proper composition of degree curricula; university departments of organizational behavior will struggle for larger budgets so that they can employ professors representing the full range of ever-increasing specialties.

Pragmatic engineering problems will presumably revert to the no-nonsense hands of operating managers. Admittedly, assessments of managers' past contributions to organization theory suggest that one should be skeptical of their future achievements (Dutton and Starbuck, 1963; March,

1965). But the managers of the past were handicapped by limited educations, narrow experiences, and the time pressures of operating decisions. The coming managerial generations will comprise a different culture altogether (Bennis, 1970).

Already, masters degrees are so commonplace that young people who seek to distinguish themselves must acquire doctorates as well, and even the masters curricula have replaced pedestrian subjects like production management and salesmanship with theoretical statistics, nonlinear programming, and market research. An ambitious manager expects to shift to a new organization every 3 years, and to change job assignments every year or so, to avoid being type-cast as some kind of esoteric specialist. Progressive business firms and government agencies give sabbatical leaves so that their most promising executives can return to the university, broaden their cultural experiences, or pursue thoughtful analyses of strategic options. And it is only a matter of time until computers take over all routine decisions (Leavitt and Whisler, 1958) and allow the human managers to spend their time developing their leadership skills in encounter groups.

Technological progress is breeding a vagabond race of philosopher kings, and they will weave organizational designs of breathtaking intricacy and wondrous subtlety. Either that, or they will do away with the bloody things altogether.

SUGGESTIONS FOR FUTURE READING

JOSEPH BEN-DAVID, "Roles and Innovations in Medicine," *American Journal of Sociology,* Vol. 65 (1960), pp. 557–568.

JOSEPH BEN-DAVID AND ABRAHAM ZLOCZOWER, "Universities and Academic Systems in Modern Societies, *European Journal of Sociology,* Vol. 3 (1962), pp. 45–84.

WARREN G. BENNIS, "A Funny Thing Happened on the Way to the Future," *American Psychologist,* Vol. 25 (1970), pp. 595–608.

MARTIN BRONFENBRENNER, "The Structure of Revolutions in Economic Thought," *The History of Political Economy,* Vol. 3 (1971), pp. 136–151.

V. GORDON CHILDE, *Social Evolution* (London: Watts, 1951). Second edition in 1963 by Fontana Library.

TERRY N. CLARK, "Institutionalization of Innovations in Higher Education: Four Models," *Administrative Science Quarterly,* Vol. 13 (1968), pp. 1–25.

WILLIAM R. DILL, "Desegregation or Integration? Comments about Contemporary Research on Organizations," pp. 39–52, in W.W. Cooper, H.J. Leavitt, and M.W. Shelly II (Eds.), *New Perspectives in Organization Research* (New York: John Wiley & Sons, Inc., 1964.

ROBERT DUBIN, "Theory from on High, pp. 258–282, in Robert Dubin (Ed.), *Theory Building* (New York: The Free Press, 1969).

JOHN M. DUTTON AND WILLIAM H. STARBUCK, "On Managers and Theories," *Management International,* No. 6 (1963), pp. 25–50.

FRED E. EMERY AND ERIC L. TRIST, Socio-technical Systems," pp. 38–97, in C.W. Churchman and C.W. Verhulst (Eds.), *Management Sciences, Models and Techniques,* Vol. 2 (London: Pergamon Books, 1960).

Claude S. George, *The History of Management Thought* (Englewood Cliffs, N.J.: Prentice-Hall, Inc., 1968).

Gerald Gordon and Sue Marquis, "Freedom, Visibility of Consequences, and Scientific Innovation, *American Journal of Sociology*, Vol. 72 (1966), pp. 195–202.

Lee W. Gregg and Herbert A. Simon, "Process Models and Stochastic Theories of Simple Concept Formation," *Journal of Mathematical Psychology*, Vol. 4 (1967), pp. 246–276.

Warren O. Hagstrom, *The Scientific Community* (New York: Basic Books, 1965).

John H. Hoagland, "Historical Antecedents of Organization Research," pp. 27–38, in W.W. Cooper, H.J. Leavitt, and M.W. Shelly II (Eds.), *New Perspectives in Organization Research* (New York: John Wiley & Sons, 1964).

Thomas S. Kuhn, "The Structure of Scientific Revolutions," *International Encyclopedia of Unified Science*, Vol. 2, No. 2 (1962), pp. 1–172.

Harold J. Leavitt and Bernard M. Bass, "Organizational Psychology," *Annual Review of Psychology*, Vol. 15 (1964), pp. 371–398.

Harold J. Leavitt and Thomas L. Whisler, "Management in the 1980's, *Harvard Business Review*, Vol. 36, No. 6 (1958), pp. 41–48.

James G. March, "Introduction," pp. ix–xvi, in J.G. March (Ed.), *Handbook of Organizations* (Chicago: Rand McNally, 1965).

E.J. Miller, "Technology, Territory, and Time: The Internal Differentiation of Complex Production Systems," *Human Relations*, Vol. 12 (1959), pp. 243–271.

National Academy of Sciences and Social Science Research Council, *The Behavioral and Social Sciences: Outlook and Needs* (Englewood Cliffs, N.J.: Prentice-Hall, Inc., 1969).

Donald Pelz and Frank M. Andrews, *Scientists in Organizations* (New York: John Wiley & Sons, 1966).

Karl R. Popper, *The Logic of Scientific Discovery* (New York: Basic Books, 1959).

Derek de Solla Price, *Science since Babylon* (New Haven: Yale University Press, 1961).

Derek de Solla Price, *Little Science, Big Science* (New York: Columbia University Press, 1963).

James L. Price, "Design of Proof in Organizational Research," *Administrative Science Quarterly*, Vol. 13 (1968), pp. 121–134.

John Price, "Corporate Cornelius: What Winds His Motor?" *Business Management*, Vol. 40 (June, 1971), pp. 12–15 and 38.

D.S. Pugh, "Modern Organization Theory: A Psychological and Sociological Study," *Psychological Bulletin*, Vol. 66 (1966), pp. 235–251.

D.S. Pugh "Organizational Behavior: An Approach from Psychology," *Human Relations*, Vol. 22 (1969), pp. 345–354.

Robert P. Quinn and Robert L. Kahn, "Organizational Psychology," *Annual Review of Psychology*, Vol. 18 (1967), pp. 437–466.

Clagett G. Smith, "Scientific Performance and the Composition of Research Teams," *Administrative Science Quarterly*, Vol. 16 (1971), pp. 486–495.

William H. Starbuck, "Some Comments, Observations, and Objections Stimulated by Design of Proof in Organizational Research." *Administrative Science Quarterly*, Vol. 13 (1968), pp. 135–161.

Eric L. Trist and K.W. Bamforth, "Some Social and Psychological Consequences of the Longwall Method of Coal-Getting," *Human Relations*, Vol. 4 (1951), pp. 3–38.

Is Chaos Necessary and Functional, and Should We Hope That the Present State of Organization Theory Will Always Be the Same?

Sherman R. Krupp

Professor
Department of Sociology
Queens College

Mr. Starbuck has presented some of his ideas on the past, present, and future of organization theory. His presentation, unfortunately, is poorly organized and diffuse. This looseness has made it difficult to pinpoint with precision what Mr. Starbuck has said. Nor am I very sure of what he intended to say. Yet despite the frustrations of pondering this extremely uncrisp essay, there are still some points worth the work.

The essay makes four points. (1) Organization theory is old but has recently come into its own. (2) The field is fragmented and there are few themes that are recurrent, or that yield a common core. (3) There are few unifying social institutions that tie the people who work in organization theory into a unified community. (4) The most important recent unifying *paradigm* comes from the application of behavioral science, but even this has significant shortcomings. Might not the victory of behavioral science breed a race of vagabond kings?

The main thrust of Mr. Starbuck's essay has been to describe, but not to explain, the fragmentation of modern organization theory into inumerable thought systems, practical programs, and kinds of theorists. This proliferation was propelled into being by the rise in modern times of large-scale military, industrial, and government bureaucracies. Mr. Starbuck is correct in pointing to this great diversity. But how to account for it? And is his hesitant conclusion that a unified value-neutral and scientific behavioral theory can emerge at all justified by the nature of the problem of organizations in the modern world.

One issue in the physical sciences, long unresolved, has been whether there can be a single unified theoretical system. Among the many positions hostile to this possibility is the argument that a "physics of the universe" and a "physics of the microcosm" must forever be explained by different laws. Thus, the macro-universe is subject to the laws of gravity whereas micro-particles behave according to electromagnetic and nuclear forces. This has led to the justification of two disparate sciences—a micro- and a macro-physics. In the social sciences a related difficulty has been that of connecting a holistic social order of totally integrated parts to the logic of a micro-world composed of unique, freely choosing individuals. In the theory of organizations this pivotal difficulty arises in the distinction between the organization in its relation to the larger society and simultaneously as a micro-social system maximizing its own goals and creating its own private efficiencies. From a larger holistic social point of view, the theory of organization deals with the power of bureaucracy in society, the nature of a social and economic world of large organizations, the distinction between private profit and social welfare, the effect of organizations on war and peace, the dilemma of individual development in a world of big institutions, or the possibility of individual freedom when power is concentrated in government, police, or the military. These are the macro-problems in the theory of organizations. The people who work on these problems and the theories that increase their understanding are not identical with the world of micro-organizational settings. In micro-organizational settings organizations are often seen as entities that contain people who are motivated by profit or by private goals, who join groups, whose expectations are fulfilled or unfulfilled, who are rational or affectual, or who find themselves or their nearby groups living in small integrated or atomized environments. Micro-organizational theory is frequently behavioral, utilizing the research and theory of psychology, utility-maximizing preference functions, or small-group studies of cohesion, leadership, or status achievement. A fundamental difficulty in human understanding arises. Is the macro-social science of societies seen as wholes, of governments envisioned as a balance-of-power, of institutions rising and falling in historic settings, made up of the same theoretical stuff as theories of utility preference? I believe the answer to this question is presently NO and, perhaps, permanently so. To this extent, organizational theory does and will have two disparate domains. Yet two areas do not exhaust the kingdom of organizations. There are many others.

Consider the view that organizations are system maximizing or goal integrating. Clearly, the effort of one system to achieve its goals, if all goals are not mutually supportive, must result in less than goal fulfillment for other related systems. A consequence of this is that the integrating, unifying processes in one organization inevitably conflict with other organizations that are also attempting to achieve their ends. Here the logic of integrating goal achievement, by implication, leads to another kind of theory—the logic of systems in conflict. A micro-theory of organization and a macro-theory of organization may be forced to develop lines of reasoning significantly different one from another.

Another issue, weaving in and out of modern organization theory, is the problem of values. If a micro-theory is developed in which organizations are regarded as systems achieving or not achieving their goals, the goals as starting points can be taken for granted or treated as single and unitary. However, I would find appalling any theory of society that prescribed a unitary goal for the macro-system. Clearly, when we live in the micro-private world of individuals, small groups, and small organizations; a biological metaphor in which a single purpose or goal is ascribed to the system may be extremely useful in explanation. But in the macro-world of total societies such a metaphor can be misleading and values cannot be taken for granted. The relationship of organizations to society cannot be meaningfully viewed from the vantage point of ethical neutrality. Large organizations declare war, create poverty, organize elites, and produce waste and inefficiency. More often than not they do all these things at the same time. Behavioral and ethical theory merge at some points and are independent at others. In a world of varied values can there be a simple unified social theory that all accept? Or does such an integrated theory normally derive from the dictatorship of a minority or the majority?

Finally, organizational ideas derive from the Western heritage in social philosophy. In this tradition there has been a significant branch of thought that holds that ideas must be varied and disparate. Hence, the existence of economics, psychology, sociology, management science, or organizational theory as branches of knowledge unintegrated and made up of different heritages. Is difference not a natural feature of all human knowledge? Integrated idea systems, unfortunately, are often byproducts of excessively integrated societies. Variety in human thought—a sociology, economics, or management science that reveals different axioms—is a necessary condition for intellectual progress in a free society. This variety probably ought to be preserved. How is one to know precisely the point at which integration stifles ideas more than common axioms advance them. At what point is uniformity suppressive of the creative iconoclast? To what degree is the fragmentation in organization theory natural and productive in human intellectual endeavor?

The questions raised by Mr. Starbuck are probably not answerable in principle and certainly not in practice. I would have preferred a different manner of treatment. But then one can also agree with many of the points without being attracted to the argument. Fortunately, in a world of many positions there may be little cause to worry about philosopher kings.

An Open Letter on Organization Theory

Craig C. Lundberg

Associate Professor
School of Business Administration
Southern Methodist University

On a first reading of this chapter, I was amazed and amused—amazed at the author's perspective on, insight into, and general erudition about, the field of organization theory; amused with the biting phrases, gripping metaphors, subtle irony, and caustic idealism. A second reading, however, left me overwhelmed: on the one hand the author imparts so much to his readers (it *is* "rich"), and on the other hand, so little for the intended audience. I admire the author's bold analytical skills, his staunchly held scientific values, and his high standards of professional competence. Knowing this about him frees me to be candid and to try to live up to his mark. My intention in the following pages is to do three things: first, to comment directly on the chapter; second, to suggest to readers how they might sift through it so as to enhance their learning from it; and third, to present some of my views on the present state and probable future of organization theory.

BETWEEN ERUDITION AND "PUTTING ON" YOUR AUDIENCE

I would have preferred to have the author tell us at the beginning what the chapter was going to be all about and how he was going to go about presenting his case. As it is, I had to go along to find out, evolving some expectations as I went along. I wonder how many readers will readily do this. I assume that the chapter has been laced with technical and sophisticated terms to provoke people to read and talk and think. Actually, the non-expert will be "snowed" by references to "conceptual paradigms, cohesive subcultures, maximizing subjective expected utilities, nepotistic hierarchies, systems properties, and decomposing quadratic programming problems." When references to fantastic fantasized devices such as folded-J semi-interval scales and cubic causal structural analysis are interwoven with fantastic sounding but actual devices such as Biomed control cards and Organization Climate Description questionnaires, it requires a refinement of discrimination rather rare in this world. The author's use of metaphor is powerful and compelling—e.g., when the victim is "caught" staring into the eye of a cobra and going into a hypnotic trance, and the careful and more literary-minded reader will no doubt experience what he is communicating. His penchant for sarcastic irony delights me as a quasi-expert in organization theory, and I catch most of it (I hope), and I believe it adds spice to a long and complex chapter—however the finesse of the irony will probably confuse and confound most readers. Let's examine a couple of examples. The author states, "As all academia knows, anyone who investigates applied problems must be less intelligent and interesting than those who pursue learning for its own sake. . . ." What if this is taken literally and not recognized as overdrawing a point for emphasis? To take another example, the author mentions that the average number of paradigms per organization theorist is 6.7813492. Although this "fact" is preceded by the statement that stating it is the finding of a "casual census," and seven decimal places surely ought to prompt skepticism, people's awe of numbers will very likely not let them sense that the example is facetious. The author is an enormous tease, dropping juicy tidbits spiced with big words right and left. One example will have to suffice. When he states that many organization theorists have never really become sophisticated enough in mathematical modeling to understand why algebraically convenient assumptions take precedence over conceptually realistic ones, I for one would like to know why. Although not wishing to belabor these points of style, level of erudition, or subtle intellectual gambits, I think that although the chapter will excite the truly curious and already somewhat knowledgeable, its potential for being viewed as a "put on" will "turn off" all but the hardy—and organization theorists need a lot of nuturent understanding, as the author is at pains to point out.

HINTS ON PANNING FOR NUGGETS, OR HOW TO TELL THE PEARLS FROM THE OYSTERS

The chapter ostensibly describes the dynamics of development of an occupational specialty–organization theory. Perhaps it should have been subtitled, "How an Occupation Grows up Absurd." In times to come I have no doubt that it will be known as one of the most perceptive studies in the sociology of occupations. However, for the reader interested in getting in touch with the present state of the art, there are many difficulties. I would here like to suggest some hints for readers, for there is a lot about organization theory in the chapter if one knows how to winnow the mass of material it contains. What if someone wanted to delve into the substantive literature on his own? I'd suggest that the people named would comprise a rather comprehensive, even excellent, bibliography. What if someone wanted to get a feel for the array of concepts available in organization theory? Well, again, going through the chapter and listing the concepts mentioned would provide an extensive and rather representative sample. What if someone wanted to acquire a model with which to diagnose an organization? The chapter section entitled "Today" contains a rough but useful beginning, for the sequence of ideas, and especially the subheadings, in this section provide much analytical leverage if rigorously applied in order. Thus such a model for diagnosis begins by questioning the organization's domain, its status, and its identity. Following this, one would inquire into subsystem specialities, their job descriptions, which are deviate, as well as the degree of cooperation among them. Subsystem cohesion, intercommunication, ideology, and leadership are the next topics to diagnose. This would bring our hypothetical diagnostician up to the subheading, "Environmental Acceptance and Rejection," and he would be well on his way.

What if someone wished to comprehend how far organization "theory" had advanced? Here there are two sorts of material to glean from. By reading the statements that include or are near to the word "theory," as well as any methodological references, the curious and the fledgling philosopher of science would find most of the issues of concern—e.g., the various sources of productive problems, the issue of interdisciplinary research, the argument over acceptable predictability, the prostitution of research, the problem of "objectivity" in social science, the desirability of multiple, even conflicting methodologies, and so on. A second reading of organizational theory's advance could come from gleaning the "propositions" or scientific sound ing statements that are liberally included. Examples of what I allude to appear about two-thirds of the way through the chapter, where the plethora of conceptual paradigms and samples from Simon, Lewin, Weber, Argyris, Dahl, and Kaufman are mentioned. Other examples are plentiful, if more disguised, as when in the first pages on ancient history, in a passing reference to the Great Wall of China, the proposition is made that bureaucratic structures impede change; and a few lines later, the reference to the Romans indicates that the more an organization is geographically dispersed, the more difficulties there will be maintaining consistency of statuses.

SOME THEMES TO BELIEVE IN

The more I studied this chapter the more I began to see some of the strands used to weave the story. Let me point out some of these strands—themes, I believe, that are worth reinforcing in the minds of readers. One is that the old industrial engineering myth of "the one best way" is slow to die and in fact still impedes a lot of organization theory. Another is the real, but seldom understood and thereby continuously debated, congruence in function among managers and organization theorists. I refer here to their common concern (shared purpose?) for solving problems, or better put, for understanding phenomena well enough to accurately predict intervention consequences. On the one hand this theme encourages managers to be more scientific and experimental in their practices, and on the other hand suggests that organizational theorists keep their conceptual efforts constantly related to empirical reality. Another theme I have detected says that the normative-prescriptive theories and the empirical-descriptive theories are not really polar opposites but can, nay need, to be combined or integrated. I interpret this as a plea for synthesis along both an axis of abstraction and an axis of conceptual scope. Other important themes include the reminder that organizations are both a subject for study as well as the context for and a factor in behavior, and the theme that organizations are dynamic systems even though they are typically cast as static structures. This "systems" theme alerts us to the organization's interface with its environments and how it depends on, transacts with, and adapts to these "external publics," and makes organization change a major theme in itself. Not even a partial listing of such themes should conclude without mentioning the "biggie": organization theory is rightly becoming truly theoretical, if albeit haltingly. There are three sorts of additional commentary I want to add—what some of the developing, contemporary conceptual issues and emphasis are, some illustrative, recent organization designs, and my opinions about the current and future direction of research strategies.

ADDENDA I: CONCEPTUAL TRENDS AND ISSUES

Two definitional lessons require clarification. One is what an "organization" is; the other is a more explicit response to the query, What is organization theory? Although what follows are not definitive responses, I offer them in the belief that the reader of the chapter does legitimately deserve some orientation. An organization (in my view) is a purposive social system, deliberately designed to coordinate the activities of many persons so as to facilitate achievement of a set of explicit objectives. Thus there is a more or less stable patterning of relationships, systems for acquiring and using resources, plans for operating and sometimes for changing, and often devices for maximizing mutual goal attainment and member satisfaction while minimizing undesirable side effects. Given this view of what an "organization" is, organization theory becomes a matter of understanding the phenomena just referred to, the explanation of how inputs are transformed into outputs under a variety of internal and external conditions such as alternative structures, processes, and contexts.

Contemporary issues in organization theory reflect the above. There is concern for understanding goals (Perrow, 1970), differentiating goal and system models of organization (Etzioni, 1964), delineating effectiveness from efficiency (Ghorpade, 1971; Price, 1968), defining the nature of an organization's environment (Lawrence and Lorsch, 1969), conceptualizing environmental dependencies (Thompson, 1967), understanding the degree of formalization and especially the degree of rational formality we call bureaucracy (Hall, 1962), the difference that differing sizes and technologies (Woodward, 1965) makes, and so forth. Speaking somewhat more abstractly, current theoretical concerns appear to be refocusing around the issues of how to identify the organization's boundary (the problem of entivity), how to compare and contrast organizations (the problem of typology, Sells, 1964), how to describe and conceptualize the organization-environmental interface (the problem of context), how to construe inter-organizational relations (the problem of organization set, Evan, 1966), how to analytically describe an organization as a general whole (the problems of organizational climate and character), how to disentangle the paralleling requirements for differentiation and integration (the problem of contingency), how to model the processes that tend to preserve or maintain an organization and the processes that tend to elaborate or change an organization form or state (the problems of morphostasis and morphogenesis, respectively, Buckley, 1967).

Lately, certain concepts have emerged into prominence and deserve mention for they become the ideas that constrain and channel theoretical efforts. Power, role, task, values, conflict, exchange and bargaining, and the ubiquitous "system" (Miller, 1972) are prominent candidates for being the most research productive concept. The whole topic of change (Hage and Aiken, 1970), however, is finally capturing the attention it so fundamentally deserves, reflecting both a growing attention to process theorizing (Weick, 1969) as well as a growing set of practical strategies and techniques for organization change —e.g., the specialty of organizational development (Bennis, 1969; Margulies and Raia, 1972; Argyris, 1971).

ADDENDA II: INNOVATIONS IN DESIGN

Organization theorists have tended to follow the lead of managers in innovating new organization designs. Although the shifts in managerial philosophy (values, beliefs, and assumptions) that occur (McGregor, 1960, 1967; Tannenbaum and Davis, 1969), may be attributed in part to academia, changing social-cultural circumstances no doubt account for most of the observable shifts. Changes in the variety and priority of goals and in environmental conditions demand, and shifts in philosophy permit, experimentation with new organizational designs. Today we find organizations breaking from stable, rigid, homogenizing, simplistic structures to temporary, adaptive, complex, heterogeneous ones, from an ideal of bureaucratic structures to an array of designs with interesting names, such as matrix (Mee, 1964), project (Sayles and Chandler, 1971), collateral, socio-technical (Rice, 1958), and so on. The name of the game for organizational design has changed from trying to discover the ideal one best way to what is an *appropriate* design given a discrete set of goals, known material and human resources, a more or less turbulent environment, and captive technologies and programs. We can expect even more diversity of designs in the years to come as the matrix of factors affecting design increases in size, and as we continue to learn how to influence these factors.

ADDENDA III: FADS, FANCY, AND FORMALIZATION IN RESEARCH

The chapter rather splendidly describes the fads in research that have reflected the successive interest in organization theory by the basic disciplines; major writers and personages; the changing professional payoffs; and the evolving development of new analytical techniques and technologies. At the present time it is safe to say that all research strategies and methods have been applied to organization theory. The earliest emphasis was on case studies and intensive field work, which was later supplemented by survey work, field and laboratory experiments, and finally simulations. What's new perhaps is that the classical order of utilizing these methodologies—e.g., case-survey-experiment—has been fruitfully reordered and combined. Current research strategies also reflect exciting and fruitful changes. Long overdue comparative, longitudinal efforts and cross-sectional efforts now appear with more regularity in the literature. Multivariant models also keep cropping up, reflecting the ever-growing concern of organization theorists not to leave variance in findings unaccounted for. Simulation advances have offered opportunities for exploration, modeling, and relatively inexpensive testing of alternative sets of factors only dreamed of a couple of decades ago. The work that pleases me most these days are the attempts at formalization, both the proposition builders and the mathematical model builders. It's a sign of organization theory's "coming of age"—there is now something to say and some scientific conscience about how to say it. This is not to say that most attempts do not now fall short. I agree wholeheartedly here with the author's views, but our colleagues are *trying* for synthesis, parsimony, and logical-deductive formats.

There are five types of research efforts that I wish to single out as vital for organization theory if we are going to continue to advance our understanding of organizational dynamics and patterning. Each of these sorts of efforts currently exist; I'm simply suggesting that we need more of each. The first is more myth and proverb testing (Simon, 1946). So much of our knowledge is in the form of interesting rules of thumb, conventional wisdoms, and just plain assumptions. We need to make these sorts of thing explicit and then to systematically confirm, disconfirm, or state the limiting conditions for them. A second reemphasis I suggest is for more descriptive research—a plea made often enough before but not adequately acted on in my opinion (Scott, 1965). Such descriptive efforts would most usefully be expended on comparative cases. A third effort would be the establishment of a major data base on organizations, once again a frequent suggestion but not as yet in existence. My fourth suggestion encourages more field experiments (Evan, 1971). No other research method can compete with experiments in producing information of such unequivocal nature or in bringing to the fore issues of causality. My last suggested direction for research is action science (Argyris, 1970). The cycling of study, intervention, restudy, etc., has so much utility for unraveling causal and change variables that we can expect to find it reported more and more. This method demands much of the investigator, yet its promise is compelling (Torbert, in preparation). With action science the researcher as a sensitive index/instrument, constantly relating several levels of consciousness, propels science one more step forward from the extreme empiricism of Locke, the dialectics of Hegel and Marx, the ethical-scientific integration of Churchman, toward the "holistic experiment" of Mitroff (1971).

I can't help but think that organization theorists are going to be replaced soon by organization scientists, or as Yanouzas (1970) has labeled them "orgametricians" (I predict systemetricians), persons practicing a sophistication of organization measurement, with an extensive empirical familiarity, and possessing a gift for elegant, abstract formulations of the "middle-range," neither grand and sweeping nor overly specialized. Come to think of it, the author might represent the arch-type. Before I get completely carried away, however, let me invite would-be managers into the growthful occupation of organization theorist, for all it requires, to quote Percy Bridgman (1945), ". . . is nothing more than doing one's damnedest with one's mind, no holds barred." Management and organization theory, and science,

> . . . like all creature activity is exploration, gambling and adventure. It does not lend itself very well to neat blueprints, detailed road maps and central planning. Perhaps that's why it's fun (Simon, 1964).

SUGGESTIONS FOR FUTURE READING

CHRIS ARGYRIS, *Intervention Theory and Method* (Reading, Massachusetts: Addison-Wesley, 1970).

CHRIS ARGYRIS, *Management and Organizational Development* (New York: McGraw-Hill Book Co., Inc., 1971).

WARREN G. BENNIS, *Organization Development: Its Nature, Origins, and Prospects* (Reading, Massachusetts: Addison-Wesley, 1969).

PERCY W. BRIDGMAN, "The Prospect for Intelligence," *Yale Review*, Vol. 34 (1945), pp. 444–461.

WALTER BUCKLEY, *Sociology and Modern Systems Theory* (Englewood Cliffs, N.J.: Prentice-Hall, 1967).

TOM BURNS, "The Comparative Study of Organizations," pp. 113–165, in Victor H. Vroom (Ed.), *Methods of Organizational Research* (Pittsburgh: University of Pittsburgh Press, 1967).

WILLIAM M. EVAN, "The Organization-Set," pp. 175–191, in James D. Thompson (Ed.), *Approaches to Organization Design* (Pittsburgh: University of Pittsburgh Press, 1966).

WILLIAM M. EVAN, *Organizational Experiments: Laboratory and Field Research* (New York: Harper & Row, 1971).

AMITAI ETZIONI, *Modern Organizations* (Englewood Cliffs, N.J.: Prentice-Hall, Inc., 1964).

JAISINGH GHORPADE, *Assessment of Organizational Effectiveness* (Pacific Palisades, California: Goodyear Publishing Co., 1971).

JERALD HAGE AND MICHAEL AIKEN, *Social Change in Complex Organizations* (New York: Random House, 1970).

RICHARD H. HALL, "Intraorganizational Structural Variation: Application of the Bureaucratic Model," *Administrative Science Quarterly*, Vol. 7 (1962), pp. 295–308.

PAUL R. LAWRENCE AND JAY LORSCH, *Organization and Environment* (Homewood, Illinois: Richard D. Irwin, Inc., 1969).

NEWTON MARGULIES AND ANTHONY RAIA, *Organizational Development: Values, Process and Technology* (New York: McGraw-Hill Book Co., Inc., 1972).

DOUGLAS MCGREGOR, *The Human Side of Enterprise* (New York: McGraw-Hill Book Co., Inc., 1960).

DOUGLAS MCGREGOR, *The Professional Manager* (New York: McGraw-Hill Book Co., Inc., 1967).

JOHN F. MEE, "Matrix Organization," *Business Horizons*, Vol. 7 (1964), pp. 70–72.

JAMES G. MILLER, "Living Systems: The Organization," *Behavioral Science*, Vol. 17 (1972), pp. 1–182.

IAN MITROFF, *On the Methodology of the Holistic Experiment*, Working paper, University of Pittsburgh, Philosophy of Science Center.

CHARLES PERROW, *Organizational Analysis: A Sociological View* (Belmont, California: Brooks/Cole Publishing Co., 1970).

JAMES L. PRICE, *Organizational Effectiveness* (Homewood, Illinois: Richard D. Irwin, Inc., 1968).

A.K. RICE, *Productivity and Social Organization—The Ahmedabad Experiment* (London: Tavistock, 1958).

LEONARD R. SAYLES AND MARGARET CHANDLER, *Managing Large Systems: Organizations for the Future* (New York: Harper & Row, 1971).

W. RICHARD SCOTT, "Field Methods in the Study of Organizations," pp. 261–304, in James G. March (Ed.), *Handbook of Organizations* (Chicago: Rand McNally, 1965).

S.B. SELLS, "Toward a Taxonomy of Organizations," pp. 515–532, in W.W. Cooper, H.J. Leavitt, and M.W. Shelly (Eds.), *New Perspectives in Organization Research* (New York: John Wiley & Sons, 1964).

HERBERT A. SIMON, "The Proverbs of Administration," *Public Administration Review*, Vol. 6 (1964), pp. 53–67.

HERBERT A. SIMON, "Approaching the Theory of Management," p. 85, in Harold Koontz (Ed.), *Toward a Unified Theory of Management* (New York: McGraw-Hill Book Co., Inc., 1964).

ROBERT TANNENBAUM AND SHELDON DAVIS, "Values, Man, and Organizations," *Industrial Management Review*, Vol. 10 (1969), pp. 67–83.

JAMES D. THOMPSON, *Organizations in Action* (New York: McGraw-Hill Book Co., Inc., 1967).

WILLIAM R. TORBERT, *The Struggle Towards a School-in-Life: First Glimpses of an Action Science* (in preparation).

KARL E. WEICK, *The Social Psychology of Organizing* (Reading, Massachusetts: Addison-Wesley, 1969).

JOAN WOODWARD, *Industrial Organization* (London: Oxford University Press, 1965).

JOHN N. YANOUZAS, "Crosscurrents of Organization Theory: Some Comments in Recent Research," pp. 38–50, in William Frey (Ed.), *Management Research and Practice* (Amherst: University of Massachusetts, 1970).

DISCUSSION QUESTIONS

1. What is your opinion of Starbuck's history of organization theory? Do you believe he is entirely serious?
2. What are the two "mental aberrations" that apparently afflict organization theorists?
3. Do you believe that organization theorists are naturally more liberal

than their colleagues in management schools? Why?

4. Do you agree that the types of persons that Starbuck claims become organization theorists include the whole field? What other types might be included?
5. Is there a difference between organizational theory and organizational behavior?
6. Why do you think Starbuck believes organization theorists have inferiority complexes? Or does he believe this?

7

Organizational and Individual Objectives

Fremont E. Kast

Professor
Graduate School of Business Administration
University of Washington

Formal organizations are contrived social systems designed to accomplish specific purposes. The tendency to organize or cooperate in interdependent relationships is basic in human nature. Through nearly all man's history, his social institutions were primarily on an informal face-to-face basis. Within the past several centuries, the growing importance of large groups or organizations has been one of the most pervasive phenomena.[1]

Man in modern society is increasingly a participant in more complex organizations. Government, business, hospitals, unions, the military, and other organizational types have become pervasive in man's life. These organizations have been created in order to achieve objectives that could not be accomplished by the individual or more informal groups. Getting to the moon, staging a massive effort to meet our health problems, and creating a multinational business require complex and sophisticated organizations. However, although organizations are created by man to help him accomplish his purposes more effectively, they may generate many conflicts and problems for him.

There are many different definitions of organizations, but all reveal certain common elements. Organizations are oriented toward accomplishing goals. Knowledge and techniques are used in achieving these goals. Organization implies structuring and integrating activities—that is, people working or cooperating together in interdependent relationships. The notion of interrelatedness suggests a social system. Therefore we can say that *organizations* are (1) *goal-oriented,* people with a purpose; (2) *psycho-social systems,* people interacting together; (3) *technological systems,* people using knowledge and techniques; and (4) *an integration of structured activities,* people working together.

This definition implies that organizations may be viewed in two distinct ways. As Selznick says, "On the one hand, any concrete organizational system is an *economy*; at the same time, it is an *adaptive social structure*."[2] As an economy, the organization is concerned with the effective and efficient transformation of resources. However, it is much more than a mechanistic system; it is staffed by people whose cooperation is imperative to its functional success.

THE ORGANIZATION AS AN OPEN SOCIO-TECHNICAL SYSTEM

Throughout this discussion organizations will be considered as socio-technical systems in interaction with their environment. Traditional management and organization theory used a highly structured, closed-system approach. The bureaucratic model emphasized the development of a rational organization structure based on authority. Scientific management concentrated on improving the performance of technical tasks. Both took a very limited and closed view of the organization.

Modern theory has moved toward the open-system approach.[3] Drawing on the contributions of many modern writers, we can view an organization as an open, socio-technical system composed of a number of subsystems, as illustrated in Figure 12. The open-system view recognizes that the organization is in dynamic interaction with its environment and receives inputs, transforms these inputs in some way, and returns outputs.

The organization can be viewed as an aggregate of several major subsystems. The organizational *goals and values* are one of the more important. The *technical system* refers to the knowledge required to transform inputs into outputs. Every organization has a *psycho-social* system that consists of individual behavior and motivation, status and role systems, group dynamics, and influence systems. The *organization structure* can be considered as another major subsystem intermeshed between the technical and the psycho-social subsystems. Structure is concerned with the ways in which the tasks of the organization are divided (differentiated) and with the coordination of these activities (integration). The *managerial system* spans the entire organization by directing the technology, organizing people and other resources, and relating the organization to its environment.

This open-systems view sets the framework for considering organizational and individual goals. The goals and values subsystem is of key im-

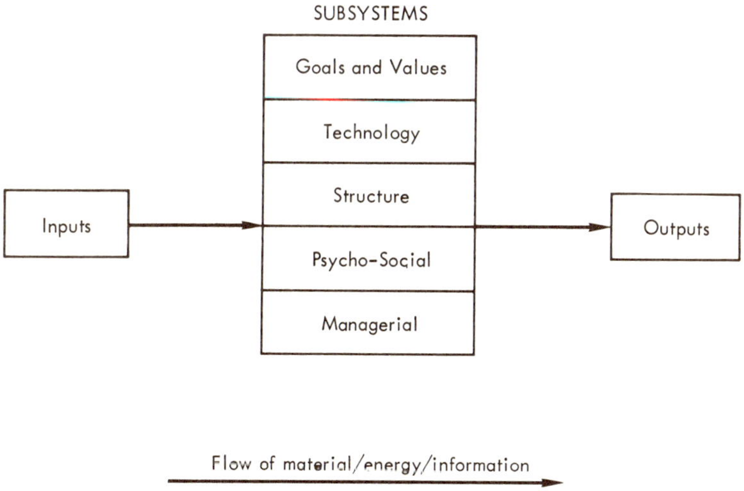

FIGURE 12. The Organization as an Open Socio-technical System

portance in relating the organization to its environment, in determining the nature of the technology and structure, and in establishing the relationships among people in the organization.

WHAT ARE GOALS?

Simply stated, goals are the desirable results of organizational or individual activities. In this sense, goals include objectives, purposes, missions, deadlines, standards, targets, quotas, and so on. However, the concept of a "goal" has acquired a variety of meanings, depending on the perspective of the writer. It is sometimes used to legitimize the role of the organization in society (the goal of General Motors is to make automobiles), or to provide a motive for the organization's activity (General Motor's goal is to make a profit). A goal may also be a specific accomplishment, such as manufacturing so many automobiles during a given time period. In another sense, goals may be considered as the set of constraints that the organization must satisfy; i.e., making profits for the stockholders, meeting governmental safety standards, pacifying the environmentalists, and satisfying customers.[4]

We need a more elaborate definition of goals that encompasses these various perspectives. Gore says that goals are:

> The objects toward which organizations direct their energies and concerns. If organization is a means of accomplishing ends beyond the capacities of individuals, goals are collective ends translated into socially meaningful terms. Often represented as being defined by action, goals also influence organized activity, for a well-established goal serves the vital function of legitimatizing action.[5]

One of the major problems in the analysis of organizational goals is the distinction between the *official* goals and the actual *operational* goals. Official goals are often stated in broad, ambiguous terms to legitimize the activities of the organization. For example, the official goal of a mental institution may be to treat mental illness. However, the operational goals are those actually pursued. The mental hospital may provide little in the way of treatment and be geared instead to custodial care of patients.

> The type of goals most relevant to understanding organizational behavior are not the official goals, but those that are embedded in major operating policies and the daily decisions of the personnel. . . . These goals will be shaped by the particular problems or tasks an organization must emphasize, since these tasks determine the characteristics of those who will dominate the organization.[6]

In studying organizational and individual goals, we face many additional conceptual difficulties. Do organizations have goals or are goals the composite of individual goals? How are goals established and modified? Who establishes the goals? Despite these and other questions we can agree on the importance of goals in organizational analysis. The efforts to achieve goals affects the ability of the organization to receive resource inputs from the broader society and thus legitimize its existence. They focus the attention of participants on actions that are organizationally relevant. They provide the standards for measuring success. They help determine the technologies and tasks required and also provide the basis for specialization of effort, authority patterns, communication and decision networks, and other structural relationships. The nature of the goals vitally affect the psycho-social relationships within the organization. In effect, the goals set the basic character of the organization. Perrow says:

> They reflect more readily the uniqueness of organizations and the role of specific influences within the more general technological and structural categories. For goals are the product of a variety of influences, some of them enduring and some fairly transient. To enumerate some of these influences: the personality of top executives, the history of the organization, its community environment, the norms and values of the other organizations with which it deals (e.g., the "mentality of the steel industry"), the technology and structure of the organization, and ultimately the cultural setting.[7]

Management is vitally affected by the nature of organizational and individual goals. Chief executives generally establish the broad institutional goals that help relate the organization to its environment. Management then translates these broad goals into operational objectives. It provides means of control to measure the extent of goal accomplishment. It must continually deal with goal conflicts and find ways of satisfying the interest of many internal and external groups. Thus, management is vitally concerned with goal formation and implementation, and conflict resolution. But it is not omnipotent. Many goals and constraints are imposed on the organization by the external society and internal participants.

This chapter will look more completely at a number of the issues raised in this introduction. The following topics are considered.

Organizational Goals—Three Levels of Analysis
Environmental Determinants of Organizational Goals
Organizational Systems Goals
Individual and Organizational Goals
Integration of Individual and Organizational Goals
The Role of Management in Setting and Implementing Goals
Managing Goal Conflicts

ORGANIZATIONAL GOALS—THREE LEVELS OF ANALYSIS

Organizational goals can be considered from three primary perspectives: (1) the environmental level—the goal constraints imposed on the organization by society; (2) the organizational level—the goals of the organization as a system; and (3) the individual level—the goals of organizational participants. There obviously may be many goal conflicts among these three levels. However, there must also be a certain degree of goal compatibility if the organization is to survive. Each of these three levels is considered in detail in the following discussion. However, it is first necessary to consider whether or not organizations have goals distinct from those of individual participants.

Do Organizations Have Goals?

Organizations have already been defined as specific goal-seeking systems. This reification of the organization—attributing a concrete reality to a social system—is reflected in much of the thinking about organizational goals. Perhaps the origins of this view stem from the classical economic theory of the firm, which considered the organization as a single entrepreneur—the goals of the firm and the entrepreneur are identical. Similarly in public agencies, the classical approach assumed that goals were determined by legislative action and the primary function of the agency was goal implementation. However, in reality there are many organizational participants—stockholders, executives, staffs, and other employees whose individual goals shape the activities of the organization. The goal structure of organizations is much more complex than that postulated by traditional economic and administrative theory. But we are left with a dilemma. If we do not accept the entrepreneural goal as the organization goal, what is the organization goal? Cyert and March set forth this problem as follows:

1. People (i.e., individuals) have goals; collectivities of people do not.
2. To define a theory of organizational decision making, we seem to need something analogous—at the organization level—to individual goals at the individual level.[8]

They also suggest a solution to this problem by conceptualizing the organization as a coalition.

> In a business organization the coalition members include managers, workers, stockholders, suppliers, customers, lawyers, tax collectors, regulatory agencies, and so on. In the governmental organization the members include administrators, workers, appointive officials, elective officials, legislators, judges, clientele, interest-group leaders, and the like. In the voluntary charitable organization there are paid functionaries, volunteers, donors, donees, and others.[9]

These organizational members have different and frequently conflicting goals. Thus the actual goals of the organization result from a continuous bargaining-learning process by coalition members.

> Goals arise in such a form because the firm is, in fact, a coalition of participants with disparate demands, changing foci of attention, and limited ability to attend to all organizational problems simultaneously.[10]

This approach is followed throughout this article. Organizations *do have* multiple goals that arise out of the continual learning-bargaining process of internal and external coalition members. These goals are frequently not officially stated and are often in conflict. There may be inconsistencies and ambiguities. The goal set of the organization is continually changing as a result of this learning-adapting process.

> In practice, goals are often set in a complicated power play involving various individuals and groups within and without the organization, and by reference

to values which govern behavior in general and the specific behavior of the relevant individuals and groups in a particular society.[11]

The question remains, Who are the various members of the coalition and how do they influence the goal structure of the organization? The open-systems model will be utilized as a framework for discussing this question. The organization is a subsystem of the broader society but it also contains internal subsystems of groups and individuals. We will therefore consider a hierarchical order moving from the environment, to the organization, to the individual levels. The boundaries between these systems levels are not absolute and there is a high degree of interaction among them, as Blau suggests:

> Social systems are typically part of broader ones that encompass them and simultaneously constitute the environment of narrower systems they encompass. Work groups are the environment in which individuals act out their roles; the organization of the department is the context within which work groups develop their structure; the total organization sets limits to the ways in which departments can be organized; and the society, including the political order, other institutions, and the state of the technology, provides the social setting that conditions the character of the organizations in its boundaries. Whereas the larger system restricts the development of those it encompasses, there are also feedback effects from the subsystems to the more encompassing ones, because subsystems are not infinitely pliable but tend to have a minimum of autonomy to which the encompassing system must adjust.[12]

Environmental Determinants of Organizational Goals

The open-system view suggests that the organization receives resource inputs, transforms these inputs, and then returns outputs to the environment. The university receives appropriations, research grants, and students; transforms these inputs through its teaching, research, and service activities; and turns out trained graduates of many types, new research information, and a great variety of services. Every organization is in constant interaction with its environment. Even more important, it depends on this environment for its very survival. The goals that society prescribes for the organization are of vital importance.

An important conceptual model for viewing the relationship between the organization and the broader society has been developed by Talcott Parsons.[13] He used a systems viewpoint to conceptualize society as a complex of interlocking systems ranging from individual personalities and small groups, through more complex organizations, to whole societies. The organization is a subsystem of the broader society and its goals must be legitimized by that society. He says:

> It seemed appropriate to define an organization as a social system which is organized for the attainment of a particular type of goal; the attainment of that goal is at the same time the performance of a type of function on behalf of a more inclusive system, the society.[14]

In this view the organization can survive only by meeting certain goals imposed by the society that legitimizes its activities. The organization is viewed as an instrument to accomplish society's goals, whether it be a business firm or some other organization.

> In achieving its generalized objectives of stability and growth, in providing for its current activities and future-oriented projects, and in making its routine and strategic decisions, society makes use of the business firm as an instrument. This is only another way of stating that private operations are public assets, to be used in accordance with social goals. Their privacy is protected only because it derives from the culture's value set and is looked on as itself contributing to social ends.[15]

Environmental Constraints on Organizations

The environment imposes many constraints on the organization. It can limit the amount of inputs the organization receives and also accept or reject the outputs. It can restrict many of the internal activities of the organization (for example, safety regulations, zoning restrictions, working standards, etc.).

In our society, with its strong emphasis on a market economy, business firms are granted a large degree of autonomy in the pursuit of their objectives. The traditional competitive model provided a form of social control that legitimized the activities of the business firm. The business firm is increasingly subject to other constraints, such as governmental regulation and pressures from environmentalists. The growing professionalism of management provides another form of externally imposed social control. In modern organization theory there is growing consideration of the interrelationships between organizations and their environment.[16]

Organizational Exploitation of Environment

At the same time that the society imposes certain goal constraints on the organization, it also serves as a field of exploitation for the organization. "To society, the firm is an instrument to be used. To the firm, society is a field to be exploited."[17] This is particularly true for business firms operating in a market economy. Environmental changes, such as technological developments and population expansion, provide new opportunities for the firm.[18]

This process of utilizing society as a field of exploitation leads to a continual modification and elaboration in the goal structure of the organization, public as well as private. The growing elaboration of goals of universities in the twentieth century is a case in point. The expansion in activities and formulation of new goals by large community hospitals is another example. The survival of the organization depends on its ability to adapt to and utilize social resources. Seashore and Yuchtman say: "We define the effectiveness of an organization as its ability to exploit its environment in the acquisition of scarce and valued resources to sustain its functioning."[19]

Social Indicators of Organizational Goal Performance

If organizations must meet social goals, how do we measure their effectiveness in accomplishing these ends? For the business firm with a tangible product, the market mechanism provides a means for measuring its success in adapting to new social goals. However, for organizations such as universities, hospitals, and many governmental agencies in which the outputs (products and services) are more intangible, the problem of measuring effectiveness from the social viewpoint is much more difficult. Thompson and McEwen suggest this difficulty:

> In sum, the goals of an organization, which determine the kinds of goods or services it produces and offers to the environment, often are subject to peculiar difficulties of reappraisal. Where the purpose calls for an easily identified, readily-measured product, reappraisal and readjustment of goals may be accomplished rapidly. But as goals call for increasingly intangible, difficult-to-measure products, society finds it more difficult to determine and reflect its acceptability of that product, and the signals that indicate unacceptable goals are less effective and perhaps longer in coming.[20]

Although this problem of measuring the organizational performance of social goals is most important in the nonbusiness sector, it does have implications for the business firm. Many problems facing business are not purely economic but have psycho-social ramifications. Many problems facing the automobile industry arise because of ecological and environmental factors that are difficult to define and make organizational performance difficult to measure.

Much of our past thinking in the business sector has been associated with the economic-technical performance of the organization. The development of internal accounting systems at the firm level and national economic accounting are reflections of this emphasis on measuring organizational performance in purely economic terms. It can be questioned whether economic performance is a sufficient standard to use in determining whether or not a business firm is meeting its social goals. It is even more inappropriate to measure the social performance of organizations in the nonbusiness sector in economic terms. Many organizations are developing more sophisticated administrative techniques for measuring performance. For example, in government agencies systems analysis, cost-effectiveness analysis, and the planning-programming-budgeting system (PPBS) are approaches used to help establish goals, evaluate alternative means for achieving these goals, and to help measure the organization's performance in accomplishing its goals. These newly developed techniques will become more sophisticated and important in the future.

New measurements of performance are being developed for the macro-level of society. In the past, sophisticated measurements in the economic-technical sector have been developed (National Income Accounts and Products) and interest currently is growing in the development of national social indicators and a program of social system accounting.[21] Development of such a system of social accounts will help in evaluating the performance of organizations (business as well as public) in the accomplishment of social goals. Although detailed discussion of this development is beyond the scope of this paper, this trend will have major significance in relating organizational activities to social goals. A system of national social accounting would aid in providing information concerning organizational performance in many sectors. This development follows the establishment of national economic accounting during the earlier part of this century and is a natural evolution toward rationalizing the relationship between organizational performance and social goals.

We have suggested that the broader socio-cultural environment imposes certain constraints on organizations to insure that they accomplish social purposes. This legitimizes the activities of the organization and requires it to set its operational goals within this framework. We will now turn to the next level of analysis—the organizational systems goals.

ORGANIZATIONAL SYSTEMS GOALS

Organizational systems goals pertain to the purposes and desired conditions of the organization as a distinct entity.[22] Self-perpetuation, a high rate of profit, stability of operations, growth, satisfaction of participants, enhancement of position in its field, technological leadership and innovation—all are examples of systems goals. Systems goals are thus those states or conditions to which the organization aspires.

It was suggested earlier that organizations have multiple goals rather than a single goal and that this goal set is determined by bargaining among coalition members. Organizational goals cannot be understood merely by accepting officially stated goals but only by observing the actual policies of the organization and how they are implemented. Typically, official goals are stated in broad and ambiguous terms to allow for substantial discretion in operational goals. Organizations, like other open systems, exhibit equifinality—they generally have many alternative means for accomplishing systems objectives.[23] The organization has substantial discretion concerning the goals that it attempts to reach and also many alternative transformation functions to accomplish them. It must operate within the constraints established by environmental forces and by the need to maintain the contributions of individual participations (to be discussed in more detail later).

The Organization as an Adapting, Goal-Satisficing System

It was suggested earlier that organizations are learning, adapting systems that have multiple, sometimes conflicting, goals. This view is in contrast to that of the organization as a rationally oriented, single-goal maximizing system. Cyert and March provided the most comprehensive treatment of this approach in *A Behavioral Theory of the Firm*.[24] They developed a comprehensive behavioral theory of organizational decision-making, one part of which is consideration of organizational objectives. For our purposes here their most essential views of organizational goals are:

Organization as a Coalition. The organization is a coalition of individuals and subgroups. These coalition members have both common and conflicting interests. The inducements necessary to ensure the participation of these individuals and groups make for a variety of organizational goals. The goals of these coalition members are constraints on the organization.

Basic to the idea of a coalition is the expectation that the individual participants in the organization may have substantially different preference orderings (i.e., individual goals). That is to say, any theory of organizational goals must deal successfully with the obvious potential for internal goal conflict inherent in a coalition of diverse individuals and groups.[25]

Formulating Goals Through Bargaining. The actual operational goals of the organization are formed through the process of bargaining for inducements by the various coalition members. These "side payments" or inducements for participation take many forms: money, authority and power, personal satisfaction, and so on. Thus stockholders require profits, employees want decent wages and favorable working conditions, managers require power and prestige, customers demand quality products. Because the coalition and power of the various members change over time, the goals of the organization are continually shifting to reflect these changes.

> It is primarily through bargaining within this active group that what we call *organizational objectives* arise. Side payments, far from being the incidental distribution of a fixed, transferable booty, represent the central process of goal specification. That is, a significant number of these payments are in the form of policy commitments.[26]

Satisficing Multiple Goals. Goals of coalition members are frequently in conflict. Therefore it is never possible to maximize the goal of any individual or group. Rather, the organization seeks to satisfy the goals of all coalition members in order to maintain their participation.

Modifying Goals Through Experience. Individuals and organizations have aspiration levels for the attainment of their objectives. These aspiration levels are influenced by past performance in relationship to goals, past aspiration levels, and comparisons with reference groups. The individual or the organization attempts to satisfy goal aspirations that can be changed in terms of past learning experiences. As an individual example, the university student who is successful in his studies may raise his aspirations—he may decide to go on to graduate school. Similarly, the organization that has achieved its sales goals within a given year will usually adjust its sights upward. Lack of success in goal achievement usually results in a downward adjustment in aspirations—both for the individual and for the organization.

Sequential Attention to Goals. With a multiple, frequently conflicting goal set, the organization cannot maximize all its goals. Generally, individuals and organizations devote sequential attention to goals. They endeavor to upgrade accomplishment of goals that have not yet been satisfactorily attained. (Students will sacrifice many other goals to cram for final examinations.) Organizations will embark on cost reduction programs or safety programs without considering all the consequences in terms of downgrading other goals. In the Cyert and March model, particular goals receive attention only when achievement falls below the aspiration levels. This is one way for the organization to minimize goal conflict. Much of the time, the conflict remains latent because the focus is on different goals at different periods of time.

Organizational Slack. The concept of organizational slack is useful in understanding how organizations maintain equilibrium in the face of multiple goal demands and changing conditions. Slack can be defined as the difference between total organizational resources and the payments necessary to maintain the contributions of the coalition members. "Slack consists in payments to members of the coalition in excess of what is required to maintain the organization."[27] When environmental conditions are very favorable, the coalition members' aspiration levels do not rise so rapidly as the available resources. These excess resources become organizational slack. Conversely, when environmental conditions become unfavorable, the slack becomes a cushion, permitting the organization to survive in the face of adversity. "Organizational slack absorbs a substantial share of the potential variability in the firm's environment. As a result, it plays both a stabilizing and adaptive role."[28] Conceptually, slack helps the organization maintain a dynamic equilibrium in the face of environmental turbulence.

Managing the Coalition. The primary executive function is to manage the coalition. Management, because of its authority position in the hierarchy and ability to allocate resources, has the key role of balancing the pressures from the various coalition members. It must satisfy their goals sufficiently well to retain their active participation. Management does not direct all organization activities toward the maximization of one omnipotent goal—such as profit maximization. Rather, it operates within the constraints of demands for goal satisfaction from many groups. It must strive to maintain the dominant coalition to insure the survival, growth, and well-being of the organization.

The Cyert–March model suggests why organizations have difficulty in setting forth specific overall goals. It is frequently impossible to get all members of the coalition to agree on specific objectives unless the overall objectives are stated in ambiguous, general, and rather broad terms. Most university presidents proclaim their organizational goals to be creation of knowledge through research, dissemination of knowledge through teaching, and service to the community. These statements are sufficiently vague to keep all coalition members happy. However, they don't help much in explaining why certain universities consistently make the top ten in the national football poll whereas others are recognized for their intellectual contributions.

Means-Ends Chain

We have suggested that overall goal statements are usually very general. They are not operational in that there are no established criteria for determining how particular programs or activities contribute to these goals. These broad statements of purpose must be translated into operational objectives. Understanding the means-end chain helps us to see how broad goals are translated into operational objectives.[29]

In analyzing goals it is also necessary to decide how they are to be accomplished, or what *means* will be used to attain them. In the organization, the relationship between means and ends is hierarchical. Goals established at one level require certain means for their accomplishment. These means then become the subgoals for the next level, and more specific operational objectives are developed as we move down the hierarchy. A fire department's primary goal is to reduce fire losses by such means as preventing and extinguishing fires. These means then logically become the goals of the next level in the organization and lead to the creation of a fire prevention unit and a fire fighting unit. The means for carrying out these units' goals might be the establishment of specific programs for locating water hydrants, educating the public, and geographically decentralizing fire stations.

The hierarchy of goals and the means-ends chain have important implications for organizational structure. Generally, the division of labor and functional specialization within the organization is based on the means-ends chain. The business organization may have a sales department, finance department, and production department that have specific subgoals related to their functional areas.

Theoretically, in a rational organization, the means-ends chain would be perfectly integrated with the hierarchy and departmental specialization. In the real organization this integration cannot be achieved. It is impossible to have sufficient knowledge to effect perfect integration. There is usually competition among the organizational units about how to achieve goals. Personal viewpoints and biases influence the integration of the means-ends chain. Simon says:

> It is also as true of organizational as of individual behavior that the means-end hierarchy is seldom an integrated, completely connected chain. Often the connections between organization activities and ultimate objectives is obscure, or these ultimate objectives are incompletely formulated, or there are internal conflicts and contradictions among the ultimate objective, or among the means selected to attain them.[30]

Goals at Different Levels

Through the means-ends chain general goals are translated into increasingly specific operational goals. Complex organizations have several administrative levels with differing goals and activities. Parsons suggests that there are three levels in the hierarchical structure of complex organizations: the technical or production level, the managerial or intermediate level, and the institutional or community level.[31]

The *institutional* level relates the activities of the organization to its environmental system. The goals at this level are broad and provide substantial flexibility concerning the means for their attainment.

The second level, the *managerial,* coordinates and integrates the task performance of the technical system to meet requirements set forth by the institutional level. The goals at this level are still fairly broad but can be stated in operational terms where performance can be measured, such as sales and production goals, budgets, and goals for program activities.

The third level concerns the *technical* subsystems that are involved in actual task performance. The goals at this level are usually very specific, short term, and measurable.

As we move from the institutional to the technical levels, goals and the means for their accomplishment become more specific, short-range, and measurable. The organization attempts to reduce the uncertainties in its basic technical operations by setting forth specific goals and means of accomplishing them. The managerial level performs a vital mediating function between the institutional and technical levels. Thompson suggests this role:

If the organization must approach certainty at the technical level to satisfy its rationality criteria, but must remain flexible and adaptive to satisfy environmental requirements, we might expect the managerial level to mediate between them, ironing out some irregularities stemming from external sources, but also pressing the technical core for modifications as conditions alter.[32]

Interdepartmental Goal Conflict

In addition to differentiating and specifying subgoals through the means-ends chain on a hierarchical basis, subgoals are established for different functional units within the organization. In the correctional institution there are certain subunits whose primary responsibility is the confinement of inmates, whereas other subunits are charged with rehabilitation. In the business firm, the sales department's goal is to increase sales, the production department's goal is efficient, low-cost production, and the research and development department's goal is the development of new products. There is substantial differentiation of activities based on subgoals for different functional units. This leads to differences in structure, attitudes, and behavior; time perspectives; and interpersonal orientations for these different subunits.[33]

This differentiation frequently leads to substantial interdepartmental conflicts within the organization. Maximizing the goal accomplishments of one functional department may entail sacrificing the goals of another department. Thus, maximizing the confinement goal in correctional institutions may be in direct conflict with other subunits that are seeking to rehabilitate inmates. This, again, is another reason why the goal structure of the organization is never perfectly rational. The actual goals of the organization are a result of the power interplay among different organizational units and individuals. They are also continually being modified by environmental forces. The goal set is continually modifying and changing to reflect these forces.

Goal Displacement

One of the most difficult problems involves measuring how effectively goals are being met. When goals can be precisely stated, as frequently is the case at the technical level, goal accomplishment can be relatively simple. However, with more general goals, the measurement becomes more difficult. For example, how do we measure how effective the university is in disseminating and creating knowledge? By number of graduates? By analysis of their life-time earnings? By the volume of research publications? By the win-loss record of the football team?

Another of the difficulties that organizations face is overmeasuring specific quantitative goals and underemphasizing more abstract, less easily measured goals.

> Most organizations under pressure to be rational are eager to measure their efficiency. Curiously, the very effort—the desire to establish how well we are doing and to find ways of improving if we are not doing as well as we ought to do—often has quite undesired effects from the point of view of the organiza-

tional goals. Frequent measuring can distort the organizational efforts because, as a rule, some aspects of its output are more measurable than the others. Frequent measuring tends to encourage over-production of highly measurable items and neglect of the less measurable ones.[34]

There are other forces that distort the goal structure of organizations. One of the more important is displacement of goals. Goal displacement stems from the need for the organization to differentiate activities and from the process of downward delegation of authority and responsibility. Sills describes this process as follows:

In order to accomplish their goals, organizations establish a set of procedures or means. In the course of following these procedures, however, the subordinates or members to whom authority and functions have been delegated often come to regard them as ends in themselves, rather than means toward the achievement of organizational goals. As a result of this process, the actual activities of the organization become centered around the proper functioning of organization procedures, rather than upon the achievement of the initial goals.[35]

Through this process, the official goals of the organization are neglected in favor of goals associated with building or maintaining the organization. Many writers on organizations have noted this process. Michels, in his study of socialist parties and labor organizations in Europe, pointed out how the original goal of creating a democratic society was displaced by the desire to maintain the organization and the position of the leaders. The original means become the actual ends of organizational activity. He refers to the "Iron Law of Oligarchy" in which the leaders achieve an oligarchical power position and seek to maintain that position in order to direct and control the activities of the organization. This led to the subversion of the organization's original democratic goals. In this view democratic social action is possible only through bureaucratic organization and bureaucracy entails the destruction of democratic values and goals.[36] Merton says that goals are displaced because the bureaucratic organization affects participants' personalities and causes them to adhere rigidly to rules and regulations for their own sake. "Adherence to the rules, originally conceived as a means, becomes transformed into an end-in-itself; there occurs the familiar process of *displacement of goals* whereby an instrumental value becomes a terminal value."[37]

This phenomenon of goal displacement is most apparent in those situations in which the organizational goals are abstract and intangible.

Intangible goals are expressions of intended states of affairs that do not adequately describe the desired states or the activities that would constitute their achievement. Such intangible goals do not provide adequate guidance for group action, and as a consequence, more tangible substitutes are developed.[38]

Participants stress adherence to rules and regulations (means) rather than adherence to the more abstract and less measurable goals. This problem is apparent in many social welfare agencies. For example, strict adherence to the rule of no welfare payments if there is an employable male in the household may actually create many adverse social and family problems and defeat the overall goals of the agency.

This problem is not easily resolved. If organizational members are bound by rigid role prescriptions, rules, and regulations to guide their activities, and strong sanctions are used to enforce adherence, goal displacement will occur.[39] The organization might work to more adequately develop the means-ends chains so that individual activities are related to ends. Attempts to translate the intangible, abstract goals into more meaningful desired states of affairs can be helpful. One such approach, management by objectives, will be discussed in a later section of this paper.

INDIVIDUAL AND ORGANIZATIONAL GOALS

We turn now to the third level of analysis; the goals of individual participants and their relationship to organizational goals. Organizations are established to accomplish human purposes, purposes that could not be accomplished by individual action. It would be simple to assume that organizational goals and individual participant goals are complementary. This, in effect, was the assumption in classical economic theory and most traditional management theories. Employees were compensated through monetary and other inducements for their participation in meeting organizational goals, thus "presumably *assuring* that employees will adhere to the organization's goals except in exception, i.e., theoretically pathological, cases."[40] This simple assumption of compatibility failed to recognize many bases for conflict between organizational and individual goals. First, man is much more complex than the rational economic man assumption. He has many needs and aspirations that are not easily met in purely economic terms. Second, the organizational goal set is not ideally rational; it is bounded by many discontinuities and ambiguities, as we saw in the preceding section.

The early human relationists saw the need for greater emphasis on human satisfaction as well as on organizational technical effectiveness. "An industrial organization may be regarded as performing two major functions, that of producing a product and that of creating and distributing satisfactions among the individual members of the organization."[41] Although they saw the need for ensuring greater human satisfaction, the need was viewed as a *means* for achieving better organizational effectiveness rather than as an *end* in itself. Greater human satisfaction would lead to more effective organizational goal accomplishment. Management should turn from emphasizing satisfaction of lower level physiological and safety needs and instead direct its attention toward satisfying higher-level social, status, and self-actualization needs in order to obtain more effective employee participation *toward accomplishing organizational goals.* Human satisfaction was a *means* to the organizational *ends.* This approach has been criticized as human manipulation and even more severely as a further inroad of technological determinism. Ellul, for example, sees organization as an application of *La Technique* in the effort to make social, economic, and administrative life more efficient.[42] From this viewpoint the trend toward industrial humanism and greater employee satisfaction is a means for more rationally accomplishing organizational objectives.[43]

We raise an even more critical issue when we question whether or not organizational goals and human needs are compatible.

> Thus, one of the major dilemmas of organizational psychology arises because policies and practices which insure organizational effectiveness often may leave an individual's needs unsatisfied, or worse, may create problems above and beyond the ones the person brought with him. He may become alienated, insecure, and bitter if the organization fails to fulfill minimum needs for security, maintenance of self-esteem, and opportunities to grow and develop.[44]

We should not overemphasize the possible conflicts between organizational goals and human satisfaction. As Etzioni suggests,

> Within limits, happiness heightens efficiency in organizations and, conversely, without efficient organizations much of our happiness is unthinkable. Without well-run organizations our standard of living, our level of culture, and our democratic life could not be maintained. Thus, to a degree, *organizational rationality and human happiness go hand in hand.* But a point is reached in every organization where happiness and efficiency cease to support each other. Not all work can be well-paid or gratifying, and not all regulations and orders can be made acceptable. Here we face a true dilemma.[45]

In the following discussion, we are not going to assume either that (1) organizational and individual goals are compatible, or that (2) organization and individual goals are contradictory. To a major extent they are both. Without a minimum degree of compatibility, organizations could not exist. But, total agreement is impossible and conflicts do exist.

The Inducement-Contribution Concept

The Barnard-Simon inducements-contributions model provides a basis for understanding the relationship between personal motives and organizational goals. The basic aspects of this model are:

1. An organization is a system of interrelated social behaviors of a number of persons whom we shall call the *participants* in the organization.
2. Each participant and each group of participants receives *inducements from* the organization in return for which he makes *contributions to* the organization.
3. Each participant will continue to participate in an organization only as long as the inducements offered him are as great or greater (measured in terms of *his* values and in terms of the alternatives open to him) than the contributions he is asked to make.
4. The contributions provided by the various groups of participants are the source from which the organization manufactures the inducements offered to participants.
5. Hence, an organization is "solvent"—and will continue in existence—only as long as the contributions are sufficient to provide inducements in large enough measure to draw forth these contributions.[46]

The individual will continue to participate in the attainment of organizational goals only as long as the organization provides inducements that meet his personal goals. This inducement may be direct if the goals of the organization have direct personal value for the individual—such as church membership or participation in a voluntary charitable organization—or indirect if the organization offers personal rewards—money, status, position—to the individual in return for his contribution. The latter case is probably true for most employees in business organizations.

In this model, once the individual has made the decision to participate, he accepts an organizational role. Thereafter, his role-enacting behavior is determined by the organizational goals rather than his personal motivations.[47] The role prescriptions require that his actions be guided primarily by organizational goals. Organizational goals become internalized—automatically evoked and applied during performance of the role.

> By whatever means the individual was originally motivated to adopt the role in the first place, the goals and constraints appropriate to the role become a part of the decision-making program, stored in his memory, that defines his role behavior.[48]

Reciprocation Between Individual and Organization

Others have suggested an even stronger bond between the individual and the organization. There is a psychological contract between the individual and the organization that fulfills the goals of each. Levinson says,

> This process of fulfilling mutual expectations and satisfying mutual needs in the relationship between a man and his work organization was conceptualized as a process of *reciprocation*. Reciprocation is the process of carrying out a psychological contract between person and company or any other institution where one works. It is a complementary process in which the individual and the organization seem to become a part of each other. The person feels that he is part of the corporation or institution and, concurrently, that he is a symbol personifying the whole organization.[49]

He suggests that in modern industrial society there has been a loosening of family, small social group, and other psychological ties and that the work organization becomes increasingly important to man. "In a man's movement from one neighborhood or community to another, the work organization is his thread of continuity and may well become a psychological anchor point for him."[50]

This view is somewhat similar to the inducement-contribution model, but recognizes even further the psychological needs for affiliation that the organization provides. It suggests that the psychological bond between man and organization helps provide goal integration.

Several recent research studies suggest the extent of this reciprocation. Morse found that managers adapted to and found personal goal satisfaction in organizations with very different structures, interpersonal relations, and environmental forces. The organization that was appropriately designed to meet its task requirements and the demands of its environment provided important psychological rewards for members of the organization and led to a high sense of personal competence. There was a close relationship between personal motivations and satisfaction of organizational goals.[51] Porter and Lawler found that managers were motivated toward organizational goals when they perceived a high probability of rewards based on performance and when they had an appropriate perception of their organizational role. When managers perceived inducements as rewards for good performance, they performed more effectively. High performers also reported significantly greater fulfillment and satisfaction.[52]

The importance of reciprocation becomes apparent when the psychological contract is broken. When the aerospace industry suffered a severe downturn, organizations discharged many long-term employees, including managers and professionals. These employees had developed a high degree of loyalty and attachment to their organizations and the results of the lay-offs were devastating (both psychologically and economically). We might hypothesize that the stronger the bonds of reciprocation, the more severe the problems of adjustment for the individual when these bonds are destroyed. Many managers, engineers, scientists, and other professionals had great difficulty accepting the fact of their dismissal. The importance of reciprocation might also explain the strong and unrelenting demand by faculties for the maintaining the university tenure system.

Internalization of Goals

Internalization of organizational goals occurs when the individual develops a personal commitment in meeting organizational goals. This internalization is one of the most effective means of integration for it removes conflicts between organizational goals and individual motivation through the development of an organizational personality.

> In this way, through his subjection to organizationally determined goals, and through the gradual absorption of these goals into his own attitudes, the participant in organization acquires an "organizational personality" rather distinct from his personality as an individual. The organization assigns to him a role; it specifies the particular values, facts, and alternatives upon which his decisions in the organization are to be based.[53]

Although this internalization represents the ideal match between organizational goals and individual motivations, it is rarely fully achieved. Few participants make a full commitment toward meeting organizational goals. There may be conflicts among the organizational role and other roles that the individual tries to fulfill. This conflict is particularly apparent among scientists and other professionals. Traditionally, in professions such as medicine and law, activities were carried out in a nonorganizational context in close interpersonal relationship with clients. Early literature on professionalism focused on the pattern of behavior of these independent professionals and how this differed from that of bureaucrats or "organization men." This traditional view of independence and autonomy is no longer appropriate for most modern scientists-professionals. They are organization men affiliated with businesses, hospitals, governmental agencies, large law firms, and other complex institutions. "No profession has escaped the advancing tide of bureaucratization."[54]

Numerous studies of scientists-professionals in organizations suggest the problems of role conflict and motivation.[55] These participants place high value on intellectual pursuits, specialized technical task performance, and autonomy. They have a deep-seated need for achievement and self-actualization. These values may create many conflicts. The desire for autonomy runs counter to the organization's need for integration. The individual is more likely to internalize the goals of his profession rather than the goals of the organization. At best, he is likely to make only a "conditional commitment" to organization goals. The same limited commitment may also be true of other participants, such as unionized employees. It is most likely that the "managerial elites" are the participants who develop the highest degree of internalization of organizational goals.

The Continuing Dilemma

Many modern behavioral scientists see a continuing conflict between organizational role requirements and individual satisfactions. McGregor was among the first to suggest this conflict.[56] He said that the traditional managerial approach (Theory *X*) imposes external controls on the individual through close supervision, structuring of behavior, and an atmosphere of constraint. This approach creates conflict between the organization goals and individual motivation. He proposed a new managerial approach (Theory *Y*), which provides an opportunity for individual growth, satisfaction of higher-level needs, and integration of personal and organizational goals.

> The central principle which derives from Theory *Y* is that of integration: the creation of conditions such that members of the organization can achieve their own goals *best* by directing their efforts toward the success of the enterprise.[57]

Argyris sees an even more fundamental conflict between individual and organizational goals. He suggests a basic incompatibility between the structural and technological requirements of organizations in fulfilling their purposes and the needs of mature individuals. Organizational efficiency and goal accomplishment are achieved at a sacrifice to the human participants. He says that the psychologically mature individual in our society grows from being passive as an infant to active as an adult; from being dependent to being relatively independent; from being in a subordinate position to achieving equality of position; and is moving continually toward self-actualization. In contrast, the formal organizations with their norms of rationality and emphasis on structure, formally designated roles, chain of command, task specialization, rigidly defined authority patterns, and administrative controls require the individual to work in a situation in which he is dependent, subordinate, and submissive. He says:

> The formal organization (which *includes* the technology) and the administrative control system typically used in complex formal organizations may be viewed as part of a grand strategy to organize human effort to achieve specific objectives, and this strategy is based on such "principles" of administration as specialization of work, chain of command, unity of direction and span of control. The strategy creates a complex of organizational demands that tend to require individuals to experience dependence and submissiveness and to utilize few to their relatively peripheral abilities.[58]

According to this view, the requirements of the organization for goal achievement are in conflict with the individual's basic needs for development and self-actualization. Although Argyris does suggest certain modifications in organizations to minimize some of the more adverse consequences to the human participants, one senses that this may only be partially possible.

In a sense it is unrealistic to expect a perfect compatibility and optimal satisfaction of individual and organizational goals. The individual *must* give up some of his individual autonomy and self-expression to participate (and gain the advantages of membership) in the organization. This is as true of participating in the informal group or family as it is in the formal organization. Organization thus reduces personal autonomy in some spheres, but it also enhances opportunities for satisfaction in other areas. It is a trade-off—never optimal for either the organization or the individual. For example, it could be argued that forced participation in our social security system reduces personal autonomy and individual discretion. However, doesn't it also increase independence and autonomy for the retiree?

INTEGRATING INDIVIDUAL AND ORGANIZATIONAL GOALS

Many modern writers interested in organizational behavior are concerned with the problem of integrating individual and organizational goals. Many of their concepts were dealt with in Chapter 2, "Behavioral Sciences for Management." This section will examine very briefly some of the suggestions for more effectively meeting both organizational goals and individual needs.

Power Equalization

Most modern behavioral scientists emphasize the importance of more democratic, less authoritarian, less hierarchically structured organizations as a means for integrating individual and organization goals. They stress the need for "power equalization" among organizational participants. McGregor's Theory *Y*, Likert's interaction-influence system, Argyris' emphasis on self-actualization, Shepard's collaborative-consensus system, and Bennis' suggestion of the inevitability of democracy in organizations all have an underlying emphasis on power equalization, participation, and more democratic leadership styles as a basis for integrating organizational and individual goals. They have a humanistic orientation that places high value on participant satisfactions rather than purely economic-technical rationality. Leavitt describes power equalization as follows:

> Besides the belief that one changes people first, these power-equalization approaches also place major emphasis on other aspects of the human phenomena of organizations. They are, for example, centrally concerned with effects; with morale, sensitivity, psychological security. Secondly, they value evolutionary, internally generated change in individuals, groups, and organizations over externally planned or implemented change. Thirdly, they place much value on human growth and fulfillment as well as upon task accomplishment; and they often have stretched the degree of causal connection between the two. Finally, of course, the power-equalization approaches, in their early stages at least, shared a normative belief that power in organizations should be more equally dis-

tributed than in most existent "authoritarian" hierarchies. Operationally this belief was made manifest in a variety of ways: in encouraging independent decision making, decentralization, more open communication, and participation.[59]

Power equalization and more participative, democratic organizations are thus fundamental for many writers. The question remains, however, how they can be accomplished.

Changing the Individual, Group, and Organization

Many behavioral scientists advocate restructuring and organizational change as a means for integrating individual and organizational goals. In their attempts to change individuals, groups, and organizations for better goal integration, they have developed many new approaches. Laboratory or T-group training is an attempt to make the individual more aware of his own behavior and the way he is perceived by others. This "people changing approach" helps the individual develop new attitudes, understanding, and behavior patterns. In the early development of laboratory training, individuals were sent to special training centers away from their organizations. More recently, these programs are taking place "in house" within the organizational setting.

The Management Grid developed by Blake and Mouton incorporates many of the laboratory training approaches but integrates them with the organizational efficiency goals.[60] Their grid recognizes the need for (1) concern for production, and (2) concern for people. The goal of their program is to bring about the system on their grid that they describe as, "A basic aim of 9,9 management, then, is to promote the conditions that integrate creativity, high productivity, and high morale through concerted team action.[61] Their development program is long-term, lasting several years, and attempts to integrate organizational and individual goals through the use of sensitivity training, group processes, focus on task accomplishment, and conflict resolution.

The Management Grid is one example of the approach toward integrating individual and organizational goals that can be termed *organization development*. Organization development programs emerged from the theory, research, and experiences at the National Training Laboratory (NTL) with their earlier emphasis on laboratory training (sensitivity or T-group). Organization development has taken as its main objective the resolution of the conflict between the organization goals and individual needs. As Beckard suggests,

> Enterprise managers today are deeply concerned with the dilemma of how to (a) fully mobilize the energy of the organization's human resources toward achievement of the organization's performance objectives, and (b) at the same time, so organize the work, the work environment, the communications systems, and the relationships of people that individuals' needs for self-worth, growth, and satisfaction are significantly met at work.[62]

In the organization development approach, the goal-setting process involves a large number of participants who actively engage in setting goals and determining how they will be implemented. Conflicts between organizational members are confronted and worked out. Ideally, through the use of such a program the individual internalizes the organizational goals and a high level of reciprocation is realized.

These approaches—laboratory training, the management grid, and organization development—recognize the inevitability of goal conflicts and establish a means of confronting conflicts based on interpersonal and group processes. Goal integration is not left to chance but is actively sought through a clearly planned and long-range action program of change. "Planned change" is the by-word, with the behavioral scientists serving as the "change agent."

Human Asset Accounting

The search for ways of relating individual and organizational goals ultimately involves the problem of measuring organizational performance. There are many problems associated with measuring how effective an organization is in accomplishing its goals.[63] The problems of measuring the achievement of participant goals within the organization are even more difficult.

There is a growing concern that traditional financial accounting measures only certain aspects of the performance of the organization and does not adequately consider many other vital factors. Likert, for example, suggests that in evaluating organizational performance, much greater consideration should be given to the psycho-social system of the organization.[64] Although there are many statements suggesting that "our people are our most important asset," there is little or nothing done in the traditional managerial accounting and reporting system to reflect this viewpoint. The typical balance sheet, profit and loss statements, and budgetary system do not reflect the value of the human assets nor the organization's effectiveness in accomplishing participant's goals. Likert and others have suggested the need for a system of human asset accounting that would measure the current value of human asset and also indicate whether these are increasing or decreasing.[65] There are many difficulties associated with integrating human asset accounting within traditional accounting systems that cannot be covered in this brief discussion. However, this can be a very important development in measuring organizational goal accomplishment. Organizations and individuals do stress those goals that are measurable and for which they can be held accountable. A well-developed system of human asset accounting would provide the organization with more definitive and quantitative information on how effective it was in meeting participant's goals and would provide the basis for more effectively integrating organizational goals and human satisfactions.

These, then, are just a few of the current steps taken to deal with the issue of integrating individual and organizational goals. The issues are complex and progress has not been rapid. However, these developments do indicate important trends for the future. We will next look more specifically at the role of management in goal setting and implementing and in conflict resolution.

THE ROLE OF MANAGEMENT IN SETTING AND IMPLEMENTING GOALS

Goals result from the learning-adapting response of the organization and are influenced by the various coalition members. Management plays a major role in actually setting operational goals and providing the resources for their implementation. The managerial system is the key decision-making and integrating force for the organization. It must respond to environmental forces and to demands of internal participants in order to maintain a viable coalition. In the complex organization, power is dispersed to the various internal and external groups and top management is constrained in setting and implementing goals. Thompson suggests that the role of administration is co-alignment of these various forces:

> The basic function of administration appears to be co-alignment, not merely of people (in coalitions) but of institutionalized action—of technology and task environment into a viable domain, and of organizational design and structure appropriate to it. Administration, when it works well, keeps the organization at the nexus of the several necessary streams of action. Paradoxically, the administrative process must reduce uncertainty but at the same time search for flexibility.[66]

This suggests that management has a vital role to play in charting the organization's course and in responding to various forces. However, it is a mistake to suggest that the goals of management and the goals of the organization are one and the same. Certainly, management is one of the major elements in the coalition, but it is not the only element. Management's power is never absolute. In the past we have mistakenly attributed the only goal of the business organization to be the profit maximization goal of owners. We should not make a similar mistake by associating organizational goals and managerial goals as one and the same.

Studies by Monsen and his colleagues suggest how management can influence the operational goals of business organizations. His studies of owner-controlled and manager-controlled firms in the same industries suggest that there are important differences in the actual operational goals of these firms. The owner-controlled firms had significantly higher rates of return on investment and lower dividend pay-outs than did manager-controlled firms within the same industry. It might be suggested that the owner-controlled firm is simply more efficient than the manager-controlled firm. Or (and from one viewpoint more logically), it might be argued that the manager-controlled firm responds to different goals and considers the stockholders interest as only one (albeit an important one) in the goal formation and implementation process. Monsen suggests this difference:

> The answer that seems most convincing is that two quite different motivational incentive systems are at work, emanating from the pursuit of different goals. It would seem that our business system is not generally structured to provide the same set of motivations or goals for both owners and managers. As a result, the behavior of our largest firms differs widely depending upon what group controls them.[67]

These findings are consistent with our previous discussion. The professional manager is responding to a *different* set of influences (including his own motivations) from the owner-manager. Because of these differences in actual (rather than publicized) goals, the behavior of the organizations are different.

Setting General and Specific Goals

At the institutional level in most organizations, statements of objectives tend to be very general. Frequently, there is a demand that these goals be made clearer. For example, in universities it is frequently suggested that we should be able to specify more clearly broad goals, thus ensuring support from constituent groups and greater efficiency in accomplishment. Yet, there may be some functionality in maintaining a degree of vagueness in the overall organizational goals. If goals are stated in general terms, there is room for organizational participants to fill in details according to their own perception. Ultra-precision can destroy flexibility and make it more difficult for individuals and organizations to adapt to changing conditions. Some vagueness makes it possible to work toward goals by many different means. It may also facilitate compromise on the part of participants with diverse value systems. As long as people can read into organizational goal statements their own interpretation of the ends to be achieved, compromise is feasible. Thus tacit agreement is often reached with regard to both ends and means. At the institutional level, mediation and compromise are essential ingredients in coordinating activity.

However, it is necessary to translate these broad, general goals into more specific objectives at the organizational and technical levels. A major part of the managerial function is to translate these broad goals into more specific operational objectives for various functional areas and participants within the organization. This process helps to simplify the complexities and ambiguities and to reduce uncertainties. "Subgoals may replace broader goals as a part of the whole process of replacing a complex reality with a simplified model of reality for purposes of decision and action."[68]

Management by Objective

Many approaches have been utilized to integrate functional and individual goals with overall organizational goals. "Management by objective" attempts to structure this relationship by setting forth established individual objectives and relating these to overall goals.

Management by objective was first popularized by Drucker who suggested that "Objectives are needed in every area where performance and results directly and vitally affect the survival and prosperity of the business."[69] He stressed the importance of establishing clearly defined objectives that guide and measure the performance of managers. Odiorne describes this approach as:

> The system of management by objective can be described as a process whereby the superior and subordinate managers of an organization jointly identify its common goals, define each individual's major areas of responsibility in terms of the results expected of him and use these measures as guides for operating the unit and assessing the contributions of each of its members.[70]

Over the past 2 decades many business corporations have adopted management by objective programs.[71] Many of these programs started initially as a managerial performance-appraisal mechanism. However, many organizations have advanced to a much broader approach encompassing long-range planning, a system of control, and a primary basis of integrating the objectives of the organization with the objectives of individual managers. Although "management by objective" sounds deceptively simple, in practice organizations adopting this approach have had to spend considerable time in modifying their structure and managerial system in order to make it effective.

Studies of specific management-by-objective programs suggest that such programs do improve communications, increase mutual understanding, improve planning, create more positive attitudes toward the evaluation system, help in utilizing management abilities, and promote innovation.[72] However, there are also many problems associated with these programs. Many organizational adjustments are necessary if the program is to be successful. It requires long-term effort and is not a short-run panacea. It includes only managerial personnel and does not provide for other employees. In particular, it is often difficult to encompass the efforts of many staff groups within such a program. There is a tendency for managers to direct their efforts toward meeting only those objectives on which they are measured. Other, less quantifiable, objectives may be short-changed. It is often difficult to set forth clearly definable objectives under conditions of rapid change or environmental turbulence. There are many difficulties tying performance appraisal into the program. Finally, there may be many difficulties in requiring objective accomplishment under uncertain and adverse conditions. Executives of companies that have established a management-by-objectives program declare that the program worked very well when environmental and competitive forces were favorable. However, during a business downturn, many managers thought they were held strictly accountable for accomplishing objectives over which they had limited control. Their programs did not adequately respond to new environmental conditions and instead of being a basis for positive motivation, the programs became a source of major conflict.

In spite of these difficulties, management-by-objective programs have been used successfully by a number of business organizations to integrate organizational and individual goals. Similar programs seem to be catching on in other types of organizations. For example, within school systems similar types of programs have been advocated for setting goals and measuring accomplishment.

Planning, Programming, and Budgeting System

Numerous programs have been initiated in the public sector to more specifically tie in goal setting, planning, and measuring organizational performance. The Planning, Programming and Budgeting System (PPBS) developed by the Department of Defense and introduced into civilian agencies of the Executive Branch of the federal government is a primary example of such an approach. The purposes of PPBS are to:

1. Make the goals and objectives of each important area of government activity an explicit concern for agency analysis and documentation;

2. Enforce agency analysis of past and future programs so that program outputs can be related to specific objectives;
3. Require definitions of objectives and formulations of programs for a time span substantially longer than the single year to which annual budget submissions apply;
4. Insure the development of useful estimates of *total* program costs—i.e., not just for the budget year in which programs are proposed to be begun;
5. Require the definition and analysis of alternative plans for achieving program objectives;
6. Establish this set of procedures as an essential, systematic part of the annual budget preparation and review process.[73]

Essentially, this system provides for a more clear-cut development of organizational goals, planning for their accomplishment, long-term budgeting of program costs, and measurement of results.

A great deal of controversy has surrounded the use of PPBS. Much of this controversy stems from the difficulties involved in setting clear-cut program goals. The Subcommittee on Economy in Government of the Joint Economic Committee in its study of PPBS indicated the problem of goal setting:

> The subcommittee is of the firm opinion that PPBS represents a substantial forward step in budgetary techniques. At the same time, it is our opinion that much more work is needed in the definition of national objectives and the determination of priorities in the allocation of public funds. If the Nation had a little clearer notion of its goals and national priorities (bearing in mind that they are apt to be continuously shifting in a society like ours), it would ease the task of PPBS inasmuch as it would give rise to definable objective programs which could then be subjected to a systems approach.[74]

PPBS has not only been used extensively in federal agencies but also it and similar systems have been used by numerous states, universities, and other institutions. It is usually necessary to make many adjustments in order to reflect special conditions and unique problems of the user agency. However, the use of such a system does reflect the attempt to more rationally link goal-setting, planning, and budgetary processes in complex organizations. Any such administrative system can only be partially successful. It can never be the final solution to the complex problems associated with defining and implementing goals in an uncertain and complex environment.

MANAGING GOAL CONFLICTS

A rising level of conflict within our organizations and in other social interactions is an apparent phenomenon in modern society. Part of this conflict arises because of different perceptions of the need for organizational and social change. Existing goals and values are being seriously challenged and we have not developed new mechanisms for resolving conflict and integrating diverse goals. This view is reflected in a recent Committee for Economic Development policy statement:

> There is now a pervasive feeling in the country that the social order somehow has gotten out of balance, and that greater affluence amid a deteriorating environment and community life does not make much sense.
>
> The discontinuity between what we have accomplished as procurers and consumers and what we want in the way of a good society has engendered strong social pressures to close the gap—to improve the way the over-all American system is working so that a better quality of life can be achieved for the entire citizenry within a well-functioning community.[75]

The increased awareness, education, and desire to influence the direction of our organizations and our society by many people are partial causes of this social conflict. Ways suggests that more people in our society are demanding the right to participate in *all* matters that affect their lives and they increasingly have the *power* to demand participation. "The general trend of twentieth-century society; particularly in the U.S., is toward a wider distribution of power, a broadening of participation by individuals in controlling their own lives and work."[76] With differing individual and group values and goals, these demands for greater participation are bound to lead to greater conflicts within organizations and in society in general.

It should be emphasized that these conflicts do not always arise because of differences in goals. They are frequently the result of different perceptions of reality, different role requirements for individuals within organizations, and conflicts over means rather than ends. Nevertheless, management and administration in all types of social institutions must deal with these conflicts and find new ways to solve them.

Throughout this chapter we have suggested many approaches for conflict resolution. Much of the work of the behavioral scientists is directed toward changing the organization to be more compatible with participant goals (and also changing participant values, attitudes, and behavior to be more compatible with organizational goals). Laboratory training, organization development, management by objective, and other specific programs take this approach.

In conclusion, we return to the basic dilemma with which we began this article. Every organizational activity, from the small informal group to the large-scale business, governmental, or religious organization, requires that the individual subordinate some of his independence and discretion to organizational requirements. He pays a price for his involvement in the hope of obtaining off-setting benefits. Although the organization is a means for the fulfilling of the individual's goals, it also requires him to direct his activities toward its ends. Any assumption that the business or any other organization should be able to satisfy *all* the goals of its participants and still accomplish its goals is in direct conflict with the requirements of organized behavior.

Management must use effective motivation to secure cooperation from organizational participants and should give greater recognition to the satisfaction of higher-level needs. Total reliance on monetary rewards, fringe benefits, and employment security as the only vehicle for motivation drastically limits the inducements that the organization can offer. Yet it does not follow automatically that management can and should take on the responsibility for total fulfillment of all participant goals. The objectives of uniformity and efficiency in the business organization mitigate against the operation of a truly democratic administration. Without democratic processes, the corporations attempting to satisfy all human goals could easily become paternalistic, monolithic structures. When the business organization, with its hierarchical structure and less than full power-equalization, seeks to meet the total goals of the individual, it runs the grave risk of completely subordinating the individual's freedom—not only in his work life but in his total life. Perhaps we would do better to recognize that man has many goals, some fulfilled by his participation in the business organization, some by other organizations such as educational institutions, churches, social groups, and families; some will not be fulfilled but will continue to be powerful motivators to higher levels of achievement.

FOOTNOTES

[1]For a discussion of this trend toward the development of complex organizations see Arthur L. Stinchcombe, "Social Structure and Organizations," in James G. March (Ed.), *Handbook of Organizations* (Chicago: Rand McNally & Company, 1965), pp. 142–193.

[2]Philip Selznick, "Foundations of the Theory of Organization," *American Sociological Review*, Vol. XIII, No. 1 (February, 1948), pp. 25–26.

[3]Some of the more important contributors to this approach are Chester I. Barnard, *The Functions of the Executive* (Cambridge, Massachusetts: Harvard University Press, 1938); George C. Homans, *The Human Group* (New York: Harcourt, Brace & World, 1950); Daniel Katz and Robert L. Kahn, *The Social Psychology of Organizations* (New York: John Wiley & Sons, 1966): James G. March and Herbert A. Simon, *Organizations* (New York: John Wiley & Sons, 1958); Talcott Parsons, *Structure and Process in Modern Societies* (New York: The Free Press of Glencoe, 1960); Philip Selznick, *Leadership in Administration* (New York: Harper & Row, 1957); Paul R. Lawrence and Jay W. Lorsch, *Organization and Environment* (Boston: Harvard Graduate School of Business Administration, 1967); Herbert A. Simon, *Administrative Behavior*, 2d ed. (New York: The Macmillan Company, 1959); and James D. Thompson, *Organizations in Action* (New York: McGraw-Hill Book Co., Inc., 1967).

[4]This view is expressed in Herbert A. Simon, "On the Concept of Organizational Goal," *Administrative Science Quarterly*, Vol. IX, No. 1 (June, 1964), pp. 1–22.

[5]William J. Gore, *Administrative Decision-Making* (New York: John Wiley & Sons, 1964), pp. 184–185.

[6]Charles Perrow, "The Analysis of Goals in Complex Organizations," *American Sociological Review*, Vol. XXVI, No. 6 (December, 1961), p. 854.

[7]Charles Perrow, *Organizational Analysis: A Sociological View* (Belmont, California: Wadsworth Publishing Company, 1970), pp. 171–172.

[8]Richard M. Cyert and James G. March, *A Behavioral Theory of the Firm* (Englewood Cliffs, N.J.: Prentice-Hall, Inc., 1963), p. 26.

[9]*Ibid.*, p. 27.

[10]*Ibid.*, p. 43. Simon has a similar view. He views the organization goals as the whole set of constraints that must be satisfied for survival. "It is doubtful whether decisions are generally directed toward achieving *a* goal. It is easier, and clearer, to view decisions as being concerned with discovering courses of action that satisfy a whole set of constraints. It is this set, and not any one of its members, that is most accurately viewed as the goal of the action." Herbert A. Simon, "On the Concept of Organizational Goal" *Administrative Science Quarterly*, Vol. IX, No. 1 (June, 1964), p. 20.

[11]Amitai Etzioni, *Modern Organizations* (Englewood Cliffs, N.J.: Prentice-Hall, Inc., 1964), pp. 7–8.

[12]Peter M. Blau, "The Comparative Study of Organizations," *Industrial and Labor Relations Review*, Vol. XVIII, No. 3 (April, 1965), pp. 329–330.

[13]For an overall view of Parsons' model see Talcott Parsons, *The Social System* (New York: The Free Press of Glencoe, 1951).

[14]Talcott Parsons, "Suggestions for a Sociological Approach to the Theory of Organizations–II, *Administrative Science Quarterly*, Vol. I No. 2 (September, 1956), p. 238.

[15]Neil W. Chamberlain, *Enterprise and Environment* (New York: McGraw-Hill Book Co., Inc., 1968), p. 139.

[16]For examples see Alfred D. Chandler Jr., *Strategy and Structure* (Cambridge, Massachusetts: The M.I.T. Press, 1962); Michel Crozier, *The Bureaucratic Phenomenon* (Chicago: The University of Chicago Press, 1964); Paul R. Lawrence and Jay W. Lorsch, *Organization and Environment* (Boston: Harvard Graduate School of Business Administration, 1967); Tom Burns and G. M. Stalker, *The Management of Innovation* (London: Tavistock Publications, 1961); Robert Presthus, *The Organizational Society* (New York: Alfred A. Knopf, Inc., 1962); A. K. Rice, *Enterprise and Its Environment* (London: Tavistock Publications, 1963); and Shirley Terreberry, "The Evolution of Organizational Environments," *Administrative Science Quarterly*, Vol. VII, No. 4 (March, 1968), pp. 590–613.

[17]Chamberlain, *op. cit.*, p. 144.

[18]Chandler provides a comprehensive study of the ways in which industrial firms have responded by adapting their strategies and structure to environmental opportunities. Chandler, *op. cit.*

[19]Stanley E. Seashore and Ephraim Yuchtman, "Factorial Analysis of Organizational Performance," *Administrative Science Quarterly*, Vol. XII, No. 3 (December, 1967), p. 393.

[20]James D. Thompson and Wiliam J. McEwen, "Organizational Goals and Environment," *American Sociological Review*, Vol. XXIII, No. 1 (February, 1958), p. 24.

[21]For a discussion of these trends see Bertram M. Gross, *The State of the Nation* (London: Tavistock Publications, 1966); Raymond B. Bauer, *Social Indicators* (Cambridge, Massachusetts: MIT Press, 1966); U.S. Department of Health, Education and Welfare, *Toward a Social Report* (Washington, D.C.: Government Printing Office, 1969); Nestor E. Terleckyj, "Measuring Progress Towards Social Goals: Some Possibilities at National and Local Levels," *Management Science*, Vol. XVI, No. 12 (August, 1970), pp. B-765–777; and "Social Goals and Indicators for American Society," *The Annals of the American Academy of Political and Social Science*, Vol. 1, May, 1967, and Vol. 2, September, 1967.

[22]Perrow, *Organizational Analysis*, p. 144.

[23]Daniel Katz and Robert L. Kahn, *The Social Psychology of Organizations* (New York: John Wiley & Sons, 1966), pp. 26–27.

[24]Richard M. Cyert and James C. March, *A Behavioral Theory of the Firm* (Englewood Cliffs, N.J.: Prentice-Hall, Inc., 1963). Their book is a comprehensive extention and elaboration based on a number of writings in the field such as: Chester I. Barnard, *The Functions of the Executive* (Cambridge, Massachusetts: Harvard University Press, 1938); Herbert A. Simon, *Administrative Behavior*, 2d ed. (New York: The Macmillian Company, 1959); and James G. March and Herbert A. Simon, *Organizations* (New York: John Wiley & Sons, 1958).

[25]Cyert and March, *A Behavioral Theory of the Firm*, p. 27.

[26]*Ibid.*, p. 30.

[27]*Ibid.*, p. 36.

[28]*Ibid.*, p. 38.

[29]For further discussion of means and ends see Simon, *Administrative Behavior*, pp. 62–66; March and Simon, *Organizations*, pp. 190–193; Joseph A. Litterer, *The Analysis of Organizations* (New York: John Wiley & Sons, 1965), pp. 139–142; Martin K. Starr, *Management: A Modern Approach* (New York: Harcourt Brace Jovanovich, Inc., 1971), p. 208; and R. W. Morell, *Management: Ends and Means* (San Francisco: Chandler Publishing Company, 1969), pp. 5–37.

[30]Simon, *Administrative Behavior*, p. 64.

[31]Parsons, *Structure and Process in Modern Societies*, pp. 60–69.

[32]Thompson, *Organizations in Action*, p. 12.

[33]For a discussion of the basis of differentiation in organizations see Paul R. Lawrence and Jay W. Lorsch, "Differentiation and Integration in Complex Organizations," *Administrative Science Quarterly*, Vol. XII, No. 1 (June, 1967), pp. 1–47.

[34]Etzioni, *Modern Organizations*, p. 9.

[35]David L. Sills, "Preserving Organizational Goals," in Oscar Grusky and George A. Miller (Eds.), *The Sociology of Organizations* (New York: The Free Press, 1970), p. 227.

[36]Robert Michels, *Political Parties* (New York: The Free Press, 1949).

[37]Robert K. Merton, *Social Theory and Social Structure*, rev. ed. (New York: The Free Press, 1957), p. 199.

[38]W. Keith Warner and A. Eugene Havens, "Goal Displacement and the Intangibility of Organizational Goals," *Administrative Science Quarterly*, Vol. XII, No. 4 (March, 1968), 540.

[39]For an insightful discussion of goal displacement and related issues see Michel Crozier, *The Bureaucratic Phenomenon* (Chicago: The University of Chicago Press, 1964), pp. 175–208.

[40]Peer Soelberg, "Structure of Individual Goals: Implications for Organizations Theory," in George Fisk, (Ed.), *The Psychology of Management Decision* (Lund, Sweden: CWK Gleerup Publishers, 1967), p. 16.

[41]Fritz J. Roethlisberger and William J. Dickson, *Management and the Worker* (Cambridge, Massachusetts: Harvard University Press, 1939), p. 552.

[42]Jacques Ellul, *The Technological Society* (New York: Alfred A. Knopf, Inc., 1964). This theme is also expressed in Charles A. Reich, *The Greening of America* (New York: Random House, Inc., 1970).

[43]For an analysis of this viewpoint see: William G. Scott, "Organization Government: The Prospects for a Truly Participative System," *Public Administration Review*, Vol. XXIX, No. 1 (January/February 1969), pp. 43–53.

[44]Edgar H. Schein, *Organizational Psychology* (Englewood Cliffs, N.J.: Prentice-Hall, Inc., 1965), p. 10.

[45]Etzioni, *Modern Organzations*, p. 2.

[46]March and Simon, *Organizations*, p. 84.

[47]Simon, "On the Concept of Organizational Goal," pp. 11–19.

[48]*Ibid.*, p. 13. Simon recognizes that this concept is an abstraction and that personal motivations do have an important impact on role-enacting behavior. However, he sees this separation of organizational role from personal goals as being very useful in understanding organizational decision-making.

[49]Harry Levinson, *The Exceptional Executive* (Cambridge, Massachusetts: Harvard University Press, 1968), p. 39.

[50]Harry Levinson, "Reciprocation: The Relationship between Man and Organization," *Administrative Science Quarterly*, Vol. IX, No. 4 (March, 1965), p. 373.

[51]John J. Morse, "Organizational Characteristics and Individual Motivation" in Jay W. Lorsch and Paul R. Lawrence (Eds.), *Studies in Organization Design* (Homewood, Illinois: Richard D. Irwin, and the Dorsey Press, 1970), pp. 84–100.

[52]Lyman W. Porter and Edward E. Lawler, III, *Managerial Attitudes and Performance* (Homewood, Illinois: Richard D. Irwin, and the Dorsey Press, 1968).

[53]Simon, *Administrative Behavior*, p. 198.

[54]Howard M. Vollmer and Donald L. Mills, (Eds.), *Professionalization* (Englewood Cliffs, N.J.: Prentice-Hall, Inc., 1966), p. 264.

[55]For example, see Simon Marcson, *The Scientists in American Industry* (New York: Harper & Row, 1960); William Kornhauser: *Scientists in Industry: Conflict and Accommodations* (Berkeley, California: University of California Press, 1962); George A. Miller, "Professionals in Bureaucracy: Alienation among Industrial Scientists and Engineers," *American Sociological Review*, Vol. XXXII, No. 5 (October, 1967); and Gloria V. Engel, "Professional Autonomy and Bureaucratic Organization," *Administrative Science Quarterly*, Vol. XV, No. 1 (March, 1970), pp. 12–21.

[56]Douglas McGregor, *The Human Side of Enterprise* (New York: McGraw-Hill Book Co., 1960) and *The Professional Manager*, Warren G. Bennis and Caroline McGregor (Eds.) (New York: McGraw-Hill Book Co., Inc., 1967).

[57]*The Human Side of the Enterprise*, p. 49.

[58]Chris Argyris, *Integrating the Individual and the Organization* (New York: John Wiley & Sons, 1964), p. 58.

[59]Harold J. Leavitt, "Applied Organizational Change in Industry: Structural, Technological and Humanistic Approaches," in March (Ed.), *Handbook of Organizations*, p. 1154.

[60]Robert R. Blake and Jane S. Mouton, *The Management Grid* (Houston, Texas: Gulf Publishing Company, 1964) and *Corporate Excellence through Grid Organization Development: A System Approach* (Houston, Texas: Gulf Publishing Company, Houston, 1968).

[61]*The Management Grid*, p. 142.

[62]Richard Beckhard, *Organization Development: Strategies and Models* (Reading, Massachusetts: Addison-Wesley, 1969), p. v.

[63]For a discussion of these problems see Ephraim Yuchtman and Stanley E. Seashore, "A System Resource Approach to Organizational Effectiveness," *American Sociological Review*, Vol. XXXII, No. 6 (December, 1967), pp. 891–903.

[64]Rensis Likert, *The Human Organization* (New York: McGraw-Hill Book Co., Inc., 1967), pp. 146–155.

[65]For further discussion see R. Lee Brummet, William C. Pyle, and Eric G. Flamholtz, "Human Resource Accounting in Industry," *Personnel Administration*, Vol. XXXII, No. 4 (July–August, 1969), pp. 34–46; Rensis Likert and David G. Bowers, "Organizational Theory and Human Resource Accounting," *American Psychologists*, Vol. XXIV, No. 5 (May, 1969), pp. 585–592; and John Grant Rhode and Edward E. Lawler III, "Human Resource Accounting: The Accounting System of the Future?" in Marvin Dunnett (Ed.), *Work in the Year 2001* (Belmont, California: Wadsworth Publishing Company, in Press).

[66]Thompson, *Organizations in Action*, pp. 157–158.

[67]R. Joseph Monsen, "Ownership and Management," *Business Horizons*, Vol. XII, No. 4 (August, 1969), p. 47.

[68]March and Simon, *Organizations*, p. 157.

[69]Peter F. Drucker, *The Practice of Management* (New York: Harper & Row, 1954), p. 63

[70]George S. Odiorne, *Management by Objectives* (New York: Pitman Publishing Corporation, 1965), pp. 55–56.

[71]For a discussion of the operations of a number of these company programs see Walter S. Wikstrom, *Management by—and with—Objectives, Studies in Personnel Policy, No. 212* (New York: National Industrial Conference Board, Inc., 1968).

[72]Stephen J. Carroll and Henry L. Tosi, "Goal Characteristics and Personality Factors in a Management-by-Objective Program," *Administrative Science Quarterly*, Vol. XV, No. 3 (September, 1970), pp. 295–305.

[73]Nicholas E. Colovin, "Social Change and the 'Evaluative Function' in Government," *Management Science*, Vol. XV, No. 10 (June, 1969), p. B-465.

[74]*The Planning-Programming-Budgeting System: Progress and Potentials*, Report of the Subcommittee on Economy in Government, Joint Economic Committee, 90th Cong., 1st Session (Washington, D.C.: Government Printing Office, December, 1967), p. 10.

[75]*Social Responsibilities of Business Corporations*, A Statement on National Policy by the Research and Policy Committee of the Committee for Economic Development (New York: Committee for Economic Development, June, 1971), p. 13.

[76]Max Ways, "More Power to Everybody," *Fortune*, Vol. LXXXI, No. 5 (May, 1970), p. 174.

The Environment, Values, Culture and Organizational Goals

Fremont A. Shull, Jr.

Research Professor of Sociology and Management
College of Business Administration
University of Georgia

As with previous reviews, this critique should be read in terms of the context of the associated chapter.[1] Yet space restrictions preclude a full review of the chapter. Moreover, the topic area itself transcends the chapter and critique together.

Professor Kast should be congratulated on his writing style and his coverage of a complex topic. His extensive footnote references, especially, are to be commended and there will be no attempt to elaborate on them here. The bibliography calls attention to the interest in "organizational and individual goals" as neither a new nor a fleeting concern in the management literature, as the following breakdown of sources in the chapter indicate: five items in the bibliography were published prior to 1950; with ten items dated between 1950 and 1959; with sixty between 1960 and 1969 (demonstrating that the materials in the chapter were most current); and ten items were published after 1970. The latter suggests growing attention to the topic for the future.

The chapter by Professor Kast presents largely a micro-view of goals and the setting of goals; in the chapter, he examined:

1. Various definitions of goals at different levels of analysis and their limitations,
2. Operational meanings of relevant variables, both independent variables (e.g., coalition formation) and dependent variables (e.g., structural), and
3. Reciprocity among goals (e.g., interaction between personal motivation and organizational objectives), especially through the concept of "fusion."

A macro-approach to the analysis of goals, which is the perspective of this critique, will lead to concerns different from the above, as incumbent members are viewed as carriers of culture into the organization. Other areas discussed here will include: (1) the nature and magnitude of organizational involvement with its environment (e.g., a reactive versus a pro-active stance); and (2) selected cultural trends that may influence future organizational goals (e.g., increasing environmental turbulence).

In addition, a major focus here will be on organization structure as a dependent variable, in which environmental goals and personal predilections are viewed as independent variables. To the extent that rational means-ends analyses are followed in specifying goals, translating and communicating goals (e.g., from operational objectives to performance standards) are functions of structure. To the extent that ascribed roles differ from prescribed roles and

[1]Profound appreciation is thankfully given to Robert L. Wells, Research Associate, Department of Management, University of Georgia, for his contribution to both the forming and communication of ideas presented here as well as for the clarity given to this author in thinking about organizational and individual goals. However, deficiencies and limitations in the gross design are not to be associated with him.

that these differences are activited, personal predilections influence organizational goals through a hierarchical structure. In affect, structure is the primary link between organizational and individual goals and, thus, bears attention in this analysis.

ENVIRONMENTAL CONTEXT AND ORGANIZATIONAL GOALS

A critical assumption about organizational goals and their environmental relationships has to do with whether or not the organization is open or closed to environmental influences (see Chapter 10). If the system is closed, tasks can be routinized and roles standardized more easily than if it is open; system openness is assumed here. But, in either case, individual motivation and expectations are affected.

If an organization is open to its environment, whether the openness is perceived by its members or not, various kinds of conditions must be considered that relate to the individual:

1. Is the environment benevolent or malevolent? If benevolent, the ready availability of resources may enhance organizational growth and increase opportunity for its members.
2. Is the organization exposed to, or insulated from, competition? The protection afforded by a monopolistic situation may subsidize organizational slack (wherein inducements to exceed contributions from members).
3. Are environmental dynamics uncertain or predictable? If unpredictable, the entrepreneurial nature of the organization may be attractive to members who are high risk-takers.

Another aspect of organizational goals has to do with the stance or strategy toward the environment (see Chapter 12)—whether the posture is aggressive or defensive. If the organization pro-acts against its environment, it is seeking to expand its opportunities rather than merely to exploit existing advantages; it may be striving for competitive advantage and growth rather than adaptation and mere self-perpetuation. If an organization attempts aggressively to modify its environment, particular care must be given to the use to which society's scarce resources are used and the manner in which they are used because of the general impact on membership motivation: incumbent members may be highly sensitive to the ethical and moral image of their organization as it proclaims and implements its goals, especially in its aspiration for growth.

An organization's efforts toward absolute or comparative growth affects its ability to attract and maintain employees. Growth may increase not only the number of roles in the system but also the variety of roles and, thus, increase its attractiveness to existing or potential members. Growth may be an imperative to maintaining membership if competitors in the "labor" pool are themselves increasing in size. Comparative advantages of a stable or declining organization may lead an individual to think that his potentials are incapable of being fulfilled.

Two additional aspects of the environment-goals complex are worthy of mention here. They have to do with the cultural determinism of organization technologies (see Professor Perrow's comments) and with cultural socialization of members' attitudes and beliefs. Although more is said about the latter subsequently, it cannot be completely ignored here. Cultural conditioning of the individual in terms of "inner-other" directedness, cosmopolitan-local orientations, or leadership-followership tendencies (see Chapter 13) may shift the values of organizational inducements as the individual perceives them (e.g., with regard to notions of the "organization man").

Although the organization's technological base may be described as "fixed" organizationally, over time it is determined by the cultural environment and, accordingly, affects goal definitions and individual motivations. The perceived nature of the task (e.g., standardized or varied) as posed to the individual by the technology and the rate of technological change and its concommitant impact on goal definitions (e.g., general-purpose versus single-purpose functions) are related to individual motivations. The individual may be more or less tolerant of, or satisfied with, task variety and goal ambiguity.

Although the author of this chapter was concerned with direct linkages between organizational and individual goals (i.e., he looked primarily inside the system), this review has examined both indirect (e.g., structural influences) and direct (e.g., goal ambiguity) relationships as well as external (e.g., cultural benevolence) and internal variables (e.g., goal communication) and has treated goals and motivations as bilateral. More specifically, this section has suggested what forces affect individual motivation as organizational goals reciprocate with their environmental context. In essence, attention was given to the impact of goal definitions on organizational survival and growth and how these interact with individual motivation. In this regard, organizational capacity was seen as determined by goal specification (as the function of money is defined so as to provide a medium of exchange or a store of value or both) and organizational relevance is constrained by historical definitions of goals (as the American Tuberculosis Association recently found out). Both of these factors are closely associated with membership motivation, as discussed in the next section.

MOTIVATIONAL VALUES OF ORGANIZATIONAL GOALS

Organizational goals may relate to individual motivation indirectly as well as directly. They are related directly to the extent that targets are provided the member that affect his aspiration levels and indirectly to the extent that he is positively reinforced through the reward system when goals are attained. Goals and motivation are also related when personal identity is established through organizational relevance to cultural needs as defined by the individual.

Economic benefits and working conditions have been considered most closely associated with individual motivation because they can be controlled. Thus there have been a myriad of attempts to relate remuneration to goal accomplishment through incentive-pay programs, bonus systems, and merit-rating systems with varying degrees of success (see Chapter 17). Various confounding variables, however, are associated with this relationship, such as: (1) increases in economic benefits may not be sufficiently large to change performance; (2) factors other than wages may dominate aspiration levels; (3) economic rewards may not be perceived as directly relating to individual performance or they may "wear off"; and (4) lengthy time periods between stimulus and response may further decrease their viability.

As with economic remuneration in an affluent society, working conditions may be a "hygienic" rather than a "motivating" determinant of individual performance. Working conditions may be perceived as sufficiently inferior to the extent that they reduce the individual's propensity to perform; thus, they may be called "hygienic" factors because superior conditions may not be related to high performance; but some minimum state of conditions must be met to elicit acceptable behavior. Similarly, generally affluent economic conditions may require inordinate increments in economic rewards to evoke significant changes in performance.

Another set of incentives, social and task satisfactions, are usually discussed in terms of their intrinsic value, from the fact that any satisfactions gained are inherent to the individual's role within the organization. Nonetheless both may have external value, for certain tasks may carry high social status (e.g., those tasks associated with professionalism) and social relations in the organization may extend into the larger community. (Another subtlety has to do with the fact that task expertise and social relations relate to incumbent power within the organization; and, the exercise of power itself is satisfying.) As organizational goals determine the structure of social relations and the technology of task requirements, they thus become related to individual motivation.

Goals may also relate to individual motivation, whether intrinsic or extrinsic, through the direction (structure) and identification (self definition) that they offer the individual. Organizational goals have symbolic characteristics and "target" dimensions that affect members directly as well as indirectly through the reward system that is designed to activate behavior toward goal accomplishment.

Moreover, organizational goals may provide a "rallying point" to help complete a definition of self and, thus, offer a psychological tie to the organization and thereby reduce anomie or alienation. In addition, specified goals may create bounded targets that help define complex conditions and provide comparative referants for feedback on the nature of a member's behavior. Both of these characteristics influence individual motivation.

Such goal characteristics are in part related to man's sense of mission, his concept of meaningfulness (more is said about this later) and have an extrinsic value as well: a member may bask in an organization's image when its pursuit of certain prestigious social aims enables it to attain status in the community at large. These concerns, although somewhat speculative and intangible, nonetheless may be very important for the future.

Organizational goals, on the other hand, may have a debilitating effect on individual motivation. In the first place, an individual may regard them as constraining, i.e., as resulting in inordinate psychological costs. Cultural division of labor and institutional specialization reduce the possibility that the goals of a single organization will encompass the gamut of individual values. In addition, reward systems are not generally conceived to fulfill the full range of individual needs. To this extent, goal specification may be perceived as confining and debilitating.

In the second place, goal definitions may partially provide the lens through which the incumbent views complex reality. Such an imposed perspective may have unintended consequences, including organizational dysfunctions. As historical goals are internalized by the individual, his behavior may become fixed and inappropriate to environmental changes. Moreover, goal definitions create selective perceptions as well as "tunnel vision," which may also result in dysfunctions to the extent that he discards appropriate search and heuristic problem-solving techniques. From all of this, it can be seen that the viability of setting organization goals is related to their internalization by the individual, the inducements offered to him for their accomplishment, and the direction afforded his behavior.

In this section, an organizational reward system was viewed as an intervening variable between goals and motivation. This was similar to the intrusion of structure in the section dealing with environment. Yet neither section has emphasized the notion of individual differences, and this should not be left to the inference of the reader. Individuals will respond differently to both direct and indirect associations with their organization's goals: man is assumed to be variously motivated. To generalize in the abstract is dangerous at best.

THE IMPLICATIONS OF CULTURAL TRENDS FOR GOAL DEFINITIONS

This section examines selected cultural trends as they affect the individual and the environmental context in which organization goals are defined (see Chapter 20). The pattern of analysis follows the concept of "fusion," which is conceived to be bilateral in nature, involving the individual's accommodation to the organization ("socialization") and the organization's accommodation to the individual ("personalization"), both of which may be acting at the same time and on each other.

The format of this section will be, first, to set forth a set of cultural trends (speculating that they will continue) as they relate to individual attitudes and values and to discuss associated structural implications for individual roles. Second, an attempt will be made to explain the effects of size and complexity on the structure of organizations. Finally, cultural changes in beliefs and norms will be suggested that may affect different priorities in organizational survival needs.

If available evidence is accurate, micro-organizations are becoming more "open" and visible to social actions. Assuming openness, the following logic can be developed:

1. The rising concern with the exercise of the democratic ethic, especially as it flows into the micro-organization (e.g., "maximum feasible participation") is making the norm of "individualism" more viable.
2. Technological advances and cultural dynamics make for increasing organizational complexity and task expertise, thus expanding the actual discretion in role (through delegation) available to the specialist.
3. Growing pluralism and diversity as demanded by creative behavior increases the strategic leniency offered to the professional incumbent by the administrative system.

In essence, then, latitude exists for disparity between individual values and organizational goals if these trends do evolve as major cultural forces. They will be enhanced, organizationally, as proprietorship goals (e.g., those related to entrepreneurial and risk-bearing motives) differ from administrative goals (e.g., organizational growth and security). The disparity will also be a function of (1) the nature of the "employment" contract; (2) inducements offered for conformity; and (3) the direction of the individual's own volition. At first approximation, the third variable would seem to be most critical to the extent of the disparity and would depend on the aggressiveness of the individual as he asserts his intelligent selfishness in attaining power and status and as his efforts coincide with or diverge from means that serve organizational purposes.

A second series of deductions can be made about individual impediments to goal identification in the way of social and structural variables. On the one hand, as organizations become more open to cultural influences, their containment of the individual weakens. Individuals maintain multiple group attachments both within and outside the organization. External "reference" groups offer both intrinsic and extrinsic satisfactions to the individual and reflect and mold his value system. Moreover, the interrelationships among people in an organization are not completely prescribed by its formal design; relationships are characterized by interactions over and above formal expectations (the "informal organization"). Thus the extent of the conflict among values of these reference groups and the formal purpose of the organization depends on the normative culture of the referent group and the degree to which these values influence those of the individual. The growing pluralism of our culture and the increasing openness of the organization would suggest a greater difference between the purpose of the organization and individual behavior.

On the other hand, the very nature of the increasing complexity of organizations may impede organizationally rational behavior. Selected elements of structure as they reflect increased complexity and possible malfunctions include:

1. *Communication (translation) of goals:* Although general directives communicated to successive tiers of hierarchical roles may coincide with organizational goals, specific instructions at lower levels may deviate from them. This deviation may occur for a variety of reasons, including (1) the tendency of a relay point to deemphasize or distort information that it feels is inconsistent with other organizational data or reflect unfavorably on it; and (2) the dynamics of the environment, such as a delay in transmissions, may create a temporary bias in the communication.

2. *Allocative mechanisms (budgets):* Measurement problems associated with individual or departmental contributions to organizational goals create vagueness and differences in the way organizational

requirements are perceived. In addition, personal orientations vary in response to budgets that symbolize organizational goals—e.g., the prestige associated with an inordinately large allocation or with "budget busting." The effectiveness of the budget thus relates to the association that it has with the organization goals and the perceived rewards and punishments intrinsic to its application.

3. *Functional division (segmentation)*: Efforts to gain the advantages of specialization result in the development of areas only partial to the total organization. These "partials," each having a close network of social affinities and each confronted with performance standards and rewards different from the others, create segmentation tendencies within the organization. To the extent that the individual feels a responsibility to his suborganization unit, his values may reflect more fully his identification with that organizational "partial" than with overall organizational goals.

If each subunit of an organization is judged by different standards, previous friction and social segregation will result in divergent and conflicting value premises held by individuals. The growing complexity of organizations, given the present state of management practice, would indicate that these organizational impediments to goal identification will not diminish significantly.

A counter-balancing tendency would seem to suggest that the disparity between goals and motivation might lessen. Cultural affluence and managerial attitudes may shift goal priorities partly from clientele toward membership satisfactions. If so, and if the barriers to goal identification described above can be reduced, individual associations with the organization may grow.

Survival needs of an organization and as they relate to potential individual satisfactions can be classified as:

1. Instrumental performance: attempts to efficiently meet latent or expressed demands of a clientele: short-run goals whose accomplishments provide resources for continuing operations. (They may be related to the economic benefits of the employment contract and task satisfactions for the individual.)
2. Internal maintenance: efforts to establish morale and organizational cohesion: longer-run goals (since morale and performance may not be positively related in the short-run) rationalized in terms of maintaining an effective constituent body. (These are associated with the provision of a satisfying organizational climate, including a structured setting.)
3. External coping: energies expended in order to elicit cultural support and social legitimation: typically long-run goals related to perpetuating environmental tolerance, if not support. (These survival needs are associated with membership desires for security and organizational continuity.)

Without external subsidy or monopolistic advantages, the imperatives of efficiency and short-run survival for organizations have given greater weight to instrumental performance than to either internal maintenance or external coping. Certainly, the maturity of the organization, the existence of organizational slack, and its environmental legitimation all vary the priorities of these survival needs, so their relative weights may change over time. The future, however, may hold a more permanent change in terms of how important they are perceived to be.

The seeds of such a change seem to reside in the possibility that (1) managerial attitudes will shift priorities toward internal maintenance; and (2) cultural notions of resource scarcity may lessen the emphasis on the efficiency norm. In terms of the former, cultural insistence on humanism may invade the confines of micro-organizations, wherein membership needs may be met even at the expense of those of the clientele. Management may accept maintenance costs as legitimate in their own right. Material abundance and demonstrated productive capacity, although having different impacts on organizations in the Western World, would seem to support this position.

Such a tendency may be further enhanced by changing assessments of scarcity. As man's nature is perceived as unlimited and cooperative and as natural resources are not bounded by national nor earthly constraints, the importance of instrumental efficiency to organizations may decline. To the extent that such possibilities are realized, maintenance as a survival need may challenge the importance of organizational performance. Whether or not the nexus of membership identification with organizational goals will become sharper and more proximate in the future, however, remains problematic.

SUMMARY AND CONCLUSIONS

As a response to the chapter, "Organizational and Individual Goals," this review has been more of an appendix than a critique. The macro-perspective, as taken here, generated concerns not fully disclosed in the micro-approach followed in the chapter. Although many of the ideas presented here were not uniquely different from those in the chapter, their exposure through this different perspective permitted associations and elaborations not made there.

Nonetheless, I must agree with a position taken by Professor Kast that the nature of goals and any discussion of them create ambiguity and conflict. Goals, as a concept of organizational behavior, especially as inferred from individual behavior, are manifested in a variety of forms as, for example, formal documents and articulated personal rationalizations. Conflicts among them, whether real or fancied, exist, and their definitions are made most vacuous because of measurement problems. Accordingly, this review has presented largely a series of propositions about goals and their relationships, many of which require empirical validation.

However, and in conclusion to this review, two positions inherent to its message must be emphasized. First, analyses of goals are not offered for manipulative purposes. Socialization, for example, is deemed acceptable only to the extent that the human dignity of the individual is protected and, if possible, enhanced. Second, and in like manner, defining and setting goals are evolutionary, if not mutational, processes in organizational life. Therefore, vagueness and ambiguity in personal and organizational goals may be desirable if for no reason other than to leaven the creativity of man.

On the Centrality of the Concept of Goals

Wilmar F. Bernthal

Professor
Graduate School of Business Administration
University of Colorado

The concept of goals is central to any explanation of behavior, whether of individuals acting alone, acting in natural groupings, or acting in formal organizations. At the same time, it is an elusive concept. In one sense, one may argue that only persons have goals. We then ascribe to organizations such goals as result from the bargaining-learning process of people in coalitions, with some individuals' personal goals more dominantly represented than others, because of these individuals' bargaining power in the coalition. The influence of elite members of organizations on its goals is clear in owner-managed business firms and in totalitarian public organizations. This influence becomes more diffused in organizations that represent a large number of owners or that operate to serve public purposes in a democratic society. In these organizations the managerial elite play a significant role in shaping organizational goals to serve "the balanced best interests of many claimants," and in modifying goals to conform to demands from the environment or to take advantage of emerging opportunities provided by changes in the environment.

Professor Kast's paper on "Organizational and Individual Goals" provides an excellent survey of the treatment of these concepts both in organization theory in general and in the empirical research studies from which the theories have developed. It also illustrates the principle that in folklore sometimes has been called "Fred Allen's Law," that things are more complicated than they seem. Whether this is a blessing or a curse depends on the point of view of the reader. For the scholar with his inquiring mind, complexity provides a challenge, and a high level of abstraction makes it possible for him to incorporate a wider range of complex phenomena into his models, and "make sense out of them." The open-systems view rules out the more traditional *ceteris paribus* assumptions that "all other things can be considered equal or constant," and lends an air of realism to the study of a complex world. On the other hand, open-systems models seldom lend themselves to determinate solutions since the nature of many of the factors affecting organizational behavior in complex systems prevents their being quantified except through use of subjective probabilities, and the relationship between factors is complex and interdependent.

For the pragmatic reader, whether he is a student of management or a practicing manager, more limited, and perhaps more prescriptive, models may seem desirable. Professor Kast's treatment of the subject provides the broadest possible perspective on the question of organizational and individual goals. Since integrating individual goals and the formal goals of organizations is a continuing responsibility of managers at all levels in organizations, even the most pragmatic reader will find the treatment of Kast's "third level of analysis, the goals of individual participants and their relationship to organizational goals," a practical review of the uses and limitations of various current management practices in attempting to maximize complementarity of individual and organizational goals. However, if the manager is confronted with a changing and non-routine technology and with a turbulent environment from which he cannot readily insulate his organization, his level of analysis must necessarily shift to Kast's second and third levels, viewing the organization as a system, and recognizing goal constraints imposed by the larger environment. Thus, Kast's open-system approach will alert even the most pragmatic reader to factors that he may be forced to consider when and if the more limited and simplistic models no longer serve him adequately in the management role in which he finds himself.

FROM SIMPLE TO COMPLEX GOAL MODELS

In the interests of parsimony, an explanation ought not be more complex than the problem demands or the situation requires. The evolution of management and organization theory illustrates the development of goal models from a closed-system mechanistic model to a modern concept of organizations as socio-technical systems in interaction with a potentially turbulent environment. The practical manager will incorporate into his decision-making only those factors that to him appear critical in solving his immediate problems, and will more or less reluctantly modify his model to adapt to a wider set of influences when he finds his simpler and more determinate model no longer adequate for his purposes. The scholar, on the other hand, will try to conceptualize the most inclusive set of factors and their relationship, often at the risk of over-complicating the problem for a student or client with more limited purposes in mind.

OFFICIAL AND OPERATIVE GOALS IN THE RATIONAL MODEL

Classical management and organization theory focused on the internal operation of organizations, assuming a placid environment and "given" goals. The "given" goals were the rational statements of organizational purpose, stemming from formal corporate charters, from missions ascribed by legislation in public organizations, or from the "natural" goal of profit-maximization in owner-managed firms. Proponents of these rational models take official statements of formal goals at face value, and see the managerial elite as implementing rational means for achieving these rational ends. Sometimes implied is the "rabble hypothesis" that managers act rationally whereas non-managers need to be directed and controlled toward rational behavior, since their non-logical behavior may be incompatible with the requirements of the rational model. In this sense, proponents of modern management science models sometimes are guilty of an "irrational passion for dispassionate rationality," since their models are less adequate in dealing with rational-emotive behavior.

Classical definitions of management stressed "getting things done through people," or "matching men and jobs." In these models, converting the goals of individuals to the goals of the organization was given top priority. Technology was an independent variable, applying efficiency concepts from industrial engineering to the design of work. Formal organization structure was an independent variable, applying the rules of the bureaucratic model for effective hierarchical control. Even managerial role was an independent variable, applying principles of management—the rational actions of a managerial elite—to planning, organizing, and controlling. The object of management action in relation to lower-level participants was to induce them to act according to the rational model by making the organization's goals more rewarding than their personal goals. The means employed were reward and punishment through performance review and personnel decisions of superiors in the hierarchy over their subordinates. The conditions under which individuals are willing to subordinate their goals to predetermined organizational goals and means are either extreme dependency conditions (poverty, ignorance, fear) in utilitarian or coercive organizations, or extreme loyalty to charismatic leaders and organizational purpose in normative organizations. The model was, and is, adequate under conditions of simple technology, a placid environment, and a culture that accepts subordination in dependency roles as legitimate.

MODIFICATIONS OF THE RATIONAL MODEL

The rational model has been criticized for its over-rationalistic view of managerial behavior. Non-rational behavior of managers resulting in organizational goal displacement or in satisficing rather than maximizing official organization goals is a favorite subject of writers in popular sociology (the critics of bureaucracy) and of novelists writing on the behavior of the organization man. The same thesis, in a more fundamental manner, has been incorporated into the modifications of the rational model proposed by human relations and industrial humanist writers. Their thesis, essentially, is that the development of complex technology, the higher level of information and education among organizational participants, as well as our culture in general, no longer provide the dependency conditions necessary to make man subordinate his goals to those of an organization. Nor can the organization function effectively if it suppresses the higher abilities and motivations of individuals in the interests of maintaining the mechanistic controls of the rational model.

Conceptually, the industrial humanist's model states that in organizations using complex technology and in a culture in which submission to arbitrary authority is no longer a norm, organizational goals may best be served by employing "the whole man," and by permitting informal organization to develop in a natural or organic manner, in order to provide work conditions under which the work itself becomes a major motivator. Thus, many of the programs for integrating the individual and the organization now include work design, organization design, and managerial role as dependent variables, responding to the requirements of the technology, to the motivational needs of individuals, and to the conditions for effective performance of natural groups. This strategy for achieving organizational goals views the organization as a socio-technical system. The tactics include experimenting with job enrichment, decentralization, management by objectives, group dynamics, participative leadership, and organizational development programs. It is at this level that the practical manager, perhaps reluctantly, searches for the appropriate trade-off between controlling behavior of organizational participants by extrinsic means on the one hand, and creating the conditions for individual voluntary commitment to organization goals and using self-control to enhance organizational performance on the other hand.

NEW DIMENSIONS IN THE OPEN-SYSTEMS APPROACH

Although the modifications of the rational model discussed above were made in response to changes in technology and environment, organization theory and most management practice still treated them essentially within the traditional closed-system framework. Professor Kast's paper, however, starts with the broadest dimension, the open-system approach. This approach views the organization as a subsystem of a larger supersystem to which organizational goals may have to adapt in order for the organization to survive, and to the constraints to which even the organization's internal operations may need to be adjusted.

The traditional American business ethic views the free market system and a supportive government as part of the American creed, and views with alarm any cultural and social changes that may question this creed. Thus, classical management and organization theory had strong normative overtones concerning what the larger society should be, and its proponents actively supported ideological causes for maintaining favorable market conditions, preserving property rights, and protecting management prerogatives against encroachment by government, labor, consumers, or society in general.

An open-systems approach also attempts to be analytical, rather than normative, about forces in the larger environment. Both technology and environment are considered as intervening variables. In a rather stable environment, these factors can be considered as "givens" at least in the short run, and attention can be focused on internal organization to effectively exploit the environment in pursuing the organization's goals. However, in a turbulent environment, the degree of certainty or uncertainty in an organization's environment will determine the degree to which it will need to constantly reappraise its goals. Such reappraisal is particularly important for organizations whose products are less tangible, more in the service category. These organizations spend considerable energy in boundary-spanning activities, developing strategies for dealing with the environment either through aggressive competition or through some form of cooperative strategy, such as bargaining, co-operation, or coalition.

An analytical open-systems approach, therefore, may consider also as variable such hallowed institutional arrangements as the market system, business-government relations, the Protestant work ethic, cultural values, life styles, and ecological factors. In a turbulent environment, these become crucial factors, even in the short run, for organizational survival and performance, and organizations must develop mechanisms for sensing changes and modifying organizational goals in order to remain compatible with the shifting demands and constraints of a changing society.

In the matter of organizational and individual goals, things are indeed more complex than they seem. It is helpful, therefore, to be clear about the perspective from which goals are being discussed, and to specify the assumptions concerning individual and organizational behavior implicit in the discusson. For these purposes, the Kast paper has given us a good and useful framework.

DISCUSSION QUESTIONS

1. Define operational goals and official goals. Are goals the same as objectives? Do, or can, organizations have goals independent from the goals of the individuals that are associated with them?
2. It is said that organizations (and individuals) have multiple goals. How are the differences in goals reconciled?
3. How are general goals translated into operational goals in an organization?
4. Why does Kast use three levels of analysis to explore goals?
5. What is the inducement-contribution concept? How is it related to the reciprocation concept?
6. Discuss the nature of the conflict between organizational role requirements and individual satisfactions. How can these be reconciled or integrated?
7. What is management by objectives? Is this operational?
8. Discuss the environment-goals complex.
9. Discuss goals in the context of open systems.

8

Communication and Information Systems

Van Court Hare, Jr.

Professor
School of Business Administration
University of Massachusetts

In order to select plans and to supervise them we require information and the ability to manipulate and communicate it. In this sense, successful management practice, both day-to-day and long-range, depends on information processing capability.

First, to select a plan, we must have at hand a number of alternatives, scan them, and pick one from the many by given criteria. Measures of information processing are defined formally by just such a selection process. (Shannon and Weaver, 1949.)

Second, with a plan in hand, we must make sure that what is wanted is accomplished. Since it is rare indeed that actions precisely follow any plan, we must monitor what is going on, detect any error that occurs between our plan and actuality, then attempt to reduce that error by any means at our disposal. (Indeed, if the error is severe and cannot be reduced, we may necessarily have to re-select our plan.)

To obtain the control outlined above, observations, comparisons, calculation processing, and return transmission of correcting instructions will be needed. This corrective cycle, found in all forms of goal-seeking organisms from the human body to the modern corporation, is known technically as *negative feedback* correction, since the process seeks to *reduce error* rather than to aggravate it. (Wiener, 1948: Ashby, 1956.)

Plan selection and feedback control may be either simple or complex. Selecting a room's temperature and maintaining (or regulating) that temperature by a wall-mounted thermostat is simple. Conversely, the planning and control sequence required to launch and to return astronauts from the moon is complex. The planning and control philosophy at both extremes is the same, but timing, planning, and execution require much greater communication and information processing capability in the latter than in the former case. Specifically, the thermostat requires only one simple, independent, corrective communication loop or cycle; the launch and return requires many, often interdependent feedback and communication cycles, many of which must occur in precisely timed sequences within a global hierarchy of men and machines.

So, one way to make sense of management information and communication systems is to classify such systems broadly by their complexity. The most transparent and helpful classification for our present purpose is shown in Table 1.

Notice the three classifications, *A, B* and *C*, in the table. The more complex system (e.g., *B* as opposed to *A; C* as opposed to *B*) assumes the existence of supporting "lower level" systems (e.g., *A* and *B* supporting *C*). Notice also that as we move from *A* to *C* the level of uncertainty, selection scope, and seriousness of error *increase*; whereas the repetitive nature of decision-making, the degree of determinism, and the mechanical guidelines that can be used to automate error correction *decrease*.

Corresponding to Table 1, Figure 13 provides a schematic view of the three-level hierarchy. (Deutsch, 1966, see appendices, proposes similar diagrams for studying government structure; and Boulding, 1956, proposes a nine-level hierarchy for classifying systems in general.)

Better than 90 per cent of installed information systems considered successful are at the operating level, with declining success as attempts are made to formalize systems and procedures at the higher levels. For example, in his review of computer results in the year 1971, Beckman (1971) cites several areas in which computer applications, have had disappointing results, and notes first:

> Much thought in the past had gone into the planning of total management information systems that would permit an effective, and to a large extent, automated and scientific approach in the management of large, complex or-

TABLE 1. A HIERARCHY OF SYSTEMS LEVELS

A. Operations. Standards fixed. Mostly deterministic data, deterministic logic. Stable situation. Little or no prediction or choice needed. Single plan of action, although many sub-conditions and options may be possible. Corresponds to application program in data processing.

B. Tactics. Standards involve some uncertainty. Data subject to error. Logic involves complexity beyond capability of brute force methods. Selection and simplification required. Analytical techniques may, or may not, be available. Tactical objectives subject to change. Possible instability in processing, or in priorities, values, or goals. Many alternate plans may be available in memory. Short-range prediction or choice needed. Corresponds to supervisory control programs in data processing.

C. Strategy. Standards, values, goals, depend on personal or political choice in addition to fixed constraints. Almost infinite choice combinations to consider. Selection problems at all points predominate. Rational logic and stability cannot be assumed. May innovate not only alternate plans of action but also goals and values used to evaluate plans. May be removed from reality by intermediate filtering of (or time delays in) lower-level information feedbacks or scans of environment. May be overloaded by information volume and variety. Possible pathological, self-destructive choices and actions. Lower-level systems may have to be bypassed to maintain external and internal realism. Long-range prediction and choice needed—combined with wide scan and awareness while present plans are fixed. Corresponds to human development of new programs, both application and supervisory (including redesign of total information system), in data processing.

ganizations. Systems that were produced in many cases did not come anywhere near the expectations of their originators.

A review of Table 1 and Figure 13 indicates why this situation is not surprising. At the tactical and strategic levels the variety and/or uncertainty is often too much for our present techniques of analysis and control to handle. And even at the operating level, many deterministic problems elude us.

As Boulding (1956) points out for his first hierarchical level, which he calls the "level of frameworks," or static structures, fairly adequate descriptive models are available. Yet, even at this simplest level, he notes, the problem of adequately describing complex structures is still far from solved.

The theory of indexing and cataloguing, for instance, is only in its infancy. Librarians are fairly good at cataloguing books, chemists have begun to catalogue structural formulae, and anthropologists have begun to catalogue culture trains.

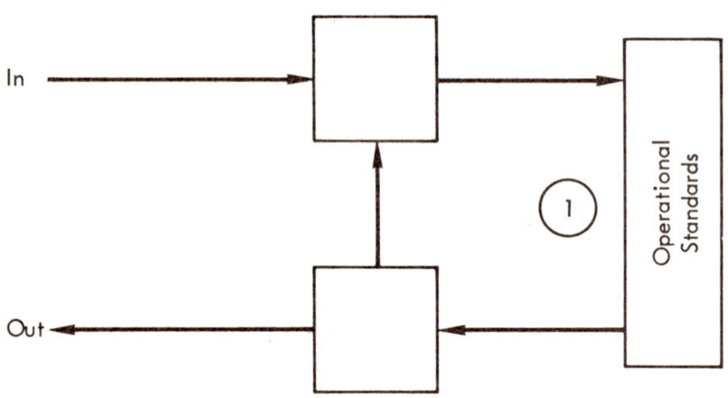

(A) Operating Level

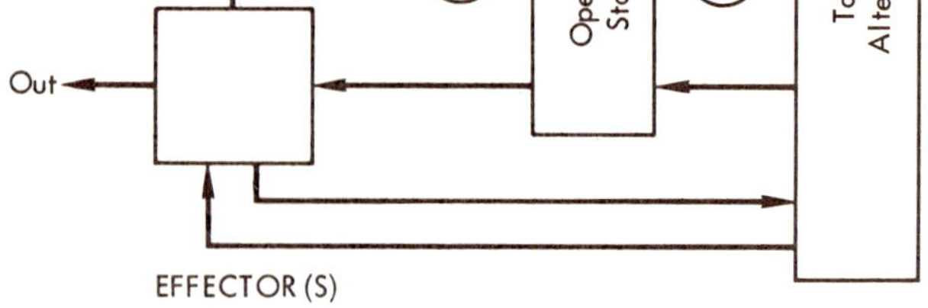

(B) Tactical Level

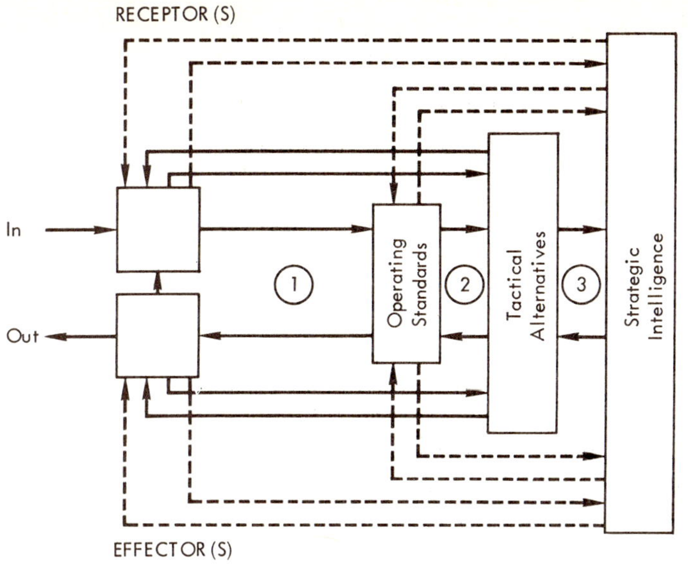

(C) Strategic Level

FIGURE 13. Communication Flow Chart Illustrating Control Hierarchy as Outlined in Table 1.

1. *Diagram of Operating System.* Simple feed-back control loop. Information processed against given standards within a single plan.

2. *Addition of Tactical Capability.* Reserve of alternate plans available. Monitor ongoing operations plus scan of input possibilities and output effectiveness—as operating system works on present plan. Plans changed as necessary. Notice more complex feed-back monitoring and correction. Tactical level can be buffered from much detail by operating system, although access to detail available. Operating system can supply summary data to tactical level for manipulation.

3. *Strategic Level Added.* New level monitors selected input/output detail, operations, and tactical adjustments. Notice longer direct communications links (solid lines) with chance of erroneous filtering at each stage, and more numerous monitoring possibilities. New plans and policies developed at this level. Processing often highly symbolic or generalized.

> The cataloguing of events, ideas, theories, statistics, and empirical data has hardly begun. The very multiplication of records as time goes on will force us into more adequate cataloguing and reference systems than we now have. This is perhaps the major unsolved theoretical problem at the level of the static structure.

Yet the last form of cataloguing and information processing is what is needed as we move up the hierarchy.

With this background in mind, we now turn to a discussion of the operating, tactical, and strategic levels, in that order.

THE OPERATING LEVEL

We can identify the operating level by its reliable structure.

Many routine, simple, and deterministic process steps can be found in most information systems. Limited logic and arithmetic is the rule. Thus, these steps, the sequence of their execution, and standards for their correctness can be fixed. This reliable structure permits automation of data processing and control.

Fortunately, clusters of highly predictable, repetitive activity can be found in almost all systems. And, such clusters represent the largest percentage of activities most systems exhibit.[1]

With this bulk of all activities taken care of routinely, we gain economy, speed, and stability. Then, we may progress to larger concerns—but not before. This is why formalization of the operating level is important in information system design.

For example, if a manufacturing or sales organization receives a customer order, that order starts a chain of events that will include both information and material processing. Figure 14 shows an operating level flow chart for a retail firm. There the order, which provides *variable* information identifying (1) the customer, (2) the number of units wanted, and (3) the products wanted can be combined with *fixed* information stored in files and keyed to the order by customer and product identification codes. This fixed information such as customer address, product unit price, product

[1]The highly skewed distribution of activity volume by activity type has been noted in many fields, and often is a product of human choice. Zipf (1949) provides exhaustive empirical data and argues that human choice of "least effort" alternatives produces the clustering noted above.

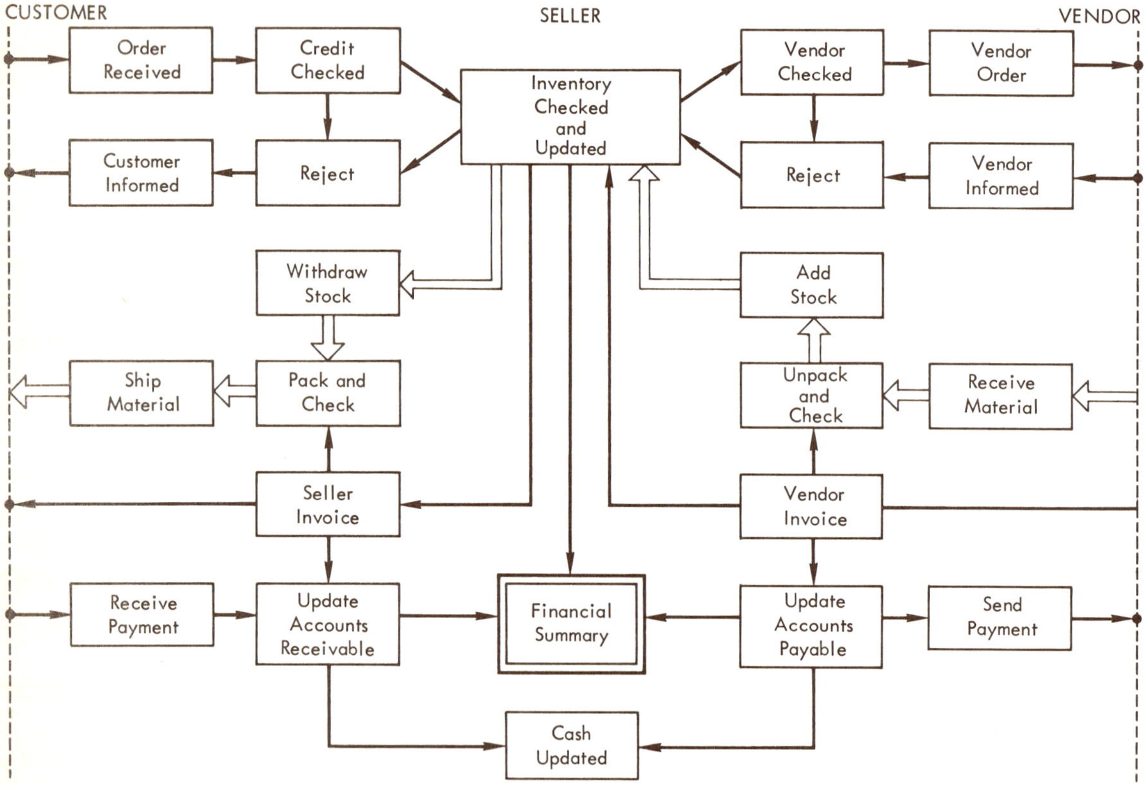

FIGURE 14. Operating Level Flow Chart for a Retail Firm

description, and inventory available permits us to write the order, update accounts receivable and inventory status, and initiate shipping and billing activities.

Through reference to inventory status and vendor records, inventory reordering rules can initiate vendor orders, update inventory on-order status, and later accounts payable. In this process, the time sequence of both external and internal events generated by the order fulfillment procedures spins off historical data that may be used for sales analysis, credit, inventory control calculations, vendor performance audits, and the like, as well as for periodic financial reports, such as balance sheets and income statements.

Except for inventory control, most of the operations described are deterministic. The "system" in Figure 14 may thus be integrated into a working whole by carefully constructing files, forms, and procedures to obtain objectives, such as a given profit level or return on investment, that are relatively easy to agree on.

Table 2 lists a classification of entities and subheadings typical of those found in the files of fixed information used in operating level processing systems of the type just discussed. Accurate identification of such data items permits a variety of information combinations to be generated by the system—e.g., sales analyses by customer or by product, or by product and customer, or vice versa. Furthermore, a given event, say, an order received, often will link one or more information categories, say a customer, with the products he desires. Such data links provide many possible extensions of the basic processing system.

Although the simple order-processing/inventory-control sequence described above may be made more conditional (by providing tests to handle exceptional cases of wide variety such as rejected credit, inventory shortages, partial shipments, receipts, payments, etc.) such exceptions do not alter the

TABLE 2. SOME TYPICAL FILE CATEGORIES NEEDED FOR INTEGRATING A TYPICAL OPERATING LEVEL SYSTEM

Coded Customer	*Coded Product*	*Coded Vendor*
Name	Name	Name
Address	Inventory	Address
Credit	Manufacturing Standards	Delivery Record
Sales	Routing	Alternates
Accounts Receivable	Sales	Accounts Payable
Coded Employee	*Coded Other Resources*	*Coded Analysis Centers*
Name	Equipment	Divisions
Address	Depreciation	Establishments
Payroll	Space	Departments
Commission	Cash Accounts	Work Centers
Incentive		Various Financial Accounts
Skill		
Work Station		
Tax Held		

basic picture. The variety of alternatives is still well within the limits of what can be done with even modest processing equipment.

Reliable processing, however, is essential. Should procedures fail, or perform erratically, the organization itself quickly faces a crisis, because its very existence is threatened by operating level failure. Even small errors can demand management attention, detracting from the supervisory resources that can be applied to the higher levels of information handling. Therefore, operating level procedures should be as automatic and as reliable as possible, much as our hearts beat and our breathing continues without disturbing our conscious thought.

Considerations in Operating System Design

It is not possible here to discuss operating system design in detail. However, several subjects are of general interest, and we will review them briefly, with references for those who wish to go further. We will discuss (1) Identification, Transmission, and Data Storage Codes; (2) File Organization and Data Structure; and (3) Error Control, Security, and Privacy. (What is said in these sections applies with even greater emphasis at the tactical and strategic levels, since, as we shall see, decisions made at these higher levels will have increasingly profound effects on the organization as a whole.)

Identification, Transaction, and Data Storage Codes

In 1868, the U.S. Army assigned Lt. Henry Metcalfe to the Frankford Arsenal to organize its paperwork and control procedures. The arsenal near Philadelphia had grown during the Civil War from a small production facility to the Union's major arms source. During this period, capacity and supervision were strained beyond their limits and record keeping, cost control, and material flow became chaotic.

Metcalfe's survey revealed records, such as they were, kept in bound ledgers, by work-center or production function—not by production item, project, or order. Thus, it was tedious or impossible to trace work flow, expedite orders, check mistakes, or control costs. Moreover, terms used to describe production items were inconsistent, often varying with the whim of local recordkeepers. Thus, consolidated statistics or historical information about a given item or order were inaccurate or misleading.

So, to improve matters, Metcalfe set forth three principles of systems design:

1. Each order and subsequent step in the manufacturing process should be initiated and confirmed at completion by individual documents, or "unit records." These were to be cards. (It was said Metcalfe was inspired by a librarian.)
2. The unit records were to be collected at a central office, where the individual records could be grouped together, sorted, and compared to show deviations between orders and results.
3. To permit accurate classification of the detail on specific items, nomen-

clature was to be standardized so that all recordkeepers would use the same words to describe the same item or process step.[2]

Metcalfe's three precepts, which solved his problem, are still the cornerstone of data processing organization. And today, as then, standardization of categories is usually the most difficult phase of system implementation.

Metcalfe devoted much of his time to constructing term dictionaries and listings to be used by all employees. He used English, since the records were written by hand. But as record-keeping machines, and later computers, replaced human processors, efficiency and accuracy demanded numeric or other forms of coded identification.

Often such coding schemes grew up as historical accidents, or were hastily conceived to get some system working. Yet identification codes directly influence file methods, processing ability, communication cost, and human interpretation. For this reason, both theory and experiment are used to develop and test identification codes used in modern, well-planned data processing.

For widely used items, such as electronic parts, common industry-wide part number codes have been standardized. Similar standardization, widely used, is used in book publishing inventory numbers, ZIP codes, even telephone numbers. Information Theory (Shannon and Weaver, *op. cit.*) provides guides to code development for technical efficiency. For example, heavily used codes should be short, rarely used codes may be longer, code symbols should appear with equal frequency for greatest brevity, and so on.

In applications wherein special security, human, processing, or historical precedents are foremost, code development is often based on experiment and empirical evidence. Thus, credit card identification codes, magazine subscription codes, and error-correcting codes are not usually publicly disclosed for given applications.

Fano (1961), Peterson (1961), Bourne (1963), Gallager (1968), and Lucky *et al.* (1968), provide technical information on code development. *Control Engineering* (1962), Fulton (1964), Spring (1966), and Chase (1966), illustrate typical industry standards and empirical development rules. Table 3 provides a selected group of code examples, with advantages and disadvantages.

[2]Metcalfe later became a private consultant and described his methods in an early systems analysis text. See Metcalfe (1885).

TABLE 3. SAMPLE IDENTIFICATION CODES

1. *Pure Serial* (e.g., a list of names)
   Example: Each item to be identified is given a number starting with "1," etc.

No.	*Name*
1	Able
2	Baker
3	Charlie

   Advantage: short, unique. Disadvantage: difficult to add or delete in listing. No meaning for serial number.

2. *Pure Block* (e.g., The postal address, or ZIP code)
   Example: Each item to be identified is given a number, each position of which has a meaning according to position as well as value.
   ZIP Code (For Amherst, Mass.)

   0 10 02
   - *02* ← Local Address
   - *10* ← Sectional Sorting Center
   - *0* ← Major Region

   Advantage: Positions and values have meaning. Can be analysed by position and value. Disadvantage: long, can cause duplicates, difficult to change selected categories.
3. *Blocked Serial* (e.g., Digit change on first letter of name)
   Example: Each item is serialized, but first (major) category is blocked.

No.	*Name*
10	Able
11	Adams
20	Baker
21	Bartlett
30	Charley
31	Chico

   Advantage: Shorter than pure blocked, unique, some meaning, easier to add and delete if blocks leave space between progressions for serial identification. Disadvantage: Blocks of serials may overflow, limited meaning.
4. *Serialized Block* (e.g., Addition of serial number for unique identification)
   Example: Identification of clothing item.
   Clothing Code

   44 L 26 70 29
   - *29* ← Unique Serial
   - *70* ← Color
   - *26* ← Style
   - *L* ← Cut
   - *44* ← Size

   Advantage: Unique, has meaning, can be analyzed by position and value, easy to add or delete. Disadvantage: longest code, serial field can overflow. (Compare to Dewey Decimal System of book classification in the library, probably the most popular form of commercial identification code.)
5. *Derivation from Input* (e.g., From a customer's name)
   Example: A given name is analyzed according to certain rules, and a code is generated. Frequently used for inquiry by phone or mail, or if a numerical account number has been forgotten. The purpose is to provide approximate, if not exact, location for a given customer's data even if slight spelling or reporting errors exist. Here is the "Soundex" code developed by Remington Rand.
   A. Given a name, retain its first letter.
   B. Delete the letters A E I O U Y W and H
   C. Assign the following numbers to the remaining consonants

1	B F P V
2	C G J K Q S X Z
3	D T
4	L
5	M N
6	R

D. In case of insufficient consonants (short names) assign the number zero (0) to make up one letter plus three digits, to total four positions. (By this method, the name RODRIGUEZ would become code R362, as would RODRIGUES.)

This procedure divides the telephone book, for example, into $26 \times 7 \times 7 \times 7$ — 8,918 blocks. The one selected is then searched serially for an exact match, based on additional information. (All digits, 0–9, have been used in other versions of this code to reduce block size.) Advantages: Places similar sounding names together, length can be controlled. Disadvantages: May not be unique and require serial search, additional information may be needed to determine match.

6. *Error Checking* (e.g., Use of extra check digit)

Example: Given any of the codes above, check it for accuracy of transmission. To illustrate, consider a numerical serial number 12345, and the "prime number weighting method" suggested by Friden, Inc., a Singer subsidiary.

A. The account number is	1	2	3	4	5
B. Multiply by	17	13	7	5	3
C. Add the results	17 + 26 + 21 + 20 + 15 = 99				

D. Subtract total from next higher or equal, multiple of the number 11, e.g.

multiple	99
check total	99
check digit	0

E. The new serial number with check digit is now 12345–0

F. Perform same computation at each stage of processing; if check digits do not match, stop and look for error.

Advantages: Very sensitive to transposition and substitution of wrong number. Disadvantages: Requires more positions, more processing. May require deletion of certain serial numbers, i.e., in this method, all serial (or code) numbers that lead to a check digit equal to the number 10 (which is possible here) must be invalidated.

The final selection of an identification code structure for a particular case, however, may include consideration of many factors, among them:

1. processing hardware to be used
2. transaction rates against identified items in a file
3. the ratio of inquiry to update (add/delete) operations
4. communication volume and methods
5. types of data analysis desired or predicted
6. potential error types and frequencies
7. response time in processing desired by transaction type
8. level of data reduction permitted in summary reports
9. complexity of inquiry or transaction (multiple or single key)
10. security or privacy desired
11. degree of "clustering" by application of file categories and transaction types
12. likelihood of future code and file changes with time
13. supervisory control programs available

14. technological trends in hardware, software, management use, etc.
15. organization method used in external statistics and data banks to which links may be desired, e.g., census figures, economic statistics, etc.

Once adopted and implemented into a system through training, file organization, processing routines, and user habit, identification and transaction codes are not easily changed. For example, once the ZIP codes used for routing mail are learned by the general population and postal workers, that code becomes fixed. Even though imperfections may be found in the standard code structure, tradition and cost prohibit their correction.

We may conclude, therefore, that the choice and design of identification and transaction codes should not be a casual undertaking, since the commitments made therein will have pervasive effects influencing later applications of the information system.

File Organization and Data Structure

Manual files in most offices have an alphabetical, date, or serial number ordering. We may usually enter such files at any point in their sequence for fast retrieval, but our ability to do so depends on strict observance of the ordering scheme. To disarray the file categories and lose their order destroys the file.

So, we do not hire disorganized clerks, nor employ disorganized methods in the file room. There, order must prevail. We must know where our papers physically are located.

With such order to provide structure, some random or sequential searching for a given item within a small, locatable file class may be tolerable. So may a few cross references in a chain of between-class looks. Nevertheless, the fastest search is direct, to a known location. Bypass all intermediate interpretations, random examinations, and multiple-search links, and we can go from question to answer in one step.

The one-step ideal, however, is not always possible. Information on a given item (or item characteristics) may be in several, physically different file categories. If the major file ordering is by date, for instance, orders received throughout the year from a given customer will be scattered (by date) throughout the file, and individual orders cannot be found without first looking at an order index by customer (or by examining every file record). Such unavoidable requests lead to more complex (and more lengthy) file retrievals.

Although complex file searches and summaries *can* be made manually, the time, cost, and skill required to do so are often prohibitively high in all but the simplest cases. Automated file-handling techniques, on the other hand, permit (1) fast summary retrievals, (2) the segmentation of large data blocks into small units that can be recombined in many ways, and (3) the use of multiple, conditional search "keys" and dictionaries to guide the search process. In short, the major difference between manual and automated file handling is high speed and low cost per "look" at data entries afforded by automated file handling. Even if the one-step ideal still holds for automated file searches, the disparity between this ideal and multiple-step searches is drastically reduced, thereby making complex computer data structures and file searches feasible in practice.

The choice of file-handling and organizational methods in automated communication and computer equipment depends on many of the factors that influence code choice, as described in the preceding section. In addition, the type of physical memory media employed by the system must be taken into account.

Three general classes of memory media are incorporated in such hardware, either singly or in various combinations.

Serial media (magnetic tape) is usually the least inexpensive information storage form. Tape, like a scroll, requires purely sequential processing and so is not suitable for fast random inquiry or updating. However, many applications can be pre-sorted and "batch processed" sequentially (payroll, summary inventory, and marketing statistics). And very large files are often stored on tape because other memory forms are too expensive.

Various semi-random media forms (magnetic drums, disks, cards, etc.) afford direct access to a small block of data in a file. That block is then scanned sequentially, much as a book is withdrawn from the library, then scanned for wanted detail. Semi-random media offers relatively inexpensive storage combined with great organizational flexibility, and is thus widely used for inquiry and updating when millisecond response times can be tolerated.

Pure random access media (magnetic coves, solid-state memories, etc.), although the most expensive, permit direct access to a given character, or even to the detailed computer code structure of a given character. Such media provides the main computational memory of most computers.

Information is usually swapped from sequential or semi-random media to pure random media for processing. In addition, the greatest flexibility of organization is available in pure random media memory form. Only cost prevents pure random its universal use. Response time is measured in millionths or billionths of a second. With this said, we can illustrate several forms of file organization in typical use.

Figure 15 illustrates three basic data organizations, which may be combined or extended to produce highly complex data structures.

Although routine batch processing may use a purely sequential organization and highly conditional inquiries, complex interrelation of files (and the data contained within them) requires an elaboration of the forms shown in Figure 15, (B) and (C).

Finally, two additional ways of organizing data for access appear in Figure 15, (D) and (E). There we see a list that provides direct access to file items having a common characteristic. These concepts may be extended at will.

Advanced forms of information retrieval and updating, which may involve searching on multiple keys, processing in alternate sequences, complex cross-referencing, and rapid file reorganizing usually demand sophisticated media and file organization types, regardless of cost. Any additional discussion of data structure details is beyond our present scope, but Dodd (1969) provides an excellent coverage of the subject with numerous references; surveys of the state of the art may be found in annual reviews, such as Cuadra (1971), and texts, such as Flores (1970).

It is important to note, however, that many attempts have been made to generalize the file management problem so that a variety of data structures can be available to the user as his needs and equipment change with time or application. Such generalized data base management systems have

BASIC FILE STRUCTURES

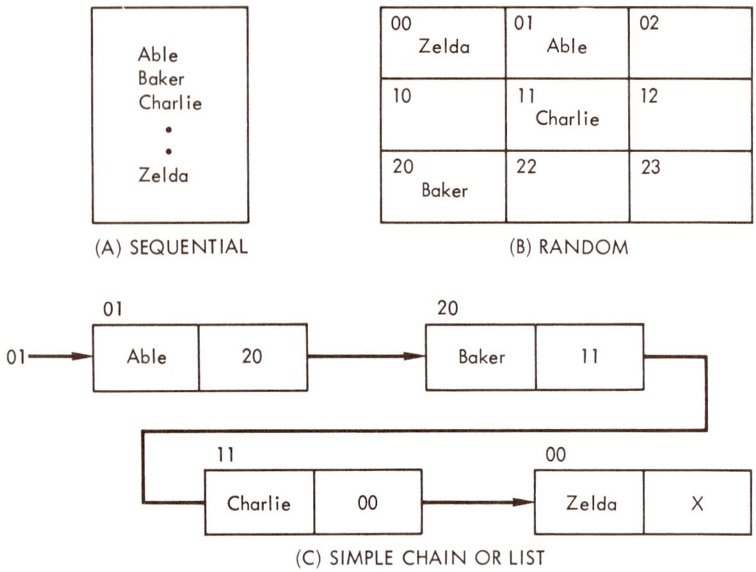

NAME	SEX
Able	M
Baker	M
Charlie	M
Mary	F
Paul	M
Zelda	F

(D) Alphabetic item order, one characteristic.

SEX	NAME
F	Mary
	Zelda
M	Able
	Baker
	Charlie
	Paul

(E) "Inverted" order on characteristic, in-class alphabetic order.

FIGURE 15. Basic File Structures

been surveyed in two important documents, one which compares ten generalized, currently available data management "packages," COCASYL (May, 1971), and another that proposes industry standards for such systems, CODASYL (April, 1971). Trade and technical journals actively report progress in this critical area of information system development. The objective of this current research and standards work is to reduce the costs of installing a data management system at the outset, and to obviate technological and applications obsolescence that could discourage any initial excursions of management into massive data management projects, which will (most observers note) be required to counter increasingly complex operational requirements. Although the reader should be aware that some technical background is needed to follow the trends described here, he will find that whatever attention he devotes to them now will be rewarding in the future.

Error Control Security, and Privacy

There are high error rates in most data-handling systems. Such errors may arise at input/output and/or processing stages, and if not controlled carefully can lead to serious output errors. Often "correctly" produced output is misleading or incomprehensible to the recipient because of cryptic abbreviations, unfamiliar formats, or incorrect assumptions about the nature and accuracy of the data-processing operation. Wide acceptance of automated data-processing demands that such errors be removed.

For example, a 4-year study at the University of Pennsylvania Hospital indicated that of the average ten independent transaction steps in processing blood-test data the probability of error was 1 to 2 per cent (per transaction). Since these probabilities are (roughly) additive, the chances were about 20 per cent (1 in 5) that a test report would be erroneous in one or more details.[3] The correct test could be reported to the wrong patient, the wrong test to the correct patient; tests could be forgotten, unnecessary tests run, and so on. The extreme actions required to reduce this error rate to acceptable levels included moving key punch machines to the laboratory itself, where lab technicians who conducted tests were responsible for entering the data, verifying test results, and identifying patients. (Raymond *et al.*, 1971.)

Similarly, studies at one insurance company showed that 5 per cent of all transaction cards punched contained one or more errors—even after verification. This rate was reduced to 0.2 percent by replacing key punch equipment with more sophisticated input terminals that could edit input, correct immediately, and identify terminal operators who were making errors, a feature easily automated on the new equipment. (Young, 1971.)

In both cases, the ability to isolate the source and type of error in the processing stream and to correct it at its source of responsibility was a major improvement strategy.

Professional systems designers always devote special attention to input and output editing, using computer tests to detect a wide range of error types. A commercial data-processing computer program, for example, may devote 80 per cent of program lines to input and output editing to assure that few errors enter the system, and that if they do they do not lead to unacceptable output. Such caution, although costly, is justified by both the economics of system protection and erroneous later action based on falsehood.

Usually the system designer must be thoroughly familiar with the practical details of the application at hand and its distribution of probable errors (often gained historically) to write such error-detecting routines. Thus, to design a retail sales application, the designer usually needs some retail sales experience to anticipate common errors, frauds, and special sys-

[3]Strictly, the probability of an erroneous report in which one or more independent elements has an error probability of 0.02, is $1 - (0.98)^n$, where n is the number of report elements. For $n = 10$, that probability is 0.183. Raymond *et al.*, provide average figures for illustration, in which n varies from test to test. Clearly, as n increases, the probability of obtaining a report correct in all particulars approaches zero.

tem demands. Such specialization has become evident in the employment market.

Security of the information system and its files also requires attention to:

1. Hardware malfunctioning
2. Environmental hazards, such as power supply variation, dirt, moisture, vibration, air conditioner failure, magnetic fields, and strong radio or radar signals that can cause processing failures or file loss
3. Disaster protection, such as precautions and emergency procedures against fire, flood, explosion, riot, vandalism, structural failures at the computer site, and similar catastrophies
4. Human intervention, carelessness, or sabotage.

Programmer and operator error, by mistake or intent, unauthorized file access or alteration, tapped communication links, and similar activities have been known to produce financial loss (embezzlement, loss of critical decision data, etc.) or system malfunctions that halt or incorrectly alter ongoing operations.

Random system audits, separation of operator, programmer analyst, librarian, maintenance, and user functions to pinpoint responsibility, and several levels of duplicate program and file copies are common precautions in well-run information systems.

For example, duplicate copies of files may be created hourly, daily, weekly, and monthly, and stored in different physical locations so that operations can at least be partially recovered without delay. Similar maintenance of transaction files or original documents for an interim period permits reconstruction of current master files from backup files in case one or more levels of file duplicates is lost. Alternate available backup hardware, identical with one's own configuration or compatible with it (say, a larger system that will accept a smaller system's programs and files) is desirable in case of hardware disaster. Unique hardware configurations are often avoided for this reason, even though some efficiency may be sacrificed thereby for the sake of security.

To illustrate, when a well-known mail order house burned to the ground in the mid-1960's, only the programs and magnetic tapes containing customer and vendor records were saved. With these data and the use of alternate computer facilities, the firm promptly resumed operations. Customers did not know of the disaster, except for a slight delay they experienced in receiving orders. Critical customer mailing lists were intact. Without program and file processing backup, plus the saved current customer and inventory files, the firm would have failed or suffered serious financial loss.

Privacy, as opposed to security, refers to the individual's protection from unauthorized access and use of files he may not wish to share with others, as well as the individual's interest in monitoring entries made in such files for necessary uses.

Credit, payroll, bank, medical, legal, police, income tax, and similar data sources are usually considered of individual as well as of organizational and social interest, so a balance must be struck between the demands of the individual and those of the group.

Thus, privacy protection requires many security precautions plus policies that strike a compromise between private and public interest.

Discussion of this topic involves many legal and social questions beyond our present scope. However, several excellent surveys of the subject exist. Hoffman (1969) summarizes security and privacy precautions and their implications; the Spring Joint Computer Conference (1967) was devoted to the subject; Hamilton (1967) surveys security problems from a commercial viewpoint, as does Greene (1966); Westin (1967), provides legal background. Brown (1967), details wire-tapping and other electronic invasion methods, and Fair (1966) speculates on the ultimate future of corporate data bank construction and competitive data collection as diplomatic and military intelligence methods move into commerce. Beardsley (1972) provides a computer security survey, with bibliography.

Finally, it should be pointed out that input/output and processing errors as well as security and privacy problems usually increase drastically as information systems move to communication-oriented, geographically dispersed configurations—the current technological trend.

In such dispersed networks, interception of transmissions and surreptitious file perusal or alteration are easier, whereas user identification and control are more difficult. Communications lines can be monitored, a user code or password thus obtained, and then direct entry into the system may be used to scan memory content, capture programs, or even alter a computer's supervisory functions—often without detection unless military-level security measures are invoked to thwart such intrusions.

An interesting result of such computer security and privacy dilemmas is the increasing use of cryptographic and similar techniques in commercial data transmission and storage, following diplomatic and military precedents. Girsdansky (1971) provides a survey of this topic, with references.

THE TACTICAL LEVEL

The subject of this section is treated elsewhere in this book by Professor Starr, so only a brief discussion follows.

The tactical level is the realm of operations research and management science techniques. Optimization, simplification, and selection methods, the definition and diagnosis of systems problems, and scrutiny of their implementation and treatment are professional concerns here.

Formulating goals and effectiveness measures can cause major problems. For example, in the game of football it is not sufficient for a team to know it will win by getting the highest score by the end of the four quarters: both teams must also know how the components of that score are rated and combined. Thus, if touch downs bring 6 points, and field goals bring 3, the total weighted score may be computed (as it is) by knowing how many of each have been attained. One may guess, however, what a coach would do if the weights were reversed, making field goals more valuable than touchdowns. Certainly the game itself, the techniques and skills required to win, would change. Kickers would be more valuable than runners, and tactics on the field would be graded differently too.

Such effects hold for plan selection and organizational evaluation in all goal-directed organisms, although the more complex the organization, the more difficult the choice of measures. If a concensus cannot be reached on traditional or clearly desired results or if measures are not independent and additive (as they seldom are in complex organizational structures) the choice of measures is critical.

Effectiveness measures may be incorrectly chosen, leading to bizarre decision-making schemes and action; they may be inconsistent, unstable, in conflict, absent, or not apparent. Policies cannot be implemented or administered under such conditions. Worse, if side effects are not carefully evaluated, the plans put into effect may produce outcomes directly contrary to what is wanted.

Two examples will suffice. In the 1960's when officials placed a high premium on medical care in Saigon, construction of medical facilities spurted. Many construction workers came from the garbage collection crews, who received lower pay, thereby leaving garbage uncollected. The rat population then increased, epidemics of plague arose, and the population's general state of health deteriorated. The "rat effect" had not been rated as a negative measure. Again, as considerable money and resources are allocated to the fight against heart disease and cancer, the larger, older population will strain the social security budget and other sources of retirement income. Will longer life lead to extreme retirement poverty?

Hitch and McKean (1967) discuss such problems with both general and military illustrations. Other references are given therein. See also Hare, 1967, Chapter 8.)

THE STRATEGIC LEVEL

As we add the strategic level to the information system (Level *C* of Table 1 and Figure 13(3)), the range of problem types reaches its greatest potential. Here we often confront one-time decisions of great importance under conditions of almost total uncertainty. And, "interesting" problems are not the same from time to time.

As a consequence, the popular notion that global and infallible information systems or generalized automated question answering schemes can be developed at this level is an illusion.

For example, most strategic information organizations—government or private—may be compared to the daily newspaper's functional parts. The need to have at hand the background information that in all likelihood will be required for future fast-breaking stories is one point to consider. The question is, What specific information might be needed? To illustrate, the New York *Times* maintains dossiers on about 2.5 million "newsworthy" individuals. But the world's population is nearly 4 *billion*. Overnight one of the undocumented personal histories in the total may be critically needed, yet be absent from the files.

Since it is not possible to store files on all living individuals (items in the file) nor to update such a listing to account for births and deaths even if such storage volume were available, we see the first form of severe selection required at the strategic level, *item selection*.

A more subtle question is what *characteristics* of a particular item should be included for those items actually filed. Thus, suppose we create a file listing all the females in a given large organization, the objective being to screen this list for an "ideal" wife. We must first decide how to describe each female, physically, emotionally, intellectually, according to her family background, and so forth. The list of characteristics for even one girl could be infinite, but it cannot be in practice; we must select some descriptive items and reject others at the outset. The file designer interjects his value judgements, or those of his clients, in the file design choices and, once that selection has been made, it is not easily changed.

To illustrate, suppose one inquirer hopes to find girls in the file with small feet, an aspect of female beauty he personally admires. If the file designer excluded that attribute, the female file is of little use to our ardent inquirer; he must seek elsewhere for a small-footed mate. To go back and reconstruct the whole file for this one missing attribute would be prohibitively expensive, time-consuming beyond our inquirer's endurance, or even impossible.

As time passes, of course, not only do the items of interest change, but so do the interesting characteristics of a given item. It is patently hopeless to design a perfect wide-scope file content and structure that will usefully endure for all time, or, indeed, even be satisfactory to any large number of inquirers today.

Furthermore, consider the *relations* between or among items and their attributes in such a strategic file. The case becomes even more difficult, since the cross-reference categories of interest are hardly ever stable or obvious. Such multiple cross references, or data links, not only slow access times and congest memory facilities, but also must be known in order to be included in the data base.

In particular, a critical pattern of cross reference may be overlooked. The pieces of data input required to illuminate a time sequence of events, or a set of concurrent, geographically dispersed events may be available, but scattered in time and place throughout the information system. So, a "key" fact, unimportant by itself, is rejected to prevent information overload. The data base is not cross referenced to show a critical emerging pattern. Attention and action are lost.

The culprit is the scope of information and evaluation at the strategic level, and the large organization of men and equipment required to counter that load. The communication links are too long, too numerous, too subject to variable delay and uncoordinated filtering. (The many dotted lines in Figure 13(3) illustrate this point graphically.)[4]

[4]Winston Churchill often mistrusted the delays and filtering imposed by the complexity of his intelligence services, and therefore arranged to see the raw data inputs of a few selected field agents whom he trusted.

In early 1941, for numerous reasons, British Joint Intelligence held the belief that Hitler and Stalin would get together, that Germany would not invade Russia. It was not until June 5 that the JIC thought there was a real possibility of an invasion, not until June 12 that they were sure. (The invasion was on June 22, 1941.)

Churchill, however, had so decided in March, based on reports that three of the five Panzer divisions moving toward Greece and Yugoslavia had been re-routed to Poland after a peace agreement with Prince Paul of Yugoslavia, then had been quickly moved back to the Balkans when Yugoslavia revolted.

To Churchill that field report illuminated the whole Eastern scene and convinced him Hitler meant to invade Russia in May but that the Belgrade revolt would delay the Germans until June. He immediately arranged that warning be sent to Stalin. (Churchill, 1950, pp. 354–361.)

Comparing the newspaper and the intelligence service, we find only a few "cross-reference" organizational possibilities. We could, for example, organize our primary data input stations geographically, functionally, or by mission. Thus, we could (1) organize "desks" by country, i.e., the "Korean" desk, the "French" desk, or (2) organize by intellectual topics, i.e., the "economics" desk, the "political science" desk, or (3) organize by product or special topic, i.e., the "oil industry" desk, the "gold smuggling" desk. Most strategic intelligence systems use a geographic structure at the lowest level because of language, cultural, field agent control, and similar operational demands. These "vertical input sources" (see Figure 16) are then backed up by the "horizontal" movement and cross reference of both functional generalists, such as economists, and technical specialists, such as aircraft metallurgists. Similar structure may be found in corporate marketing and long-range planning staffs.

At some point, however, the shifting pattern of inputs must be assembled, or monitored as a whole, for "pictures" of importance to the users of the intelligence service. Hopefully, the "horizontal" cuts made through the input stream by the secondary functionalists and experts, and even cross communication among geographical desks, will reveal such important patterns. But when many diverse trends occur at once, their combined effects may not be sensed in time for action, regardless of organizational structure.

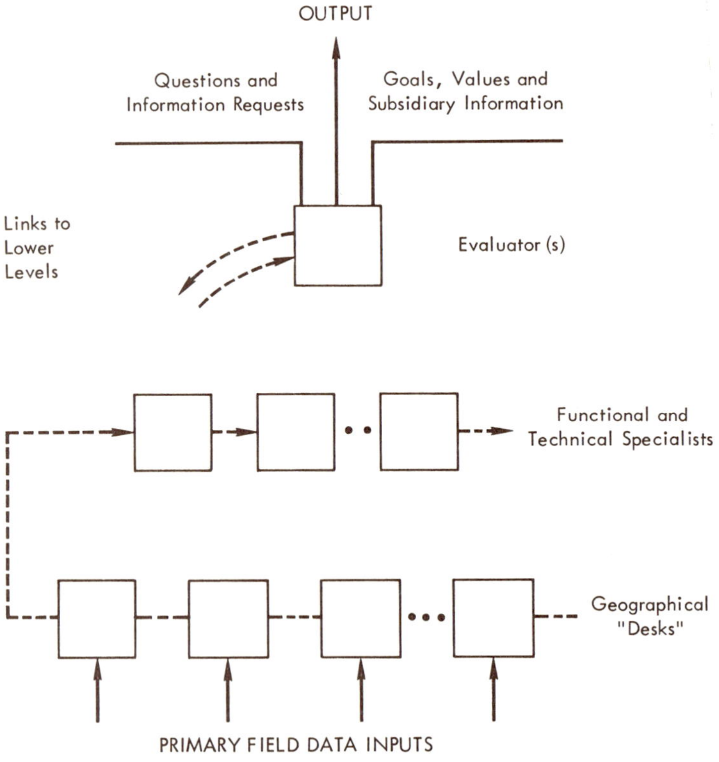

FIGURE 16. Schematic Diagram of Common Strategic Intelligence System Design. For clarity, links between levels are not shown in detail.

For example, many universities and other educational systems now use computer programs to assign students to classes and classes to instructors and space under the assumption that (1) courses offered, (2) student requirements or choices, (3) physical facilities, and (4) staff are given. (Often a variant problem is to determine staff and facility requirements far in advance, or otherwise study relationships among rigid constraints, those that can be altered, demand, and various measures of educational effectiveness.) Available computer routines usually can provide a matchup under given, currently accurate conditions. But to determine the given inputs far in advance requires strategic information.

In the early 1970's some universities suspended historical liberal arts language requirements, increased mathematical requirements in business and engineering, and allowed more Pass/Fail grades to count toward graduation. Student subculture also shifted to a more personal orientation. This combination of factors drastically altered student transitions from course to course, changes in major field, and the distribution of teaching loads. Often such patterns were not anticipated strategically, so assignment computations became worthless. Language courses were empty, yet many tenured faculty members were on the staff to teach them. Both business and engineering enrollment was off. Yet, psychology, sociology, criminology, anthropology, life-and-the-family, and similar courses were "unexpectedly" oversubscribed by factors as high as 10. Often there was no staff to handle the demand shift—much of which an institution may have brought on itself by a sequence of uncoordinated policy changes, fixed physical and employment constraints, and little appreciation for shifts in student values, often beyond the control of the institution but not beyond their strategic anticipation and evaluation. Many book publishers similarly found their inventories and print schedules scrambled by the same chain of events.

Finally, developing or even past patterns of input (or stored data) may not be uniformly *perceived* by evaluators, who are necessarily remote from the data sources (because they cannot encompass all the input detail personally, nor could any computer or communication system). Ten men look at a vague ink blot and come away with different interpretations of the same identical and specific physical picture. Ten men consult a physically identical file of females and cannot agree on criteria for selecting a wife.

Aberrations at this point include lack of realism, group or individual attention fixation, goal and value fixation, or, conversely, vascillation in attention, goals, or values.

For example, history may either teach or glue us to obsolete ways of thinking. As a young military officer between World War I and World War II, Charles DeGaulle wrote a book entitled *The Modern Army*. In it he described theories and strategies for the successful use of armored vehicles in future hostilities and predicted that such use would be decisive. His French superiors rejected DeGaulle's ideas, but his words were not lost on the German General Staff. Ironically, the German armored *blitzkriegs* in Poland, Czechoslovakia, *and* France during World War II followed DeGaulle's precepts almost to the letter.

A particular and unresolved question as it involves strategic intelligence evaluations is whether (or not) those who evaluate should also be responsible for carrying out action—e.g., should your auditor also keep your books, or would you bet on the long-range success of a family-arranged marriage as opposed to one you contracted for yourself? One side says the evaluator/operator is best; he knows the case and the operating details required to handle it. The other says no, the evaluator/operator can never be dispassionate because he seeks to justify his aims and later actions regardless of how they turn out. This conflict, for example, has continued for decades in the services of both U.S. and foreign intelligence operations. At any time the choice has been political, as it has also been in most industrial organizations.[5]

If all we have said is true, then, is it hopeless to design and operate a strategic management information system? The answer must be yes and no.

Any proposal for a system to handle all eventualities for all time clearly will fail. But a more limited strategic approach that permits flexibility, monitors a few major trends, and exploits selected historical and operating data is not only feasible, but desirable. The amount of detail to be carried at each of the three levels, (operating, tactical, and strategic) and the ratio of processing required at each level become critical questions in practical design, and can only be resolved by reference to the facts of a given case. Yet highly useful (if imperfect) strategic intelligence systems abound in both government and industry.

The following description of one industrial man/machine strategic intelligence system illustrates a typical application in 1971.

Employed successfully by IBM World Trade Corporation, the system combines two computerized data banks and a team of human evaluators. A large marketing data bank contains over a decade of detailed history on equipment rental and sales. Statistics on each product show country, customer, customer industry class, item serial number, and similar facts so organized that they may be correlated with economic indicators, industry intelligence, political forecasts, and the like. Mathematical forecasting models are used to analyze trends and produce product, industry, country, and similar sales projections.

An experienced team of product line, industry, and country specialists then sifts through this output, asking for alternate reports as necessary. External factors anticipated by this group, and patterns of change seen by them in technology, economics, politics, and customer use are used to modify the sales forecasts for both near-term and long-range sales estimates. When final agreement has been reached, the human results are again passed to the computer.

The next step compares the evaluators' estimates to a production and resource capability data bank that contains manufacturing standards, facilities available, personnel skills, and similar resource factors by location. This comparison shows what surpluses and shortages may be expected by resource type and location far enough in advance of need so that corrective

[5]In November, 1971, the various U.S. intelligence services were reorganized under the single coordination of Richard Helm, then Director of the Central Intelligence Agency. Helm was to report directly to President Richard Nixon.

"At first glance," noted analyst Joseph Kraft, "this looks like a mere administrative tightening. The producers of raw intelligence are simply being made more responsive to the consumers in the White House.

"But the Nixon Administration is no more free than most of the itch to enforce conformity. Unless very carefully watched, the new set-up could be one more device for destroying independent centers of analysis and information inside the government." (San Francisco *Chronicle*, November 11, 1971, p. 43.)

adjustments in the resource system can be made. The same data bank can also be used to create *pro forma* production schedules, cash flow analyses, personnel hiring and training plans, facilities, acquisition and capital requirements, and similar management reports.

Although the strategic planning system described above requires the expenditure of millions of dollars annually, such costs can be justified by the orderly management decision-making that can be based on this comprehensive man/machine analysis. The entire sequence of events above is repeated periodically (or on request) to create moving annual and 5-year advance "looks" into the future. Also, the data banks used are constantly updated, so accurate spot inquiries can be made to answer detailed management questions as they arise.

In the author's opinion, most of the interesting literature at this level comes from government practice. Kent (1949, reprinted 1965) provides a classic survey of intelligence problems and methods of organization. Hilsmann (1956) and Dulles (1963) offer other insights in the same vein.

Other sources include various management texts. Most of this management literature, however, centers on long-range planning methods and philosophy without discussing the inherent problem of communication and information handling in a complex organizational setting, nor on the even more difficult problems of pattern-recognition and realism that lie behind such work.

Regretfully, those sources that treat the technical problems of such information handling are either classified, too technical to discuss here, or simply unwritten. As indicated at the outset of this chapter, our knowledge, our theory, and our methods fail here to keep pace with the need.

Thus, the discussion above was limited to those topics of general interest, largely following Kent.

CONCLUSION

Nothing has been said here about specific economic trends, nor forecasted technique development in the information-handling fields. Purposefully so, since specific costs and specific methodology change so rapidly that detailed projections would be dated on publication.

However, a few long-range outlooks can be covered.

1. *The cost of communication and processing devices will decline.* Present economic "learning curves" in the semi-conductor industry run 50 to 70 per cent. Thus, when the production base doubles, a device formerly costing $10 costs $5 to $7. Furthermore, the power and complexity of the components is at the same time increasing, so end-product cost may be expected to decline more rapidly. Similar reductions appear at hand in the communication tariff field, making dispersed interconnected information systems more reasonable. (See Martin, 1971.)
2. *Greater attention will be paid to non-human data input and output devices.* Optical character and page readers, voice output, a coupling of information-handling and power control devices will become more wide-

spread, both to reduce cost and lessen error. Various graphical devices, such as light-emitting diodes and liquid crystals will appear in consumer as well as industrial products, such as automobiles. Advanced air traffic control demands such sensors, effectors, and displays for its success, as does modern medical practice. For example, Caceres, Weihrer and Pulliam (1971) state:

> Computer techniques with appropriate interfaces that automatically gather data directly from a patient for practical clinical use will, we believe, make the big difference and contribution to this century's medicine.

Fortune in 1970 forecast a $200 *billion* medical account in the Gross National Product by 1980, making medical service and care by then the largest single item. Funds and pressures for medical cost reduction should further foster the general trend noted above.

3. *The average person will be more inclined to automated information-handling procedures in the next decade because of both trends above.* As more electronic devices, and methods for their use, appear in his home, his car, his place of work, and in the services rendered to him, the citizen will come to expect more innovation at lower cost, and through the market and political processes to demand it. Reliable operation is a must before such acceptance can be gained, and market sources will become internationally competitive. (Over 50 per cent of semi-conductor production in 1970 was outside the United States.)
4. *The development of new "software" techniques, on the other hand, will not necessarily be so uniform, nor so bright.* Just as most of the developments mentioned above are at what we have called the operating level in the equipment area, we may also expect more technique production there, too. As we move to the tactical and the strategic levels, the problems of poorly structured data, information overload, and shifting data relevance persist, so less progress can be expected. Even at lower levels, high information densities must be overcome by techniques yet unknown. For example, Macy (1965), cites a medical experiment in which a 1-hour recording of several analog (continuous) measurements filled over eighty computer tapes as the measurements were converted to numbers for processing. Highly effective data-reduction techniques are needed even here to make wide use practical.

SUGGESTIONS FOR FUTURE READING

ASHBY, W. ROSS, *An Introduction to Cybernetics* (New York: John Wiley & Sons, 1963, Science Editions, originally Chapman & Hall, Ltd., London, 1956).

BEARDSLEY, C. W., "Is Your Computer Secure?" *IEEE Spectrum*, Vol. 9, No. 1 (January, 1972), pp. 67–78.

BECKMAN, F. S., "Computers," in *1972 Britannica Yearbook of Science and the Future* (Chicago: Encyclopaedia Britannica, Inc., 1971), pp. 223–227.

BOULDING, K. E., "General Systems Theory—The Skeleton of Science," *Manage-*

ment Science (April, 1956), pp. 197–208. Also available in Bower, J. B., and W. R. Welke, *Financial Information Systems* (Boston: Houghton Mifflin Co., 1968), pp. 7–19.

BOURNE, C. P., *Methods of Information Handling* (New York: John Wiley & Sons, 1963).

BROWN, R. M., *The Electronic Invasion* (New York: John F. Rider Publisher, 1967).

CACERES, C. A., A. L. WEIHRER, and R. PULLIAM, "Information Science Applications in Medicine," Chapter 10 in C. A. Cuadra (Ed.), *Annual Review of Information Science and Technology*, Vol. 6 (Chicago: Encyclopaedia Britannica Reviews, 1971), pp. 325–368.

CHASE, W. L., "The Use of Transaction Codes in Operating Report Preparation," *Management Accounting* (March, 1966), p. 61.

CHURCHILL, W. S., *The Grand Alliance*, Vol. 3 of *The Second World War* (Boston: Houghton Mifflin Co., 1950), pp. 354–361.

Codasyl Programming Languages Committee, *Report of the Data Base Task Group*, Association for Computing Machinery, 1133 Avenue of the Americas, New York, N.Y., 10036, $6.00, April, 1969. (Do not confuse with DBTG report dated October, 1969, which the April, 1971, report replaces.)

Codasyl Systems Committee, *Feature Analysis of Generalized Data Base Management Systems*, Association of Computing Machinery, 1133 Avenue of the Americas, New York, N.Y., 10036, $8.00, May, 1971.

Control Engineering, "In Coding It's Structure That Counts" (October, 1967), p. 100.

CUADRA, C. A. (Ed.), *Annual Review of Information Science and Technology*, Vol. 6 (Chicago: Encyclopaedia Britannica Reviews, 1971). (Previous volumes are available from the same publisher.)

DEUTSCH, K. W., *The Nerves of Government* (Glencoe, Illinois: The Free Press, 1966).

DODD, G. G., "Elements of Data Management," *Computing Surveys*, a publication of the Association for Computing Machinery (June, 1969), pp. 117–133.

DULLES, A., *The Craft of Intelligence* (New York: Harper & Row, 1963, Signet Books, 1965).

FAIR, W., "The Corporate C.I.A.," *Management Science* (July, 1966), pp. B489–B503.

FANO, R. M., *Transmission of Information* (New York: John Wiley & Sons, 1961).

FLORES, I., *Data Structure and Management* (New York: John Wiley & Sons, 1970).

FULTON, J., "Designing Identification Codes," *Automation* (October, 1964), p. 89.

GALLAGER, R. G., *Information Theory and Reliable Communication* (New York: John Wiley & Sons, 1968).

GIRSDANSKY, M. B., "Cryptology, The Computer, and Data Privacy," *IBM Research Reports*, Vol. 7, No. 4 (1971), reprinted in *Computers and Automation* (April, 1972), pp. 12–19.

GREENE, R. M., JR., *Business Intelligence and Espionage* (Homewood, Illinois: Dow Jones–Irwin, 1966).

HAMILTON, P., *Espionage and Subversion in Industrial Society* (London: Hutchinson, Ltd., 1967, and Humanities Press, New York, 1967).

HARE, V. C., JR., *Systems Analysis: A Diagnostic Approach* (New York: Harcourt, Brace & World, 1967).

HILSMANN, R., *Strategic Intelligence and Rational Decisions* (Glencoe, Illinois: The Free Press, 1956).

HITCH, C. J., and R. N. MCKEAN, *The Economics of Defense in the Nuclear Age* (Cambridge, Massachusetts: Harvard University Press, 1960, paper, Atheneum, 1967).

HOFFMAN, L. J., "Computers and Privacy: A Survey," *Computing Surveys,* a publication of the Association for Computing Machinery (June, 1969), pp. 85–103.

KENT, S., *Strategic Intelligence for American World Policy* (Princeton, N.J.: Princeton University Press, 1949, (reprint, paper, 1965).

LUCKY, R. W., J. SALZ, and E. J. WELDON, JR., *Principles of Data Communication* (New York: McGraw-Hill Book Co., Inc., 1968).

MACY, J. JR., "Analog-digital Conversion Systems," in R. W. Stacy and B. D. Waxman (Eds.), *Computers in Biomedical Research,* Vol. 2 (New York: Academic Press, 1965), pp. 3–34.

MARTIN, J., *Future Developments in Telecommunications* (New York: John Wiley & Sons, 1971).

METCALFE, H., *The Cost of Manufacturers and The Administration of Workshops, Public and Private* (New York: John Wiley & Sons, 1885).

PETERSON, W. W., *Error-Correcting Codes* (New York: John Wiley & Sons, 1961).

RAYMOND, S. *et al.,* "Laboratory Identification of Patient Identity," *Proc., 1971 Spring Joint Computer Conference,* Atlantic City (Montvale, N.J.: American Federation of Information Processing Societies, 1971), pp. 265–270.

SHANNON, C. E., and W. WEAVER, *The Mathematical Theory of Communication* (Urbana: University of Illinois Press, 1949).

SPRING, J., "Industry Product Codes are Required for Universal EDP Input," *The Office* (April, 1966), p. 102.

WESTIN, A., *Privacy and Freedom* (New York: Atheneum, 1967).

WIENER, N. *Cybernetics or Control and Communication in the Animal and the Machine* (Cambridge, Massachusetts: M.I.T. Press, paper, 1961, original edition, 1948).

YOUNG, D. V., "Sharing a Data Entry System," *Datamation,* (October 15, 1971), pp. 30–31.

ZIPF, G. K., *Human Behavior and the Principle of Least Effort* (Cambridge, Massachusetts: Addison-Wesley, 1949).

Systems and Progress

Adrian M. McDonough

Professor
Wharton School of Finance and Commerce
University of Pennsylvania

Typically, writers and practitioners have underestimated the difficulties associated with information and communication systems. Van Court Hare has not been typical. He has faced this problem squarely and the result is a realistic statement for those who would seek improvements in this area of management. In a short space, he has provided a useful structure and he has used this structure to demonstrate the depth and breadth of information planning and control. He has practiced what he preaches. There is much potential information in his statement.

The word "potential" is significant, for information must be tested at the point of receipt. Does the message inform—somebody? Does the receiver understand the problem? Of all the data that are collected, stored, processed, and sent to someone, how much is information? There is not a one-to-one relationship. Ten copies of the same newspaper do not give us ten times as much information. Running our Xerox operations around the clock does not necessarily make us rich with information. As Dr. Hare says, "The selection process itself is an information processing activity." In his own selecting, he has emphasized two scales: the scale of complexity and the scale of degree of uncertainty. Figure 17 shows these two scales at a right angle moving out from a zero point of no knowledge. We make progress as we are able to move out from the corner and handle problems of increasing complexity and uncertainty.

This is a simplified, but very mean-

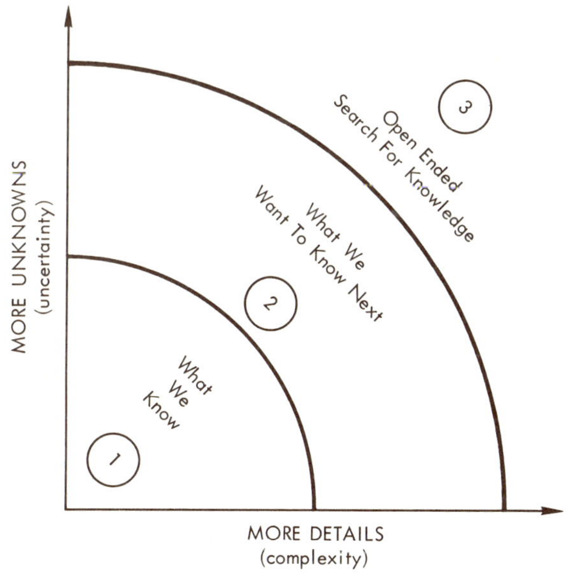

FIGURE 17. The Scales of Progress

ingful, way of looking at the past, present, and future of information and communications systems. The field of information study is not yet a science, it is not yet a technology. At this time, however, it is an aspiration of the highest priority. As such, it deserves the attention of the highest priority. Information is the complement of knowledge. To inform is to add to what we know. To want to know more and to be more confident in our knowledge is a common denominator of all disciplines. Van Court Hare has, in this chapter, generalized three types of information situations:

1. Operating Level—routine, deterministic data processing
2. Tactical Level—practical seeking of alternative methods and measures of effectiveness as support for management decisions.
3. Strategy Level—exploratory seeking of conceptual frameworks and selecting values and perspectives.

The three circled numbers in Figure 17 show the relationships of these levels to the scales of uncertainty and complexity. Realism means that we must work with the different situations at these three levels.

The figure shows, for example, that when we work with strategic problems we must be extremely selective because of the open-ended choices. At these extremities of our knowledge, we need a special type of information associated with the *questions* related to problem definition. At the lower level of operating systems, we already know the questions and are merely processing to get *answers* to these questions. The intermediate, or tactical, level involves a combination of tentative questions and tentative answers.

To repeat, it has been typical to underestimate the difficulties associated with information and communication systems. One of the problems has been that we have no way to think about measuring the size of our systems. The material presented by Dr. Hare on classifications and codes demonstrates this measurement problem. Consider the blocks on his diagrams and the lists of classifications and code numbers. Even though these are examples, the number of identified items is large. Item count, however, is not enough. A system implies relationships and the real question is, How do we isolate and measure relationships? Any relatively small number of system items has the potential of an astronomical set of relationships—for example, 48 pieces of data in a file has the potential for producing 276 trillion different reports. The fear of being drowned in reports is sufficient reason to carefully select any classifications and codes.

Irwin Bross has said that, "Classification is a prerequisite to measurement." If we want to put data on scales and use such scales to support decisions, the scales must first be identified. This is often a difficult and tedious job. There is a tendency to shy away from this work and to concentrate on the processing—even though the classifications of input data are not understood or tested.

It is no wonder that there has been so much dissatisfaction with the results of recent information analysis. Too much has been expected too soon. Great expectations, unfulfilled, can make even the most talented analyst appear stupid.

This situation is most apparent at the level of strategic systems design. Dr. Hare has stated it well:

> The popular notion that global and infallible systems, or generalized automated question answering schemes, can be developed easily or inexpensively at this level is in error. . . . As we move to the tactical and strategic levels the problems of poorly structured data, information overload, and shifting data relevance persist, so less progress can be expected.

A basic question could be asked: Why bother attempting to develop these more sophisticated systems? Life is certainly more simple and comfortable in the corner representing the operational level in Figure 13. Why not stay there?

The answer is quite clear. If society wants what it calls progress, it cannot stay in the corner. Rather, society as a whole will encourage the search for new knowledge and the accompanying information and communications systems.

This context has been cited to give an approximation of the extent to which information and communication systems affect our society. Such systems are no longer some small part of our overall activities. Rather, these are our primary activities, directly or indirectly. Activities of this magnitude do not grow overnight. We have been moving in this direction for some time.

Today we have a $1,000 billion Gross National Product and over half of that sum is accounted for by salaries and other monies that are paid to white-collar personnel. This is work that in no way involves the use of muscles. For the first time in history over half of our labor force is in the brainwork, or knowledge, industry. For the first time in history white-collar workers outnumber the total of farm and factory workers. This in itself is a significant change—but the predictions are even more interesting. Recent estimates indicate that in a few decades only 2 per cent of all Americans, as farmers and factory production workers, will be able to produce all the food and manufactured goods the whole population will need.

We are, at last, in a position to break out of the restraints that have forced us in the past to give most of our attention to the production of food, shelter, and clothing. People who assume that work is limited to the production of food, shelter, and clothing are now predicting all sorts of calamities. These are the people who are pointing out that the solution is to train people to use their coming leisure. Forced leisure can very well be necessary for dislocated blue-collar workers, but it will not be the case for the increasing majority of white-collar workers. This is the group that I have labeled as producers of knowledge.

Assume that even the above-mentioned 2 per cent of workers no longer are needed on the farm and in the factories. In other words, assume the extreme case wherein all food and products are produced untouched by human hands. The question then is, Just what will occupy the attention of all people who work for a living?

A large part of the answer to this question depends on our ability to recognize that the production of knowledge can itself be used to create new job positions. Let me give some evidence that this movement is already well under way.

The emphasis on computers and on data processing today is but a superficial indicator of the shift to the production of knowledge. More fundamental evidence is shown in the record that some $75 billion per year are being spent for salaries to research and technical personnel. Another $75 billion goes to executive and supervisory salaries. And, $200 billion dollars are paid at the clerical white-collar level in the processing of 150 billion paper transactions per year.

All of these efforts are associated with the need to know—with knowledge in the specific sense. These figures do not give the whole picture of the scope of production of knowledge for they do not include the white-collar workers in government, education, or in the communication services industry. When these positions are included, the total dollars already being paid for "need to know" add to over half of our Gross National Product.

In a society that is well housed, clothed, and fed, the "need to know" marketplace can be as large as the curiosity of that society. Einstein said that imagination is more important than knowledge. I am sure he meant that imagination sparked by curiosity is the means to achieving new knowledge. He was emphasizing the additions to knowledge as compared to the existing body of knowledge.

The heart of the matter is the universe of human curiosity. Curiosity is expressed in terms of "want to know," and "want to know" can be scaled from extreme "need to know" to ephemeral "nice to know." The largest market in the United States is the market for information. It is in this market that Van Court Hare has identified the categories of operational, tactical, and strategic systems. It is at these levels that progress will be made.

What are the scales of progress? What are their magnitudes? For example, there can be Assumption *A:* We know very much, and there is little left to learn. There can also be Assumption *B:* We know very much, but this is just a small part of what there is to know.

Under Assumption *A* there is little, if any, incentive to plan for a future of expanded effort in building better systems. Under Assumption *B* the case is the opposite. Opportunities are great and investments in information-seeking systems are justified.

With physical muscle work decreasing and the number of white-collar jobs increasing, Assumption *B* has certain attractions. (Assumption *A*, of course, has the attraction of nostalgia for the past.) If we can extrapolate the recent past, Assumption *B*, applied in moderation, is a necessity for our society. Challenges must be moderated by the magnitude of the task. Frustration, caused by underestimating difficulties, can be replaced by a more realistic step-by-step approach to progress.

Dr. Hare has not only identified problems, he has spelled out opportunities—for problems are the opportunities for progress. The problems he identifies will require more and more information analysis—but this is the way white-collar jobs are created. This is the labor market of the future. When was the last time you saw someone digging a ditch by hand? We will dig deeper and wider. Stronger foundations will be laid for information and communications systems.

We need better ways (early warnings) to identify priority problems. Surveillance refers to those selected activities by which a better perspective of an organization and its environment can be obtained. If we do not know where we want to go, it does not matter how we get there. Surveillance has its own information requirements. These requirements are the leading edge of the strategic analysis for an organization. There is much opportunity for improvements at this level, and improvements here can benefit work at each succeeding level down to operating systems.

Classifications determine the useful vocabulary of any information system. All information depends on classification, yet we have very little knowledge about how to design good classifications. Classification is the very beginning of organizing facts and, therefore, of any system. It is appropriate that the problem of classification be looked at much more carefully.

A particular type of classification is involved in selecting criteria. Criteria are the words in which standards are expressed. To measure, we must have standards. Selecting standards is a prerequisite to setting priorities among the varieties of information that can be produced. Such analysis can provide challenging jobs for talented people for a long time.

One other example of opportunity and work to be done is associated with documentation. It is not enough to make progress by adding to knowledge. That knowledge must be preserved and communicated. Documentation involves explaining the problem, the information requirements, and the logic of the processing systems. The amount of effort now going into the search for ways of preserving knowledge indicates that we are not very advanced. Many times we just give up and start all over again rather than trying to use existing documentation.

These are a few examples of the ways that problems can be viewed as progressive opportunities. There are many more that have not yet come into view.

It has taken all of our recorded history to achieve our present state of physical well-being. Just as the capacity of physical energy is now being organized to benefit everyone, so the power and the pleasure of knowledge can be available to provide the energizing force of the future. This is my interpretation of Van Court Hare's statement. We are at an important point of change in history and he has not let it go by unnoticed.

Are There No Behavioral Variables?

Rocco Carzo, Jr.

Professor, and Chairman
Department of Management
School of Business Administration
Temple University

This writer has an unpleasant task. He must critique the work of an author who has earned credits for outstanding performance in the past but has done a poor job in meeting the challenge of this volume. Generally, the chapter contains no issues and few viewpoints and falls short of presenting a comprehensive view of information systems.

Rather than survey all the issues that could have been covered, this paper will dwell on the behavioral one. This issue was chosen because it is missing from much of the literature on information systems and it should be included. Characteristically, Van Court Hare's paper also has this deficiency. He describes, prescribes, and projects characteristics of information and communication systems without referring to behavior variables. In the past, when technological developments and behavioral science moved along different paths, this condition may have been understandable. Contemporary developments, however, indicate convergence and there is no valid reason for discussing one without referring to the other.

In the literal sense, the title "Information and Communication Systems" does connote a merger between technical and human variables—that is, between the transmission and understanding of information for decision-making and action. Despite this connotation, Dr. Hare chooses to belabor the technical side by spending considerable time on matters such as codes, files, and security.

If there is to be consolidation between technical and human considerations, design of information systems and organization design must become a single process. Several problem areas have been selected to illustrate this need for a merger of information and organization design. The areas, listed below, are not exhaustive and they are in need of theoretical development and research.

1. The author's approach, classifying information needs according to system levels, is commendable. In this regard, he seems to follow the works of Deutsch (1966), Boulding (1956), and Thompson (1967). Thompson, for example, identifies technical, managerial, and institutional levels, which are very similar to Van Court Hare's operating, tactical, and strategic levels.[1] After making this breakdown, Dr. Hare generalizes his material by implying that information needs are the same for all organizations at these levels. His presentation would have been more meaningful if he had classified the material further to reflect differences in the technology and the environment of organizations. It is understandable, for example, that the information needs and the design of systems will differ depending on the degree of interdependence (pooled, sequential, and reciprocal, according to Thompson) among organizational units and whether task environments are homogeneous or heterogeneous, and stable or rapidly shifting.

2. Another factor that should be critical to the determination of information needs is the style of management used by an organization. The system designer would need to know the answer

[1]Thompson, James D., *Organizations in Action* (New York: McGraw-Hill Book Co., 1967).

to questions such as: Does the organization plan to use a centralized or decentralized management style? Will operational personnel participate in the decision process? Then, there are structural considerations involving span of control, line and staff, boundaries, a tall or a flat configuration, and departmentation. Of course, these considerations are not mutually exclusive, but they are dependent. Accordingly, the designer is obliged to take a total or systems approach when performing his task.

3. Still another consideration involves the social psychological phenomena of power. Oftentimes, people who process information acquire power that is greater than the administrative authority allocated to their position. They become powerful because others are dependent on them for accurate and timely appraisal of facts. March and Simon (1958, pp. 165–166) call this condition "uncertainty absorption."

> Uncertainty absorption takes place when inferences are drawn from a body of evidence and the inferences, instead of the evidence itself, are then communicated.
>
> By virtue of specialization, most information enters an organization at highly specific points. Direct perception of production processes is limited largely to employees in a particular operation on the production floor. Direct perception of customer attitudes is limited largely to salesmen. Direct evidence of the performance of personnel is restricted largely to immediate supervisors, colleagues, and subordinates.
>
> In all of these cases, the person who summarizes and assesses his own direct perceptions and transmits them to the rest of the organization becomes an important source of informational premises for organizational action. The "facts" he communicates can be disbelieved but they can only rarely be checked. Hence, by the very nature and limits of the communication system, a great deal of discretion and influence is exercised by those persons who are in direct contact with some part of the "reality" that is of concern to the organization. Both the amount and the locus of uncertainty absorption affect the influence structure of the organization.
>
> Because of this, uncertainty absorption is frequently used, consciously and unconsciously, as a technique for acquiring and exercising power.[2] Given the effect of uncertainty absorption and the importance of the influence structure on organizational affairs, it seems appropriate that the systems designer show some concern for desired outcomes or the directions contemplated by managers.

4. The author gives no recognition to statistical sampling techniques. Is the reader to assume that the system must gather and analyze all available information? He seems to answer this question in the negative but he offers a "strategic approach which permits flexibility in monitoring a few major trends," which hardly sounds like a sampling.

There is also a problem with respect to the cost of information. Is data gathering, analysis, and dissemination justified because it facilitates order? In his description of one strategic planning system, the author says that the expenditure of millions of dollars was justified because it produced "orderly management decision-making." Although a cost-benefit analysis may be inferred from this statement, its vagueness and the other parts of the text leave doubts that this was the intent.

The costs involved are not restricted to economic costs. Behavioral scientists would argue that there also are social costs. Imposed structure, rules, procedures, and supervision, when carried to extremes, tend to produce malfunctioning and indifferent attitudes. In effect, they argue, the rules or prescribed patterns of behavior become the

[2]James G. March and Herbert A. Simon, *Organizations* (New York: John Wiley & Sons, 1958).

ends rather than the means to achieve objectives.

The designer, then, must make some assessment of the costs and benefits before prescribing the procedures and structure of any system. The statistical technology is well developed, especially Bayesian statistics. The behavioral technology is less well developed but this condition does not diminish the importance of behavioral considerations.

DISCUSSION QUESTIONS

1. List and discuss some of the drawbacks and benefits of codes.
2. Point out at least five difficulties associated with information and communication systems. What has been done (or can be done) to overcome these problems?
3. Why does Dr. Hare divide information situations into three types (or levels)? Does this categorization actually help to understand information? Is it operational for management?
4. Why must information systems become sophisticated?

9

Organizational Change

Kenneth D. Mackenzie

Edmund P. Learned Distinguished Professor
School of Business Administration
University of Kansas

INTRODUCTION

The brilliant essay on social change by Alvin Toffler (1970) contains many examples and speculations about the acceleration of change in industrialized societies.[1] He says:

> . . . if the last 50,000 years of man's existence were divided into lifetimes of approximately sixty-two years each, there have been about 800 such lifetimes. Of these 800, fully 650 were spent in caves. . . .
>
> Only during the last seventy lifetimes has it been possible to communicate effectively from one lifetime to another—as writing made it possible to do. Only during the past six lifetimes did masses of men ever see a printed word. Only during the last four has it been possible to measure time with any precision. Only in the last two has anyone anywhere used an electric motor. And the overwhelming majority of all the material goods we use in daily life today have been developed within the present, the 800th lifetime. (p. 14).

It is easy to find comments today about the changes occurring in the quality and quantity of our scientific output, our social arrangements, technology, ideology, and focuses of concern. The problems of change seem so compelling and there are so many of them to deal with that many disciplines and areas of concern have developed in this 800th lifetime. There are simply too many problems to do more than just mention a few as illustrations. One can worry about the process of invention and the diffusion of invention (Rogers, 1962). One can study technological change and the economics of technological change (Lave, 1966 and Salter, 1966). One can study attitude change (Coleman, 1964) and changes in interpersonal be-

[1]The research in this chapter was sponsored by Canada Council Grant S70–0022 and National Research Council of Canada Grant A-7413 while I was at the University of Waterloo, Waterloo, Ontario, Canada. The descriptions of adoption and diffusion processes are a short summary of the joint work I share with Professor I. Bernhardt.

havior (Bennis, 1966; Blake and Mouton, 1968; Argyris, 1965), and Lerner's (1958) concepts of empathy. One can worry about resistance or being a change agent (cf. Spicer, 1952). A vast amount has been written about attempts to provide frameworks with which to structure theories of social change. Among these are the works of Appelbaum (1971), Moore (1963, 1968), and Smelser (1968). There are subfields within the area of social change, including the psychology of creativity, the change agent (Hoffer, 1951 and 1964), field studies of industrial firms undergoing technological change (Burns and Stalker, 1961 and Woodward, 1965), brand switching in marketing, consumer behavior (Nicosia, 1966), achievement motivation (McClelland, 1961; and Atkinson, 1964), guerrilla warfare, manpower planning (Lewis, 1969), political change, and many more. The few cited here are just a tiny sample. In fact, it is difficult to find any social science in this 800th lifetime that is not concerned with change of some sort. Furthermore, it is inconceivable that any change studied by any social scientist would not eventually have an impact on an organization.

Organizational changes are not limited to the 800th lifetime and Western civilization. As phenomena, they are more universal and pervasive than a response sequence activated by a particular technological, ideological, cultural, or military event. Organizational change is studied primarily because it concerns the human capacity to make social adaptations at a pace far more rapid than biological adaptations occur. But in our recent past, the importance of the problem has increased, probably because of the current trend toward large organizations, with strong intra-organizational and inter-organizational interconnections. Failure of such organizations to adapt affects more people than ever before, outside as well as within the organization. Many types of organizations have a vested interest in promoting change. There is a sense that changing moral and social values and problems of public order are related to the capability of organizations to manage change. There is a sense that the pace of change itself is increasing.

The pervasiveness of change, the "constant" impacts on organizations of "external" changes and the effects of "internal" organizational changes on "external" organizations make studies of change fascinating to the social theorist. Theories are needed to make economical use of the myriad facts and relationships. The reduction of complex phenomena to systems of causal or logical relationships provides frameworks for analysis and diagnosis. And at any given time there are many contending theories and theorists. Their debate and application of scientific methods tend to sharpen issues that discredit some theories; limit their applicability, and subject most to an almost Darwinian struggle for survival. Theories are pursued in the belief that they help organize analysis and eventually will aid in adaptation. One of the most useful effects of theory is the realization that causes of an event may be multiple and some of these are likely to be different from those assumed. Theory can also force critical distinctions in concept and measurement.

For example, small technological innovations can have enormous effects and large ones can have a relatively minor impact. L. Sharp (1967) reports the devastating social impact caused by the introduction of steel axes to the Yir Yoront group of Australian aboriginals. The axe was technically only a substitute for polished stone axes hafted in short handles. "The result was a mental and moral void which foreshadowed the collapse and destruction of all Yir Yoront culture, if not, indeed, the extinction of the biological group itself" (p. 85–86).

The impact of the introduction of the steel axes was socially "like a bullet smashing into a pane of glass" (Toffler, p. 300). It shattered the Yir Yoront culture. What would, to us, be regarded as a very minor technological change had set off processes that ended in organizational collapse. Conversely, there are examples of major changes having relatively minor effects on primitive societies. One such is the adoption of social rules imposed by foreigners on Palau (Useen, 1967). Major changes also can have major effects, as illustrated by the introduction of the horse to the North American Plains Indians. The horse transformed their way of life in two generations. They became warlike raiders after centuries as fairly peaceful farmers. Mansfield (1961), on the other hand, has shown that simple and rational decision processes can account for the rate at which producers adopt producer durables, which are often major technological innovations.

Many innovations are not adopted, some are adopted and then discarded, some are adopted after the innovation has been altered to be more acceptable. Some innovations are competing with counter innovations. About every conceivable combination of innovation type and adopter response has occurred. To make sense out of all these cases, it is necessary to consider the concept of change itself more carefully.

THE CONCEPT OF CHANGE

Some changes can probably be discussed solely in terms of the physical properties and laws that are incorporated into a device or innovation. However, such an approach would fail to explain why in some cases neolithic tribes may adopt a change like a steel axe easily and some like the Yir Yoront, might not. Another problem with such an approach is that the "innovativeness" of any innovation is relative to the adopting group. For example, it may be easier for a professor of business administration to adopt operations research techniques than for a small building contractor. A technological description of an innovation also fails to distinguish differences in the knowledge required to use an apparatus from the technology of the apparatus itself. For example, many intelligent people use the computer without much knowledge of how a computer works. Functional illiterates can use solid-state color television and persons ignorant about radar can use it to navigate. Many devoted and intelligent people are employed to reduce systematically the impacts of technological change on the user. Much of what we use is "designed by geniuses to be used by morons." Finally, a technological description of a change may ignore the often major social changes that can result from the use of an innovation.

It would seem more reasonable to take care to define a change in terms of the changes in *actual behavior* of the adopter of the change. Given an innovation, it is obvious that the change in the adopter's behavior will vary with the individual and the circumstances under which it is introduced. The change in behavior will be called the *nature of the change.* The nature of the change is defined with respect to what it replaces. If the behavior is described in terms of activities, a change may result in some old activities being dropped, some remaining unchanged, and some new ones being performed. For the adopter there will be economic and social consequences. Calculating these consequences will involve uncertainty because the precise nature of the change may be unclear to him and, given the nature of the changes, he may be uncertain about their consequences. These uncertainties create risk in his mind. If the anticipated consequences are clearly negative, he will resist the change. If the changes appear to be such that their consequences will be advantageous, he may adopt with little resistance. If the consequences are perceived to be generally advantageous but, under some circumstances, detrimental, the potential adopter may set out to investigate the consequences more carefully. This search reduces the risk associated with the decision to adopt or reject. As the search process proceeds, both the nature of the change and its consequences may vary. Such search behavior may take a very long time and may involve considering both economic advantage and social legitimacy. In the course of time the innovation itself or that which it replaces may also change. Different potential adopters differ in how they search for consequences, in their awareness and assessment of the nature of change, and in the time it takes them to adopt changes. Change agents, relationships with other adopters and potential adopters, the norms of the adopting group, and the social structure of the group and the particular social status of the adopter will affect the adoption process. Rogers (1962) presents a useful summary of those many effects. Processes by which the adoption decision of one is related to those of other potential adopters are called *diffusion processes.* It is very important to emphasize that the individual adoption process is, in part, determined by the potential adopter's social group. One of the effects of the larger group is to alter the perceived nature and consequences of a particular innovation.

The nature of the change can be divided into two classes: (1) dropping old activities, and (2) adding new activities. The consequences of these two types of changes tend to be evaluated differently. If there are either economic or social benefits and costs associated with each change, the potential adopter will tend to *differentially evaluate* them. An adopter is more certain about economic or social benefits and costs associated with those activities to be dropped than he is about new ones. Consequently, to reduce risk, the potential adopter tends to discount the benefits more than the costs associated with the new activities. Benefits tend to be discounted more than costs for both types of change and those benefits involving new activities are discounted more than the old to-be-dropped activities. The adopter acts as if he has a "safety margin," which acts to reduce the net benefits to lessen the probability of making a mistake by adopting.

The line of argument suggests ways to reduce resistance to change. An obvious method is to attempt to reduce the nature of the change. This can be done by planning and anticipating changes so that the nature of the change is minimized. For example, if a university wishes to install a new computer system, the smaller the number of programming changes required by the user, the less likely he is to resist it. To do this, many specialists work very long hours to work out the "bugs" in the system and devise methods to make the new system maximally compatible with the old. If many changes are contemplated, specialists are used to minimize the nature and consequences of such changes. Efforts are simultaneously made to reduce the conversion costs of the user by attempting to educate him, to maintain parallel facilities during the transition, or to provide direct consultative help.

Another procedure is to introduce an innovation in stages. By segmenting the innovation, there is a reduction in the nature of the change. The result is a lower differential evaluation and less search by the potential adopter. If the first stage has been adopted, and the change is considered beneficial to the adopters, there is less differential evaluation associated with the second stage, and so on. Thus, it is possible to secure adoption in a sequence of steps faster than if the entire innovation were introduced as a single change. Slow escalation of the Vietnam conflict could be viewed as an example of this strategy. However, such a strategy can backfire if the end result is perceived to be objectionable. This may affect the chances of introducing yet another change by the same change agent. In short, the change agent himself is evaluated positively or negatively with respect to his credibility in calculating benefits and costs.

Another strategy is to arrange for the nature of the change to affect different people differently so that most are only dealing with a part of the change, and different persons are with different parts. This reduces the differential evaluation for each. It may make it harder for resistance to organize and may create an illusion that there are many adopters, which tends to reduce the social costs of adopting for each one by spreading these costs and benefits unevenly over more adopters. In an organization in which there are "specialisms" but not specialists structured rigidly in a mechanistic organization structure (cf. Burns and Stalker, 1961), it is easier to cope with change by using this strategy. This strategy tends to reduce both the nature and consequences of a change for each individual.

The rapid-style changes in the Los Angeles area furniture industry have fostered the development of many small manufacturers who specialize in manufacturing furniture components. Cut and dimension stock manufacturers produce pieces to be later used in drawers, tables, chests, and other items. Others assemble frames for upholstered furniture. Some specialize in manufacturing round tapered table legs, others square tapered table legs, one in manufacturing seats for wooden furniture. There are many other specialists who assemble furniture components. The manufacturers maintain a large display warehouse where the different finished furniture pieces are displayed. All it takes to alter production from Early American furniture to Danish Modern is to make a list of component parts required, order them from the various specialists, and then assemble them. Many firms can change products overnight. A shift in style can result in different finishes and different parts. Because there are so many styles and so many shifts in style demanded by a large diverse population, man can continuously produce a special part—like bar stool seats (not the whole chair, just the seat)—over a long period of years. This specialist is an expert in gouging out the shape required by the human rear. If the style changes from Danish Modern to Spanish, he buys oak instead of walnut or teak from a specialty lumber broker and applies the old process to the new wood. He delivers the seats, which are then assembled by the chair manufacturer. An upholsterer would purchase new fabrics and spray the exterior wood component with a color consistent with the new style. The industry is further serviced by specialists in furniture design who "free lance." The existence of many specialities enables the Los Angeles area furniture manufacturers to be especially nimble in adapting to a rapidly changing and volatile market. Considering this industry as an organization, it is very "organic" in the Burns and Stalker (1961) use of the word. These observations were made in 1963. It is perfectly conceivable that one large manufacturing firm could do the same thing in one large facility where apparent economies of scale could be gained by applying modern computer and operations research techniques.

Another technique is to reduce the consequences of change by using specialists whose function is to absorb some of the risk and uncertainty. Many consulting firms have sprung up to help plan and introduce modern management techniques. This requires a lower investment in specialists (who are often high priced) and reduces the amount of change for each person. The consultants have consultants. Some firms have staff members who function as brokers or middlemen between innovators and adopters.

Another strategy in coping with change is to form committees or temporary subunits to analyze temporary problems that require research and planning. Such units may become institutionalized if the problems appear to be recurring. Examples are research and development groups.

There are many other techniques or combinations of techniques used to cope with change. The various strategies attempt to reduce or buffer both the nature and the consequences of a change for the adopter. Some work to reduce these for an individual and some across individuals to reduce the attendant repetition of organizational changes caused by individual changes. The particular strategy or combination of strategies varies with the situation. In every case it is important to understand the underlying idea of minimizing differential evaluation associated with changes.

It is often stated that one "cannot make an omelet without breaking eggs." Some persons may be hurt by change. Their skills may become obsolete or no longer required. The threat of change can evoke strong worker resentment, which can spill over to other working arrangements. Strikes, "work-to-rule," slowdowns, absenteeism, high turnover, sabotage, or political infighting may occur. The probability of change may force management to take greater care to institute due-process procedures regarding employment conditions and to rationalize training and retraining of employees and managers in order to reduce the differential evaluation of a change. That such humaneness also serves management's long-run self-interest makes it all the more likely to occur.

This section has focused on the problems of gaining acceptance of an innovation or change. The techniques can also be reversed to delay acceptance of change. At some point one may want to resist change in order to modify it. Many changes may appear unwise and one's ethics may require resistance. Changes may also be resisted in order to obtain policy or financial commitments (Woodward, p. 194, and pp. 222–224).

ORGANIZATIONAL CHANGES

So far the discussion has centered on the nature and consequences of change. The nature of a change has been described in terms of the alteration in behavior caused by an innovation and the consequences in terms of net benefit (economic and social) to the potential adopter. Adoption and diffusion processes have been discussed. The main point is that the evaluation of the nature of a change and its consequences to an individual is strongly affected by his social group membership. Following this line of reasoning, several strategies for gaining adoption of an innovation are suggested. These strategies derive from the central notion of minimizing differential evaluation.

The argument up to this point has been general and not directed specifically to the more precise descriptions of the processes of organizational change. In this section the discussion narrows to what is involved in an organizational change. We shall employ concepts derived from laboratory experiments that are precisely defined. Since key concepts such as structure have been used in so many ways, the usage in this paper will be confusing to some. The reader is cautioned to pay very close attention to the definition given here so as to avoid misreading what follows. It is helpful to introduce some rather simple notation in order to simplify the analysis.

An organization is a system containing, like all systems, parts, structures, and processes. Parts consist of groups of individuals or are the individuals themselves. The choice of what to consider the parts of an organization depends on the unit and purpose of analysis. Let a vector $X=(x_1, x_2, \ldots, x_i, \ldots, x_n)$ describe the list of the n parts. In the case of a 5-man group, x_1 is the way we designate the first person, x_2 the second, . . . and x_5 the fifth. The parts perform activities. The activities performed by each part determine its role. The role, although describing the behavior of a part, also carries with it normative expectations that it not only exhibits certain behaviors but also that it should behave in these ways. The role of a part may vary with experience and changing circumstances. Although roles are central to the analysis, they will be represented in patterns of role behaviors called structures and processes. We shall define structures and processes in terms of roles. For the purpose of discussion, let us assume that an organization, G, containing the n parts described by $X=(x_1, x_2, \ldots, x_i, \ldots, x_n)$, performs activities that can be catalogued or listed by a vector of activities, α, where for convenience we write $\alpha=(A_1, A_2, \ldots, A_\alpha, \ldots, A_\alpha)$. If there are twenty-five different activities in G, then $\lambda=25$. To define the role of a part, say, x_i, we ask whether x_i performed activity A_1, or A_2, . . . , finally to A_λ . If the answer is yes, x_i performed A_1 once, then we state $r_{i1}=1$. If x_i does not perform A_1, then $r_{i1}=0$. If x_i performs the αth activity three times then $x_{ia}=3$, and if he does not, $x_{ia}=0$. Thus we can define the role of each part by asking questions and tabulate all this information in a table or matrix, which is called a *role matrix*, R. The rows of the role matrix, R, designate the parts, X, and the columns designate the activities, α, such that the entry in the ith row and the αth column, designated r_{ia}, is 1 if x_i does a and 0 if x_i does not do a. If x_i performs a 5 times, $r_{ia}=5$. Matrix R looks like this:

Activities

		A_1	A_2	. . .	A_α	. . .	A_λ
	x_1	r_{11}	r_{12}	. . .	$r_{1\alpha}$	. . .	$r_{1\lambda}$
	x_2	r_{21}	r_{22}	. . .	$r_{2\alpha}$	. . .	$r_{2\lambda}$
	.	.	.		.		.
	.	.	.		.		.
$R=$Parts of G	.	.	.		.		.
	x_i	r_{i1}	r_{i2}	. . .	$r_{i\alpha}$	. . .	$r_{i\lambda}$
	.	.					
	.	.					
	.	.					
	x_n	r_{n1}	r_{n2}	. . .	$r_{n\alpha}$	. . .	$r_{n\lambda}$

Now suppose activity A_1 means that person x_1 sends a communication (verbal, written, body gesture, etc.) to person x_2 about sharing information. Suppose activity A_2 means that person x_2 sends a message to person x_1. If $r_{11}=1$ and $r_{21}=1$, then x_1 and x_2 exchanged information. If $r_{11}=1$ and $r_{21}=0$, then x_1 sends to, but does not receive a communication from, x_2. It is easy to see how one can examine R to define each of the $n(n-1)$ pair relationships between any two parts (x_1 to x_2, x_1 to x_3, x_1 to x_4, . . . , x_1 to x_n, x_2 to x_1, x_2 to x_3, . . . , x_2 to x_i, . . . , x_2 to x_n, . . . , x_n to x_1, x_n to x_2, . . . , x_n to x_i, . . . , x_n to x_{n-1}). Sometimes it is convenient to summarize all of this information contained in R in another table, Γ. Although R has n rows and λ columns, Γ has n rows and n columns. All the pairwise relationships derivable from R can be summarized in Γ.

If we can conceive of a channel of communication between two parts, say x_i and x_j, then we may speak of a communications channel between them as being made up of the ij^{th} *half-channel* from x_i *to* x_j and the ji^{th} half-channel from x_j to x_i. The degree of the interaction on the ij^{th} half-channel is Γ_{ij} and the degree of the interaction on the ji^{th} half-channel is Γ_{ji}. In many cases $\Gamma_{ij} \neq \Gamma_{ji}$. If the parts are individuals, we say $\Gamma_{ii}=0$. The value of Γ_{ij} corresponds to the entry in the role matrix, R, involving role i and the appropriate column representing an interaction with person j. If, in our example, $r_{11}=6$, then x_1 sent 6 messages to person 2 and $n_{12}=6$. We write, Γ, as:

$$\Gamma = \text{Sender} \quad \begin{array}{c|cccccc} & \multicolumn{6}{c}{\text{Receiver}} \\ & x_1 & x_2 & \cdots & x_j & \cdots & x_n \\ x_1 & 0 & \Gamma_{12} & \cdots & \Gamma_{1j} & \cdots & \Gamma_{1n} \\ x_2 & \Gamma_{21} & 0 & \cdots & \Gamma_{2j} & \cdots & \Gamma_{2n} \\ \vdots & \vdots & \vdots & & & & \\ x_i & \Gamma_{i1} & \Gamma_{i2} & \cdots & \Gamma_{ij} & \cdots & \Gamma_{in} \\ \vdots & \vdots & \vdots & & & & \\ x_n & \Gamma_{n1} & \Gamma_{n2} & \cdots & \Gamma_{nj} & \cdots & 0 \end{array}$$

The *structure of the organization* G, denoted S_G, is the combination $S_G=(X;\Gamma)$. The structure S_G, represents the *pattern of interactions* among all pairs in G. Attempts have been made to describe structures and their main properties. For example, if all interactions are directed either to or from one position and all these half-channels are used, the structure is said to be *a wheel*. The center (who receives from all and responds to all) is the *hub* and the remainder are called *spokes*. A wheel group is *centralized* (Mackenzie, 1966). At the other extreme, if all persons send to every other person, the structure is called an *all-channel structure*. An all-channel is the most *decentralized* group structure. Technically (Mackenzie, 1966b), the participation is maximum in an all-channel with equal entries in Γ. The level of participation in a wheel is considerably lower. A *hierarchy* is essentially a concatenation of wheel subgroups; spokes on the second level interact with the one person at the top level in a wheel. Those spokes, in turn, become hubs to their subordinates on level 3, and so on. An index of hierarchy is more complex to define (Mackenzie, 1971), but its characterization as a wheel of wheels of wheels, and so on, is a necessary condition.

In defining structure, we used the example of persons sharing information. Suppose there are other *dimensions* of interactions, such as sharing answers, selecting structure for the group, and nontask oriented activities. A structure can be defined for each dimension. In the case of multiple dimensions (the usual case in the author's experience), a group possesses multiple structures. This is why we use the plural, organizational structures. If Γ_1 is the structure with respect to dimension 1, Γ_2 is the structure with respect to dimension 2, . . . and Γ_r is the structure with respect to dimension r, then the organization structures, S_G, is given by

$$S_G = (X; \Gamma_1, \Gamma_2, \ldots, \Gamma_r)$$

An organization may have different structures for different dimensions, such as wheel for answers and all-channel for social activities.

It is clear that the definition of structure contains the organizations parts. The next feature of an organization is its processes. In general, a *process* is any time-ordered means-end chain of more than one link. Suppose that a group is solving a problem involving stages. As the group progresses from the beginning to the end, it moves successively over intermediate stages. Some stages can be reached by an individual and some must be reached by the entire group. Some stages involve necessary steps, some may appear unnecessary or redundant, and some may involve processes related to error and error-correcting processes. Some steps involve discussion and the process of selecting a structure. The choice of the stages to be analyzed will depend on the purpose of analysis. Given a purpose and the relevant stages, we describe each stage as a *"milestone."* The *actual process* of a group is described as a *path* through the milestones. Let the beginning milestone be denoted M_1, the second by $M_2, \ldots,$ and the final milestone by M_f. There is a list or vector of milestones, M, in which $M = (M_1, M_2, \ldots, M_f)$. The activities associated in leaving one milestone and arriving at another are *subprocesses*. The graph of the milestones and subprocesses can be written as a *process structure*, S_P, wherein

$$S_P = (M; P)$$

and the list of milestones, M, corresponds to the parts, X, of an organization, G, and the matrix P describing the pair relationships among milestones corresponds to the interactions matrix, Γ.

$$\text{Destination Milestone}$$

$$P = \text{Origin Milestone} \quad \begin{array}{ccccccc} & M_1 & M_2 & \cdots & M_m & \cdots & M_f \\ M_1 & 0 & P_{12} & \cdots & P_{1m} & \cdots & P_{1f} \\ M_2 & P_{21} & 0 & \cdots & P_{2m} & \cdots & P_{2f} \\ \cdot & \cdot & \cdot & & \cdot & & \cdot \\ \cdot & \cdot & \cdot & & \cdot & & \cdot \\ \cdot & \cdot & \cdot & & \cdot & & \cdot \\ M_k & P_{k1} & P_{k2} & \cdots & P_{km} & \cdots & P_{kf} \\ \cdot & \cdot & \cdot & & \cdot & & \cdot \\ \cdot & \cdot & \cdot & & \cdot & & \cdot \\ \cdot & \cdot & \cdot & & \cdot & & \cdot \\ M_f & P_{f1} & P_{f2} & \cdots & P_{fm} & \cdots & 0 \end{array}$$

Usually a group proceeds in an orderly or *timely* fashion. In which case, for any three milestones, M_k, M_m, and M_o, $P_{km} = 1$ if M_k precedes M_m and $P_{mo} = 1$ if M_m precedes M_o and if $P_{km} = 1$ and $P_{mo} = 1$, then $P_{mk} = 0$, $P_{om} = 0$, and $P_{ok} = 0$. All other processes are untimely.

The relationship between process and structure is deeper than their mere defined similarity as structures. The milestones are defined as being reached in terms of activities completed. Thus, as the role matrix becomes filled out, we know the organization's milestone position. Only when certain activities have been completed do we know the precise milestone location. However, if each milestone represents a dimension of interaction, then we can also examine the relevant dimension of structure to see whether sufficient activities for this dimension have taken place for us to declare the attained milestone. Thus, we examine the structure corresponding to the dimension of the organization's structures for the milestone according to some criterion. The *parts, M,* of S_P *are structures in* S_G *that have satisfied some completion criterion.* Consequently, S_P is a structure of structures and a problem-solving sequence can be viewed as a series of steps from milestone to milestone wherein we judge our achievement of a particular milestone by applying a criterion to a substructure corresponding to the dimension describing the subprocess of reaching a particular milestone. Hence, if we know the dimensions of an organization's structure and the time sequence, we also know the actual processes. Since more than one structure may achieve criterion for a given milestone, knowing only the processes is insufficient to define the structures. Hence, structure is the more basic concept. Finally, knowing the substructures and their sequence, we know all the three elements of an organization: parts, structures, and process.

Theoretically, then, the problem of organizational change is that of structural change. Thus, in order to have a theory of organizational change, we need to describe a theory of structural change.

THE THEORY OF STRUCTURAL CHANGE

The preceding section explained the meanings of structure and process in terms of a role matrix. In particular, a structure is described as a pattern of interaction among members of an organization. There usually is more than one structure in a group; there is one structure corresponding to each dimension of interaction. Structure is defined by its parts and the pair relationships among parts. Structural change occurs whenever either the parts or the pair relationships change. In this essay we shall consider the parts as constant and concentrate on explaining changes in the relationships.

Let us assume that persons join and maintain membership in a group in order to satisfy some needs, be they economic, emotional, or social. We shall not presume that we know these needs precisely; we merely assume their existence and satisfaction by the members' roles. Let us also assume that a member is allowed to enter and remain in a group, provided his role can help satisfy needs of the other group members. We shall also assume that interactions occur in order to satisfy individual and group needs. Thus, we say that a structure represents a mutually satisfying interaction pattern. This does not mean that the needs of each member are maximized but rather a much weaker condition—given the problem, incentives, other member roles, norms, and the like, the interaction pattern satisfies more than alternative structures, considering the perceived "costs" of setting up one of them (which may be considerable in some circumstances). If the interaction pattern does not satisfy this condition, it will change. As the needs, incentives, and problems change, so will the structure. A group structure that remains stable represents a sort of equilibrium across the needs of the various members and the situational demands placed on the group.

Recalling that $S_G = (X; \Gamma)$, we should examine changes in Γ to explain structural change. The interactions initiated by any member of G represent his use of his half-channels to each other member. Assuming that there is no physical barrier preventing his use of any half-channel in any intensity, it follows that x_1 has *absolute control* over the use of x_1's half-channels. That is, x_1 has absolute control over the first row of Γ. He does not have such control over any other entries. Similarly, x_2 has absolute control over the entries in the second row of Γ. Likewise, in turn, each person has absolute control of his row of Γ. It may be detrimental to exercise this control or it may be advantageous depending on the circumstances.

However, if each person has absolute control over his use of his half-channels, then a stable structure represents a *consensus* across all the members. For example, in a five-man group there are twenty half-channels. To form a wheel group about person one, say x_1, four people have to agree to send only to x_1 and no one else and x_1 agrees to send to the other four. Only eight of the twenty half-channels are *open* and twelve are *closed.*

The processes associated with the opening (use) or closing (non-use) of any half-channel, then, represent a composite process of first determining the state of each half-channel and the means by which the individual's absolute control is moderated to obtain the consensus required to form a stable structure. This analysis is required for each dimension of structure in order to explain the group's structures.

It is unusual that a group will deliberately set out to define its functioning structures precisely. It may have a "leader" or "boss" on paper but if one examines the actual interaction pattern, the "leader" will be the leader only if this structure is satisfactory to each member. By defining structure in terms of actual interactions, it is not necessary to differentiate between formal and informal structures. There are structures, period. Consistency of these structures to some ideal may be useful in making certain diagnoses of organizational problems. One might wish, for example, to explain departures from the structure suggested by the organization chart. If the structure differs from the organization chart, the structure represented by the organization chart is incorrect, but the explanation of the differences may be very revealing. We define structures in terms of what is, not in terms of what ought to be. Our definition of structure is inherently dynamic, not static.

It is tempting to state that the value of Γ_{ij} is proportional to the marginal advantages of x_i interacting with x_j. If there are factors, say w_1, w_2, and w_3, it would be tempting to argue that

$$\Gamma_{ij} = f_{ij}\ (w_1,\ w_2,\ w_3)$$

Then, given f_{ij} and the values of w_1, w_2, w_3, we could compute Γ_{ij} and eventually Γ. However, if w_1, w_2, w_3, and so on, represent needs or "benefits" and "costs" to x_i in interacting with x_j, the problem of obtaining consensus implies that the values of w_1, w_2, and w_3 are partly affected by the other members. This raises formidable estimation problems in defining the necessary "structural" equations and determining the "reduced" form equations.

The author has conducted many experiments that demonstrate that as the incentives and social pressures are manipulated, one can control Γ_{ij} and hence, Γ, wherein control means that one can usually arrange incentives, tasks, and social pressures to evolve structures that are those predicted (Mackenzie, 1973). However, the exact expression of the values of f_{ij} are unknown and would require too many repetitions of any experiment to identify and estimate statistically. At this point, it suffices to state that as the means to achieving needs are altered, the structures will change in the direction of a need-satisfying interaction pattern.

We don't know the utility functions to define f_{ij} and even if we knew the form, it is probably impossible to identify and estimate them in the context of a freely interacting group of individuals. Subjects in experiments usually do not speak in the terms required for a utility theoretical analysis. If one observes groups, one can obtain accurate and detailed transcripts of actual sequences of interactions. The problem is to infer from the content of the messages how a particular half-channel was opened or closed and how consensus across the absolute controllers is reached. Another approach is required.

Assume that each message sent, regardless of its obvious task content, represents an attempt by the sender to convey information concerning opening, closing, or not changing the state of a half-channel. Each message, then, is some sort of a *ballot.* The ballot contains positions with regard to the use or non-use of one or more half-channels. These positions are called *votes.* Votes get tabulated with respect to a sender, a receiver, the content, and half-channel according to *vote tabulation rules.* These vote tabulations change as messages are sent and received. The result of a sequence of votes is determined by a *voting rule.* Voting rules result in half-channels becoming *elected closed or open.* A contrary vote concerning an elected half-channel results in a *recall.* Recalls are the cause of subsequent explicit or implicit elections. When all half-channels are elected and there are no more recalls, the structure is said to be *inaugurated,* at which point the election process terminates. Subsequent events in the experiment or in the group itself can cause a new election process.

This sort of election process is quite different from the formal voting that takes place on election day. It is more like the processes by which opinions are formed before the election. A current problem in this type of research involves defining a theory of constitutions from which the various voting processes investigated by the author can be logically derived.

It is very possible that what appears to be noise and randomness in committee meetings results from the observer's lack of understanding of the patterns of social processes. Similarly, a non-naturalist walking through a meadow misses the fine sense of order seen by a trained naturalist. Canny committee chairmen learn to accurately decode these signals. Although many decisions are reached prior to the commencement of a meeting, sometimes, as a result of debate, positions change. By the conversation and by knowing something about the persons involved, one can apply voting-process concepts to predict the outcome of the recorded vote. This outcome is sometimes easy to predict exactly.

One interesting empirical result reported in Faucheux and Mackenzie (1966) is that the groups formed wheel structures for one task and then decentralized into all-channels for a new, more difficult task. A wheel group of five persons has a hub whose span of control is 4. As the group proceeded through a set of problems, they were able to solve problems more quickly, with fewer messages and fewer errors. The problems varied somewhat in complexity. A typical pattern was what appeared to be a sudden centralization. Working backward from the assumptions that the group's goal was to minimize time per trial and that a wheel structure formed when the hub was able to solve problems sufficiently fast to satisfy the needs of those in groups, it is possible to define deterministic models that predict the exact time at which the structure stabilizes. The rapid decentralization of the structures following the introduction of the more complex task is consistent with calculations that demonstrate the old leader could not solve the new problems fast enough to warrant the group's maintaining the old structure. These calculations imply that the group reset its norm of how long to allow the coordinator to function as hub. When the norm is violated, election processes to recall the old structure occur almost immediately. Thus the needs to be satisfied are changing along with the structures.

Recent calculations with these and related data demonstrate the group tends to form increasingly hierarchical structures as experience increases (Mackenzie, 1971). This is especially significant because of the extremely high correlation reported between the degree of hierarchy and efficiency. Together, these suggest that structures that are need satisfying (assuming a group goal is efficiency) tend to form.

The main ideas of a half-channel voting model that have been described are consistent with the assumptions of absolute control by the origin of a half-channel. We need now to examine in more detail a mechanism by which consensus among absolute controllers is reached.

In a paper by Mackenzie and Barron (1970), a mathematical model for structural change shows that the rate of change of the number of adopted channels follows a logistic function, which is the basic function used to describe the diffusion process for adopting an innovation. For example, if a group of five begins in an all-channel, there are twenty open half-channels. If after the election process the group evolves into a wheel structure, twelve of these half-channels are adopted closed. If the structures are those for sending data and broadcasting an answer, there are only four open half-channels for each dimension at the conclusion of the election process. There are four that represent the sending of data to the hub and there are four that represent the sending of answers from the hub to the four spokes. If the number of half-channels remaining open is four and there are twenty half-channels, then sixteen are adopted closed. Let n_t be the number of adopted half-channels at time t from the first vote. Then the rate of adoption of half-channels is

$$\frac{dn_t}{dt} = (k_1 n_t (\mathrm{N} - n_t))$$

where if $t = 0$, $n_0 = 4$. $N = 20$.

The solution to this equation is the logistic function that has an "S" shape. There is a slow rise at first, followed by rapid adoption of half-channels, and finally a leveling off as no more remain to be adopted. The slope of the diffusion curve is determined by the value of k_1. The larger the value of k_1, the more rapid the adoption of a structure. The logistic curve owes its shape to the interaction between adopter and non-adopters (in this case the controller of the half-channels). Assuming that the greater the intensity (votes per minute) in favor of the final structure, the greater the value of

k_1 and the greater the intensity of votes against the final structure, the lower the value of k_1, an attempt was made to define a model to "explain" the different values of the slope k_1 in terms of the relative intensities of the voting. The results confirm the assumption of a diffusion process to describe the adoption of a structural change. The values of k_1 varied by a factor of approximately 26. Thus, rather simple mechanisms can be employed to define a theory of structural change in the example cited.

The results are not too surprising if one considers the need for consensus. Initially, all twenty half-channels are open and are voted on. Eventually, one person adopts the closing of a few half-channels. The person at the other end also closes his end of the channel. The two then send messages to the others to obtain consistency. They send stronger vote intensities in favor of the final structure and weaker ones against the final structure. If another adopts a consistent set of states for his half-channels, the relative intensity of favorable to unfavorable votes increases even more and is directed more intensively at those not yet adopting. The process continues to accelerate until consensus is reached. It would appear that the adoption of a change in structure is not different in principle from the adoption of any other innovation.

Adoption-diffusion processes are useful in explaining the causes and rates of adoption of a change in structure. Voting processes explain the mechanisms and calculus by which influence efforts among the members of a group result in a structural change. Vote intensities underlie the explanation of rates of adoption. However, these calculations are specific to the conditions under which the groups worked. A natural set of questions for more general analysis of organizations concern the effects of incentives and social pressures in the change in structures. Specifically, to what extent can management intervene to create conditions that will alter a structure to a desired state without controlling individual behavior directly?

Presumably there would be less resistance if management attempted to control the instrumentality of interactions rather than the interactions themselves. Groups develop many internal controls over member behavior. Can development of these controls be controlled? To intervene directly at the interaction level instead of controlling the conditions under which the internal controls develop is analogous to pushing someone through a door instead of leading him through. The job of a manager would be easier both for him and those managed if he would seek to create the conditions under which a self-regulating group can manage itself to do what must be done without direct and continuous intervention. Indirection is often the preferable strategy (B.H.L. Hart, 1954).

Applying the theory of structural change, the primary problem is to arrange conditions so that needs can best be satisfied in the desired structure. The less desirable the structure to be adopted, the more it will take to obtain adoption. The greater the costs to each member of not adopting the desired structure, the more likely they are to adopt it. If conditions are set correctly, one should be able to obtain adoption without either a long adoption process or expressions of resentment about those controlling the conditions. Although little is really known about how much and what type of indirect control should be applied under what conditions for different purposes, there are some laboratory results that do suggest the essential correctness of an indirect approach.

Data from the Faucheux-Mackenzie (1966) experiment demonstrated that for the complex, non-routine problem requiring inferences, groups always worked in decentralized structures even if they had experience in a centralized structure for another task. In fact, their five-man groups always used all available half-channels to solve these problems. A subsequent set of experiments showed (1) that if given longer time (8 hours vs. about 2) groups did not centralize for this task; and (2) groups could perform these problems as effectively in a centralized wheel structure. Given a choice, groups always adopted an all-channel structure. Investigations have been made to learn what amount and what type of indirect controls could be applied and under what conditions to obtain a prespecified structure without actually intervening directly in the adoption process (Mackenzie, 1973). Two of these are reported here.

The first involved a combination of economic and social pressure to obtain wheel structures. The second involved the same combination to obtain a circle structure. In a circle structure, each member interacts only with two persons and the number of communication channels equals the number of persons. The wheel structure is easier to understand and easier for a group to operate. The circle appears to require too many information relays and these can occur in many different, confusing combinations. It never occurred naturally in any previous trial by any previous group. It would appear to be a less desirable structure. Hence, we would expect that it would require a greater amount of economic and social pressure to obtain conformity to it than to the wheel.

The economic and social pressure applied consisted of allowing each group free use of those channels matching the desired structure (the wheel or the all-channel). The other channels were rented to each group and the channel rental fee was fixed for each channel and group, but different groups were charged different rents. The rental costs were deducted from the fixed salary paid to the subjects for solving four problems. This economic cost was, however, partially transformed into a social cost by allowing each member, before each trial, to decide anonymously and independently what channels he thought the group needed, with his decision being binding on all other subjects. Thus, if one subject rented two channels, all others had to pay this rental fee even if they did not choose it. Channel renting, in this case, amounted to one student subject spending another's money. This violated student norms and violators incurred a social cost. The channel rentals were 50 cents, 25 cents, 10 cents, 5 cents, and 1 cent per channel per trial. When channels were free, all were "rented." When no channels could be rented, the channel rental was "infinite" and none were rented. The data are given in Table 4.

At 25 cents per channel, the wheel groups were never willing to pay money to avoid the wheel structure whereas the circle groups were willing to pay approximately 65 cents per trial to break out of the circle. These data clearly show that subjects are more willing to pay to avoid a circle structure than a wheel structure. The structure selected in both cases is a function of the costs associated with not conforming, and it takes a much smaller amount of pressure to obtain conformity to the more reasonable structure.

Many other variants of structure, incentive, and social pressure have been conducted. These data demonstrate that structure and process can be controlled by indirect methods and that changes in group structures and

TABLE 4. AVERAGE PERCENTAGE OF CHANNELS RENTED PER GROUP PER TRIAL

Rental Cost per Channel per Trial	Desired Structure *Wheel*	*Circle*
∞	0	0
50¢	not run	16%
25¢	0	52%
10¢	6%	75%
5¢	10%	96%
1¢	83%	94%
0¢	100%	100%

processes can be systematically studied. These results, albeit limited in context and scope, also suggest that organizational change can be controlled. The more satisfying or the less dissatisfying a structure or process, the easier it is to control. Although it will be easier to control organizational changes, as they are regarded as more beneficial, conflicts will arise where it may be necessary to impose changes that are less than beneficial. A changer ought to try to match the degree of control to that minimum required by the problem. It is wasteful to employ excessive pressure. As well as being poor human relations, it may even be counter-productive in the long run.

Although the use of unobtrusive controls seems preferable to direct intervention, it is interesting to investigate direct intervention techniques to learn more about the postulated voting processes. The author and several of his students have been conducting investigations of direct intervention. The argument is that if we have a model of the voting processes and these processes, in conjunction with other parameters, explain structural change, then we ought to be able to intervene directly to control a structure. One recent experiment conducted with A. C. Silcox at the University of Waterloo attempted to organize an all-channel group into a wheel structure and then reorganize it about another hub and then again about the original hub in the course of a 2-hour experiment. Armed with a precise knowledge of the voting processes for a particular task (the routine, deductive problem in the Faucheux-Mackenzie experiment), and controlling two confederates in a group containing three naïve subjects, such control was easily managed.

An analysis of data from business game teams, in which groups had an operations research graduate student operating as an experimenter's confederate, provide data on adopting decision-making processes. The confederate's duty was to introduce and attempt to gain implementation of optimal operations research based on solution techniques for three types of decisions the group had to make in regard to prices, economic lot size, and economic order size for three products. Results for the rate of adoption of an optimal decision-making process indicate that a diffusion process is sufficient to explain these data and that process change and structural change are highly related, as one would expect from a theory of structural change (Mackenzie and Barron, 1970b).

CONCLUSIONS

We began this essay with a discussion of the pace, extent, and nature of social change. Social change requires adoption of something new, which we called an innovation. The nature of the change and its consequences were discussed in terms of the behavior of an adopter rather than in terms of the technological qualities of the innovation. From there we discussed, briefly, the theory of the adoption and diffusion of an innovation.

An organizational change is one type of social change. Since organizations consist of parts, structures, and processes, those components were related to the fundamental notion of structure based on the roles of its constituent parts. Structure was conceived as representing a need-satisfying pattern of interactions among the parts. A theory of structural change, then, was considered the core problem in developing a theory of organizational change. After summarizing a theory of structural change, several examples of this theory were presented from laboratory investigations. These findings suggest that although the approach may be useful, it is just a beginning.

Aside from attempts to isolate several key issues in organizational change and to suggest theoretical approaches, there are broader implications that ought to be discussed. Agreeing with Katz and Kahn (1966, pp. 390–391) and others that there is, in the organizational change literature, an overemphasis on individual change, it may be instructive to reconsider why this may be so and why organizational change might well be studied by investigating the behavior of laboratory groups.

Suppose that in some far-distant future the sciences of genetics and molecular biology have progressed so far that there exists a specialty called bio-genetic engineering. The field is so advanced that by some routine process a complete human being can be reproduced in some miraculous vat. Suppose further that this replica is so precise that it, as an individual, is absolutely identical to the original. Let us also assume that there is a language that can describe such an individual by a long list of "traits." So, let person 1's replica be a vector of traits, T_1. Suppose that there are also persons 2, 3, 4, and 5, whose corresponding trait vectors are T_2, T_3, T_4, and T_5, Suppose further that all five are brought together in the psychological laboratory to be subjects in an experiment in which they are to form a group, T, and perform a sequence of related tasks. What can we say about the structures and processes of T even if we know $T_1, T_2, \ldots, T_5$ precisely? That is, on what calculus is the aggregation of individuals formed from the individuals? Do we add the vectors? Should we average them? How about multiplying them or performing Boolean arithmetic? We simply don't know! We suspect, however, that the aggregation problem is not a mathematical problem of combining vectors. We suspect that there are more serious substantive issues. These issues should form the nucleus of a theory of groups.

Presumably, the replicas have personal goals, and to satisfy them they agree to consent to participate in the experiment. The five replicas are led into a room where the psychologist explains the problems that must be solved by the joint efforts of the five replicas working together as a group.

The type of problem is, of course, completely new to these replicas. One can imagine T_1 sitting in his chair wondering what to do. He probably will form some hypothesis that if he performs a certain activity in a certain way it ought to help him achieve his goals. Suppose he then behaves by communicating an act to T_2, who by this time is also trying to decide what to do. If T_1's behavior seems helpful to T_2 and T_2's helpful to T_1, the responses may encourage them to repeat this behavior. A less favorable reply may result in a new hypothesis and behavior. By this time T_3, T_4, and T_5 are also exhibiting behaviors. Slowly, perhaps, consensus forms concerning what each replica should do. The roles become more differentiated. If the differentiation is satisfying, it will tend to become stable. Norms develop. Departures from individual roles may be perceived as dissatisfying. Sanctions to maintain consistency with the norms evolve. And after a period of time, each replica has given up a little of what he would have done alone by adjusting to the demands of the group. After a while the problems may become routine, with the costs associated with departure from the norms greater than the benefits of maintaining them. Over a long period of time, attitudes may even change.

Now we ask two questions: (1) Are the replicas still replicas? (2) Can we describe the structure and processes of the group only in terms of the original vectors? The answer to each is probably no. These questions then raise the question of how individual is the member of a group? The demands of the problems, goals, and requirements in adjusting to the others mean that only a very small fraction of his total capacities are being exhibited. With respect to his role in the group, he may *appear like* an *automaton.* Even though he is really much more, it doesn't show while he is participating. For example, to an observer from a vantage point high in the sky, the behavior of a driver on a turnpike is very predictable, almost machine-like, even though the driver may be a poet dreaming of love and success. But if from the aggregate view of the whole group he appears to be an automaton, what about the others? Does not a group of five interacting "automatons" resemble a machine?

Are there not properties of groups and laws of group behavior that suggest that knowing individual characteristics is insufficient to understand the functioning of the group as a group? Are not the problems of aggregating individuals into a group like the problems of aggregating groups into organizations? In which case, the main problems of analyzing aggregation lie in aggregating individuals into a group. Hence, the small-group laboratory experiment may be an effective means of studying aggregation and change in aggregates.

An organizational change is a change in the structures and processes of the organization. These problems, although very complex, seem to be attempting to re-program automata with the least effort or cost.

Hard, scientific knowledge of organizational change is scant. Clearly the field is in its infancy. The problems are fascinating. Attaining more knowledge about the responsiveness of structures to different types, degrees, and combinations of controls will require years of research both in and out of the laboratory. Although the problems appear important and their solution potentially very useful, they pose serious moral and ethical questions. To what future use may they be put? Mastering the scientific problems could usher in social control methods that could be used to free men or to enslave them. Because current theory suggests these techniques only work to the extent that needs are satisfied, the author is cautiously optimistic.

SUGGESTIONS FOR FUTURE READING

APPELBAUM, R. P., *Theories of Social Change* (Chicago: Markham Publishing Co., 1971).

ARGYRIS, C., *Organization and Innovation* (Homewood, Illinois: Richard D. Irwin and The Dorsey Press, 1965).

ATKINSON, J. W., *An Introduction to Motivation* (Princeton, N.J.: D. Van Nostrand, 1964).

BAVELAS, A., AND G. STRAUSS, "Group Dynamics and Intergroup Relations," in BENNIS, W. G. BENNE, KENNETH D., CHIN, ROBERT (Eds.) *The Planning of Change* (New York: Holt, Rinehart and Winston, 1961).

BENNIS, W. G., *Changing Organizations* (New York: McGraw-Hill Book Co., Inc., 1966).

BLAKE, R. R., AND J. S. MOUTON, *Corporate Excellence Through Grid Organization Development* (Houston, Texas: Gulf Publishing Co., 1968).

BURNS, T., AND G. M.. STALKER, *The Management of Innovation* (London: Social Sciences Paperbacks, 1961).

COLEMAN, J. S., *Model of Change and Response Uncertainty* (Englewood Cliffs, N.J.: Prentice-Hall, Inc., 1964).

FAUCHEUX, C., AND K. D. MACKENZIE, "Task Dependency of Organizational Centrality: Its Behavioral Consequences," *Journal of Experimental Social Psychology*, Vol. 2 (1966), pp. 361–375.

HART, B. H. LIDDELL, *Strategy* (New York: Frederick A. Praeger, 1954).

HOFFER, E., *The True Believer* (New York: Harper & Row, Perennial Library, 1951).

HOFFER, E., *The Ordeal of Change* (New York: Harper Colophon Books, 1964).

KATZ, D., AND R. L. KAHN, *Social Psychology of Organization* (New York: John Wiley & Sons, 1966).

LAVE, L. B., *Technological Change: Its Conception and Measurement* (Englewood Cliffs, N.J.: Prentice-Hall, Inc., 1966).

LERNER, D., *The Passing of Traditional Society* (New York: The Free Press, 1958).

LEWIS, C. G., (Ed.), *Manpower Planning: A Bibliography* (London: The English Universities Press, 1969).

MCCLELLAND, D. C., *The Achieving Society* (Princeton, N.J.: D. Van Nostrand, 1961).

MACKENZIE, K. D., "Structural Centrality in Communications Networks," *Psychometrika*, Vol. 31 (1966a), pp. 17–25.

MACKENZIE, K. D., "The Information Theoretic Entropy Function As a Total Expected Participation Index for Communication Network Experiments," *Psychometrika*, Vol. 31 (1966b), pp. 249–254.

MACKENZIE, K. D., "Organization Theories: State of the Art for the Problem of Bureaucracy," *Proceedings of the 1971 NATO Conference on Manpower Planning Models*, D. J. Clough (Ed.) London: English Universities Press, in press.

MACKENZIE, K. D., *A Theory of Group Structures* (New York: Gordon and Breech, 1973, forthcoming).

MACKENZIE, K. D., AND F. H. BARRON, "Modelling Change in Behavior," *Working Paper No. 25*, Department of Management Sciences, University of Waterloo, Waterloo, Ontario, 1970a.

MACKENZIE, K. D., AND F. H. BARRON, "Analysis of a Decision Making Investigation," *Management Science*, Vol. 17, No. 6 (1970b), pp. B-226–B-241.

MANSFIELD, E., "Technological Change and the Rate of Imitation," *Econometrica*, Vol. 29 (1961), pp. 741–766.

MOORE, W. E., *Social Change* (Englewood Cliffs, N.J.: Prentice-Hall, Inc., 1963).

MOORE, W. E., "Social Change," *International Encyclopedia of the Social Sciences*, Vol. 14 (New York: Macmillan-Free Press, 1968), pp. 365–375.

NICOSIA, F. M., *Consumer Decision Processes* (Englewood Cliffs, N.J.: Prentice-Hall, Inc., 1966).

ROGERS, E. M., *Diffusion of Innovations* (New York: The Free Press, 1962).

SALTER, W. E. G., *Productivity and Technical Change*, 2d ed. (Cambridge: Cambridge University Press, 1966).

SHARP, L., "Steel Axes for Stone Age Australians," Case 5 in E. H. Spicer (Ed.), *Human Problems in Technological Change* (New York: John Wiley & Sons, 1967), pp. 69–90.

SMELSER, N. J., *Essays in Sociological Explanation* (Englewood Cliffs, N.J.: Prentice-Hall, Inc., 1968), pp. 192–280.

SPICER, E. H. (Ed.), *Human Problems in Technological Change* (New York: John Wiley & Sons, 1967).

TOFFLER, A., *Future Shock* (New York: Bantam Books, 1970).

USEEM, J., "Democracy in Process: The Development of Democratic Leadership in the Micronesian Islands," in E. H. Spicer (Ed.), *Human Problems in Technological Change* (New York: John Wiley & Sons, 1967).

WEBER, M., *From Max Weber: Essays in Sociology*, translated by H. H. Gerth and C. W. Mills (New York: Oxford University Press, 1946).

WEBER, M., *The Theory of Social and Economic Organization*, translated by A. M. Henderson and T. Parsons (Glencoe, Illinois: The Free Press, 1947).

WOODWARD, J., *Industrial Organization: Theory and Practice* (London: Oxford University Press, 1965).

Conceptual Trade-offs in Studying Organizational Change

Karl E. Weick

Professor
Graduate School of Business
and Public Administration
Cornell University

Three options are open to the person who wishes to study organizational change.[1] He can study it in its full-blown complexity, he can systematically scale it down and examine it in miniaturized replicas, or he can exclude portions of the complexity and study it piecemeal. Any of these approaches has its merit if it is done and interpreted within the same category. The trouble starts when a person works in one category and claims that he is working in another one. It would appear that Mackenzie believes he is working theoretically and empirically on a scaled-down version of organizational change that has retained the complexities of the full-scale process. However, both his theory and experiments suggest that he has excluded vital elements of organizational change and therefore is working on only a portion of the problem.

Let us examine some of the elements of change that have been excluded both theoretically and empirically. At least four serious omissions seem to have occurred: the conflict between internal and external selection criteria, the relationship between adaptation and adaptability, the meandering, ing, incremental quality of change, and reaction and disillusionment following change.

The internal-external criterion problem derives from a long tradition in group psychology of theorists distinguishing between the problems internal to a group and the problems that are external to a group (Homans, 1950). The problem stated simply is that solution of internal problems may work at cross-purposes to the solution of external problems. Since internal problems are concerned mainly with the stability of the group, and are "solved" by reward and punishment principles, it is very possible that the application of criteria to establish smooth internal functioning may provide group members with the illusion that all is going well when in fact the group is in deep trouble relative to its environment. This process is discussed by Campbell (1965):

> A process of habit meshing takes place within any organization, in that each person's habits are a part of the environment of others. Encounters which are punishing tend to extinguish; . . . rewarding encounters increase the strength of behavioral tendencies on the part of both parties. Thus any social organization tends to move in the direction of internal compatability, independently of increased adaptiveness (p. 33).

Thus any theory of organizational change must pay close attention to the cost of achieving internal compatability at the expense of external adaptation. I mention this point because Mackenzie continually argues that structures form to satisfy needs, a postulation that clearly is paying more attention to internal group processes than to the group's adaptation to its environment. In his experiments as well as in his theory, it would appear that Mackenzie has eliminated at least half of the dilemma that

[1]Preparation of this paper was supported by the National Science Foundation through Grant GS 28353.

a group faces when it must decide whether to change and how to implement and embed that change. Most change activities have to blend, balance, alternate, or take account of two problems—namely, maintaining stability within the group and flexibility relative to the environment.

Notice that in the majority of Mackenzie's experiments, there is no unpredictable, malevolent, puzzling, or competitive environment to which the group must accommodate. Conceivably, one could argue that whether a group is assigned a complex or a simple task constitutes the environment for them, but it is really more accurate to say that any group in real change situations is working on a task and their final decision about how they will work on the task primarily solves the internal problem but can easily undercut the appropriateness of that task *output* for an environment whose demands are fickle, shifting, and unstable. If all the members have to worry about is getting along with one another, then it is not particularly surprising that structures seem to develop in ways that satisfy needs. If, however, organizations face the dual problem of satisfying the members sufficiently so that they will remain in the group and of developing structures that have an impact on the outside world, then any attempt to change structures is more complex than Mackenzie assumes.

The dilemma between adaptability and adaptation is closely related to the issue of internal versus external criteria, but it focuses on two kinds of external criteria. Stated compactly, the argument is that adaptation precludes adaptability (see Service, 1960, p. 96, and his discussion of the Law of Evolutionary Potential). A group that maximizes its fit to immediate circumstances may find that this adaptative specialization is a cruel trap that is irreversible when the environment changes.

There is considerable disagreement over whether there is a negative correlation between adaptability and adaptation and if so, how large that correlation might be. A proponent of the possibility that there is either no correlation or a very low correlation is Dunn (1971).

> Adaptation of the social group to an external physical environment is not as deterministic a correlation of social behavior with physical environment as characterized phylogenetic branching in the biological realm. Nor is the attendant stabilization so apt to terminate the history of the system. Overcoming stabilization in this kind of cultural specialization may be difficult and in fact, may not be achieved in a particular case. However, there exists in every culture (even though specialized and isolated) the potential capacity for individual human learning that may produce generalizing ideas. It may be less likely to occur than in less specialized cultures but it is possible. Furthermore, through idea diffusion the specialized culture may have access to more general adaptative ideas from other cultures. The specialized culture may be redeemed from specializations that tend to terminate social history (p. 88).

Whether a potential capacity for change is concealed within a specialized group becomes an absolutely vital question when one is trying to assess the likelihood and consequences of organizational change. Mackenzie consistently plays down the question of hidden resources within a group that might aid adaptation to either a group or environmental change. But his example of the highly specialized Los Angeles furniture industry makes this a crucial issue (for example, given the high degree of specialization that he has detailed, what would happen to this industry if conservationists successfully reduce the amount of lumbering activity, foreign competitors flood the United States market, people decide to build their own furniture or buy second-hand furniture, or do away with furniture in the interest of being more mobile). Organizational change needed to cope with any of those modifications could be impossible or possible only at staggering costs if adaptation precludes adaptability. The obvious point is that we simply don't know the answer to that crucial question. But simply because we don't know the answer is no reason to exclude the issue of group resources. And to say that people resist change is to miss the point of this comment. The point is that people may resist change simply because they cannot make the change. They can't make the change partly because specialized adaptation has reduced the resources available to them and has so stabilized and reinforced the existing organizational structure that new ways of behaving are unavailable. It does no good to borrow someone else's idea if you do not retain the skills or repertoire to use that idea.

A common theme in much of the change literature is the meandering, incremental course that change follows. A good example of this point of view is found in Hirschman and Lindblom (1962), who assert that "a rational problem solver wants what he can get and does not try to get what he wants except after identifying what he wants by examining what he can get." The incremental point of view contends that change is continuous rather than discrete, considerable ambiguity surrounds the choice of means, the means available oftentimes define the end one is working toward, and that foresight and planning may be of questionable value.

The reason for citing this alternative view of change is that it contrasts sharply with the one presented by Mackenzie. My chief worry is that Mackenzie's formulation and experimental settings do not contain sufficient slack or intentional looseness such that the meandering and fragmented aspects of the change process could intrude, be discovered, and be represented. In other words, if change as it unfolds in real life has considerable irrationality about it, and if the presence of this irrationality is crucial to predicting the course and outcome of change, then there seems to be no way that it can affect either Mackenzie's experiments or his theory.

Perhaps the most obvious place in Mackenzie's work where this point is illustrated is in the discreteness of the categories in his theory. For example, when he describes the *nature of the change,* he points out that some activities are dropped, some remain unchanged, and some new ones are performed. But activities are seldom that clear cut and from the fragmented view of change it is much more likely that activities are grafted on to one another rather than reduced. Costello (1971), in commenting on his experience in the New York City municipal government, remarked that "Vested interests are so quickly built up around urban programs, and pressures for their maintenance become so strong that change most often must be the *addition* of things, not program substitution or the elimination of old programs. As a result, the range of change decisions is narrowed" (p. 137). Furthermore, when Mackenzie talks about *adoption processes* his usage of this phrase has the aura of an all or none character about it. Little mention is made of the possibility that adoption is oftentimes partial, hedged, and that what is adopted is seldom mutually exclusive compared to what went before. This discreteness concern must be tempered by the reality that if one wishes to model change processes, then explicit definitions and demarcations are essential. My concern is that in marking off these boundaries, most of the dynamics and predictors of the results of change and resistance to change have been excluded. Similarly, the discreteness of trials in Mackenzie's experiments does not allow a continuous flow of activity and a continually changing situation that would seem necessary if one wishes to create the plausible parallels of organizational change (McGrath, 1964). Discrete trials in a laboratory experiment chop the behavioral stream into tidy, clear-cut segments and what is done earlier has a relatively modest effect on what happens later. Add to this the fact that the experimental means-activities are clear cut and the ends are well specified, and it then becomes apparent that organizational change is not being studied in a scaled-down version but rather that a small portion of it is being examined, and those portions that are excluded have a good chance of recasting the proposals that Mackenzie makes.

Once people have been through a change episode several dynamics emerge that can either solidify or undo the change. Neither in the theory of organizational change nor in the experiments discussed by Mackenzie do we find the change process extended far enough temporally to pick up these crucial dynamics.

A possible belated outcome of change is discussed by Barnett (1953) and is labeled by him The Second Disaffection:

> Disaffection can be compounded and so produce a complex pattern of attraction and repulsion. Men . . . revolt first against their cultural heritage and then in disillusionment recoil from the conflicts produced by their anomalous position. Their rebounds may take an erratic course: but unless there is some third choice, their revulsions have a reverse component so that the second disaffection has a reactionary result; . . . reversion resulting from disillusionment is a very common reaction (p. 398).

Data we have collected recently (Weick and Gilfillan, 1971) in studies of culture histories in a laboratory setting support this point. We found that when a change occurred in a culture, if this change caused disruption, then people used the fact of disruption to justify a return to the old ways of behaving. And surprisingly, they made this justification and reversion even when the new way was as efficient as the old way and was easier to comprehend. The point I am concerned with is that there may be significant forces at work to undo a change once it is apparently implanted, and any viable theory of organizational change must pay closer attention to the durability of a change once it is introduced and the ways and adequacy with which it is embedded. Mackenzie's failure to look at this problem is temporary, since by simply extending the duration of his experiments after a change had been introduced, and by varying the pressures on members to revert to their original ways of behaving, he should be able to get valuable information about which kinds of changes and which kinds of intervention tactics lead to embedded rather than transient changes.

So far I have tried to indicate four variables affecting organizational change which seem sufficiently powerful that their omission from either a framework or an experiment will limit the value of that work. I want to emphasize that making trouble for Mackenzie on these four dimensions is not simply a shrill and conventional indictment of modeling and laboratory experiments because they fail to contain the blood, sweat, and tears present in the real world. Instead, I think the problems involving internal versus external system functioning, the question of whether adaptation to current circumstances lowers the chance of adapting to a changed circumstance, the ambiguity of means-ends relationships in change episodes, and finally the likelihood of reversals once a change has been implemented will affect such crucial items in the Mackenzie formulation as differential evaluation, social and economic costs, and the likelihood that structural changes will be guided primarily by considerations of need satisfaction.

Throughout the Mackenzie paper one has the feeling that his propositions would improve if richer metaphors were used. For example, rather than talk about search behavior and try to get from that to predictions of adaptation to change, he might use as his metaphor the assimilation of a stranger (Schutz, 1964). The stranger experiences many of the same bewilderments when he enters an unknown group as people do when they are undergoing change in their own groups. The stranger is uncertain of the ground he is standing on and it is difficult for him to orient himself, a plight that is quite similar to what happens to a habituated group that finds itself suddenly without old familiar routines. The plight of a group immersed in change and that of a stranger approaching a new group seem quite similar. The use of a stranger metaphor might be doubly helpful because much organizational change does involve shifts of personnel or interactions (this is the principle definition of organizational change used by Mackenzie), and in this sense how the stranger orients himself and how a group orients itself toward a stranger would seem to move Mackenzie closer to the actual world to which he hopes to generalize.

The voting model of consensus building could be improved and there seem other models equally suitable for this same process that could move the Mackenzie formulation closer to some of the realities of organizational change.

I find it hard to view each message sent by a person over his half-channel as a ballot and easier to view this process as a nomination. The way Mackenzie describes the process makes it appear as if what a person is actually doing is nominating himself for a position of importance within the role structure. And as is true of nominating conventions, after coalitions and bargaining have occurred the nomination is either ratified or rejected. If structures are presumed to be need satisfying, then one fairly prominent need one could postulate is that people have a need to maintain the control that they start out with and to have some say in the group decision. They are unlikely to send as their initial messages a relatively passive ballot that asks the other members simply to check off whether the sender can have an influential position or not. Rather, one would expect that a person would state his case more aggressively and it is this sense in which a nominating speech or being put in nomination seems the more accurate portrayal of the initial stage of consensus building.

The whole voting analogy seems somewhat strained, however, and to be making more of the decisions about channel opening and closing than may be there. Other metaphors seem more appropriate. One way to view the initial activity among members is that they are trying to negotiate a reality which they can work with (Scheff, 1968; Emerson, 1970). Members are trying to figure out what the reality of their circumstance is and how they will construct it for the duration of their interaction. They probably are negotiating such basic things as ground rules about how they will work, what they will pay attention to, and basically what their present circumstance is. If one uses the metaphor of a ballot, this carries with it the presumption that the issues are clear and that all one needs to do is register his approval or disapproval of a clear-cut circumstance. But if the reality negotiation metaphor is unhelpful, then one could substitute the idea that members are bidding for control and are engaged in a process of making offers and counter-offers before reaching a final agreement.

The concept of initiating a half-channel in the hopes that the sender will find this initiative reciprocated and that a channel will be open between two people involves some sticky psychological problems. For example, it is commonplace in the literature on superior-subordinate relationships to find that communication typically goes from subordinates to superiors rather than in the reverse direction. In other words, most communications in any kind of hierarchical organization move from lower levels toward higher levels. Conceivably in a communication network the first person to open his half-channel tacitly is signifying that the person to whom the message is directed is in a superior position and that the initiator is both lower than and dependent on the person to whom the message is directed. Notice that this formulation is opposite to one introduced earlier in this paper where it was suggested that people try to nominate themselves as centers of power. I am aware of this possible contradiction but wish simply to illustrate that *either* possibility may be present in an experimental situation *if* one takes account of psychological dynamics. It gets even more complicated if one begins to probe deeper into the dynamics of the exchange processes that Mackenzie is discussing. One of the common features of an exchange is that the first person who makes overtures essentially obligates the receiver to respond in some way. Since people typically seem to be bound by a norm of reciprocity, reciprocation of overtures is to be expected. It is expected not because of voting processes but simply because of prevailing norms. This being the case, it is not altogether clear what we would make of sender-receiver matrices if they indicated that a given number of messages or activities had not been reciprocated. Mackenzie mentions this as one possibility. If anything but reciprocation occurs this would raise serious questions about why the reciprocity norm could be violated under these conditions (e.g. no sanction available?), and whether the activity actually did need to be reciprocated or whether it was self-contained. I am simply not sure that full-blown exchange processes are adaptable to a matrix format.

Mackenzie's concept of milestones on the way to the solution of the problem seems to give insufficient attention to the concept of equifinality—namely, that there are many ways to accomplish the same end. The milestone concept reads as if there is one and only one pathway that will produce an outcome and I find this constraint both severe and unrealistic. The reason for pointing to this problem is that a change in organizational structure as defined by Mackenzie could mean nothing more than adopting an alternative pathway through the milestones for the sake of variety, to relieve boredom, or for other reasons that have no great bearing on organizational change. In other words, change that is responsive to psychological dynamics such as satiation or boredom or variety, using receiver-sender matrices, could not be singled out from structural changes that are of more consequence and interest.

The concept of need is a useful one but it carries with it a host of fringe issues. If Mackenzie wishes to use need formulations, then he should be alerted to some of the problems involved. For example, the content of the need will make a difference if he is trying to predict which people will pair with which other ones. A person with a high need for approval will probably open all of his half-channels and keep them open as long as possible simply in the hope that he will get back that scarce commodity that he needs in great supply—namely, approval and assurances of worth. In other words, depending on the nature of the need, and the composition of the people in the group as regards need, very different structures will be initiated. But more important, as these needs are satisfied and satiated, then new needs may be activated and exert pressures on members to arrange the structure. Thus, if one uses the concept of need satisfaction, then I am not certain that he can predict a stable group structure if a satisfied need drops out as a control over behavior and is replaced by others that remain unsatisfied. A related point is the fact that Mackenzie is continually concerned with stable structures and the fact that a stable structure will occur if it is need satisfying. One problem is that he seems to play down the importance of task considerations. People do satisfy their needs in other places than work groups (the concept of partial inclusion) and if that is the case, then structures may be much more responsive to task demands and much less responsive to need satisfaction than this formulation suggests. Furthermore, the idea of a stable structure seems to conflict with the kind of structure one sees more frequently. It is common to find that people develop a workable, satisfactory-for-the-*moment*, temporary, and intermittently changing structure. This has a number of implications for organizational change, one of which is that change may not occur against quite the background of stable structure that the theory contends. Or at least the ties among pairs of people may not be of the intensity that the concept of a stable group would imply.

There are several interesting issues buried in Mackenzie's discussion of differential evaluation. Basically, he is postulating that when people are faced with the decision of whether to drop an old activity in favor of a new one, their evaluation process downgrades, benefits, and exaggerates costs, both of dropping and of adopting. Others who work in the tradition of dissonance theory would argue that this exaggeration and downgrading does not occur prior to the decision but rather occurs subsequent to making it. It does appear that during the pre-decision period people pay more attention to the alternative that is eventually not chosen (Jones and Gerard, 1965, p. 195), but the evidence does not suggest that this differential attention is accompanied by concurrent evaluation. Among the many reasons for this neutrality toward the alternatives during the pre-decisional phase is that the person is actually trying to establish what the costs and benefits are and then establish some values so that he can arrive at some cost-benefit summary prior to making the decision. Now the interesting twist that is added to this problem area by Mackenzie is the fact that in his choice situations, the choice consists of an ongoing old activity and the question of whether it should be dropped in favor of a new activity. This is not a common choice dilemma studied by dissonance theorists and it may well be that when the alternatives consist of a current practice versus changing to a new activity, evaluations of the activities *do* occur in the pre-decisional phase. This would be a fascinating point to pursue, since there is a growing concern with conceptualizing activity as something that is continuously going on rather than something that starts up and stops (see Atkinson, 1969). For the moment the only thing we can say is that Mackenzie may have raised a fascinating theoretical puzzle. But it should also be pointed out that existing data do not totally support the idea that costs are given greater attention in the pre-decisional phase.

I am also intrigued by Mackenzie's use of a rental fee charged to manipulate the difficulty of structural change in a network. As described, that seems like an exceedingly useful procedure to enrich laboratory networks. Also, the manipulation of social costs such that one student's decision binds the other members and they too must pay money without having a say is a plausible manipulation of social costs. I think Mackenzie might be able to nudge this manipulation even closer to organizational change by increasing the risk in the rental fees. If there were a bonus for a very fast solution of the problem, such that by buying extra channels a group has some increased probability of getting this bonus, then this might capture more of the risk involved in organizational change without a radical change in the experimental procedure. This would also allow Mackenzie to determine prior to renting the channel, whether it is true that costs are given more attention than benefits (his differential evaluation formulation).

A few concluding remarks will summarize the intent of this essay. The invitation to comment on Mackenzie's work stated that we were free to disagree with an author's emphasis. Prior to reading Mackenzie's paper I anticipated that disagreements would be minimal since I regard Mackenzie as a first-rate experimenter who thinks clearly. Obviously, the disagreements were more substantial than I anticipated. What should not get lost is the fact that I learned more about organizational change by trying to explain why I would set this problem up differently than Mackenzie did. I would never have learned these things about change without Mackenzie's help. And I'm grateful to him for that assistance. Comparing our two approaches, the reader may also be benefited in clarifying his own thoughts about change. If that happens, then both Mackenzie and I have accomplished what we intended.

SUGGESTIONS FOR FUTURE READING

ATKINSON, J. W., "Change of Activity," in T. Mischel (Ed.), *Human Action* (New York: Academic Press, 1969), pp. 105–133.

BARNETT, H. G., *Innovation, the Basis of Cultural Change* (New York: McGraw-Hill Book Co., Inc., 1953).

CAMPBELL, D. T., "Variation and Selective Retention in Socio-Cultural Evolution," in H. R. Barringer, G. I. Blanksten, and R. Mack (Eds.), *Social Change in Developing Areas* (Cambridge, Massachusetts: Schenkman Publishing Company, 1965), pp. 19–49.

COSTELLO, T. W., "Change in Municipal Government: A View from the Inside," *Journal of Applied Behavioral Science,* Vol. 7 (1971), pp. 131–145.

DUNN, E. S., JR., *Economic and Social Development* (Baltimore: Johns Hopkins University Press, 1971).

EMERSON, JOAN P., "Nothing Unusual is Happening," in T. Shibutani (Ed.), *Human Nature and Collective Behavior* (Englewood Cliffs, N.J.: Prentice-Hall, Inc., 1970), pp. 208–222.

HIRSCHMAN, A. O., AND C. E. LINDBLOM, "Economic Development, Research and Development, Policy Making: Some Converging Views," *Behavioral Science,* Vol. 7 (1962), pp. 211–222.

HOMANS, G. C., *The Human Group* (New York: Harcourt, Brace, 1950).

JONES, E. E., AND H. B. GERARD, *Foundations of Social Psychology* (New York: John Wiley & Sons, 1967).

MCGRATH, J. F., "Toward a 'Theory of Method' for Research on Organizations," in W. W. Cooper, H. J. Leavitt, and M. W. Shelly (Eds.), *New Perspectives in Organization Research* (New York: John Wiley & Sons, 1964), pp. 533–556.

SCHEFF, T. J., "Negotiating Reality: Notes on Power in the Assessment of Responsibility," *Social Problems,* Vol. 16 (1968), pp. 3–17.

SCHUTZ, A., "The Stranger," in A. Brodersen (Ed.), *Collected Papers,* Vol. II (The Hague: Martinus Nyhoff, 1964), pp. 91–105.

SERVICE, E. R., "The Law of Evolutionary Potential," in M. D. Sahlins and E. R. Service (Eds.), *Evolution and Culture* (Ann Arbor: University of Michigan Press, 1960), pp. 93–122.

WEICK, K. E., AND D. P. GILFILLAN, The Sway and Decay of Tradition. University of Minnesota, 1971, unpublished manuscript.

Alternative Approaches to Organizational Change

Alan C. Filley

Professor
Graduate School of Business
University of Wisconsin, Madison

It is my understanding that the chapters in this volume are supposed to summarize the present state of the art with respect to topics presented and to suggest possible new directions in the field of management. As reviewer of this chapter I proposed to do the following: (1) summarize the thesis presented by Mackenzie, (2) comment on strengths and weaknesses in the thesis, (3) suggest some other approaches to the topic of growth and development, and (4) discuss one of these alternative approaches in more detail.

MAJOR THESIS PRESENTED

As I read it, the paper suggests the following:

1. Many things are changing, and many topics might be included under the subject of "change."
2. Aside from changes in physical properties, one might usefully deal with the issue of change in terms of:
   - a. the behavior of the change adopter;
   - b. the kind and degree of the behavioral change ("nature of the change");
   - c. processes involved in the adoption decision;
   - d. processes involved in moving a change from the initial to subsequent adoptors ("diffusion processes").
3. The anticipated resistance to change may be reduced through several strategies:
   - a. using planners to minimize change effort by participants;
   - b. segmenting changes into temporal units;
   - c. dividing change into differential responsibilities;
   - d. adjusting the real or perceived cost/benefit balance in the minds and actions of those affected.
4. One may, through matrix algebra, model organization structure and process by:
   - a. displaying activities associated with parts (individuals or groups) to show roles;
   - b. displaying the structure of interactions between parts;
   - c. displaying start and completion of subprocesses;
5. One can represent change by displaying the effect on 4a and 4b above (the third matrix is dropped from further discussion) of, say, a restructuring of communication patterns; that is, structure, as shown, may become the dependent variable for experimental purposes.

SOME COMMENTS

If one is to make a judgment, one must state the basis of comparison. In the case of Mackenzie's paper, one might consider comparing it with other theoretical approaches, with the stated goals of the chapter, with the work of others on the same subject, and with the somewhat arbitrary tastes of the reviewer himself.

Before making such comparisons

I think it helpful to place Mackenzie's discussion in the context of alternative approaches to theory. In relating theory to data, there are at least four modes of theory construction that might be identified (Marx, 1963, p. 10). The first is a *model* that presents an analogue of real-world phenomena, often in physical or mathematical terms. The second is *deductive theory*, which is a logical arrangement of explicit formulations of explanatory propositions, emphasizing internal consistency and logical elegance. The third is *functional* theory. Such theory is provisional, emphasizing its tool value in recording the relating research findings and in generating hypotheses for further research. Finally, *inductive theory* is little more than summary statements regarding empirical findings, with a minimum of inference or deduction.

The first part of Mackenzie's chapter, dealing with the concept of change, seems to be deductive and functional in character whereas the last part and the bulk of the thesis presented relates to a model that might be used in studying change. The early discussion of change concepts does not deal with empirical realities. Rather, it introduces logical elements that might fruitfully be tied to some kind of model of change dealing with system, goals, structure, process, participants, or merely the calculative balance between a present and future state.

The change concepts become the basis for discussing "techniques" ("strategies," "methods," "procedures") utilized in reducing resistance to change. Such resistance might well be defined if it is to be in the discussion, specifying the balance of utilities or disutilities involved, the nature and source of resistance (individuals, systems, structures), and appropriate empirical evidence about alternative techniques. Furthermore, I do not see much difference between the first method suggested in which "many specialists work many long hours to work out the 'bugs' in the system . . ." and a later method in which one finds ". . . specialists whose function is to absorb some of the risk and uncertainty . . ." through planning.

Behavior effect, or attitudes aside, it might be useful to explore the structural arrangements that facilitate or impede change. The literature is rich with information concerning how rules, hierarchy, departmentalization, task forces, integrating specialists, and manipulation of resources affect the responsiveness of people to change in organizations (Burns and Stalker, 1961; Dutton and Fitch, 1966; Galbraith, 1968 and 1969; Hall, 1962; Lawrence and Lorsch, 1967; Lorsch and Lawrence, 1968; Reeves and Turner, 1972; Walker and Lorsch, 1968; Thompson, 1967; Woodward, 1965).

Finally, Mackenzie seems to base the thrust of his thesis on the matrices representing activities, interactions among organizational parts, and benchmarks of subprocesses. One might applaud this effort either on the basis of an innovative new approach containing a certain amount of theoretical elegance or for its tool value in generating empirical findings. Unfortunately, the use of matrix algebra for modeling various dimensions of organizations is not uncommon (see, for example, Starbuck, 1965; Stinchcombe, 1961; Carzo and Yanouzas, 1957). As a matter of fact, the particular matrix dealing with subprocesses, which is introduced in the paper and then dropped from further discussion, is not unlike the typical computer matrix used to process critical path schedules.

The experimental evidence presented at the end of the paper does not persuade me of the tool value of the model. The structural processes described need not depend on the matrix and, as the author seems to suggest, empirical prediction is as yet limited by "formidable estimation problems."

SOME OTHER APPROACHES TO CHANGE

Since organization growth and development is a subcategory of "organization change," some other approaches to the subject raised by Mackenzie may be illustrated. Here a brief overview of the literature is presented as well as some further detail about one model of growth and change.

In his rather heroic review of the literature on the subject, Starbuck (1965, 1972) identifies four basic models of growth. The first is the *cell-division model.* Such approaches often treat the firm as a biological analogy and conceive of growth and change in much the same way as an organism grows through cell division. For example, Haire (1959) drew on Thompson's work (1952) dealing with biological growth to consider the interrelationship among size, shape, and function in the firm. He argued (pp. 277–279) that "the rate of increase (in company size) can be determined from the first few generations," in practice the first 3 years, to be limited as environmental constraints began to operate. Cell-division models emphasize the prediction of total size over time and pay little attention to adaptation processes.

The second is the *metamorphosis model.* These focus on the patterns of structure that appear as the firm changes in *kind* as well as degree. Just as the human differs in structure and function from infancy, to adolescence, to adulthood, so the organization is frequently considered in terms of sequential stages or ideal types. For example, describing union organizations and the growth of the labor movement, Lester (1958) identified a pre-growth period as was common prior to 1932, a period of rapid growth and development from 1933 to 1946, and a period of institutional middle-age after 1947. Although in the thirties and forties nearly every national union was organizing militantly and was led by visible, charismatic individuals, the later period was characterized as one of corporate-like operations with staffs of experts and professional leaders. Such metamorphosis models are poorly suited to identifying cause and effect, but they do facilitate classification and comparison of organizations. We shall return to this type later.

The third model for growth is the *will-o'-the-wisp.* Here growth is a process of pursuing some kind of resource or advantage. For example, Edith Penrose (1959) suggests that in planning growth a firm considers its inherited resources—that is, its available factors of production, including management—and the resources that must be obtained from the market. Growth or expansion will draw on services of present management and such services constitute the limit on the rate of growth. Unlike economists, who have assumed management to be a fixed factor, Penrose argues that, additions to management aside, present management becomes an increasing resource through improvements in its own ability.

As indicated, will-o'-the-wisp models are more concerned with cause-and-effect relationships and tend to focus on a limited number of processes related to growth and development.

The fourth type is the *decision-process model.* Here the model builder attempts to reproduce the basic characteristics of a single decision process in enough detail to permit actual prediction of decisions made. Once an accurate simulation is demonstrated, it then becomes possible to test the outcome of possible alternative decision strategies. For example, Clarkson (1963) constructed a model of the trust investment process employed by trust officers of a bank that rather closely approximated decisions actually made on portfolio selection. Such models clearly set forth causal factors in the process of change.

The four models presented above hardly do justice to the variety of issues involved in the process of growth, development, and change but they do suggest the scope of the literature related to the topic of the chapter and that could have been advantageously included in the chapter.

VALUES AND LIMITS OF METAMORPHOSIS MODELS

My own interest and experience are with metamorphosis models and I should like to suggest some characteristics in more detail. The literature dealing with institutional growth exhibits a number of common strains. Stage theories or ideal typologies have been suggested by a number of writers. Max Weber (1947) described types of political and economic organizations as "traditional," "charismatic," and "bureaucratic"; Lippitt and Schmidt (1967) describe organization growth in terms of crises associated with "birth," "youth," and "maturity." National growth has been characterized in Western nations in terms of a progression from "feudal culture," to "dynamic politico-economic expansion," to "consolidation" by Bennett and McKnight (1956); and by Rostow (1960) for nations in general as stages starting with the "traditional" and passing through "pre-conditions for take-off," "the take off," "the drive to maturity," and "maturity." Eric Hoffer (1958) has described mass social movements in terms of leadership by the "man of words," "the fanatic," and finally by "the practical man of action." There are others as well.

This writer has also proposed a metamorphosis model dealing with three types of firms identified as a *craft stage, a promotion stage,* and an *administrative stage* (Filley and House, 1969). The model is limited to internal growth in firms with a single product base and does not assume that all stages must occur or that they necessarily occur in one order. Stages are determined by a syndrome of structural and managerial characteristics and appear to be associated with different rates of change within the firm.

The *craft stage* may be briefly characterized as one in which institutional goals are comfort to owners and survival. Policies are fixed by past practice and are not highly adaptable. Leadership is exerted by the owner-manager, who is likely to be skilled in the technology of the firm and whose position is established through his ownership of resources. Morale is not a problem because limited mobility of members and stability of roles keep expectations consistent with reality. The craft firm typically emphasizes a single function such as production or sales and structures itself into levels of power rather than into roles or positions. Since the firm does not seek growth or adaptation, it makes little use of staff services for planning or control, assuming a continuation of past practices. Such firms evidence little adaptability or innovation and decisions are made by the owner-manager under conditions he perceives as certain.

The *promotion stage* is built around a strong central leader and the exploitation of an innovative advantage. Objectives are high levels of achievement and rapid growth, with policies improvised by the leader as tactics change. The leader displays a high need for achievement, a low fear of failure, and a charismatic influence on organization members. Morale in this stage is based on reinforcement of high expectations, accompanied by a high degree of interaction among a heterogeneous group of members. Functional development occurs with successive emphasis on production, sales, financial control, staff support, and a separation of administration from operations. Such firms seem to structure themselves informally, like a field of force around the leader, with the promoter intruding into all aspects of the organization. The staff services are limited to personal assistants to the leader and technical or housekeeping services. In the promotion stage members are proactive and innovative. They act on, rather than adapt to, the environment. Since there is little experience base to draw on, decision-making occurs under conditions of uncertainty rather than risk. Economies in this stage are heavily weighted to those of the growth process rather than size or scale. Successful termination of the stage depends on a shift, then, from external exploitation to internal efficiency.

The *administrative stage* is one in which the firm develops an institutional character apart from its members, and, if successful, relies on adaptation to the market and environment. Institutional goals of profitability, growth, adaptation, and the like, are separate from those of organization members. Policy becomes stable and known, representing a rule of law. Leadership is based on professional ability to perform requirements of specified positions. Morale is based on achievement of differentiated member goals and is associated with limited interaction and a more homogeneous work group. Although dependent on technology, indirect labor constitutes a large proportion of the membership, and functional balance and integration are displayed. Staff engages in planning, control, and development activities, permitting decision-making under conditions of risk rather than uncertainty and product development rather than innovation.

Transition into the administrative stage from the craft or promotion stage involves planning, restructuring, establishment of internal controls, and the addition or development of professional management skills. Thus, the transition may occur gradually over several years. The transition from the craft to the promotion stage requires a significant change in leadership style, expectations, and technology that occur rapidly in a matter of months, probably no more than a year. Thus craft firms, if they change at all, will more likely become administratively structured than move into a promotion stage.

In considering this and other metamorphosis models, we should examine their values and limits. By design, such models emphasize changes in kind as well as degree. In part, this is a function of having more than two types or stages. They also suggest that strategies endemic to, and perhaps contributing to, success in one stage of development may be seriously dysfunctional in another. Metamorphosis models contain a high degree of internal consistency within a type or stage that demonstrates interdependency of parts.

There are difficulties as well. Like some other models the metamorphosis models seldom attempt to differentiate among changes resulting from age, size, technology, and internal changes in character. In addition, some suggest an unalterable evolution of stages whereas others are more likened to classes of types. Finally, such models often suggest or imply normative aspects, based on the assumption that growth or change is good.

Metamorphosis models have tool value empirically by incorporating findings as they are present, through explaining phenomena with brevity, and by suggesting hypotheses for further testing. In comparing a metamorphic explanation with other models of growth in the history of ten firms, Starbuck (1968) demonstrated the unique explanatory value of the former, though suggesting that many forces external to the firms instigated the changes involved. The models have also been shown to relate to predictable patterns or rates of growth (Rostow, 1960; Filley and House, 1969; Schroeder, 1953).

The evolutionary character of institutions (i.e., change in kind as well as degree) has also been demonstrated through the use of Guttman scaling techniques. Although assuming unidimensionality and not arranged into stages per se, such scalings display the successive addition of organizational characteristics as an institution evolves. Carneiro and Tobias (1963) have shown political, social, and structural developments in 100 societies. Udy (1958 has presented the development of twenty-five prediction-oriented organizations, and Hall and Tittle (1966) used a Guttman scale of perceived bureaucratization derived from twenty-five organizations. It would seem that such models provide a useful method of explaining change and development.

CONCLUSION

The preceding discussion concerned a critique of the explanation for organization change offered by Professor Mackenzie and suggested other approaches to the subject. Mackenzie has chosen to summarize his own work on the subject. This would be most defensible if it represents the leading or only work on the method described. Yet, as suggested earlier, there are others who have worked in the same vein and their work might well have been included in what is intended as a review chapter. The other forms of remodeling change cited also have shown themselves useful in describing organizational change.

BIBLIOGRAPHY

Bennett, J. W., and R. W. McKnight, "Approaches of a Japanese Innovator to Cultural and Technical Change," *Annals of the American Academy of Political and Social Science,* Vol. 305 (May, 1956).

Burns, Thomas, and M. Stalker, *The Management of Innovation* (London: Tavistock Publishers, 1961).

Carneiro, R., and S. Tobias, "The Application of Scale Analysis to the Study of Cultural Evolution," *Transactions of the New York Academy of Sciences,* Ser. II, Vol. 26 (December, 1963).

Carzo, R., and J. Yanouzas, *Formal Organization* (Homewood, Illinois: Richard D. Irwin and the Dorsey Press, 1967).

Clarkson, G. E., "A Model of Trust Investment Behavior," in R. Cyert and J. March (Eds.), *Behavioral Theory of the Firm* (Englewood Cliffs, N.J.: Prentice-Hall, Inc., 1963).

Dutton, J., R. Walton, and H. Fitch, "A Study of Conflict in the Process, Structure and Attitudes of Lateral Relationships," in A. H. Rubenstein and C. J. Haberstroh (Eds.), *Some Theories of Organization,* rev. ed. (Homewood, Illinois: Richard D. Irwin, 1966).

Filley, A. C., and R. J. House, *Managerial Process and Organizational Behavior* (Glenview, Illinois: Scott, Foresman and Co., 1959).

Galbraith, Jay, "Achieving Integration Through Information Systems," *Proceedings of the Academy of Management* (December, 1968).

Galbraith, Jay, "Organization Design: An Information Processing View," Working Paper, Massachusetts Institute of Technology (October, 1969).

Haire, M. (Ed.), *Modern Organization Theory* (New York: John Wiley & Sons, 1959).

Hall, R., "Intra Organizational Structure Variation," *Administrative Science Quarterly* (December, 1962), pp. 295–308.

Hall, R. H., and C. R. Tittle, "A Note on Bureaucracy and its Correlates," *American Journal of Sociology,* Vol. 72 (1966).

Hoffer, E., *The True Believer* (New York: The New American Library of World Literature, 1958).

Lawrence, P., and J. Lorsch, *Organization and Environment* (Boston: Division of Research, Harvard Business School, 1967).

Lester, R. A., *As Unions Mature* (Princeton, N.J.: Princeton University Press, 1958).

Lippitt, G. L., and W. H. Schmidt, "Crises in a Developing Organization," *Harvard Business Review,* Vol. 45, No. 6 (November–December, 1967), pp. 102–112.

Lorsch, J., and P. Lawrence, "Environmental Factors and Organization Integration," Paper read at the Annual Meeting of the American Sociological Association, August 27, 1968, Boston, Massachusetts.

Marx, M. H., *Theories in Contemporary Psychology* (New York: Collier-Macmillan, 1963).

Penrose, R., *The Theory of the Growth of the Firm* (New York: John Wiley & Sons, 1959).

REEVES, T. K., and B. TURNER, "A Theory of Organization and Behavior in Batch Production Factories," *Administrative Science Quarterly*, Vol. 17, No. 1 (March, 1972), pp. 81–98.

ROSTOW, W. W., *The Stages of Economic Growth* (Cambridge, Massachusetts: Harvard University Press, 1960).

SCHROEDER, G., *The Growth of Major Steel Companies* (Baltimore: Johns Hopkins University Press, 1953).

STARBUCK, W. (Ed.), *Organizational Growth and Development* (Baltimore: Penguin Books, 1971).

STARBUCK, W., "Mathematics and Organization Theory," and "Organizational ganizational Growth and Development," in J. March (Ed.), *Handbook of Organizations* (Chicago: Rand McNally & Company, 1965).

STARBUCK, W., "Organizational Metamorphosis," in R. W. Millman and M. P. Hottenstein (Eds.), *Promising Research Directions* (New York: Academy of Management, 1968).

STINCHCOMBE, A. L., "On the Use of Matrix Algebra in the Analysis of Formal Organization," in A. Etzioni (Ed.), *Complex Organizations* (New York: Holt, Rinehart and Winston, 1961).

THOMPSON, D., *On Growth and Form*, 2nd ed. (Cambridge, Massachusetts: Harvard University Press, 1952).

THOMPSON, J., *Organizations in Action* (New York: McGraw-Hill Book Co., Inc., 1967).

UDY, S. H., "Bureaucratic Elements in Organization," *American Sociological Review*, Vol. 23, No. 4 (1958), pp. 415–418.

WALKER, A. H., and J. LORSCH, "Organizational Choice: Product vs. Function," *Harvard Business Review*, Vol. 46 (November–December, 1968), pp. 129–138.

WEBER, MAX, *The Theory of Social and Economic Organization*, translated and edited by Am. M. Henderson and T. Parsons (New York: Oxford University Press, 1947).

WOODWARD, J., *Industrial Organization: Theory and Practice* (London: Oxford University Press, 1965).

DISCUSSION QUESTIONS

1. What does the "nature of change" mean?
2. Define and describe adoption and the diffusion processes.
3. List and define three "structures of organization."
4. Discuss the three options open to a person who wishes to study organizational change.
5. What is your impression of Mackenzie's experimental methodology? Why? What is Weick's impression?
6. Discuss and contrast the cell-division, metamorphosis, will-o'-the-wisp, and decision-process models of change.

10

Organizations and the External Environment

Gerald D. Bell

Associate Professor
Graduate School of Business Administration
University of North Carolina

INTRODUCTION

The degree to which an organization thrives depends to a great extent on how well it adapts to it's external environment. If the customers of a retail firm change their preferences for styles of clothing, for example, and the firm continues to stock only the styles that have been popular in the past, the customers lose their loyalty to their old store and search for alternatives.

Today's environment presents organizations with shockingly rapid changes in knowledge, technology, communications, and transportation. Furthermore, organizations are becoming more international, products have shorter life cycles, and work is becoming more professionalized. Consequently, organizations must monitor and adjust themselves to situations that are much more complex than in the past.

Recently a textile firm closed its doors. The interesting point was that it was the largest textile firm in the United States during the 1930's. In contrast, Burlington Industries was started in the 1930's and it has grown to be the largest textile company and one of the biggest firms in the world. In examining what happened to the company that died, one factor stood out clearly—the firm had changed very little since its founding days. Management practices, product lines, marketing strategies, and personnel policies were "out of touch" with the changes that had occurred in the firm's environment. On the other hand, Burlington Industries has adapted effectively to the environmental conditions that it has encountered. Because of the rapid changes in our society, organizations are more dependent on effective adaptation to their environments than ever before.

The question we are interested in here is, How do organizations adapt effectively to their external environments? To answer this question we will examine (1) the key dimensions of organizations' external environments, (2) the major aspects of organizational design, (3) six major types of environmental systems and how they affect organizations' operations, and (4) the mechanisms organizations use to adapt to their environments.

WHAT IS AN ORGANIZATION'S ENVIRONMENT

An organization's external environment consists of those things outside an organization such as customers, competitors, government units, suppliers, financial firms, and labor pools that are relevant to an organization's operations. As one can readily see, often there is not a clear distinction between what is inside or outside an organization.

For example, do you consider a university's students as falling inside or outside the organization? This type of dilemma introduces the concept of an organization's *boundary*.[1] An organization's boundary is that line or fence that distinguishes the inside of an organization from its external environment. Boundaries of organizations vary on how visible, firm, expansive, or easily penetrable they are. Accordingly, environments vary on how complex, changing, powerful, and homogeneous they are. We have formulated a model of six basic types of external environments and will discuss these shortly.

THE KEY DIMENSIONS OF AN ORGANIZATION

All organizations, from very small groups to large firms, depend on and thus are open to their external environments for survival. They are not self-sufficient nor self-contained. Each organization imports some form of *input* from the environment. Raw materials, money, labor, and energy are examples of inputs into the organizational system. Once an organization acquires inputs, it transforms or modifies them. This transformation process is called the *throughput* of an organization. After throughput processes have occurred, an organization exports some product into the environment in the form of an *output*. When an organization exports its output to its external environment, the transaction returns to the organization as *feedback* or new inputs. An organization, therefore, is open to be influenced by and to influence its environment because it is in a constant recycling process with its environment.

Organizations have four major internal subsystems or components—technological, structural, normative, and human.

Technical Subsystem

An organization's technical subsystem refers to the main work techniques carried on to reach its major goals. Each job, department, and organization has a variety of techniques of work to perform in order to pro-

[1] J. S. Adams, Behavior in Organization Boundary Roles. Unpublished manuscript, 1971.

duce its main products and to reach its objectives. Workers on the assembly line in a production plant, most physicians and nurses in a hospital, professors and secretaries in a university are carrying out major productive tasks by using certain work techniques. Their techniques vary in complexity, homogeneity, and repetitiveness, and in the extent of training and judgment required to perform them adequately.

Structural Subsystem

The structural subsystem refers to the ways in which the relationships among the members of the organization are patterned. Organizations vary on how formalized the relationships are, how decentralized or centralized the points of decision-making are, and how the different jobs in the throughput process are divided up. Jobs can be grouped according to common processes, products, or locations.

Normative Subsystem

The normative subsystem of an organization consists of its guiding traditions, values, philosophies, and goals. New members of an organization quickly learn what they should and should not do. In one large textile firm, for example, the norms are strongly religious. Therefore, employees are not allowed to smoke or swear at work, and twice a day production is stopped for a one-minute prayer.

Human Subsystem

The human subsystem refers to the types of personalities, group relations, and leadership styles that the members of an organization possess. Some organizations select and train their people to be friendly and cooperative, whereas others seek more aggressive, competitive types. Accordingly, individuals vary in the degree to which they seek to participate with their subordinates or to dominate them.

ORGANIZATIONS AS SYSTEMS

Each of these components is significantly interdependent. Because of this interdependence, we refer to organizations as *systems*.[2] Whenever there is a change in one of the components or *subsystems*, the change causes alterations in the other subsystems. If a firm were to completely automate its technology, for example, the change would have important effects on the organization's structure in the form of new possibilities for measuring performance, reducing labor costs, and training management. There might be new *norms* of rationality and planning, and fewer *people* with different

[2]Daniel Katz and Robert L. Kahn, *The Social Psychology of Organizations* (New York: John Wiley & Sons, 1966).

personalities hired. Since the interdependence of the subsystems of an organization is important for understanding the relationship between an organization and its environment, this topic will be analyzed more carefully.

THE INTERDEPENDENCE OF AN ORGANIZATION'S SUBSYSTEMS

Effects of the Technical System

The technical or productive activities encourage management to shape the structural components in particular ways. One investigation suggests, for example, that the more complex the tasks of production workers, the less inclined management will be to establish rules or close supervision.[3] In other words, the more unpredictable the work demands are, the more decentralization and flexibility there will be.

The technical activities also are closely related to the *human system.* Many bemoan, for example, the loss of variety in many workers' jobs.[4] Social commentators say that lack of novelty in work is producing a robot-like society.[5] And research suggests that job satisfaction and productivity suffer when variety is taken out of work.[6] In the view of an auto assembly-line employee:

> My job is to see that the body fits properly, and to clean the steering column. After the body is dropped on the chassis, I put in four bolts; I spray rubber dough on the toe plates, I hook up a striplight wire; I clip speedometer cables in two places, place a cover shield on the steering column. That's about it in a minute and a half. . . . Anybody that wants to work on a moving line has got rocks in his head. . . . It's rough. It's too steady, too much of a pace.[7]

Dislike of routine jobs is not the exclusive preserve of skilled and unskilled workers, however, for many supervisors and staff personnel also seem to be unfavorably disposed toward repetitive activities.[8] Correspondingly, Andrews reports that scientists who perform several different tasks, such as teaching and administration, along with their research, tend to have higher performance rates than those who work full time only at research.[9]

[3]Gerald D. Bell, *Formalism Versus Flexibility In Complex Organizations: A Comparative Investigation Within A Hospital.* Ph.D. Dissertation, Yale University, 1964.

[4]Eric Fromm, *The Sane Society* (New York: Holt, Rinehart and Winston, 1955).

[5]George Orwell, *1984* (New York: New American Library of World Literature, Inc., 1955).

[6]Nancy C. Morse, *Satisfaction in the White-Collar Job* (Ann Arbor: Institute for Social Research, University of Michigan, 1953); Chris Argyris, *Understanding Organizational Behavior* (Homewood, Illinois: The Dorsey Press, 1960); F. C. Mann and L. K. Williams, "Some Effects of the Changing Work Environment in the office," *Journal of Social Issues,* Vol. 18 (1962), pp. 90–101.

[7]Thomas M. Lodahl, "Patterns of Job Attitudes in Two Assembly Technologies," *Administrative Science Quarterly,* Vol. 8 (March, 1964), pp. 482–520.

[8]Frank Friedlander and Eugene Walton, "Positive and Negative Motivations Toward Work," *Administrative Science Quarterly,* Vol. 9 (September, 1964), p. 193.

[9]Frank M. Andrews, "Scientific Performance and Time in Teaching or Administration," *Administrative Science Quarterly,* Vol. 9 (September, 1964), p. 193.

In a similar vein, with the advance of automation and technology, the growing specialization of tasks is producing numerous occupations for which we have no names. Consequently, many workers' occupational titles lack social significance outside of their trade or company. As Robert K. Merton comments, "The splintering of work tasks involves loss of public identity of the job. Who but a chosen few, for example, can distinguish a fin sticker in an automobile plant from some other radiator-core assemblers."[10]

Finally, technical activities have an important, yet subtle, impact on the *normative subsystems* of an organization; the goals and traditions of an institution are constantly being reshaped as technological changes in both machinery and knowledge occur. For example, as we acquire more knowledge and skill in retraining criminals, many of the prisons whose goals have traditionally been only to protect society have adopted new policies for rehabilitating society's deviants.[11]

Effects of the Structural System

The structural component of an organization also has important effects on the other three categories—technical, human, and normative. When workers are dissatisfied with their jobs, administrators often reshape the nature of technical *processes*. They expand workers' responsibilities, make their tasks more difficult to perform, and consequently alter the types of products, services and machinery of the technical system.[12]

The effects of structuring activities on the *human relationships* of employees are probably quite familiar to readers. The structure your professor uses in conducting his class affects your attitude toward him. When your supervisor rewarded you by telling you that your work was very good or by giving you a raise, you undoubtedly felt highly gratified—a response that signifies the impact of administrative activities on your personal life at work. Similarly, you probably have been in situations in which you had to wait in line for a long time or had to get "four copies of a form filled out and signed by twelve people." The anger that you may have felt toward these structural conditions again demonstrates the close connection between administrative structure and human adjustments.

The *normative characteristics* of an organization are molded by management's efforts in many, often subtle ways. Several of the early glass-manufacturing establishments formed in the 1800's in America were started by entrepreneurs of European descent. The cultures of their corporations quickly took on the values of the managers: their goals were to produce quality products; their leisure time was devoted to European recreational pursuits. When mass production started to appear, these companies were

[10]Robert K. Merton, *Social Theory and Social Structure*, rev. ed. (New York: The Free Press of Glencoe, 1957), p. 564.

[11]Gerald D. Bell, *Organizations and Human Behavior* (Englewood Cliffs, N.J.: Prentice-Hall, Inc., 1967).

[12]Gerald D. Bell, *Formality Versus Flexibility in Complex Organizations: A Comparative Investigation Within a Hospital.* Unpublished doctoral dissertation, Yale University, Department of Sociology, 1965.

often the slowest to change their operational patterns. For example, quality and craftsmanship remained high in priority, and quantity (mass production) was accorded little importance. Consequently, new technological developments were not readily adopted by these firms.

Effects of the Human System

The satisfaction an individual experiences in his work, the sentiments he holds toward his supervisors, and the warmth he feels toward his co-workers are important determinants of his life within an organization. One's personal adjustment has significant effects, first of all, on the *technical* activities: If a worker is highly dissatisfied with his job, for example, he may damage machinery, slow down his output, or perform his tasks erratically.

Workers' personal sentiments also have important effects on the *structuring* of activities. Employees' feelings are expressed to administrators by various means—through union grievances, work slowdowns, subtle comments, and/or more direct communications. Managers usually seek the positive commitment of employees and invest a great amount of time, energy, and money to gain it. If employees are discontented, administrators often alter the communication networks, reward structures, and styles of leadership to increase satisfaction and commitment.

Finally, the feelings and personal relationships of employees are translated over time into *normative traditions* and policies of the organization. When new members are brought into a work group, they are taught by the older employees the history of their relationships with various supervisors, the feelings generally held about specific jobs, and so forth.

Effects of the Normative System

The norms of an organization influence the *techniques* of work the employees are willing to use. In some firms, for example, salesmen learn that they ought to try to use a "hard sell" approach, whereas in others the "soft sell" approach is stressed. Similarly, if an organization's norms embrace democratic and equalitarian beliefs, the *structure* of relationships will be molded in more decentralized patterns. Accordingly, the *human* relationships, personalities, and leadership styles that will be sought and rewarded within a democratic normative system will be more open and achievement-oriented than in a normative system that encourages authoritarian beliefs.

THE EXTERNAL ENVIRONMENTS' SUBSYSTEMS: A MACRO-VIEW

How do organizations relate to their external environments? To examine this question it is helpful to break down environments into the same four broad components—technical, structural, normative, and human, and then to examine the relationships of organizations to each of these components.

Technology

Every society has a technological base of skills, tools, and knowledge that its members and formal organizations use to provide for their needs. Each society differs in the degree of development of technology. The United States, for example, has a more advanced level of technology in such things as space exploration and medicine than do countries such as Pakistan or India. Thus, the kinds of productive activities that can be carried on in space centers and hospitals in America will be much different from comparable activities in India. The structures of organizations within a society, then, are highly dependent on the levels of technology existing in that society.

As a society becomes more industrialized, the rate of technological innovation increases. Similarly, the larger organizations within a society tend to develop relatively higher levels of technological change than do the smaller units. Consequently, larger enterprises experience greater pressures for reorganizing their structural, human, and normative systems.

Current developments in automation and computers symbolize the rapid rate of technological change in the Western world. Automation refers to the development of productive equipment that no longer needs to be designed to fit the physical and mental capacities of man (that is, where machines control their own operations, they correct their own errors and move products throughout the entire production cycle). Automation has created numerous changes in occupations and organizations within our society. In Esso's refinery at Fawley, England, for example, six men on every shift process 5.5 million gallons of crude oil a day.[13]

The electronic processing of information by computers has also had significant effects on patterns of work. In the kitchens of the Sara Lee Company in Deerfield, Illinois, the computer system not only mixes and bakes twelve different kinds of cakes, but also packages them, freezes them, stores them, starts them on their way to the store, and even handles some of the bookwork. These computers direct operations at about 15,000 points in the plant, issue 180,000 instructions every 3 seconds, monitor some 300 variables in the cake-baking process, and scan 200 incoming messages per second. The kinds of occupations that exist, the patterns of supervision, and the worker relationships are significantly altered by these types of changes in technology.

A potential disaster that many see as a consequence of automation is unemployment. Although there is no clear evidence, the balance of arguments suggests that automation is reducing the number of jobs available in our society more rapidly than it is creating new ones. In farming, for example, in 1949 one man could produce enough food for fifteen people, but in 1960 one man could produce enough for twenty-four. Since 1945 productivity in bituminous coal mining rose 96 per cent, but employment fell by 262,000. Railroad productivity has increased by 65 per cent, and employ-

[13]Arnold B. Barach, *U.S.A. and Its Economic Future* (New York: The Macmillan Company, 1964).

ment has declined by 540,00.[14] Although all these changes do not result solely from automation, a large part of the decrease in number of jobs does stem from the elimination of unskilled jobs by automatic machinery.

Automation, furthermore, makes work physically easier, thereby permitting more older people to work with automatic machinery. Such a development may be a mixed blessing, however, since unions and management are encouraging earlier retirement because of unemployment and older individuals—often the most difficult to re-educate—need to be retained for new jobs.

Automation has potentially positive benefits, however, since it creates new jobs that require higher education and occupational skills. It frees human hands from physical labor and increases leisure time. These consequences must remain in the "potential benefits" category because, although there are increased demands for highly trained employees, society's ability to produce enough trained individuals often lags behind the demand. Similarly, with physical labor having been taken out of most jobs, we are now confronted with problems of keeping people physically fit. And finally, even though free time for leisurely pursuits has grow,n, many people are unhappy with extra time on their hands. With these thoughts in mind, let us now direct our attention to the structural components of society.

Structural Activities

The mechanisms by which (1) natural and human resources are allocated to different industries, organizations, and occupations, (2) productive and social activities of individuals are coordinated, and (3) participation in society's activities are rewarded and punished are much less clearly defined in a society than in formal organizations. Yet, in most societies, mechanisms of government or administrative control develop that attempt to structure the above types of problems.

Societies, usually in the form of governmental units, differ in the degree to which they formalize their attempts to solve problems of allocation, coordination, and rewards. Russia, for example, has an explicit, pervasive governmental apparatus, whereas certain underdeveloped countries have merely informal government networks. The occupations and formal organizations in Russia, correspondingly, are significantly affected by governmental rules, whereas in the emerging nations the organizations and occupations are less intensely circumscribed.

The operations of governmental units also determine the very existence of many types of organizations and occupations. For example, when the war on poverty expanded in America, so did the growth of public-service agencies and occupations.

The Human Factors

Research suggests that the more satisfied an individual is with his family life, the more happy he is with his job. In turn, when individuals are

[14] *Ibid.*

asked how satisfied they are with life in general, their answers are closely associated with their satisfactions in family and occupational roles.[15] Thus, one's personal adjustment at work is closely related to his participation in other major societal activities.

Several investigations also suggest a close association between a person's mental health and his vocational success. J. P. LaPlace gave personality tests to forty-nine major-league baseball players (they were designated as being successful in their occupation) and to sixty-four minor-league players (they were labeled as being less successful). When LaPlace compared the personality profiles of the two groups, he found that the minor-league players showed a greater tendency to take personal offense, a lower ability for self-discipline, and less capacity to adjust to activities requiring initiative.[16] In another study, although the reasons for the relationships are not clear, L. G. Wispe and K. E. Lloyd found that among the forty-three insurance agents who made up a district force of a life insurance company, the salesmen who preferred a more democratic type of relationship with their supervisors had better sales records than those who preferred authoritarian relationships.[17]

The above investigations suggest the close connection between human characteristics and adjustments on the job. Let us turn our attention now to the final dimension of society within which formal organizations exist—the normative, or cultural, aspects.

Normative System

Each society has a culture with unique normative patterns in which the work organizations operate. For example, in our society the belief in democracy is carried into the plant, and employees expect to be given opportunities to participate in making decisions about work activities. And the "good" supervisor is one who controls his subordinates in a democratic fashion.

A significant contrast to these patterns is displayed in other societies, however. In Germany before World War II employees wanted their supervisors to be domineering. Leaders who sought subordinates' suggestions were disliked and thought to be weak, unfit supervisors.[18] In Japan (although this practice is currently undergoing revision) employees are hired for life and are seldom fired even if they are poor workers. In a sense, when an individual is hired, he becomes a member of a large family. Pay and promotion are based on the number of children the employee has and on his seniority.[19] These examples illustrate the tendency of employees reared

[15] *Ibid.*

[16] J. P. LaPlace, "Personality and Its Relationship to Success in Professional Baseball," *Research Quarterly of the American Association of Physical Education, and Recreation*, Vol. 25 (1954), pp. 313–319.

[17] L. G. Wispe and K. E. Lloyd, "Some Situational and Psychological Determinants of the Desire for Structured Interpersonal Relations," *Journal of Abnormal and Social Psychology*, Vol. 51 (1955), pp. 57–60.

[18] Kurt Lewin, *Resolving Social Conflicts* (New York: Harper & Row, 1948).

[19] James C. Abegglen, *The Japanese Factory* (New York: The Free Press of Glencoe, 1958).

in a given culture to carry values consistent with that culture into organizations and occupations in which they participate.

ENVIRONMENTAL INFLUENCES ON ORGANIZATIONAL DESIGN: A MICRO-VIEW

Each environment influences an organization along lines that make it conform. Members of an organization naturally design their organizational systems to fit or complement their environmental situations. The more an organization adapts to its environment, the more effective it will be and the greater will be its chances of long-term survival. It is important, therefore, for an organization to understand accurately the characteristics of its environment and the most effective organizational design that will fit its unique environmental circumstances. There appear to be six main types of environmental situations that confront most organizations. An analysis will be presented below of these six types and how they affect organizational design.

SIX TYPES OF ENVIRONMENTS AND THEIR INFLUENCE UPON ORGANIZATIONAL DESIGN

The six types of environmental systems to be described below are ideal types. Seldom do you find an environment that fits exactly into one of the types. Rather, environments are usually combinations of these six types. It is important, however, to have some models in mind when trying to understand an organization's external environment, because the models provide you with the tools to perform a more specific analysis for a given organization. The six types of environmental systems are the commander, attacker, avoider, pleaser, performer, and achiever.[20]

THE COMMANDER ENVIRONMENTAL SYSTEM

The commander environmental system presents an organization with a stable, homogeneous, repetitive, and relatively non-influential environment.

The Technical Component

The types of technology and techniques of work prevalent within a commander environmental system are mostly repetitive and orderly. For example, production or manufacturing departments of organizations often deal with commander technical components in their environments. The technical characteristics that many older textile firms deal with, for instance,

[20]Gerald D. Bell, *The Achievers* (Chapel Hill, N.C.: Preston-Hill, Inc., 1972).

use very standardized methods of production, stable types of machinery, and a small variety of techniques for carrying out productive activities. Furthermore, the basic processes involved in manufacturing their products have not changed greatly in many years.

The Structural Component

The organizations that compose the commander environment for a specific organization are quite stable and dispersed. Therefore, the focal organization is relatively independent from the forces in its environment. The organization can buy its supplies from many different suppliers at competitive prices, delivery schedules, and specifications. Labor pools are relatively plentiful, easily trained, and substitutable. On the output side, the organization can sell its products or services to a variety of different customers and can increase or decrease sales quickly by merely varying prices slightly. These factors allow an organization to deal with its environment in relatively certain terms and to control the environment's impact on the organization.

The Normative Component

The norms and cultural patterns within a commander environmental system encourage order, precision, planning, and stability. Organizations are rewarded by a commander environment for following standard customs and procedures and are punished for innovations or deviations that are unique.

The Human Component

The human component of a commander environment consists primarily of people who prefer orderly, definite, patterned relationships. They think in terms of clear-cut categories, rules, and policies. Change and creativity are valued little. Conflicts are resolved quickly according to standardized procedures. Lines of authority among people within the environmental system and those who relate to the focal organization are clearly defined and carefully adhered to.

A COMMANDER ORGANIZATION

An organization that is surrounded by a commander environment tends to react to it by evolving a *commander organizational design*. This organization develops *techniques* of work that are routine, highly specialized, and highly systematized. Operations management and manufacturing skills are highly valued. The *administrative structure* is clearly defined, lines of responsibility are carefully documented and followed, there are extensive rules and policies established to govern most inputs from the environment, and decision-making is highly centralized. Central administrators are able to predict accurately and explain their environmental contingencies and therefore can formulate relatively accurate decisions to solve their environmental relationships effectively.

Norms evolve within a commander organizational system that urge consistency, discipline, and efficiency. Accordingly, the *human* component requires employees with personalities that are self-controlled, orderly, and detail-oriented. They prefer standardization to innovation and clarity to creativity.[21]

When a commander environment is met by a commander organizational design, the organization usually is very effective and thrives within its environment. The organization has reached its *best-fit-adjustment*. The organization controls, responds, and adapts appropriately to its environmental demands, and the four subsystems within the organization mutually complement one another and their specific counterparts within the external environment.

THE ATTACKER ENVIRONMENTAL SYSTEM

The attacker environmental system presents an organization with highly contradictory, inconsistent occurrences that are often hostile and difficult to deal with. The organization, however, is allowed to be fairly independent from its environment.

The Technical Component

The work techniques found in an attacker environment are highly competitive, aggressive, and allow individuals to come and go as they please. Few long-term commitments are expected or found. Instead, short-term relationships dominate. Critical analysis is highly emphasized as a skill within an attacker environment.

The Structural Component

There is little cohesiveness in the structural components of an attacker environment. There are few consistent, stable procedures to be followed. Rather, the organizations that compose the attacker environment change frequently, and are therefore unpredictable.

The Normative Component

The norms that pervade an attacker environment reward aggression, defiance, independence, and constant upheaval. Revolutionary organizations that defy traditions and resist controls are examples of organizations that are compatible with such an environment.

[21] *Ibid.*

The Human Component

People within an attacker environment need to release considerable hostility and aggression and therefore are negative and argumentative in their relationships. They dislike being made dependent and responsible to other units and therefore keep moving from one relationship to another.

AN ATTACKER ORGANIZATION

An organization that deals with an attacker environment develops an attacker organizational design. This type of organization establishes *techniques* of work that demand independence, competitiveness, and drive. Hard-nosed selling would be an example of this type of technology. A salesman in a tough, competitive environment must be independent, able to fight aggressive competition, and overcome a seasoned buyer's resistances. A movie or social critic and a sarcastic comedian would also be illustrative of the independence and thrust found in occupations that deal effectively with an attacker environment. Social organizations whose purposes are to fight "injustices" by gathering evidence with which to ridicule or shame another organization would also exemplify attacker units.

Administrative *structures* of attacker organizations set few stable guidelines to follow and jump from one plan to another frequently. Reacting to events is preferred over establishing directions for the organization. In this regard, the *norms* that exist within an attacker organization reinforce negative, cynical behavior, and the *human* component is represented by individuals who switch from one assignment to another frequently, who dislike being dependent on anyone or any situation within the environment. They prefer aggressive, hostile relationships in which they can release their negative feelings.

When an attacker environment is matched by an organization with an attacker organizational design an effective interdependence results—*best-fit-adjustment* has been reached. The types of demands the attacker environment places on the organization are fulfilled very well by the types of technologies, structures, norms, and human qualities within the attacker organization design.

THE AVOIDER ENVIRONMENTAL SYSTEM

An avoider environment is orderly and predictable and places few serious risks or demands on the organizations within it.

The Technical Component

The work techniques prevalent within an avoider environment are routine, repetitive, and risk-free. Little initiative or self-responsibility is required from the organization members to deal effectively with the technologies within the environments.

The Structural Component

The structural components of the environment are quite orderly and precise, yet not too influential. Guidelines are clearly established to direct the organizations within an avoider environment.

The Normative Component

The norms within an avoider environment encourage safety, procrastination, non-measurement of performance, and stability of relationships. Members within the organizations that deal with an avoider environment are rewarded for conformist behavior and are punished for deviance.

The Human Component

The individuals who work within an avoider environment shirk responsibilities, conflicts, and decisions. The less their personal exposure, the more satisfied they are.

THE AVOIDER ORGANIZATION

Organizations that are engulfed by an avoider environment evolve *techniques* of work that are routine, repetitive, and mass-production oriented. Key-punch operators, bookkeepers, and production people often perform these relatively simply tasks. The *structure* of relationships and work consists of extensive rules, regulations, and directives for employees to follow so that they do not have to rely on their own judgements to complete their tasks. The *norms* reinforce stability and routine and discourage innovation or assertiveness among its members. Accordingly, the *human* components to avoider organizations are filled with people who need to evade risks, and personal responsibilities, to escape from making decisions and to work on safe, unmeasured assignments. Management-by-objectives and job enrichment are shunned. The major differences between a commander and avoider design is that the commander organization is quite dominant over, and competitive with, its environment, whereas the avoider organization is very dependent on, and risk-averse toward, its environment.

When an avoider environment is matched by an avoider organization, an effective adjustment is made between the organizatoin and its environment. The organization changes only to the degree that the environment demands; it is faced with few risks from its environment and operates quite conservatively. The organization neither significantly affects, nor is affected by, its environment.

THE PLEASER ENVIRONMENTAL SYSTEM

The pleaser environmental system is cooperative, easy-going, and non-demanding. Organizations that operate within it feel accepted and wanted.

The Technical Component

The types of work techniques carried out most effectively in the pleaser environmental situation involve social skills, making others happy, solving tensions, and developing close relationships.

The Structural Component

Little structuring is provided by the environmental situation. Relationships are allowed to evolve relatively freely and unencumbered by rules and regulations. Work relationships are loose and flexible.

The Normative Component

The norms within a pleaser environment encourage friendship, kindness, consideration, and cooperation. Conflicts are shunned.

The Human Component

The individuals who work primarily within a pleaser environment need to be liked and accepted. To satisfy these needs, they develop special talents for pleasing others.

THE PLEASER ORGANIZATION

The pleaser organization forms *technical* skills that involve building close, warm relationships. Skills such as using proper manners, telling jokes, relieving tensions, and performing kindnesses become the work techniques in pleaser organizations. Receptionists, some public relations kinds of jobs, and soft-sales assignments that involve maintaining good customer relations are examples of pleaser types of occupations.

Pleaser organizations are *structured* quite loosely. Decisions are made informally and on a group basis. Few rules and regulations are established that cannot be modified to fit the immediate needs of the organization members. The goals that are set are relatively easy to attain. The *norms* reinforce these informal characteristics. Cooperation, kindness, and friendliness are highly rewarded whereas aggressiveness and competition are devalued.

The *human* component consists of people who need to be accepted, and accordingly, who design their efforts to gain full acceptance by their groups. They exert little self-initiative and take few risks, because both of these actions would produce conflicts.

In those circumstances in which a pleaser organizational design operates within a pleaser environment a highly effective adaptation occurs between the organization and its external environment, because the two are mutually very compatible. They have reached a best-fit-adjustment.

THE PERFORMER ENVIRONMENTAL SYSTEM

The performer environmental system rewards those organizations that are able to maneuver effectively, to play politics well, to build an impressive image, and to strive for results.

The Technical Component

The work techniques that are found most frequently within a performer environmental system consist of skills in presenting favorable first impressions, artful sales approaches, and an appearance of sincerity.

The Structural Component

The design of a performer environment is moderately structured, primarily in terms of what is proper and improper behavior. A certain amount of flexibility exists to allow the organizations to maneuver themselves into the most advantageous positions to achieve their goals.

The Normative Component

The norms of the performer environment stress respectability, prestige, and maintaining a good image. Consequently, candor and interpersonal honesty are discouraged.

The Human Component

The individuals who work within a performer environment need to gain recognition and prestige and aim their actions toward making successful appearances. They are artful politicians.

THE PERFORMER ORGANIZATION

The performer organization responds to its environmental stimuli by engaging in *technical* activities that emphasize shrewd maneuvering of individuals and situations, artful communication, skillful presentation of winning arguments, and successful image management to gain advantageous positions.

Relationships are *structured* along the lines of what should and should not be done, but still allow enough flexibility for the manipulators to move within the structure.

The *norms* that guide the organization's operations emphasize manners, customs, and traditions. In turn, the *human* dimensions of the organization reveal individuals who desire recognition, who enjoy making deals, and who are skilled in keeping in the middle of things to maximize their image.

When an organization that operates within a performer environment is able to organize itself in the style of a performer design, then its abilities to reach its goals are greatly enhanced. The organization design matches the demands of the environment and thus facilitates an effective adaptation of the firm with its environment.

THE ACHIEVER ENVIRONMENTAL SYSTEM

The achiever environmental system is very complex, changing, and dynamic. Creative challenges are constantly presented to the organizations that operate within the achiever environment.

The Technical Component

The work *techniques* prevalent within an achiever environment require creative, innovate efforts to overcome moderately risky obstacles. Marketing, general management activities, and other jobs that require self-initiative and self-responsibility are examples of achiever work techniques.

The Structural Component

The environment is relatively *unstructured* and flexible. Many alternatives are available for organizations to select from in their efforts to attain their objectives, and constant changes confront the organizations within achiever environments.

The Normative Component

The norms that are found within achiever environments stress quality in performance, the desire to improve, hard work, and willingness to take reasonable risks.

The Human Component

The individuals who operate within an achiever environment need to find challenges to overcome and require concrete feedback about their performance and ways of introducing novelty into their work.

THE ACHIEVER ORGANIZATION

Work *techniques* in achiever organizations are highly complex, changing, and demanding of discretion. Creativity and training are integral parts of this type of technology. The jobs are *structured* only slightly in order to allow the work activities to match the dynamic nature of the environmental demands. Decision-making is decentralized to the point closest to the environmental changes in achiever organizational designs.

The *norms* within the achiever organization stress hard work, excellence in results, meeting competition, and task orientation rather than friendship orientation. Closely related to these norms is the *human* component of achiever organizations, which includes mostly individuals who like to master difficult assignments and who perform better when under stress. They are self-confident, somewhat disorderly, willing to take risks, seek novelty in their work, and desire results more than prestige or money.

Again, when an organization is faced with an achiever external environment, it tends to be most effective if it formulates an achiever organization design.

MISMATCHES OF ENVIRONMENTAL NEEDS AND ORGANIZATIONAL DESIGNS

If one of the six types of environmental systems is not met by a complementary organizational design, the result is a mismatch or conflict between the two systems and ineffective performance by the organization. If, for example, an avoider environmental system is met by an achiever organizational design, serious inappropriate relationships occur. The avoider environment demands stability, routine, and low risk-taking action; however, the achiever organization is active, changing, and eager to take risks.

In one organization I studied, this mismatch was readily apparent. The environment that surrounded a large clerical department in an insurance firm was an avoider environment. A young, aggressive, achievement-oriented manager took over this suborganization and proceeded to create an achiever organizational design for it. Through his many innovations and lack of interest in detail, however, he soon brought the department's effectiveness down to its lowest all-time level. This achievement manager was a very effective person, but simply had been placed in the wrong environmental context and tried to establish an inappropriate organizational design for it. He was soon switched to an achiever environmental context, into marketing, and he performed well in this environmental situation.

Another mismatch occurred when an individual who preferred attacker organizational designs became the manager of public relations for a large manufacturing firm. The environmental situation for the public relations department was a combination of a pleaser and a performer environment. The new manager established an attacker organizational design to assault aggressively his department's environment, to defy authority and traditions, and to be counter-productive rather than polite and constructive. Obviously, this mismatch was neither effective nor long-lasting.

The cases illustrate (1) that there is no one appropriate organizational design to fit all environments, and (2) that different types of environments require different kinds of organizational systems to produce maximum adaptation between the two.

MOST ORGANIZATIONS FACE ALL SIX TYPES OF ENVIRONMENTS

The question of effective adaptation between an organization and its environment becomes more difficult when we realize that most large organizations do not operate in a single type of environment, but encounter all six of the types discussed above and probably many unique combinations of these types. This means that most organizations have a highly *differentiated* external environment.[22] Organizations are simultaneously confronted by demands for order and change, for friendship and aggression, for a strong impression and for "pure" results.

HOW DO ORGANIZATIONS ADAPT EFFECTIVELY TO SUCH DIFFERENTIATED ENVIRONMENTS?

First of all, this problem is reduced somewhat by the fact that organizations often attempt to form suborganizations or departments to fit and adapt to each different environmental type. This allows each department to *integrate* or coordinate the organization more effectively with the separate environmental systems.[23] For example, production departments often deal with commander environments, marketing with achievement environments, public relations with pleaser environments, bookkeeping or clerical with avoider environments, and so forth.

To the extent that an organization has a separate suborganization or department that has just one type of environmental system with which to deal, the department has a relatively easy time of adapting effectively to its external environment. Each department establishes a different organizational system to match its environmental type. If each department is allowed to have a unique organizational design that matches perfectly its unique environmental situation, then effective adaptation occurs.

If this type of *decentralized departmentation* occurs within an organization, however, an additional problem results—extensive *internal* differentiation within the organization. Each department has a different organizational design.

[22]Paul R. Lawrence and Jay W. Lorsch, *Organization and Environment: Managing Differentiation and Integration* (Boston: Division of Research, Harvard Business School, 1967).

[23]*Ibid.*

These dilemmas are highlighted, for example, in the administrative units that are responsible for coordinating the different departments within the parent organization. Since the departments that the administrative units must coordinate are extensively differentiated, they are much more difficult to integrate. This point is well illustrated by the traditional battles that occur between manufacturing and marketing departments. The differences in personalities, in orientation toward time, order, creativity, and risk-taking, for example, make it difficult for these two units to coordinate their activities effectively.[24]

The conclusions that can be drawn from these dilemmas are: (1) even if a suborganization (or department) properly matches its environmental system, ineffectiveness might occur within the total organization's operation because of the high degree of differentiation that exists in the variety of organizational designs of each subunit; and (2) the more differentiation in the external environment with which an organization is confronted, the more likely the differentiation of departments and the more the problem stated in the first conclusion becomes a critical factor in overall effectiveness.

When an organization faces a great number of different types of environments, it has a much more difficult time adapting effectively to them. For an organization to adapt effectively to each different part of it's environment then, it must establish different departments and give them the responsibility and authority to perform the adaptation.[25] Accordingly, each department evolves a unique organization design to fit it's particular environment. This produces an organization with a large number of departments with many *differentiated* organizational designs that are highly *integrated* with their respective environments.[26]

In this case, then, the organization as a whole has a significant problem. Each department, although it is "inside" the organization, acts as an internal environmental force on the other departments. To the degree that the departments within an organization are different, they have difficulty in integrating or cooperating with one another. The administrative departments within the organization must somehow integrate these highly differentiated departments to insure that the inputs to the organization are smoothly coordinated with the throughputs and outputs. Thus, the technology of these administrative units becomes very complex and their major objectives revolve around resolving conflicts and managing pluralism effectively.

One solution to this problem is to reduce the degree of internal differentiation by designing all departments along the same lines. If this is done, however, the departments will not adapt effectively to their respective environments and the total organization will be out of touch with its environments. The internal operations will run smoothly, but the external relationships will suffer. There is a trade-off, then, between the degree to which an organization can adapt effectively to its environmental needs and the degree to which it can coordinate smoothly its internal operations.

Both external environmental integration and internal departmental

[24] *Ibid.*

[25] James D. Thompson, *Organizations In Action* (New York: McGraw-Hill Book Co., Inc., 1967).

[26] Bell, *The Achievers.*

coordination are necessary for an organization to reach maximum levels of effectiveness. The more the one is accomplished, the less the other is achieved, for they are significantly interdependent. For an organization to maximize it's overall effectiveness, it must reach a balance between these two alternatives.

Types of Interdependencies

Even if an organization faces a highly differentiated environment, it must be significantly interdependent with its environment for the above problems of adaptation and internal coordination to occur. We can break down the types of interdependencies involving an organization and its environment into three major categories—pooled, sequential, and reciprocal.[27]

Pooled interdependence exists when two workers or departments can perform their jobs with very little effect on each other. For example, two insurance salesman who cover different territories, although for the same company, work virtually independently. *Sequential interdependence* refers to those activities that occur in a sequence. For example, each department in a production line is sequentially interdependent, because first one department performs its tasks, then passes the product on to the second department, which then performs its tasks. The second department must wait for the first department to do its job before it can complete its assignments, so it is dependent on the first department. *Reciprocal interdependence* occurs when two departments or persons depend on each other to carry out assignments. Two surgeons operating on a patient adjust their behavior to each other as the operation progresses. Marketing and production must mutually adapt their behavior because marketing can sell only what production can produce and there is little sense in producing a product that cannot be sold. In these instances the activities of one department influence and are influenced by the other. Reciprocally interdependent departments, then, deal with the most unpredictable environments.

When an organization has *pooled* interdependence with part of its environment, it has little need, and thus finds it relatively easy, to integrate or adapt to its environment. In those cases wherein a department is *sequentially* related to its environment, the department must plan carefully and make special efforts to schedule connections with its environment.

A department that is *reciprocally* related to its environment is highly dependent on its environment to reach its objectives. Accordingly, this department must establish articulate procedures to fine tune its adaptations to its environment.

MECHANISMS ORGANIZATIONS USE TO ADAPT TO THEIR ENVIRONMENTS

Organizations utilize a variety of techniques to adapt effectively to their environments and to minimize the uncertainties and fluctuations that

[27]Thompson, *Organizations in Action.*

environments create for them. Since the inputs and outputs of organizations seldom flow continuously or smoothly from or to their environments, organizations develop mechanisms for regulating exchanges with their environments. We will now discuss the major types of adaptation techniques.

Buffering Techniques

Buffering techniques soften the effects of the environment.[28] Buffering on the input side is illustrated by stockpiling materials, preventive maintenance, and training and indoctrination of personnel.[29] Buffering on the output side takes the form of warehousing inventories and long-order periods for delivery of products.

For avoider and commander types of organizational designs and environments, buffering takes the form of *standardization*.[30] In this case detailed rules and procedures are established to make activities routine and consistent. *Planning* is another form of buffering, used mostly by pleaser and attacker organizational-environmental systems because they are more unpredictable. Therefore, general schedules and policies are established to adjust activities.[31]

A third buffering technique, one used mostly by performer and achiever systems, is *coordination by feedback*. This is a mutual adjustment process that involves the transmission of information between the organization and its environment almost instantaneously following any activities in either system. Since these two types of organizational-environmental systems usually are confronting constant change, the mutual adjustment process is frequent.[32]

Leveling Techniques

Leveling techniques are a slight modification of buffering activities. Leveling refers to attempts to smooth out or to reduce fluctuations in the environment whereas buffering absorbs or softens the impact of the environment.[33] Examples of leveling would be the efforts by a firm to attract customers for its products in off seasons by offering them special inducements or charging premiums during peak periods, somewhat like the airlines or resorts do.

Rationing Techniques

Rationing refers to a careful allocation of resources according to a system of priorities.[34] For example, the post office assigns priorities to first-

[28] *Ibid.*, p. 20.
[29] *Ibid.*
[30] *Ibid.*, p. 56.
[31] *Ibid.*
[32] *Ibid.*
[33] *Ibid.*, p. 21.
[34] *Ibid.*, p. 23.

class mail and rations the manpower, time, and effort devoted to different services. Companies whose products suddenly become popular ration deliveries to their distributors. Rationing is usually not a very happy solution, because by definition it means not serving or adapting to some parts of an organization's environment.

Dominating Techniques

In some cases an organization can adapt effectively to its environment by dominating it. Dominating techniques refer to an organization's efforts to control events in its environment and to reduce its dependency on it.[35] When an organization can set the prices for its products without worrying about what competitors will do, it has significant power over its environment. Similarly, in company towns, the organization that "runs" the town usually exerts important power over its labor force.

Maintaining alternatives is one of the means organizations use to dominate their environmental relationships.[36] Developing many suppliers and customers is a standard practice that most organizations follow to free themselves from depending on their environment. Another dominating technique is developing *cooperative exchanges* with the environment.[37] In this case the organization agrees to exchange some product or service with a segment of the environment if it agrees to do the same for the organization. Cooperative exchanges often take the form of *contracting*.[38] Formal agreements between labor and management and suppliers and customers reflect contracting. *Cooperating* is an exchange effort that involves absorbing part of the environment into the organization.[39] Cooperating can take the form of subtle persuasion or more formal efforts at establishing joint ventures or partnerships.

Changing Boundary Techniques

If an organization has a very difficult problem with a specific segment of its environment, it can change products or services and thereby change its boundaries to try to avoid relating to that segment. Another method is to expand the organization's boundaries around the trouble spot in the environment. A jewelry retail chain, for example, might have a difficult time getting a sufficient supply of diamonds at proper delivery dates and prices and in acceptable styles if it has only one supplier. In an actual case like this, the organization's solution was to start their own diamond-supply company. Organizations are likely to change boundary techniques especially when the environmental relationship is crucial for the organization.[40] The vertical integration of grocery chains and bank mergers are also illustrative of these processes.

[35] *Ibid.*, p. 31.
[36] *Ibid.*, p. 32.
[37] *Ibid.*, p. 35.
[38] *Ibid.*
[39] *Ibid.*
[40] *Ibid.*, p. 36.

Anticipation Techniques

When environmental changes are highly unpredictable, such as is frequently the case in achiever environments, organizations set up techniques to study and anticipate environmental fluctuations.[41] Long-range planning, forecasting, and research and development are examples of anticipation techniques. Similarly, organizations will often establish *boundary scanning units* to observe environmental changes closely. This can take the form of appointing a *boundary role person* to become an expert in dealing with the environment, or hiring an outside organization, like an advertising agency or public relations firm, to perform these activities for the organization.[42]

SUMMARY

The question of how an organization relates to its environment becomes more significant as our society grows more complex. Our entire social system changes more rapidly each year, and consequently, organizations also must change more quickly to keep up with their environments.

As environmental changes increase and become more complex, the types of environments and organizations that develop are more frequently achiever or performer systems. In these cases environmental adaptation is more complex and difficult to attain. Indeed, those organizations that survive will be those that are able to develop effective ways of integrating their operations effectively with their environments. Those that die assuredly will be out of adjustment with their environments.

[41] *Ibid.*, p. 21.
[42] Adams, "Boundary Role Persons."

On the Applicability of Environmental Models

Alvar O. Elbing

Professor
IMEDE
Management Development Institute
Lausanne, Switzerland

The external environment of organizations is a subject of increasing challenge for today's managers. In fact, the managers of societies' major organizations —business, education, government—have been forced by recent events to place an increasing focus on a rapidly changing environment and its effect on the internal organization.

The manager looks at the environments of his organization through some mental concept or model that is fundamental to his decision-making processes. The manager who wishes to improve his effectiveness will want to systematically assess his model of the environment to determine its appropriateness to reality. Professor Bell in his chapter "Organizations and the External Environment" has offered one such environmental model. In the short space allotted here, a few basic criteria for the decision maker will be presented for testing environmental models such as Bell's. Although Professor Bell's article will be referred to as the example throughout, the criteria and and charts presented here may be applied for the systematic analysis of any environmental model.

Professor Bell in his model presents four sets of categories:

1. four aspects of the internal organization;
2. six types of environments, each subdivided into four organizational aspects;
3. three kinds of interdependency;
4. seven adaptative mechanisms.

In total, there are thirty-eight subcategories to Bell's model. Although no evidence is provided to explain why one should accept these particular categories, it is, nonetheless, implied that the categories are inclusive. In terms of the purpose of practical decision-making, it is possible that the environment may be more complex to diagnose with the model than without it. A question a manager must answer for himself is whether the use of a highly complex model for diagnoses results in a net gain in his clarity of insight.

TESTING MODELS

Professor Bell indicates that he is dealing with the question, "How do organizations adapt effectively to their external environment?" He answers this with the claim that: "The more an organization adapts to its environment the more effective it will be and the greater will be its chances of long-term survival." Two key questions emerge from this presentation:

1. For decision-making purposes, is the model practically *applicable* to the environment?
2. Is the claim growing out of this model (that *adaptation* is the necessary behavior for successful organizations) justified?

These questions are two important criteria by which this model or any model may be tested.

CRITERION OF APPLICABILITY

The manager can test any behavioral model, including his own, against the criterion of its applicability. A model with awesome suggestive appeal may be found to be useless to a particular manager when he sets about applying it systematically to the specifics of the situations he faces. The critical question for practical management purposes is: Does the model apply to the *specific* environments of *this* organization?

Asking this question confronts the manager with another issue. In order to *compare* any model with any specific environments, it is necessary to *specify* just which "environments" are being referred to. It is an important psychological issue of management that we all have mental models of the "environment"—of the "out there"—frequently without having matched our models with specified environments.[1] To see how to go about testing the applicability of an environmental model, we can use the model presented by Professor Bell.

The first step is to determine whether he has already done this job for us. Has he clearly specified just what environments his model can be practically applied to? It is, in fact, difficult to identify what Professor Bell means by the term "environment." He provides no one clearly specified referent for the term. What he does refer to as "environment" often shifts in a way that leaves in doubt just *what* "environment" means in each particular context.

Nevertheless, the manager can test Bell's model (or his own model) by constructing two simple diagrams of the organizations actual environments—the organization's "direct-action environments" and the organization's "indirect environments."

DIRECT-ACTION ENVIRONMENTS

The following chart specifies the "direct-action environments" of an organization, so called because they act on the organization, and are acted on by it, *directly* as a part of the organization's primary function.

This chart is a rudimentary guide that can be used as a reference tool for

[1]See Alvar O. Elbing, *Behavioral Decisions in Organizations* (Chicago: Scott, Foresman and Co., 1970), Chapters 2 and 4.

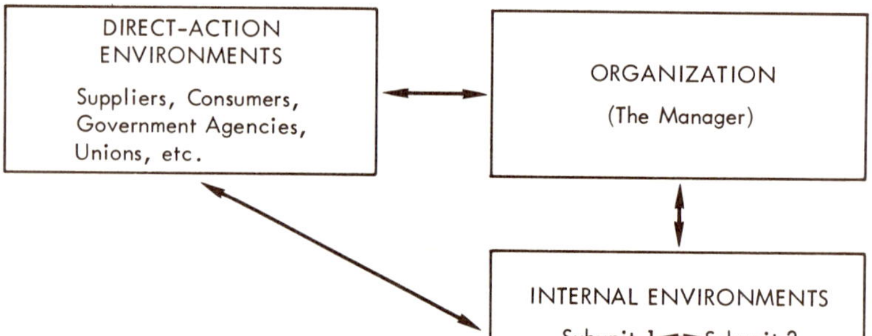

FIGURE 18. Direct Action Environments

This is a guide for clarifying specific reference for the direct-action and internal "environments" of organizations.

the manager in drawing up his own chart of his organization's specific environments. It simply paves the way for the manager to systematically specify what data he is referring to when he considers the nebulous term, "the environment" of the organization. It is only when the manager has clearly specified the environments he means that he can go on to test the *applicability* of a diagnostic model of "environment."

The applicability of Bell's model can now be tested by matching it with the specific environments clarified above. Are the classifications of Bell's model applicable to the *external* environments of the organization? To review, Bell states that six types of environments are: "commander," "attacker," "avoider," "pleaser," "manipulator," and "achiever." With a diagram of the specified environments of his own organization, the manager can pose specific questions of the model, such as:

1. Can the organization's *customers* or *clients* be classified as "commander" environments, "achiever" environments, etc.?
2. Is it practically applicable to classify the *government agencies* with which the organization (and the manager) deal as "attacker" environments, "pleaser" environments, etc.?

The above two questions are but two examples of specific questions by which the manager can compare his model with specific environments.

It is indeed difficult to think of external environments for which any of Professor Bell's labels is directly applicable. Bell suggests the hospital environment, but can a hospital's clients be said to be commanders, attackers, avoiders, pleasers, manipulators, or achievers? Can the government or any other of the hospital's external environments be so classified? Actually, it is only the manager himself who can judge if any of these classifications has practical application to these specific environments of his organization, and hence aid his diagnoses of conditions.

One possible danger in using such ready-made classifications when referring to the groups that constitute the external environment is that they constitute stereotyping at the outset. Stereotyping incites selective diagnoses designed to fit the preconceived classifications, which, in turn, incites selective actions that can serve to reinforce the stereotype. If, for example, we label a particular group as an "attacker" environment, we might look only for the behavior that supports our stereotype, thereby reinforcing the stereotype. A second danger is that labels are essentially static and may lock the manager into regarding conditions as relatively fixed, and less amenable to management, rather than viewing them as dynamic, manageable systems. Finally, there is the danger that the labels have no sound empirical basis. By what systematic empirical process does the manager go about assigning such labels to various groups? No methodological tools are provided.

The above dangers can be avoided if the manager builds his own model; if he asks diagnostic questions rather than matches situations to ready-made labels:

1. What evidence is there of the specific goals currently being pursued by a particular group in the external environment?
2. What evidence is there of the group norms currently being acted out in the relationship?
3. How do the group norms and goals of particular environments coincide with the organization's goals and norms?
4. By what means does one impute motives to the behavior one observes in the groups in the environment?[2]

It is preferable for the manager to get behavioral data about the groups that constitute the direct-action environment of the firm before he attempts to

[2]For a discussion of group and inter-group behavior, see Muzafer Sherif (Ed.), *Inter-Group Relations and Leadership* (New York: John Wiley & Sons, 1962).

label those specific groups. If the manager can get the behavioral data he needs to answer those basic questions, he already has a sound basis for diagnosis and decision-making—even if he cannot devise a characterizing label for the groups. However, if he starts with a label that assigns a specific trait to a group without having attempted to get data about that group's goals and norms, that label may only serve to distort or even block realistic gathering of data and diagnosis.

JUSTIFICATION OF CLAIMS

Once the manager has tested the applicability of the model to the data—to specified environments—he can go on to test the applicability of claims made through the model. With reference to Professor Bell's model, it is claimed that organizations adapt more successfully to environments of the same type. Bell states that an organization will adapt to and be more effective in an environment that is similar to the organization's own environment. He states: "If one of the six types of environmental systems is not met by a complementary organizational design, the result is a mismatch or conflict between the two systems and ineffective performance by the organization. If, for example, an avoider environmental system is met by an achiever organizational design, serious inappropriate relationships occur."

Is this claim justified? Let us suppose that it is possible to classify a particular consumer as a "commander consumer" (let us say, the navy). According to Bell, a "commander" organization would be more successful in selling to the navy than, for example, a "pleaser" or an "achiever" organization. Is this true? Might not a "pleaser" organization get as many orders from the navy as a "commander" organization, which sticks to its traditional specification despite the Navy's changing demands? Might not an "achiever" organization be chosen by the navy to design its new rockets? Or, let us take another example of a "commander" organization manufacturing cake mixes. Might not a "commander" cake mix producer as effectively sell to a "pleaser" organization (e.g., a restaurant chain) as to some other classification? More evidence is needed to make Bell's claim convincing. Again, it would seem useful to diagnose existing relationships rather than to give them labels.

APPLICABILITY TO INTERNAL ENVIRONMENTS

The systematic manager will want to go on to test the practical applicability of any environmental model to the organization's *internal* environments (see Figure 18). Again, the necessary first step is to clarify just what he is referring to when he uses the term "environments." For any particular decision-making problem, the manager must know precisely what groups he wishes to consider as "environments" of what other groups. Otherwise, his reasoning about "environments" may continuously and nebulously shift ground.

There is not one single way to specify the groups that constitute "the" internal environments of the firm. Groups may overlap so that one person or even many persons may identify with or be a part of more than one formal or informal group. The important thing is that the manager be clear about his analytic purpose. In terms of his specific decision-making problem and purpose at hand, he must have a clear picture of just what groups he has under consideration as "environments" of what other groups.

Although Professor Bell's article is entitled "Organizations and the External Environment," he discusses internal environments as well, remarking that ". . . each department within an organization forms part of the other departments' environment . . . ." At first glance, it would seem that Professor Bell's model is more applicable to the internal divisions of an organization than it is to its external environment. If it is useful for the manager, perhaps he can label the research and development department as an "achiever" environment, the production department as a "commander" environment, the insurance unit as an "avoider" environment, accounting as a "commander environment," laboratories and food services as "commander" environments (or "pleaser" environments?). Some departments or informal groups, however, may be harder to classify. It would seem quite possible that in a particular organization, all the groups might be a mixture of all the classifications, in which case the labels would seem to be of doubtful value, as Professor Bell would doubtless agree.

If the manager finds these classifications particularly applicable and useful in his diagnoses and decision-making with respect to internal organizations, he can, by all means, use them. In any case, the only sound *basis* on which the manager can decide whether the label is realistically applicable is to gather substantial empirical data about the groups in question. If he does that, however, the labels may be superfluous.

INDIRECT ENVIRONMENT

Today the concern of most managers goes beyond the traditional environments just charted. In fact, the very word "environment" now calls forth a vastly wider milieu of physical and social forces. Although the manager must still occupy himself with the day-to-day problems of dealing with supplies and suppliers, products and consumers, research and production, the challenge is always with him in this new era to manage—to make decisions—in this larger world. How can the manager conceptualize this larger environment? Should he conceptualize decision-making in this larger world as "adaptation"? Does one "adapt" to groups doing research on ecology and pollution, to groups making various presentations of social problems, to public protest and demands? Does the multinational organization "adapt" to the mores of every culture in which it operates?

Is it possible to characterize environmental groups in the larger world according to some model such as Bell's (as "attacker," "pleaser," etc. groups) and then go on to adapt to them in terms of these labels? This is certainly what some groups in today's society are demanding of organizations. Should management always adapt to the other groups' style or approach?

Although Professor Bell's article is entitled "Organizations and the External Environment," his model is clearly not intended to apply to this enlarged sense of the term "environment." The question nevertheless remains: Would it be possible to "adapt" to the larger environment—or even desirable?

Here again a chart that specifies the larger environment would be helpful. However, the larger—indirect—environment is not so easily charted as is the direct-action environment, and there are no traditional charts to turn to. Yet this larger environment is more in need of clarification for the purposes of decision-making. Figure 19 is an initial attempt to conceptualize the larger environment surrounding an organization.

The thesis embodied in the chart is that the most realistic and practical way of denoting environments for practical decision-making purposes is to denote them as *groups*. It is more useful to the manager to conceptualize the broad indirect environment in terms of specific groups than to use more vague and abstract terms such as systems, institutions, or ideas, because these terms are not managerial action concepts; the manager cannot directly act on and interrelate with abstractions. Denoting groups as environments is preferable, too, to denoting "data" about physical objects in the physical world, because such "data" are, in any case, produced and interpreted by groups. In Figure 19, the arrows signifying relationships among groups do not touch the organization (i.e., they are not in direct intergroup confrontation), because once they do touch, they become part of the organization's direct-action environment. The

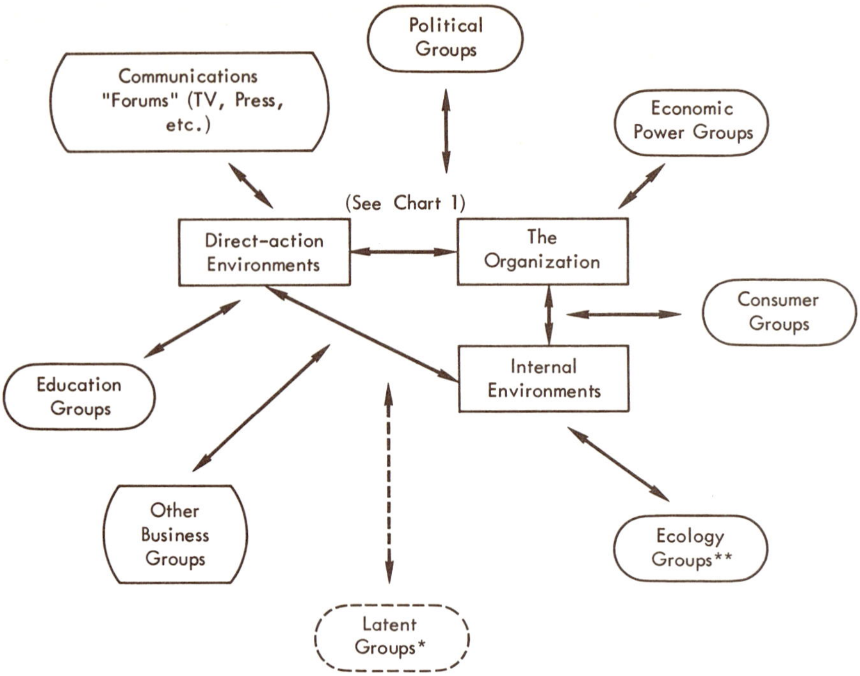

FIGURE 19. Indirect Environments

*"Latent Groups" refers to unaffiliated people who may form into cohesive groups as a response to the actions of the organization or of other groups.

**"Ecology Groups" refers to influential groups producing and interpreting "data" about the physical environment.

chart, then, shows real, acting groups of people that influence the organization and have the potential of interacting with the organization. Whether the manager enters into direct action with these groups, or avoids it, is a matter for conscious and systematic decision-making.

The question before us, then, is: Is the concept of "adaptation" applicable to the larger environment? The traditional concept of adaptation today is fraught with question marks. Not only do various public groups make conflicting demands for adaptation, but an even greater difficulty is that nobody has a definitive answer to just what *effective* adaptation to the larger environment might be. The manager must choose which environmental problems consciously to act on, decide what are meaningful facts and sound interpretations, and create his own course from start to finish. He must then pursue his own course in situations wherein he will reap mostly anxious criticism for whatever course he has invented, and in which the only satisfaction is his own internal hope that he may be helping to stave off some fatal crises, or that, in any case, he is identifying with those who act. This kind of creativity, however, hardly falls under the traditional form of "adaptation." More appropriately, it should be termed "creative decison-making."

The concept of "adaptation," therefore, is no longer applicable to the process of (1) solving today's environmental problems, (2) managing environmental change, or (3) even dealing with the direct-action environment on a day-to-day basis. The concept is too limited by the image of the status quo, can be irresponsible in terms of the issues of the day, and implies that someone else initiates the character of relationships.

The term "adaptation" fixed itself

in the scientific and popular consciousness in the period when Darwin pictured vividly to the human mind the struggle of each species to cling to its rock, to reach out to the adjacent leafy shoots, to seize other animal species—in short, to "adapt" to its ecological setting. Man's environment today is not analogous to that model.

Man himself now constitutes the single most important environmental force for man. And what constitutes that force are, above all, the driving symbolic concepts—the assumptions—behind his behavior. It is too feeble today to speak of man having adapted to his environment; he is the primary force in his environment and the primary obstacle to the solution of environmental problems. From a modern behavioral standpoint, it is meaningless to speak of men "adapting" to other men. What has evolved beyond the Darwinian model are two significant situations: (1) men co-creating one another and their social-conceptual environment through their responses to one another; and (2) men hence co-creating "for good or ill" the significant trends in their total environment.[3]

From the manager's standpoint as well as from the behavioralist's standpoint, the term "adaptation" is far too passive in the light of today's crises. Whether consciously or not, the manager (and the organization) is not an adapter but a co-creator of the future environment.

[3]See Alvar O. Elbing and J. Carol Elbing, *The Value Issue of Business* (New York: McGraw Hill Book Co., Inc., 1967).

Typology and Environment

Walter Hill

Professor
College of Business Administration
University of Florida

The importance of an organization's external environment to its ability to survive and grow always has been implicitly recognized. Organizations, whether they were political, military, or economic, always have had to acquire their resources from their environment, transform them into products and services desired by their environment, and provide these outputs to environmental customers of one type or another. The efficiency with which these functions were performed determined the extent to which customers accepted the products and services of one organization rather than another. When customers purchased an organization's outputs, they provided the wherewithal to acquire additional resources, and as the operations researchers say, the process was iterative—i.e., more inputs were acquired, transformed, and sold. The transactional nature of organizations has been spelled out more explicitly in recent years by systems theorists who describe the organization's relationships to its environments in terms of inputs, transformations, outputs, and feedback mechanisms.

The increased interest in the organizational environment stems not from the fact that organizations must exchange resources with their external environments but from the fact that the nature and magnitude of these exchanges are changed. As Terreberry has pointed out, contemporary changes in organizational environments are such that they increase the ratio of externally induced change to internally induced change and that other organizations are increasingly becoming the important components of the focal organizations environment.[1]

Most organizations originally were formed to provide only a limited number of products and services. Thus Dupont produced explosives; prisons isolated undesirables from the public; schools educated the rich; and the army fought battles. A specific organization generally dealt with only a limited, well-defined, stable environment. Today, as environmental customers have demanded more services and products, these same organizations, in an effort to survive and grow, have diversified and expanded their outputs. Thus Dupont makes plastics, paints, and synthetic fibers as well as explosives; prisons perform rehabilitative functions, which may include manufacturing products, developing education, medical, and psychiatric programs, as well as custodial functions; schools develop programs to educate all segments of the population in diverse fields ranging from art to zoology as well as perform research for business, public, and military organizations. Even the army has expanded its traditional role to include occupational training; building and maintaining sophisticated space systems, dams, and navigation projects; and, more recently, educating the underprivileged and performing other community services.

As these organizations have expanded the nature and scope of their products and services, they have begun to exchange resources with new environmental customers whose interests and evaluative criteria often are conflicting. Thus, the need to examine more thoroughly the organizational environment stems from two major considerations: (1) organizations must now deal with an increasing number of external environments that possess conflicting expectations concerning the organizations' performance and (2) the exchange that now occurs between any two organizations is increasingly affected by the organizational pattern in which they find themselves. As Warren has pointed out, the interaction between two organizations—department stores, for example—will differ depending on whether they are the only stores in a medium-sized city or just two of some twenty stores in a large city.[2]

Table 5 presents an example of the conflicting demands that different external groups can place on a business firm. It is easy to see that the allocation of an organization's resources to maximize stockholders' claims can easily lead to not meeting the claims of other external forces. It is perhaps more difficult to see that modifications in government policy, such as the recent wage and price freeze, can affect union requests for pay increases, pricing policies of competitors and suppliers, as well as customer and stockholder expectations of returns. Thus, the actions of one external claimant can and do influence the demands of other claimants on the focal organization.[3]

[1]Shirley Terreberry, "The Evolution of Organizational Environments," *Administrative Science Quarterly*, Vol. 12 (March, 1966), pp. 590–613.

[2]Roland L. Warren, "The Interorganizational Field as a Focus for Investigation," *Administrative Science Quarterly*, Vol. 12 (December, 1967), pp. 396–419.

[3]Warren provides an interesting illustration of the variety of claimants who can influence a community decision organization in Roland L. Warren, "The Interaction of Community Decision Organizations: Some Conceptual Considerations and Empirical Findings," paper presented at the 4th Annual Conference on *Interorganizational Models: Conflict Resolution and Change*, Comparative Administration Research Institute, Kent State University, May 27–28, 1971.

TABLE 5. Systems Criteria for Judging Company Performance

Superordinate systems	*Criteria*
Stockholders	Price appreciation of securities
	Dividend payout
Labor force (union)	Wage levels
	Stability of employment
	Opportunity
The market: consumers	Value given
The market: competitors	Rate of growth
	Innovation
Suppliers	Rapidity of payment
Creditors	Adherence to contract terms
Community	Contribution to community development
Nation (government)	Public responsibility

Source: Seymour Tilles, "The Manager's Job: A Systems Approach," *Harvard Business Review*, Vol. 41 (January–February, 1963), p. 78.

The above discussion has suggested the growing importance and complexity of environmental groups to the survival and growth of modern organizations. It is, therefore, important that organizations learn more about their environment and how it influences their operations.

One compelling reason why organizations must learn more about their environments has its genesis in the research conducted by Burns and Stalker, Woodward, and Lawrence and Lorsch, among others, who have suggested that certain structural properties of organizations seem to be more effective than others, given a unique environmental focus. Burns and Stalker concluded on the basis of four separate studies of Scottish and English firms that the effective organization of industrial resources does not conform to one ideal pattern but varies in important proportions with changes in external factors such as different rates of technical and market changes.[4] They outlined two polar organizational forms and suggested that mechanistic management systems were appropriate for stable environmental states and that organic management systems were more appropriate for changing conditions.

Woodward's study of 100 manufacturing firms in England concluded that "firms in which organization structure reflected an implicit acceptance of what has become known as classical management theory were not always the most successful from a commercial point of view."[5] She suggested that the more successful firms were those who were able to meet the demands of different technologies through appropriate organization structures. Her later writings set forth the control system as a mediating variable between technology and structure.[6]

Lawrence and Lorsch, expanding on the works of Burns and Stalker, Woodward, and others, studied firms in three different industries that differed in the degree to which they were characterized by economic and market uncertainty.[7] These authors concluded that

[4]Tom Burns and G. M. Stalker, *The Management of Innovation* (London: Tavistock, 1961).

[5]Joan Woodward, *Industrial Organization: Theory and Practice* (London: Oxford University Press, 1965), p. vi.

[6]Joan Woodward (Ed.), *Industrial Organization: Behaviour and Control* (London: Oxford University Press, 1970).

[7]Paul Lawrence and Jay Lorsch, *Organization and Environment; Managing Differentiation and Integration* (Boston: Division of Research, Harvard Business School, 1967).

the degree of differentiation as well as the nature of integration that characterized successful firms varied with environmental uncertainty. Organizations operating in highly uncertain environments, such as the plastics industry, required not only a higher degree of differentiation but also that integration occur at a lower organizational level to be successful. On the other hand, successful organizations operating in a more stable environment, such as the container industry, were characterized by lower degrees of differentiation and by integration at higher organizational echelons.

More recently, Pugh and his associates have provided evidence that an organization's structure is a function of variables such as size, technology, dependence, location, origin and history, charter, resources, and ownership and control.[8]

The above studies lend credence to the now recognized fact that there is no one best way for an organization to structure itself. Appropriate structural designs depend, to a large extent, on the environment in which the organization functions. Indeed, different parts of an organization generally operate within different contexts, so that the organization must be viewed both as a collective and as separate units; e.g., divisions or even departments. The collective must deal with the total environment whereas parts of the organization must deal with those aspects of the total environment that are most relevant to them. The last point has been corroborated by the studies of Allen[9] and Pollert[10] who suggested that conglomerates and vertically integrated organizations, respectively, must allow their various divisions flexibility to deal with their own unique environments in order to perform effectively.

Thus, while we are observing that the environment is becoming increasingly important to the organization, we also are learning that different forms of organization structure are more appropriate for different environmental conditions. Professor Bell's paper thus provides an important ingredient when it attempts to develop an environmental typology, because if we can learn to classify environments that organizations are likely to face, and if we are able to sense what environment presently confronts the organization and its various divisions, then we can suggest structural forms that will more likely be effective for that organization and its various divisions.

THE BELL TYPOLOGY

Professor Bell's attempt to build an environmental typology is an ambitious one. He tries to depict the environment on multiple dimensions that are distinguished by questions such as (1) is the firm relatively dependent on or independent of the environment? (2) is the environment influential or non-influential? (3) is the environment friendly or unfriendly? (4) is the environment demanding or non-demanding? (5) is the environment stable and predictable or dynamic and unpredictable? and (6) is the environment homogeneous or heterogeneous? Although Bell's typology could be improved by describing more precisely each type of environment on each of the above dimensions, several important, unanswered questions would still remain. For example, how does an organization (or even who in an organization) determine where it stands on each of the dimensions vis-à-vis each of its external claimants and what effects do the various combinations of these dimensions in each of the claimants have on the organization as a whole as well as on its divisions?

[8]D. S. Pugh, D. J. Hickson, C. R. Hinings, and C. Turner, "The Context of Organization Structures," *Administrative Science Quarterly*, Vol. 14 (March, 1969), pp. 91–114.

[9]Stephen A. Allen, *Managing Organizational Diversity: A Comparative Study of Corporate-Divisional Relations.* Doctoral Dissertation, Harvard Business School, 1969.

[10]William R. Pollert, *Managing Differentiation and Integration in Full Integrated Steel Firms.* Doctoral Dissertation, University of Florida, 1971.

Although viewing an organization on multiple dimensions enables a more discerning picture to be drawn (albeit a more difficult and complex one), it also complicates the statistical analyses of the relationships between the total environment and any facet of an organization's structure. With our present state of knowledge, resolving this complication may be beyond our capabilities.

AN ALTERNATIVE TYPOLOGY

A less ambitious but more pragmatic approach might be to isolate one or more of Bell's dimensions as being more important and then to examine existing empirical evidence to explore what structural alignments seem to work best given designated values of these dimensions. As our empirical evidence grows, we could add more environmental dimensions to improve our analysis.

Given the paucity of our existing data base, any typology must be simple. It also should be stated in terminology that is familiar to and accepted by practicing managers as well as academicians. One alternative environmental typology, based almost entirely on the work of Emery and Trist,[11] as well as the nature of some structural elements thought to be appropriate to each part of the typology, are presented in Table 6.

The use of this typology requires that managers assess two dimensions of their environment: (1) Are the external claimants independent or interconnected? (2) Is their relationship to the focal organization stable or unstable? These questions are important because they have structural implications. For example, if claimants are interconnected such that the focal organization's reaction to one affects its relations with the others, a more centralized overall strategy is appropriate. If, on the other hand, the claimants are independent of one another, a more decentralized structure would enable each division to develop unique tactics for dealing with each of its claimants separately. Likewise, if the relationships among exogenous claimants and the focal organization are stable, more standardization, specialization, and formalization are possible than if the relationships were

[11]F. E. Emery and E. L. Trist, "The Causal Texture of Organizational Environments," *Human Relations*, Vol. 18 (June, 1965), pp. 21–31.

TABLE 6. AN ALTERNATIVE TYPOLOGY

Relationship Between External Claimant and Focal Organization	Relationship Among External Claimants	
	INDEPENDENT	INTERCONNECTED
STABLE	Decentralized authority High degrees of specialization, standardization, and formalization	Centralized authority High degrees of specialization, standardization, and formalization
UNSTABLE	Decentralized authority Low degrees of specialization, standardization, and formalization	Centralized authority Low degrees of specialization, standardization, and formalization

unstable. The last condition would call for a higher degree of organizational flexibility so that reactions could be tailored to the demands of the situation.

Although the suggested typology is easy to understand and there is empirical evidence that the structural properties listed for each typological case are appropriate, much more work will be required before organizational designs can be matched satisfactorily with various environmental conditions. Pugh and his associates already have developed satisfactory measures for structural components such as specialization, standardization, formalization, centralization, and configuration, but similar measures of environmental dimensions either do not exist or exist only on dichotomous rather than continuous scales.[12] The absence of reliable and valid measures of environmental dimensions is a recognized deficiency in the proposed typology, and this problem will become much more serious as the number of dimensions are expanded. Fortunately, managers have a "feel" for the proposed dimensions so they can be operational if appropriate linking mechanisms with the environment are established. As Lynton has pointed out, linking mechanisms such as ad hoc study groups, market research, and public relation departments are necessary not only to detect future changes in environmental forces but also to predict whether such changes are temporary or permanent, frequent or infrequent, and differentiable or not, because these factors will influence the appropriateness of various structural responses. If, for example, it is predicted that an environmental change will occur that will be permanent, frequent, and differentiable, it may be advisable to establish a separate organizational unit to deal with the change. On the other hand, a temporary, infrequent, indifferentiable change may warrant only an ad hoc committee to deal with it.[13]

This author has pointed out previously that successful adaptation to environmental pressures depends on the identification of relevant environment claimants; the determination of the form, focus, and intensity of their expectations as well as their power to impose such demands, and a measurement scheme to help predict the impact of each of their expectations on organizational outputs and on other identified outside claimants.[14]

The development of an environmental typology assumes the first two points and attempts to deal with the last. This is a necessary and important task but it should not be forgotten that a typology can serve little practical use if an organization is unable to identify its claimants and their demands.

DISCUSSION QUESTIONS

1. Define the environment of an organization. Is the line that separates the "inside" from the "outside" clearly marked?
2. What are the four major subsystems, or components, of organizations? Why are these the "key" dimensions of organizations?
3. What is a "commander environmental system"? Illustrate your answer. Why

[12]D. S. Pugh, D. J. Hickson, C. R. Hinings, and C. Turner, "The Dimensions of Organization Structure," *Administrative Science Quarterly*, Vol. 13 (June, 1968), pp. 65–105.

[13]Rolf P. Lynton, "Linking an Innovative Subsystem into the System," *Administrative Science Quarterly*, Vol. 14 (September, 1969), pp. 398–417.

[14]Walter Hill, "The Goal Formation Process in Complex Organizations," *Academy of Management Proceedings*, 27th Annual Meeting, December 27–29, 1969, pp. 169–177.

would a "commander" organization fit best into such an environment? Or would it?

4. Do you agree that the match of environmental types with similar organizational designs ensures organizational success?
5. How do organizations adapt to their environments? What happens if they do not?
6. Discuss the differences between pooled, sequential, and reciprocal interdependence.
7. Do you agree with Elbing's tests of Bell's models? Why?
8. Is the manager an "adapter," as Bell suggests, or a "co-creater," as Elbing claims?

11

International Management

Richard N. Farmer

Professor
School of Business
Indiana University

INTRODUCTION

It is sometimes argued that there is a field called international management. This management is somehow different from other domestic kinds; it arises only when firms cross national frontiers and operate in two or more countries. A closely related field is comparative management, which attempts to observe management in two or more different environments. Often a multinational firm will practice comparative management as it handles its various divisions or branches.

International management is also called a myth, since there is only one management theory, and it is universal. One practices management in about the same way in Buenos Aires as in New York, and although there admittedly are environmental differences, there really are no managerial differences. If we have a domestic management theory jungle, full of the rich complexity of competing fields,[1] then we also have a similarly lush international management theory jungle,[2] which in the end turns out to be the same thing. In short, management is universal, and international management is merely one interesting variant on a familiar theme.

Our first task is thus to determine if there is a task. Is international management alive and well, or is it just a figment of some wilder academics' imaginations? Certainly various things have been called international management, and many major business schools have courses in the field. Presently, thousands of multinational firms are managed so well in many cases that these firms are the fastest growing and most profitable of all private

[1]See Harold Koontz, "Making Sense of Management Theory," in Harold Koontz (Ed.), *Toward a Unified Theory of Management* (New York: McGraw-Hill Book Co., Inc., 1964), pp. 1–17. The jungle still exists—it appears lusher than ever.

[2]See Hans Schollhammer, "The Comparative Management Theory Jungle," *Academy of Management Journal*, Vol. 12, No. 1 (March, 1969), pp. 81–98, for coverage of one dimension of this problem.

enterprise anywhere on earth. But are these firms merely doing what they do at home, only more so? Good managers may well be able to manage anywhere with considerable effectiveness.

A follow-on question relates to operationality. Good theory should be useful to someone, and it should be applicable to real-world situations. If there is some special international management theory, then we should be able to use it in real-world situations. Hence, a part of this chapter will consider if anyone is using what is alleged to be international management theory, and if so, what good or harm it may be doing to its users.

And finally, there is a question of what appears to be happening in international management, both in practice and theory. It is clear that international business in all its dimensions is growing rapidly; it would seem logical to expect that there is some trend in thinking about these multinational activities, including where they might be going in the future, and how they might be managed.

WHAT IS INTERNATIONAL MANAGEMENT?

In observing both what managers in multinational situations do, and what is written about their activities, it becomes clear that much international management is about the same as domestic management. We find production management, marketing management, financial management, and all the other functional managerial areas in international as well as local firms. And we also find the usual planning, control, staffing, directing, and organization work going on. The same mathematical models used in Iowa are (or could be) used in Moscow or Paris (Illinois or France). Although it is clear that individual and group behavior is quite different in different cultures, the same types of sociological and psychological work can be done everywhere. Various behavioral theories can be tested and perhaps used in a wide variety of cultural situations.

Managers and scholars, observing this conventional managerial activity in various countries, have at times concluded that there is no real difference between domestic and international management. They point to demand analysis, production flow problems, or personnel practices and planning as being similar everywhere. Of course, variations in managerial effectiveness are extreme, but conceptually the problem seems the same. Figure 20 suggests how one could perceive the problem. Various inputs flow into a firm; they are processed and transformed into usable outputs; and then they are sold in various markets. The places of various managerial and functional specialties are shown in the diagram.

If this is all there is to the problem, this would be a short chapter indeed. Readers will see that other chapters of this volume cover every item in Figure 20. No one would argue that these are not complex and difficult areas to manage efficiently, but conceptually they are the same everywhere. The only question would be how efficiently each is handled, and how well various subdivisions are integrated into the whole.

It was observed in Biblical times that countries and cultures were different, often strikingly so, and firms around the world operate in various

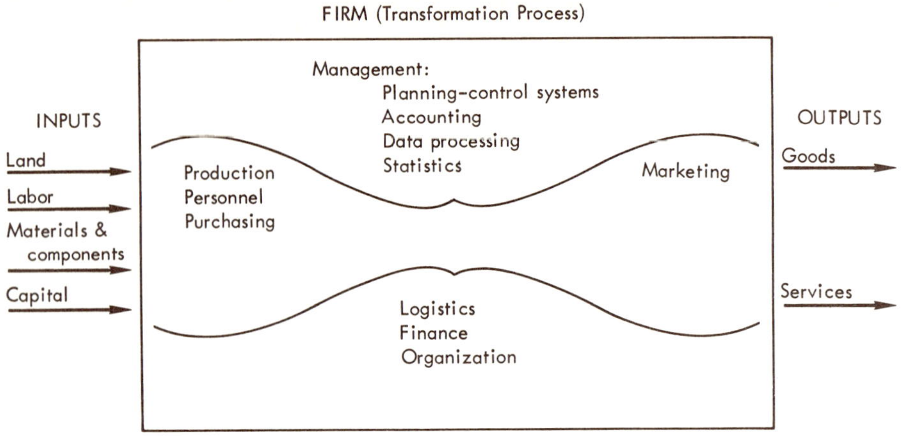

FIGURE 20. The Firm Management Process

business environments.[3] For centuries scholars and men of affairs have studied international economics, politics, cultural differences, military affairs, and related problems dealing with such environmental differences. Except peripherally (as in economics), such studies had relatively little to do with management or business, although most senior managers responsible for any international dimension of his firm usually knew a great deal about them. But until the 1960's, relatively little interrelating was done, and even then most such work was concerned with specific problems or cases rather than with general theory.[4]

By 1960, a few writers were beginning to point out various problems that internationally oriented firms were having in strange environments.[5] Of course, marketing management and all the rest was conceptually the same as at home, but the results within firms often turned out to be wildly different. The means were the same; the ends were decidedly not. Others noted that when strictly domestic, "by the book" types were sent to exotic places to manage, they often failed. Somehow, those rules and regulations and management by the book that worked so well in Kokomo didn't work at all in Rio.

Practitioners were also having their problems. Those who somehow managed to mesh a bit better with whatever strange environment they encountered abroad did a better management job than those who ignored the local culture. Those neat rules in the best management texts never seemed to work out right in alien cultures, so new rules had to be developed.[6] It

[3]The first business story was an international one. Try *Genesis*, 39041:1–57.

[4]See, as one excellent early example, John Fayerweather, *Management of International Operations* (New York: McGraw-Hill Book Co., Inc., 1960), 604 pp.

[5]Special credit here belongs to John Fayerweather and Richard D. Robinson, who were the early scholars in this field, and who were responsible for stimulating interest in international business theory. All of their writings (both early and later) merit careful attention by all serious scholars and practitioners in this field.

[6]This author learned his international and comparative management the hard way, managing a trucking company in Saudi Arabia (1959–61). Even a doctorate and a complete set of excellent American texts in all functional and general management fields did little

was gradually becoming clear that there was more to working and managing internationally than the American books related.

Research in something called international business or management was well under way by this time, but close examination of such work suggests that it was largely the older environmental fields being explored once more.[7] Thus, studies in international economics were loosely tied to business problems; political problems and processes were looked at from the standpoint of a firm; and so on. Yet rarely did any writers attempt to relate in any direct way their environmental studies to internal management and operations.

Farmer and Richman's *Comparative Management and Economic Progress*[8] was an early effort (1964) to put the pieces together in some systematic fashion. This study took pretty much as given the various managerial theories and fields, and it also took as presented earlier various environmental materials. The difference between this and earlier work on both the micro- and macro-levels was an effort to interlock the environment and the internal management processes of the firm.

Figure 21 suggests one part of the analysis. Here the firm is the same as in Figure 20. We still find the usual managerial and firm functions. But we now add environmental categories, which impinge on the firm in various ways. The argument is that if the environment in one country is sufficiently different from the environment in another, a firm may well manage in the same way, but come out with very different results. Thus if one country has an annual inflation rate of 3 per cent, whereas a second country has an annual rate of 40 per cent, the financial management function will conceptually be the same in both places, but actual results will be quite different. The question is not one of absolute managerial differences, but rather one of degree.

This whole schema can be reduced to a matrix, as shown in Table 7. Here the environment is classified across the figure, and managerial and

---

good in that alien environment. See Richard N. Farmer, and Barry M. Richman, *Comparative Management and Economic Progress*, rev. ed. (Bloomington, Indiana: Cedarwood Press, 1970), Appendix A, for 1 per cent of what really went on.

7See John Fayerweather, *op. cit.;* Howe Martyn, *International Business* (New York: The Free Press of Glencoe, 1964), 287 pp.; Richard D. Robinson, *International Business Policy* (New York: Holt, Rinehart and Winston, 1964) 252 pp.; and particularly Charles F. Stewart and George B. Simmonds, *A Bibliography of International Business* (New York: Columbia University Press, 1964).

8Farmer and Richman, *op. cit.*, pp. 1–73.

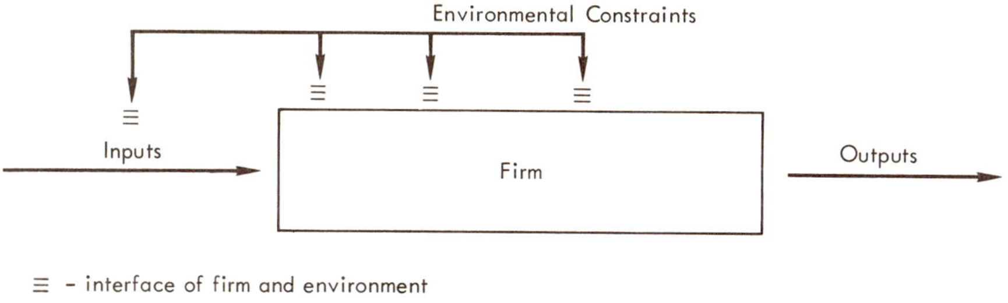

FIGURE 21. The Environmental/Internal Firm Model

LOCAL ENVIRONMENT CONSTRAINTS

FIRM AND MANAGERIAL FUNCTIONS	Educational	Behavioral	Legal-Political	Economic
Planning	a_1	a_2		
Control				
Organization				
Staffing				
Direction				
Marketing				
Production & Procurement				
Research & Development				
Finance				
Public & External Relations				a_{40}

Each block a_1, a_2 --- a_{40} is a potential interface problem between the firm and its environment.

TABLE 7. FIRM/ENVIRONMENT MATRIX

firm functions are classified vertically. There are forty blocks where environment and management interlock and interrelate.[9]

To this point, we are suggesting comparative differences, which are useful for practical managers who have branches in different countries. How does one manage abroad? The same way he does at home, except that it is useful and practical to keep in mind how any given environmental difference could lead to extensive internal firm management differences. These would be differences in results, not in techniques or management conceptualizations.

Use of the matrix begins to be operational in analyzing why some foreign operations went sour. On reflection, it almost invariably turns out that a manager forgot where he was, and tried to apply the same rules and frames of reference he used at home. At home he could assume that decentralized middle management worked well; abroad he found that there were too few middle managers with the ability to work in this way to make the operation go. At home, he could assume that there were competent and efficient suppliers of components for his product; abroad he loaded warehouses full of half-finished product because such suppliers just weren't there. Indeed, post mortems typically suggest that the biggest single cause of foreign managerial failure is the tacit assumption that something in the alien environment is the same as at home, and hence the managers do not

[9]See Farmer and Richman, *op. cit.*, pp. 74–324, for detailed examination of these various blocks and interrelationships.

have to pay much attention to it.[10] If this assumption is wrong, the company is in trouble.

But there is another dimension to this problem. Much international business is conducted across country lines, as when firms export or import, obtain capital in other countries, remit profits from foreign subsidiaries, or try to obtain entry visas for key personnel to suspicious new nation states. In these situations, the international environment also becomes very relevant. Since countries often have special rules of the game for international flows as compared to domestic ones, the firm also must interrelate such constraints to its various domestic operations. Thus if a country restricts certain imports of components, the firm may have to restructure its entire local operation to make these in the country, or try to get another local firm to make them. If profit remissions are restricted, the firm may have to replan its financial situation, and so on.

Table 8 shows these international constraints classified as in Table 7.[11] Again, the internal firm managerial functions are classified vertically, and on this diagram we find thirty more possible interlocks between the firm and the environment. Of course, all of these have to be interrelated to the forty domestic ones for every country concerned. Since every country can

[10]One classic example of this is covered in Jack Baranson, *Manufacturing Problems in India: The Cummins Diesel Experience* (Syracuse: Syracuse University Press, 1967). 146 pp.

[11]See Richard N. Farmer and Barry M. Richman, *International Business: An Operational Theory* (Homewood, Illinois: Richard D. Irwin, 1965), pp. 45–165, for detailed examination of these international constraints; also see Farmer and Richman, *op. cit.*, pp. 373–392.

INTERNATIONAL CONSTRAINTS

FIRM AND MANAGERIAL FUNCTIONS	Behavioral	Legal-Political	Economic
Planning	b_1	b_2	
Control			
Organization			
Staffing			
Direction			
Marketing			
Production			
R & D			
Finance			
Public Relations			b_{30}

Each block b_1, b_2 --- b_{30} is a potential interface problem between the firm and its environment.

TABLE 8. INTERNATIONAL CONSTRAINTS AND FIRMS

set whatever international constraints it pleases in this nationalistic world, the whole problem can quickly become extremely complicated.

It may now be clear what international management may be. Essentially, it is the systematic study of management in situations wherein both local and international constraints may differ considerably, to the point at which key managerial problems within firms are seriously affected. When such critical internal areas are isolated, the process of proper management becomes quite like any managerial problem. Management *is* universal; only the outcomes are strikingly different.

This may be almost a trivial point, but observation of managers in many countries always suggests how culture bound we all are. Examination of any domestic management theory book will suggest many taken-for-granted assumptions about the culture in which the studies are made. Since most of them are American, what happens is that much of what passes for universal truth turns out to be American truth—which may or may not be valid elsewhere.

Since 1964, studies in international management have taken this general direction, although not every student would agree with the precise Farmer-Richman model or taxonomy.[12] But the general pattern of environmental-firm interrelationships is increasingly showing up in the literature. Since there are many ways to interrelate managerial problems to an environment, no one lacks for interesting materials, and no one ever will. The permutations and combinations of various environmental factors, however classified, with various internal managerial and firm functions, are enormous.

Figure 22 suggests finally what international management is. Here the various earlier figures are consolidated into one unit. Only two countries are shown—there are 140 such pairs (in all possible combinations, or 40!), thousands or even millions of firms in each country, and numerous subcultures within larger nation states that often are different enough to merit close examination.

International management theory has now branched off into two distinct parts, which are interrelated. Comparative management deals with comparisons of managerial situations in various cultures, and numerous studies have attempted to analyze why various results (e.g., profitability, growth, overall economic efficiency) are so different in various countries.[13] International management deals mainly with the management of multinational firms, along with various managerial problems stemming from flows of men, money, or goods across national frontiers. The usual focus of such studies is how to manage better (however defined) in such transnational situations.

[12]Other classifications differ in detail, but are generally similar in structure. See John Fayerweather, *International Business Management* (New York: McGraw-Hill Book Co., Inc., 1969), pp. 57; Roy Blough, *Internation Business Environment and Adaptation* (New York: McGraw-Hill Book Co., Inc., 1966), pp. 1–292; Endel J. Kolde, *International Business Enterprise* (Englewood Cliffs, N.J.: Prentice-Hall, Inc., 1968), pp. 3–86; and Richard D. Robinson, *International Management* (New York: Holt, Rinehart and Winston, 1967), 178 pp., for some recent examples.

[13]See Schollhammer, *op. cit.*, pp. 81–97, for a comparative study of comparative and international management theories. Of particular note are studies by Granick, Richman, Lauterbach, Hartman, Geiger and Armstrong, Neghandi, and Estafen, cited on p. 91 of this article.

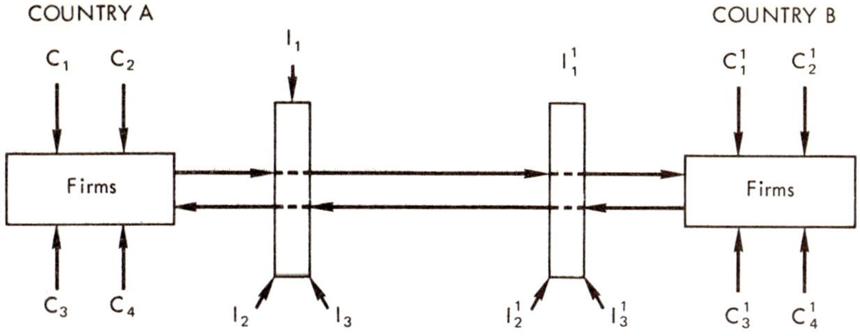

C_1 --- C_4: Local environmental constraints, Country A

I_1 --- I_3: International constraints, Country A

C_1^1 --- C_4^1: Local environmental constraints, Country B

I_1^1 --- I_3^1: International constraints, Country B

FIGURE 22. **The International Management Process**

When using this definition of international and comparative management, it turns out that a lot of materials called international management are not. Many studies and theories deal only with environmental problems, as when an economist studies balance-of-payments problems[14] Although interesting and possibly very significant to an international manager, the study itself is not international management, unless some systematic interrelationship of the firm and the environmental factor is considered. Many other studies of firms in given countries also turn out to be considering only a given firm in a given country, without comparative or international implications. Such studies are usually management-oriented in some way, but they are not international or comparative management.

Interest in international and comparative management appears to be growing geometrically at about the same rate as American investments abroad. As more major and many minor firms struggle with seemingly intractable problems in strange places around the world, considerable interest has developed in some theory or frame of reference that will sort out all the mysterious and often confusing facts and structure them in some way amenable to top management analysis. Virtually all modern (e.g., post-1964) international and comparative management theory attempts to do this by first classifying the environment in some way; then classifying the internal firm management problem; and then putting the two together.[15] This is done schematically, graphically, verbally, and even at times mathematically, but a common thread runs through all theory.

[14]Most pre-1965 studies were of this type. See Lee C. Nehrt, J. Frederick Truitt, and Richard W. Wright, *International Business Research: Past, Present & Future* (Bloomington, Indiana: Indiana University Graduate School of Business, Bureau of Business Research, 1970), p. 7. The authors note a steady trend in international business research to material as defined in this paper since 1965.

[15]See citations in footnote 12, for examples.

Like all other management theory, international and comparative theory is a major borrower from any discipline that has anything to offer. As suggested above, virtually all business and management theory developed earlier is used in one form or another in international and comparative theory; moreover, this theory also now borrows heavily from various environmental disciplines, such as economics, political science, the behavioral sciences, pedagogy, and law. Other forms of management theory also did much borrowing of this sort, but typically in a more intuitive way than is found in international-oriented theory. This follows from the culture boundedness of the theory. After all, we Americans *knew* what the behavioral patterns were, and there was no need to spell them out; we *knew* what the legal structure was, and so on. Only when managers and firms wandered off to strange new lands did the need to spell out more precisely these environmental constraints become more obvious. Virtually all American managers have some good working knowledge of contract and antitrust law, but very few of them know what such law is in Tanzania or Lebanon. Hence, "obvious" managerial decisions suddenly become not so obvious, and we all become comparative lawyers—or try to be.

WHAT IS INTERNATIONAL MANAGEMENT GOOD FOR?

Any theory ought to be useful to someone. It would seem that the great recent interest in international management implicitly suggests that someone is in fact getting something useful out of work being done.

On the micro-side, which would include the various types of business management theory, there is relatively little new insight applicable to the real world. Many firms and scholars have studied various worldwide operations, and comparative management workers have looked in many ways at a wide variety of management problems and compared them among cultures. But the management theory used here has been relatively conventional, following the various formats and concepts discussed in other chapters of this book. The newness here is more in using such materials in cultures where they have not been applied before. Indeed, this may turn out to be the real American gift to other cultures. The export of quite conventional American managerial techniques has been widely noted and copied abroad. In most countries, such techniques are seen as quite revolutionary in terms of impacts on system efficiency, so much observation, debate, and concern is common.

At the macro-level, firms now, as before, are paying close attention to economic, political, behavioral, international, and educational variables in countries where they have an active business interest. Since more firms are now internationally or multinationally oriented, such interest could be expected, even if no one had ever talked about international management.

But increasingly firms and managers are making linkages of the sort mentioned above. They not only look at the macro-country variables, but they proceed to link these up with critical internal firm elements, trying to build a managerial structure that will mesh as best as possible with whatever environment they find themselves in.

This type of work drives conventional wisdom types up the wall. If it really is true that any firm or managerial function may change because the environmental situation is different, then those managers who insist on iron-clad policy manuals, universally applicable the world around, are in for trouble. It is precisely because such types have been in deep trouble abroad that many firms are beginning to shift to a more flexible, environmental-internal firm variable mesh. If it really matters that a given company policy or decision has to mesh with the environment, then either the policy changes, or the firm does not perform as well as it might.

Much of the very practical international managerial work being donc is performed by individuals who have never been near an international management text, but who have the necessary wisdom, wit, and insight to make necessary adjustments to the real problems they face. The field is made somewhat more complicated than it might be by absence of any agreed-on classification of the problem; by taking into many environments all the confusion of local management theories; by the baffling complexities of dozens of countries, hundreds of products, and thousands of variables for every simple problem; and by the usual problem that managers do not have any common body of wisdom and knowledge to cover before they manage.

It also appears that gaps among the best international business practice, average practice, and the worst practice are extremely wide. The field is so new, and so many firms and individual managers are so recent arrivals to the scene, that taken-for-granted activities in one firm may be complete mysteries to others.

Thus it is common to find that one firm has a very elaborate system of exchange-rate forecasting, complete with skilled analysts, economists, and an information intelligence service capable of providing and summarizing all relevant information. This system is linked into the firm's financial planning system, so that expected exchange rate values can influence where money is kept, what is done with currency holdings in various parts of the world, how different branches can borrow from one another, and so on. Notice again the use here of quite conventional and excellent financial planning techniques, this time linked to the international environmental fact of currency value changes.

But a visit to the next firm, perhaps even in the same industry, shows that the top international people don't even know for sure what a devaluation is. They have no staff to plot potential currency changes; their financial management has nothing to do with possible currency values; and their rate of return from overseas operations may be 5 to 20 per cent lower as a result. Yet their managers are equally intelligent and presumably equally competent at home. What is happening is that this second firm has only been in multinational business in a serious way for perhaps 5 to 10 years, and the managers have yet to sort out all the possibilities and options open to them. The first firm might also be a newcomer to multinational business, but by some historic accident, one or two key persons convinced top management that this international financial planning was valuable and necessary.

Such performance deviations are common and suggest similar deviations in local management in the 1920's and 1930's. One can find extremely good management performance in almost any international management dimension; but we also can find total ignorance as well.

Intuitively or explicitly, the top performers appear to follow the international management methodology suggested earlier, simplified to meet the needs of the specific problem. In the above foreign currency example, the problem is to manage sources and uses of funds as efficiently as possible. To do this, firm managers must develop linkages between relevant environmental constraints and internal firm functions. Once these linkages are in place, the problem becomes one of conventional (and perhaps quite sophisticated) financial management. Financial managers do what they always have done (if they were good), but now they have a new international dimension to consider.

Table 9 suggests what these linkages are. Here is a typical mini-matrix in an international setting.[16] That is, instead of handling the total environment for the firm (which in this case would include all local environments for all countries the firm operates in, plus all international constraints among all pairs of such countries), the international manager merely uses the part of the environment that applies to this particular financial problem. And instead of looking at the entire management of the firm, with all its rich complexity, managers examine closely only the financial aspects.

A further dimension of practical complexity is suggested by these mini-matrices. If the problem were one of selecting proper product mixes for a consumer goods producing firm for the thirty-four countries in which it operates, then managers would still construct similar mini-matrices—but in this case, many environmental variables might be different than in Table 9. We all know that brand monopolies are useful, profitable, and well worth obtaining if the firm can manage them—yet there may well be many situations in which the environment is such as to preclude this useful strategy. Suppose that trade-name legal protection is poor—what then? Or suppose that price controls are very tight, and brand-name products cannot raise prices rapidly in a highly inflationary local economy? The winner in either case might be a firm that abandoned the brand-name concept and did something quite different. In this case, the mini-matrix would appear as in

[16]See Barry M. Richman, "Empirical Testing of a Comparative and International Research Model," *Academy of Management Proceedings* (1967), pp. 34–65; Richard N. Farmer, "Further Explorations in Comparative Management," in Anant R. Negandhi (Ed.), *Comparative Administration and Management: Conceptual Schemes and Research Findings* (Kent, Ohio: Kent State Bureau of Economic and Business Research, 1969), pp. 89–118, for elaborations on this mini-matrix idea.

ENVIRONMENTAL VARIABLES

	Local Inflation Rates	Political Pressures	Balance of Payments Situation
Types & costs of financing	C_1	C_2	
Sources of capital			
Uses of capital			C_9

C_1, C_2 --- C_9: Potential critical interfaces with firm and environment

TABLE 9. MINI-MATRIX FOR AN INTERNATIONAL FINANCE PROBLEM

Table 10. Notice that this analysis frames the problem somewhat differently than for a local firm, operating in a known and familiar environment. What happens in international management is that many environmental constraints become variables. Really good international managers have learned this and have tried to apply it in a wide variety of problems.

The above examples of international management also suggest real possibilities of suboptimization on two levels. One level is common to all firms. This is optimizing a marketing or financial solution at the expense of something else within the firm, and such suboptimizations are common in local management as well as international. But there is also a second-level suboptimization, which is to optimize the branch profits at the expense of the total corporation. In the above financial problem, what is best for the German branch manager, given a high probability of revaluation of the mark, may not be the optimal solution for the global corporation. Explorations in various international management problems suggest that such global optimizations are as yet rather rare.[17] Few firms have been at it long enough to put all the pieces together correctly.

PREDESTINATION OR FREE SOULS?

A lively debate now raging in international and comparative management is whether or not managers really manage, or whether they are pushed along by unfriendly environments to some pre-determined fate. Farmer and Richman initially inferred that the environment is determining; others have argued that any manager can perform significantly better than his environment would suggest, if he is good enough.[18] Those who

[17]Stefan Robock, "Overseas Financing for U.S. International Business," *The Journal of Finance* Vol. 21, No. 2 (May, 1966) pp. 297–307, pointed out that at that time no American finance text contained any substantive materials on international finance. Only in 1969 did an integrated international finance text appear. See David B. Zeoff and Jack Zwick, *International Financial Management* (Englewood Cliffs, N.J.: Prentice-Hall, Inc., 1969), 550 pp. See especially the preface.

[18]Schollhammer, *op. cit.*, p. 86; Anant R. Negandhi, "A Model for Analyzing Organizations in Cross-Cultural Settings: A Conceptual Scheme and Some Research Findings," in Negandhi, *op. cit.*, pp. 60–61.

ENVIRONMENTAL VARIABLES

MARKETING VARIABLES	Copyright Law	Price Controls	Inflation Rate
Product Line	d_1	d_2	
Pricing Policy			
Sales Promotion			d_9

d_1, d_2 --- d_9: Potential environmental interface with the firm.

TABLE 10. MINI-MATRIX FIRM'S MARKETING PROBLEM

see managers as Schumpeterian heroes naturally enough tend to support the latter view; grim Calvinist types would tend to support the former.

There appears to be some agreement that the environment in which firms operate does matter. A manager clearly cannot operate quite so well in a primitive country, without communications, experts, or social overhead capital facilities as can one in an advanced country with all of these advantages. Two equally good managers, placed in different environments, would undoubtedly not perform exactly as well in each. But the follow-on question is whether or not a good manager cannot in fact perform far better than the average for the culture in which he finds himself. The answer is that he can—but how much better? At once the debate gets bogged down in both rich environmental complexity, along with equally rich complexity concerning how managers are selected and trained in given environments. Added to the debate is the role of the outsider, typically American, who may well be managing cross culturally, oblivious to many local behavioral constraints that might inhibit good local managerial performance. Questions of how rapidly local managers can learn become extremely relevant—and this question, in turn, leads to studies of management skills transfer. Increasingly, it is becoming clear that the skills transfer problem is a two-way street—even the best managers from the advanced cultures can learn much from counterparts in other lands.

Such debates are fun, and they lead not only to managerial insights, but also to serious studies of how managing actually is done, and how well, around the world. In the comparative dimension, these questions have raised issues about how the productive job of any culture gets done, and what might be suggested to improve always inadequate performance. Such questions also have posed important problems at the national level about management information, skills, and technique transfer across national frontiers. If it is perceived that one culture (say, the United States) has superior management performance, and hence greater wealth creation possibilities, then how might such skills be transferred to another culture (say, France), where they are badly needed? Consideration of such questions has barely begun, and in spite of Servan-Schrieber's initial work,[19] we as yet do not know too much about even what is to be transferred, let alone how it might be transferred efficiently.[20]

MACRO- AND MICRO-MANAGEMENT

Most management theorists have focused on or within the firm, since this is where the typical action is. But as soon as scholars and practitioners begin to ponder the implications of environmental impacts on firm effectiveness, the question of environmental change also becomes significant. Internationally oriented firm managers quickly perceive that certain environ-

[19] J. J. Servan-Schrieber, *The American Challenge* (New York: Avon Books, 1969), 254 pp.

[20] See Richard N. Farmer, *New Directions in Management Information Transfer* (Ruschlikon-Zwick; Gottlieb Duttweiler Institute, 1968), 70 pp., for further discussion of this point.

mental constraints are wrong, in that they impede firm efficiency. If they were changed, all firms could be better. At this point, the field moves from the micro-considerations within the firm to national policy questions. Many constraints, particularly the legal and economic ones, can be changed by government. If governments are interested in higher incomes and wealth, why not do the job the easy way, by simply changing key constraints that impair all firms' performance?

Such environmental analysis has been done for centuries, and properly belongs to relevant fields such as law and economics. But notice the difference here—whereas in the traditional macro-economic analysis, it was assumed that firms would respond to various stimuli (such as interest-rate changes) properly, now international and comparative management types suggest that exact effects within firms of various environmental changes can be traced. Instead of assuming that management is done more or less correctly, we can figure out with some precision, given the environment, firms, and changes, what is likely to happen.

Rapid development of multinational firms, along with many examples of foreign managers in action all over the world, have helped here. Instead of reading about what an American or British manager does at home, one can observe their activities right in the country. And if he and his firm appear to be doing extremely well indeed, cocktail party conversation, when it turns to what's wrong, may well take an environmental change twist. The American manager may point out that he could do much better, if only this or that constraint were changed.

Nothing succeeds like success, and political leaders, acutely conscious of their country's poverty and need for more income and wealth, may well ponder such words of wisdom and may even do something about it.

This analysis has just begun, in part because most persons interested in management have quite enough to do within the firm, and in part because it is extremely difficult to trace with any detail or certainty how internal firm efficiency will improve if some environmental change occurs. As with internal firm activities, possibilities of suboptimization here are very high, and no one really understands the full implications of such analysis. But in any country, real income and value added are created by firms, which are managed in some way or another; every country in the world wants more income; and if countries are to achieve their economic goals, they in the end have to figure out how to make all firms, public and private, more efficient.

Economists, who are most concerned with such macro-issues, are beginning to come to this issue from yet another door. It is common to find that development policies, carefully worked out for various poorer countries, don't work nearly as well as expected.[21] Post mortems on such macro-planning often suggest that the wrong variables are being considered.[22] What really seems to matter is organizational efficiency, which can have incredibly wide ranges (from value added figures of perhaps $40,000 per year per man in some modern American industry to perhaps $10 per year per

[21]Robert S. McNamara, "The True Dimensions of the Task," *International Development Review* (January, 1970), pp. 3–9.

[22]See Harvey Leibenstein "Allocative Efficiency vs. 'X-Efficiency'," *American Economic Review*, Vol. LVI, No. 3 (June, 1966), for one economist's view of this key problem.

man in primitive situations). Hence if efficiency is increased, other things equal, then income rises. But now we find that we are discussing management, not economics, since questions of efficiency and productivity within firms is what managers and management theory deal with. Since international and comparative management theory straddles the line between macro and micro, it may turn out that both national and firm questions eventually become a part of the field.

TAKING OFF THE CULTURAL BLINDERS

If nothing else, the practice and theory of international and comparative management has forced many persons to remove their cultural blinders. We all are culture bound, but few of us realize how much we are until we get into international situations in which we must deal with persons from other cultures. Since even the most powerful international firms must deal with other persons on a bargaining basis, and since you rarely can have it all your own way, some compromise must be achieved; and various managers, politicians, technicians, and what not, have to sit down and figure out mutually advantageous deals.

When this happens, we normally find that there are lots of things, managerial and otherwise, that are quite different in other lands. One of the peculiarities of making deals, rarely noticed, is that some degree of tolerance has to be present, or conversation is impossible, let alone consummation. A good and proper Presbyterian, facing a charming Moslem with three wives, cannot let his own value perceptions botch the job, nor can a good Catholic Italian official emote much when dealing with a thrice-divorced American executive. Since the deal will be mutually advantageous to all, we have to treat one another as equals. Tolerance and empathy are really the essence of the game. And, after some years of working with various characters from all over the place, one discovers to his surprise that it really doesn't matter all that much anyhow.

Similarly, international managers operate in all sorts of environments, with all sorts of local peculiarities. These are annoying, absurd, ludicrous, or whatever, but after all, you are a guest there, so you live with them. And when the opportunity presents itself, you can gently point out just how silly some things are, and just how expensive, in terms of inhibiting productive firm performance.

But the blinders are on both sides. Americans abroad discover, as they investigate and work in other environments, that the American environment has lots of blinkers and blinders and absurdities as well. The trick is to try to put together the optimum environment that would achieve whatever one has in mind. It is common these days to discover in the popular American press serious studies of how the English, French, or Swiss work out problems of relevance to Americans, such as city planning, antitrust law, or whatever. Maybe they do have a point, after all.

If international business does nothing more than slightly diminish all the varieties of jingoism present around the world, it will probably be worth while in the end. One overlooked thing that international and comparative management does is to present many of us with models of what might be, distilled from examples all over the world. Maybe they are presently too crude and too simplistic to be workable, but at least we are beginning to realize that our own cultural blinders may have precluded quite workable solutions to many pressing internal firm and external environmental problems.

CHANGING PERCEPTIONS OF ONE WORLD

The very rapid rise of the multinational firm in the past 2 decades has generated lots of excitement, theory, interest, fear, and admiration. Although some form of international business has been around since Genesis, this new breed appears to be something quite different, something never before seen in world affairs. And in the end, the development may turn out to be very important in dimensions not now perceived or seen as particularly important.

It is really quite incredible that multinational firms can even exist in a nationalistic world. After all, few countries are willing to give up their precious sovereignty or wealth to a bunch of crazy foreigners. But such firms do exist, prosper, and expand. They can do this because they are the only institutions around in the international scene who are playing a positive sum game.

This means that any multinational firm, if it is to get into a country and prosper, has to give its host country something in return. A deal has to be made that will guarantee that the host country, or its citizens, will be better off by the presence of the company than if it did not exist. Of course, the multinational firm must gain too, which is why the game is positive sum. The winners far outnumber the losers. Gains typically (though not always) are measured in money, and the way you get positive sums is to be more productive with given resources than before. In short, the multinational firm is productive, and it shares its gains with its hosts.

This does not mean that everything is smooth sailing, as any study of almost any bargaining session would suggest. It does not necessarily mean that gains are equally distributed the country may get 10 per cent and the firm, 90 per cent. But no one makes a deal without expecting to get something out of it, and in the multinational firm case, the company does not have gunboats any more to enforce an unfair deal. If the initial agreement is bad, renegotiation is inevitable. Everyone is always complaining, but somehow the job gets done, and the multinational firms manage to survive and prosper.

Multinational firms can offer positive sum deals because they are productive—and greater productivity leads directly to greater gross national product for the host country. Because they can, countries gulp, sigh, and deal, even though the firm may be bigger than the country. One can understand some reluctance to work with such monsters, but what else does a small country have? The options, including the sterile, unproductive nineteenth-century Marxism, don't look too attractive. Who wants to be an Albania?

Multinational firms, along with international management theory, also have another revolutionary seed built into them. Virtually all of our conventional economics, politics, nationalism, and cultural analysis are essentially provincial, concerned mainly with petty local problems. Petty nationalism or hyper-nationalism is rampant in many places, including the United States, and when various issues come up, they are seen by most people in a purely provincial way.

But multinational firms, managers, and theory view the world in quite another way. Their orientation is transnational, and they visualize the world as a unit, pockmarked here and there by various local booby traps, pitfalls, and constraints set up by provincials who seem to feel that such things are very important. If these local pitfalls are important, there is money to be made and things to do someplace else. If one country doesn't want the new assembly plant, we can put it in another; if one country refuses to train technicians because the training will interfere with local cultural sensibilities, there are plenty of other persons elsewhere who will jump at the chance; and so on. In short, transnational firms treat the local peasants as locals or provincials. Given the need for empathy and tolerance noted earlier, no one will be rude about such things; it just turns out that if a country or culture really wants to be itself, it pays the price. The price is economic—incomes are lower. The price is cultural—somehow your citizens are out of the world game, and no one really cares much what you think or feel. The price is educational—your citizens don't get educated in ways that get them into the world mainstream.

And, in the end, the price is being an Albania—no one knows or cares what happens within the country, because it is totally irrelevant.

It is, of course, possible that long after the multinational firms and world powers are gone, the Albanias of this world will still be chunking along in good shape. However, few individuals or leaders appear to want to pay this kind of price, or wait for two or three generations to find out if this isolationist option is in the end the wise strategy.

Thus, curiously, transnational business turns out to be a major integrative force in world affairs. Even the Russians now want in on the game, as they search for Ford or some other Western truckmaker to give them the ability they need for local purposes. The countries that have accepted transnational firms turn out to be the ones where the action is, where economic growth is highest, where people want to be. Those taking the other course turn out to be the stagnant backwaters of the world, where nothing happens except brain drains, dreary Kafka-like bureaucratic stiflings, and endless grim boredom. How long has it been since anyone suggested that Eastern Europe had anything to offer the rest of the world? Twenty-five years ago, these Communist countries were seen as the wave of the future.

Multinational firms are certainly not immune from criticism, nor have they ever seen very clearly this particular role they play. They frighten to death the petty bureaucrats, local religious and cultural leaders, politicians, two-bit local businessmen of the old school (high markups, low volume), students, radicals, and many others. These people are quite correct in their concern—if the multinational firms really do their jobs, the local world will be different forevermore, and those holding real power will be quite different from the present wielders of influence. Who is more important—

the president of some small African republic, or the manager of the local copper mine with world sales ten times as big as everything else put together in the republic? Indeed, one major reason for academic concern about international business is just this power takeover that is occurring. Serious scholars rarely study irrelevant things.

But these weird multinational firms are way ahead of all other significant international groups as an integrative force in world affairs. They work with the world as their beat, and they regard local problems as interesting, significant, possibly costly, but nothing really to get very excited about. Something can always be done. In the end, the goal is a totally integrated world firm, able to maneuver through whatever political, diplomatic, or economic thickets ingenious locals are able to devise. And as a few politicians and countries begin to realize the productive potential in truly world-level integrated corporations, such thickets may not be too critical anymore. Changes will be more positive than negative in many areas.

Now, all of this is done for all the wrong reasons. Anyone who seriously argues that all he is trying to do is to make money is not likely to be in the mainstream of world ethics, philosophy, and politics. But somehow, the options don't look so very attractive. Gunboat diplomacy doesn't work too well any more; nor does the Marxist deal of the totally isolated state, eagerly planning its own destiny. Models available for this activity are not too attractive. And the power politics option, with its real dangers of atomic war, are even less attractive. As usual, in the somewhat imprecise and messy state of human affairs, the available options are all bad for one reason or another.

But the transnation business option looks a bit better than the rest. I would rather argue with some rabid nationalist any day across a business table than take some shots at him—or worse, have him take some shots at me. If all international business ever does is create large amounts of loud bargaining, accompanied in the end by some shady agreement whereby we both can survive, it may be worth while. And if, in the process, those vulgar business types discover to our surprise that they have pushed the world a bit further toward total integration for all the wrong reasons, I'm with them—and I'll diligently try to develop some more imperfect theory to help them on their way. The practical options to this path on our troubled planet don't appeal to me at all.

The Nature of International Business

Jean Boddewyn

Professor
Graduate School of Business Administration
New York University

Professor Farmer defines international management as "The systematic study of management in situations wherein both local and international constraints may differ considerably, to the point at which key managerial problems within firms are seriously affected." In many ways, this is a workable definition because the differences among the American and foreign *environments* (physical, economic, political, social, and cultural) are usually significant and therefore bound to affect the performance of the *management process* (planning, organizing, staffing, directing, and controlling), of the *business functions* (production, financing, marketing, accounting, etc.), and of their outcome. I would also agree that effectiveness in international management (I really prefer the term "international business," and will use it from now on) depends on "the development of linkages among relevant environmental constraints and internal-firm constraints."

Yet, this definition of international business can be still improved, because Professor Farmer stresses the analysis of the *environment* (which is obviously very important) at the expense of that of the international *firm* itself.[1] Hence, the following discussion complements Professor Farmer's with an analysis of the nature of the international firm, and relates these additional considerations to the problems of careers and training for international business.

INTERNATIONAL BUSINESS CAREERS

All sorts of participants are found in international business (meaning here business involving the crossing of a national border by goods, services, people, firms, capital, patents, ideas, etc.). Nowadays one hears readily of such giant multinational firms as IBM, Shell, and Mitsubishi that have invested and operate in many countries. However, for a few hundred of those giants, there are tens of thousands of small and medium companies—all the way down to the one-man business such as is run by a friend of mine who is a consultant on international market research for the container industry and advises a score of firms on both sides of the Atlantic.

This example also illustrates the fact that there is much more to international business than manufacturing abroad. For one thing, international production must be supported by all sorts of *subsidiary services* such as management and marketing, consulting, banking, shipping, legal advising, lobbying, and so on, where all sorts of firms find profitable niches. Besides, most international firms do not engage in foreign production but focus mostly on the *exporting and importing* of goods, capital, patents, and other services. There

[1] I am using the term "international" in a fairly general way although a variety of distinctions have been made among "international" (mainly focused on exports), "multinational," or "plurinational" (operating plants in several countries), and "transnational," "supranational," or "global" (without any real home country) firms.

is also a fairly sizable army of so-called *"expatriates"* who have left their country to work abroad—for various lengths of time or even for good. They constitute some sort of a "foreign legion" of technicians and managers who sell their services to international and foreign companies and governments after having acquired some experience abroad in the army, the Peace Corps, or international organizations.

This brief enumeration suggests that there is a large variety of international career opportunities and patterns, and many paths to them. Too often, students interested in such a career think only of a few scores of very large international manufacturers and fail to consider their numerous smaller and/or auxiliary brethren.

Moreover, it is well to realize that large firms seldom recruit people directly for international assignments—and the reason is relatively simple. In the first place, a large organization (or any organization for that matter) needs to appraise the new recruit to see if he "belongs" before sending him overseas at great cost. Furthermore, he needs to be trained in some skills, and this usually requires assignment in some home office or plant. Finally, only a few thousand Americans are sent abroad by large international firms for any great length of time. Many more, of course, go abroad on trouble-shooting assignments, but this is different from making a career overseas in a large corporation.

The often-quoted figure of 40,000 overseas Americans must thus be understood to include the roving technicians, engineers, and managers of fortune, as well as the one-man businesses (Harry's Bar in Paris!)—not just the personnel of large international companies.

On the other hand, stateside, there are many more tens of thousands of staff and line people involved more or less directly in international business at headquarters, in the international division, and in all the other parts of a large firm affected by its international dimension (planning, finance, auditing, legal, marketing, etc.). These people may only go overseas for short trips, but theirs are international careers too.

In any case, a career in international business requires some preparation and training—in fact, it is a never-ending process because of the constancy of change and of the large variety of environments involved. Although space does not permit us to develop the possible contents of such a learning process,[2] one can better visualize it in terms of what international business is all about.

SOME FURTHER THOUGHTS ON THE NATURE OF INTERNATIONAL BUSINESS

As promised, let us expand on Professor Farmer's definition of "international management," particularly in the context of a large multinational corporation that represents today the epitome of the complexity of modern business.[3] Four criteria can be used to

[2]For further details about international business education, see S. H. Robock and L. C. Nehrt (Eds.), *Education in International Business* (Bloomington, Indiana: Indiana University, Graduate School of Business, Bureau of Business Research, 1964); John Fayerweather, Jean Boddewyn, and Holger Engberg, *International Business Education: Curriculum Planning* (New York: New York University, Graduate School of Business Administration, 1966); *The Professional School and World Affairs; Report of the Task Force on Business Administration and Public Administration* (New York: Education and World Affairs, 1967); S. F. Otteson (Ed.), *Internationalizing the Traditional Business Curriculum* (Bloomington, Indiana: Indiana University Graduate School of Business, Bureau of Business Research, 1968); and Vern Terpstra (Ed.), *International Business Course Descriptions* (Ann Arbor, Michigan: University of Michigan, Institute for International Commerce, Graduate School of Business Administration, 1970).

[3]These concepts are elaborated in somewhat different form by John Fayerweather in his *International Business Management: A Conceptual Framework* (New York: McGraw-Hill Book Co., Inc., 1969).

distinguish it from the "domestic" variety.

"Things Are Different"

This first dimension refers to the variety of materials, services, laws, regulations, political systems, climates, technologies, credit facilities, and so on around the world. For the one-man business, there are work permits to obtain when there may be none in his own country. For the exporter, there are special instruments such as the letter of credit and consular invoices and different packaging and labeling requirements. For the firm intending to manufacture abroad, there are new production and marketing costs to figure and compare. These are just examples, but there are volumes written by legal, financial, accounting, marketing, and engineering experts on foreign systems and international transactions. A particularly relevant body of theory here is international economics, which analyzes the rationale for countries specializing in certain productions and engaging in exchange relations; but other international business courses also provide relevant factual information about such "thing" differences.

"People Are Different"

Although our business education does not make much of the fact that southerners differ from midwesterners, Californians or New Yorkers, such "people" differences are hard to overlook abroad. The term "culture" is often used as a shorthand expression for the "learned and shared ways of life" found in each country or region: how individuals view themselves, their superiors, peers, and subordinates; how societies are divided into classes and castes, and how these segments interact; how economic pursuits are valued in contrast to other personal and societal goals; how authority is perceived and shared; who is likely to engage in business and management, and what prestige they have; and so on.

One recognizes readily here the stuff on which management and organization are built, and cross-cultural similarities and differences are relevant in organizing and managing firms. In this context, comparative courses and training programs are most relevant for developing the proper knowledge, attitudes, and skills needed to deal with the people of different cultures.[4]

"The Organization Is More Complex"

Geographic extension complicates the management of multinational corporations, which, like other business organizations, must also cope with their functional and product dimensions. To quote Fayerweather,[5] many "gaps" appear when the far-flung parts of an international company (export department, international division, fully-owned subsidiaries, licensees, partners in joint ventures, beneficiaries of a management contract, etc.) plus all the "domestic" units must be coordinated:

1. The *cultural gap* associated with the communication problems among people from groups having different values, social mores, and attitudes;
2. The *nationality* gap, which refers to the fact that most people identify with their own country rather than with the host or home country of the corporation;
3. The *environmental gap*, which pertains particularly to the problems of

[4]See J. Boddewyn, *Comparative Management and Marketing* (Glenview, Illinois: Scott, Foresman and Co., 1969); J. Boddewyn (Ed.), *Comparative Management Teaching, Training and Research* (New York: New York University Press, 1970); R. A. Webber (Ed.), *Culture and Management* (Homewood, Illinois: Richard D. Irwin, 1969); S. M. Davis, *Comparative Management; Organizational and Cultural Perspectives* (Englewood Cliffs, N.J.: Prentice-Hall, Inc., 1971); and A. R. Negandhi and S. B. Prasad, *Comparative Management* (New York: Appleton-Century-Crofts, 1971).

[5]Fayerweather, *op. cit.*, pp. 173–81.

individuals in one country attempting to make decisions that are best for another country, and without really understanding the foreign situation fully;

4. The *distance gap,* which comes about from geographic distance together with imperfections in existing communication media, resulting in impediments and obstructions to the flow of information.

These gaps certainly make the coordination of a multinational enterprise much more complex than for most purely domestic firms. There is by now an abundant literature on the management of such monster firms,[6] but international firms are still a long way from having mastered such a coordinative skill.

"Legitimacy Must Be Acquired"

The constant criticism of private business since its appearance in the late Middle Ages, together with more recent discussions of business social responsibilities toward the physical environment and the consumer, should remind us that even in their home country, U.S. business firms must represent (and appear to represent) a legitimate and meaningful way of conducting economic activities,[7] and that they must obtain the support of society at large, and more particularly of government, which embodies the task of ensuring the general welfare.

Acquiring such legitimacy is even more difficult abroad because every country and person is *nationalistic* to some extent—that is, tends to react against "foreign bodies" simply because they are foreign. Besides, as Professor Farmer points out, international companies have a lot to offer, but still their views do conflict at times with what foreign governments consider to be in the *national interest* (e.g., shutting down a plant may make sense to a company trying to streamline its worldwide production facilities, but does conflict with the host or home country's goal of full employment, increased exports, etc.). Furthermore, there are conflicts of *national sovereignties* when one country insists that its laws be applied abroad, as when the U.S. government forbids American subsidiaries abroad to export certain goods to Communist countries.[8]

Acquiring such legitimacy is difficult in today's turbulent world where expectations and political regimes change rather frequently. Courses are just appearing along these lines, but training in economics and political science is particularly relevant here.

CONCLUSION

As Professor Farmer points out, there are still people who see international business or management as fundamentally the same as the domestic vari-

[6]For a sample of such studies, see John Fayerweather, *Management of International Operations* (New York: McGraw-Hill Book Co., Inc., 1960); J. S. Ewing and Frank Meissner (Eds.), *International Business Management; Readings and Cases* (Belmont, California: Wadsworth Publishing Co., 1964); E. J. Kolde, *International Business Enterprise* (Englewood Cliffs, N.J.: Prentice-Hall, Inc., 1968); and Ashok Kapoor and P.D. Grub (Eds.), *The Multinational Enterprise in Transition* (Princeton, N.J.: Darwin Press, 1972).

[7]There is an abundant literature on "business and its environment" and "business and society." See, for example, J. W. McGuire, *Business and Society* (New York: McGraw-Hill Book Co., Inc., 1963).

[8]For further analysis of these issues, see Raymond Vernon, *Sovereignty at Bay* (New York: Basic Books, 1971); R. D. Robinson, *International Business Policy* (New York: Holt, Rinehart and Winston, 1964); J. N. Behrman, *National Interests and the Multinational Enterprise* (Englewood Cliffs, N.J.: Prentice-Hall, Inc., 1970); C. P. Kindleberger, *American Business Abroad* (New Haven, Connecticut: Yale University Press, 1969); and Ashok Kapoor, *International Business Negotiations; A Study in India* (New York: New York University Press, 1970).

ety. Personally, I think that the four dimensions outlined above add up to a significant difference. It is true that one needs to be a good manager or staff specialist at home before one can contribute something to foreign economies and societies. However, these managerial and business knowledges, attitudes, and skills must be overlaid by another layer of competence. The foreman, the division head, and the president may all be managers, but the latter are managers on a higher plane, which requires further training and experience. Similarly, international management demands an additional set of abilities to further broaden and heighten the manager's competence and put him in a different league—one to which more and more people will be called in our increasingly interdependent world.

Multinational, Comparative, and International Management

William Voris

President
Thunderbird Graduate School of International Management

From all evidence there is probably not a field of theory called international management. It seems clear from a survey of the literature[1] that the widely accepted field of scientific management theory is applicable to all environments. In other words, theory is theory whether it is applied in the United States, Latin America, or the Far East. A company has an organization structure, it has employees, it has a financial side, it has a distribution side, and it has a production side if it is in manufacturing. It does not matter in which locale it finds itself. A student, therefore, who is interested in studying for an international career is probably just as well off to attend any sort of management theory courses that are applicable to his needs and wishes. All will serve him well. This does not mean that by acquiring this kind of scientific management knowledge he will be equipped immediately for applying this knowledge in an international environment. The point being made here is that there is both a science and an art of management.[2] The science of management is universal, what-

[1]See Ralph Davis, *The Fundamentals of Top Management* (New York: Harper and Bros., 1951), p. 5. He discusses ably the nature of scientific management.

Harold Koontz and Cyril O'Donnell, *Principles of Management*, 3rd ed. (New York: McGraw-Hill Book Co., Inc., 1965), p. 4. The authors state that the thesis of their book is essentially the universality of management theory.

Peter F. Drucker, *Preparing Tomorrow's Business Leaders Today* (Englewood Cliffs, N.J.: Prentice-Hall, Inc., 1969), p. 169. Drucker says, "The tasks of management are increasingly becoming 'non-national.' It is the same task everywhere."

[2]See William Voris, *Production Control*, 3rd ed. (Homewood, Illinois: Richard D. Irwin, 1966), pp. 1–2. The distinction between the science and the art of management is made relatively clear.

ever the environment. The art, or the practice, of management varies because of many different situations. One of the possible situations is an international locale. The art of management is practiced differently in Chicago than it is in Birmingham, Alabama, and, of course, is practiced much differently in Lyon, France, than in either Birmingham, Alabama, or in Chicago.

A course in international management at Indiana University, New York University, or Thunderbird Graduate School would be composed primarily of management theory of the same sort that could be picked up in a management theory course at the University of California, Berkeley, or at the University of Chicago. The difference in an international management course would be that the applications, the descriptions, and the cases would be devoted to international situations, and hence would require different application of the same theory because of a different environment. This is Professor Farmer's main point and is very valid.

COMPARATIVE MANAGEMENT

There is definitely a field of inquiry called comparative management. It seems to this author that this is a field that offers valuable research opportunities for building a pragmatic approach to international situations. Farmer and Richman have made a significant start in this field.[3] What comparative management does is not compare the sciences of management, but the practice of management from one region to another. This approach has great practical value.

Anyone practicing management in any part of the world, including various parts of the United States, should be a student of comparative management, because he must take the theories and temper them with environmental inputs and constraints, such as educational level, behavioral systems, legal and political environment, the economic situation—all of which is very carefully spelled out in Farmer's chapter. The practicing manager on an international scale must become a student of the environment in which he is to operate. To be successful he requires a breadth of knowledge, empathy, and insight that the typical graduate of a graduate school of business administration would not have. To be truly successful as a practitioner in transnational organization it seems clear that the manager must have an intimate knowledge of the languages, the behaviorial patterns, and the history of the region where he is to work. This, of course, is the approach of the Thunderbird Graduate School and is practiced extensively in the major multinational companies that are sending families into international locales to manage their far-flung offices. They are sending them to language schools and giving them courses in international studies. Of course, they probably were picked originally by the company because of their detailed knowledge of scientific management.

INTERNATIONAL MANAGEMENT AND COMPARATIVE MANAGEMENT

To this author, international management is merely the art of leading others in a foreign environment. It has its roots originally in economics, psychology, and sociology, and most immediately has emerged from scientific management theory. It has no particular theory of its own, but is primarily an application of management theory to various international problems and locales. It can primarily be taught and learned through case studies, descriptive lectures, and situational problems. To this author, comparative management is

[3]See Richard Farmer and Barry Richman, *Comparative Management and Economic Progress* (Homewood, Illinois: Richard D. Irwin, 1965). A pioneering effort in the field of comparative management.

an effective field for studying international management after a solid basis of universal management theory has been acquired.

THE KNOWLEDGE NECESSARY FOR SUCCESS

It is probable that Professor Farmer was exaggerating when he said, "Much of the very practical international work being done is performed by individuals who have never been near an international management text, but have the necessary wisdom, wit, and insight to make necessary adjustments to the real problems they face." If one counted all the minor supervisors around the world, this statement would probably be true. However, most of the men and women with major responsibilities being sent out to offices by multinational firms are thoroughly grounded in the management theory they need to do the job. They are going to know monetary theory, they are going to know development economics, they are going to understand some of the contributions of the behavioral scientists to management. It certainly will help if they have wisdom with insight, but one can't always count on that and this author is not sure that it is always necessary for success on the international scene. If they have the management knowledge coupled with insight, it will certainly be a help to them. Without one or the other, they are definitely in trouble. It is certainly clear that insight alone will not be enough. It is not enough for the manager to know his people and the political situation in Paris. He also must understand the planning function, the organization function, and the control function. Any company that sends an executive to a foreign post without providing him extensive background through education and training, through scientific management, languages, and area studies is courting a failure. In the past this has happened more often than not. The pioneering multinationals have faced this problem and are handling it very well at the present time. Some of the large pioneering American banks have come a long way in this direction—the First National City Bank of New York, the Chase Manhattan Bank of New York, the Bank of America, all have extensive recruiting efforts, training programs, and screening processes that come as near as possible to providing the insight and scientific management knowledge that is necessary for their overseas representatives. This sort of reasoning and practice is spreading rapidly to firms around the world who are involved in transnational business.

THE TRANSFER OF MANAGEMENT SKILLS

Professor Farmer alludes to the burgeoning problem of skill transfer. Of course, the United States has been a significant leader in trying to transfer management skills from one culture to another, in trying to open a two-way street between the developing culture and the developed. Peter P. Gabriel has an interesting little book on the international transfer of corporate skills.[4] In this book, a doctoral dissertation at the Harvard Graduate School of Business Administration, he discusses the use of management contacts in less-developed countries.

The author of this critique was involved in a situation in Teheran, Iran, some years ago, in which he and his counterpart both learned about an equal amount about management in the Iranian milieu. This mingling of managerial personnel with different national backgrounds coming from different cultures and environments is a significant achievement and should be practiced on

[4]See Peter P. Gabriel, *The International Transfer of Corporate Skills* (Cambridge: Harvard University Press, 1967), Chapter 8. Transfer of skills can be brought about through management contacts.

a much larger scale than it is. American management applications science may or may not be effective in a different environment, but the inputs of a person with a management science background and an indigenous upbringing can be of great value to the company that is seeking to establish a foothold in a foreign land. Farmer is quite correct when he says that we do not know too much about transferring management skills and sciences, but we are learning, and what has been done has been effective. The counterpart situation may be an answer to many problems in achieving culturalization.

THE WORLD IS GROWING CLOSER TOGETHER

The world seems to be becoming increasingly homogeneous. This is very evident from a comparison of Europe in 1945 and 1955, and now in the seventies. If anything, the customs, the habits, the value systems of people in Europe are becoming more like those of Americans and Japanese. The implications of this trend toward homogeniety among cultures will tend to make the practice of management much more universal. Farmer is probably correct when he says that the efforts of foreign management personnel to improve their performance may very well result in the continuing development of this cultural homogeneity. The international manager will realize that his ability to perform as a manager will be much enhanced by improvements in the political, economic, and social environment of the country in which he is attempting to be efficient and effective. If countries wish to continue to develop, they will heed this sort of criticism and pressure by foreign officials. Difficulties will be overcome. Things will get done and the lot of the people will be greatly improved, partly as a result of the efforts of management personnel of transnational companies.

In many ways this increasing homogeneity between cultures is a sad thing. Theorists must be ready to face the possibility that nations and groups of people may suddenly decide they do not want to progress any further or to be like someone else. Apparently, the peoples of developing nations want to be exact copies of their counterparts in the developed nations. They want to wear the same clothes, drink the same beverages, eat the same food, drive the same cars as a middle-class individual in the United States, Japan, or England. The people of the United States are just now learning that this kind of achievement and accomplishment is not always what it is "cracked up" to be. The reason for bringing this up is that this movement toward homogeneity could be forestalled by changes in values, such as is currently being experienced among many of the young in the United States. The people of India might over a period of time decide that they do not want to be like the British, that they do not want to become an industrialized nation. This is not likely, but it is possible. One could hardly disagree with Professor Farmer, however, when he says that if international business does nothing more than slightly diminish jingoism around the world, it probably will be worth while in the end. The reverse of this is true, also, it seems to this author, and if exposure to different cultures, different value systems, and different climates can make better human beings out of Americans, it also will be worth while.

THE MULTINATIONAL COMPANIES

The direction the multinational company takes in the future and its impact on the world at large will command a considerable amount of attention on the part of scholars and practitioners of management. Prognostications on the future impact of the multinationals range all the way from predictions about the assumption of vast economic and military by Perlmutter down to the possibility of the complete extinction of the multinational company.

The second trend has been predicted by some recently because of the growing trend toward nationalization of the divisions of multinational companies in some parts of the world—namely, in Latin America and Africa. As in all things, the actuality probably is somewhere in between. The multinational company does supply a little bit of something for everyone. Before it can gain a foothold in any country, it must work out some sort of deal with that government, as suggested by Farmer. It has a great advantage in being able to use the international monetary system to its advantage by manipulating different foreign currencies, and by selling and buying among its many divisions and organizations around the world. Schollhammer says that U.S. based multinational firms tend to set definite limits on the discretionary authority given their many divisions around the world.[5] European-based multinationals tend to give considerable autonomy to their foreign operating units. It seems that the European approach to this organization problem will be the long-range tendency, because of the relationships between the multinational companies and the nations where they establish branches and divisions. Nations will probably further stipulate in the future that a greater share of the profits of multinations be left in the participating country rather than being returned, as a standard procedure, to headquarters in New York, or Geneva, or Paris. The editors of *Fortune* magazine, December, 1971 edition, state that multinational companies based in the United States can possibly benefit greatly from the new economics being practiced by Americans. The fact that they operate in the currency of the country in which they have a plant and office and the fact that tariff and other restrictions among nations will be lowered are all plus factors in the future of the multinational concern.

In summary, the future of the multinational corporation seems to be rosy. There are problems, of course, especially of nationalization, the opposition of American labor unions, the protectionist attitudes of many Americans, and other factors. Farmer's point about how multinational firms view the world is very important. These companies and their personnel are thinking globally. They do visualize the world as a whole and tend less and less to think of small segments and their petty problems. Over the next 100 years, the peoples of the world will probably become more and more one people. The practice of international business management will probably have a lot to do with development.

[5]See Hans Schollhammer, "Organization Structures of Multinational Companies," *Academy of Management Journal*, Vol. 14, No. 3 (September, 1971), pp. 345–66.

DISCUSSION QUESTIONS

1. Is there really such a thing as "international" management? Is it different from "management"? If so, how? And what is international management?
2. Can management performance be transferred from one country to another?
3. Do international managers just have to worry about culture, language, and techniques, and that's all?
4. What would it really mean to be an Albanian in Farmer's terms? Would this be good? Why?
5. What are some of the careers in international business? How should people prepare for these?
6. What does the "universality" of management mean?
7. What is "comparative" management? How does it differ from international management?
8. What is a "multinational" company?

PART THREE

THE MANAGEMENT "CORE"

12

Comprehensive Managerial Planning

George A. Steiner

Professor and Director
Division of Research
Graduate School of Management
University of California, Los Angeles

INTRODUCTION

A new comprehensive managerial planning system, called by many different names, has developed and has spread rapidly around the world during the past 15 years.[1] It has ripened into a major management tool. At the heart of the process is strategic planning. Although the process can be done informally, more and more companies, particularly the larger ones, find that it is best conducted in a more formal fashion.

At the outset, it is important to point out that there is no one way to introduce and use this new planning system. Each company is unique. We do know, however, those fundamental principles and practices that are essential to success. This chapter will summarize the nature of this system, how it operates, its importance to business, and the major pitfalls to be avoided in its operation. The literature in this field has been growing rapidly and now includes hundreds of articles and several hundred books. This chapter is a distillation of this literature.[2]

[2]I have leaned heavily on my book *Top Management Planning* (New York: The Macmillan Co., 1969). This book contains a bibliography of about 700 items which, I think, included the best literature at the time of writing. For an earlier annotated bibliography of about 500 references see Melville C. Branch, *Selected References for Corporate Planning* (New York: American Management Association, 1966). For a more recent brief résumé of the best literature in the field, see Robert J. Mockler, "Theory and Practice of Planning," *Harvard Business Review*, Vol. 48 (March–April, 1970), pp. 148–150, 152–158. To this should be added a reference to the only journal in the world devoted exclusively to long-range planning. It is *Long Range Planning*, published by Pergamon Press, Ltd., on behalf of the Society for Long Range Planning, Terminal House, Grosvenor Gardens, London, England. It first appeared in 1968.

Special reference should be made to surveys about what really is being done in business with respect to the formal planning process. Two of the earliest substantial studies were, first, David I. Cleland, *The Origin and Development of a Philosophy of Long-Range Planning in American Business*, Doctoral Dissertation, The Ohio State University, 1962. The second was William T. Newell, Jr., *Long-Range Planning Policies and Practices:*

Although comprehensive managerial planning systems cover the complete spectrum of plans from what to do tomorrow to the far distant future, its newness and emphasis is focused on the long range and on adaptation to changing environments. The discussion in this chapter follows this emphasis.

INTUITIVE-ANTICIPATORY VERSUS FORMAL LONG-RANGE PLANNING

Fundamentally, there are two types of comprehensive long-range corporate planning. The first is intuitive-anticipatory planning. Although no one really knows the precise mental processes by which it is accomplished, it has several discernible major characteristics. Generally, it is the work of one person. It may or may not, but often does not, result in a written set of plans. It generally has a comparatively short time horizon and reaction time. It is based on past experience, the "gut" feel, the judgment, and the reflective thinking of a manager. It is very important. Many managers have extraordinary capabilities to intuitively devise brilliant strategies and methods to carry them out.[3]

In contrast, the formal planning system is organized and developed on the basis of a set of procedures. It is explicit in the sense that people know what is being done. It is research-based, involves the work of many people, and results in a set of written plans.

These two systems of planning often clash. A manager who has been successful with his intuitive judgments is not likely to accept completely the constraints of a formal system. He may be uneasy with some of the new language and methods incorporated by sophisticated staff in a formal plan-

---

Selected Companies Operating in Texas, Research Monograph No. 25, Austin, Texas, The University of Texas, Bureau of Business Research, 1963. A more recent publication is Kjell-Arme Ringbakk, *Organized Corporate Planning Systems,* doctoral dissertation, The University of Wisconsin, Graduate School of Business, 1968.

Long-range planning in foreign countries has not been examined as extensively as in the United States. There are, however, exceptions. One is Toyohiro Kono, "Long-Range Business Planning in Japan," mimeographed, Tokyo, Japan, Japan Management Center, 1967. Another is Bernard Taylor and Peter Irving, "Organized Planning in Major U.K. Companies," *Long Range Planning,* Vol. 3 (June, 1971), pp. 10–26. Yet another is Raoul M. Elias, "State of the Art of Canadian Corporate Planning," mimeograph résumé of MBA dissertation, McGill Faculty of Management, Montreal, Quebec. Special mention should be made of a large data bank of information concerning formal planning systems that is developing at Harvard University under the direction of Professor Richard F. Vancil. See Richard F. Vancil and Lewis B. Ward, "Formal Planning Systems: The 'Data Bank' Project," in Francis J. Aguilar, Robert A. Howell, and Richard F. Vancil (Eds.), *Formal Planning Systems: 1970,* mimeographed (Cambridge, Massachusetts: Harvard University Graduate School of Business Administration, 1970).

[3] I am using synonymously several words associated with creativity. Actually, there are differences among such things as intuition, judgment, hunch, instinct, invention, innovation, and entrepreneurship. See *Top Management Planning, op. cit.,* pp. 353–355. This footnote provides the occasion to make the comment that there is no general agreement on the many words and phrases used in planning. There is evolving, however, some consensus on some definitions.

ning system. Or, he may feel a challenge to his authority as those participating in the system engage in the decision-making process.

There should be no conflict, however, between these two systems. They should complement each other. The formal system should help managers to sharpen their intuitive-anticipatory inputs into the planning process. At the very least, the formal system should give managers more time for reflective thinking.

In a fundamental sense, formal planning is an effort to replicate intuitive planning. But formal planning cannot be really effective unless managers at all levels inject their judgments and intuition into the planning process.

FORMAL COMPREHENSIVE MANAGERIAL PLANNING DEFINED

In its early history the words "long-range planning" were used to describe the system that is the subject of this chapter. Other names have subsequently been coined. Long ago, for reasons that will be developed in this chapter, I abandoned the words "long-range planning" and began using synonymously these words: comprehensive corporate planning, comprehensive managerial planning, total planning, long-range planning, integrated planning, formal planning, overall planning, corporate planning, and other combinations of these words.

Corporate long-range planning should be defined in at least four ways, each of which is vital to its understanding. First, long-range planning deals with the futurity of current decisions. This means that long-range planning looks at the chain of cause-and-effect consequences over time of an actual or an intended decision that a manager is going to make. If he does not like what he sees ahead, he then will change the decision. Long-range planning also looks at the alternative courses of action that are open in the future, and when choices are made they become the basis for making current decisions. The essence of long-range planning is a systematic identification of future opportunities and threats that, in combination with other relevant data, provide a basis for a company's current decisions to exploit the opportunities and avoid the threats.

Second, comprehensive corporate planning is a process. It is a process that begins with the development of objectives, defines strategies and policies to achieve objectives, and develops detailed plans to make sure that the strategies are carried out to achieve the objectives. It is a process of deciding in advance what is to be done, when it is to be done, how it is to be done, and who is going to do it.

Third, it is a philosophy. Many businessmen talk about corporate planning as being a way of life. Executives speak of assuring the proper climate in their enterprise to guarantee effective corporate planning. This climate is a function of many forces, among which is an attitude of wanting to do effective planning.

Fourth, comprehensive corporate planning may be defined as a structure of plans. It is a structure that integrates strategic with short-range operational plans. In this structure are integrated, at all levels, major objectives, strategies, policies, and functions of an enterprise.

All these characteristics of corporate planning will be further examined. Before looking at them, however, it is important to make a few comments on what long-range planning is not.

WHAT LONG-RANGE PLANNING IS NOT

Long-range planning does not attempt to make future decisions. Rather, planning involves choosing the more desirable future alternatives open to a company so that better current decisions can be made.

Comprehensive corporate planning is not forecasting. It is not forecasting product sales and then determining what should be done to assure the fulfillment of the forecasts, with respect to such things as material purchases, facilities, manpower, and so on. Corporate planning goes beyond present forecasts of current products and markets and asks such questions as: Are we in the right business? What are our basic objectives? When will our present products become obsolete? Are our markets expanding or eroding? For most companies there is a wide gap between a simple forecast of present sales and profits and what top management would like its sales and profits to be. If so, there is a gap to be filled by comprehensive corporate planning.

Comprehensive long-range planning is not attempting to blueprint the future. It is not the development of a set of plans that are cast in bronze to be used day after day into the far distant future. Indeed, long-range plans are obsolete the very minute they are completed, because the environment assumed in their preparation has already changed. On the other hand, long-range planning permits a company to "invent" its future. This means that a company, through the corporate planning process, tries to foresee the future it wants for itself. It then, very often, can fulfill the targets it sets for itself by developing wise strategies and detailed plans.

CORPORATE PLANNING MODELS

Figure 23 shows my conceptual model of the structure and process of corporate planning. It further elaborates the meaning of comprehensive planning, particularly strategic planning, and explains how the process can be carried out. Over a number of years I have examined planning systems of many companies and conclude that those that do effective comprehensive planning follow this model explicitly or implicitly. Yet, paradoxically, I have never found an operational system diagramed in precisely the same way as Figure 23. Operational flow charts vary depending on differences among companies, but underneath, the basic elements of Figure 23 are found in the better systems. If one element of the model in Figure 23 is missing, either explicitly or implicitly, the system will not operate effec-

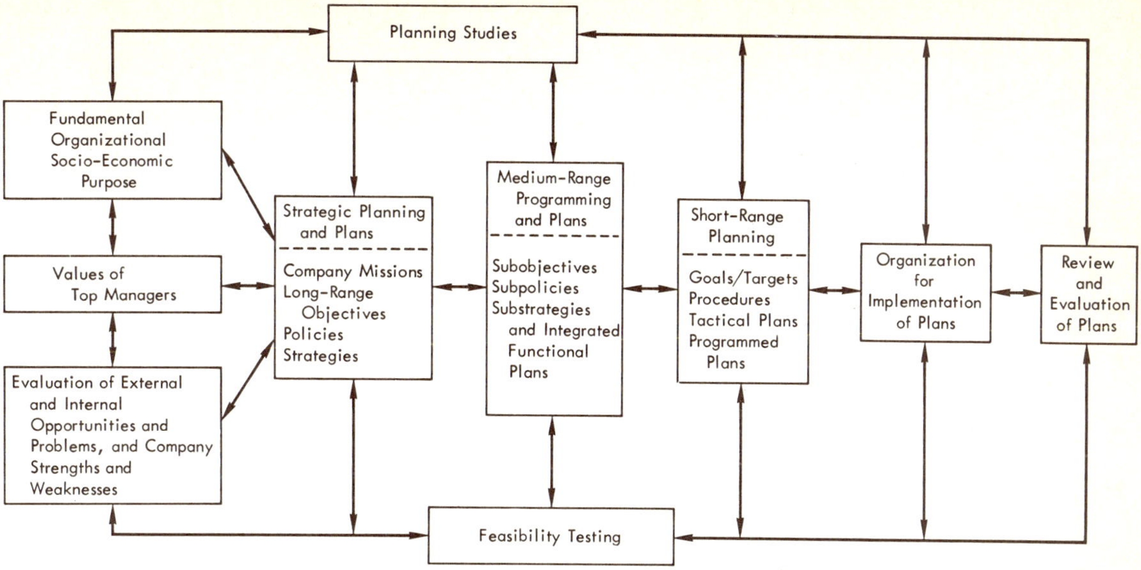

FIGURE 23. A Structure and Process of Business Planning

Source: Adapted from George A. Steiner, *Top Management Planning* (New York: The Macmillan Co., 1969).

tively. Conceptual models of leading authors in the field are quite comparable to this model.[4]

In the following exposition Figure 23 is used to explain the planning process. It should be pointed out, however, that in actual practice the process is repetitive and may begin at different points. In practice, there is much back-and-forth analysis before decisions are made. For instance, a tentative objective may be established and then strategies are examined to achieve them. Depending on the analysis of strategies, the objectives may be changed, and vice versa.

THE STRATEGIC PLANNING PROCESS

The strategic planning process includes the four blocks to the left of the model shown in Figure 23 and may extend to the blocks to the right of the model, as illustrated in Figure 27. The activity in the block marked "strategic planning and plans" results in a determination of a company's fundamental missions, objectives, policies, and strategies that govern the acquisition, use, and disposition of resources to achieve its basic aims. In doing this, of course, the understanding of the socio-economic purpose of the enterprise is important; the values of top managers must be considered;

[4]See, for example, Robert N. Anthony, *Planning and Control Systems: A Framework for Analysis* (Boston: Harvard University Graduate School of Business, 1952); Frank Gilmore and R. G. Brandenburg, "Anatomy of Corporate Planning," *Harvard Business Review*, Vol. 40 (November–December, 1962), pp. 61–69; and Robert F. Stewart, "A Framework for Business Planning," Report No. 162, Long Range Planning Service, Menlo Park, California, Stanford Research Institute, February, 1963.

and facts about future opportunities, threats, and company strengths and weaknesses are significant data inputs.

Several other characteristics of the strategic planning process should be pointed out. First, the time spectrum covers ranges from the very short range to infinity. Although the general thrust and content of strategic planning is long range, a decision can be made to stop producing *X* product tomorrow or to start building tomorrow a new plant to produce product *Y*.

Another important characteristic is that although the process may produce a written document on a periodic basis, such as once a year, the process is a continuous activity of top management, as illustrated in Figure 28. Top management cannot, of course, develop a strategic plan once a year and forget strategy in the meantime.

Another important characteristic of strategic planning, as compared with medium-range and short-range planning, is that the results are not usually neatly incorporated in a prescribed form. Medium-range and short-range planning result in numbers for specific functions for a prescribed period of time, as shown in Figure 26. Strategic planning covers any element of the business that is important at the time of analysis and embodies details that are of sufficient scope and depth to provide the necessary basis for implementation. The format for strategic plans generally is much more flexible than for other type plans and varies in content from time to time.

Attention in both the business and academic world is moving more and more to the strategic planning process. This is so simply because of the growing significance of this process to business growth and survival. Most of the literature in the field, however, is of recent origin and is growing slowly.[5] The work of scholars has been delayed not only because of the recent attention to business strategy, but also because it involves difficult and messy unstructured problems.

In the following discussion a few highlights of the nature of each of the major elements in the strategic planning process will be presented. This discussion will combine concept, methodology, and operational principles to the extent that space permits.

EXPECTATIONS OF MAJOR OUTSIDE INTERESTS

Up to a few years ago, in the academic as well as in the business world, a business was said to have but one major interest and that was to use the resources at its disposal as efficiently as possible in producing the goods and services that consumers wanted at prices they were willing to

[5]One of the first good books in the field was Igor H. Ansoff's *Corporate Strategy* (New York: McGraw-Hill Book Co., Inc., 1965). This was followed by an excellent treatment in J. Thomas Cannon's *Business Strategy and Policy* (New York: Harcourt Brace and World, 1968). An earlier unique contribution to the field was A. D. Chandler, Jr. *Strategy and Structure: Chapters in the History of the Industrial Enterprise* (Cambridge, Massachusetts: The M.I.T. Press, 1962). This was an historical analysis and not operational, as was Ansoff's and Cannon's analysis. Important work has been done recently in the application of new quantitative tools to strategic planning. Reference will be made later to this literature.

pay. Many people in both the educational and business world still think this is business' only responsibility. But more and more, especially for the larger companies, other interests are exerting an important influence on the business decision-making process. Stockholders want higher per share earnings and rising market prices for their shares. Customers want lower-priced products of higher quality. Suppliers and creditors have their own set of expectations. Of rising concern to business managers are the general expectations of society. Edward N. Cole, President of General Motors Corporation, has made the following observation in this connection: "The big challenge to American business—as I see it—is to carefully evaluate the constantly changing expressions of public and national goals. Then we must modify our own objectives and programs to meet—as far as possible within the realm of economic and technological feasibility—the new demands of the society we serve."[6] Any large company that begins its long-range planning solely on the basis of the short-range profit maximization principle as its only objective will inevitably wind up in a heap of trouble.

EXPECTATIONS OF MAJOR INSIDE INTERESTS

Among the most important inside interests that affect the planning program are the values of top managers. These are basic and fundamental premises in any comprehensive corporate planning system. Sometimes executive values are written out, but most of the time they are not written nor even articulated. Many of these values cannot be validated or invalidated on the basis of numbers or even logic, yet they may determine basic long-range objectives of a company. For instance, a chief executive may say: "I want my company to be the biggest in our industry in ten years." Or, he may say: "I want my company to be the technologically best in the industry." Or, he may say: "My goal is to make my company the biggest and the technically best company in my industry in the next decade." Each of these objectives provides a very different frame of reference for corporate planning. Each is rooted in the value system of the chief executive officer in the company.

Value systems not only influence objectives but also all sorts of decisions made in the planning process. For instance, one executive may wish to do business with the Mexicans because he likes them. Another in the same industry may prefer not to extend his operations to Mexico. The reasons of both managers may have nothing to do with sales and profits but may be solely determined by the values that each holds.

As many companies are coming to realize, the expectations of other managers, hourly workers, and staff also are important in what a company plans to do. Increasingly, these interests are reflected in the basic premises on which planning proceeds.

[6]Edward N. Cole, "Management Priorities for the 1970's," *Michigan Business Review*, Vol. XXII (July, 1970), p. 1. See also Committee for Economic Development, *Social Responsibilities of Business Corporations*, New York, June 1971; and George A. Steiner, *Business and Society* (New York: Random House, 1971), Chapter 9.

The Current Position and Future Environment

Figure 24, which is a modification of Figure 23, illustrates in the two left blocks the range and variety of subject matter involved in assessing current strengths and weaknesses and in identifying future opportunities, threats, and risks. It also shows that operationally and conceptually the planning process can begin with this assessment. A large part of the analytical work of corporate planning staffs is performed in this area. Analysis in this area can be done before, during, or after objectives and strategies are formulated.

The number of environmental factors that may be important to a company, either as opportunities or threats, is so great that it is necessary to determine those that are most significant and to spend as much time and effort as possible in studying them. Consumer disposable income is very important to an automobile company but not to an aerospace company. Threats to a beer producer are far different from those to a steel company.

Figure 25 illustrates different ways a company can identify opportunities, threats, and risks. Problem identification in the upper left-hand corner refers to results of simple observation or deep analysis. For instance, a company may note that its profit margin for product X is falling. This is a problem and the next step is to define precisely what is causing it. When that is understood, what can and should be done in the future to correct it becomes clearer. Some companies begin the planning process by identifying opportunities and threats in this way.

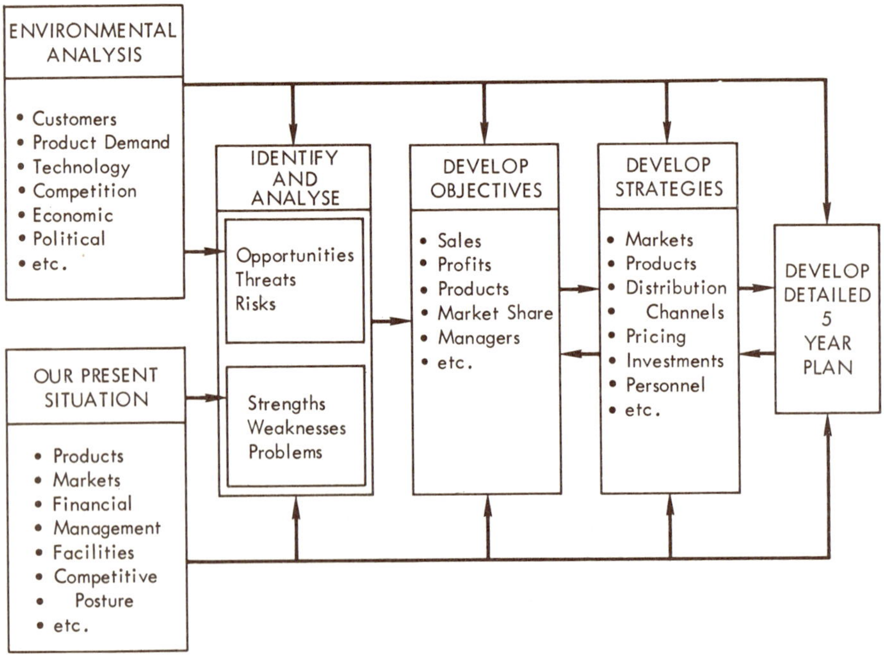

FIGURE 24. A Model for Business Long-Range Planning

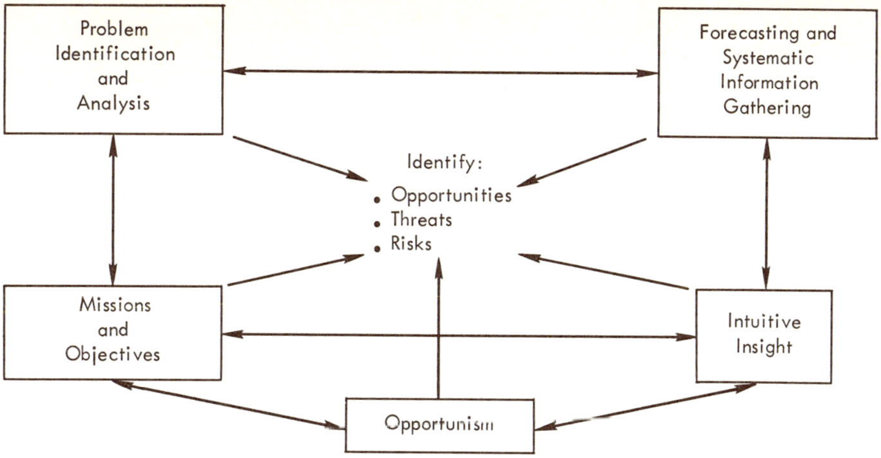

FIGURE 25. Opportunity-Threat-Risk Analysis

Another approach is to ask what are the basic missions and objectives of the company and then determine what are the opportunities ahead to achieve them or the threats that may thwart their fulfillment.

Opportunism is a third approach. For example, the analysis of diversification opportunities of some companies depends on "what comes over the transom." In other words, they wait to see what offers are made and then analyze each one. This differs from a careful examination of opportunities in the environment to find the best possibilities for diversification. McDonald-Douglas's movement into computer software systems resulted from such a systematic study.

Instinctive feel or intuitive insight into the future is always, of course, a potentially powerful approach.

Finally, luck may play a role in opening opportunities or creating threats. Magic Chef, for instance, years ago developed stoves using bottled gas. The large appliance manufacturers were not interested. When the mobile housing market boomed in the past few years, Magic Chef found itself in an enviable position and now commands about one-third of that market. Luck is, of course, important, but one cannot rely on it.

All of these approaches can result in a determination to make sophisticated forecasts and to gather masses of other information. They also can follow this activity or parallel it.

There are five major types of forecasts made in and for the planning process. First are survey-research type forecasts that involve integrating many different areas of knowledge. For example, a quality forecast of the automobile market will rest not alone on economic analysis but on changes in social values, technology, politics, and pollution standards. Second are economic type forecasts, most often of sales. Although there is no standard methodology for making survey-research forecasts, the tool kit of sales forecasters is very rich.[7]

[7]See, for instance, William F. Butler, and Robert A. Kavesh, *How Business Economists Forecast* (Englewood Cliffs, N.J.: Prentice-Hall, Inc., 1966); Robert S. Reichard, *Practical Techniques of Sales Forecasting* (New York: McGraw-Hill Book Co., Inc., 1966); and Norbert Lloyd Enrick, *Market and Sales Forecasting: A Quantitative Approach* (San

Technological forecasts are a third type of futures information which are being made by more and more companies. In recent years important advances have been made in technological forecasting. The methodology ranges from mathematical formulas to informed judgment.[8]

Forecasting what competitors are likely to do is something that all companies should do systematically, but few do. For a large company a questionnaire to informed personnel is a simple and effective method for acquiring such information.

Two other types of forecasts are now being made by very large companies but will be made increasingly, especially by larger companies, in the future. They are forecasts of social values and social indicators. Social values refer to attitudes and views that people hold about such matters as social justice, comfort, human dignity, materialism, national pride, and so on. Everyone knows that values are changing dramatically. A large company that can forecast changes in society's values that will affect its fortunes will obviously have an advantage.[9] Social indicators are measures of phenomenon associated with quality of life, such as personal safety, medical care, and pollution.[10]

Forecasts in these last two areas will increase among the larger businesses and, for some, they will in the future stand beside the traditional economic forecasts as major considerations in corporate decision-making. Important strides have been made in the past few years in making such forecasts.[11]

Return now to "Our Present Situation," in Figure 24. There is no single way to identify and analyze a company's strengths and weaknesses. These can, of course, cover a wide range from management talent to salesmen in the field. It is hardly necessary to comment that a company should act from its strength and avoid its weaknesses, and it should understand that a strength today may become a weakness in tomorrow's environment. Yet companies fail because they ignore their weaknesses. Many have failed because they had a success syndrome that blindly assumed that present

---

Francisco: Chandler Publishing Co., 1969). See also John C. Chambers, Satinder K. Mullick, and Donald D. Smith, "How To Choose the Right Forecasting Technique," *Harvard Business Review*, Vol. 49 (July–August, 1971), pp. 45–74.

[8]Mention should be made of *Technological Forecasting*, a journal that began in 1969 and that is devoted to the methodology of the subject. Three good books on the subject are Erich Jantsch, *Technological Forecasting in Perspective* (Paris: Organization for Economic Cooperation and Development, 1967); James R. Bright, *Technological Forecasting For Industry And Government* (Englewood Cliffs, N.J.: Prentice-Hall, Inc., 1968); and Robert U. Ayres, *Technological Forecasting and Long-Range Planning* (New York: McGraw-Hill Book Co., Inc., 1969).

[9]See Kurt Baier and Nicholas Rescher (Eds.), *Values and the Future* (New York: The Free Press, 1969).

[10]See *Toward A Social Report*, Washington, D.C., U.S. Department of Health, Education and Welfare, 1969; and Nestor E. Terleckyj, "Measuring Progress Towards Social Goals: Some Possibilities at National and Local Levels," *Management Science*, Vol. 16 (August, 1970), pp. B-765–778.

[11]For different forecasting methods see John McHale, "Typological Survey of Futures Research in the U.S.," mimeographed (Binghamton, N.Y.: Center for Integrative Studies, School of Advanced Technology, State University of New York at Binghamton, 1970). For future forecasts see *The Futurist*, a journal that was created in 1967 to cover forecasts, trends, and ideas about the future.

success was based on a strength that would continue. Not enough companies systematically examine their strengths; fewer systematically study their weaknesses.

This is a much too brief and inadequate examination of how a manager can identify the right problem, opportunity, and threat. The literature on how to solve a problem once it is discovered is mountainous. The literature on how to be sure to identify the right problem and the best opportunity is extremely small. This is unfortunate, because a business man runs a far greater risk in not finding the right problem or opportunity than in determining how to solve the problem or how to exploit the opportunity once it is identified.

Developing Basic Business Missions

On the basis of premises developed in the above steps, the strategic planning process then hammers out basic missions, long-range objectives, and policies and strategies to achieve them. Each of these will be treated in turn. But first it is useful to point out that, contrary to so many elementary economics textbooks, there is no such thing as the single goal or objective of a company. Each firm has a network of aims that includes the basic socio-economic purpose of the company, value objectives of top managers, business missions, long-range objectives, and short-range targets and goals.[12] Each of these is different, has a different purpose in the planning process, and is developed in a different fashion. A surprising number of companies have developed creeds or philosophies for general distribution that encompass the basic ends that the top managements of these companies seek to achieve and, sometimes, how they wish them to be achieved.[13]

Basic missions should be stated in both product and market terms. A company may say that it is in the business of producing air conditioners. However, it will be in entirely different businesses if it chooses to make air conditioners for office buildings, or for home cooling, or for automobiles. Deciding on a basic mission is a fundamental step in planning. If the Baldwin Locomotive Works had decided that its mission was to make tractive power for railroads, instead of sticking to the manufacturing of steam locomotives, it probably would still be in business. A company that says it is not in the business of making bricks for construction but is in the clay products business for construction widens its opportunities as well as its threats. Too broad a mission, however, may be dangerous. For instance, it is doubtful whether a company making lead pencils should change its mission to making communications equipment. There is a sort of iron law of product-market development which states that the farther a company moves from its present products and markets, the less likely it will be to make a profit. But if the product and market are very narrow, growth and prosperity can be enhanced by a judicious widening of the mission.

[12]Charles H. Granger, "The Hierarchy of Objectives," *Harvard Business Review*, Vol. 42 (May–June, 1964), pp. 63–74.

[13]Stewart Thompson, *Management Creeds and Philosophies*, Research Study No. 32 (New York: American Management Association, 1958).

Long-Range Objectives

Objectives are desired results to be achieved, usually in a specific time. They are very important in the planning process because they are guides to the development of actions to assure their fulfillment. Behavioral scientists point out that they also are important motivators of people in organizations, because generally people in organizations like to try to achieve the objectives set for the organization. The more people in organizations participate in the objective-setting process, the greater is their motivation to achieve them. Objectives can be used effectively, of course, as standards for measuring performance.

Objectives may be expressed for every element of a business that is considered important enough to be the subject of plans. There is no standard classification of objectives nor of the number of objectives that a company should have.

All companies that have a planning process set objectives for profits and sales. In addition to objectives in these areas one generally finds in planning systems of larger companies objectives for the following: marketing (e.g., share of market); finance (e.g., debt retirement, dividend objectives, new financing); stability (e.g., sales, profits, employment); personnel (e.g., developing managers, working conditions, employment levels); research and development; and survival. This does not exhaust the list and many subobjectives may exist in each category.

Peter Drucker says that objectives are needed in every area of a business in which performance and results directly and importantly affect the survival and prosperity of the enterprise. Following are the areas in which he says objectives ought to be set: market standing, innovation, productivity, physical and financial resources, profitability, manager performance and development, worker performance and attitude, and public responsibility.[14]

Objectives can be based on different considerations. They may be dictated by top management without any research analysis, or they may be based on thorough analysis. They may be extrapolations from the past or may be set to exploit a foreseen opportunity or avoid a perceived threat. They may be derived from a settled strategy or designed to support other objectives.

However derived, objectives should exhibit a few major characteristics. First, they should be able to lead and motivate, and the more concrete and specific they are the more likely are they to be directive. To say that "our company seeks to make a good profit," is far less effective than to say, "our objectives is to make $4 million in profits three years from today." Second, objectives should be action-oriented. Goals that are far too high or far too low do not inspire action. Objectives should be a little aggressive and should require imagination and hard work to achieve. Third, objectives should be understood by those who are to develop means to achieve them. Fourth, objectives should conform to ethical and social codes accepted by

[14]Peter F. Drucker, *The Practice of Management* (New York: Harper & Bros., 1954), p. 63.

society and by the business. Finally, objectives should correlate and be mutually supporting, to the extent possible. For instance, if the objective is to achieve a return on investment of 15 per cent after taxes by the end of 5 years, the target is much more likely to be achieved if sub and sub-subobjectives are linked to it. Thus, subobjectives might be: increase sales to $10 million in 5 years, raise gross profits to $2.5 million in 5 years, build modern facilities and operate them at capacity over the next 5 years, and upgrade and maintain a skilled work force in specified ways. These objectives might also be linked to sub-subobjectives. For example, an increase in sales might be sought by setting specific objectives for market share, advertising expenditures, market penetration, product redesign, and research and development in specific directions. Similarly, sub-subobjectives might be set for achieving the subobjectives of gross profits, facilities, and work force. If the sub and sub-subobjectives are achieved, the achievement of the dominant objective is inevitable.

Developing Policies and Strategies

Once objectives are established, the logical sequence is to develop policies and strategies to achieve them. Policies are broad guides to action, such as a decision to allow divisions to acquire other companies, after approval from headquarters; or a decision not to require one division of a company to buy the products of another division unless it wishes to do so. Strategies are specific important actions, usually but not always involving the deployment of resources to achieve an objective. In mind are major actions to distinguish them from minor tactics.[15]

Strategies, of course, can be associated with all kinds of activities in a business—markets, products, financing, diversification, pricing, and so on. There is no classification that has any common acceptance. Most writers would agree, however, that two broad classifications of strategies are personal and business. Personal strategies can influence business strategies, and vice versa. Karl von Clausewitz, speaking about military success, commented that "The best strategy is always to be very strong, first generally, then at the decisive point." This rule, of course, can apply to both personal affairs as well as to military and business strategy.

The most successful strategies turn out to be clusters of strategies. A strategic decision by a company, for example, to expand its foreign operations will result in substrategies for geographic area, financing, marketing, management, and so on.

A systematic strategic planning process in a formal planning system is a preferred approach to developing effective strategies. The following specific approaches can be incorporated in a formal planning process or can be conducted in the absence of a formal system. Intuition, as pointed out earlier, is an excellent approach if it is brilliant. For some activities, such

[15]Much confusion often exists in the use of these words. One reason is that different authors have different definitions for them. Another more important reason is that the words are used in different connections in the planning process. For a good examination of this source of confusion see Bertram M. Gross, *The Managing of Organizations*, Vol. II (New York: The Free Press, 1964), Chapter 19, "The Matrix of Purposes."

as acquisitions, some companies use the ad hoc, trial-and-error approach. A successful invention is an unexcelled strategy. Another approach is to determine the really significant factors that are important in the success of a particular business and concentrate major decisions on them. For instance, a new imaginative toy is a critically strategic factor in the success of a toy company, but superior technical and fail-safe qualities are of dominant importance to the success of an airplane manufacturer. Finding a particular spot, a propitious niche, where a company can give a customer an irresistible value that is not being satisfied and at a relatively low cost is a strategy that has made many companies rich. Finally, some companies are satisfied to follow the lead of other companies.

Two concluding points of importance should be added about strategies. What is a successful strategy for one company may turn out to be another's poison. Chances are that if Avon exchanged strategies with Revlon, neither would do as well as they are doing. Also, timing is very important. The Edsel automobile filled a niche for the Ford Motor Company, but the company's timing was bad and the product failed.

MEDIUM-RANGE PROGRAMMING

Medium-range programming is the process whereby specific functional plans are related for specific numbers of years to display the details of how strategies are to be carried out to achieve long-range objectives and company missions. Many companies prepare manuals of procedures that instruct the divisions how to prepare their medium-range programs and plans. Typically, the planning period is for 5 years, but there is a tendency

DIVISION FIVE-YEAR PLANS

Item	Last Year	This Year Forecast	Next Five Years				
			First Year	Second Year	Third Year	Fourth Year	Fifth Year
Sales							
Marketing Expenditures							
Advertising							
Distribution							
Unit Production							
Employees							
Total							
Direct							
Indirect							
R & D Outlays							
New Products							
Product Improvement							
Cost Reduction							
New Facilities (Total)							
Expansion							
New Products							
Cost Reduction							
Maintenance							

FIGURE 26. Division 5-Year Plans

for more technically advanced companies to plan ahead in some detail for 7 or more years. In most companies the medium-range plans cover only the major functions and are quantified on comparatively simple forms, as shown in Figure 26. In most companies the functional plans are translated into financial terms in the form of a *pro forma* profit and loss statement, as shown in Figure 27. Sometimes a *pro forma* balance sheet is also prepared. Sometimes, depending on its importance, detailed forms are prepared for selected elements, especially for facility programs.

SHORT-RANGE PLANNING AND PLANS

The next step, of course, is to develop short-range plans on the basis of the medium-range plans. In about half the companies that do formal planning, the numbers for the first year of the medium-range plans are the same as in the short-range yearly operational budget summaries. Some companies feel that tightly linking budgets and medium-range plans will help to make long-range plans realistic. Others feel that a tight relationship will divert attention from the long range to current matters, such as return on investment. This is especially so if a manager's compensation is based principally on yearly return-on-investment performance. If the linkage is very loose, the long-range plans still can be reflected in, and be very important to, current budget-making.

The current operating budgets will, of course, be much more detailed

FINANCIAL SUMMARY

Division: ____________________

	This Year	19__	19__	19__	19__	19__
Sales - Units						
Gross Sales - Dollars						
Allowances						
Net Sales						
Cost of Goods Sold						
Gross Profit on Sales						
G & A Expense						
Selling Expense						
Advertising Expense						
R & D Expense						
Total Operating Expense						
Other Charges, Net						
Interest on Long Term Obligations						
Other						
Income before Depreciation						
Depreciation						
Income before Overhead Allocation						
Allocation of General Overhead						
Net Income before Taxes						
Rate of Return on Assets						

FIGURE 27. Financial Summary

than the budgets in the medium-range plans. Also, many more subjects will be covered. The numbers of subjects will depend on what management wishes to control in the short run. Some elaboration of this point is shown in Figure 28.

One should not leave this subject without at least commenting on the scope of short-range planning. Although strategic and medium-range plans may provide the framework within which short-range planning is done, the different types of short-range plans that can be affected covers a wide range. In mind are production plans such as plant location, layout of facilities, work methods, inventory plans and control, employee training, job enrichment, management education, and negotiations with unions. Space limita-

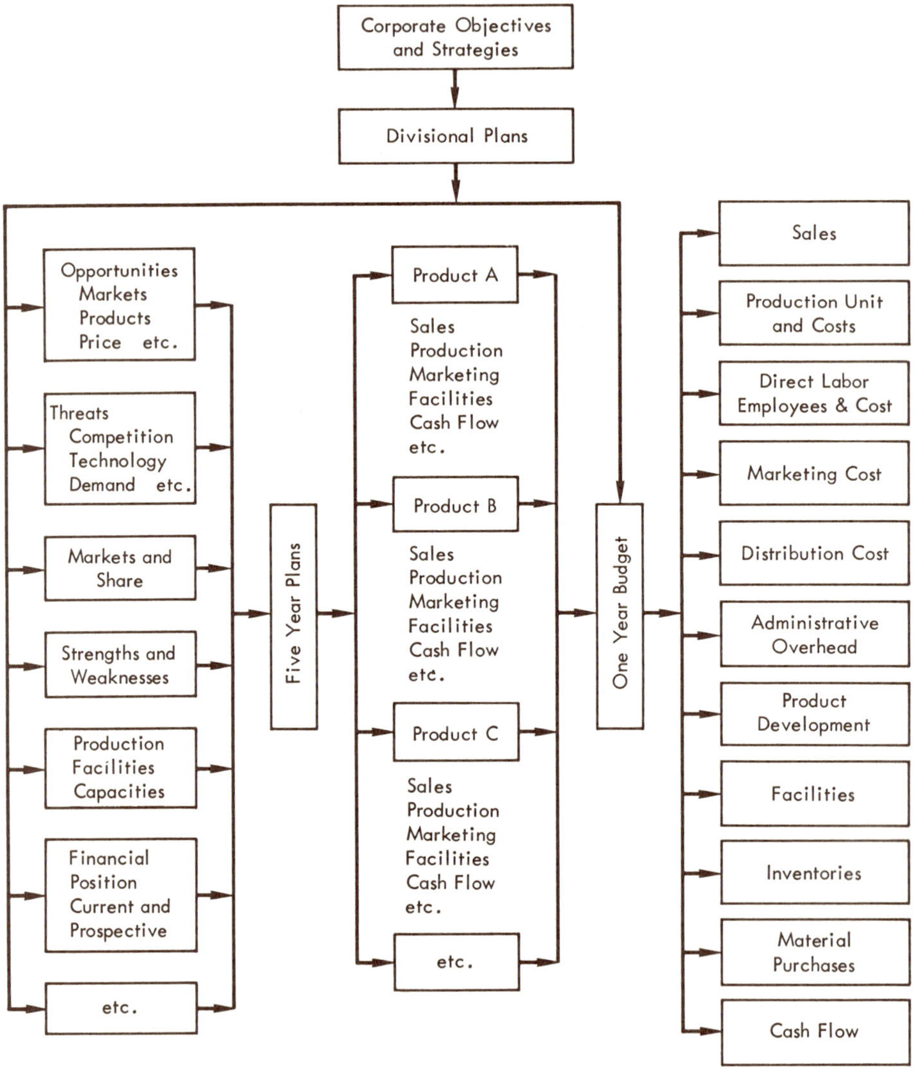

FIGURE 28. Relationship Between Strategic and Tactical Plans

tions prevent any further examination of these types of short-range plans, their nature, or how they are prepared.

TRANSLATING STRATEGIC PLANS INTO CURRENT DECISIONS

Figure 28 shows that corporate strategies can be deflected immediately in current plans or used as a basis for developing medium-range plans, which in turn are the basis for annual or shorter plans. There are several additional features of Figure 28 worth examining. In a divisionalized company where there is decentralized authority, the general manager will be obliged to make studies of the environment for his product. This information will be used, with whatever directions he gets from headquarters about objectives and strategies, to make his medium-range plans. There should be, therefore, a close linkage between top management objectives and strategies, and subobjectives and substrategies forged by the divison manager.

Also, the details of the 1-year budget are considerably different from the main categories of the 5-year plans. The two can be the same, but the budget is more concerned with coordinating and controlling critical internal flows of resources. The subject matter of the short-range plans, therefore, will be focused on these concerns rather than on the more aggregative functions in the medium-range plans. The aggregates of the short-range plans, however, can relate to medium-range plans, as mentioned above.

In the formal planning process there is not a sharp distinction between strategic planning at one extreme and tactical planning at the other, or of planning at one end and control tat the other. Each has a graduated impact throughout the planning process, as shown in Figure 29. This chart shows that traces of strategic planning are found in detailed short-range planning. Also, strategic planning, and particularly medium-range programming, is conducted with some degree of control over operations in mind.[16]

PLANNING STUDIES AND FEASIBILITY TESTING

Planning studies can, of course, be made throughout the planning process. I have mentioned how important such studies are in examining the environment. They also, however, can be important in analyzing such matters as current inventory replacement policy, or suitability of the present organization for planning.

Feasibility testing takes place throughout the planning spectrum. For instance, when lower-level managers are examining different alternative choices, one may comment: "Method A has great profit potential but I do not think the top management would like to use this method." He is obviously applying a feasibility test by appraising an alternative against the values of top management, as he understands them. At lower levels the

[16]For distinctions between strategic and tactical plans see Steiner, *Top Management Planning, op. cit.*, pp. 37–41.

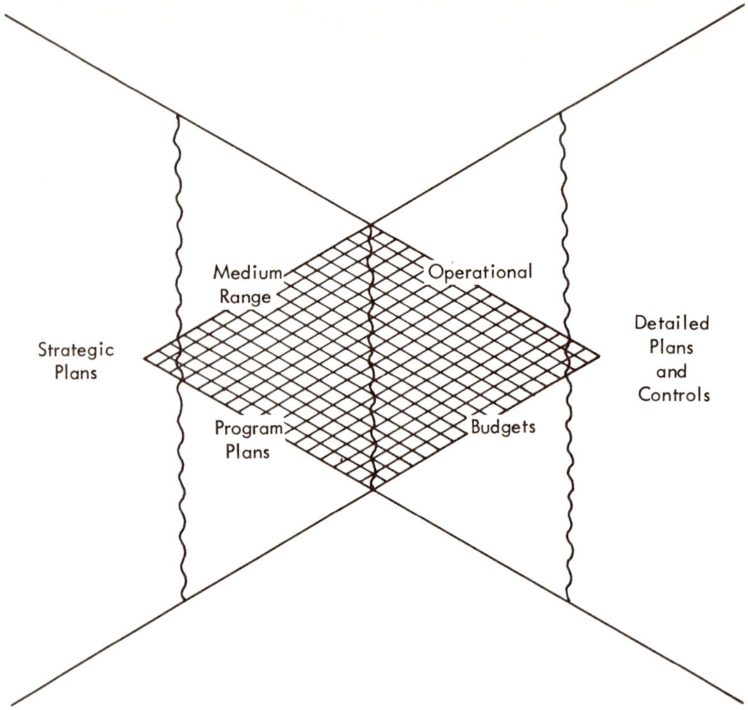

FIGURE 29. Intermeshing Long-Range Planning and Operational Control

testing can become completely quantitative and sometimes very sophisticated, as for instance in the applying of a linear programming model to test distribution routes for products to their markets.

REVIEW AND EVALUATION

Plans that are developed should be reviewed and evaluated. There is nothing that produces better plans on the part of subordinates than for the top managers to show a keen interest in the plans and their results. When comprehensive formal planning was first developed some 15 years ago, there was a tendency for companies to make written plans and not revise them until they became obviously obsolete. Now, the great majority of companies go through an annual cycle of comprehensive planning in which the plans are reviewed and revised.

PLANNING TOOLS

The range of tools available for making "rational" decisions in the planning process is very broad. It covers a spectrum ranging from nonquantitative tools, such as intuition, judgment, and hunches, to very complex and highly sophisticated methods, such as systems analysis and computer simulation. In between are older quantitative tools, such as conventional accounting techniques and newer quantitative methods like probability theory and linear programming.

This subject cannot be treated fully here, but there are several points that should be added to the present analysis. First, the applicability of different tools varies considerably depending on where and when they are applied in the planning process. For example, a sophisticated quantitative forecasting technique such as exponential smoothing is not very effective in making a forecast involving broad unknowns, such as the market for aspirin in China. Second, it is very important for technicians to concentrate on major business problems that their methods can solve for managers rather than to try to find problems that their tools can solve easily. Third, there is currently a virtual groundswell in the use of more sophisticated quantitative tools at higher levels of corporate planning. For instance, computer simulation and risk analysis is being used widely in strategic planning.[17] Most of the computer simulation models are deterministic. They answer "what if" types of questions. But, increasingly, probability theory such as David Hertz's risk analysis[18] is being used in top-level decision-making. At the end of this chapter are a few more comments concerning the tools of analysis.

ORGANIZING THE FORMAL PLANNING PROCESS

There is no single method, or formula, or standard way to start and conduct a formal corporate planning system. What is done is a function of such factors as managerial style, size of organization, whether the firm is centralized or decentralized, managerial authority extended to decentralized managers, types of problems the company faces, managerial knowledge, types of products, and other comparable factors. So each system is fitted to each company.

There are two fundamentally different approaches to doing formal planning. The first is the top-down approach. Comprehensive planning in a centralized company is carried out at the top of the corporation, and departments and outlying activities are pretty much told what to do. In a decentralized company the flow of activity is shown in Figure 30. The President gives the divisions guide lines and asks for plans. The plans are reviewed at headquarters and sent back to the divisions for modification or with a note of acceptance. If the division plans do not add up to what top management wishes, additional corporate plans are then prepared that may provide for acquisitions, divestment, or refinancing.

In the bottom-up approach top management gives the divisions no guidelines and asks them to submit plans. Information such as the following may be requested: major opportunities and threats, major objectives,

[17]James B. Boulden and Elwood S. Buffa, "Corporate Models: On-Line, Real-Time Systems," *Harvard Business Review*, Vol. 48 (July–August, 1970), pp. 65–83.

[18]David B. Hertz, *New Power for Management* (New York: McGraw-Hill Book Co., Inc., 1969).

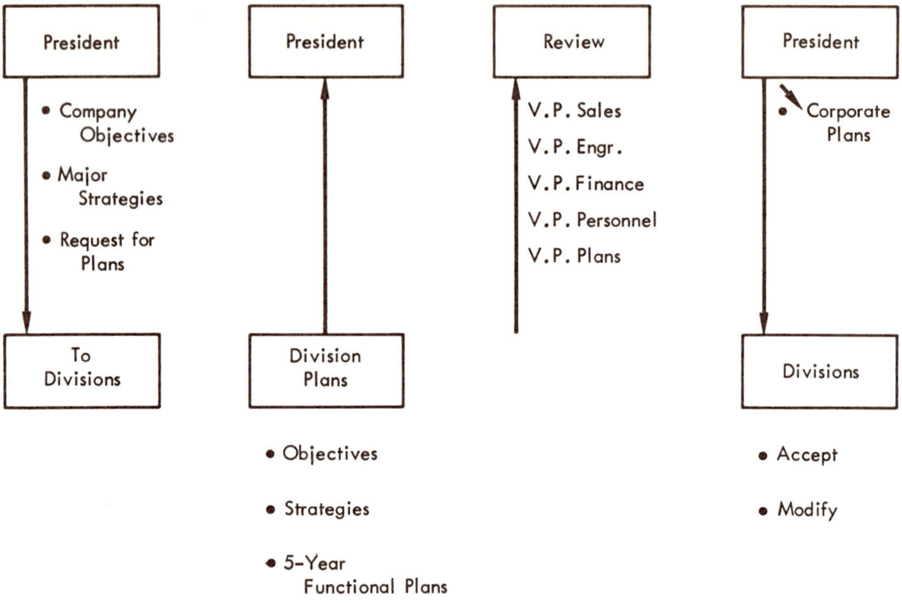

FIGURE 30. Top-Down Approach

strategies to achieve the objectives and specific data on sales, profits, market share sought, capital requirements, and number of employees for a specified number of years. This information then is reviewed at top-management levels and the same process as outlined in the preceding paragraph is followed.

A third approach, of course, is to develop a mixture of the top-down and bottom-up approach. This is the method used in most large decentralized companies. In this approach, top management gives guidelines to the divisions. Generally, they are broad enough to permit the divisions a good bit of flexibility in developing their own plans. Sometimes a top management may hammer out a basic objective by dialogue with division managers. Such objectives as return on investment may be derived in this way, empirically if the performance of the division manager is measured according to this standard.

In smaller centralized companies the chief executive will often use his main line managers as staff in helping him to develop formal plans. In some very large companies the president will use his line managers in the same fashion. In many companies the president has a group of executives with whom he meets on a regular basis to deal with all the problems facing the company. In some companies, part of the time of this group is spent on long-range planning. Over time, the group will develop written long-range plans.

Another organizational dimension is the scope of information accumulated. Some companies start the process simply by asking divisions and department heads to develop 5-year objectives for selected functions (e.g., sales, profits, markets, etc.) and major strategies to achieve the objectives.

Better results seem to flow, however, when enough information is requested so that decisions can be made and the plans can serve as a basis for preparing current operating plans. Also, it is better to initiate planning on a regular cycle, such as preparing written plans once a year.

Larger companies may appoint a director of planning, and give him a small staff, to start and maintain the planning system. He should report to the top management. His basic functions are to help others, particularly line managers, to do an effective planning job and to coordinate the plans developed by different parts of the organization when that is desirable. He may help top management formulate goals, policies, and strategies to guide the planning process. When plans are received from others, he may help top management evaluate them. He may make forecasts for others to use, help weak divisions make plans, show others how to develop effective plans, assist top management in making current decisions on the basis of long-range planning, and make recommendations concerning product development. He does not assume responsibility for doing the planning for either the top management or other line managers. Long-range planning is a line function and cannot be delegated to staff.[19]

One final observation on organization is that in all companies it is desirable to do a little "planning to plan" before actually starting the process. In larger companies this may result, and should, in a set of procedures which will tell everyone what is going to be done, how it is to be done, and when. Generally speaking, it is better to prescribe as little as possible in order to permit those who are doing the planning a maximum of flexibility. But a minimum of procedure is required. In manuals it is desirable to define important words used in the planning process. This will very much improve communications. Figure 31 shows a typical time schedule for comprehensive planning in a large decentralized company.

THE VALUE OF FORMAL CORPORATE PLANNING

Comprehensive formal long-range planning has been growing in use throughout the world simply because managers find that it is valuable. There are many reasons why this is so, a few of which are briefly noted below.

To begin with, the times demand it. Business environment is changing ever faster and becoming much more turbulent. In the product area, for instance, the typical life cycle is shrinking rapidly; but the average research and development time is lengthening and the costs to prototype are increasing. Technological threats to products are growing and coming from areas other than the industry to which they are related. Everyone is aware of shifting population movements, more and highly complex government regulations, changing consumer demands, and many other forces that make

[19]George A. Steiner, "Rise of the Corporate Planner," *Harvard Business Review*, Vol. 48 (September–October, 1970), pp. 133–139; and Richard F. Vancil, ". . . . So You're Going to Have a Planning Department!" *Harvard Business Review*, Vol. 45 (May–June, 1967), pp. 88–96.

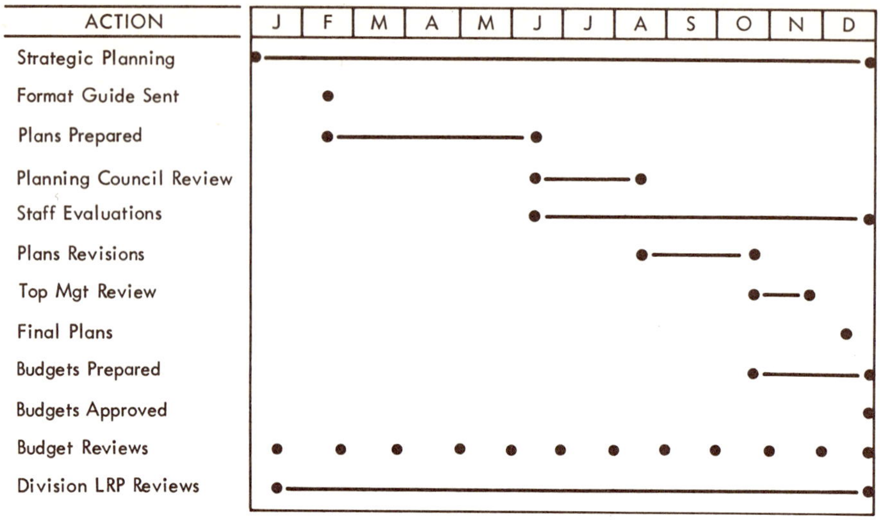

FIGURE 31. A Planning Time Schedule

the evolving environment at one and the same time a world of opportunity and threat to every company.

Long-range planning is essential to discharging top management's responsibilities. Marvin Bower, a management consultant, wrote a book to describe the functions of chief executives and much of the book dealt with formal planning, particularly strategic planning.[20] Some companies that have job descriptions for their chief executive officer say explicitly that the chief executive is the chief planner of the company.

As mentioned earlier, planning enables a company to simulate the future, on paper. If it does not like what it sees, it erases the plan and starts over. This is much less expensive than letting the future evolve on an ad hoc basis. It applies the systems approach. It looks at a company as a system composed of many subsystems. Looking at the company in this way prevents suboptimization of parts. It forces a company to set objectives and clarifies future opportunities and threats. It links decision-making between top and lower-level managers. Lower-level management decisions are much more likely to be made in conformance with the wishes of top management because plans are written and available to them. It sets standards of performance.

Formal planning answers some very significant questions for a manager, such as: What is our basic line of business? What are the company's long-range objectives? What products are or are not going to be obsolete? How will we replace these products and when? What will be our cash flow over the next few years? What and where are our markets? What share of the market do we wish to get? How will we get it?

Long-range planning is a new and significant communications system. It permits people to participate in the decison-making process. People are more adaptable to change because they participate in making the change.

[20]Marvin Bower, *The Will to Manage* (New York: McGraw-Hill Book Co., Inc., 1966).

It is a learning and mind-stretching exercise that increasingly is being recognized as a major tool for training managers.

Finally, a few recent studies are providing concrete evidence that long-range planning really pays off in cash. One study compared the 5-year performance of firms that introduced formal planning with those that did not. It also compared the performance of the firms for the 5 years before introducing long-range planning with 5 years of long-range planning. Results were measured for sales, earnings per share, stock price, earnings on common equity, and earnings on total capital. In each instance those companies that did long-range planning showed significantly better performance than companies in the same industry that did not formally plan. Also, in each case the record of the firms that did long-range planning was better after than before introducing the system.[21] Another study concluded that on virtually all relevant financial criteria companies that made acquisitions by a systematic planning approach did much better than those that went about it on an unplanned opportunistic basis.[22]

In sum, there are two types of values in comprehensive long-range planning—substantive and behavioral. Either set should be sufficient to convince management of the value of this new tool. When both are considered it is easy to see why formal long-range planning has been introduced into most medium-sized and larger companies.[23] More and more managers are agreeing with an old military assertion that says: "*Plans* sometimes may be useless but the planning *process* is always indispensable."

LIMITS OF FORMAL PLANNING

Comprehensive corporate planning is not, of course, without its shortcomings. It is an intimate part of the managerial process and if other parts of management are weak the planning process itself may be less than satisfactory. Long-range plans may not turn out well sometimes because of unexpected changes in the environment. Of fundamental importance, also, is the fact that long-range planning is virtually worthless in getting a company out of a major current crisis. Aside from such shortcomings, there are all sorts of problems that can arise in the development of a planning system. Many of these are suggested in the following array of pitfalls in planning.

[21]Stanley S. Thune and Robert J. House, "Where Long-Range Planning Pays Off," *Business Horizons* (August, 1970), pp. 81–90.

[22]H. Igor Ansoff, Jay Avner, Richard G. Brandenburg, Fred E. Portner, and Raymond Radosevich, "Does Planning Pay? The Effect of Planning on Success of Acquisitions in American Firms," *Long Range Planning*, Vol. 3 (December, 1970), pp. 2–7.

[23]From 1956, when the first survey was made of how many companies did formal planning, until the latest surveys, the number of companies purportedly doing formal long-range planning has increased rapidly. (See Steiner, *Top Management Planning, op. cit.*, pp. 14–15 for a résumé of this data.) The most recent survey I have seen was made in 1970 by Marvin J. Cetron and concluded that 95 per cent of the 1,114 companies surveyed had some sort of formal long-range planning activity. The range of comprehensiveness and coverage undoubtedly varied immensely among these companies. See Marvin J. Cetron, *Industrial Applications of Technological Forecasting* (New York: John Wiley & Sons, 1971).

PITFALLS IN COMPREHENSIVE LONG-RANGE PLANNING

Following are fifty major common pitfalls in starting, doing, and using long-range planning. They are the most important ones that I have detected. They vary in significance, but each can adversely affect the planning system and its value. Some of them were mentioned in the preceding discussion, but many were not. Space does not permit any comment about them.[24]

A. Pitfalls in Getting Started:

1. Top management's assumption that it can delegate the planning function to a planner.
2. Rejecting planning because there has been success without it.
3. Rejecting formal planning because the system failed in the past to foresee a critical problem and/or did not result in substantive decisions that satisfied top management.
4. Assuming that the present body of knowledge about planning is insufficient to guide fruitful comprehensive planning.
5. Assuming that a company cannot develop effective long-range planning in a way appropriate to its resources and needs.
6. Assuming that comprehensive corporate planning can be introduced into a company and overnight miraculous results will appear.
7. Thinking that a successful corporate plan can be moved from one company to another without change and with equal success.
8. Assuming that a formal system can be introduced into a company without an "agonizing reappraisal" of current managerial practices and decision-making processes.
9. Ignoring the power structure of a company in organizing the planning process.
10. Failing to develop a clear understanding of the long-range planning procedure before the process is actually undertaken.
11. Failing to create a climate in the company that is congenial and not resistant to planning.
12. Failing to locate the corporate planner at a high enough level in the managerial hierarchy.
13. Failing to make sure that the planning staff has the necessary qualities of leadership, technical expertise, and personality to discharge properly its responsibilities in making the planning system effective.

B. Pitfalls Related to a Misunderstanding of the Nature of Long-Range Planning:

14. Forgetting that planning is a political, a social, and an organizational, as well as a rational, process.

[24]Partly derived from Steiner, *Top Management Planning*, *op. cit.*, pp. 720–722. For other planning problems see E. Kirby Warren, *Long-Range Planning: The Executive Viewpoint* (Englewood Cliffs, N.J.: Prentice-Hall, Inc., 1966).

15. Assuming that corporate comprehensive planning is something separate from the entire management process.
16. Failing to make sure that top management and major line officers really understand the nature of long-range planning and what it will accomplish for them and the company.
17. Failing to understand that systematic formal planning and intuitive (opportunistic, or entrepreneurial) planning are complementary.
18. Assuming that plans can be made by staff planners for line managers to implement.
19. Ignoring the fact that planning is and should be a learning process.
20. Assuming that planning is easy.
21. Assuming that planning is hard.
22. Assuming that long-range planning can get a company out of a current crisis.
23. Assuming that long-range planning is only strategic planning, or just planning for a major product, or simply looking ahead at likely development of the present product (in other words, failing to see that comprehensive planning is an integrated managerial system).

C. Pitfalls in Doing Long-Range Planning:

I. Managerial Involvement

24. Top management becomes so engrossed in current problems that it spends insufficient time on long-range planning, and the process becomes discredited among other managers and staff.
25. Long-range planning becomes unpopular because top management spends so much time on long-range problems that it ignores short-range problems.
26. Failure to assure the necessary involvement in the planning process of major line personnel.
27. Too much centralization of long-range planning in the central headquarters so that divisions feel little responsibility for developing effective plans.

II. The Process of Planning

28. Failing to develop company goals on which long-range plans can be formulated.
29. Assuming that equal weight should be given to all elements of planning (i.e., that the same emphasis should be placed on strategic as on tactical planning, or that the same emphasis should be accorded to major functional plans).
30. Injecting so much formality into the system that it lacks flexibility, looseness, and simplicity, and restrains creativity.
31. Inability to avoid overoptimism and/or overcautiousness in committing resources.
32. Extrapolating rather than rethinking the entire process in each cycle (i.e., if plans are made for 1972 through 1976, adding 1977 in the 1973 cycle rather than revising all plans from 1973 to 1977).
33. Developing such a reverence for numbers that irreverence for

intuition and value judgments predominates the thinking going into planning.

34. Seeking precision of numbers throughout the planning horizon.
35. Assuming that older methods to choose from among alternatives should be discarded in favor of newer techniques.
36. Assuming that new quantitative techniques are not so useful as advertised.
37. Doing long-range planning periodically and forgetting it in between cycles.

III. Creditability of Results

38. Failing to develop planning capabilities in major operating units.
39. Failure of top management, and/or the planning staff, to give departments and divisions sufficient information and guidance (e.g., top management interests, environmental projections, etc.).
40. Attempting to do too much in too short a time.
41. Failing to secure that minimum of system and information to make the process and its results creditable and useful.

D. Pitfalls in Using Long-Range Plans:

42. Failure of top management to review with departmental and divisional heads the long-range plans that they have developed.
43. Forgetting that the fundamental purpose of the exercise is to make better current decisions.
44. Assuming that plans once made are in the nature of blueprints and should be followed rigorously until changed in the next planning cycle.
45. Top management's consistently rejecting the formal planning mechanism by making intuitive decisions that conflict with the formal plans.
46. Assuming that, because plans must result in current decisions, it is the short-run that counts and planning efforts as well as evaluations of results should concentrate on the short run.
47. Failing to use plans as standards for measuring managerial performance.
48. Forgetting to apply a cost-benefit analysis to the system to make sure advantages are greater than costs.
49. Failing to encourage managers to do good long-range planning by basing reward solely on short-range performance measures.
50. Failing to exploit the fact that formal planning is a managerial process that can be used to improve managerial capabilities throughout a company.

Planning Processes and Criteria

David I. Cleland

Professor
Department of Industrial Engineering
Systems Management Engineering
and Operations Research
University of Pittsburgh

INTRODUCTION

The title of Professor Steiner's paper—*Comprehensive Managerial Planning*—gives a hint of the subsequent thorough treatment the author gives the subject. Four fundamental ideas for the planning student are contained in the paper:

1. Comprehensive planning systems are concerned with the futurity of present decisions.
2. The identification and dissemination of strategic values and objectives is a major responsibility of managers; the other management functions (organizing, motivating, control) depend ultimately on effective planning.
3. The initiation and continued success of a comprehensive planning system depends on the guiding conceptual framework that has been built to provide a "strategy" for developing strategy.
4. The outcome of a planning system is reflected in a complex of plans that establishes the future direction of the organization.

Professor Steiner has left little undone in his scholarly treatment of the subject. What follows is a series of viewpoints that augment, or take a slightly different viewpoint from his approach.

THE PLANNING FUNCTION OF MANAGEMENT

Planning is one of the two major functions of management and is associated with the "deciding" aspect of the manager's job. The other function—execution—involves implementing decisions. Thus, "deciding" and "doing" are inseparable parts of the manager's job; indeed, developing and operating a comprehensive planning system involves these two parts: Deciding what to do—and then doing it. It is much easier to design a planning system than it is to implement it. Most of the literature that has evolved in the past 15 years neglects the planning for the implementation phase of strategic planning. Steiner has wisely avoided this pitfall; his paper reflects both the nature of the planning philosophy and the realities of implementing actual planning.

A PLANNING PROCESS MODEL

At the outset, it is important to suggest a planning model to use as a basing point for subsequent discussions. Figure 32 reflects such a generic model that is relevant to any type of organization, be it industrial, military, or educational.[1]

[1]This model and its subsequent explanation is drawn from David I. Cleland and William R. King, *Management: A Systems Approach* (New York: McGraw-Hill Book Co., Inc., 1972).

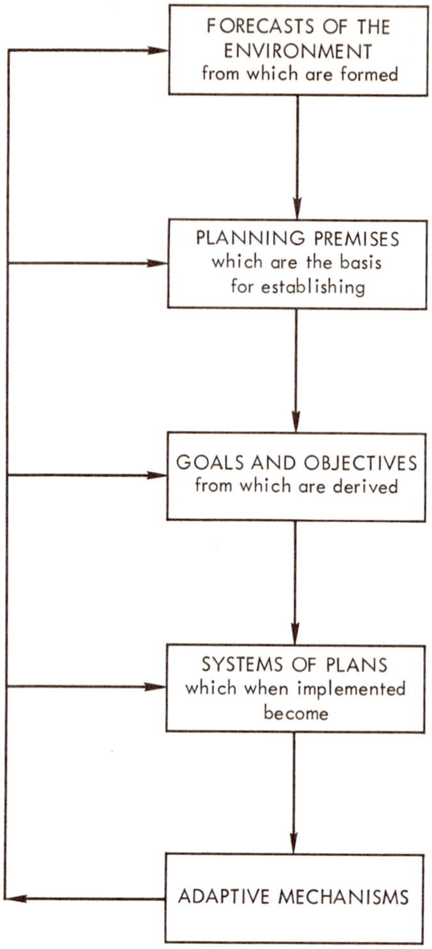

FIGURE 32. The Adaptive Planning Process

(From D. I. Cleland and W. R. King, *Management: A Systems Approach* (New York: McGraw-Hill Book Co., Inc., 1972), p. 207.

This model reflects the repetitive relationship of forecasts, premises, goals, and objectives and a system of plans that, taken together, provides a philosophical perspective from which to view the "systems" nature of the planning process. It is within the framework of this model that a comprehensive planning activity can be carried out.

Forecasting

Planning starts with forecasting—ranging from the "gut" feel a manager has to sophisticated economic modeling. Both the "gut" feel and the economic model have their place, and one should not confuse the two. Forecasting has as its key purpose the development of a qualitative/quantitative data base that enables the planner to build a representative model of an expected future environment. The type of forecast depends on the business the organization is in or would like to be in cast in terms of future expectations. Steiner has identified the complex range of general forecasts of concern to a manager. Quite clearly, the growing concern of businessmen with social and environmental matters will necessitate developing an expertise in forecasting "demand" in these areas.

Planning Premises

Planning premises augment the forecasts that have been drawn up for the environment. Premises permit the planner to build an assumed model of the future that can be used as the basis for evaluating and selecting strategic objectives. Premises follow the subject matter of the forecasts and play a particularly important role in building a future environmental model.[2]

Goals and Objectives

Contemporary planning literature tends to mix up goals and objectives. For our purposes they are to be defined as follows:

[2]According to Harold Koontz and Cyril O'Donnell in *Principles of Management* (New York: McGraw-Hill Co., Inc.), p. 94: "Premises, then are planning assumptions, the future setting in which planning takes place—in other words, the environment of plans in operation."

A *goal* is a desired accomplishment whose achievement can be measured in a specified time period.

An *objective* is a broad, general, and timeless purpose that specifies the organization's relationship to its environment.[3]

Strategic objectives establish a desired "state of affairs" for an organization at some future time, whereas goals are the stepping stones along a path to that strategic objective. Strategy defines an organization's products "in terms more functional than literal, saying what they do, rather than what they are made of."[4] Stating objectives in this manner permits the flexible development of goals. In fact, as one defines objectives in a 10- to 15-year time dimension, the product nature of those objectives often becomes difficult to discern, yet the market need can be expressed in a functional mode. For example, an aerospace firm affirmed its continued intent to stay in the space business by stating a strategic objective in this manner:

> Design, develop, and operate a reusable space vehicle repair capability.

Does the statement of objectives precede the environmental forecasting? This is the proverbial chicken-and-egg question. Forecasting and setting objectives are inseparable in practice, yet we tend to speak of them as separate things. This is done to facilitate the myriad of action and thought processes necessary to proceed from a tentative statement of objectives through to a final statement that has been accepted by the organization. How should these goals and objectives be established? How should one "organize" for developing and "testing" organizational goals and objectives?

Two organizational forces often operate to the detriment of an integrated approach to setting goals and objectives—*organizational* and *disciplinary* parochialism. Organizational parochialism reflects a tendency to emphasize planning for the extension of an existing product line in which an element (e.g., a product division) of an organization is currently successful to the neglect of alternative products. Disciplinary parochialism results in objective setting for a particular functional area to the neglect of overall organizational strategies.

The risk of disciplinary and organizational parochialism can be alleviated by the use of ad hoc task forces. Membership on a particular task force is drawn from the various organizations that have primary responsibility or knowledge of the subject of the task force's effort. For example, a task force set up to establish tentative objectives for a new product development effort would have members representing such areas as engineering, marketing, finance, plant and equipment, and production *and* would be drawn from different levels in the organization. Obviously, such an interdisciplinary team would bring about "conflict," but out of such "conflict" should come a cooperative statement of goals and objectives. The use of task forces tends to foster a built-in "checks and balances" by bringing about a high degree of personal involvement. The task force approach also permits a high degree of participation by people who otherwise might not have the opportunity to influence the future direction the organization should take. Of course, the output of a task force should be forwarded through the appropriate line executive for evaluation.[5]

One could say that the task of setting objectives has been relatively simple in the past when the profit motive

[3] I have paraphrased these definitions from Edmund P. Learned *et al., Business Policy* (Homewood, Illinois: Richard D. Irwin, 1969).

[4] *Ibid.*, pp. 16–17.

[5] The task force approach is also a way of organizing interdisciplinary groups of people outside of a particular formal organization who have something to contribute to the setting of goals and objectives. Membership on a task force also provides an opportunity to develop managers and those who aspire to managerial positions.

dictated the choice of strategic alternatives. In today's world, in which organizations are more complex and interdependent, a statement of organizational goals in terms of one criterion (such as return on investment) is to deny the growing involvement representative of modern times. Today's industrial organization faces a myriad of vocal "claimants" such as stockholders, customers, suppliers, employees, unions, creditors, governments, community, and the public, all desiring some role in the affairs of the organization. To be responsible to such a diverse group of claimants requires a multiplicity of conflicting organizational goals, which require continuous negotiation in order to maintain overall organizational effectiveness.

System of Plans

The output of the planning system is a system of plans that encompasses planning *for all organizational activities and all relevant time periods.*[6] Taken in this context, the question of how far ahead to plan is academic, for the system of plans contains these types of plans:

Strategic Plan. This plan outlines the broad objectives and strategies that the organization wants to achieve in the long-run future. The strategic plan establishes the direction that subsequent planning should take in the organization.

Development Plan. The development plan deals in the time period of 1 to 5 years and determines the activities necessary for the next generation of products or services. At the same time, development plans map in greater detail the route toward a desired future strategic position.

Operational Plan. This plan supports the current generation of products. It is the blueprint for current organizational actions. The operational plan reflects each functional area of effort—production, marketing, finance, and so on.

Project Plan. Project plans support higher-level plans and deal with an ad hoc activity such as:

1. Developing new products.
2. Realigning or relocating the organization.
3. Building and starting up a new plant.
4. Developing and installing a management information system.
5. Effecting an organizational merger.

Project plans are the basic building blocks of organizational strategy; consequently, they have short, intermediate, and long-range implications.

The relationship among the system of plans is illustrated in Figure 33. These relationships are expressed in terms of typical time horizons and specific content of the various plans. The terminology in Figure 33 is applicable to the system of plans for an educational organization rather than a business firm.

ORGANIZATIONAL PLANNING SCHEMA CRITERIA

The essence of a planning schema for an organization is a planning approach which contains the following:[7]

[6]I have paraphrased from *A Framework for Business Planning*, Stanford Research Institute, Report Number 162, Menlo Park, California, February, 1963.

[7]Criteria one and two have been paraphrased from E. Kirby Warren, *Long-Range Planning: The Executive Viewpoint* (Englewood Cliffs, N.J.: Prentice-Hall, Inc., 1966), pp. 29–31.

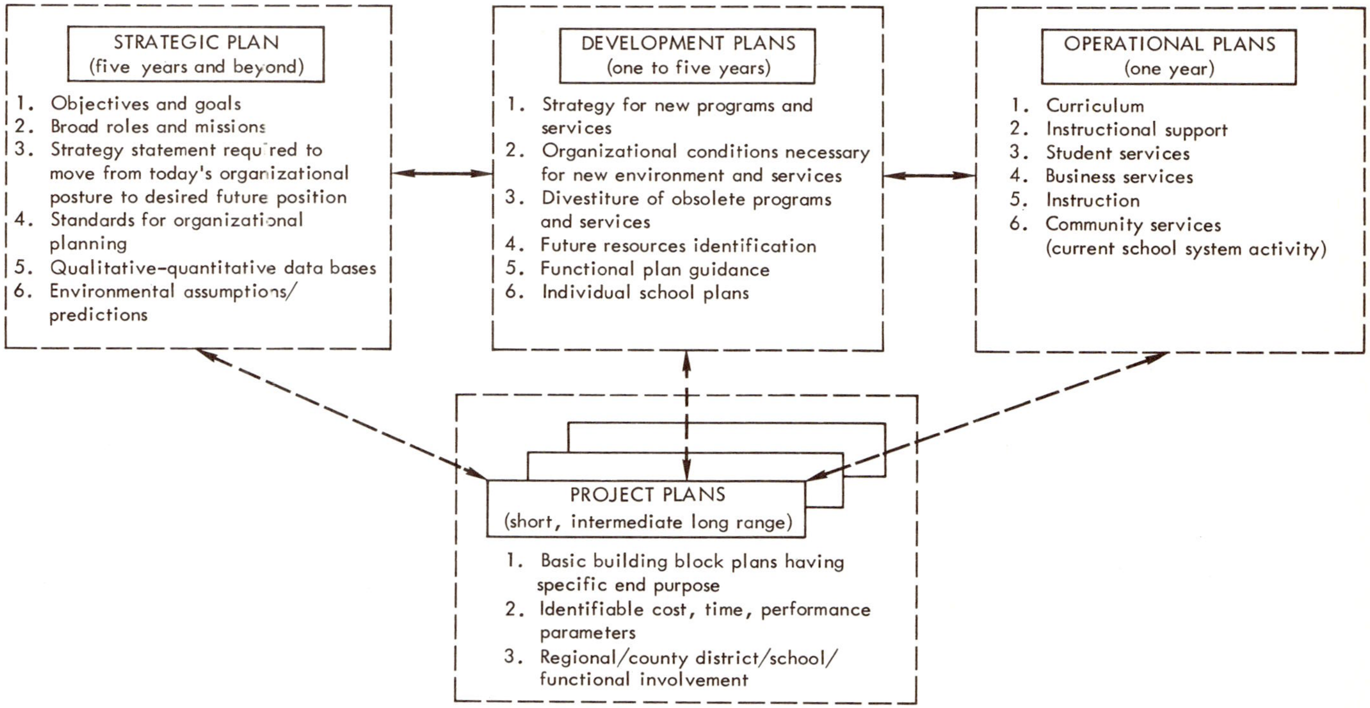

FIGURE 33. A System of Plans

From D. I. Cleland and W. R. King, *Management: A Systems Approach, op. cit.,* p. 270.

1. A means for studying and evaluating those areas of future opportunity that require current decisions.
2. A prediction of how current decisions will affect future actions.
3. An indication of information requirements in the form of a qualitative/quantitative data base to use in making forecasts and building assumptions.
4. A system of plans that reflects planning for all organizational activities and all relevant time periods.
5. The decentralization of planning authority and responsibility to the lowest possible level in the organization. Top-level planning should deal mainly with the development of strategic and development plans and facilitating planning activities at lower levels in the organization.

SUMMARY

The purpose of this critique has been to present some ideas of planning that would have been put forth had I written the chapter. The planning process model that I suggest provides an overall view of planning and emphasizes the strategic aspects of the planning function. In so doing, I have neglected the *planning for implementation phase* of the process, an important matter that cannot be ignored by the practitioner.

The literature reflects a growing awareness of planning philosophies, particularly those of a long-run strategic nature. The time horizons for which we must plan are being pushed farther out into the future. For the manager, the need becomes quite clear—to become a "manager of change" in tomorrow's complex social, political, and economic milieu.

A Critique of "Comprehensive Managerial Planning"

Raymond Radosevich

Associate Professor
Graduate School of Management
Vanderbilt University

I would like to begin this critique with a statement of purpose, as I perceive it, for George Steiner's chapter in order that we may judge how well he accomplishes that purpose. The purpose is twofold—to establish the state of the art and the trends in comprehensive managerial planning and to guide the interested reader to more extended and comprehensive sources. In view of the difficulty of treating the chosen subject in one chapter, the second purpose is extremely important and very capably accomplished by Professor Steiner. As far as providing a summary state of the art and probable areas for significant advances in comprehensive managerial planning, I feel compelled to take issue with Professor Steiner in several regards.

My most general disagreement is with his overemphasis on rationality in the planning process. His process description does not sufficiently emphasize the human and organizational contexts within which the process occurs.

PLANNING IN ORGANIZATIONS

To explain the relationship of planning and organizational systems, a taxonomy of planning processes should recognize the difference between processes of organizational change and processes of efficient exploitation of the firm's current product/market/technology posture. Organization theorists have long recognized the efficiency of bureaucratic structure for firms with stable environments and the dysfunctional aspects of bureaucratic rigidity and inflexibility for firms that are closely linked to dynamic environments. Designers of formal management systems, particularly planning systems, must also recognize the differences between efficient management of current activities and management of change activities intended to find and develop new businesses. To justify this contention, let me digress for a brief moment.

In the not-too-distant past, when the life cycles of products and services were measured in years and even decades, the prime concern of management was efficient day-to-day operation. Significant environmental changes necessitating a strategic repositioning occurred relatively infrequently. The emphasis was on the use of *performance plans*—standing, periodic, regular procedures through which higher levels of the organization direct routine activities of lower levels. These performance plans were used primarily to promote standardization and efficiency in operations. Sizable changes in the organization and the subsequent routinization of operations occurred primarily in a serial manner—a short period of change and then long efficient production runs.

The last decade has seen a plethora of documentation that indicates accelerating change in the environment of the organization. As a result, the use of strategic planning processes has increased to continually reposition the organization in its product, market, technology, and resource relationships with the environment. Ad hoc plans, single-use plans, are increasingly used to direct unique activities for introducing change or development into the organization at regular intervals.[1] We commonly refer to these planning processes as programmatic, project, or venture planning. Schematically, one can superimpose these planning processes on the hierarchial structure of organizations as follows.

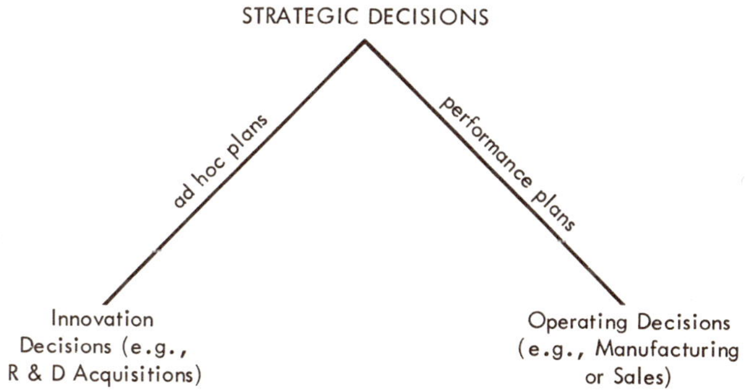

FIGURE 34. Strategic Decisions

[1]The distinction between *performance planning* and *ad hoc planning* is recognized in James C. Emery, *Organizational Planning and Control Systems: Theory and Technology* (New York: The Macmillan Co., 1969). A more detailed description of the differences in planning systems for innovation and operations is contained in Raymond Radosevich and Robert L. Hayes, "Management Systems for Organizational Innovation," Report No. 1, Institute for Management Innovation, Graduate School of Management, Vanderbilt University, September, 1971.

Table 7 relates the structure of planning processes to the organizational hierarchy along several dimensions.

If one remains cognizant of the dichotomy between ad hoc and performance planning, the conceptualization of the overall planning process can accommodate more behavioral and technological variables. For example, for operating activities the plans are often generated by people who do not implement the plans. In one instance, industrial engineers and production controllers plan the methods and rates for workers. For innovative activities, the planning process is highly participative. Plans more often take the form of expressing desired results rather than explicit procedures for accomplishing them. Continuing the example, the planning "tools" mentioned by Professor Steiner are most appropriately applied in operating activities. Tools for planning innovation activities are not mentioned in the chapter but might include PERT, Convergence Programming, or Synectics.[2]

PLANNING AS A MANAGEMENT SUBSYSTEM

A second omission is explicit emphasis on the relation of the planning subsystem to the overall management system. Some brief discussion of the interface of planning, control, and information systems would seem to be appropriate.

THE RELATIONSHIP OF PLANNING TO CONTROL

The most obvious interface between planning and control occurs when responses must be made to deviations from plans. In other words, what are the alternatives when performance as measured by criteria specified in the plans does not match levels specified in the plans. The response hierarchy contains at least four levels. The first is to simply ignore the deviations because they are insignificant (management by exception). The second alternative is to modify implementation procedures, perhaps by trying alternatives specified in contingency plans. The third level of response would be to re-plan, to trigger the planning cycle or instigate ad hoc planning activities perhaps based on new assumptions or forecasts. The fourth level of response is to change the planning process or related aspects of

TABLE 7. THE RELATIONSHIP OF PLANNING AND ORGANIZATIONAL STRUCTURES

	Organizational Level	*Time Horizons*	*Management Perspective*	*Level of Detail*
Performance Plans				
Strategic	High	Long	External to organization	General
Operating	Low	Short	Internal to organization	Specific
Ad Hoc Plans				
Programmatic	High	Long	External	Specific
Project	Low	Short	Internal	General

[2]The reader may not be familiar with the last two; they are described in Louis Carrese and Carl G. Baker, "The Convergence Technique: A Method for the Planning and Programming of Research Efforts," *Management Science* (April, 1967). William J. J. Gordon, *Synectics: The Development of Creative Capacity* (New York: Harper & Bros., 1961).

the organization. Perhaps line managers need new planning tools or should change their attitudes toward planning. Managers with planning experience in innovative activities frequently develop control systems to utilize all four levels of response. Control systems for operating activities rarely use more than the first two.

PLANNING INFORMATION

Adding formality and rationality to the planning process as described by Professor Steiner necessitates commensurate and consistent changes in the information and communication processes. Planning innovative activities requires different information than planning for operations.[3] The futurity dimension of information becomes more critical and formal forecasting and prediction procedures must be added to the information processing. Using existing operating information systems for strategic planning is like driving an automobile by watching only the rear-view mirror. Another dimension of significant difference is the source of primary data. Strategic planning information originates more frequently from sources external to the firm. Other dimensions of information systems must also be accommodated simultaneously with changes in the planning processes.

Professor Steiner's chapter also contains a number of assertions that I find ambiguous or misleading. I will next examine these and present my viewpoint in each case.

INTUITIVE VIS-À-VIS FORMAL PLANNING

Professor Steiner's statement that "formal planning is an effort to replicate intuitive planning" is most confusing. He says that intuitive and formal systems should not conflict but complement each other. Adding formality to planning makes it less intuitive, and hence formality and intuition are basically incompatible. Perhaps Professor Steiner means that some elements of the planning process (such as the planning of innovative activities) currently must remain relatively more intuitive because the benefits from added formality are outweighed by the associated costs.

PLANNING TRIGGERS FOR FUTURE DECISIONS

I also disagree with the statement that "long-range planning does not attempt to make future decisions." In one very important sense it does—without long-range planning the need to make certain decisions at specific points in the future will never be recognized. Formal planning systems assure that decisions will be made in the future that otherwise would not be made.

PLAN OBSOLESCENCE

The statement that "long-range plans are obsolete the very minute they are completed because the environment assumed in their preparation has already changed" is incorrect. Long-range plans are based on assumptions about trends and changes in the environment, not the current state of the environment, and thus plans do not become obsolete until these assumptions become false or outdated. If the environment is forecasted and monitored properly, this may occur as much as several years after the completion of plans.

[3]An elaboration of these different characteristics and the implications for information and planning systems is contained in Robert L. Hayes and Raymond Radosevich, "Designing Information Systems for Strategic Decisions," Report No. 4, Institute for Management Innovation, Graduate School of Management, Vanderbilt University, January, 1972.

THE PLANNING NONPROCESS

Mr. Steiner depicts the planning process with what he calls a flow chart. It is not a flow chart because it does not give any insight into the process flow among planning activities. Since all of his flows are two-way, it is possible in the chart to go anywhere or nowhere. For example, one process might proceed, in his chart, from "Fundamental Purpose" to "Planning Studies" to "Review and Evaluation of Plans." Another process might go back and forth between "Values of Top Managers" and "Strategic Planning" for two or two hundred iterations. Thus the chart depicts an infinite number rather than "the" process. Other authors cited by Professor Steiner (for example, Gilmore and Brandenburg) do describe an explicit flow in their conception of planning processes. Although there is considerable repetition in the planning process, I believe the conceptual process should delineate the flow and logical ordering of activities.

VALUES OF TOP MANAGERS

Why not mention the importance of recognizing the values of all organizational participants in the planning process. Certainly one must be cognizant of the power structure of the organization when designing planning systems, but to exclude mention of the importance of the values (and value conflicts) of research and development scientists, salesmen, assembly-line workers, and others implies that the values of users of plans is of little importance. If plans are to guide the behavior of all members of the firm, the values and needs of all participants, not just top management, should be accommodated to the greatest extent possible.

STRENGTHS AND WEAKNESSES

Professor Steiner claims that "not enough companies systematically examine their strengths; fewer systematically study their weaknesses." In my experience, the reverse is true in that systematic examination of crises, problems, and failures (a more common activity than systematic examination of successes) is always aimed at detecting and analyzing weaknesses. The systematic analysis of the strengths of the organization is a popular step in many prescriptive planning processes but it is extremely difficult to do. That which is a strength in one strategic alternative may well be a weakness in another. Thus, without a comprehensive specification of strategic alternatives *a priori,* one cannot list a generic statement of strengths, and hence it is rarely done well.

RISKS AND PROFITS IN NEW BUSINESSES

In Professor Steiner's words "there is a sort of iron law of product-market development which states that the farther a company moves from its present products and markets, the less likely it will be to make a profit." I prefer a lead law (malleable enough to accommodate the many counter-examples to this kind of generalization) that recognizes a greater risk but not a lower probability of making a profit; there is an important difference here. The farther one gets from current products and markets, the greater the range of possible losses (and profits)—i.e., the possible losses may be large but the *expected profit* may be as high or higher than with current product/markets. Often there are very good chances for very large profits to offset the risks; this is the very basis for organizational entrepreneurship.

THE HIERARCHY OF OBJECTIVES

Professor Steiner asserts that "if the sub and sub-subobjectives are achieved, the achievement of the dominant objective is inevitable." This is true only if the subobjectives are consistent with, and properly linked to, the dominant objective. It is very rare if they are; this is one of the major problems in good planning practices. A classic example is a profit objective that is translated to lower levels in terms of maximizing revenue (the sales function goal) and minimizing cost (the production function goal). As personnel in each function try to accomplish their subobjective, they make many decisions that suboptimize the profit objective.

QUANTITATIVE MODELS IN THE PLANNING PROCESS

Professor Steiner states that the testing of some alternatives can be completely quantified and cites a linear programming example. This is a common misconception of many top managers who do not understand quantative techniques, their limitations, and potential. In the cited example, there are many factors that cannot be accommodated in an LP model. Thus the answer provided by this quantitative model must be subjectively tempered in terms of qualitative factors by a manager who understands the model and the technique.

LINE AND STAFF FUNCTIONS IN PLANNING

Professor Steiner tells us that "Long-range planning is a line function and cannot be delegated to staff." Obviously, many parts of the planning function are and should be delegated to staff specialists, both in terms of designing planning systems and providing support for the planning process. They cannot, however, support line management without active participation by the line. This lack of clarity in the respective roles is one of the chief reasons why so many planning difficulties are reported in surveys of existing planning systems.

Formalized planning processes have undoubtedly contributed significantly to the effective management of many firms, particularly the larger ones. However, the potential for improvement is tremendous and the study of the planning process in a wider organizational context will require contributions from scholars in many disciplines and managers in many firms.

DISCUSSION QUESTIONS

1. What, precisely, is formal comprehensive planning? What is it not?
2. Define and distinguish between long-, medium-, and short-range planning.
3. What is the strategic planning process?
4. Describe and discuss Cleland's planning model.
5. Why does Professor Radosevich disagree with Professor Steiner's "overemphasis on rationality in the planning process." Who do you agree with and why?

13

Leadership and Management

Fred E. Fiedler

Professor
Department of Psychology
University of Washington

Martin M. Chemers

Professor
Department of Psychology
University of Utah

Leadership, essentially, means power over other people; and power over others enables a man to do things, to get things, to accomplish feats that he cannot attain by himself. But power over others also usually implies some measure of their consent, or at least some willing compliance for which the leader and his organization must pay a price. How to obtain this compliance and how to use it effectively is the topic of this chapter.

There can be very little question that an organization's success and failure—indeed, its very survival—depends in large part on the leadership it is able to attract. As a result, we heap rewards and honors on our leaders for the success of their organizations, and we make them bear the brunt of failure. If the team loses, the coach gets fired. On the other hand, we are willing to pay some of our leaders 10, 20, or even more times the salary of the non-supervisory employee. And we also spend billions of dollars yearly on recruitment, selection, and training of leaders, managers, and supervisors. Clearly, the problems of leadership are far from academic.

WHAT IS A LEADER?

Some Definitions

There are nearly as many definitions of leadership as there are leadership theories—almost as many as there are theorists. A few important definitions are reproduced here just to show what various writers have meant by the terms, "leadership" and "leader."

> Leadership is the exercise of authority and the making of decisions (Dubin, 1951).
>
> Leadership is the initiation of acts which result in a consistent pattern of group interaction directed toward the solution of mutual problems (Hemphill, 1954).

The leader is the man who comes closest to realizing the norms the group values highest; this conformity gives him his high rank, which attracts people and implies the right to assume control of the group (Homans, 1950).

The leader is the person who creates the most effective change in group performance (Cattell, 1951).

Leadership is the process of influencing group activities toward goal setting and goal achievement (Stogdill, 1948).

We shall here define the leader as the individual in the group who has the task of directing and coordinating task-relevant group activities. In groups that do not have a designated leader, he is the one who carries the primary responsibility for performing these functions in the group.

One point on which there is considerable agreement among leadership theorists is that there are no leaders where there are no followers. Above all, leadership is a relationship. More specifically, it is a relationship based on one person's power and influence over others. We shall confine our discussion to leaders who interact in face-to-face situations—that is, in groups or organizations.

Groups and Organizations

By a group we generally mean a set of individuals who share a common fate—that is, individuals who are interdependent in the sense that an event that affects one member is likely to affect all (Campbell, 1958). Typically, the human group shares a common goal, and its members interact in their attempt to achieve this goal. As a rule, the members are rewarded as a group for achieving their purposes; they are punished or they experience a sense of failure if their group does not perform well.

The term "organization" will be used to mean two or more groups that are interdependent and related to one another in order to accomplish certain common goals. Most of our working life is spent in organizations. Work groups, crews, boards, committees, delegations, panels are almost without exception subunits of organizations. Task groups typically are creatures of larger organizations rather than isolated units. In most cases, the organization selects the members of the group, assigns the leader, and specifies the task. If the group performs poorly, the organization might dissolve it or change the leader.

There are some groups that exist specifically for furthering the goals of the individual members rather than for furthering organizational purposes. This is true of psychotherapy groups, encounter groups, training classes, or social organizations. Our main concern in this chapter, however, will be with task groups within organizations—i.e., those established for the purpose of performing specific assignments or performing various services.

WHO BECOMES THE LEADER?

Modern leadership theory has had two major concerns. The first involves who becomes a leader or how one attains a position of leadership. This concern has resulted in hundreds of studies devoted to searching out leadership traits. The second major problem pertains to the question of leadership effectiveness—or how one becomes an effective leader. This second concern has spawned numerous studies of leader selection, leadership tests, research on effective and ineffective leader behavior, and leadership styles. It has influenced the philosophy and method of leadership training for supervisors and managers in business and industry. In discussing the theories and research on leadership, it is important that we clearly distinguish between leadership *position* and leadership *effectiveness*. Whether we like it or not, it is important to recognize that the attainment of a leadership position may be purely fortuitous. A person may be the leader because he is the most charming or able member of the group, because his family owns 51 per cent of the stock or simply because he was the only person available at the time. Whether he will be comparatively more successful than others is a distinct and separate question.

Who Wants to be a Leader?

Although there may well be a shortage of good leaders, there is rarely if ever a shortage of people who are willing to take over the leadership of a group. Obviously, being a leader provides very important satisfactions. The fact that leaders tend to get paid better than followers is undoubtedly one reason, but there is ample evidence that the leadership position is sought even if the tangible rewards are small or absent. Mann's (1959) review of leadership traits points out that, on the whole, leaders tend to be more dominant than nonleaders. Leadership not only entails power over others, but also affords the individual greater control over his own destiny.

The most comprehensive answer to the question of why people seek to lead comes from studies by Hemphill (1961), who found a variety of circumstances that motivate an individual to aspire to leadership. Hemphill suggests, first of all, that there must be a promise of large personal rewards for the leader if and when the task is accomplished. Second, the leader must believe that he can, in fact, accomplish the task if he tries. Third, the leader must feel that the group will accept him and that his previous attempts to assert leadership in the group have been accepted. Finally, the individual must believe that he has the required abilities or competence to get the job done.

Why, then, do others not try to lead? One major reason emerging from Hemphill's study is the fear that the group might reject the individual who tries to assert himself. In addition, the individual might believe that he has less chance to get the job done than others in the group, or that he is less competent.

It is important to realize, however, that the difference between leaders and followers is considerably less than one ordinarily assumes. The person who plays the leader role at one time might play the follower role at another. In fact, Hollander and Webb (1955) found that individuals who would be preferred as followers also tend to be preferred as leaders. McClintock (1963) reported that the leaders and active followers were more similar in behavior than were the followers who were active and those who were nonactive. The difference, then, is not so much between leader and follower

—both may be active participants in the group process—but rather between being an engaged participant in group action or a nonparticipant in the group.

Is Somebody Following You?

How do you get to be a leader? The simplest answer is to get someone to follow you. This is accomplished by having material or psychological resources that the followers want—superior intelligence, a strong personality, money to hire employees, or control over organizational resources, such as a military commander might have. Although the trend in the United States is against nepotism, most leaders throughout the world attain leadership positions at least in part by being born into the right family (Domhoff, 1967). Warner and Abegglen (1955) reported that 48 per cent of American business executives came from families that owned substantial stock in the company. The proportion in many countries outside the United States is undoubtedly higher.

Also, consider the many supervisory positions in American government and industry that require specific types of training and education. How many managers of a highway department do not have a degree in civil engineering? Many production managers have to have college training, it is almost impossible to become a judge without being a lawyer, and it is difficult, if not impossible, to rise to high positions in the military services without college or military academy training.

Personality attributes clearly do play a part in determining who becomes a leader. However, we should be fully aware of the fact that the attainment of a leadership position may be as much a factor of a person's education, economics, politics, or genealogy as of his personal attributes.

Personality Attributes of the Leader

What, then, are those personality factors that help a person to rise to a position of leadership? This is a question that engaged the efforts of social psychologists well into the 1940's. It is probably fair to say that almost every conceivable personality measure and trait has been related at one time or another to leadership behavior, leadership status, or leadership performance. These attempts to establish consistent relationships, however, have not been very fruitful.

In one of the most important studies of leadership, Stogdill (1948) reviewed existing studies of leadership traits—that is, studies of stable personality attributes that are relatively independent of the specific situation in which an individual is observed. Some of the personal attributes that he found to correlate with leadership status were the individual's intelligence, his height, weight, rated personal adjustment, social poise, and dominance. However, his most important finding was that the correlations were quite small and that it would hardly be practicable to utilize any of these measures as predictors of leadership. This finding was supported in a subsequent review of the literature by Mann (1959). The most important single conclusion that emerged from these studies was that the leader's abilities and aptitudes or his background tended to be related to the particular and specific goals the group was trying to achieve. Thus, a bowling team was more likely to choose as captain a good bowler rather than a poor one, a person elected to the presidency of a scientific organization tended to be a good scientist rather than a poor one, and the leader of a group charged with solving intellectually demanding problems tended to be intelligent rather than dull.

Nevertheless, some personality attributes do correlate with leadership status. According to Stogdill, leaders exceed members in (1) "capacity"—i.e., intelligence, alertness, verbal facility, originality, judgment; (2) "achievement"—i.e. scholarship, knowledge, athletic accomplishments; (3) "responsibility"—i.e., dependability, initative, persistence, aggressiveness, self-confidence, desire to excel; (4) "participation"—i.e., activity, sociability, cooperation, adaptability, humor; (5) "status"—i.e., socio-economic position, popularity; as well as (6) factors "due to the nature of the situation"—i.e. mental level, status, skills, needs and interests of followers, or objectives to be achieved.

Stogdill concludes by saying,

> A person does not become a leader by virtue of the possession of some combination of traits, but the pattern of personal characteristics of the leader must bear some relevant relationship to the characteristics, activities, and goals of the followers. Thus, leadership must be conceived in terms of the interaction of variables that are in constant flux and change. . . . The persistence of individual patterns of human behavior in the face of constant situational change appears to be a primary obstacle encountered not only in the practice of leadership, but in the selection and placement of leaders. . . . It becomes clear that an adequate analysis of leadership involves not only a study of leaders, but also of situations. [Gibb (Ed.), 1969, p. 125.]

Recently, a number of researchers have attempted to predict leadership or the attainment of managerial positions in specific organizations by detailed assessments of individuals on various patterns of personality test scores (i.e., Gough, 1969; Cattell, 1951; Bray and Grant, 1966). These studies have revealed interesting results, which suggest that the patterning of a sufficiently large number of attributes might predict who will become a successful executive in specific organizations. It seems doubtful, however, that there are general personality attributes that lead inevitably to managerial success, regardless of the organizational factors that define the job.

It should be borne in mind in this connection that the functions of an executive are considerably broader than the functions of a leader. They involve ability to write reports, give speeches, keep records, and negotiate with other supervisors, as well as directing subordinates. All executives are leaders, but not all leaders are executives.

To sum up, it seems fair to say that the leadership trait approach is not at this time a live issue. It has a certain limited theoretical importance in showing stable relations between various personality attributes and leadership status, but these relations are weak. Personality attributes will loom large mainly in situations in which all other important variables are controlled, and hence they may predict well within a particular organization.

Situational Factors in Leadership Attainment

Are there, then, other factors that account for leadership achievement? The answer to this question is clearly yes. A few examples will serve to make this point.

One of the most important and significant advances in social psychological experimentation was made by Bavelas (1948), who developed a paradigm for communication network studies. Small groups were placed around a table and permitted to communicate in certain ways while attempting to solve various problems. These problems, at least in the early studies, consisted of piecing together a puzzle of which each member had only certain parts.

The major importance of this line of research for leadership was the clear although somewhat incidental finding that those who were at the hub of the communication net also tended to become the decision makers (Leavitt, 1951). Thus, the person through whom all communications had to be channeled soon became, in effect, the leader of the group.

Dorothy McBride Kipnis (1957) showed that the place an individual occupied in the communication system of a B-29 bomber crew determined to a large extent the number of choices he obtained from other crew members for a leadership position. Likewise, Steinzor (1950) and Howells and Becker (1962) have shown that seating arrangement determines leadership position to some extent (see Gibb).

Leadership, then, does depend to a considerable degree upon being at the right place at the right time. It also helps to be visible. In a very ingenious series of studies, Bavelas, Hastorf, Gross and Kite (1965) designed several experiments that permitted them to reward or penalize various group members for speaking during group discussion sessions. The members were told that observers, presumably sitting behind one-way mirrors, were watching them, and that they would periodically indicate whether the statements made by a particular group member helped or disrupted the discussion. In actuality, the signals were given in purely random order. As expected, the individuals who were rewarded for speaking did, in fact, talk more than those not so rewarded. However, regardless of the substance of their contribution to the discussion, they were regarded by more group members as leaders than were those who had spoken less because that behavior had not been rewarded. The importance of these studies, supporting the facetiously-called "blabbermouth theory of leadership," is that the visibility and participation of the individual determined to a large extent his leadership status.

Who, then, becomes a leader? Two major generalizations are in order.

1. People tend to become leaders if they are somewhat superior to other members in their group in the particular abilities, skills, or control over resources which assist group members to satisfy their needs or the group to achieve its goals.
2. People tend to become leaders if their particular assignment or personality attributes make them more visible than others in the group.

HOW DO LEADERS BEHAVE?

It is obvious that leaders behave differently from members. If we happen to enter a room in which a group is meeting, it usually takes only a moment to figure out who sits on top of the totem pole. Likewise, when we enter a factory or office it is easy enough to spot the foreman or supervisor of a work group. Although these statements might seem obvious enough, they also demonstrate quite clearly that leaders behave differently from members. We have different expectations of leaders and they have different expectations of group members. The fact that these expectations are so well understood in our society makes it possible for groups to function without our writing elaborate rules. When we call a committee meeting, the members will almost automatically turn to the chairman for directions on how to proceed. If a member starts to give these directions, it is often regarded as an illegitimate attempt to usurp power or to undermine the leader. Several different techniques to isolate and identify leader behavior have been employed.

Critical Incidents

There have been a number of successful empirical approaches to describing leadership behavior. Preston (1948), using Flanagan's technique (1949), attempted to identify "critical requirements" of successful leaders. The study was based on interviews with 640 air force officers whose ranks and jobs differed widely. These officers were asked to describe "critical incidents," indicating how their leaders behaved in various circumstances. A classification of these incidents led to six categories of leadership behavior. These are:

1. Supervising personnel
2. Planning, initiating, and directing action
3. Handling administrative details
4. Accepting personal responsibility
5. Showing group cohesion and loyalty to the organization
6. Performing professional or technical specialty

Behavior Observations

A study by Carter (1953, p. 16) identified three main factors of leadership behavior:

Factor I: *Group Goal Facilitation*—the dimension of behavior that is interpreted as being effective for achieving the goal toward which the group is oriented. Efficiency, insight, cooperation—all seem to facilitate group action in solving the task.

Factor II: *Individual Prominence*—the dimension of behavior that makes an individual stand out from the group. The behavior associated with influence, aggressiveness, leadership, initiative, and confidence seems to inspire recognition by the group of a member's individuality.

Factor III: *Group Sociability*—the dimension of behavior that indicates the positive social interaction of an individual in the group. The traits heavily loaded in this factor—sociability, striving for group acceptance, co-operation, and adaptability—all signify friendly interpersonal patterns of behavior of the individual toward the group.

Leadership Behavior Descriptions. The most comprehensive and important research on leadership behavior was conducted at Ohio State University. In one major research effort, Hemphill (1950) obtained ratings of leadership behavior on over 1,800 items. An analysis of these descriptions isolated two factors that accounted for most of the variance in leadership behavior. Halpin and Winer (1952) summarized these factors as follows:

1. *Consideration:* . . . the extent to which the leader, while carrying out his functions, is considerate of the men who are his followers. There is no implication, however, of laxity in the performance of duty, or of superficial human relations behavior. Individual items indicate that the positive pole of this factor is characterized by warmth of personal relationships, mutual trust, readiness to explain actions, and willingness to listen to subordinates and allow them to participate in decision-making.

2. *Initiating structure:* This dimension represents the extent to which the leader organizes and defines the relation between himself and his subordinates or fellow group members. Scale items with high positive loadings here include "maintains definite standards of performance," "makes his attitude clear to the crew," "asks that the crew follow standard operating procedures," and "assigns crew members to particular tasks."

If we want to describe how leaders behave, measuring (1) how considerate they are and (2) how much they structure the interaction will give us most of the picture. Subsequent studies by a number of investigators (Fleishman, Harris, and Burtt, 1955; Halpin, 1955), as well as studies outside the Ohio State group, have supported the importance of these two dimensions. Their identification constitutes one of the most important achievements in the area of leadership research.

Although behavioral definitions of leadership are elusive and behavioral descriptions are susceptible to some forms of bias, the advantages of these approaches are considerable. There is substantial reliability, especially when a relatively large number of members is asked to rate the leader's behavior. The ratings are relatively easy to obtain, especially for groups in field studies in which observations of leaders are frequently impossible to obtain. And above all, as we shall see, these descriptions supply useful information for understanding leadership.

Another method that has enjoyed wide acceptance is Bales' Interaction Process Analysis (1951). This method was designed for studying small problem-solving groups in the laboratory. Observers were trained to identify and categorize twelve different types of behaviors. Three of these indicate positive reactions: showing solidarity, tension release, and agreeing with another. Three reflect negative reactions: showing disagreement, tension increase, and antagonism. Three of the behaviors are active task-oriented, i.e., "problem solving attempts"—gives information, gives opinion, gives orientation—

whereas three are "questions"—asks orientation, asks for opinions, asks for suggestions.

The method has led to a differentiation between "task specialists" and "social specialists," a classification that has had considerable impact on leadership theory. Effective groups, according to Bales, need both types of leadership although both might be provided by the same person. This finding was supported in a study of Korean combat rifle squads (Clark, 1955). Clark showed that the effective squads were those in which all important leadership roles were filled whether by the leader or by the other members of the group. Thus, someone had to perform the command and modeling functions, the therapeutic functions, the household functions, and the like, if the squad as a whole were to perform well.

Leadership role studies, and in particular Clark's (1955), make clear that the leader must perform a wide variety of functions or see to it that others will perform these functions. Not surprisingly, the role expectations that group members may have of a leader may not always be compatible with one another. Hollander (1955) has pointed to one very intriguing and theoretically important conflict inherent in the leader's role. The leader must serve as a model, and therefore embody or exemplify the group's norms and expectations. At the same time, leadership also implies creating new roles and new group structures, and initiating new directions for group action. Thus, the leader must be the conservator of group norms as well as the initiator and modifier of these norms. In order to reconcile this conflict, Hollander points out that the leader must first gain the confidence of the group members by doing what is expected of him. In effect, the leader's conformity and achievement earn "idiosyncracy credits" that allow him occasionally to depart from the group's norms.

WHO IS THE EFFECTIVE LEADER?

Let us now turn to the second major question in leadership theory—namely, how to be an effective leader. As you will recall, we define the leader's effectiveness in terms of his group's performance.

Some writers have maintained that we should consider morale and job satisfaction, as well as the employee's personal growth, as criteria of performance. It is certainly reasonable to take this position. Argyris (1964) and others have argued, for example, that industry should enable employees to reach higher levels of personal fulfillment. One might also argue that high morale is an organizational output in its own right, and that it is desirable, regardless of whether the group does or does not perform well.

The alternative that we adopt here is to say that the task group exists primarily for the purpose of accomplishing a goal or a set of tasks. Almost always these goals and tasks are assigned by the organization of which the group is a part. The morale of the group usually is a byproduct and not the group's major purpose. It may assist (or hinder) the group in achieving its stated objectives, but it is not, as a rule, the leader's major assignment. Although many organizations explicitly or implicitly recognize that they have social responsibilities for the welfare and development of their employees, this is a secondary aim. For better or for worse, executive bonuses are not based on morale scores or the amount of character a department builds.

Two Approaches to Effective Leadership

In grossly oversimplified form, there have been two major approaches to teaching effective leadership. The first and traditional one derives from Taylor's *Scientific Management* (1911), which called on the leader to direct and control the group and to assign and exactly specify what the subordinate had to do. This approach requires the leader to diagnose the situation and to plan and supervise appropriate action. The essential formula of this approach might be stated as, "I'll do the planning and you carry out the orders."

At the other end of this continuum, we find the more recent positions that stem from the so-called human relations movement. These exhort the leader to engage his group members' interest in the task, which he does by involving the members in the decision-making process and by developing an interpersonal relationship with them that will motivate the members to work with the leader on the task at hand.

McGregor (1967) elaborates two major managerial styles. The orthodox style, which he calls, Theory *X*, is based on the traditional view that the average human being has an inherent dislike of work and will avoid it if he can; that most people must be coerced, controlled, threatened with punishment, and that the average human being prefers being directed and wishes to avoid responsibility since he has relatively little ambition. In contrast, the Theory *Y* manager assumes that work is as natural as play and rest, that man will exercise self-control and self-direction, and that the average human being, under proper conditions, seeks responsibility. The ideal manager must, therefore, create conditions such that the members of the organization can achieve their own goals best by directing their efforts toward the success of the enterprise.

The Management Grid, a well-known method of management training developed by Blake and Mouton (1964) is based on the McGregor theory. It postulates two dimensions of leadership behavior. These are described as "Concern for People," and "Concern for Job or Mission Performance." A leader can be classified in terms of the emphasis he places on each item in terms of a scale from 1 to 9. Different leadership styles can then be expressed by indicating the point on which the leader falls on the 9 x 9 grid. The ideal leader, a "9, 9," integrates highest concern for job performance with highest concern for people. Although the Management Grid is a very attractive and popular theory among business and military executives, there are no substantial empirical data that support the claim that the method improves organizational performance. Nor have we found evidence in other studies that one type of leadership approach is consistently better than the others. The same leader may be highly effective in one situation but relatively ineffective in another.

For example, Voiers (1956) found that the performance of air crews in radar bombing exercises was completely unrelated to the performance of these same crews in visual bombing. A study of army tank crews showed that the time in seconds to hit a target was unrelated to the time the crew required to recognize the target or to travel from target to target (Fiedler, 1955). An experiment that utilized ninety-six three-man teams composed of Belgian sailors (Fiedler, 1966) involved four different tasks consisting of writing a recruiting letter, routing a ship through ten and then twelve different ports, and showing men how to disassemble and reassemble a .45-caliber pistol. The median intercorrelations of performance among these four tasks was 0.14; that is, essentially zero. Thus, group leader performance was unrelated across tasks. Other examples could easily be enumerated to make the same point.

The findings that leadership performance over different tasks is uncorrelated also supports the conclusion that leadership traits do not predict leadership performance. First, they show that the performance of the group cannot be attributed primarily to the leader's characteristics, his style, his attitudes, or his personality. Otherwise, we would expect groups under one leader to be consistently good, and groups under another leader to be consistently poor on different tasks.

Second, since some leaders are effective in situation *A* but not in situation *B*, the situation must play a substantial part in determining how well the group will perform.

Third, these findings contradict the commonly heard notion that the effective leader is "flexible"—that is, that he changes his behavior, his style, or his relationship toward subordinates depending on the situation. If this were the case, we would again expect that some individuals will be more flexible than others; hence, that they would be better leaders regardless of the situation. The fact that leadership performances over different types of tasks are uncorrelated indicates, however, that this is not likely to be the case. Moreover, training individuals to be more sensitive and aware of their interpersonal relations with subordinates has not led to systematically better performance of these trained leaders (Dunnette and Campbell, 1968; House, 1967).

International Theories

Several recent theories have attempted to develop a model for the interaction of leader attributes and situational factors. One of the theories that explicitly recognizes the situational factors as well as leadership variables is Floyd Mann's (1965) Skill Mix Theory. Mann postulates four important skills. These are (1) human relations skills involved in working with people; (2) technical skills required for performing and directing the work activities of the group; (3) administrative skills for coordinating the work of the group, making job assignments, planning, and the like; and (4) institutional skills required for relating the organization to its environment, developing appropriate policies, and representing the group or the organization to other agencies outside the organization.

At the lower organizational levels, technical skills are relatively more important than human relations and administrative skills. At higher organizational levels the administrative skills become more important. Institutional skills are more necessary at the top level as technical and human relations skills become less critical. A similar point of view emerges in Katz and Kahn's theory (1966), which argues that leadership requirements systematically vary as we consider different levels of the organizational hierarchy. Still another theory that stresses the interaction of leader and situation was developed by Hersey and Blanchard (1970). These authors stress ". . . as the level of maturity of one's followers continues to increase, appropriate leader behavior not only requires less and less structure (task) while increasing consideration, but eventually it should entail decreases in socio-emotional support (relationships)."

In sum, most leadership theorists today recognize the important part that the situation plays in determining leadership performance. Probably the most explicit statement of how the leader's personality and the situation interact is, at this time, the Contingency Model (Fiedler, 1964, 1967, 1971).

THE CONTINGENCY MODEL

This theory, like most other current theories in the leadership area, tries to answer the question, "What kind of leadership is required for what kind of situation?" The problem basically consists of (1) classifying personality attributes of the leader, (2) classifying leadership situations, and (3) matching a particular type of leadership to a particular leadership situation. We will here describe briefly the measures of leadership motivation and a method for classifying groups before considering the substantive findings to which the theory has led.

Leadership Motivation

By leadership motivation we mean here a motivational system that expresses itself in various goal-seeking behaviors that the individual perceives as rewarding or perhaps even as necessary for his emotional wellbeing. Notice that we need to differentiate clearly between leadership motivation and leadership behavior. Different kinds of behavior may be employed to achieve the same goal.

We have identified two motivational patterns that are here labeled "relationship-motivated" and "task-motivated." These are measured by means of a simple bipolar adjective scale that asks the individual (1) to think of everyone with whom he has ever worked, and (2) to describe the one person with whom he could work *least well.* This description of his "least preferred coworker" or LPC is made by marking sixteen to twenty items such as the following:

friendly	: ___	: ___	: ___	: ___	: ___	: ___	: ___	: ___ :	unfriendly
	8	7	6	5	4	3	2	1	
cooperative	: ___	: ___	: ___	: ___	: ___	: ___	: ___	: ___ :	uncooperative
	8	7	6	5	4	3	2	1	

The sum of the item scales constitutes the individual's LPC score. A relatively high score indicates a high LPC or relationship-motivated person whereas a low score indicates a low LPC or task-motivated person.

We must think of the LPC score as an index of a goal or motivational hierarchy. The high LPC person has, as his primary goal, the establishment and maintenance of close interpersonal relations—he needs to be related and socially connected to others. He will show concern for good interpersonal relations when the situation is tense, when his relations with co-workers seem tenuous, and when the situation is generally anxiety-arousing. However, this person does not have to behave in this way when his goals of being related are already secured. This is analogous to Maslow's (1943) well-known statement, "needs which are satisfied are no longer motivators." If I have completely satisfied my hunger, more food will not entice me until I am again hungry. The relationship-motivated, high LPC person who has secured his goal of being related to others will then seek the satisfaction of secondary goals. These secondary goals appear to be the approval and admiration of others, and the attainment of a position of prominence. A leader of a task-group can achieve these self-oriented goals by acting in a leaderlike fashion or by being officiously concerned about the task.

The low LPC person has as his major goal the accomplishment of a task or assignment. His self-esteem seems to depend on doing a good job (Bishop, 1964). When he feels, however, that the accomplishment of the task will present no problem, he, too, will pursue his secondary goal, which appears to be having good interpersonal relations with his co-workers. In fact, the low LPC person believes that good interpersonal relations are conducive to task accomplishment (Fiedler, 1972). Thus, when the task appears to present no difficulties, the low LPC leader will have pleasant, friendly, and considerate interactions with his co-workers.

Categorizing the Situation

Let us now ask, How we shall go about developing a category system for situations? Consider here, for a moment, that a leadership situation is, in effect, a power relationship. In other words, we may speak of leadership as the issue of who is able to influence whom to do what. If we now want to categorize leadership situations, it seems reasonable to look at the degree to which the situation makes the exercise of power and influence easy or difficult.

It is relatively easy for a leader to control people if they like and trust him, if they feel a personal loyalty to him and desire to follow him. Conversely, it will be difficult to lead when the group dislikes, distrusts, or rejects its leader.

A second important aspect of the situation that will influence the leader's power and influence is the nature of the task. The leader who knows more than the members, or has at his disposal a step-by-step procedure for performing the task, will find it relatively easy to control and influence the group. He will be able to tell his group members exactly what to do. Moreover, the organization can give the leader support. If a man does not follow explicit orders, he can be punished. This is not possible if the task is vague and unstructured. Consider, for example, the task of a committee charged with writing a new policy for governing student housing. The members will be as knowledgeable as the chairman, and each member could easily challenge the chairman's ideas and suggestions, or his instructions on how to proceed. Furthermore, how can the leader prove that the group member is not so creative as he could be?

Finally, it is obvious that the leader will have greater power if he can reward and punish, or if he can promote or demote. A leader who has been given "fate control" over his members obviously will be in a more powerful situation than will someone who has no formal or legitimate power. The captain of a ship has more power and influence by virtue of his position than does the chairman of a PTA committee.

We have identified three major aspects of the situation that provide the leader with power and influence, that make the situation "favorable" or "unfavorable" for him. These are, specifically, leader-member relations, task structure, and leader's position power. Although there are clearly other situational components that play a role, the three that we have here described are probably the most important.

This three-dimensional scheme can, no doubt, be improved but it does enable us to scale the favorableness of the leadership situation. One method for doing this is to divide groups roughly at the median of each of the three major dimensions. This will give us groups in which the leader-member relationship is relatively good and groups in which it is relatively poor. Likewise, we can divide the groups into those that have relatively structured tasks and those with relatively unstructured tasks. Finally, we can divide the groups into those that give the leader high position power and those in which the leader position is vested with relatively little power. Research has shown that the leader-member relations dimension is the most important of the three and groups are, therefore, first divided on the basis of how well the leader feels, or is, accepted by his group.

The classification system thus consists of eight cells, octants, which are shown on the horizontal axis of Figure 35. Octant 1 represents the most favorable situation, since the groups falling into this octant would have (1) accepted and trusted leaders with (2) a structured task and (3) high position power. Octant 2 would be somewhat less favorable since the leader, although he is liked and has a structured task, does not have very much position power, and so on, until we come to Octant 8, in which groups have a leader who (1) is not accepted, (2) has an unstructured, vague task, and (3) low position power. At this point, it is important to notice that the favorableness of the situation affects the way in which leaders behave and perform but it is not, *by itself*, highly related to leadership performance. On the whole, trusted leaders or liked leaders are no more effective than distrusted or disliked leaders, and powerful leaders are no more effective than leaders with little legitimate power (Fiedler, 1967).

Which Type of Leadership for Which Situation?

Given a meaningful system of classifying situations, what specific kind of leader personality or leadership motivation do each of various situa-

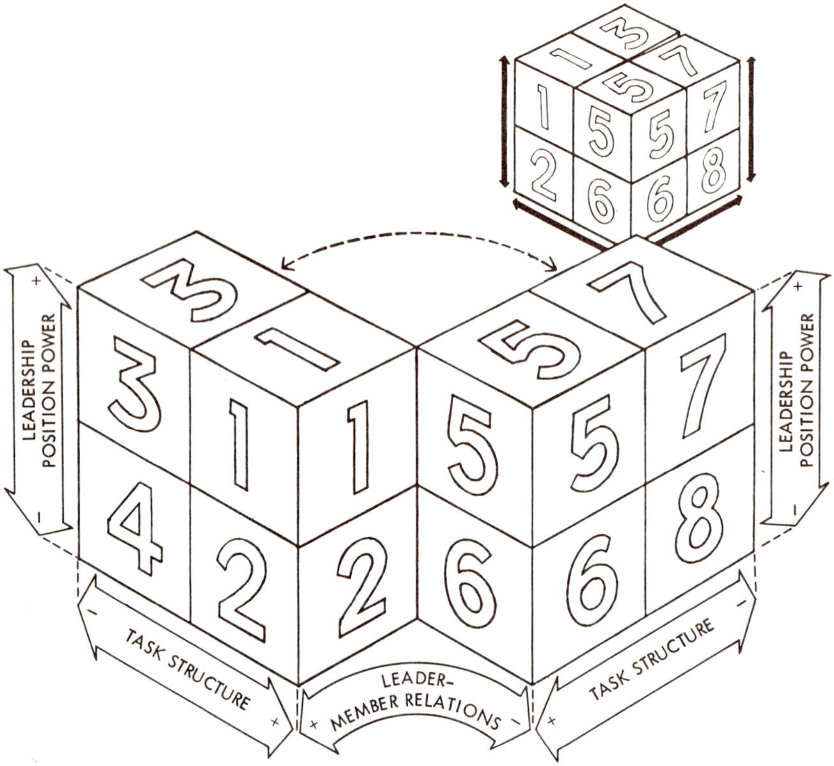

FIGURE 35. Classification of Leadership Situations

tions call for? The Contingency Model was developed by re-analyzing data that had been obtained in earlier years. These data included studies of high school basketball teams in which the proportion of games won in league play constituted the criterion; surveying parties in which the accuracy of land measurement was the criterion; air force bomber crews, in which we used measures of bombing accuracy; and tank crews, in which we used the number of seconds required to hit a target. Other groups had the task of writing a story or an advertisement or solving a problem wherein judges rated the creativity of the products and other factors. Also included were boards of directors, managers, and foremen of various business and industrial concerns, with criteria based on net income figures and production records.

The critical question is which leadership style or motivational pattern is required by which kind of situation. Each set of groups was categorized so that it could be assigned to a particular octant of the system for classifying the situational favorableness. We then correlated within each of these sets of groups the leader's LPC score and the effectiveness measure of his group. The various correlation coefficients for groups within an octant can then be plotted, and are shown in Figure 36.

The figure shows the favorableness of the situation on the horizontal axis, with the most favorable octant 1 to the left and the least favorable octant 8 to the right of the axis. The vertical axis shows the correlation

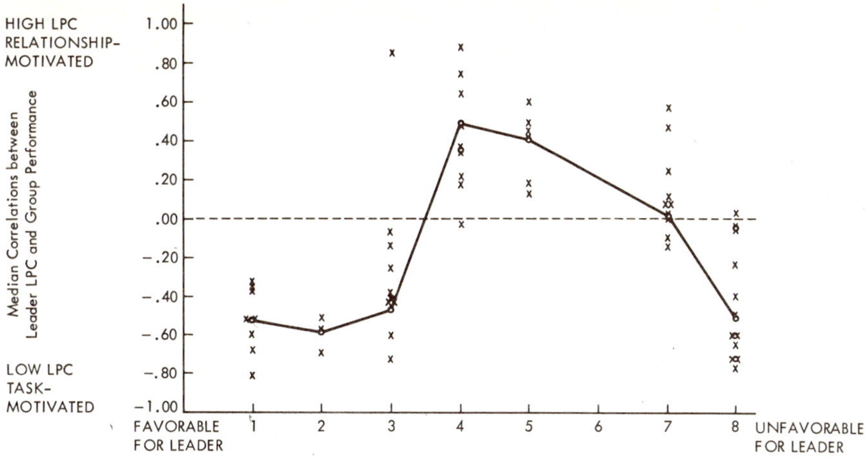

Leader-member Relations	good	good	good	good	mod. poor	mod. poor	mod. poor	mod. poor
Task Structure	str.	str.	unstr.	unstr.	str.	str.	unstr.	unstr.
Leader Position Power	strong	weak	strong	weak	strong	weak	strong	weak

FIGURE 36. Relationships Between LPC and Group Effectiveness

coefficients, which indicate whether the relationship-motivated (high LPC) leaders or the task-motivated (low LPC) leaders were more effective. Since a high LPC score indicates a relationship-motivated leadership style, a *positive* correlation (shown as a point above the mid-line) indicates that the relationship-motivated (high LPC) leaders were more effective than the task-motivated leaders. A *negative* correlation (shown as a point below the mid-line) indicates that the task-oriented (low LPC) leaders tended to be more effective than were the relationship-oriented leaders. The larger the correlation in either the positive or the negative direction, the stronger was the relationship; hence, the greater would be our confidence that we are not dealing with chance findings.

How Good is the Model?

Before going further it is essential to know whether the Contingency Model is valid. To what extent does it predict performance in other types of groups; to what degree can we generalize from it?

A number of studies have been conducted within the past few years by our laboratory as well as by other investigators to test the prediction of the theory. Studies that adequately tested the model show that the theory predicts quite well (Fiedler, 1971). For example, Hunt (1967) conducted research on departments of a large physical science research laboratory, a chain of supermarkets, and a heavy machinery manufacturing plant. Hill (1969) reported studies in a large electronics firm and with assembly line instructors. Fiedler, O'Brien, and Ilgen (1966) worked with public health volunteer groups in Honduras. In all of these studies, the groups were classified on the basis of their leader-member relations, task structure, and position power. The leader's or manager's LPC score was then correlated with group performance measures.

In addition, a number of experiments and controlled field studies have been conducted to test the model (Fiedler, 1966). Studies were conducted by Shima (1968) using Japanese student groups, by Mitchell (1970) using participants of a church leadership workshop, and by Fiedler (an unpublished study) using trainees of an executive development program. In addition, a carefully controlled experiment was conducted by Chemers and Skrzypek (1971) at the Military Academy at West Point. The leader was chosen on the basis of sociometric choices by the members—i.e., the experimenters ascertained in advance whom the members would choose as a leader and then assembled half the groups with preferred and accepted leaders and half with non-preferred leaders. This study, which carefully preselected leaders, almost precisely replicated the predicted correlations. A comparison of median correlations obtained in the original and the validation studies shows considerable similarity in the results supporting the validity of the Model (Table 8).

Looking at the graph, we see that the task-motivated (low LPC) leaders tend to perform better than relationship-motivated leaders in very favorable and in relatively unfavorable situations. The relationship-motivated (high LPC) leaders tend to perform better than task-motivated leaders in situations of intermediate favorableness.

What does this mean? First of all, the data suggest very strongly that both the task-motivated as well as the relationship-motivated types of persons can be effective leaders *if they are placed in the right situation.* In other words, every leader can be effective in some situations and ineffective in others.

Second, we cannot really talk about a good or a poor leader since the data show that the effectiveness of the leader is determined in large part by the situation. Hence, we can only speak about a leader who is effective in one situation but ineffective in another. Finally, how can we apply this theory in order to improve leadership performance?

IMPROVING LEADERSHIP PERFORMANCE

Experience

The immediate and most pressing question to most top executives in business and government is, of course, how to improve leadership performance. The current efforts devoted to leadership training undoubtedly ex-

TABLE 8. MEDIAN CORRELATIONS OBTAINED IN VARIOUS OCTANTS OF THE CONTINGENCY MODEL

	Octants							
	1	*2*	*3*	*4*	*5*	*6*	*7*	*8*
Original Studies	—52	—58	—33	47	42	——	0.05	—43
Validation	—64	17	—22	38	22	10	26	—35
Field Studies	—57	—21	—29	23	21	—24	30	—33
Laboratory Studies	—72	24	—16	38	16	13	0.08	—33

ceed several billions of dollars annually. What evidence do we have that this money and time has been well spent? What evidence do we have that new approaches will yield better returns? A short review of the evidence is probably in order before we present alternatives that seem to offer more promise than methods used in the past.

Let us first look at the effect of leadership experience. Most laymen as well as most managers and business executives firmly believe that leadership experience improves organizational performance. However, anecdotal and empirical evidence suggests otherwise. To give but a few examples, Alexander the Great commanded the Macedonian cavalry when he was 16 years old, William Pitt became England's prime minister at age 24, Charles Percy became president of Bell and Howell before reaching 30, and Robert Hutchins was president of the University of Chicago at 31.

Furthermore, a study of Belgian petty officers (Fiedler, 1966) showed that years of experience did not correlate with leadership effectiveness on experimental tasks, and a subsequent study of Canadian officers similarly indicated that those with long years of experience were no more effective than the inexperienced (Fiedler and Chemers, 1968). Similarly, a study of post office managers showed no relationship between years of experience and performance, nor did analyses of chemical research teams, grocery and meat markets, or production departments in a heavy machine plant. The summary analysis of the relationship between performance and leadership experience, based on twelve different types of managers ($N=385$) yielded a median correlation of -0.12, hardly significant in the positive direction (Fiedler, 1971). Subsequent analyses of the performance of school principals (McNamara, 1968) and of police sergeants have produced identical results.

Leadership Training

The findings concerning leadership training are more confused but hardly more encouraging. A recent review of leadership training by Campbell *et al.* (1970, p. 325) states, "Thus with regard to the *bulk* of the literature on training effects, it remains to be demonstrated whether the changes in the criteria used to measure training effects have any importance for the organization's goals." These authors found that behavioral changes have occurred as a result of training but there is little evidence that they do any good. Others (Odiorne, 1964) take an even less charitable view. Recent research (Fiedler, 1971) on the overall effects of leadership training provides us with no reason for disagreement with Campbell and his associates.

The previously mentioned Belgian study (Fiedler, 1966) compared the leadership performance of petty officers with that of newly inducted recruits. The recruits performed as well as the petty officers who had had two years in petty officer training school. No differences were found in leadership performance between the trained and untrained leaders. Another study (Fiedler and Chemers, 1968) compared officers with four years of military academy training and men who had just finished basic training. Again, no substantial or significant differences in leadership performance appeared. In fact, in one of the three tasks, the recruits performed somewhat better than did the officers. In a study of post office managers that correlated the amount of training with rated managerial performance, the correlations were on the whole slightly negative.

To these dismal results should be added the well-known study by Fleishman, Harris, and Burtt (1955) that involved the leadership training of plant foremen at International Harvester Company. Although training during this study temporarily modified leadership behavior, the effects did not last long and did not improve organizational performance. Dunnette and Campbell (1968) and House (1967) extensively reviewed sensitivity and T-group training and concluded that some behavioral modifications occur but that these have no consistent effect on organizational performance.

TRAINING AND EXPERIENCE EFFECTS IN LIGHT OF THE CONTINGENCY MODEL

Modifying Situational Favorableness

If the Contingency Model shows that the group's or the organization's performance depends on the situation as well as on the motivational pattern of the leader, it provides certain alternatives to the usual leadership training strategies. One alternative calls for modifying the leadership situation, a program suggested in an earlier paper (Fiedler, 1966) but not empirically tested. The approach is based on the assumption that it is easier to change a man's job than to change his motivational pattern, and that some of these changes in situational favorableness are accomplished relatively easily.

Such changes in situational favorableness are, in fact, made every day. One supervisor is given the routine jobs whereas another gets the trouble-shooting and problem solving-assignments. One manager is told that anything he does will get the blessing of his superior whereas another is given to understand that he had better clear any departures from routine with his boss, or even his subordinates. Some people love working with difficult employees and are good at it whereas others cannot tolerate much interpersonal stress. Some men need constant challenge because they get bored, sloppy, and negligent under routine conditions; and the wise boss will see to it that the challenging jobs go their way. Thus, the Contingency Model provides here a theoretical basis for management decisions that up to now have usually been made on an intuitive level.

It is also obvious, of course, that we should be able to teach a man how to diagnose the conditions under which he will be effective and those under which he is likely to perform poorly. The leader who is able to avoid situations in which he is likely to fail is bound to be a success. Moreover, the ability to recognize the situational factors that lead to good performance will also enable an individual to modify his own job or assignment in order to bring about a leadership situation compatible with his personality and motivational pattern.

Reconceptualization of Leadership Experience and Training

The second approach to improving leadership performance represents a major departure from our previous thinking. We usually view leadership training and experience as changing the leader—he learns something, and this new knowledge should help him perform better. Let us now reconsider this problem. The typical leadership experience and leadership training teaches the leader (1) how to get along better with his fellow workers and subordinates, and (2) how to perform his job more effectively. The first is in fact the topic of most current management training, sensitivity and T-group methods, and the various human-relations-in-industry courses (Nealey and Fiedler, 1968). The second provides the leader with technical knowledge about his job, teaches him how to handle various usual and unusual situations he is likely to encounter, and acquaints him with new methods in his field. In other words, it makes the job more routine and structured since the leader will need to develop fewer new creative solutions to problems, and since many aspects of his job will now be routine. Moreover, Csoka (1971) has pointed out that training helps a man to utilize the potential structure in a task. The most structured task to the untrained leader will appear as unstructured. (The reader who has no cooking experience might try his hand at making crepes suzettes by following a cookbook!) Thus, *both types of leadership training, interpersonal and task, improve situational favorableness.*

If the Contingency Model is correct, training should have different effects on the performance of the relationship-motivated (high LPC) and the task-motivated (low LPC) leader. Let us now say that we have a situation that is favorable for the experienced and well-trained leader. This same situation would, of course, be correspondingly less favorable for leaders with inadequate training and experience—that is, it might be intermediate in favorableness. Hence, for the *untrained*, high LPC leaders would perform better than low LPC leaders in a situation of intermediate favorableness. If we now train these same leaders, we would make the situation very favorable. Hence, the high LPC leaders will become worse and the low LPC leaders will become better (see Figure 37). Similarly, in a situation that is

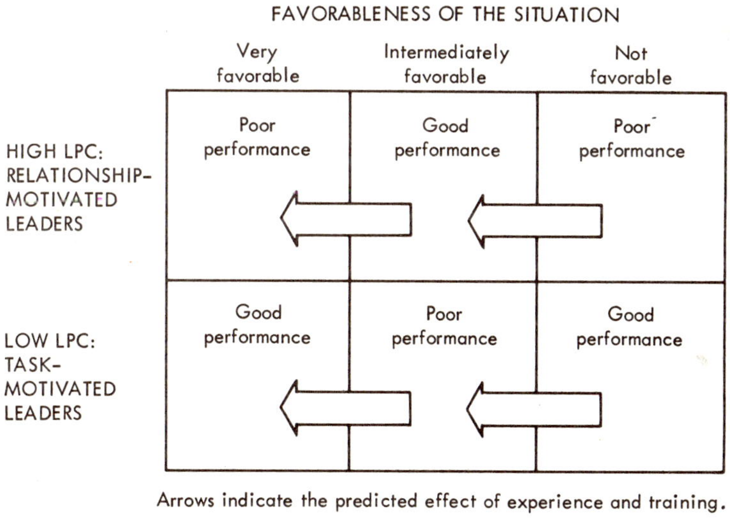

FIGURE 37. The Effect of Performance on Leaders with Different LPC Characteristics

intermediate in favorableness for the trained leader, the trained high LPC leader would perform better than the trained low LPC leader. This same situation would be unfavorable for the untrained leader; therefore, the untrained low LPC leader would perform better than the untrained high LPC leader.

The effect of experience on performance was studied by McNamara (1968) in an investigation of Canadian primary and secondary school principals. McNamara divided his principals into those with relatively little experience (less than 2-year tenure) and those with relatively high experience (more than 3-year tenure). Elementary principals in this sample had a rather favorable leadership situation. The schools were small, having five to seven teachers; the principal's position power was high: the job was relatively structured (everybody teaches from the same books); and elementary schools are not likely to present many crises that require difficult policy decisions. We would, therefore, expect that the leadership situation is favorable for the experienced principal but intermediate in favorableness for the new principal. Experienced low LPC principals should perform more effectively than experienced high LPC principals. Inexperienced high LPC principals should perform more effectively than inexperienced low LPC principals. This was indeed the case. The correlation between performance and LPC of experienced principals was -0.26 ($N = 77$, $p < 0.05$) and for inexperienced principals 0.35 ($N = 51$, $p < 0.01$).

The leadership situation of the secondary school principals should be more difficult. Although the position power is high, principals of these schools were in charge of thirty to forty teachers who were assigned to various departments. Secondary schools demand a large number of policy decisions, making the task relatively unstructured. We would, therefore, classify the situation as intermediate in favorableness for the experienced principal and as unfavorable for the principal with little experience on the job. The criterion of performance, in this case, was the average score of 11th grade students on a province-wide achievement test. As the model predicts, the established principals with high LPC performed better than those with low LPC (0.45, $N = 45$, $p < 0.01$) whereas among the new principals, the low LPC leaders were more effective ($-$ 0.48, $N = 19$, $p < 0.05$).

Figure 38 shows the average performance of high and low LPC principals in elementary and secondary schools. As the Contingency Model predicts, the inexperienced high LPC principals in elementary schools performed better than did the experienced principals. In secondary schools, the low LPC principals with little experience performed better than their more experienced colleagues with low LPC. Thus, the additional experience actually seemed to decrease the performance effectiveness of the leaders in the "wrong" octant of the model.

Our findings show that this is the case. A few studies are here briefly described. (For more extensive reports see Chemers, 1969; Fiedler, 1971; Fiedler and Csoka, 1971; Csoka and Fiedler, 1971).

Data from a study of small consumer cooperative companies (Godfrey *et al.*, 1959) were recently re-analyzed. These companies belonged to a statewide federation that provided carefully compiled data on company performance, based on the company's net income and operating efficiency. The leadership situation had been rated previously as relatively favorable. The

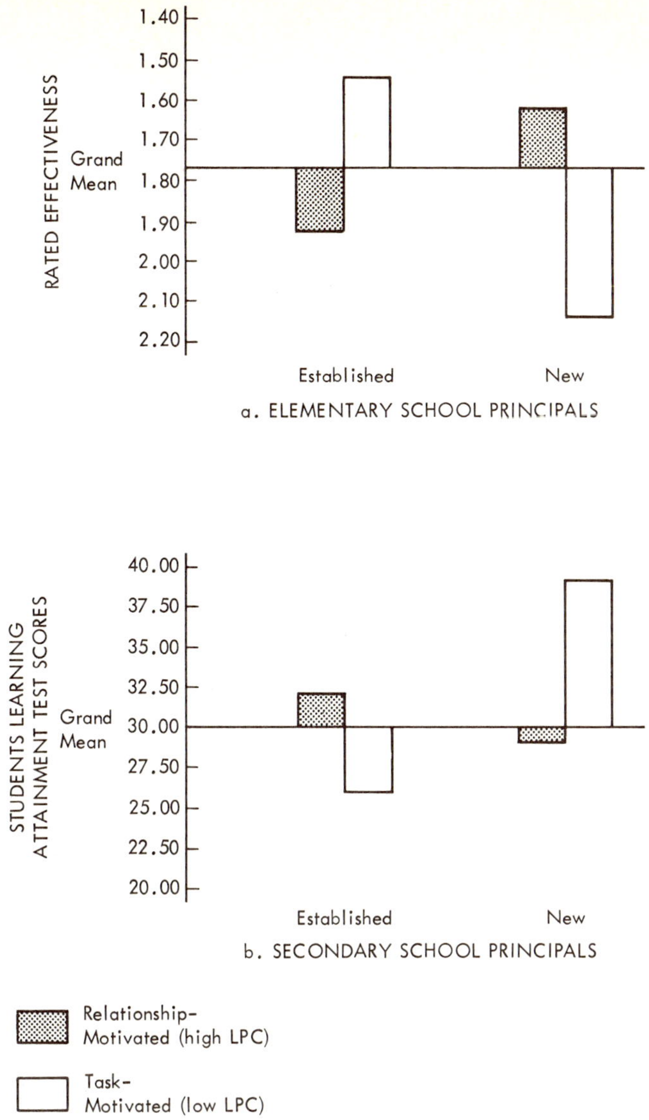

FIGURE 38. Average Performance of High and Low LPC Principals in Elementary and Secondary Schools

managers attended frequent training courses that were offered by the federation. Number of years with the company was, therefore, a measure of training as well as of experience. The managers were divided into those with relationship-motivated and task-motivated leadership patterns as well as into those with relatively high and relatively low number of years with the company. The results between experience and training with performance are shown on Figure 39. Here again, the findings conform to the predictions of the Contingency Model.

Finally, two recent studies (Csoka and Fiedler, 1971) specifically tested

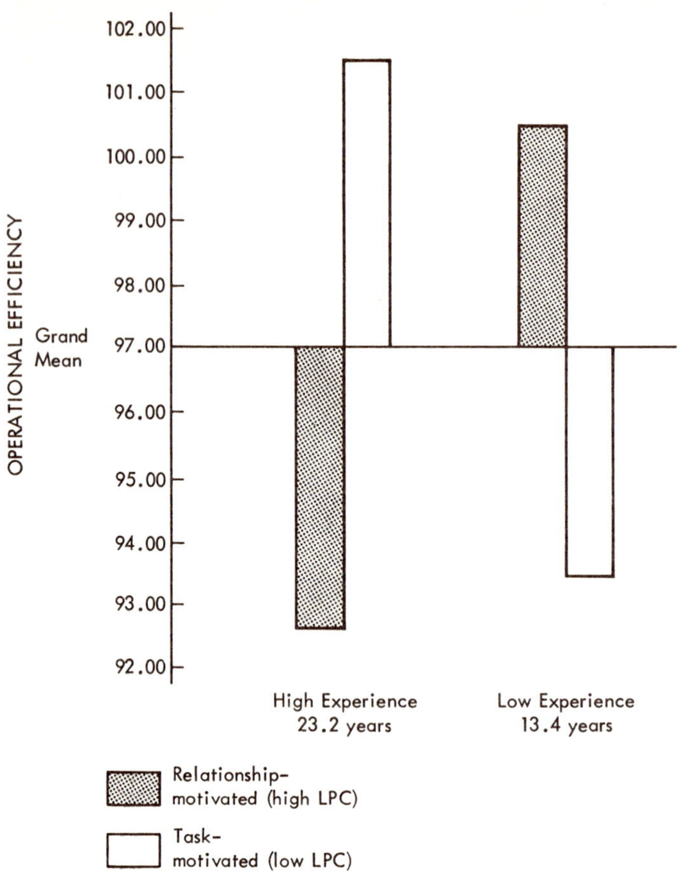

FIGURE 39. Comparison of Effectiveness (Operational Efficiency) of Experienced and Inexperienced Managers of Illinois Farm Supply Companies (N's = 5 each)

the prediction that leadership training and experience would benefit high and low LPC leaders differently, depending on the situation. These studies were conducted on section chiefs of a field artillery group as well as on supervisors of naval aviation maintenance shops. In these normally structured tasks, the Contingency Model would predict that the task-motivated (low LPC) leaders would perform more effectively in Octants 1 and 3 of the model, as well as in Octant 8, whereas relationship-motivated leaders should perform better in Octant 5 (see Figure 36). The task was defined as structured for leaders with a high degree of training, and as equivalent to unstructured for leaders with relatively little training. As can be seen in Figure 40, these hypotheses were supported. All predictions were statistically significant.

The finding that training and experience is detrimental for a substantial number of leaders may seem startling at first. On second thought, however, most executives are well aware of the fact that this may happen. The "overtrained" person who becomes sloppy, bored, and distinterested with his job is far from rare. And the individual who has his job so well in hand that he becomes arrogant and careless is also a familiar figure. These data simply support the notion that men require a job that fits their personality needs, be this for a quiet and predictable environment or the constant challenge of a soap-opera hero.

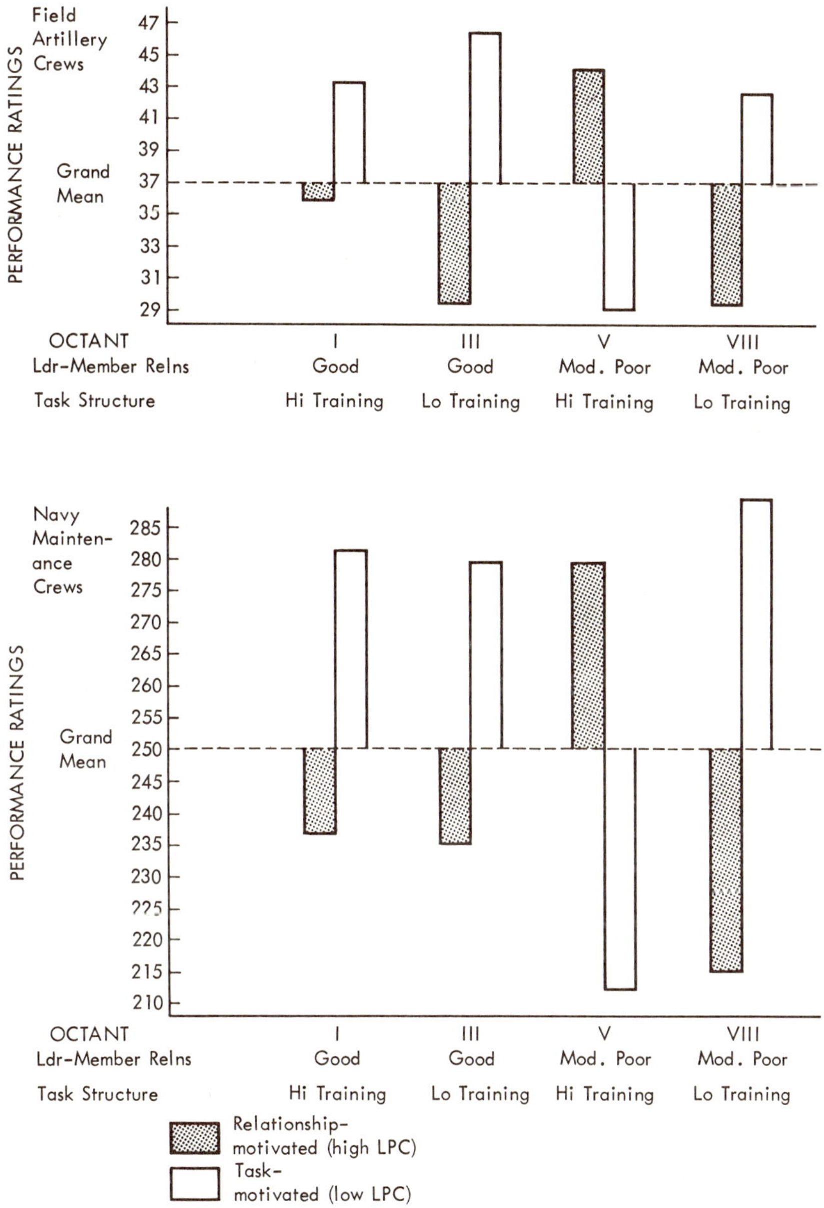

FIGURE 40. The Effects of Training Upon Leadership Performance in Tasks with Varying Degrees of Structure

Implications

The interpretation that leadership training and experience affect situational favorableness has major implications for the management of executive personnel as well as for understanding why previous methods of leadership training have yielded such dismal results. We shall briefly mention some of the changes in leadership training that these findings suggest.

The data very strongly suggest that the same training will have beneficial effects for some leaders and detrimental effects for others. It is essential, therefore, that we identify task-motivated and relationship-motivated leaders at some time in the training process. A number of alternatives are then open.

1. We can decide to give training only to some managers but not to others. This course of action is quite plausible, but might have some undesirable side effects. Specifically, being sent to training courses is frequently regarded as a reward, a symbol of success or as a forerunner of promotion. The manager who is excluded from such training courses may, therefore, feel that he has failed, or that he is being unjustly downgraded.

2. We may provide leadership training for all eligible managers, but subsequently assign certain managers to the jobs they had before, or to jobs of the same degree of situational favorableness, whereas we can assign the other managers to more challenging jobs that are lower in situational favorableness. This is probably the more appropriate course of action, as we see the problem at this time.

3. We have also seen that the effect of leadership experience has different consequences for high and for low LPC leaders. This suggests the fairly simple solution of rotating individuals with one motivational pattern more rapidly than those with the other motivational pattern. This allows some leaders to build up experience while others do not. This is, probably, the most effective and inexpensive method for providing certain types of training to management personnel.

SUGGESTIONS FOR FUTURE READING

ARGYRIS, C., *Integrating the Individual and the Organization* (New York: John Wiley & Sons, 1964).

BALES, R. F., *Interaction Process Analysis* (Reading, Massachusetts: Addison-Wesley, 1951).

BAVELAS, A., "A Mathematical Model for Group Structure," *Applied Anthropology*, Vol. 7 (1948), pp. 16–30.

BAVELAS, A., A. H. HASTORF, A. E. GROSS, and W. R. KITE, "Experiments on the Alteration of Group Structure," *Journal of Experimental and Social Psychology*, Vol. 1 (1965), pp. 55–70.

BISHOP, D. W., Relations between Tasks and Interpersonal Success and Group Member Adjustment. Unpublished M. A. Thesis, University of Illinois, 1964.

BLAKE, R. R., and J. S. MOUTON, *The Managerial Grid* (Houston: Gulf Publishing Co., 1964).

BRAY, D. W., and D. L. GRANT, "The Assessment Center in the Measurement of Potential for Business Management," *Psychological Monographs,* Vol. 80 (1966), p. 17.

CAMPBELL, D. T., "Common Fate, Similarity, and Other Indices of Aggregates of Persons as Social Entities," *Behavioral Science,* Vol. 3 (1958), pp. 14–25.

CAMPBELL, J. P., M. D. DUNNETTE, E. E. LAWLER III, AND K. E. WEICK, JR., *Managerial Behavior, Performance, and Effectiveness* (New York: McGraw-Hill Book Co., Inc., 1970).

CARTER, L. F., "Leadership and Small Group Behavior," in M. Sherif and M. O. Wilson (Eds.), *Group Relations at the Crossroads* (New York: Harper & Row, 1953).

CATTELL, R. B. "New Concepts for Measuring Leadership in Terms of Group Syntality," *Human Relations,* Vol. 46 (1951), pp. 589–595.

CHEMERS, M. M., "Cross-cultural Training as a Means for Improving Situational Favorableness," *Human Relations,* Vol. 22 (1969), pp. 531–546.

CHEMERS, M. M., and G. J. SKRZYPEK, "An Experimental Test of the Contingency Model of Leadership Effectiveness," *Journal of Personality and Social Psychology,* in press.

CLARK, R. A., "Leadership in Rifle Squads on the Korean Front Line." Human Resources Research Unit No. 2, CONARC, Fort Ord, California, 1955.

CSOKA, L. S., A Contingency Model Approach to Leadership Training and Leadership Experience. Unpublished M. A. Thesis, University of Washington, 1971.

CSOKA, L. S., and F. E. FIEDLER, "The Effect of Leadership Experience and Training in Structured Military Tasks—a Test of the Contingency Model" (Seattle: University of Washington Organizational Research, July, 1971).

DOMHOFF, G. W., *Who Rules America?* (Englewood Cliffs, N.J.: Prentice-Hall, Inc., 1967).

DUBIN, R., *Human Relations in Administration; the Sociology of Organization, With Readings and Cases* (New York: Prentice-Hall, Inc., 1951).

DUNNETTE, M. D., and J. P. CAMPBELL, "Laboratory Education: Impact on People and Organizations," *Industrial Relations,* Vol. 8 (1968), pp. 1–44.

FIEDLER, F. E., "The Influence of Leader-Keyman Relations on Combat Crew Effectiveness," *Journal of Abnormal and Social Psychology,* Vol. 51 (1955), pp. 227–235.

FIEDLER, F. E., "A Contingency Model of Leadership Effectiveness," in L. Berkowitz (Ed.), *Advances in Experimental Social Psychology,* Vol. I (New York: Academic Press, 1964), pp. 149–190.

FIEDLER, F. E., "The Effect of Leadership and Cultural Heterogeneity on Group Performance: A Test of the Contingency Model," *Journal of Experimental and Social Psychology,* Vol. 2 (1966), pp. 237–264.

FIEDLER, F. E., *A Theory of Leadership Effectiveness* (New York: McGraw-Hill Book Co., Inc., 1967).

FIEDLER, F. E., "Leadership Experience and Leader Performance—Another Hypothesis Shot to Hell," *Organizational Behavior and Human Performance,* Vol. 5 (1970), pp. 1–14.

FIEDLER, F. E., "Validation and Extension of the Contingency Model of Leadership Effectiveness: a Review of Empirical Findings," *Psychological Bulletin,* Vol. 76 (1971), pp. 128–148.

FIEDLER, F. E., "Personality, Motivation Systems, and Behavior of High and Low LPC Leaders," *Human Relations* (1972), in press.

FIEDLER, F. E., and M. M. CHEMERS, "Group Performance under Experienced and Inexperienced Leaders: a Validation Experiment." Group Effectiveness Research Laboratory Technical Report, University of Illinois, 1968.

FIEDLER, F. E., and L. S. CSOKA, "A Contingency Model Approach to Leadership Training." Proceedings of NATO Symposium, Brussels, August, 1971.

FIEDLER, F. E., G. E. O'BRIEN, and D. R. ILGEN, "The Effect of Leadership Style upon the Performance and Adjustment of Volunteer Teams Operating in a Stressful Foreign Environment," *Human Relations*, Vol. 22 (1966), pp. 503–514.

FLANAGAN, J. C., "Critical Requirements: a New Approach to Employee Evaluation," *Personnel Psychology*, Vol. 2 (1949), pp. 419–425.

FLEISHMAN, E. A., E. H. HARRIS, and H. E. BURTT, "Leadership and Supervision in Industry." Educational Research Monograph No. 33, Ohio State University. Columbus, Ohio, 1955.

GIBB, C. A., *Leadership* (London: Penguin Books, Chaucer Press, 1969).

GODFREY, ELEANOR P., F. E. FIEDLER, and D. M. HALL, *Boards, Managers, and Company Success* (Danville, Illinois: Interstate Press, 1959).

GOUGH, H. G., "A Leadership Index on the California Psychological Inventory," *Journal of Counseling Psychology*, Vol. 16 (1969), pp. 283–289.

HALPIN, A. W., "The Leader Behavior and Leadership Ideology of Educational Administrators and Aircraft Commanders," *Harvard Educational Review* (Winter 1955), pp. 18–32.

HALPIN, A. W., and B. J. WINER, *The Leadership Behavior of the Airplane Commander* (Columbus, Ohio: Ohio State University Research Foundation, 1952).

HEMPHILL, J. K., *Leader Behavior Description* (Columbus, Ohio: Ohio State University Personnel Research Board, 1950).

HEMPHILL, J. K., "A Proposed Theory of Leadership in Small Groups," *Second Preliminary Report* (Columbus, Ohio: Ohio State University, Personnel Research Board, 1954).

HEMPHILL, J. K., "Why People Attempt to Lead," in L. Petrullo and B. M. Bass (Eds.), *Leadership and Interpersonal Behavior* (New York: Holt, Rinehart and Winston, 1961), pp. 201–215.

HERSEY, P., and K. BLANCHARD,"Changing Patterns of Leadership," in *The Study of Leadership*, Vol. I (New York: U.S. Military Academy, 1970–1971).

HILL, W., "The Validation and Extension of Fiedler's Theory of Leadership Effectiveness," *Academy of Management Journal*, Vol. 12, No. 1 (March, 1969), pp. 33–47.

HOLLANDER, E. P., and W. B. WEBB, "Leadership, Followership and Friendship," *Journal of Abnormal and Social Psychology*, Vol. 50 (1955), pp. 163–167.

HOMANS, G. C., *The Human Group* (New York: Harcourt, Brace, 1950).

HOUSE, R. J., "T-group Education and Leadership Effectiveness: a Review of the Empiric Literature and a Critical Evaluation," *Personnel Psychology*, Vol. 20 (1967), pp. 1–32.

HOWELLS, L. T., and S. W. BECKER, "Seating Arrangement and Leadership Emergence," *Journal of Abnormal and Social Psychology*, Vol. 64 (1962), pp. 148–150.

HUNT, J. G., "Fiedler's Leadership Contingency Model: an Empirical Test in Three Organizations," *Organizational Behavior and Human Performance*, Vol. 2 (1967), pp. 290–308.

KATZ, D., and R. L. KAHN, *The Social Psychology of Organizations* (New York: John Wiley & Sons, 1966).

KIPNIS, DOROTHY M., "Interaction between Members of Bomber Crews as a Determinant of Sociometric Choice," *Human Relations*, Vol. 10 (1957), pp. 263–270.

LEAVITT, H. J., "Some Effects of Certain Communication Patterns of Group Performance," *Journal of Abnormal and Social Psychology*, Vol. 46 (1951), pp. 38–50.

MCCLINTOCK, C. G., "Group Support and the Behavior of Leaders and Nonleaders," *Journal of Abnormal and Social Psychology*, Vol. 67 (1963), pp. 105–113.

MCGREGOR, D., *The Human Side of Enterprise* (New York: McGraw-Hill Book Co., Inc., 1960).

MCNAMARA, V. D., *Leadership, Staff, and School Effectiveness*. Ph.D. Thesis, University of Alberta, Edmonton, Alberta, Canada, 1968.

MANN, F. C., "Toward an Understanding of the Leadership Role in Formal Organization," in R. Dubin, G. C. Homans, F. C. Mann, and D. C. Miller (Eds.), *Leadership and Productivity* (San Francisco: Chandler Publishing Co., 1965), pp. 68–103.

MANN, R. D., "A Review of the Relationships between Personality and Performance in Small Groups," *Psychological Bulletin*, Vol. 56 (1959), pp. 241–270.

MASLOW, A. H., "The Authoritarian Character Structure," *Journal of Social Psychology*, Vol. 18 (1943), pp. 401–411.

MITCHELL, T. R., "Leader Complexity and Leadership Style," *Journal of Personality and Social Psychology*, Vol. 16 (1970), pp. 166–174.

NEALEY, S. M., and F. E. FIEDLER, "Leadership Functions of Middle Managers," *Psychological Bulletin*, Vol. 70 (1968), pp. 313–329.

ODIORNE, G. S., "The Need for an Economic Approach to Training," *Journal of the American Society of Training Directors*, Vol. 18 (1964), pp. 3–12.

PRESTON, H. O., *The Development of a Procedure for Evaluating Officers in the U.S. Air Force* (Washington, D.C.: American Institute for Research, 1948).

SHIMA, H., "The Relationship between the Leader's Modes of Interpersonal Cognition and the Performance of the Group," *Japanese Psychological Research*, Vol. 10 (1968), pp. 13–30.

STEINZOR, B., "The Spatial Factor in Face-to-Face Discussion Groups," *Journal of Abnormal and Social Psychology*, Vol. 45 (1950), pp. 552–555.

STOGDILL, R., "Personal Factors Associated With Leadership: a Survey of the Literature," *Journal of Psychology*, Vol. 25 (1948), pp. 35–71.

TAYLOR, F. W., *The Principles of Scientific Management* (New York: Harper & Bros., 1911).

VOIERS, W. D., *Bombing Accuracy as a Function of the Group School Proficiency Structure of the B-29 Bomb Team* (San Antonio, Texas: Lackland Air Force Base, Air Force Personnel and Training Research Center, 1956).

WARNER, W. L., and J. C. ABEGGLEN, *Big Business Leaders in America* (New York: Harper & Row, 1955).

On Rediscovering the Leader

Eugene Emerson Jennings

Professor
Graduate School of Business Administration
Michigan State University

Leadership theory suffers from a defect —it does not represent leadership—not as historians define it and as leaders themselves practice it. Everything that Fiedler and Chemers summarize concerns management. If the reader substituted "manager" for "leader" in their report and presented the material before a seminar of executives, the audience would be none the wiser.

This fusion of leadership with management occurs partly because of the desire of early theorists to make a distinction between traditional (autocratic) management and what they believed was better management, which they called leadership. However, what was ideal management several decades ago has now become the norm that many executives attempt to practice. Meanwhile, the theorists have not rediscovered the essential difference between leadership and management and blindly perpetuate the myth that the two concepts are interchangeable. For centuries man has endowed leadership with special meaning. The manager arrived relatively lately on the scene of human debate and enterprise. The two ideas were never intended to be fused. Great leaders were seldom effective managers.

In the interest of rediscovering the essence of leadership, the author will draw on his insights acquired by studying the patterns of mobility of chief executives of our largest corporations, the positions through which they passed on the way to the top, and the experiences that they picked up along the route (Jennings, 1969, 1971). In addition to mobility auditing, the author has coached and counseled presidents and executives who experienced career crises (Jennings 1965, 1967). Both of these efforts have been underway since 1948 and represent continuing endeavors. He will take an historical view of corporate leadership.

The author wrote in 1960, "Ours is a society without leaders." He stated his honest observations about what seemed to be a decrease in the mystique of leadership and the number of presidents who embraced this mystique. A mystique is a framework of doctrines, ideas, and beliefs, or the like, constructed around a particular object or activity, endowing it with enhanced value or profound meaning. Thus, we speak of the mystique of science, or of the feminine mystique.

The author's work with company presidents and executives in the early fifties revealed to him that many of them had embraced this mystique of leadership and that few could be fully understood without exploring the extent to which they had attempted to ennoble their careers with the leadership mystique. The author cannot provide actual statistics, but the frequency with which he encountered this leadership mystique forced him to acknowledge it as a vital part of his counseling program.

Leadership had the most profound meaning to those chief executives who had changed drastically the character and direction of their corporations, or who were attempting to do so. To them, the leader was the vital force of change. He inherited an organization in a particular condition and he employed his resources and the resources of others to create an entirely different organization. To do this, the leader had to have an objective and a game plan.

The chief executive who embraced the mystique did not call his commitment to change an objective. He called it his mission. The leader had a vision of a future possibility to which he became committed. Hence, the vital aspect of the mystique was the heroic image. He saw himself as a man prepared to give his whole life and to sacrifice many pleasurable and worldly rewards to achieve his mission. Some of the missions of the chief executives that the author knew were to make nutritious cereal for every household, to electrify the whole nation, to produce arable land with inexpensive inorganic fertilizers, and so on. These missions were not cheap gimmicks. They were integrated with the ego and were expressed with the passion of a true believer.

Fiedler and Chemers report that leadership means power over people. But this generalization misses the mark. People who have power over others may not necessarily become change agents. The leader believes that power is a means to his noble mission. His purpose for climbing the ladder is to acquire the necessary resources, including power. Most men who emerge at the top do not yet have their missions in focus.

However, they privately believe that they were expected to become leaders when they emerged at the pinnacle. Leadership alone would justify the many personal and family sacrifices they had made to get to the top. Some took more time to find their mission and evolve their dedication than others. Some never did really acquire a vision and spent most of their tenure attempting to find it.

The seekers of their mission were most often extremely frustrated. They were under self-induced stress because they had embraced the leadership mystique early in life or in their careers. Then, our culture more uniformly embraced the mystique. Children were raised to believe that men at the top were extraordinary men—or they should be—who took in their own hands the responsibility of doing great and beneficial things for their world. Leaders enhanced the value and meaning of life for all those who were touched by their efforts. To be just an executive who maintained the essential organization as he inherited it was a sign of failure. The purpose of placing vast powers at the top was to allow the chief executive to move the organization in a direction it was not going nor would probably not go. Each president who embraced the mystique looked forward to some day becoming recognized as the man who showed others the way to progress and greater happiness. Thus, we had few managers and many aspiring heroes.

The successful implementation of the leadership mystique required more than a sense of mission and a realistic acquisition of power. The presidents who moved their organizations the most uniformly revealed that several times they almost had given up their causes. Few leaders escaped the agony of reappraisal. Visions of the type that the author found in the early fifties were obstructed by all kinds of hostile forces, including stockholder groups, bankers, competitors, financial restrictions, and inertia within the firm itself that sent it along its merry way despite the leader's thrust.

The author does not know of one leader who did not have to finally face his own self doubt. The loneliness, isolation, and the trials of testing his commitment produced an integration of the ego with the mission. From this period of testing the leader emerged with a third quality—a will to persevere against a discourteous, unbelieving world of sometimes total opposition. Without the courage of their convictions, their missions failed. No doubt there was more to their leadership, but these three aspects were common and vital—a sense of mission, a capacity for power, a will to survive and persevere.

Near the end of the sixties, the author noticed that few chief executives embraced the leadership mystique. The principal concern of presidents was maintaining and enhancing a viable organization. They were managers, not leaders, in aspiration and capability. The leader was dedicated to using the corporation to produce a culturally beneficial breakthrough. The manager was concerned with building an effective, profitable, well-functioning organization.

Hence, the manager talked about what Dubin, Hemphill, Cattell, Stodgill, and Fiedler report. They conceived of themselves as problem-solvers, decision-makers, motivators of people, arbitrators of conflict. The array of definitions was seemingly infinite and depended more on their corporate experiences than their sense of history and of the world in which they lived. It was obvious that they were hard-headed realists, men of narrow focus, of limited vision. Few arrived at the top with the makeup to become cultural heroes.

For some time the mystique of leadership had been on a collision course with the reality of the corporate organization. It seemed only a matter of time before the mystique would become virtually extinct. The managers first arrived at the top in the corporations that practiced mobility. In the early fifties only a few corporations utilized geographical and hierarchical mobility to compress time and experience and produce younger, more skillful practitioners of management.

Mobility spread like a brush fire. Many of the executives who normally would have been selected for top jobs were bypassed by the mobile types. Mobile executives moved from job to job with specific projects or assignments that organized their time and energies, and disciplined their minds to the immediate and the clearly possible. No room for vision here. Long-range planning converted presidents into project types who, on completing their objectives, turned their batons over to the next guy behind them in this endless relay race. Presidents stayed on for 5 years on the average and were carefully matched to the specific objective spelled out by the master plan and to how well they could fit into the existing team. They were the contingency managers.

Seldom did presidents provide the chief input for their long-range plans. The input came from specialists and research programs in marketing, finance, and social-cultural forces. Also, the corporation next discovered the financial type and these men of determinate minds moved into the executive suite. Then, also, came profit-centered management and later management by objectives. The bottom line, the equity debt ratio, the price-earning ratio, and the setting of specific objectives that were realistic and entirely possible dulled the spirit of leadership.

But foremost of these forces inimical to the mystique of leadership was the total systematization of the corporate organization. The many systems of gathering, analyzing, and reporting information, when imbedded into the rigid rules, regulations, and policies of bureaucracy ground young impulsive minds into formidable realists. The possible became that which was clearly evident. Men trained on mobility, nourished on objectives, and secure with only the real, could not and did not dream. The author observed many times how the man with the facts beat out the man with a profound vision. More often than not, the realist made the dreamer look ridiculous.

The author realized with anguish that mobility was a duplicit device that could stamp out imagination while it developed tough-minded realism. He also gained the perspective of what traditional, immobile management did to the aspirants to the top. Although it did not necessarily motivate men to excel in tasks and interpersonal skills, neither did it extinguish the mystique of leadership. The mystique often acquired early in life remained untouched and dormant during the long, slow haul to the top. As a man neared the top, this urge to commit corporate power to heroic purposes was still available. But mobility in a maze of systematic routines and near-sighted objectives bred mobile maze runners. Vision, imagination, risk, and dreaming were directly confronted and largely extinguished.

During the sixties the economy grew more than in the preceding 50 years. This unprecedented and largely unheralded growth cycle put the finishing touches to the leadership mystique. Mobility became all the more widespread. Many managers did not stay in a position long enough to finish their tasks and left messes for the next guy to clean up. In many corporations, managers had to work at making mistakes or looking bad. There were so many opportunities to look good in this growth period that the mobile manager seized upon those that promised the highest, most immediate payoffs. No vision needed here.

Men with fast track records in greater numbers than ever emerged at the top to continue their exploitation of the self-evident. By 1969, when Nixon administered the recession to preserve the value of the dollar, many corporations had become thoroughly hypnotized by their spectacular successes. Many chief executives reported to the author that they had the best management team in the history of the company.

And then the thud of the recession. Corporations had to move from a growth strategy to a shrink strategy. They cut back the human, financial, and technical resources to achieve the lean, trim look necessary to weather a tight economy. Corporations soon discovered that many of the fast track managers knew little about managing non-growth. They knew more about how to invest than to divest, how to increase than decrease, how to exploit than to economize.

The recession became a managerial catastrophe. The author recorded that twice as many managers were put into the streets to look for new jobs during the 1969–70 recession than in the 1958–59 years. Corporations became uptight. Suddenly there was a shortage of good managers who could get more out of the system while putting less into it, who could motivate without resources to promote or increase salary. They rediscovered the manager who was stable, efficient, and dependable. If there were any hope for the few heroic types left by then, their chances were dashed on the rocks of a shrinking economy.

While pausing to rediscover a firm basis on which to build anew, the strange forces of another new world began to set in: consumerism, pollution, fair employment, minority laws, women's rights. Before corporations could rebound, the awareness of these powerful non-marketing forces bombarding the firm had stayed the hand of many a chief executive. For the first time in history, businessmen were being asked to provide both profitable goods and services and to clean up our world—make it more human and humane. The awesome uncertainties of the seventies, and the broad asset base of the large corporation, would seem to be the necessary condition for the reappearance of the heroic leader. Uncertainties represent possibilities and assets represent power. By the way, the managerial mind will see uncertainties as a risk and assets as constraints.

But where are the leaders? How many of our business chiefs speak with the authority of a man on a mission. Where have all the leaders gone? More important, will they return to lead the nation and their competitive rivals to the new world of quality life? And what has become of the mystique of leadership. Lindbergh was a hero to his generation, the astronauts were simply ordinary, well-trained technicians to the children of the sixties. Since Franklin Roosevelt there has been only one president in the author's opinion that embraced the mystique of leadership. He was Jack Kennedy. He had not yet been tested, his mission was still uncertain, his ability to acquire and exercise dominance over his friends and enemies had not yet been finely honed. But he had the style of a hero. In contrast is Richard Nixon, who has many of the important qualities of a manager.

Ours is an anti-heroic society. The children are for the most part without heroes. Vietnam has produced few heroes. Television has made politicians more real than imaginable. Science has destroyed mystery and its own mystique. The mystique of progress has become for many the road to human depravity. And change has lost its own mystique of automatic benevolence. Hence, our disrespect for leadership.

However, the picture is not entirely bleak. For the first time our nation has a core of young men and women who substantially changed the life of the university, of the community, of society. They gained early in life the courage and skill of street fighters. Many of them experienced the feeling and commitment of self sacrifice, of vision, and of power. With premature wisdom they now are making their way into politics, government, business, and civic organizations. They are taking their law and medical degrees into the ghetto. They are building new thought patterns, new ideals, and values. A few see so very clearly the silent opportunities into which they can direct their energies and talents. To the author they represent the front of a new age of leadership.

But many do not see their opportunities to lead. The author's study of early arrival managers is still underway and is not ready for systematic evaluation. However, he has realized that early arrival managers (men in their late twenties to middle thirties who earn more than $30,000 salary) often display a desire to be something more important than managers. In seminars these early arrival managers find the information comparable to that compiled by Fiedler and Chemers to be interesting, useful, if not necessary. But in their private moments many will seek advice from the author about a larger, deeper concern. Succinctly put, it is, "I want to do more than just manufacture or market autos, or typewriters, or computers, or what have you. I want to see if business can't solve some of the real problems of today's world." They want to be more than effective. They want to endow their lives with a heroic purpose and they want to believe that their business experience can become a force for meaningful change. What they lack is a vision and the courage to implement it by whatever means necessary. They feel powerless because of the limitations placed on them by their managerial responsibilities.

In this growing concern of young managers we can see the general outlines of the mystique of leadership—the use of the powers of organization for human benefit. This concern to ennoble their lives illustrates what leadership is really about and how presently constituted corporate organizations lay a deadening hand on such heroism. Perhaps the mystique of leadership will through our young people become once again the vital center of human aspiration. Perhaps they who are successful or unsuccessful in their attempts to change our world for the better will instill in their children the essence of heroism.

The author's major criticism of leadership theory and research is that both miss the vital essence—leadership. Most, if not all, of these efforts constitute the study of managers, and are indeed useful and relevant to men with limited resources and opportunities to produce predictable results. However, their generalizations afford little insight into the plight of these concerned early arrival managers.

Also, the author finds little help from leadership theory to explain and understand Thomas Watson, Jr., of IBM who envisioned the future of the computer as few others did and built an organization that reaches today into every sector of our society. IBM is probably the most crucial corporation in our nation, having replaced General Motors and General Electric. Nor will such leadership theory be of substantial help in understanding Harold Geneen of ITT, whose mission is to build an organization of such a multinational capability that it can survive every economic crisis save a total worldwide catastrophe. Watch leaders of this cast struggle, sacrifice, apply leverage, dominate, and fulfill the demands of the mystique of leadership. Watch leaders employ managers, transform them into true believers (Patterson of United), or watch other leaders struggle to reach disbelieving managers and fail to engage their important skills (Trippe of Pan Am). Watch leaders and managers struggle to perform in the same arena their important functions.

Only when research attempts to capture the motives and spirit of men who change completely the character and direction of their organizations and thereby grossly change the world about them will we understand the essence of leadership. The author believes that a measure of the intent to which the mystique of leadership is dormant or dead may be gauged by the degree leadership has been confused with management. The generalizations by leadership theorists represent middle management psychology at best and middle management manipulation at worst. Such information has the capability of fitting the manager to the corporate organization more than helping him to discover and embrace the mystique of leadership.

The author is also critical of the Contingency Model. As early as the Romans, some men believed that leadership was a marriage between the man and his times. But to make such a marriage work was to court disaster. The author fears that faulty, permanent stereotyping will be the result. For example, once the child is discovered to have a reading problem, he is put in a group of children with reading problems. He does not solve his reading problem but he is not anxious either. Likewise, the problem is that the manager seldom exceeds the norm when he is well matched with his group and learning situation.

The author has personal experience with the problem of stereotyping. He has seen many a manager become classified as task-oriented and precluded from the higher position requiring relationship skills because others with these skills were deemed less risky. He would like to suggest that some of our greatest corporate leaders had horrible human relationships. And may he point out that a task manager who has the right of co-option can overcome his human relations problems by his choice of crucial subordinates. It is done every day by leaders who are courageous enough not to let the situation dictate their purposes and missions.

There are less costly and less dangerous ways than those depicted by the contingency theory to breed flexible managers. In today's world, situations change rapidly as do information, people, and organizations. To make the Contingency Model work, mobility will have to be utilized. But mobility produces a high degree of flexibility in the first place. And flexibility to move among changing situations precludes the need for the Contingency Model. The author can attest to the superior flexibility of mobile managers. Although more flexibility is still desirable, the need for creative solutions and pioneering programs and a corporate environment that will make power available for their implementation are indeed more critical kinds of needs.

For that matter, a rethinking is needed by leadership theorists about whether corporate enterprise of the scale and complexity that we know today has outlived its usefulness. No doubt that if and when a new model of human enterprise appears, it will be the workings of a visionary with the courage of a hero. The author hopes that leadership theorists will not be still engrossed in contingency mazes.

Or to put it more positively, leadership research might better concern itself with causes and conditions favoring the emergence of leaders by studying them and their corporate environments both present and antecedent. Our society needs to know what and how the various institutions and organizations contribute to the development of heroic leadership. Meanwhile, Fiedler and Chemers have done an excellent job of presenting the essential ingredients of managerial effectiveness. They do not need the mystique of leadership (or the use of the word) to endow their work with special value and profound meaning. The theorist needs to regain his sense of leadership.

SUGGESTIONS FOR FUTURE READING

JENNINGS, EUGENE E., *The Mobile Manager* (Ann Arbor, Michigan: University of Michigan, Bureau of Industrial Relations, 1969).

JENNINGS, EUGENE E., *Routes to the Executive Suite* (New York: McGraw-Hill Book Co., Inc., 1971).

JENNINGS, EUGENE E., *The Executive in Crisis* (East Lansing, Michigan: Michigan State University, Bureau of Business and Economic Relations, 1965).

JENNINGS, EUGENE E., *Executive Success* (New York: Appleton-Century-Crofts, 1967).

JENNINGS, EUGENE E., *Anatomy of Leadership* (New York: Harper & Row, 1960).

The Search for a Theory of Leadership

Victor H. Vroom

Professor
Yale University

The potential importance to society of an adequate understanding of the leadership process cannot be underestimated. Any knowledge that the behavioral sciences could contribute to the identification and enhancement of leadership in organized human endeavor could be of considerable value in increasing the effectiveness of the organizations in society.

For many years, the research that has been conducted on the topic of leadership was purely of academic interest and had little if any impact on the day-to-day workings of organizations. There are some recent indications that the situation is now changing. Contributions ranging from the new profession of organization development (Bennis, 1969) to the technology of assessment centers (Bray and Grant, 1966) show promise of contributing to the effectiveness of organizational leadership. More elusive, however, has been the formulation of a theory of leadership. Such a theory should be consistent not only with the vast amount of research that has been conducted on leadership but also with general knowledge of the processes that govern the behavior of individuals and of organizations. If a general theory of leadership could be developed, it could constitute a firm foundation for enhancing leadership in organizations.

Search for a theory of this kind within the behavioral sciences has been filled with false starts, based on erroneous and oversimplified conceptions. One of the false starts stemmed from a conception of leadership as a general personality trait—i.e., a single quality that people possess in different amounts. If reliable and valid measures of this trait could be developed, they could be used in selecting people for leadership positions. However, as Fiedler has correctly pointed out in his chapter, the search for traits that distinguish leaders from followers or effective leaders from ineffective ones has been unsuccessful. His conclusion and the conclusions of most other people who have examined the evidence is that the relationships between traits and leadership varies markedly with the situation. The question, Who will be the best leader? is akin to asking, What will be the best fishing bait?. Neither question can be adequately answered as stated.

In retrospect, this conclusion is not surprising. In fact, it would be surprising to find that the nature of the group or organization, its prevalent norms and values and the critical problems it faces in its relation to its own environment, have nothing to do with the kinds of people elevated to leadership status or with those who prove to be effective in carrying out their leadership roles.

If there are no stable or invariant

personality characteristics that distinguish leaders from non-leaders or effective leaders from less effective ones, it is still possible that there are methods or styles of leadership that are more effective than others. A second approach, which also could be termed "a false start," involved looking not at the personality of the effective leader but at the way in which he behaves in carrying out his leadership role. It assumed that there were stable behavioral correlates of effective leadership. Research based on such an assumption was directed toward answering such questions as, How do leaders of effective groups behave in their leadership role that distinguishes them from leaders who are less effective?. Are they autocratic or democratic in their leadership style? Do they exhibit more initiative or more consideration than those who are less effective?

If simple answers to such questions could be obtained, they could point to ways to be an effective leader or, at least, provide a sound empirical foundation for leadership training. But once again answers were not simple. The Ohio State studies that Fiedler cites and another parallel set of studies conducted at the University of Michigan had limited success in identifying consistent correlations between patterns of leadership behavior and measures of group performance or effectiveness.

One conclusion that can be drawn from all this research is that the problems were more complicated than was originally expected. For example, it became clear that the situation was an overlooked source of influence. Initiative and other measures of leadership behavior were associated with group effectiveness in some situations but not in others. However, to conclude that "issues are complex" or that "it depends on the situation" is merely to indicate a further direction for research rather than a specific testable solution to society's need for effective leadership.

Fiedler and his Contingency Model represent one approach to this problem. In a sense, his theory is an outgrowth of the search for personality characteristics that are associated with leadership, since the measure that he employs, LPC, is a simple psychological test and its relationship to leadership behavior is a matter of some uncertainty (Graen, Orris, and Alvares, 1971). However, unlike the earlier work stemming from a conception of leadership as a personality variable, his work and that of his associates involves an attempt to classify situations and determine those in which there were positive and negative relationships between LPC and group performance.

The search process employed by Fiedler and his associates was inductive and empirical rather than theoretical and deductive. The system of octants was based on empirical results showing wide variance in the correlations that have been obtained between LPC and group performance. As the reader can see in Figure 36 in his paper, the ability of the octant system (which Fiedler terms the favorableness of the situation) to account for these differences is very high. There is, however, some controversy concerning the capacity of the theory to account for data collected subsequent to its formulation. (Graen, Alvares, Orris and Martella, 1970).

There are other empirical facts concerning leadership that are more difficult to integrate with the Contingency Model. Fiedler challenges the common notion that leaders change their behavior depending on the situation. In the view of this writer, his position stems more from the difficulty of incorporating such behavioral changes within the basic framework he has adopted rather than consideration of the evidence. Lewin's classic dictum (1951) that behavior is a function of both personal and environmental properties appears no less applicable to leadership behavior than to behavior in other settings. The situation or environment not only influences the consequences of a given pattern of leadership behavior but also plays an important role in determining that behavior. A number of recent studies have shown that certain aspects of leadership behavior previously regarded as stable elements of leadership style vary markedly with the situation. Lowin and Craig (1968) have shown that leaders exhibit less consideration, more initiative, and much closer supervision toward subordinates who are low in performance than toward those who are high in performance. In a more recent study Heller (1971) has found that the extent to which leaders share power with their subordinates varies with the kind of decision being made. For example, managers are more likely to share power in decisions affecting a subordinate's employees than in decisions affecting the subordinate himself.

Vroom and Yetton have made what appears to be a different assumption from Fiedler's—that leaders can and do vary their behavior with the demands of the situation. They distinguish between normative models of leadership that purport to prescribe behavior for different classes of situations and descriptive models that attempt to predict how leaders will behave in different classes of situations. In one paper (Vroom and Yetton, 1971) they introduce a taxonomy of leadership styles varying in the extent to which the leader provides his subordinates with an opportunity to participate in making decisions. Five leadership styles are described, ranging from autocratic, in which the leader makes the decision by himself and issues an order to his subordinates, to group decision-making, in which the leader serves as chairman of a meeting aimed at reaching consensus on the course of action to be taken. A normative model is presented that is purported to be consistent with research evidence concerning the consequences of participation. It represents a method for analyzing the properties of the problem to be solved to determine how involved subordinates should be in its solution, if at all.

A subsequent paper (Vroom and Yetton, 1972) deals with descriptive models of leadership behavior. The questions addressed concern the factors in the situation, in the personality of the leader, and in their interrelationship, which influence the extent to which leaders provide their subordinates with an opportunity to participate in decision-making. The evidence is overwhelming that leaders do vary their behavior with the situation, although the manner in which they do so varies from one leader to another.

This program of research suggests an alternative to Fiedler's conceptualization of leadership behavior. Instead of attempting to account for differences among leaders in terms of a single personality variable such as LPC, it relates these differences to programs or decision rules that leaders employ in attempting to fit their actions to the various situations that they encounter. Expressed in this way, a program for selecting and placing leaders requires matching the programs or decision rules employed by an individual to those required by his role. Similarly, a program for leadership training would involve modifying or developing such programs to better fit the critical tasks that the leader's role entails.

The issue of leadership training is also difficult to handle with the Contingency Model. LPC and the behavior patterns that it is assumed to represent are assumed to be stable leadership characteristics and consequently unmodifiable by training. If training is to have any effects, a matter about which Fiedler expresses some doubt, it must be through modifying the favorableness of the situation. This formulation appears awkward and sidesteps such issues as differences in methods and objectives of training and their appropriateness to different leaders and situations.

Fiedler's Contingency Model represents an ambitious and interesting effort to go beyond the correct but vacuous statement that, "Leadership depends on the situation" and shows on what properties of situations and of persons the phenomenon of leadership depends. To be sure, the theory is crude in its present form and the practical implications are, at this point, matters of considerable uncertainty. Like most pioneering efforts, it will undoubtedly be shown to be incorrect in detail if not in substance. If it survives the test of future research, it could prove to be a valuable aid in placing leaders in situations that match their personal qualities and, in addition, provide some rough guidelines for engineering the job to fit the leader. If the Contingency Model does not pass that test, we will have but one more indication of the complexity of the processes on which a theory of leadership must ultimately be founded.

SUGGESTIONS FOR FUTURE READING

BENNIS, W. G., *Organization Development: Its Nature Origins and Prospects* (Reading, Massachusetts: Addison–Wesley, 1969).

BRAY, D. W., and D. L. GRANT, "The Assessment Center in the Measurement of Potential for Business Management," *Psychological Monographs,* Vol. 80, No. 625, entire (1966).

GRAEN, G., J. B. ORRIS, and K. M. ALVARES, "The Contingency Model of Leadership Effectiveness: Some Experimental Results," *Journal of Applied Psychology,* Vol. 55 (1971), pp. 196–204.

GRAEN, G., K. ALVARES, J. B. ORRIS, and J. A. MARTELLA, "Contingency Model of Leadership Effectiveness: Antecedent and Evidential Results," *Psychological Bulletin,* Vol. 74 (1970), pp. 285–296.

HELLER, F. A., *Managerial Decision-Making* (London: Tavistock Publishers, 1971).

LEWIN, K., "Frontiers in Group Dynamics," in D. Cartwright (Ed.), *Field Theory in Social Science* (New York: Harper & Bros., 1951), pp. 188–237.

LOWIN, A., and J. R. CRAIG, "The Influence of Level of Performance on Managerial Style: An Experimental Object-Lesson in the Ambiguity of Correlational Data," *Organizational Behavior and Human Performance,* Vol. 3 (1968), pp. 440–458.

VROOM, V. H., and P. W. YETTON, Leadership and Decision-Making. Unpublished Manuscript, W.P. 42–71–2. Carnegie-Mellon University Graduate School of Industrial Administration, November, 1971.

VROOM, V. H., and P. W. YETTON, Some Descriptive Studies of Participation in Decision-Making. Unpublished Manuscript, W.P. 75–72–1. Carnegie-Mellon University Graduate School of Industrial Administration, February 1972.

DISCUSSION QUESTIONS

1. After reading this chapter and the critiques, what is leadership? Discuss alternate definitions.
2. In the light of your own experience, reflect on leaders you have known personally. How did they become leaders?
3. Do leaders typically possess certain personality traits? Give arguments pro and con, and give examples of such traits.
4. Must executives be leaders? Should executives be leaders? What is the difference between a manager and a leader?
5. What is expected of a leader? Of followers?
6. Is there any empirical evidence that one leadership approach is consistently better than another? What are these approaches? Do you intuitively believe that one is better than another?
7. Describe and discuss the Contingency Model of leadership.
8. What is the mystique of leadership?

14

Power, Influence and Authority

Joseph A. Pichler

Associate Professor
School of Business
University of Kansas

> From this arises the question whether it is better to be loved more than feared, or feared more than loved. The reply is, that one ought to be both feared and loved, but as it is difficult for the two to go together, it is much safer to be feared than loved, if one of the two has to be wanting.
>
> Niccolo Machiavelli

INTRODUCTION

Much of history is explainable in terms of man's drive to control his physical and social environment.[1] This motivation has been directed toward myriad goals—some noble and creative, others brutal and destructive. It has led scholars to grope for the laws that govern this universe and has driven conquistadors to obliterate alien cultures in order to extend the limits of their own. The acquisition of control over any resource is generally accompanied by rewards that are both physical and psychological. These are especially great when the resource is human. For this reason, there is a particular fascination about the study of processes by which interpersonal power is attained and exercised.

This chapter begins with a definition of social power and a discussion

[1]The author expresses his appreciation to Professor F. Douglas Tuggle and Professor Howard Baumgartel, both of the University of Kansas, for their comments on an earlier draft, and to Mr. Clinton Richards and Mrs. Sara Wallace for their research assistance.

of the processes by which it is exerted. Particular emphasis is placed on power relationships that are characterized by interaction between two or more parties. A theoretical model is used to analyze the conditions that generate and limit such interactive power. The second section explores various dimensions of power processes that refine or qualify conclusions that were deduced from the model. The third and fourth segments consider two forms of power—influence and authority—in terms of the framework and concepts introduced in the first half of the chapter. The discussion of both power forms is supported by frequent references to empirical research regarding specific sources of power and the effects of its exercise. The final section provides an overview of the chapter's key elements by considering their implications for managerial behavior.

SOCIAL POWER

The concept of social power may be defined in a variety of ways, so as to focus particular attention on one or another facet of the underlying relationship.[2] The term will be used here to mean "individual or collective ability to affect the thoughts, emotions, or actions of one or more other persons." Several implications of this particular definition should be pointed out. First, it does not require that one party *intend* to affect another, but only that the effect occurs.[3] Second, the definition contains an implicit test for the existence of power: differences in the response of one party to two stimulus situations that differ only by the perceived presence of a second party indicate that the second possesses social power. This formulation includes a broad range of behavioral changes, such as learning, which are excluded by many authors. Third, power may reside in more than one party within a given relationship. Indeed, some degree of power may be simultaneously exercised by every party. For example, bilateral monopoly implies balanced power dictated by the unavailability of alternative exchange partners to both the seller and the buyer. Finally, there is no requirement that any party *resist* the exercise of power by another. Although the idea of resistance is central to other definitions of power,[4] it is excluded here to permit the discussion of relationships in which one party willingly subjugates himself in order that his behavior might be changed. This would include, for example, apprentice relationships wherein a worker temporarily binds himself by contract to an employer (plus a union in many instances) in order to learn a trade.

The processes by which power is exerted may be divided into two categories: interactive and non-interactive. Non-interactive processes consist of one-way communications from the power-wielder to the party whose

[2]Robert L. Peabody, *Organizational Authority: Superior-Subordinate Relationships in Three Public Service Organizations* (New York: Atherton Press, 1964), p. 5.

[3]The term "party" will be used throughout this chapter to include groups as well as individuals.

[4]Max Weber, *The Theory of Social and Economic Organization*, translated by A. M. Henderson and Talcott Parsons (New York: The Free Press; London: Collier-Macmillan Limited [1947]), p. 152; and Richard M. Emerson, "Power-Dependence Relations," *American Sociological Review*, Vol. 27 (1962), p. 32.

behavior is affected.[5] One party sends a communication to the other but receives none in return. It is not necessary that the "message" be intentionally sent or that the power-wielder even be aware of the other's existence. Included in this category are the writings, speech, and actions of one party that are read, heard, or observed by another, and that produce some effect on the second party's behavior. Non-interactive power may be subdivided into referent power and expert power.[6] Consider two parties, *X* and *Y*. The measure of *X's* referent power over *Y* consists of the degree to which *Y's* behavior is modified because of his "feeling of oneness" with *X* or his desire for such a feeling.[7] Specifically, this desire causes *Y* to behave in the way that he believes *X* would act under the same circumstances, to associate with or feel positively toward those objects or persons that give him some identity with *X*, and to reject that which he believes *X* would reject.[8] The tendency of youngsters to mimic the mannerisms of television heroes provides a common illustration of referent power. The imitative behavior, triggered by a one-way communication, enables the youthful viewer to identify with and vicariously partake of the heroes' exploits. Expert power consists of *X's* ability to affect *Y's* behavior because of *Y's* belief that *X* possesses special knowledge and competence in a given area. This belief may be based on reputation or demonstrated evidence that *X* is indeed an expert whose behavioral prescriptions should be heeded. Expert power may be exerted through a variety of non-interactive media such as books, lectures, and film.

The principal concern of this chapter will be with power that is exerted through interactions between two or more parties. Interaction exists when all parties send and receive communications. The concept of "social exchange" is essential to the analysis of interactive power. Blau postulates that individuals enter a social relationship because they expect to obtain rewards that are either intrinsic (inherent in the very act of association; e.g., companionship) or extrinsic (all other possible rewards; e.g., money).[9] Each party has such prior expectations, and the relationship will be maintained only if it proves to be *mutually* satisfying. That is, there must be a continued "social exchange" of rewards consistent with both parties' expectations if the association is to remain stable. In order for one party to provide rewards for others, he must command some type of resource. "Resource" is used in its broadest sense to include personal characteristics, physical objects, and access to social networks that can be used in a manner that will satisfy the needs of others.[10] It is important to keep in

[5]Throughout this chapter, behavior will be used in its broadest sense to include thoughts, emotions, and actions.

[6]These categories were devised by John R. P. French, Jr., and Bertram Raven, "The Bases of Social Power," in *Studies in Social Power*, Dorwin Cartwright (Ed.) (Ann Arbor: University of Michigan Research Center for Group Dynamics, Institute for Social Research, 1959), pp. 161–165.

[7]*Ibid.*, p. 161.

[8]For a rigorous analysis of the conditions that produce such "balanced" attitudinal relationships, see Fritz Heider, "Attitudes and Cognitive Organizations," *Journal of Psychology*, Vol. 21 (1946), pp. 107–112.

[9]Peter M. Blau, *Exchange and Power in Social Life* (New York: John Wiley & Sons, 1964), pp. 19–20.

[10]Notice that expert and referent power are also based on resource ownership and that these resources may be used in interactive as well as in non-interactive power processes.

mind that the designation of some property as a "resource" *and* its valuation in terms of satisfaction potential is made by possible exchange partners rather than by the owner himself. The sum of the resources commanded by a party may be thought of as a capital stock that can be invested or consumed to yield a rate of return. Investment alternatives consist of the various social exchanges that might be entered, and the returns to capital are the rewards obtained through these transactions. Each party attempts to satisfy his needs by inducing others to allocate their resources in a certain way. The inducement takes the form of a reciprocal allocative offer. For example, firms induce employees to allocate their skills, strength, and time in specified ways by offering monetary resources in exchange. Interactive power is exercised whenever one party successfully induces another to allocate resources in a manner that rewards the first party.

Although a party can possess power only if he commands resources valued by others, it does not follow that his power over another is measured by simply summing the reward value of the resources at his command. The measurement of power requires that the rewards available to the second party from *alternative* exchanges also be considered. The interaction of these two factors may be expressed as a formula adapted from Chamberlain's model for measuring power in collective bargaining relationships.[11] The power of *X* over *Y* may be defined as:

$$(1) \qquad P_{X/Y} = \frac{Y\text{'s Net Cost of Disagreement with } X}{Y\text{'s Cost of Agreement with } X}$$

$$(2) \qquad = \frac{(X\text{'s Offer}) - (\text{The Best Alternative Offer Available to } Y)}{\text{The Best Alternative Offer Available to } Y}$$

The "offers" equal the satisfaction value of the resources that are available to *Y* by *X* and by alternative exchange partners. In union-management exchange relationships, *Y's* Net Cost of Disagreement (N.C.D.) and Cost of Agreement (C.A.) are usually measured in monetary terms, often with a high degree of accuracy. Application of the formula to other social transactions requires that these costs be more broadly defined to include social-psychological variables that may not be readily quantified. Nevertheless, the formula is of value because its succinct expression of the relationship between the factors that are relevant to the measurement of power permits us to draw important conclusions that are independent of the precision with which those factors may be measured.

Y's Cost of Agreement with *X* equals the benefits that he foregoes by not investing the same quantity of his resources in the most profitable alternative exchange. There can be a value of zero only when three stringent conditions obtain. First, *Y* can achieve no satisfaction by consuming his own resource.[12] Second, the resource is of no value to second parties other than *X*. Third, the conclusion of an exchange of specified resources with *X* does

[11]Neil W. Chamberlain, *Labor* (New York: McGraw-Hill Book Co., Inc., 1958), Chapter 6. Chamberlain's formulation utilizes the Total rather than the Net Cost of Agreement. We have used the second expression because its results can be immediately interpreted as a rate of return.

[12]Although it is not specified in the formula, the consumption value of some resources; e.g., leisure time, is often of great importance for allocation decisions.

not preclude *Y* from entering alternative exchanges based on other resources that he commands. If only the first condition is relaxed, the C.A. equals the loss in satisfaction that *Y* incurs by not consuming the resource himself. If only the second condition is relaxed, the cost equals the value of the resources that could have been obtained from the most profitable alternative exchange. If only the third is relaxed, the cost equals the satisfaction that could have been obtained from the most profitable exchange of *Y's* other resources. If all are relaxed, the Cost of Agreement equals the most profitable alternative that is foregone, considering *Y's* entire resource stock and including consumption as an alternative. The stringency of these assumptions may be more clearly seen through the following example. Assume that *Y* has been trained as an electrician. His Cost of Agreeing to employer *X's* offer of one day's work at a stated salary equals zero only if *Y* can derive no benefits from consuming that day (e.g., in leisure), if there are no alternative employers of electricians, himself included, and if *Y* can simultaneously invest his non-electrical resources in the most satisfying alternative exchange while he works for *X*.

Students of economics will recognize that the concept of cost being used here is "opportunity cost," the loss incurred by foregoing the best alternative opportunity. This is also the relevant concept for discussing the numerator of $P_{X/Y}$. *Y's* Net Cost of Disagreement with *X* equals the difference between the reward that would be obtained if an exchange were concluded with *X* and the reward obtainable from the most satisfying alternative exchange (or from consumption). This may be less than, equal to, or greater than zero. There will be negative costs if the exchange in question is less profitable than some alternative. Returning to the earlier example, assume that *Y* may work as an electrician only for *X* or *Z*, that *X* will pay $1 per day, but that *Z* will pay $2. If these are the two most profitable alternative exchanges available to *Y*, then his N.C.D. with *X* equals —$1. Thus, *Y* incurs a *negative* cost—positive revenue—by disagreeing with *X's* terms. Notice that *Y's* C.A. in this example equals the $2 that would be foregone by not agreeing with *Z* so that $P_{X/Y}$ is calculated as $-\$1/\$2 = ½$. The negative sign indicates that *X* has no power over *Y*. That is, *X* is unable to satisfy his needs by inducing *Y* to enter an exchange at the specified terms.

Positive Disagreement Costs occur if the exchange in question is the most satisfying alternative available. In the above example, *Y's* N.C.D. with *Z* equals +$1—the difference between *Z's* and *X's* offers; *Y's* C.A. with *Z* equals the $1 that he forgoes by not agreeing with *X*; and $P_{Z/Y}$ equals 1 ($1/$1). *Z's* terms are sufficient to induce *Y* to allocate his resources in the desired manner.

The Net Cost of Disagreement may equal zero in either of two cases. If a party has only one possible exchange partner, and can derive no benefit from any resource controlled by that potential partner or from consumption, then he incurs no cost by rejecting every offer. For example, if *Y* has no interest in golf and *X* offers to lend him some clubs in exchange for a day's work, then *Y* will suffer no loss by rejecting *X's* offer if this is the only possible exchange, the clubs are the only resource that *X* can provide, and *Y* can gain no benefit from consuming the day. *X* cannot affect *Y's* behavior. $P_{X/Y}$ is undefined because the Costs of Agreement and Disagreement both equal zero and there is no rational (utility maximization) basis for exchange. *Y's* acceptance or rejection of the *X–Y* transaction is a random event. The second case in which the *N.C.D.* equals zero occurs if there are at least two potential exchanges that offer the *maximum* return for a given investment of resources. The net opportunity cost of rejecting one of these offers equals zero because the same return is available elsewhere, and the cost of acceptance equals the (non-zero) value of the exchange that must be forgone. In terms of the earlier example, if electrician *Y* is offered $1 by *X*, $2 by *Z*, and $2 by *S*, the *Y's* Net Cost of Disagreement with *Z* becomes $0 because the opportunity cost of working for *Z* at $2 exactly equals the $2 that was forgone by not working for *S*. If these bids are independent, neither *Z* nor *S* *individually* possesses the power to induce *Y* to behave in the desired manner. If the $2 maximum offer resulted from collusion between *Z* and *X*, then they have *joint* power over *Y* because they have increased the probability that *Y* will allocate his resources in a manner desired by one of them rather than by *X*. In economic terms, *Z* and *S* have formed a cartel. If there is no such collusion, the equally attractive offers of *Z* and *S* nullify the power that either would possess in the other's absence, and *Y's* choice among these exchanges will again be random. This case of multiple-maximum alternatives is more fully developed below.

Specifying *X's* power over *Y* is not sufficient to express the power *relationship* between the two parties that will ultimately determine whether there will be an exchange. This requires an analysis of the Differential Power of the two parties. The Differential Power of *X* over *Y* may be expressed as:

$$(3) \qquad DP_{X/Y} = P_{X/Y} - P_{Y/X}$$

where

$$(4) \qquad P_{Y/X} = \frac{X\text{'s Net Cost of Disagreement with } Y}{X\text{'s Cost of Agreement with } Y}$$

It is important to keep in mind that the terms in equation (4) are independent of those in equation (1). *X* possesses resources that differ from *Y's* and generally has a range of exchange alternatives other than those that are available to *Y*. Which this *caveat* in mind, we may proceed to a consideration of the values over which $DP_{X/Y}$ may range.

The Differential Power of *X* over *Y* equals zero if $P_{X/Y} = P_{Y/X}$. This equality occurs if the Net Costs of Disagreement for both parties equal zero and the Costs of Agreement do not equal zero or if the ratios of the Net Disagreement Costs to the respective Agreement Costs have equal values other than zero. The first case exists if the most satisfying alternative exchanges available to both parties have reward values equal to those obtainable from the *X–Y* exchange. This is the multiple-maximum case discussed above. Neither *X* nor *Y* incurs an opportunity cost by forgoing the *X–Y* exchange because the same benefit-cost ratio is available elsewhere. Because the definition of resources and rewards includes *all* intrinsic and extrinsic factors, there can be no differentiation among the multiple-maximum exchanges and selection among them will be random. Thus, neither party can induce the other to enter the *X–Y* exchange, and the Differential Power of both parties equals zero.

It is clear that the limits of a party's power are determined by the alternatives available to potential exchange partners. This has long been understood by economists who have championed competition as a market structure that minimizes any party's economic power. Perfect competition requires that so many parties offer the use of a resource that collusion is impossible, no party owns a disproportionately large share of the total quantity of a given resource, any party may enter any exchange that he chooses, and exchange partners know the terms of trade available from all potential exchanges. Given these conditions, the system yields multiple-maximum alternatives for every party so that none possesses differential economic power. In Friedman's words:

> So long as effective freedom of exchange is maintained, the central feature of the market organization of economic activity is that it prevents one person from interfering with another in respect of most of his activities. The consumer is protected from coercion by the seller because of the presence of other sellers with whom he can deal. The seller is protected from coercion by the consumer because of other consumers to whom he can sell. The employee is protected from coercion by the employer because of other employers for whom he can work, and so on.[13]

These same comments may be applied to non-economic forms of social exchange wherein the existence of multiple-maximum alternatives results in zero Differential Power. Whether the resources to be exchanged are measured in units of money, love, knowledge, or beauty, the power of any party is limited by the competition of others who possess the same resources for exchange on like terms.

The Differential Power of *X* over *Y* also equals zero if $P_{X/Y}$ and $P_{Y/X}$ have equivalent values other than zero. Such a relationship requires that the ratio of the benefit from the *X–Y* exchange to both parties' best alternative exceed unity, but be equal. Like the multiple-maximum reward case there is zero Differential Power. Unlike the multiple-maximum case, the reward from the *X–Y* exchange exceeds that of the best alternative so that there is power on both sides of the exchange. If each party seeks to maximize his rewards, he will enter this exchange rather than any other, the choice will not be random, and each party affects the behavior of the other. Emerson comments as follows on such equal power relationships:

> A moment's thought will reveal the utility of the argument that balance does not neutralize power, for each party may continue to exert profound control over the other. It might be more meaningful to talk about the parties being controlled by the relation itself.[14]

These "balanced" or "countervailing" power relationships may arise under various circumstances. In some cases, the same resources possessed

[13]Milton Friedman, *Capitalism and Freedom* (Chicago: University of Chicago Press, 1962), p. 15.

[14]Emerson, *op. cit.*, p. 34.

by X and Y may also be possessed by other parties who will make them available on terms that are proportionately less satisfying to X and Y than those of the X–Y exchange. In others, X may be the only "buyer" and/or "seller" of given resources and Y the only "seller" and/or "buyer" of the same resources, but there is equal differential power because each may conclude alternative exchanges for *other* types of resources that have proportionately equal value as compared to an X–Y exchange. Thus, equal differential power may exist even under conditions of monopoly or monopsony for one resource if each party may also trade in other types of resources and receive equivalent rewards. Zero Differential Power occurs in the strict bilateral monopoly case if neither X nor Y possesses resources other than those of the potential X–Y exchange, neither can gain satisfaction by consuming his own resources, and neither desires resources other than those possessed by the other. This "death marriage" case implies indeterminately large power for both parties because their Costs of Agreement equal zero. Not only is the X–Y exchange the most desirable, it is the only one possible. Obviously, such cases are rare. Perhaps the closest industrial approximation occurs for a unionized work force in a "one-industry" town. Even under these circumstances, both parties normally have some alternative exchanges available no matter how undesirable they might be.

When $P_{X/Y}$ is greater than $P_{Y/X}$ and both exceed zero, equation (3) states that X has Differential Power over Y because X's alternative exchanges are *relatively* more satisfying than Y's. It would appear that X is not only able to induce Y to enter an exchange but that he might force Y to provide more resources than were originally offered. In economic terms, a positive value derived from equation (3) indicates that Y's rate of return from the X–Y exchange exceeds that of X. It is tempting to conclude that X would be able to force a change in Y's terms because Y's relative loss from a failure to conclude the transaction would exceed that incurred by X. However, such a conclusion is open to question. When the values of $P_{X/Y}$ and $P_{Y/X}$ both exceed zero, the Differential Power formula only indicates that an exchange will occur; it is not sufficient for determining the terms of trade. For the case in question, X would jeopardize his own access to the X–Y exchange—which is the most favorable one available to him—if he threatened to withhold his resources in an attempt to induce a change in the terms offered by Y. Whether he will in fact do so depends on other factors such as his taste for risk, his knowledge of Y's alternatives, and his perception of Y's risk preference.[15] For any definable value of $P_{Y/X}$, X's Differential Power over Y approaches infinity as the value of the resources that Y can obtain from *any* alternative exchange approaches zero. X moves toward a position of monopoly or monopsony for *all* the resources commanded by Y. In the limiting case, X could dictate any terms of exchange if he has full knowledge of his differential power. The reverse holds true if $DP_{X/Y}$ is less than zero, in which case the limit is minus infinity, and Y controls the exchange.

Finally, if either $P_{X/Y}$ or $P_{Y/X}$ is less than zero, there will be no exchange unless the proposed terms are altered. If only $P_{X/Y}$ is negative, Y has

[15]The consideration of risk goes beyond the scope of this paper. Interested readers should refer to J. Pen, "A General Theory of Bargaining," *American Economic Review*, Vol. 62 (1952), pp. 24–42.

alternatives that are equal or superior to the X–Y exchange and he may withhold his resources from X without risk in an effort to induce X to increase his offer. The reverse is true if only $P_{Y/X}$ is negative.

The foregoing analysis indicates that parties may attain incremental power over potential exchange partners by operating on their own resources, on their own alternatives, or on their potential partners' alternatives.[16] Acquiring valued intrinsic or extrinsic resources either by exchange processes or by private investment, such as study, and differentiating resources from those controlled by competitors provide access to profitable new exchanges that may permit the terms of present exchanges to be favorably altered. Similarly, investing resources in the search for new potential exchanges may increase the number of alternatives and thereby increase a party's power in an existing exchange.[17] Finally, the formation of "cartels" with alternative suppliers or users of a given resource yields group power by reducing the number of alternatives available to potential exchange partners. The formation of such a group constitutes an exchange in itself, and parties will be induced to enter only if their expected share of the group reward exceeds that which they could obtain by continuing to operate as individuals. Examples of alternative-reduction via group formation include labor unions and the football draft system.

DIMENSIONS OF POWER RELATIONSHIPS

The preceding section discussed power relationships in rather theoretical terms as if social interaction consisted of "bid and asked" communications possessing all the emotion of a bond quotation. Obviously this is not the case. The exchange model clarifies the sources of power and provides a means of measuring power differentials only by stripping away all the nuances of interpersonal relationships. Power may be wielded ruthlessly or fairly from the subordinate's viewpoint. Differentials may be clear or hazy. The terms of trade may be precisely specified or only vaguely communicated. The relationship may involve a series of transactions rather than a single exchange. Such variations have important implications for the nature of the relationship.

Complete certainty about the terms of trade seldom exists, and it is more correct to say that each party enters the exchange with *expectations* regarding the terms. This is true for most commercial/legal transactions as well as for personal exchanges, such as friendships. For example, a newly hired accountant may not know in advance whether the office's mean temperature is 68° or 75°, whether blue spread-collar shirts are permitted or white button-downs required, whether his starting salary falls above or below the average for beginners. If one party's expectations are not completely fulfilled, he must balance the newly understood benefits from that

[16]More accurately, the party can alter his power over another by altering his perceptions or the second party's perception of resource values.

[17]For a rigorous analysis of the economic value of search, see George J. Stigler, "The Economics of Information," *Journal of Political Economy*, Vol. 69 (1961), pp. 213–225.

exchange against the *expected* benefits from his best alternative, estimate the power differential, and decide whether he can change his present partner's behavior, must submit to his terms, or should break the relationship. In other cases, both parties may enter a relationship on mutually understood terms, but one or the other may subsequently request or demand a change. Again, the outcome will be determined by the parties' estimates of differential power.

Relationships also differ in expected longevity, a factor that greatly affects both differential power and the degree to which it is fully exploited in a single transaction:

> In a long-term relationship, when A knows he must go on living or working with B after he has tried to change B's behavior, he may proceed with caution no matter what his personal ethics. His own dependency on the others in the relationship serves as a built-in governor on his influence techniques, even if his conscience doesn't. But in short-term, one-shot relationships, when A never expects to see B again—after the door-to-door sale—the range of influence techniques A may use is limited by his own conscience and his fear of the law.[18]

The "governor" in the long-term relationship is, of course, the benefits that *A* hopes to obtain in *future* exchanges if the association is continued. *A* may find it desirable to discount the stream of future rewards that *B* can provide, and this present value becomes part of *A's* expected net benefit from the first transaction. If *A* views the world in a manner that is consistent with equation (3), he will perceive that his power over *B* decreases as the expected net benefits from future exchanges with *B* increase. *A* may not press his full advantage in the first exchange because *B* might withhold future rewards by breaking the association to enter a more favorable alternative exchange. In one-shot exchanges, *B's* power is limited to the resources he offers in a single exchange, there are no future benefits for *A* to discount, and *A* suffers no loss from using every available means for raising *B's* expectations regarding the benefits he will receive. Once the exchange is concluded, *B's* dissatisfaction cannot be registered by the withholding of future benefits.

Unless there are multiple-maximum alternatives available to both parties, one exchange exceeds all others with respect to expected net benefits and rational parties will enter that transaction rather than any other. Thus, to some degree each party is dependent on the other for maximum need-satisfaction, a condition that has important psychological implications. Various authors have pointed out that ambivalent emotions generally accompany dependency relationships.[19] The exchange partner is at once "loved" for the satisfactions he provides and "hated" for the rewards that he exacts, for the additional satisfactions that he *could* supply but doesn't, and (perhaps) for the feelings of personal weakness that he engenders within the party who must rely on him for need satisfaction. Social rela-

[18]Harold J. Leavitt, *Managerial Psychology: An Introduction to Individuals, Pairs, and Groups in Organizations,* 2d ed. (Chicago: University of Chicago Press, 1964), p. 132.

[19]*Ibid.*, p. 20; Frank K. Knight, "Authority and the Free Society," in *Authority,* Carl J. Friedrich (Ed.) (Cambridge: Harvard University Press for the American Society of Political and Legal Philosophy, 1958), p. 67; and Charles W. Hendel, "An Exploration of the Nature of Authority," in Friedrich, *op. cit.*, p. 5.

tionships differ widely according to the balance between the positive and negative feelings that the parties hold toward each other. One would expect negative feelings to increase if the rewards received were lower than expected, the rewards given were higher than expected, or a change in the power differential produced an unfavorable change in the terms of trade. Additionally, negative feelings might be aroused, even if the terms were as expected, if one party perceived that the other's benefit/cost ratio from the exchange greatly exceeded his own.[20] One might also expect all positive feelings to be snuffed out when an enormous power difference is exploited. There is evidence to the contrary. In his analysis of the psychological impact of imprisonment on inmates of Dachau and Buchenwald, Bettelheim found that prisoners held positive as well as negative feelings toward the Gestapo.[21]

In view of the fact that some ambivalence will generally be felt by both parties to a power relation, Machiavelli's question may be rephrased: "Is it better to be loved more than hated or hated more than loved?" On balance, it would seem that it is better for a power-wielder to be loved more than hated, at least if he is dealing with a group rather than with isolated individuals. If the distribution and exercise of power conform to group norms of "fairness," the superior's demands will generally be met with approval. Collectively approved power is said to be "legitimated," and the superior whose demands are legitimated obtains an increment to his power from the group pressure that is exerted on subordinates who might be tempted to resist those demands or change the terms of trade.[22] On the other hand, demands that are not viewed as legitimate engender group pressures *against* compliance and may result in subtle reductions in the terms of trade or in the formation of subordinate coalitions that limit the superior's alternatives and actually shift the balance of power against him. The potential strength of group pressures and the corresponding value of legitimation as incremental power are developed more fully in the next section.

We have shown that a necessary condition for the existence of power is command over psychological, social, and material properties (resources) that have need-satisfaction value to others. The analysis also indicated that a party's power is not a fixed quantity but varies across potential exchanges according to the specific resources involved in each and the terms of trade available in alternative exchanges. The same individual may be at once master in some relationships and slave in others. Because power is partly determined by the value of resources that can be offered, some of the variation in power across relationships is explained by the fact that the same party may have access to different "capital stocks" in different situations. Some resources, such as intelligence and personal wealth, are inseparable from the person and may be brought to bear at the discretion of the owner.

[20]See George C. Homans, *Social Behavior: Its Elementary Forms* (New York: Harcourt, Brace and World, 1961), Chapter 12, for a discussion of the concept of justice in exchange relationships. I am indebted to Mr. Martin Gillo of the University of Kansas for referring me to this work and for his observation that equation (3) of the present chapter corresponds to Homan's statement of the rule of distributive justice. *Ibid.*, pp. 241–242.

[21]Bruno Bettelheim, "Individual and Mass Behavior in Extreme Situations," *Journal of Abnormal and Social Psychology*, Vol. 38 (1943), p. 451.

[22]French and Raven include legitimation as a separate category in their typology of power. *Op. cit.*, pp. 158–161.

Others are commanded by virtue of the position that an individual occupies in a formal organization. These reside in the office rather than in the individual, and their use is prescribed by regulation. They are intended for use only in "official" transactions. The term "influence" will be used here to designate power that is based on personal resources, and "authority" will refer to power derived from formal position. The next section is concerned with the first of these power forms.

INFLUENCE

All of us can recall acquaintances who have affected our lives in some way: an uncle whose athletic prowess lent special weight to his admonitions against smoking; a college sweetheart whose literary tastes caused us to drop Spillane in favor of Proust; a minister who persuaded us to cancel our membership in a segregated country club. We can also identify informal groups that have exerted similar forces. Each is an example of influence because the effect on behavior was induced through a process that involved the power figure's personal resources rather than the perquisites of office. The characteristics of this power form may be readily sketched by reference to the framework developed in the course of our general discussion of power. First, influence may be exerted through both interactive and non-interactive processes. Second, the exercise of influence is frequently unintentional, a situation that is particularly likely in the area of referent power. More mature readers will recall the letter that was sent to Dizzy Dean by an irate English teacher whose students began to imitate Dean's less-than-conventional speech habits. Finally, influence is legitimated solely by the influencee. That is, the determination that an individual or group has a "proper" right to exert influence in a given manner is made only by the party whose behavior is affected.

A party can exercise influence only if others *perceive* that he commands valuable personal resources. In interactive power relationships, this normally involves two steps: acquiring resources and communicating to others that those resources are available for exchange. Acquisition may occur through non-interactive process, such as solitary study or by social exchange. The importance of both acquisition methods has been verified by empirical research. Katz and Lazarsfeld have shown that individuals who influence the opinions of others regarding public affairs, fashion, consumer goods, and movie choices tend to read more books, more magazines, and spend more hours listening to the radio than do those who were influenced.[23] The solitary investment of time in reading and listening gives influentials control over resources—knowledge in this case—which they can exchange with others and thereby influence the recipient's behavior. The same study also revealed the importance of social exchange as a medium for acquiring resources. Highly gregarious persons are more likely to be opinion

[23]Elihu Katz and Paul F. Lazarsfeld, *Personal Influence,* A Report of the Bureau of Applied Social Research, Columbia University (Glencoe, Illinois: The Free Press, 1955), p. 310; and Herbert Menzel and Elihu Katz, "Social Relations and Innovation in the Medical Profession: The Epidemiology of a New Drug," *Public Opinion Quarterly*, Vol. 19 (1955–1956), pp. 337–352.

leaders than those with fewer social contacts.[24] Investment in large numbers of social exchanges evidently yields resources that enable the individual to influence the opinion of others. Obviously, their wider social network also affords them greater opportunities to exercise influence.

We have mentioned that the term "power" has meaning only in terms of specific relationships and resources. The resource-specific nature of power implies that one party may exert considerable influence over some behavior of a second party and have no effect on other behaviors. This was verified by Katz and Lazarsfeld who found that about two-thirds of the opinion leaders exerted influence in only one opinion area. The authors conclude: "By and large, however, the hypothesis of a generalized leader receives little support in this study. There is no overlap in any of the pairs of activities. Each arena, it seems, has a corps of leaders of its own."[25]

The second step in the influence process involves communicating to others that valued resources are available for exchange. This information may be transmitted either by attribution or observation. Attribution involves one party's learning about the other's resources by communicating with the owner himself or with a third party. Observation requires that the knowledge be gained from a personal assessment of the outcomes produced by another's actions. To illustrate, an employer may learn that an applicant has valuable skills by reading the information supplied on the application form (self-attribution), by talking to the applicant's former employer (attribution by a third party), or by the applicant's performance on an achievement test (observation).

Research has shown that influentials devote considerable energy to transmitting information about the resources in their possession. Studies of groups as diverse as juries and children's playgroups indicate that individuals who exert the most influence on group decisions also tend to initiate more interaction and more influence attempts than do those who are influenced.[26] Thus, the volume of interaction is often important at both stages of the influence process. Influentials acquire resources by their broad social network and then communicate their resource ownership by high levels of interaction. Interaction alone is not sufficient to establish influence. A high level of communication that is not accompanied by resource possession produces negative reactions but not influence.[27]

Various authors have studied the process by which one individual

[24]This observation did not hold true for movie leaders. Katz and Lazarsfeld, *op. cit.*, p. 308.

[25]*Op. cit.*, p. 334.

[26]Fred L. Strodtbeck, Rita M. James, and Charles Hawkins, "Social Status in Jury Deliberations," *American Sociological Review*, Vol. 22 (1957), pp. 713–719; Ronald Lippit, Norman Polansky, Fritz Redl, and Sidney Rosen, "The Dynamics of Power," *Human Relations*, Vol. 5 (1952), pp. 37–64; Launor Carter *et al.*, "The Behavior of Leaders and Other Group Members," *Journal of Abnormal and Social Psychology*, Vol. 46 (1951), pp. 589–595; and Jacob I. Hurwitz, Alvin F. Zander, and Bernard Hymovitch, "Some Effects of Power on the Relations among Group Members," in Dorwin Cartwright and Alvin Zander (Eds.) *Group Dynamics: Research and Theory*, 2d ed. (Evanston, Illinois: Row, Peterson and Company for Research Center for Group Dynamics, University of Michigan, 1960), pp. 800–809.

[27]Robert F. Bales, "Role and Role Conflict," in Eleanor E. Maccoby, Theodore M. Newcomb, and Eugene L. Hartley (Eds.), *Readings in Social Psychology*, 3rd ed. (New York: Holt, Rinehart and Winston, 1958), p. 446.

achieves influence within a group.[28] The scenario may be summarized in the following way. Unless there is prior attribution of resource ownership to one of the parties, informal relations begin with all participants on an equal footing. Over time, one or more members attempt to display their resources by offering recommendations, giving directives, stating opinions, and so forth. If these are accepted by the other parties, the incipient influential receives feedback that others perceive his value and he grows confident that future communications will also be favorably received. With the risk of rejection now reduced, his influence attempts increase. Negative feedback produces the opposite effect.

How is this rise to power viewed by those who are influenced? As indicated earlier, the reaction is generally one of ambivalence. On the one hand, the exercise of influence is approved insofar as it assists the other parties to achieve their desired goals. Therefore it is not surprising to find that high-power persons are better liked on the average by other group members than those with low power.[29] On the other hand, the attainment of power in an informal relationship often involves a certain amount of competition that is likely to generate hostility and uneasiness among those who lose out in the struggle.[30] There is a variety of evidence to support this assertion. First, participants in informal relationships make different choices when they are asked to select a task leader than when they are asked to choose friends.[31] Second, students of small groups are well aware of the tendency for informal groups to develop two types of leaders, one who moves the group toward completion of the task and one who "keeps the group together" by making comments that support other members and reduces the level of hostility within the group. It has been found that the "socio-emotional" leader is better liked by group members than is the task leader.[32] This splitting of functions appears to reflect the group's mixed emotions toward the individual who takes command and moves the group toward the completion of its task. He is valued for his allocation of resources in a manner that moves the group toward its objective, but his exercise of influence generates negative reactions that prevent him from being selected as the best-liked member.[33] Finally, evidence of tension is also provided by studies that indicate that those who interact least with their peers (and are therefore likely to be the least influential) are also less satisfied with the group than are those who interact the most.[34]

28George Levinger, "The Development of Perceptions in Newly Formed Social Power Relationships," Cartwright, *op. cit.*, pp. 83–98; Lippit, Polansky, Redl, and Rosen, *op. cit.*; John P. Kirscht, Thomas M. Lodahl and Mason Haire, "Some Factors in the Selection of Leaders by Members of Small Groups," *Journal of Abnormal and Social Psychology*, Vol. 58 (1959), pp. 406–408.

29Hurwitz, Zander, and Hymovitch, *op. cit.*

30Sidney Verba, *Small Groups and Political Behavior: A Study of Leadership* (Princeton, N.J.: Princeton University Press, 1961), pp. 166–167.

31E. P. Hollander and Wilse B. Webb, "Leadership, Followship, and Friendship: An Analysis of Peer Nominations," *Journal of Abnormal and Social Psychology*, Vol. 50 (1955), pp. 163–167.

32Bales, *op. cit.*, pp. 440–441.

33It has been shown that socio-emotional leaders exert considerable influence on group tasks. This may explain the apparent contradiction between the findings of Hurwitz and those of Hollander and Webb that were cited earlier.

34Strodtbeck, James, and Hawkins, *op. cit.*, p. 716.

The existence of tension may jeopardize the stability of the social relationship. Assuming that the exchange is of positive value to the influential, what steps might he take to reduce the level of hostility that is engendered by his exercise of power? The question may be answered by empathizing with the feelings of the low-power parties. One would expect that parties to an informal relationship generally *wish* to be liked by those who possess greater relative power.[35] Such a desire may be fostered, in part, by the knowledge that power figures exercise a measure of control over one's ability to satisfy certain needs. Statements of approval or affection imply that the relationship will be maintained and that future needs may be satisfied. In Maslow's terms, approval by those with greater power fulfills the security needs of the party who enjoys less power.[36] Moreover, the recipient of such indications of approval may achieve increased status (and power) among his peers as they become aware of his closer ties to the influential party. Thus, influentials may reduce negative feelings by showing positive regard toward those with less power, thereby improving the terms of exchange for those whom they influence. A second method of reducing the negative feelings is derived from the earlier discussion of interaction patterns in informal relationships. We have already observed that influentials generally have higher levels of interaction than do those who are influenced. It has also been shown that an individual's degree of satisfaction with an informal relationship is positively related to his level of interaction. It would seem to follow that the influential might induce more positive feelings toward himself by encouraging higher participation levels among those who are influenced.[37] Research has shown that the rate at which an individual expresses opinions depends heavily on the listener's reaction[38] and that the frequency of communication by a low-power figure is positively related to the volume of communication directed toward him by a high-power figure.[39] One would conclude from this that influentials may increase the interaction levels and satisfaction of those with less power by directing more communication toward them (rather than toward other power figures) and by reacting positively to their responses. This strategy would seem to be particularly valuable once the influential has firmly established his power position. Indeed, there is evidence that informal leaders do in fact "let up" on and reduce the volume of their directives once their position is secure.[40] Finally, the influential may reduce the negative feelings by exercising discretion in his choice of influence topics so that his power position is not endangered by negative feelings generated by the exercise of power over relatively unimportant matters.

35Evidence for this is provided by Hurwitz *et al., op. cit.*, pp. 806–807.

36A. H. Maslow, "A Theory of Human Motivation," *Psychological Review*, Vol. 50 (1943), pp. 370–396.

37This assertion has been verified by Bales, *op. cit.*, p. 446.

38William S. Verplanck, "The Control of the Content of Conversation: Reinforcement of Statements of Opinion," *Journal of Abnormal and Social Psychology*, Vol. 51 (1955), pp. 668–676.

39Hurwitz, Zander, and Hymovitch, *op. cit.*, p. 806.

40C. Heinicke and Robert F. Bales, "Developmental Trends in the Structure of Small Groups," *Sociometry*, Vol. 16 (1953), pp. 35–37; and James G. March, "Influence Measurement in Experimental and Semi-experimental Groups," *Sociometry*, Vol. 19 (1956), pp. 260–271, as cited by Verba, *op. cit.*, p. 167.

All of these means for reducing negative feelings involve costs to the influential. Greater participation by low-power members may prolong discussion beyond optimal time limits; increased communication toward those with lower power may reduce the amount that is directed to others with greater power; the reduction of interaction volume by the high-power figure may reduce *his* satisfaction from the interchange. These costs must be weighed against the benefits achieved from increasing the positive feelings of those who are influenced.

When an informal relationship involves more than two people, the influential's skillful use of measures to retain the approval of most group members may add considerably to his existing power. Earlier we introduced the term "legitimacy" to describe power that is collectively approved by a group's members. Legitimacy implies that other parties are not only influenced but that they also *approve* of the terms that are exacted in the exchange. The power figure who achieves such majority approval acquires an additional resource, group pressure, which may be used to affect the behavior of others in the relationship. The sanctions imposed by group members who approve of a power figure's influence attempts may induce recalcitrant parties to comply with his wishes.

Numerous studies have verified the powerful effects of group pressure on attitudes and behaviors.[41] Perhaps the most dramatic evidence is contained in Asch's experiment, which required subjects to view four lines and select the two that were equal in length.[42] When the subjects worked privately, only 5 per cent made any errors and none mismatched more than two pairs of lines in eighteen trials. However, the error rate increased markedly when the subjects were asked to publicly announce their judgments after seven confederates of the experimenter had purposely announced erroneous choices. The experimental subjects faced the unsettling choice of either making the correct match, thereby rejecting the unanimous majority choice, or bowing to group pressure. Under these conditions, 74 per cent of the subjects made at least one incorrect choice and 30 per cent made six or more incorrect choices. Discussion with those who yielded to majority pressure indicated that most made errors because they became mistrustful of their own judgments; others knew they were making a mistake but did not wish to depart from the group view; a few actually perceived the erroneous matchings as being correct. Later experiments induced the full "majority effect" even when the size of the confederate group was reduced from seven persons to as few as three. Although the Asch study did not involve legitimacy *per se,* the same formidable pressures may reinforce the influential's personal power if he has achieved collective approval of its exercise.

These findings are particularly significant in view of the conditions of Asch's experiment. The judgmental task had an objectively correct answer, no informal leader exerted influence, the group was randomly assembled

[41]M. Sherif, "An Experimental Approach to the Study of Attitudes," *Sociometry,* Vol. 1 (1937), pp. 90–98; William Foote Whyte, *Street Corner Society,* 2d ed. (Chicago and London: University of Chicago Press, 1955), pp. 20–23; and Kurt Lewin, "Group Decision and Social Change" in Maccoby, Newcomb, and Hartley, *op. cit.,* pp. 197–211.

[42]S. E. Asch, "Effects of Group Pressure on the Modification and Distortion of Judgments," in Maccoby, Newcomb, and Hartley, *op. cit.,* pp. 174–183.

to participate in the brief experiment, and the majority exerted no pressure other than the public statement of their choices. Despite this rather minimal pressure situation, about one-third of the subjects bowed to the group on at least half their statements. One would expect that submission to group pressure would be even more frequent if the task required a subtle judgment of an ambiguous issue or a public statement of opinion on a controversial matter, such as race relations; if a power figure had been present to support the majority view; if the group had existed over a long period of time and membership was highly valued; or if members who deviated from the prevailing view were subject to verbal admonitions from their peers.[43] Such "high-pressure" conditions often accurately characterize common informal relationships, such as friendship circles and social groups.

The process by which an individual's influence degenerates may be briefly sketched in terms of the earlier discussion of power acquisition. Influence declines if other parties perceive that the influential's personal resources have diminished. This may result from changes that are internal to the power figure, such as aging or illness. Alternatively, other parties may change their evaluation of the influential's personal resources on the basis of information obtained through observation or attribution. The advice of an erstwhile expert may be disregarded if he is proven or reputed to be in error on numerous occasions. A shift in the influencee's value system may also cause the decline. The athletic uncle's advice against smoking loses its force if a desire for excellence in sports is replaced by a desire for membership in a friendship group in which smoking is the norm. Finally, influence ceases to exist if exchange partners become aware of alternative transactions that will yield the desired resources on more favorable terms. The search for alternatives may be triggered by terms of exchange that are judged to be excessive or inappropriate. Thus, the maintenance of legitimacy has the important function of promoting the stability of the relationship by reducing the probability that alternatives will be sought.

AUTHORITY

The preceding section discussed power that is based on resources that are personally commanded by an individual. The resources' intrinsic link to the person implied that they were available for allocation strictly at the owner's discretion for whatever purpose and in whatever context he deemed appropriate. The discussion of the processes by which such power is acquired and exercised was necessarily confined to informal relationships in which the balance of power is determined by "competition" among the parties. Attention is now shifted to power based on resources owned by formal organizations. We shall adopt the following definitions:

[43]These expectations have been confirmed in a variety of studies. See Sherif, *op. cit.;* Whyte, *op. cit.*; Alberta Engvall Siegel and Sidney Siegel, "Reference Groups, Membership Groups and Attitude Change," *Journal of Abnormal and Social Psychology*, Vol. 55 (1957), pp. 360–364; Leon Festinger, Stanley Schachter, and Kurt Back, *Social Pressures in Informal Groups* (New York: Harper & Row, 1950), pp. 99–100.

> *Organizations* are social units consisting of a network of relations which orients and regulates the behavior among a specific set of individuals in the pursuit of relatively specific goals. An organization is said to be *formal* to the extent that positions are identified and defined and relations with other positions specified irrespective of the characteristics of the individuals occupying the positions.[44]

These definitions call attention to several important characteristics of authority. First, this power form is exercised only in the context of a social structure that has been consciously created to attain a specified goal, such as a corporation formed to make a profit by the production and sale of automobiles. Second, the structure consists of a network of positions or "job slots." The rights and duties of each position are defined by rules that are intended to orient the activities of the occupant toward the organization's goals. These rights and duties reside in the office rather than in the individual. They are acquired concurrently with appointment to the office and lost at the time of resignation or removal. Third, the network of relationships among offices is structured by regulations. The rules that define goals, positions, and structure are specified by those who fund the organization or by their representatives.

The basic resource for most formal organizations is money. Money is generally provided by an external source through some form of exchange. In the case of profit-sector corporations, stockholders allocate capital in exchange for a proportionate ownership claim on future profits; bondholders exchange funds for some stipulated rate of return. Similarly, government agencies obtain monetary resources from taxpayers who, through their elected representatives, agree to provide these funds in exchange for specified public services. These "funding" transactions provide a financial base that is then allocated in subsequent exchanges to acquire the more specific resources—buildings, equipment, and human capital—needed to achieve the funders' specified goals. In formal organizations, the responsibility for these allocational decisions is delegated to administrators who are appointed by a representative of the funding group, such as a board of directors.[45] By virtue of his appointment to office, the administrator acquires control over that portion of the organization's resources that forms the basis of his authority.

Relationships among offices generally take a hierarchical form,[46] and the rank of each office usually corresponds to the value of the resources delegated to its control. In other words, the structure consists of a chain of offices linked in the shape of a pyramid; the span of resource control widens as the pyramid narrows. Each position within the chain is defined by rules that specify both the resources that are under its control and the purposes for which those resources may be allocated. Thus, rules perform the dual function of distributing power within the structure and constraining

[44]W. Richard Scott, "Organizational Goals and Tasks," in W. Richard Scott (Ed.) *Social Processes and Social Structures: An Introduction to Sociology* (New York: Holt, Rinehart and Winston, 1970), pp. 412–419.

[45]Weber comments: "Officials, employees, and workers attached to the administrative staff do not own the non-human means of production and administration." In *The Theory of Social and Economic Organization, op. cit.*, p. 331.

[46]Robert K. Merton, *Social Theory and Social Structure*, rev. ed. (New York: The Free Press, 1957), pp. 202–204.

the use of that power to purposes that are consistent with the organization's goals.

Because authority is confined to the context of a formal organization, the processes by which this form of power is acquired, legitimated, and exercised differ significantly from those that characterize influence.[47] Acquisition necessarily occurs by exchange since the resources on which authority is based reside outside the person. The administrator acquires command over organizational resources in exchange for his agreement to allocate personal resources in the manner specified by the rules that define his position. If the organization is to maximize the probability of achieving its goals, candidates for office must be chosen on the basis of their technical competence rather than their personal affinity to those with appointive authority.[48] Considerations of referent power or of resources other than the form of expertise required to fulfill the duties of office should not be injected into the appointment transaction.

Communication that an individual controls organizational resources usually occurs by attribution rather than observation. Rules that define the resource rights of a given position also attribute those rights to the incumbent.[49] If rules are to fulfill their function of ensuring that all organizational resources are directed toward intended goals, they must allocate the entire stock among specified positions. That is, they must completely enumerate the resources that are assigned to each position, and the summation of these assignments across all positions should exhaust the entire stock. Failure to do so invites misallocation or subversion of resources to the personal use of those who achieve a claim on them by the exercise of *influence*. Misuse of resources may occur even though the rules have completely allocated the stock, but such infractions can be identified if the rules are promulgated. Those who observe a resource expenditure may refer to the regulations and determine whether the allocation was appropriate. Thus, rules permit the incumbent's actions to be monitored by comparisons of observed power with attributed power.

We have defined legitimate power as power whose existence and exercise is collectively approved. In the discussion of influence, this definition referred to approval by those who are the recipients of influence because that relationship involved only two status levels: influentials and influencees. Authority relations, however, generally involve at least three levels in the organizational hierarchy. The administrator occupies a formal position that controls those that are linked to it in a subordinate relationship and, at the same time, is controlled by those linked to it in a superior relationship. The concept of legitimation is relevant to both sets of linkages. In the context of formal organizations, an individual's power is said to be "authorized" when it is legitimated by superiors and "endorsed" when it is legitimated by subordinates.[50] Ideally, the criteria for both forms of legit-

[47]The following discussion draws heavily on Weber, *op. cit.*; Merton, *op. cit.*; Scott, *op. cit.*, pp. 311–320, 351–356, and 384–392; and Terence K. Hopkins, "Bureaucratic Authority: The Convergence of Weber and Barnard," in *Complex Organizations: A Sociological Reader*, Amitai Etzioni (Ed.) (New York: Holt, Rinehart and Winston, 1961), pp. 82–98.

[48]Weber, *op. cit.*, p. 333.

[49]*Ibid.*, p. 330.

[50]Scott, *op. cit.*, pp. 386–387.

imation are the rules that define each position's jurisdiction over resources and direct their allocation. Superiors and subordinates are expected to view the administrator's control over and expenditure of organizational resources as legitimate as long as these are consistent with positional rules. If superiors fail to authorize an administrator's power when it is exercised in a manner consistent with the rules, they deprive him of resources that are presumably necessary to perform assigned duties and he cannot be held accountable for a failure to achieve the stated goals of his position. For example, a supervisor may not rightly be subjected to discipline for the poor performance of subordinates if his positional rights to hire and fire have been consistently overridden by superiors. In such a case, the administrator would possess responsibility without authority. The failure of subordinates to endorse power that corresponds to the rules of position may reduce the likelihood that the organization will achieve its goals if non-legitimation is accompanied by such behaviors as group restriction of output or sabotage. These effects are discussed more fully in later paragraphs.

In order to coordinate the allocation of organizational resources, rules generally constrain the exercise of power to relationships among linked hierarchical positions. Exchanges outside the established network suggest that the network is deficient or that resources are being misallocated. These "illegal" transactions may be based on referent or expert power. Although it *may* be functional for a subordinate to respond to his superior out of "a desire for oneness," it is generally dysfunctional for him to make resource allocation decisions on the basis of such a relationship with those in other positions.

The exercise of expert power outside a linkage presents a more complex problem.[51] As mentioned earlier, appointments in an idealized formal organization are based on considerations of expertise. If this is the case, the individual's authority of office also achieves legitimation on the basis of his expertise and—assuming that the latter is utilized in a manner consistent with organizational goals—the exercise of both power forms is simultaneous and inseparable. In some cases, the organization provides administrators with access to additional "knowledge resources" by linking them to positions formally created to supply technical assistance. The problems created by such "line and staff" relationships are well known. The exercise of expert power by an individual over those outside a staff or control linkage generally represents a misallocation of resources. The expert is himself an organizational resource that has been allocated to a specified jurisdiction. His exercise of power elsewhere, unless authorized by his superiors on an ad hoc basis, reduces the quantity of resources that were intended to be directed toward the accomplishment of his positional goals.

The central importance of rules to the concept of authority should now be clear. They define a position's jurisdiction over organizational resources (which include the incumbents of subordinate positions), specify the personal resources that are to be evaluated in selecting among candidates for office, communicate the administrator's control over organizational resources and direct the manner in which they are to be allocated, provide rational criteria for legitimating the exercise of power within the organiza-

[51]For a more detailed discussion of this topic, see Amitai Etzioni, *Modern Organizations* (Englewood Cliffs, N.J.: Prentice-Hall, Inc., 1964), pp. 75–77.

tion, and create a network of relationships among all positions. The effectiveness of an authority system is measured by the extent to which organizational rules are obeyed.[52] If the *content* of rules allocates resources in an efficient manner, then the test of effectiveness for the authority system is identical to the test for organizational effectiveness.

We shall now consider the implications of authority for interpersonal relationships. In order to do so, the "human element" must be introduced into the framework of the rules that define the power balance among positions within the formal organization. When an individual is appointed to office, he brings along personal resources other than technical expertise. Their utilization may expand or contract the limits of his intra-organizational power beyond those defined by the rules. He also brings goals and values that are not necessarily consistent with those specified in the definition of his position. Moreover, the administrator's superiors and subordinates also possess resources, values, and goals other than those specified in their positional definitions. Each of these factors may generate *influence* forces that place an authority system under stress and elicit behaviors that are inconsistent with the organization's rules and goals. On the other hand, the authority system shapes and constrains the interplay of these "non-rational" forces so that resultant behaviors differ from those that would occur in an informal setting.

The third section of this chapter depicted the acquisition and exercise of influence as a competitive process in which each individual communicates his possession of resources and matches them against those controlled by others. Evidence was cited to support the contention that this competition produces negative feelings among the "losers," which tend to reduce the relationship's stability. One would expect less friction of this kind to occur in authority relationships because rules *define* the power balance between linked positions, thereby removing the need to establish a hierarchy via competitive scramble. Indeed, the rules specifically intend that "power plays" be foreclosed. Individuals are appointed to office with prior knowledge of their relationship to superiors, and acceptance of appointment signifies their expectation and willingness to respond to those in higher position. This proposition was verified in Berkowitz's study of seventy-two business and governmental committees, which showed that formally designated leaders did not engender negative reactions when they attempted to control the behavior of subordinates.[53] Indeed, such reactions developed only if control was *not* exerted. The distribution of power by rules may also reduce friction because there is less need for superiors to engage in behaviors that at once reinforce his position and alienate subordinates. Research by Carter and his associates indicated that appointed leaders act less aggressively than do those who achieve power on the basis of purely personal resources.[54] As compared to emergent leaders, individuals who were *appointed* to leadership roles showed lower interaction levels (which permitted subordinates to increase their own), were less argumentive and defensive, and were more likely to perform routine tasks themselves

[52]Hopkins, *op. cit.*, p. 85.

[53]Leonard Berkowitz, "Sharing Leadership in Small, Decision-Making Groups," *Journal of Abnormal and Social Psychology*, Vol. 48 (1953), pp. 231–238.

[54]Carter *et al., op. cit.*, pp. 591 and 594.

rather than delegate these to others. The authors suggest that these results may be attributable to the appointed leaders' knowledge that his position was secure and need not be continually reinforced by a display of power.

Rules operate in other important ways to increase interpersonal harmony. Merton states that the constraints that regulations impose on behavior protect subordinates from arbitrary action by their superiors.[55] In specifying the rights and duties of each position, rules place explicit limits on the content of the commands that superiors may give. The psychological security that subordinates derive from the knowledge that their obligation to obey is bounded reduces the likelihood that they will engage in defensive tactics that obstruct the functioning of interpersonal relationships. In many cases this security is enhanced by rules that establish due process procedures, such as a grievance system, for adjudicating disputes over the appropriateness of a command.[56] Subordinates are further protected from arbitrary sanction insofar as the rules that specify the duties of office also define minimum acceptable levels of performance and enable the subordinate to predict the conditions under which he is subject to sanction.[57] Finally, rules reduce interpersonal conflict by the very fact that they *depersonalize* certain aspects of relationships that are marked by a power differential. This seeming paradox results from what Gouldner terms the "screening" functions of rule.[58] Regulations that define job duties have the effect of programming subordinate behavior and reduce the frequency with which superiors must issue directives. There is considerable empirical evidence that employee satisfaction and morale increase with decreases in the closeness of supervision.[59] This may result, in part, from the fact that subordinates are not continually reminded that they are at a power disadvantage. In Gouldner's words: ". . . the rules provide the foreman with an impersonal crutch for his authority, screening the superiority of his power which might otherwise violate the norm of equality."[60]

Rules also enable superiors to cast themselves in the role of (perhaps reluctant) agents who are only implementing organizational laws, rather than imposing their personal wills, when they issue directives. This permits subordinates to obey without loss of face. Negative emotions are likely to be particularly strong when directives involve some form of punishment. In such instances, part of the hostility may be drained off if the punishment is "legitimated" by rules. As pointed out earlier, rules serve the warning function of informing officeholders of the behaviors that will call forth the application of sanctions. If such rules are consistently applied, violators have foreknowledge that they will be disciplined, and punishment is less likely to be viewed by the guilty party or his peers as an unexpected and capricious exercise of personal whim. Gouldner states that the "punish-

[55]Merton, *op. cit.*, pp. 195–196.

[56]By contrast, there are no constraints on the exercise of influence other than the influential's ethics and the terms of trade available to influencees in alternative transactions.

[57]Alvin W. Gouldner, *Patterns of Industrial Bureaucracy* (New York: The Free Press, 1954), reprinted in Scott, *op. cit.*, p. 327.

[58]*Ibid.*

[59]For a summary of such studies, see Robert L. Kahn and Daniel Katz, "Leadership Practices in Relation to Productivity and Morale," in Cartwright and Zander, *op. cit.*, pp. 554–570.

[60]Gouldner, *op. cit.*, p. 322.

ment-legitimating" function is strengthened if the rule specifies not only the behaviors that will result but also the form and intensity of punishment for each type of infraction.[61] This is particularly common in union-management relationships—a situation that is, on balance, functional from the administrator's standpoint since "illegitimate" discipline is likely to generate concerted reaction from a powerful adversary.[62]

However, rules cannot be expected to completely resolve the subordinate's ambivalence toward his superiors. Regardless of the fact that power in formal organizations is distributed, constrained, and screened by rules, subordinates are still fully aware that theirs is a dependent relationship. Dependence on the organizational resources commanded by superiors is often translated into dependence on the persons who occupy those offices. Those persons possess resources and characteristics that are unrelated to their formal position. Ideally, such personal resources would be overlooked and the administrator's right to control would be endorsed on the same rational bases that the administrator's superiors considered in authorizing him that right. Clearly, that is not always the case. Subordinates may grant or withhold legitimation on bases other than those related to organizational goals. Legitimation by subordinates cannot be dictated through rules, but must be won by the administrator. The section on influence discussed the important increment to power that is gained by legitimation. This same power—the enforcement of group norms through social pressure—may be tapped and directed toward organizational goals. Alternatively, the group may withhold this incremental power or even turn it against those goals. The following paragraphs will consider two bases of achieving endorsement of authority systems and will discuss empirical evidence regarding their effects.

A superior may attain the endorsement of subordinates by gaining their acceptance of him as a person. This might be accomplished through communications that indicate that the superior possesses personal resources, such as expertise or affective qualities, that are of value in the attainment of the work group's goals. Such resources reinforce those that are controlled by virtue of the superior's formal position and provide a basis for legitimation. The research of French and Snyder provides support for the prediction that the achievement of personal acceptance yields dividends in the form of incremental power.[63] The authors assembled four-man teams composed of three enlisted men and their superior non-commissioned officer (NCO). The enlisted men were asked to rate their NCO on two scales, one measuring personal affect and the other expertise. Each officer's ability to control the behavior of his subordinates was then observed on one task that required him to change their judgments of the length of lines in a geometric figure and on another that required him to direct their activities in a simple card-sorting task. The findings indicated that NCOs who were better liked were also more successful in changing their subordinates' opinions and were able to induce higher productivity on the card-sort task. The ability to

[61]*Ibid.*, p. 325.

[62]The complete specification is in itself an indication that the union has the power to enforce due process procedures on the employer.

[63]John R. P. French and Richard Snyder, "Leadership and Interpersonal Power," in Cartwright, *op. cit.*, p. 148.

change opinion was also found to be positively correlated with the subordinates' ranking of the NCO on the perceived expertise scale. In short, superiors who had achieved personal acceptance on either the affective or expertise dimension acquired personal power in addition to their authority. It is interesting that the authors also found that the number of control attempts by the NCO rose with increases in acceptance.[64] We have suggested elsewhere that a high volume of directives from a power figure is generally met with hostility. It is possible that such a result would have occurred in the French and Snyder study had the experiment continued over a long period of time. Alternatively, and probably more likely, legitimated directives do not produce the negative emotions that are generally associated with dependency relationships.[65]

A second method of legitimating the exercise of power is to involve the subordinate group in the process by which rules are established. This technique differs from the first in that it induces acceptance of the regulations rather than of the superior. As they participate in the rule-making process, subordinates are in effect binding *themselves* to behave in certain ways and signifying their advance acceptance of directives that are consistent with those rules. Enforcement of the rules may then be supported by group pressure as well as the superior's authority. The value of group participation for achieving group acceptance of new regulations was clearly shown in Coch and French's study of the effects of a change in production methods at a manufacturing plant.[66] Work changes of equal difficulty were introduced into four employee groups. One group was simply told that the production department had modified the process and the piece rate because of competitive conditions. A second was shown the need for change by means of a product comparison that elicited the group's informal agreement that cost reductions were necessary. This group then elected representatives who worked with management to review the job, eliminate needless operations, set new piece rates, and train the others. In two other groups the changes were introduced by a "total participation" process that was similar to the second variation except that *all* operators participated in designing the new job. The changes for all three sets of groups were then introduced and output over a thirty-two-day period was compared to the prechange standard output of sixty units. The "no participation" group's production hovered around fifty units and at no time rose above fifty-five; the "representative participation" group rose steadily after the change, and climbed to almost seventy units; the "total participation" groups' output exceeded the others' over the entire period and was above seventy units by the end of the experiment. Moreover, 17 per cent of the "no participation" group quit within forty days; there were no quits in the other groups.[67] The authors attribute at least a part of these results to group pressures. There was evidence that such pressures enforced a norm of output restriction in

[64]*Ibid.*, p. 147.

[65]Verba, *op. cit.*, pp. 170–172.

[66]Lester Coch and John R. P. French, Jr., "Overcoming Resistance to Change," *Human Relations*, Vol. 1 (1948), pp. 512–532.

[67]The benefits of participation were validated later when the "no participation group" was transferred to a new job under "total participation" conditions. The results were virtually identical to those of the "total participation" group in the first experiment.

the "no participation" group, but spurred production in the other cases. The act of participation apparently legitimated both the *need* for new work rules and the rules themselves, so that the group forces operated to ensure their successful implementation.[68]

Other evidence that participation may be used to achieve legitimation of organizational goals and rules is provided in MacGregor's analysis of the Scanlon Plan.[69] When a firm adopts the Plan, employees participate in decision-making by means of a joint management-employee board that reviews recommendations on any aspect of the firm's activities and decides whether they should be implemented. The cost savings from such a suggestion are divided among employees and management on the basis of a formula that is designated in advance. In some ways, the Plan is an extension of the "participation by representation" variation of the Coch and French study because it provides a basis for the employee legitimation of rule changes through (elected) representatives on the review board. Group forces as well as the authority and monetary reward systems then enforce obedience to the new rules. In some cases, the Plan has yielded startling efficiencies.[70]

Of course, the attempt to achieve legitimation by participation is not without its dangers. If workers reject management's contention that changes are needed, the unilateral imposition of revised rules would then be viewed as illegitimate and (possibly) cause the marshaling of group pressures against their successful implementation. The effects of such negative pressures on production have been verified in the classic study by Roethlisberger and Dickson of work groups at the Hawthorne plant as well as in the "no participation" variation of the Coch and French research.[71] In order to avoid this danger, participatory methods might be confined to the implementation stage *after* a policy change has been developed by management. Discussion with employees of the circumstances that precipitate the need for change can provide the superior with information about whether the work group views the new goals as legitimate. If the reaction is positive, the administrator may then utilize fuller participation to develop the specific goal-oriented rule changes so as to achieve their legitimation. If the reaction is negative, he must then exercise his authority to impose and monitor the changes he deems appropriate. Clearly, the key to the process is the first step in which the need for change and the goals to be pursued receive the group's endorsement. This is probably most easily achieved in crisis situa-

[68]Coch and French, *op. cit.*, pp. 530–531.

[69]Douglas McGregor, "The Scanlon Plan Through a Psychologist's Eyes," in *The Scanlon Plan: A Frontier in Labor-Management Cooperation*, Frederick G. Lesieur (Ed.) (Cambridge, Massachusetts: M.I.T. Press, 1958), pp. 89–99.

[70]Russell W. Davenport, "Enterprise for Everyman," in *The Scanlon Plan, op. cit.*, p. 18.

[71]F. J. Roethlisberger and W. J. Dickson, "Management and the Worker," *Business Research Studies*, No. 9 (Cambridge, Massachusetts: Harvard Business School, Division of Research, 1939), Chapter XVIII. There is evidence to suggest that the use of group participation in introducing change will not result in production increases when strong norms to restrict production already exist. See J. R. P. French, Jr., J. Israel, and D. As, "An Experiment on Participation in a Norwegian Factory," *Human Relations*, Vol. 13 (1960), pp. 3–19.

tions when the organization is in danger. It is perhaps for this reason that the Scanlon Plan has generally been most effective when the firm is in danger of financial collapse.[72]

It should not be assumed that failure to achieve endorsement through personal acceptance or participation necessarily results in a drastic loss of efficiency. A study by Evan and Zelditch of the behavior of employees in an experimentally created bureaucracy showed that subordinates who perceived their superiors to be experts did not achieve higher production on a routine task and were no more likely to obey purely procedural rules than those who felt that their superiors lacked expertise.[73] Moreover, virtually all participants thought that their superiors had a right to expect obedience regardless of their opinion of his technical competence. Apparently, the authority of the superior's office was sufficient to legitimate his power even without endorsement based on personal resources. On the other hand, a significantly greater number of acts of covert and overt disobedience to commands on matters that required expertise occurred among those who viewed their superior as inferior. One might conclude from this that the achievement of legitimacy is probably more essential for superiors who direct activities of a creative or non-routine nature, or who are unable to closely monitor subordinates' activities. In both cases the norm of compliance can then be enforced by group pressure and by the subject's own value system:

> . . . when the exercise of power is seen as legitimate by those subject to it—that is, when the orders issued or rules set conform to the values to which the subjects are committed—compliance with be much deeper and more effective. The subject will "internalize" the rules. He will find the discipline less alienating and he will continue to follow rules and orders when the organization's power is weakened or even absent.[74]

We have seen that authority systems—as specified in formal rules—serve the organization by constraining the allocation of its resources toward uses that are expected to maximize the probability that the specified goals will be attained. Such systems were also shown to reduce friction in interpersonal relations by reducing the need for competition, by providing a rational basis for legitimating power, and by depersonalizing its exercise. There is a well-known dictum in economics that "there's no such thing as a free lunch"—there is a cost associated with every benefit. In view of this *caveat,* it is important to consider some costs that might be borne by the organization and its officials as a result of the structuring of power relationships by formal rules. One such negative byproduct may be personal and organizational rigidity. As mentioned earlier, the test of an effective authority system is the degree to which officeholders obey the rules. If the rules are correctly specified, such obedience will also maximize the organizational goals. However, Merton argues that the devotion to regulation that

[72]George P. Shultz, "Variations in Environment and the Scanlon Plan," in Lesieur, *op. cit.,* p. 102.

[73]William M. Evan and Morris Zelditch, Jr., "A Laboratory Experiment on Bureaucratic Authority," *American Sociological Review,* Vol. 26 (1961), pp. 883–893.

[74]Etzioni, *Modern Organizations, op. cit.,* p. 51.

is demanded by the organization transforms those rules into absolutes such that obedience becomes an end in itself.[75] Because no set of rules can dictate the appropriate response to all contingencies, strict adherence to existing regulation prevents the administrator from adapting to situations that fall outside the rules or to a changed external environment that renders behavior specified by the existing rules inappropriate for achieving the organization's goals. Such a tendency is further heightened by the fact that obedience to rules protects the administrator from censure by his superiors. Behavior that does not maximize organizational goals may be "justified" simply because it conforms to regulation. Readers who have enjoyed the hospitality of the armed forces for any period can readily attest to the tendency toward rigidity that results in the sacrifice of organizational goals in favor of rigid compliance to rules.

Clearly, there is some conflict between the organization's need to coordinate behavior through imposition of rules and its need to adapt in a manner that will maximize the probability that it will achieve its goals. Organizations that are characterized by a high degree of interdependence among the functions of various offices necessarily require a complex rule structure and rather strict obedience in order that activities may be effectively coordinated. In such cases, the conflict between creativity and discipline may be at least partially resolved by creating and encouraging the use of formal mechanisms for upward communication within the hierarchy so that superiors may be continually apprised of changed circumstances that require a revision of the rules. Effective upward communication may also permit supervisors to legitimate in advance some actions of subordinates that depart from established rules but that are more efficient in terms of organizational goals. Where technology permits, adaptation may be further encouraged (indeed enforced) by evaluation rules that test the behavior of administrators' actions against the organization's goals rather than behavioral rules.[76]

The authority system is particularly likely to come into conflict with the need for adaptation in organizations such as research laboratories in which the major goal is to maximize creativity. Part of the conflict arises from the personality characteristics of the inhabitants of such organizations. Steiner states that highly creative persons are more likely to view authority as "conventional or arbitrary, contingent on continued and demonstrable superiority."[77] In addition, the organizational structure that will maximize coordination and control over activities is in direct conflict with that which is most likely to induce creativity. We have stated that effective authority systems are hierarchical and that communication among position occupants is limited to channels that are specified by the formal structure. However, the potential for creativity is maximized when there is a free flow of information among all members of the organization. This flow is impeded by communication linkages that are rigidly enforced and by barriers that result from differences in hierarchical status. Organizations engaged in crea-

[75]Merton, *op. cit.*, p. 200.

[76]For an example of such a system, see Peter M. Blau and W. Richard Scott, *Formal Organizations* (San Francisco: Chandler Publishing Company, 1962), pp. 129–131.

[77]Gary A. Steiner, *The Creative Organization* (University of Chicago, Selected Papers No. 10), p. 13.

tive activities may seek to resolve these conflicting needs by decentralization, separation of creative from administrative or production functions, and minimizing the status distances among offices.[78]

Finally, one may ask whether the impersonality and discipline associated with authority systems have serious implications for the administrator's personal behavior. Does continued employment in a hierarchical structure result in a tendency to view more non-formal relationships in terms of power differentials? Can the impersonality required of the individual-as-official be confined to organizational relationships? Can personal ethics be preserved in situations in which the norm of obedience to authority demands compliance with a morally questionable command? There is little research evidence to suggest answers to the first two questions. That which exists for the third question is decidedly gloomy. A series of studies by Stanley Milgram suggests that a substantial fraction of individuals who find themselves in a subordinate relationship are willing to obey commands that conflict with widely accepted ethical norms.[79] Although there are numerous possible explanations for this result, one is particularly frightening to students of authority. Milgram suggests that individuals can, under certain circumstances, assume a "state of agency" wherein they view themselves as instruments of others and follow directions without evaluating the implications of their behavior in terms of their personal value systems. Milgram describes such circumstances in the following way:

> To achieve this change, you have to be in a situation where there seems to be a ruling authority whose commands are relevant to some legitimate purpose. . . .[80]

The parallel between this description and that of the relationships within formal organizations is unmistakable. One recalls the statement by an official of a major industrial firm regarding the reaction of corporate executives to pressure from superiors to engage in illegal price fixing:

> (The Executive Vice-President's) theory had been live and let live, contact the competitors. He gave us this theory at every opportunity and we took it down to other levels and had no trouble getting the most innocent persons to go along . . . and if they didn't want to do it, they knew we would replace them.[81]

Some subordinates apparently saw the illegal orders as "legitimated" by the fact that they were given by superiors. Others were faced with a proposed transaction that involved rather unsettling terms of trade: ethics were to be exchanged for a job. One solution to such dilemmas may be derived from our initial discussion of power. In every power relationship, control is limited in part by the alternative transactions that are available to the subordinate. The continual development of such alternatives is an important safeguard to the individual's integrity.

[78]*Ibid.*, p. 23.

[79]Stanley Milgram, "Behavioral Study of Obedience," *Journal of Abnormal and Social Psychology*, Vol. 67 (1963), pp. 371–378.

[80]Philip Meyer, "If Hitler Asked You to Electrocute a Stranger, Would You?" *Esquire* (February, 1970), p. 132.

[81]Richard A. Smith, "The Incredible Electrical Conspiracy," *Fortune* (April, 1961), p. 137.

MANAGERIAL IMPLICATIONS: AN OVERVIEW

When an individual accepts a managerial position, he is thrust into a web of power relationships with superiors, subordinates, and occupants of lateral positions. In many cases, this web extends beyond organizational boundaries to suppliers, customers, and competitors. The manager's effectiveness, in both personal and organizational terms, is largely determined by his ability to affect the behavior of others through the social exchange process. This ability, which we have termed social power, is grounded in the value of resources commanded by the manager relative to those possessed by potential exchange partners and by rivals who seek to deal with the same partners. From the administrator's point of view, career success is measured in terms of the employment conditions which he is able to exact in exchange for his skills, knowledge, energy, and other personal resources. From the organization's point of view, the administrator's effectiveness is measured by the ratio between the benefits that he generates (sales, reduced costs, etc.) and the organizational resources that are expended on his position. Thus, the manager's association with the organization exhibits the partial conflict and partial dependency that characterize power relationships.

In his interactions with subordinates, the administrator brings to bear the organizational resources that are delegated to his position as well as his personal resources. We have defined "authority" as power based on the former resources and "influence" as power generated by the latter. Authority is exercised when subordinates are induced to behave in a certain way by the superior's offer to allocate or to continue allocating organizational resources in a manner that satisfies subordinates' needs. Organizational efficiency is maximized when the ratio of the organizational benefits that accrue from the subordinates' behaviors relative to the resources expended is at a maximum. Ideally, then, the administrator's performance would be evaluated by comparing the benefit-cost ratio he actually achieves and the maximum level attainable. In most cases, however, the latter is unknown and the evaluation generally takes the form of an implicit or explicit comparison between achieved benefit-cost ratios and some "satisfactory" ratio.

The efficiency criterion defined earlier corresponds to the power model that was presented in this chapter. Its use as an evaluation device draws attention to the fact that the manager's central function is to search for ways to improve the terms of trade with subordinates. In some cases the search may suggest that an improved benefit-cost ratio can be achieved by an actual or threatened reduction in the quantity of organizational resources allocated for the benefit of subordinates. For example, an analysis of the labor market may reveal the existence of large numbers of unemployed persons with skills equivalent to those possessed by subordinates. The knowledge of this ready alternative to the present workforce may permit the manager to induce higher output from employees at the current wage or to maintain output at a reduced wage. In other cases, the search may suggest that an improvement in the ratio can be achieved by allocating larger quantities of resources in a manner that will induce a greater than proportionate increase in output, such as the adoption of advanced technology.

Even though the manager may be continually engaged in the search for more efficient alternatives, at any point in time he must operate with the specific group of individuals who are currently on his staff. Assuming that their performance is adequate, it is to the manager's advantage to keep the work group intact. This can be accomplished only if their reward-for-effort-expended equals or exceeds the expected return from alternative employment. In some cases, employees may become aware of such alternatives through chance contacts or casual search processes that require little effort, such as the perusal of newspaper want ads. Often, however, the knowledge of other job opportunities can be gained only by significant resource expenditures in the form of registration with a private fee-charging agency or successive visits to other establishments. An employee's willingness to engage in active search is perhaps most often triggered by dissatisfaction with current employment conditions. A key element in the arousal of dissatisfaction is the failure of actual job conditions to conform with expectations. We have seen that exchanges are entered when both parties expect that the returns equal or exceed those from alternative transactions. These expectations may be altered over time, but the relationship will remain stable for as long as prior expectations are fulfilled or exceeded and expected future net benefits are positive. If the employment relationship is intended to be long term (multi-exchange) in nature, the administrator should take steps to ensure that employees enter the organization with an accurate set of expectations regarding the benefits they are to receive and the resources they will be asked to expend. As the employment relationship continues, the manager must exercise care in his own behavior to avoid raising expectations that he is not willing to fulfill. Failure to achieve such accurate expectations may generate subordinate dissatisfaction, trigger the search for alternative employment, and result in the loss of a valued work group member. The costs associated with this loss will, of course, vary with the amount of resources that must be expended to search out and train a suitable replacement.

The development of accurate expectations among subordinates is by no means an easy task. Individuals enter employment relationships with prior expectations about myriad job factors: pay, work-pace, environmental conditions, disciplinary policy, and so on. Although the administrator may be able to predict many of the factors that are of major importance to all employees, it is impossible to anticipate all of them in any specific case because of the variation among individuals with respect to needs and tastes. Thus, if the relationship is to be stable, the subordinate must also be encouraged to express his own priorities. When the spectrum of key factors has been identified, the superior may then state the organization's expectations regarding these factors so that the potential employee will have an accurate estimate of the benefits and costs associated with acceptance of the position. The conditions for such communication must be maintained because expectations on both sides of the exchange will generally be altered as the relationship continues.

The maintenance of congruent manager-subordinate expectations becomes more crucial when group dynamics are considered. We have seen that individuals interacting in a group tend to develop shared expectations regarding matters of mutual interest. In work situations, group expectations commonly develop about the employment terms of trade—i.e., about the manner in which the superior should exercise authority and about the appropriate worker response. When authority is exercised in accordance with such group expectations, the administrator's power is said to be "legitimated" and he obtains a twofold benefit. First, the individual worker who has no prior expectations regarding the appropriateness of a legitimated directive will tend to regard it positively because his perceptions will be heavily influenced by those of other group members. Second, even if the directive runs counter to an individual's expectations, he faces the prospect of being sanctioned by the group as well as by the superior if he demurs from obeying. Thus, the achievement of legitimation adds an increment to the administrator's power. On the other hand, if a manager attempts to exercise authority in a manner that is inconsistent with group norms, the same forces may be generated against compliance. This may bring about a group withdrawal from the employment relationship resulting in the necessity of hiring and training an entire work force. Alternatively, group members may form a coalition that is able to exact more favorable terms of trade (a lower benefit-cost ratio) from their superior through their combined ability to impose a greater cost of disagreement. The primary example of the latter response is, of course, unionization.

It is particularly important that employees have accurate expectations regarding the bases on which their performance will be evaluated. Uncertainty or misunderstanding regarding the evaluation scheme prevents subordinates from concentrating their resources on activities that will yield the maximum payoff for themselves and—assuming that the reward system is appropriately structured—for the organization. Moreover, the imposition of sanctions by a superior is almost certain to appear arbitrary and illegitimate under such circumstances. When the subordinate's task involves programmed activities, the communication of management's expectations regarding satisfactory performance is a relatively easy matter: step-by-step procedures can be explained in detail and the level of required output can be specified. Evaluation can then be based on the subordinate's ability to follow procedures at the required pace. The situation is considerably more difficult when the task is so complex that the subordinate must exercise a substantial degree of judgment in selecting the appropriate procedure. These conditions are common to managerial and creative occupations. In such cases, the superior must rely on "management by results" and the task of communicating expectations regarding the evaluation criteria requires an operational statement of the goals to be achieved. Such goals may be difficult to specify when the output cannot be measured in physical units.

If the performance and evaluation criteria have been fully communicated before the subordinate is employed, then the exercise of authority consistent with such prior expectations is likely to be viewed as legitimate. However, most organizations exist in an environment of constant change so that alterations in these criteria are frequently necessary. Such changes are particularly likely to produce dissatisfaction. The manager's goal in introducing change should be to achieve legitimation of the new requirements so that group forces will be generated in the direction of compliance. As discussed in this chapter, one approach to achieving endorsement of change is by involving subordinates in the change process. This generally requires two steps. First, the conditions that impel the organization to alter its requirements must be effectively communicated to subordinates so that the *need* for change and the new performance goals are viewed as legitimate. If the goals are accepted, subordinates may then be encouraged to participate fully in the development of specific procedures to achieve them. The subsequent enforcement of new policies that have been developed in this way is more likely to be viewed as legitimate because the rules are partly a creation of those who are subject to them.

It should be clearly stated that the use of participation as a means to legitimate change is not equivalent to the institution of democratic processes within organizations. The determination that alterations in market conditions, technology, legal constraints, and the like require a change in policy and the specification of new performance goals must be made by those who ultimately control the organization's resources—that is, by those with authority. Goal determination cannot be a matter for democratic choice except in those rare cases, such as cooperatives, in which organizational ownership rests with the employees. It is for this reason that employee participation must generally be limited to the implementation stage, and then only if the administrator is fairly certain that his subordinates accept the need for change and view the new goals as legitimate. If these conditions do not exist, the manager should calculate the balance of power between himself and his subordinates by estimating the costs of imposing the change relative to the costs of retaining the status quo. If the latter costs exceed the former, then the efficiency criterion demands that the change be imposed.

Finally, it is clear from the above that superior-subordinate relationships are likely to be marked by stress. We have seen that the mutual dependency inherent in every power relationship creates ambivalence. Both parties have parallel interests insofar as the maintenance of the relationship satisfies their respective needs, but both are to some degree competitors insofar as the net benefits that accrue to one partner *could* be increased by reducing those that accrue to the other. Administrators who are aware that subordinates feel such ambivalence toward them may be able to reduce the negative emotional component and thereby improve the stability of the relationship. One possibility is to establish boundaries on the superior's own power by clearly defining the rights and duties of the subordinate's position. Second, the administrator may "screen" his power differential by establishing rules that program the subordinate's repetitive duties and reduce the number of occasions on which directives must be issued. Finally, the superior may institute rules that legitimate the imposition of sanctions by specifying in advance the punishment for various infractions and by providing due process procedures in discipline cases. These possibilities, all of which are derived from Gouldner, depersonalize the relationship by interposing rules between the administrator and his subordinates. It is a curiosity of power relationships that depersonalization is often the most effective means for safeguarding personal integrity.

SUGGESTIONS FOR FUTURE READING

BOOKS

BLAU, PETER M., *Exchange and Power in Social Life* (New York: John Wiley & Sons, 1964).

———, AND W. RICHARD SCOTT, *Formal Organizations* (San Francisco: Chandler Publishing Company, 1962).

CARTWRIGHT, DORWIN (Ed.), *Studies in Social Power* (Ann Arbor: University of Michigan Research Center for Group Dynamics, Institute for Social Research, 1959).

———, AND ALVIN ZANDER (Eds.), *Group Dynamics: Research and Theory*, 2d ed. (Evanston, Illinois: Row, Peterson and Company for Research Center for Group Dynamics, University of Michigan, 1960).

CHAMBERLAIN, NEIL W., *Labor* (New York: McGraw-Hill Book Co., Inc., 1958).

ETZIONI, AMITAI (Ed.), *Complex Organizations: A Sociological Reader* (New York: Holt, Rinehart and Winston, 1961).

———, *Modern Organizations* (Englewood Cliffs, N.J.: Prentice-Hall, Inc. 1964).

FESTINGER, LEON, STANLEY SCHACHTER, AND KURT BACK, *Social Pressures in Informal Groups* (New York: Harper & Row, 1950).

FRIEDMAN, MILTON, *Capitalism and Freedom* (Chicago: University of Chicago Press, 1962).

FRIEDRICH, CARL J. (Ed.), *Authority* (Cambridge: Harvard University Press for the American Society of Political and Legal Philosophy, 1958).

GOULDNER, ALVIN W., *Patterns of Industrial Bureaucracy* (New York: The Free Press, 1954).

HOMANS, GEORGE C., *Social Behavior: Its Elementary Forms* (New York: Harcourt, Brace and World, 1961).

KATZ, ELIHU, AND PAUL F. LAZARSFELD, *Personal Influence* (Glencoe, Illinois: The Free Press, 1955).

LEAVITT, HAROLD J., *Managerial Psychology: An Introduction to Individuals, Pairs, and Groups in Organizations*, 2d ed. (Chicago: University of Chicago Press, 1964).

LESIEUR, FREDERICK G. (Ed.), *The Scanlon Plan: A Frontier in Labor-Management Cooperation* (Cambridge, Massachusetts: M.I.T. Press, 1958).

MACCOBY, ELEANOR E., THEODORE M. NEWCOMB, AND EUGENE L. HARTLEY (Eds.), *Readings in Social Psychology*, 3rd ed. (New York: Holt, Rinehart and Winston, 1958).

MERTON, ROBERT K., *Social Theory and Social Structure*, rev. ed. (New York: The Free Press, 1957).

PEABODY, ROBERT L., *Organizational Authority: Superior-Subordinate Relationships in Three Public Service Organizations* (New York: Atherton Press, 1964).

ROETHLISBERGER, F. J., AND W. J. DICKSON, "Management and the Worker." *Business Research Studies*, No. 9 (Cambridge, Massachusetts: Harvard Business School, Division of Research, 1939).

SCOTT, W. RICHARD (Ed.), *Social Processes and Social Structures: An Introduction to Sociology* (New York: Holt, Rinehart and Winston, 1970).

VERBA, SIDNEY, *Small Groups and Political Behavior: A Study of Leadership* (Princeton, N.J.: Princeton University Press, 1961).

WEBER, MAX, *The Theory of Social and Economic Organization*, translated by A. M. Henderson and Talcott Parsons (New York: The Free Press; London: Collier-Macmillan Limited, 1947).

WHYTE, WILLIAM FOOTE, *Street Corner Society: The Social Structure of an Italian Slum*, 2d ed. (Chicago and London: University of Chicago Press, 1955).

ARTICLES

BERKOWITZ, LEONARD, "Sharing Leadership in Small, Decision-Making Groups," *Journal of Abnormal and Social Psychology*, Vol. 48 (1953), pp. 231–238.

BETTELHEIM, BRUNO, "Individual and Mass Behavior in Extreme Situations," *Journal of Abnormal and Social Psychology*, Vol. 38 (1943), p. 451. (16)

CARTER, LAUNOR *et al.*, "The Behavior of Leaders and Other Group Members," *Journal of Abnormal and Social Psychology*, Vol. 46 (1951), pp. 589–595. (4)

COCH, LESTER, and JOHN R. P. FRENCH, JR., "Overcoming Resistance to Change," *Human Relations*, Vol. 1 (1948), pp. 512–532. (16)

EMERSON, RICHARD M., "Power-Dependence Relations," *American Sociological Review*, Vol. 27 (1962), p. 32.

EVAN, WILLIAM M., AND MORRIS ZELDITCH, JR., "A Laboratory Experiment on Bureaucratic Authority," *American Sociological Review*, Vol. 26 (1961), pp. 883–893.

FRENCH, J. R. P., JR., J. ISRAEL, AND D. AS, "An Experiment on Participation in a Norwegian Factory," *Human Relations*, Vol. 13 (1960), pp. 3–19.

HEIDER, FRITZ, "Attitudes and Cognitive Organizations," *Journal of Psychology*, Vol. 21 (1946), pp. 107–112.

HEINICKE, C., AND ROBERT F. BALES, "Developmental Trends in the Structure of Small Groups," *Sociometry*, Vol. 16 (1953), pp. 35–37.

HOLLANDER, E. P., AND WILSE B. WEBB, "Leadership, Followship, and Friendship: An Analysis of Peer Nominations," *Journal of Abnormal and Social Psychology*, Vol. 50 (1955), pp. 163–167. (16)

KIRSCHT, JOHN P., THOMAS M. LODAHL, AND MASON HAIRE, "Some Factors in the Selection of Leaders by Members of Small Groups," *Journal of Abnormal and Social Psychology*, Vol. 58 (1959), pp. 406–408. (4)

LIPPIT, RONALD, NORMAN POLANSKY, FRITZ REDL, AND SIDNEY ROSEN, "The Dynamics of Power," *Human Relations*, Vol. 5 (1952), pp. 37–64. (4)

MARCH, JAMES G., "Influence Measurement in Experimental and Semi-experimental Groups," *Sociometry*, Vol. 19 (1956), pp. 260–271.

MASLOW, A. H., "A Theory of Human Motivation," *Psychological Review*, Vol. 50 (1943), pp. 370–396.

MENZEL, HERBERT, AND ELIHU KATZ, "Social Relations and Innovation in the Medical Profession: The Epidemiology of a New Drug," *Public Opinion Quarterly*, Vol. 19 (1955–1956), pp. 337–352.

MEYER, PHILIP, "If Hitler Asked You to Electrocute a Stranger, Would You?" *Esquire* (February, 1970), p. 132.

MILGRAM, STANLEY, "Behavioral Study of Obedience," *Journal of Abnormal and Social Psychology*, Vol. 67 (1963), pp. 371–378.

PEN, J., "A General Theory of Bargaining," *American Economic Review*, Vol. 62 (1952), 24–42.

SHERIF, M., "An Experimental Approach to the Study of Attitudes," *Sociometry*, Vol. 1 (1937), pp. 90–98.

SIEGEL, ALBERTA ENGVALL, AND SIDNEY SIEGEL, "Reference Groups, Membership Groups and Attitude Change," *Journal of Abnormal and Social Psychology*, Vol. 55 (1957), pp. 360–364. (4)

SMITH, RICHARD A., "The Incredible Electrical Conspiracy," *Fortune* (April, 1961), p. 137.

STIGLER, GEORGE J., "The Economics of Information," *Journal of Political Economy*, Vol. 69 (1961), pp. 213–225.

STRODTBECK, FRED L., RITA M. JAMES, AND CHARLES HAWKINS, "Social Status in Jury Deliberations," *American Sociological Review*, Vol. 22 (1957), pp. 713–719. (20)

VERPLANCK, WILLIAM S., "The Control of the Content of Conversation: Reinforcement of Statements of Opinion," *Journal of Abnormal and Social Psychology*, Vol. 51 (1955), pp. 668–676.

MONOGRAPHS

STEINER, GARY A., *The Creative Organization*. University of Chicago, Selected Papers No. 10, p. 13.

Alternative Approaches to Power, Influence and Authority

Thomas A. Petit

Professor, and Coordinator
of the Management Program
College of Business Administration
Virginia Polytechnic Institute and State University

INTRODUCTION

Robert Dahl has pointed out that so many people at so many different times have felt the need to attach the label power in so many different ways that power is probably not a Thing at all but many Things.[1] It follows, then, that the usefulness of any particular approach to power depends on the end in view. Presumably the purpose of Chapter 14 is to inform the non-expert about the nature and significance of power, influence,

[1]Robert A. Dahl, "The Concept of Power," *Behavioral Science*, Vol. 2 (1957), p. 201.

and authority in contemporary management theory and practice. Therefore, the approach should be informative, general, and comprehensive. In my view, Professor Pichler's chapter does not meet these criteria entirely because of the highly specialized economic approach that he employs.

THE ECONOMIC APPROACH TO POWER

The chapter defines *power* as "individual or collective ability to affect the thoughts, emotions, or actions of one or more other persons." *Influence* is power based on resources that are personally commanded by an individual, and *authority* is power based on resources owned by the organization and allocated to officeholders as perquisites of their office. Thus influence and authority are forms of power in an organizational context. They differ in that influence is generated through informal relations and authority is prescribed by formal structure.

Professor Pichler views power as a resource that is the currency of social exchange. It is a scarce resource and therefore an economic commodity. Each powerholder attempts to develop exchange relationships that maximize the returns he receives from his initial stock of power. Considerable space is used to develop a sophisticated theoretical model to analyze the conditions that generate and limit power in interaction between two or more parties.

This economic model is valid and undoubtedly useful in analyzing certain types of management activities, such as collective bargaining. However, it treats power, influence, and authority in such a limiting way as to exclude much material that is highly relevant for the purpose of the chapter. Power is a problem as well as a resource for the business organization. The members of the organization want personal rewards from the organization, and they must be given suitable inducements to make their contributions.[2] Power is needed to influence them to perform their necessary functions in ways consistent with the achievement of overall organizational goals, because rewards alone are not sufficient to coordinate the multitude of interdependent task activities. How employees and managers respond to power is more of a behavioral than an economic matter.

THE BEHAVIORAL APPROACH TO POWER

When a behavioral rather than an economic approach is used, the relationships among power, influence, and authority are different. Now influence is the all-inclusive concept rather than power. March and Simon have argued that influence is simply a special instance of causality—namely, the modification of one person's responses by the actions of another.[3] If this be the case, influence must be seen as an aspect of the larger study of the determinants of human behavior. Katz and Kahn follow this approach:

> . . . we have considered interaction in terms of influence. To a large extent the expected activities in terms of which individual roles are defined are expressed in terms of communicative acts of an influential character. The role prescriptions specify the persons from whom one is to accept influence and expect role-related communications, as well as the persons over whom one is expected to exert such influence and from whom such information is to be provided.

[2]James G. March and Herbert A. Simon, *Organizations* (New York: John Wiley & Sons, 1958), Chapter 4.

[3]James G. March, "An Introduction to the Theory and Measurement of Influence," *American Political Science Review*, Vol. 49 (1955), pp. 431–451; Herbert A. Simon, *Models of Man* (New York: John Wiley & Sons, 1957).

The authority structure of an organization is nothing more than the pattern of such legitimized and influential communicative acts.[4]

The behavioral approach can deal with the possibility that a member of the organization may resist the exercise of power over him by another, which is a central issue in most definitions of power. Resistance is excluded from Professor Pichler's economic approach, "in order to permit the discussion of relationships in which one party willingly subjugates himself in order that his behavior might be changed."[5] The example given of the apprentice who temporarily binds himself by contract to an employer (and perhaps to a union) to learn a trade is covered adequately by the authority concept, since there is no coercion involved.

When the possibility of resistance is taken into account, *power* can be defined as control over one or more persons to promote one's own goals without their consent. *Authority* is control over one or more persons to promote collective goals with their knowledge and consent.[6] Defined in this way, the two concepts differ in goals and compliance. Power is used to promote one's own goal, but authority is used to promote collective goals. Those subject to power comply involuntarily, but those subject to authority comply voluntarily. Therefore, authority is not a form of power, but both are forms of control.

THE HISTORICAL TREND FROM POWER TO AUTHORITY

The distinctions between individual and collective goals and involuntary and voluntary compliance are important in understanding the evolution of business in Western civilization. The balance has shifted from power to authority in business as in other areas of life as society has become more democratic. The coercive power that the company had over the individual worker, who was forbidden by law from combining forces with his fellows, has been weakened substantially through the institutionalization of collective bargaining.

Authority is effective only when it is accepted by those over whom it is exercised. The subordinate has a certain tolerance range within which he will accept direction without analyzing the merits of the behavior as related to the problem at hand.[7] This "zone of acceptance" is becoming narrower as workers are more highly educated. They want to know *why* a particular course of action should be followed. Furthermore, workers actively seek ways to gain more power and improve their position relative to management.

The question of the distribution of power in organizations is particularly crucial today because of the rapidity of change in business life. Early studies of organizational change, that of Coch and French, for example,[8] held power constant and manipulated the participation of employees in bringing about the change. The next logical step was to work out the power variable, and this is being done in various power-equalization approaches. They emphasize that changes in organizations can occur only after the people in them have changed. These approaches "value evolutionary, internally generated change in individuals, groups, and organizations over externally planned or implemented change."[9] This point of view is behind

[4]Daniel Katz and Robert L. Kahn, *The Social Psychology of Organizations* (New York: John Wiley & Sons, 1966), p. 457.

[5]March and Simon, *op. cit.*, p. 3.

[6]Walter Buckley, *Sociology and Modern Systems Theory* (Englewood Cliffs, N.J.: Prentice-Hall, Inc., 1967), p. 186.

[7]Simon, *op. cit.*, p. 75.

[8]L. Coch and J. R. P. French, Jr., "Overcoming Resistance to Change," *Human Relations*, Vol. 1 (1948), pp. 512–533.

[9]Harold J. Leavitt, "Applied Organizational Change in Industry," in *Handbook of Organizations*, James G. March (Ed.) (Chicago: Rand McNally, 1965), p. 1154.

the programs to encourage participative decision-making, open communication, decentralization, and executive development techniques such as the managerial grid and sensitivity training.

LEADERSHIP AS A FORM OF INFLUENCE

Leadership is touched on only slightly in Chapter 14, for the obvious reason that it does not fit into the bargaining approach to power that runs throughout the chapter. Yet leadership is an important aspect of managing. As Sayles points out, the dictum that authority equals responsibility is hardly ever realized in business because of the interdependence of tasks imposed by modern technology.[10] Therefore, the manager depends on many other individuals and groups in and out of the organization for the resources that he needs. He has no direct power over them, and therefore he must rely on his personal abilities to get what he requires. This involves the exercise of leadership.

Leadership is best understood in terms of the manager's influence on the behavior of his subordinates. When a worker is routinely doing his job, he is not being "led." The essence of leadership is the influence wielded by the manager to get workers to perform over and above ordinary requirements. In other words, leadership comes into play only when a problem emerges that cannot be solved by routine means. Then a special effort is required, and it is accomplished because leadership is exercised.[11]

Historically, three factors have been emphasized by writers on leadership: (1) the leader himself, (2) the situation in which leadership is required, and (3) the followers. Early analyses focused on the psychological or physical traits that differentiated leaders from the led. But so many traits were suggested by writers and there was so little agreement among them that Gouldner concluded that "At this time there is no reliable evidence concerning the existence of universal leadership traits."[12] Later studies focused on the situations calling for leadership acts and the personal needs of followers and the leader's ability to satisfy them. Tannenbaum, Weschler, and Massarik take all three factors into account in their definition of leadership:

> We define leadership as *interpersonal influence, exercised in situation and directed, through the communication process, toward the attainment of a specified goal or goals.* Leadership always involves attempts on the part of a leader (influencer) to affect (influence) the behavior of a *follower* (influencee) or followers in *situation.*[13]

INTERORGANIZATIONAL POWER RELATIONS

Finally, another topic that the chapter omits is the power relationships among business firms. This is an important area of analysis today because of the recognition of the strong influence that environmental forces have on organization and management behavior.

Each firm operates in a task environment consisting of all the market elements of support and competition that affect its welfare. It depends on sources of sales, funds, personnel, raw materials, and machinery and equip-

[10]Leonard Sayles, *Managerial Behavior* (New York: McGraw-Hill Book Co., Inc., 1964), p. 42.

[11]Katz and Kahn, *op. cit.*, Chapter 11.

[12]Alvin W. Gouldner (Ed.), *Studies in Leadership* (New York: Harper & Row, 1950), p. 34.

[13]Robert Tannenbaum, Irving R. Weschler, and Fred Massarik, *Leadership and Organization* (New York: McGraw-Hill Book Co., Inc., 1961), p. 24.

ment. Dependence is the opposite of power. Therefore, the more dependent a firm is on an element in its task environment, the less power it has.

A way for a firm to acquire power is by developing exchange relationships with other organizations (in a similar way to that described by Professor Pichler's model). This can be done in a way satisfactory to both parties by employing cooperative strategies that increase the power of both organizations simultaneously. Each party is able to exchange its capacity to reduce uncertainty for another organization in return for that organization's commitment to do the same in return. For example, a company that requires large quantities of a raw material may contract with a supplier for a specified quantity at a given price over a period of time. This reduces the firm's uncertainty about an important input, and at the same time it reduces the supplier's uncertainty about its sales.

The strategic aspect of this type of cooperative strategy lies in the nature of the commitment of both firms. As Thompson points out, "commitments are obtained by giving commitments and uncertainty reduced for the organization through its reduction of uncertainty for others. Commitment thus is a double-edged sword, and management of interdependence presents organizations with dilemmas."[14] There are three cooperative strategies by which organizations can deal with these dilemmas:

1. *Contracting*—negotiating an agreement, which may or may not be legally binding, for the future exchange of performances.
2. *Co-opting*—absorbing new elements into the leadership of an organization as a means of warding off threats to it.
3. *Coalescing*—combining with another organization to undertake a joint venture.[15]

When support capacity is concentrated and balanced against concentrated demands, the organizations involved will attempt to handle their dependence through contracting. An example is collective bargaining between a moving picture projectionists' union and an association of moving picture theaters.

When support capacity is concentrated but demand is dispersed, the weaker organization will attempt to handle its dependence by co-opting. An example is a situation in which one bank in a small town serves a number of small businesses that need bank loans. Under these circumstances it is a good strategy for a small firm to ask the bank manager to become a member of its board of directors.

When support capacity is concentrated and balanced against concentrated demands, but the power achieved through contracting is inadequate, the organizations involved will attempt to coalesce. As example is the participation of American oil companies in joint ventures in developing Middle East oil fields.

CONCLUSION

To summarize, to a large extent the approach one takes to power, influence, and authority in business is a reflection of how he sees the world and of the aspects of management that interest him. I found Professor Pichler's approach interesting and valid, but not identical to my own. My remarks are not intended as a criticism so much as a difference in point of view.

[14]James D. Thompson, *Organizations in Action* (New York: McGraw-Hill Book Co., Inc., 1967), p. 35.
[15]*Ibid.*, p. 36.

Power, Dependence, and Interpersonal Comparisons of Utility in N-Person Supergames

James D. Laing

Associate Professor
School of Urban and Public Affairs
Carnegie-Mellon University

Few concepts in social science have received so much attention[1] with so little apparent payoff as have conceptions of interpersonal power.[2] Yet the dogged persistence of students of social and political behavior in the face of this adversity attests to their belief that something crucial will be lost if, in our despair, we abandon the chase. The nascent development of social exchange theory offers renewed hope that the phenomena of interest to students of interpersonal power can be subjected to rigorous theoretical analysis.[3] It is in this spirit that I comment on Joseph A. Pichler's thoughtful essay, "Power, Influence, and Authority."[4]

Essentially, Professor Pichler presents his argument in two stages. In the first stage he adapts Chamberlain's work on collective bargaining relationships[5] to develop a model of interpersonal power. In the second stage of the paper, Pichler develops a comprehensive, creative synthesis of the literature bearing on his topic. The scope of the materials he addresses is impressive, as is his integration of previous research findings within the general framework of social exchange analysis. I find little to criticize in this second stage of his essay, although I would place considerable emphasis on the role that evaluation of performance plays in authority systems and, more generally, in social exchange relationships.[6] My general agreement with Pichler's discussion of the literature allows me to devote the rest of this paper to the model he develops and to its relationship to his subsequent analysis.

The primary contribution of the first stage of Pichler's paper is to establish the general social exchange perspective he so effectively employs to integrate the literature. In contrast, the model he develops in the first part of the paper contributes (at best) little to his subsequent analysis. The second stage of his paper must, as it were, de-

[1]This paper was prepared under a grant (GS-32161) to the author from the National Science Foundation.

[2]See, especially, the excellent critique by James G. March, "The Power of 'Power,'" in David Easton (Ed.), *Varieties of Political Theory* (Englewood Cliffs, N.J.: Prentice-Hall, Inc., 1966).

[3]For the seminal works on social exchange, see Peter M. Blau, *Exchange and Power in Social Life* (New York: John Wiley & Sons, 1964); George C. Homans, *Social Behavior: Its Elementary Forms* (New York: Harcourt, Brace and World, 1961); and John W. Thibaut and Harold H. Kelley, *The Social Psychology of Groups* (New York: John Wiley & Sons, 1959).

[4]Chapter 14, this volume.

[5]Neil W. Chamberlain, *Labor* (New York: McGraw-Hill Book Co., Inc., 1958).

[6]James D. Laing, Organizational Evaluation and Authority: a Test of a Theory. Unpublished Ph.D. Thesis, Stanford University, 1967. For a more comprehensive statement of this position, see Sanford M. Dornbusch and W. Richard Scott, with the collaboration of Bruce C. Busching and James D. Laing, *Evaluation and Authority* (New York: McGraw-Hill Book Co., Inc., forthcoming).

velop most of the paper's considerable "thrust." I attribute this failure of the model to two important classes of problems. First, there is a technical defect in the model within the scope Pichler has delimited. Second, the model's scope is too limited to be of much help in Pichler's subsequent analysis. In this paper I deal with these two problems.

Pichler's model, given its scope as delimited, has a fatal defect. A careful reading of his comments in developing the model reveals that his index for the "power" of X over Y, $P_{X/Y}$, is expressed in terms of *Y's utility* for various "offers." Let $U_Y(O_i)$ denote *Y's* ("expected," if you prefer) *u*tility for I's *o*ffer to him. Then expressions (1) and (2) in Pichler's model may be stated as

$$P_{X/Y} = \frac{U_y(O_x) - \underset{i \neq x}{\text{MAX}}\ U_y(O_i)}{\underset{i \neq x}{\text{MAX}}\ U_y(O_i)}$$

$P_{X/Y}$ represents *Y's* proportionate increase in utility associated with accepting *X's* offer instead of his most attractive foregone alternative. However, the definition of a utility function is unique only up to a linear transformation, $U'_y(O_i) = a + bU_y(O_i)$. Thus, the representation of *Y's* utility function is quite arbitrary in its assignment of the parameters a and b. The problem is that the $P_{X/Y}$ expression is *not* invariant under linear transformations of *Y's* utility function.[7]

This difficulty becomes fatal to Pichler's argument when, in equation (3), he defines the *d*ifferential *p*ower of X over Y as

$$DP_{X/Y} = P_{X/Y} - P_{Y/X}$$

wherein the last term is defined by exchanging the roles of Y and X in expression for $P_{X/Y}$. In principle, the value of $DP_{X/Y}$ cannot be specified, given the arbitrariness of the parameters in the utility functions of Y and X. Yet the value of this expression assumes fundamental importance in Pichler's application of the model.

At least two directions for scientific development to take in overcoming this type of difficulty can be suggested. One is to develop a theory about how humans make interpersonal comparisons of utility. The other is to finesse the problem by building a theory that does not depend on these comparisons. Later in this paper I discuss a model of "power" that somewhat delicately avoids interpersonal comparisons of utility.

The second major deficiency of the model for Pichler's analysis of complex social exchange relations resides in the narrow scope he at least initially delimits for the model. Pichler's analysis cogently recognizes that in natural social settings, persons are engaged in complex networks of relationships with many others that continue through time.[8] Pichler attempts to account for

[7]Let $U'_y\ (O_i) = a_y + b_y\ U_y\ (O_i)$, where $b_y > 0$. Replacing the utility terms in the expression given for $P_{X/Y}$ in the text yields

$$P'_{X/Y} = \frac{(a_y + b_yU_y(O_X)) - (a_y + b_y \underset{i \neq x}{\text{MAX}}\ U_y(O_i))}{a_y + b_y \underset{i \neq x}{\text{MAX}}\ U_y(O_i)}$$

$$= \frac{U_y(O_x) - \underset{i \neq x}{\text{MAX}}\ U_y(O_i)}{(a_y/b_y) + \underset{i \neq x}{\text{MAX}}\ U_y(O_i)}$$

Thus, given the term (a_y/b_y) in the denominator, the value of $P_X/_Y$ is *not* invariant under linear transformations of *Y's* utility function.

[8]See, especially, Pichler's comments in his section titled "Dimensions of Power Relationships."

the time dimension by incorporating expected utility in his model on the basis of the actors' forecast of future consequences of present behavior. However, the only actors affecting the relationship between *X* and *Y* in Pichler's model outside of that relationship are the sources of the best alternative offers to *X* and *Y*. Pichler does not develop his model to address the complex networks of social exchange relationships, although his discussion of these networks, unaided by his model, is quite comprehensive. In order to analyze social relationships in natural settings, Pichler introduces such concepts as legitimacy and coalition formation. Yet these concepts are not recognized in his model.

In summary, Pichler's model is of little help to his comprehensive analysis of complex social behavior because it both uses interpersonal comparisons of utility and fails to account for the complexity of continuing social exchanges in networks of interdependent individuals. Unfortunately, I know of no theory that is capable of addressing the difficult analytic task that Pichler undertakes in the second stage of his paper.

However, I share Pichler's belief that the literature on social exchange processes provides a perspective from which such theory can be developed. Somewhat more specifically, the approach I have in mind assumes that individuals act as if they address complex social situations with incrementally adapted decision rules and relatively simple preferences.[9] Individuals in complex, continuing social relationships recognize that their transactions with one another are not independent events and attempt to take this as well as the others' calculations into account in choosing their strategies. In short, I propose that we attempt to develop a behavioral theory of *n*-person supergames in our efforts to model complex social exchange networks.

I next discuss some research developed within this approach that at present focuses on a continuing social situation that is far simpler than those analyzed by Pichler.[10] This research has two features that are particularly relevant to this paper. First, it focuses on interdependence of two-person transactions across a sequence of dyadic exchanges among three persons. Second, the model I outline incorporates a conception of "power" that both avoids interpersonal comparisons of utility and quite successfully predicts behavior in the situation.

The situation involves three participants in a sequence of games played in the laboratory. The three players know that the sequence of games will end without warning at a randomly chosen time, and that each player's monetary payoff depends on his final rank in the distribution of total scores accumulated across the sequence. Each game in the sequence involves face-to-face bargaining until a two-person coalition forms and decides how the two partners will divide the points available on the trial between them. At the beginning of each game in the sequence, players know the current distribution of accumulated scores and the number of points to be won by the coalition forming on that trial.

In this situation, players wish to maximize their final rank, but don't know when the sequence of games will end. The formal theory I briefly describe here assumes that, in an effort to

[9]This perspective is, in general, consistent with that used by James G. March and Herbert A. Simon, *Organizations* (New York: John Wiley & Sons, 1958); Richard M. Cyert and James G. March, *A Behavioral Theory of the Firm* (Englewood Cliffs, N.J.: Prentice-Hall, Inc., 1963); and Cyert and Morris H. DeGroot, "Multiperiod Decision Models with Alternating Choice as a Solution to the Duopoly Problem," *Quarterly Journal of Economics*, Vol. 84 (1970), pp. 410–420.

[10]For a more complete description of the laboratory situation and ("hyperopic") model discussed in the sequel, see James D. Laing and Richard J. Morrison, "Coalitions and Payoffs in Three-Person Sequential Games: Initial Tests of Two Models," School of Urban and Public Affairs working paper, Carnegie-Mellon University, January, 1972.

maximize final rank, each player acts as if he adopts certain well-specified preferences and bargaining positions that govern his behavior on each trial in the sequence, and acts as if he expects the other players to use identical preference rules and bargaining positions. Given the current distribution of accumulated scores and the value of the game to be played in the trial, each player is assumed to aspire initially to the maximum payoff he can obtain in each of his potential coalitions if his partner follows the rules. Assuming tentatively that he obtains this payoff and his partner gets the remaining points, each player can calculate the rank he would hold at the end of the trial in the resulting distribution of accumulated scores. If player I expects to achieve a higher rank with one partner, say J, than in coalition with K, then he prefers J and tentatively chooses J as coalition partner with ("attraction") probability $A_{ij} = i - \varepsilon_i$, and chooses K with probability $A_{ik} = \varepsilon_i$, where $O < \varepsilon_i < 1/2$. If a player, say I, has no rank-based preference for one potential partner, then he is assumed to choose each player in proportion to the probability his choice is reciprocated: $A_{ij}/A_{ik} = A_{ji}/A_{ki}$. Typically, the initial rank aspirations are not jointly feasible within each potential coalition since they require more points than are available in the game. The theory analyzes the structure of attractions, $\{A_{ij}\}$, among the three players to identify asymmetries that give one player a bargaining advantage over the other that he can exploit in obtaining concessions.

At this point, the theory employs a conception of dependence and bargaining advantage using the perspective of Emerson's model of power and dependence relations in the dyad,[11] a model that Pichler cites. However, in using Emerson's model, one is in grave danger of making interpersonal comparisons of utility. I next develop an adaptation of Emerson's model for this situation to show that interpersonal comparisons of utility are not problematical in this application. Consistent with the spirit of Emerson's model, define the *dependence* of player I on J as coalition partner: $D_{ij} = A_{ij}/A_{ki}$. Notice that D_{ij} varies directly with I's "attraction" to J, and inversely with the "availability" to I of K as coalition partner (for distinct I, J, K). Then I has a *bargaining advantage* (cf. Emerson's "power advantage") over J if $D_{ij} < D_{ji}$. If $D_{ij} = D_{ji}$, neither partner enjoys a bargaining advantage over the other in coalition (I, J).

The theory assumes that in any coalition whose potential members hold jointly infeasible aspirations, the player at a bargaining disadvantage concedes by lowering his aspirations one rank (if neither partner is disadvantaged, then both concede). These revised rank aspirations are then fed back to revise rank-based preferences for coalition partners, and to update the attractions and dependencies. The new tentative solution is tested for feasibility, and, if necessary, further concessions are made until all coalitions pass the feasibility tests. When this solution process terminates, we have the final values for the dependence of each player on every other player, bargaining advantage within each coalition, and the jointly feasible rank aspirations of the members of each coalition. There may be a variety of point divisions consistent with these final rank aspirations for each coalition. We call this set of payoff divisions the *negotiation range* for the coalition. Each coalition member's preferences are assumed to be monotone increasing with his share of the points for divisions within the negotiation range. The theory states that the player enjoying a bargaining advantage within the coalition has the ability to obtain up to his most preferred division within the negotiation range, and predicts that he tends to do so.

Now one might suspect that by using the parameters $\{\varepsilon_i\}$, the theory tacitly assumes interpersonal comparisons of utility in establishing bargaining

[11] Richard M. Emerson, "Power-Dependence Relations," American Sociological Review, Vol. 17 (1962), pp. 31–41.

advantages. The values of ε_i indirectly represent the relative importance each player attaches to forming a coalition in which he expects to achieve a higher rank. This suspicion is likely to become stronger if one also knows that in the basic statement of the theory, it is assumed for convenience that $\varepsilon_i = \varepsilon_j$ for all i, j. However, it can be shown that allowing each player to establish his own parameter value within the assumed open interval, (O, ½), for all attraction structures identified by the theory, the attributions of bargaining advantage depend on the values of the ε_i in only two situations. These exceptions occur only in those dyads in which both players are symmetric in holding rank-based preference for each other, or for the third member of the triad. In this event, the negotiation range consists of a single (50–50) division, so the indeterminancy of bargaining advantages in these instances is moot. Who enjoys a "bargaining advantage" is of no consequence if only a unique division is admissible. Thus, interpersonal comparisons of utility are not problematical in this application of Emerson's model of power and dependence relations. This model also predicts which coalitions form. The probability that coalition (I, J) forms is

$$P^*_{ij} = \frac{A_{ij}A_{ji}}{A_{ij}A_{ji} + A_{ik}A_{ki} + A_{jk}A_{kj}}$$

for distinct i, j, k.

The empirical results from laboratory studies are very encouraging. The concept of bargaining advantage described above is a powerful predictor of payoff allocations within the coalitions that form. Also, the theory successfully predicts which coalitions form. Moreover, the models may be used to develop successful predictions about such supergame phenomena as the initiation, maintenance, and defection from coalitions formed under multiple-trial agreements.[12] This suggests that it is too soon to abandon attempts to develop viable conceptions of "power" in continuing social relations among a large number of individuals. However, extensive theoretical development is needed if we are to treat rigorously the scope of phenomena considered in Pichler's sophisticated analysis of complex systems of social exchange.

SUGGESTIONS FOR FUTURE READING

BLAU, Peter M., *Exchange and Power in Social Life* (New York: John Wiley & Sons, 1964).

CHAMBERLAIN, NEIL W., *Labor* (New York: McGraw-Hill Book Co., Inc., 1958).

CYERT, RICHARD M., AND MORRIS H. DEGROOT, "Multiperiod Decision Models with Alternating Choice as a Solution to the Duopoly Problem," *Quarterly Journal of Economics,* Vol. 84 (1970), pp. 410–420.

CYERT, RICHARD M., AND JAMES G. MARCH, *A Behavioral Theory of the Firm* (Englewood Cliffs, N.J.: Prentice-Hall, Inc., 1963).

DORNBUSCH, SANFORD M., AND W. RICHARD SCOTT, in collaboration with Bruce C. Busching and James D. Laing, *Evaluation and Authority* (New York: McGraw-Hill Book Co., Inc., forthcoming).

[12]The basic statement and test of the theory with coalition outcomes formed under single-trial agreements can be found in Laing and Morrison, *op. cit.* For an analysis of coalition behavior under multiple-trial agreements, see James D. Laing and Richard J. Morrison, "Coalitions and Payoffs in Three-Person Supergames: Formal Theory and Evidence from a Laboratory Study," delivered at the 1971 Annual Meeting of the American Political Science Association, Chicago, Illinois, September 7–11, 1971.

EMERSON, RICHARD M., "Power-Dependence Relations," *American Sociological Review*, Vol. 17 (1962), pp. 31–41.

HOMANS, GEORGE C., *Social Behavior: Its Elementary Forms* (New York: Harcourt, Brace and World, 1961).

LAING, JAMES D., Organizational Evaluation and Authority: a Test of a Theory. Unpublished Ph.D. Thesis, Stanford University, 1967.

LAING, JAMES D., and RICHARD J. MORRISON, "Coalitions and Payoffs in Three-Person Sequential Games: Initial Tests of Two Models," School of Urban and Public Affairs working paper, Carnegie-Mellon University, January, 1972.

LAING, JAMES D., and RICHARD J. MORRISON, "Coalitions and Payoffs in Three-Person Supergames: Formal Theory and Evidence from a Laboratory Study," delivered at the 1971 Annual Meeting of the American Political Science Association, Chicago, Illinois, September 7–11, 1971.

MARCH, JAMES G., "The Power of 'Power'," in David Easton (Ed.), *Varieties of Political Theory* (Englewood Cliffs, N.J.: Prentice-Hall, Inc., 1966).

MARCH, JAMES G., AND HERBERT A. SIMON, *Organizations* (New York: John Wiley & Sons, 1958).

THIBAUT, JOHN W., AND HAROLD H. KELLEY, *The Social Psychology of Groups* (New York: John Wiley & Sons, 1959).

DISCUSSION QUESTIONS

1. Do you think it is important for managers to know about power, influence, and authority? Why?
2. Define power, influence, and authority. What distinguishes each from the others?
3. Define and discuss the concept of social power.
4. Is it better for a person with power to be loved more than hated? Or hated more than loved? Why?
5. How does influence actually operate? Illustrate several ways that you have been influenced. That you have influenced.
6. Do managers need power? Influence? Authority? Do they need rules? What are rules?
7. How is the exercise of power made legitimate?
8. Argue the merits of the "economic" vs. the "behavioral" approach to power.

15

Managerial Decision-Making

Kenneth R. MacCrimmon

Professor
Faculty of Commerce and Business Administration
University of British Columbia

INTRODUCTION

Choice and the Decision Process

The core of decision-making is *choice*. In order for a decision situation to exist, there must be two or more alternatives to choose among. Choice, however, is only the culmination of earlier parts of the decision process. Choice requires some criteria for selecting one alternative over another. These criteria will be linked to the decision maker's objectives. The criteria are applied to the possible outcomes of alternatives. The possible outcomes depend on the uncertainty in the decision environment and on the actions available to the decision maker. Through search and information acquisition, the decision maker learns about the uncertainties and generates the alternatives. The search and information acquisition are influenced by how the decision problem is recognized and defined. Hence, in this chapter, we shall be concerned with *choice* and the *decision processes* proceeding it.

Decision: Thought and Action

Decision-making is a bridge between thought and action. The decision process itself involves both *thought* and *action*. The process following choice is directed toward implementing the thought and action that preceded it (Simon, 1957a). The intertwining of thought and action are at the heart of management. If management is regarded as functional, then decision-making underlies all the functions; if structural, decision-making infuses the structure. Simon (1960) treats "decision-making" and "management" synonymously.

The terms "problem-solving" and "judgment" imply many of the same thought processes as "decision-making." Perhaps they imply somewhat less of an action orientation, but for the purposes of this chapter we shall not bother distinguishing between them. *Decision-making*, then, will mean the processes involving both thought and action that culminate in an act of choice.

A thought-oriented mode would view decision-making in terms of *information* acquisition, processing, and communication. The steps of the process could be described as a widening or narrowing of the decision maker's information set. In contrast, an action-oriented mode would view decision-making in terms of *resource* acquisition, commitment, and allocation. The steps of the process could be described as a widening or narrowing of the decision maker's resource set. Both the information processing and the resource processing modes will be used in this chapter to describe the decision-making process.

Elements of Decision-Making

The main elements of decision-making are a *decision maker* in a *decision environment* (MacCrimmon, 1970). For expositional convenience, in describing basic concepts we shall usually refer to a "decision maker," which can mean either an individual, a group, an organization, or a society. The primary considerations for a decision maker are his *values*, his *beliefs*, and his *resources*. That is, in understanding his decision processes we are interested in what he wants, what he knows, and what he has. The various theories to be considered assume differences in values, beliefs, and resources.

The decision environment can be characterized in many ways but perhaps the most pervasive dimensions are complexity and uncertainty. These are the aspects we shall emphasize in this chapter.

Placing a decision maker in a decision environment leads to a decision-making process, such as that described briefly at the beginning of the chapter. This chapter is organized in terms of the decision-making process. Many listings of the steps in a decision process are available, most of them stemming from Dewey (1933) and Wallas (1926); the one used here seems compatible with most.

In real decision situations, one seldom observes the clear, step-by-step process such as that described here. Steps in the process proceed simultaneously, some steps are skipped, steps are repeated, and so on. There are obvious interactions, feedbacks, and cycles. Also, decision situations intermingle; decisions are imbedded in decisions. All these complications are quite real and usually quite rational. In this chapter we try to allude to them within the linear constraint of chapter topics.

Theories of Decision-Making

The theories of decision-making are of two basic kinds. *Normative* theories describe how decisions *should* be made, whereas *descriptive* theories describe how decisions *are* made (Marschak, 1964). We shall consider both types here but the normative theories that are of most interest are those that can be applied and are based on solid premises. The most interesting descriptive theories are those that describe what effective decision makers do.

The decision maker is subject to information processing and other constraints that limit his rationality (Simon, 1957b). On the other hand, the constraints on effective decision makers are probably not so binding as are those that limit poor decision makers. Hence, we shall consider rational behavior subject to the bounds that a purposeful, careful decision maker would confront.

The theories we consider are drawn from many disciplines, including economics, psychology, philosophy, statistics, mathematics, and management itself. The theories will be introduced at those parts of the decision process in which they have a contribution to make. This approach has the disadvantage of fragmenting the theories, so it may be more difficult, for example, to piece together the subjective probability, utility, risk, and expected utility components of statistical decision theory. On the other hand, the process type of format seems to have the advantage of not emphasizing the existing packaging of the theories and makes more apparent the points at which particular theories make a major, minor, or zero contribution. It also allows an opportunity to bring in some minor theories or techniques that may be useful at only small stages of the process—but useful nevertheless.

Hopefully, this format will allow us to (1) pull together and organize the diverse literature on decision-making, (2) provide a concise summary of the main ideas and results useful to managerial decisions, (3) evaluate the theory and results, and (4) suggest ways that students of decisions or decision makers can piece together those components that would be of most use to them.

PROBLEM DEFINITION

Decision Problems

A decision situation can be viewed as a *gap* between the decision maker's desired state and his existing state. The *desired state* consists of the goals and objectives he is trying to attain. The *existing state* is described by the decision maker's resources at some point in time (Dunker, 1945; Newell, Shaw, and Simon, 1958).

A decision maker's desired state and his existing state (whether current or anticipated) seldom coincide exactly, yet he is not constantly involved in decision-making in all areas of his interests. A gap between desired and existing states, then, is a necessary but not a sufficient condition for decision-making behavior to occur. The conditions that determine a *decision problem* are: (1) a *gap* between desired and existing states, (2) *attention* directed to a particular gap, (3) *motivation* to reduce the gap, and (4) an *ability* to do something about it. We shall consider each of these elements in more detail in the next four subsections.

Gap between Existing and Desired States In the simplest case, the decision maker's desired state may be described by a single dimension. In the classical theory of the firm, for example, the only objective considered is maximization of profit (Marshall, 1890). Real business firms, however, pursue multiple goals—such as profitability, return on investment, share of market, managerial control, growth, and so on (Drucker, 1954; Johnsen, 1968; Carter, 1971).

There are various ways that gaps between existing and desired states can arise or be altered. The desired state may change while the existing state stays the same; the existing state may change while the desired state stays the same; or both the existing and desired states may change. The first case is characteristic of a revision in goals owing to, say, new survey information about the size of a potential market. These situations would be anticipated *opportunities.* The second case is characteristic of something going wrong in a system, such as production costs soaring. These situations are *threats* to the decision maker. The third case is a combination of the two and may occur, for example, when new product ideas come out of research and development activity (Ansoff, 1965).

Perceiving Decision Problems The many dimensions of existing and desired states imply many possible gaps. The limited capacity of a decision maker clearly precludes him from dealing with many different things at the same time (Miller, 1956; Simon, 1957). Hence, the gap will have to be above some minimal threshold in order for it to be perceived (Lewin, 1946). Cyert and March (1963) discuss the process by which attention sequentially shifts from one gap to another and how this shift can reduce internal conflict. Drucker (1963) points out that threats are more readily perceived than opportunities and subsequently become an overwhelming concern of inefficient managers.

The information about the gap may come from various sources. The differences resulting from a decision occasion being initiated by a communication from a subordinate versus a superior are discussed by Barnard (1938), along with other practical aspects of decision occasions.

Motivation to Resolve The motivation on the part of the decision maker to reduce the gap between existing and desired states will depend on the size of the gap and on how important the reduction of such a gap is in achieving further ends. The gap does not merely have to be perceived but must be above some threshold to make its reduction worthwhile (Lewin, 1946).

Controllability and Solvability Clearly it is not enough to be aware of the existence of the gap and to be motivated to reduce it. In order for a meaningful decision problem to exist, the decision maker must be able to take actions that will reduce the gap. This suggests classifying the factors in a decision situation into those that are *controllable* and those that are *uncontrollable.* Those that are partially controllable can be decomposed into their controllable and uncontrollable components (Howard, 1971). If there are no possibilities for action in the controllable class, there is not much use in the decision maker trying to "solve the problem." For even if he was able to generate a solution, there would be no way to implement it. The elements that are controllable depend on the resources that the decision maker is willing to expend in order to obtain control—and this will be part of the decision problem.

Another consideration is whether the problem is solvable even if there are many controllable elements at the decision maker's command. In the extreme, one might say that any problem is resolvable if the appropriate resources are at hand. In practical decision situations the question to ask is whether the problem can be resolved for a feasible level of resource expenditures.

Influences on the Identification of Problems

Premises and Constraints In diagnosing problems, the decision maker will bring in various premises. Sometimes these premises may be stated explicitly (e.g., no one is to be fired), whereas at other times, and more frequently, they are held implicitly by the decision maker. The premises may be based on interpretations read into the problem information. Rokeach (1960) has described how people often try to resolve problems based on unjustified implicit premises.

The premises may also be regarded as constraints that the decision maker imposes on the problem. Initially most of the constraints are open but as the decision maker proceeds to identify the problem he begins to close these open constraints (Reitman, 1964). If he proceeds judiciously, he efficiently resolves the problem. The imposition or the closing of inappropriate constraints, however, may eliminate the possibility of resolution.

Set One basis for unjustified premises and interpretations is when a psychological set has developed and a decision maker sees problems as being identical to ones he has faced in the past. Luchins and Luchins (1959) have discussed the rigidity in behavior and stereotyped response that can arise in such a situation. The business analog to this is the individual who sees all problems he encounters as being of the same type—for example, an operations researcher viewing everything as a linear programming problem no matter what the problem differences and its susceptibility to other methods.

There are cases, obviously, when great efficiencies can be attained by identifying a problem as similar to another and using the techniques that were applied to solve the first. Specialized staff and programs in business firms are testimony to this. Gardner (1967) has given examples of seemingly different problems that are similar to tic-tac-toe.

Problem Types

Well-structured and Ill-structured Problems Simon (1960) and Minsky (1961) have identified two endpoints on a continuum of decision problems. At one end are the well-structured or programmed problems that are repetitive and routine and for which a definite procedure that will yield a solution has been worked out. At the other end are the ill-structured or unprogrammed problems that are novel and important and for which there are no routine solution procedures.

Polya (1957) has subdivided well-structured problems into "problems to find" and "problems to prove." Reitman (1964) has identified six types of ill-structured problems in terms of what is known about (1) the initial (i.e., existing) state, (2) the terminal (i.e., desired) state, and (3) the solution process. Obviously, in most managerial decision situations we are dealing with ill-structured problems. Both Reitman (1964) and Emmet (1960) discuss practical examples of types of ill-structured (or "open") problems.

Quality-dominant and Acceptance-dominant Problems Maier (1963) has provided another useful distinction in problem types by considering the need for high quality and the need for high acceptance in a decision situation. If the problem is one for which quality is much more important than acceptance, then a non-participative decision seems appropriate. If, however, acceptance of the decision is more important than quality, then a group decision procedure seems desirable. Decisions that require both high quality and high acceptance are handled by combined procedures.

Diagnoses and Preliminary Steps Toward Resolution

Alternative Diagnoses Clearly, the way a decision problem is defined can have a considerable effect on the types of alternatives considered and the types of resources utilized to solve it. This is illustrated nicely in a simple experiment of Maier's in which two strings hanging from the ceiling have to be tied together, but holding the end of one and trying to walk to the other does not succeed. Consideration is given to whether the problem is defined as (1) the string is too short, (2) the arm is too short, (3) the string will not stay in the proper place, or (4) the string will not swing over. He shows how the definition influences the use of the available resources (e.g., a pair of pliers) for resolving the problem (Maier, 1931).

Diagnosis of Causes of Disequilibria The diagnosis of decision situations in which a system is temporarily out of equilibrium requires determining what the difficulty is and the steps to take to restore equilibrium. Kepner and Tregoe, (1965) present a very practical approach for dealing with such cases. The decision maker is advised to first attempt to determine what are the characteristics of the out-of-control part and what are the characteristics of the in-control part. Following such a "what is" and "what is not" determination, an attempt is made to find single *causes* that will explain the "is" part and will discriminate it from the "is not" part. Changes are systematically probed until the equilibrium restoring action can be taken. Although Kepner and Tregoe do not limit the scope of their method to these types of problems, it is difficult to see how it could be used more generally, for example, in problems involving structural changes or in open-ended problems (e.g., controlling inflation).

Working Forward or Working Backward A decision maker may approach a problem by either trying to work forward or backward. In the terms we have used earlier, he may work (forward) from the existing state to see how it might be transformed into the desired state, or he may work (back) from the desired state to see if a means for arriving at the existing state can be developed (Feldman and Kanter, 1964; Miller, Galanter, and Pribram, 1960; Feldman and Kanter, 1965). Both techniques seem to be used in actual decision-making. Working forward is the most apparent and hence most common tactic, but some techniques, such as dynamic programming, emphasize working backward (Bellman and Dreyfus, 1961).

Means-end factoring The solution of a problem implies eliminating the gap between the existing state and the desired state. The gap can be reduced by applying appropriate operators (Newell and Simon, 1961). The operators are the "means" to the "end" of reducing the gap. After the operator is applied, there may be a new gap (i.e., end) to be reduced and hence new means may be considered. A computer program, the General Problem Solver, has been constructed to operate in this fashion (Newell, Shaw, and Simon, 1960).

The resolution of most problems involves factoring them into subproblems, which in turn may be factored, and so on. This process leads to a hierarchy of means and ends. Simon (1961) has given an example of a watchmaker who by arranging his assembly in terms of subparts can be much more productive when interrupted than a watchmaker who tries to assemble complete clocks at one time (see also Koestler, 1967). Breaking up a problem into subproblems is only useful if there are not too many interrelationships among the subparts, otherwise the coordination problems would clearly outweigh the decomposition. Simon and Ando (1961) have looked at some of the technical conditions for such a decomposition. Decomposition obviously allows the use of specialization and division of labor when the decision maker's subunits have differential capabilities. It also allows for additional parallelism in resolving the problem; hence, the decision maker's sequential processing abilities (Simon, 1969) can be overcome. Braybrooke and Lindblom (1963) have also emphasized this common form of problem separation with their development of concepts of "disjointedness."

Summary: Problem Definition

As the bibliography at the end of this chapter indicates, the literatures on Gestalt psychology, cognitive processes, and management techniques are most useful in problem definition. Most economic and statistical studies pick up after the problem has been defined and so have little to contribute here. It is popularly asserted that once a problem has been correctly defined, the decision situation is essentially resolved. Either this is tautological (implying that the correct definition involves all the other steps in the decision process) or it is false. It may serve, however, to emphasize that careful attention must be given to defining decision problems. If all decision problems one encounters must be resolved "yesterday," there are obvious pressures against paying much attention to diagnosis before making choices.

ALTERNATIVES

Standard and Creative Solutions

Although it is important to take time to carefully diagnose a problem, it is also important to move as quickly as possible to a consideration of the *alternative choices* available to the decision maker. In economic and statistical theories of decision-making, the whole set of alternatives is assumed to be known to the decision maker at the outset and he must choose the best alternative from this set. In most real decision situations, however, the alternative actions are far from obvious and a great deal of effort may be required to generate feasible alternatives.

On the one hand, there will be a set of *standard responses*—that is, alternatives that the decision maker has used on such problems before. Application of a standard response, of course, is predicated on the decision maker identifying the problem he confronts as one member of a particular class of problems and then identifying the standard solutions used for that class of problems. Less directly, the standard solutions may be ones that other decision makers have used for that type of problem, and the decision maker himself may not have direct experience in applying that solution, even though others have used it before.

On the other hand, in important managerial decision problems there will be a set of non-standard responses. The interesting ones are those that are feasible in addition to being novel—that is, they are *creative solutions* to the problem at hand. Generating creative alternatives is not easy; hence, the decision maker needs general guidance and specific techniques to assist him in this part of the decision process. In this section we shall examine some of the general issues of generating alternatives in more detail and shall consider various viewpoints and methods that seem helpful.

Routine Responses

Programs A routine response to a problem involves a standard sequence of operations that has been performed before. March and Simon (1958) have emphasized how routine responses can be viewed as programs, in the same sense as computer programs. That is, situations arise for which a particular program seems appropriate, so this program is called forth from the program library, it is applied to the situation, and then is returned to the program library to be called on again when a similar situation arises. In organizations, the "program library" may be solely within the heads of the participants or may be written down in the form of individual memos, standard operating procedures, or organization manuals. March and Simon (1958) and Cyert and March (1963) discuss the efficacy of these standard operating procedures in business and public organizations. Such programs serve to minimize the variability in organizational response by assuring that different participants in particular roles will carry out a standard series of operations (Cyert and MacCrimmon, 1968). Kaufman (1960) gives an excellent description of how elaborate sets of programs are used as routine responses in the U.S. Forest Service.

The Representation of Programs Relating routine responses of a decision maker with computer programs highlights the ability to pull out, revise, and, reinsert specific parts of a sequence of routine operations (Newell, 1970). Such a correspondence also helps us to determine which types of processors (men or machines) are best suited to carrying out each part of the response sequence so that the most effective man-machine combination can be utilized. Furthermore, it suggests two methods used in computer programming—flow charts and decision tables—that are relevant to more general forms of decision-making.

Flow charts are diagrammatic representations of sequences of operations in terms of shapes representing operations, questions, and the like, connected by arrows indicating the precedence relationships. Extensive use of such flow charts to model human decision-making can be found, for example, in Clarkson (1960), Gore (1964), and Kleinmuntz (1968).

Less often used are *decision tables.* A representative one would contain a list of conditions relating to the decision (e.g., did sales revenue decrease last month?) as the top group of rows of the table, and a list of possible actions (e.g., increase newspaper advertising by 10 per cent) as the bottom group of rows. A column represents a decision rule that maps various combinations of conditions into a set of actions that should be taken. Thus, the decision maker would specify the list of conditions relating to the decision situation, then find the column (i.e., decision rule) that had the corresponding answers, then go down the column and find out which bottom rows have been check marked for this column and hence identify the actions to be taken. Decision tables have not been widely used in general decision making but the technique appears to have some potential. For a further discussion of decision tables see McDaniel (1968), and for a short description of a medical example see Wartak (1970).

Algorithms and heuristics A set of standard operations that guarantee a solution to a problem in a finite number of steps is called an algorithm. When dealing with programmed or well-structured decisions, a search for an appropriate algorithm may be quite reasonable. When dealing with unprogrammed or ill-structured decisions, however, algorithms will rarely be worked out. Even in programmed decisions, the decision maker may be able to develop heuristics or rules of thumb that provide good enough solutions rather than spending the extra effort on algorithm generation and operation. Heuristics can also be used for ill-structured decisions, and so they lie in the middle ground between standard responses and creative responses.

Warehouse location, for example, is a well-structured problem for which heuristics can be useful in the sense that they are computationally simple and flexible with respect to the parameters. Kuehn and Hamberger (1963) use heuristics such as "locate regional warehouse near concentrations of demand" to develop a heuristic program that compared quite favorably to the linear programming solution to the problem. When the game of chess is considered, however, even though it is a game of perfect information (von Neumann and Morgenstern, 1944) and an algorithm can theoretically be stated, the algorithm cannot be used because the computations required are beyond the capabilities of any foreseeable computers. Hence when chess players play, or when one designs chess-playing programs, reliance must be placed on heuristics, such as "control the center of the board" (Newell and Simon, 1972; deGroot, 1965).

Heuristic programming, then, can assist decision makers in wide ranges of problem types. Although the concepts (such as means-end analysis, breadth vs. depth search) underlying heuristic programs are quite general, the heuristics themselves are not. As pointed out, the heuristics are usually particular to a specific decision problem at hand, and so progress in the area depends very much on which decision contexts are studied. The types of situations have been broadening (Simon, 1969) and the theory too has been developing, (Newell, 1970) so heuristic programming promises to be a useful development to management decision-making. See Newell and Simon (1972) for an excellent overview.

Creative Responses

Creativity At times a standard response to a decision situation may seem inappropriate or impossible. In such cases the decision situation must be handled uniquely and the decision maker attempts to generate novel alternatives. How can creative alternatives be developed? To the extent that people differ in creative ability, creative alternatives might be more readily generated by creative people. It sems most fruitful, however, to ask if there are any procedures by which creativity can be engendered in any decision maker. The most useful procedures that have been suggested seem to fall into three main categories.

Unstructured Procedures for Creative Alternatives Brainstorming methods advanced by Osborn (1957) have received considerable attention. The process involves a group of individuals seated together, each generating and stating ideas for solving the problem. The procedure disallows criticism of any idea but encourages the modification and combination of prior ideas. Experiments (e.g., Taylor *et al.*, 1958; Dunnette *et al.*, 1963) have shown, however, that the output of such a brainstorming group when compared with the output of individuals working in isolation yields not only fewer ideas but also fewer good ideas. So in terms of both quantity and quality, it would seem preferable to have the individuals think freely on their own and then to pool their ideas later.

Structured Procedures for Creative Alternatives At the other extreme from the open-ended, unstructured brainstorming sessions are methods that advocate a systematic process of putting together combinations of subparts of alternatives into a large number of new alternatives. This approach is based on the premise that the psychological set of problem solvers makes them myopic toward some ways of combining elements into unique alternatives. Hence, decision makers are advised to follow a systematic program that will produce a large number of alternatives, most of which will be worthless but a few of which will hopefully be novel and important.

A major technique in this category is the *morphological approach* of Zwicky (1965), which has the decision maker, first, identify the key dimensions of the solution. For example, if the problem involved setting up a subsidiary in Europe, one might identify such aspects as location, size, structure, staffing, and market served. For each of these dimensions it is necessary to identify values, which are then taken in combination with one another exhaustively. In this case, an example of one alternative that might emerge is to set up in Brussels a very small organization, structured in project teams, staffed half by Americans and half by Belgians, to sell strictly to EEC countries. With just a few features for each dimension, a very large number of combinations arise, and the problem then becomes one of sorting through them to identify the creative ones from all the rest. Obviously there is no guarantee that anything creative (or even feasible) will emerge, and the procedure is very inefficient; yet whenever there are unique combinations that can be generated, this exhaustive technique will generate them and the decision maker will be made aware of an unusual combination. For a discussion of more general aspects of morphological procedures, and some sweeping claims about their applicability, see Zwicky (1969).

Another systematic procedure that involves generating combinations is the *relational algorithm* of Crovitz (1970). To date this approach has only been used for solving very simple laboratory problems (such as the two-string problem) but it seems to have applicability to at least some types of real-world problems. It is based on the observation that the solution to simple problems usually takes the form of one object taken in some relationship to some other object (e.g., the pliers and the string). All forty-two relation words in Ogden's Basic English (1938) have been identified (words such as "on," "in," "below," etc.) These words then become the connectives in forty-two sentences of the form "Take *object A* on *object B*," "Take *object A* in *object B*," and so on. The different objects in the problem environment (e.g., the pliers and string) are inserted into the object word locations and hopefully a good solution is generated. The reader is referred to Crovitz's book for more details of the procedure and its application to simple problems. The X-ray problem described in the book and the reader's own imagination should suggest some real-world uses.

Creative Alternatives through Viewpoints The *synectics* approach (Gordon, 1961) utilized both unstructured and structured processes. The procedure involves a group led by an experienced leader progressing through various ways of viewing the problem situation at hand. The main characteristics of the approach are an attempt to make the strange familiar and to make the familiar strange. Analogies are the primary mechanisms used. The problem solver is asked to play the role of some element in the problem (e.g., a missing murder weapon) in order to free himself from looking at the commonplace in a commonplace way. In addition, he is asked to develop direct analogies to the present problem from nature (e.g., the ability of chameleons and flounders to change color), to make symbolic analogies (e.g., mathematical models), and to make fantasy analogies (e.g., demons and elves). Synectics has been widely used and appears to have many of the advantages of brainstorming (viz., an opportunity to put forth some free-flowing ideas) but also incorporates some mechanisms and structure to utilize the interaction more effectively. Whether, in fact, synectics is more effective than brainstorming—or morphology or other approaches—does not seem to have been the subject of any formal investigation. It would seem particularly effective to use promising aspects of each technique and to put them together into an eclectic, creative programming procedure.

Summary: Alternatives

The more formal writing on decision-making, such as we find in economics and statistics, provides few useful concepts or techniques on alternative generation, because these theories assume that the decision maker is initially given an exhaustive list of the alternatives available to him. The cognitive process literature, on the other hand, makes important contributions to programming and heuristics. The methods for generating creative alternatives come from quite diverse sources and include techniques that have had extensive applications.

In passing, we should point out that the technique of "incubation" has been found useful in generating alternative solutions by managers and scientists alike. If the decision maker takes the time to reflect carefully on his problem and to be receptive to ideas even when he is working on other things, he may find that useful solutions pop into his head. Hopefully, he becomes part of the solution instead of just part of the problem.

UNCERTAINTY

Coping with Uncertainty

In most decision situations the decision maker is faced with considerable uncertainty. He may be uncertain about what the decision problem really is and when, or even whether, he should try to resolve it; he may be uncertain about the alternative actions he can take and whether he has the resources to carry them out; he may be uncertain about what external events will occur and how they will affect the outcomes. In each of these cases to say that uncertainty exists is analogous to saying that there is a lack of appropriate information. The only uncertainty to which any significant attention has been paid by decision scholars is uncertainty about external events over which the decision maker has no control.

Responses to uncertainty There are various ways in which the decision maker may cope with uncertainty in a decision situation. They are grouped into four classes, based on the characteristics in Table 11.

In this section we shall focus on responses to uncertainty based on the information currently available. Information collection responses (category III) will be discussed in a later section. We will emphasize category II in this section but will first deal briefly with categories I and IV.

Avoiding and Reducing Uncertainty

Avoiding Uncertainty Psychologists have studied the aversion of people to ambiguity and uncertainty (Rokeach, 1960; Adorno *et al.*, 1950). Beyond a particular level, considerable anxiety can be created by uncertainty. One way of obviating or reducing this anxiety is to simply ignore the

TABLE 11 WAYS OF COPING WITH UNCERTAINTY

	Information Processing Activity	*Action/Inaction-Oriented Activity*
No further interaction with the environment	II Formalization —probability —models	I Ignore or avoid Reduce to certainty
Attempt to reduce uncertainty by further interaction with the environment.	III Information collection	IV Negotiation Adaptation

more uncertain parts of the decision environment. For example, Kates (1962) and White (1964) describe how residents of flood plain areas disregard the threat of floods unless the floods occur so regularly that they are impossible to ignore.

Cyert and March (1963) have reported that many business firms avoid uncertainty by neglecting to consider its sources. To some extent this may result from an inability to consider all sources of uncertainty, but when it occurs in response to major factors (e.g., wage-price controls), an explicit avoidance strategy seems to be used. Carter (1971) has provided evidence of this tendency even in a dynamic computer software firm.

Ignoring uncertainty may sometimes be wise strategy, since some of the uncertainty will be resolved by waiting (Barnard, 1938). At times uncertainty will be ignored in order to expend resources in building up an adaptive capability (Ackoff, 1970; Weick, 1969). In such cases the decision maker prepares himself to respond quickly no matter what values the uncertain variables take on.

Reduction to Certainty Complete avoidance of important uncontrollable variables is rather uncommon; more often the decision maker behaves as if the uncertain events are more certain than they really are. For example, business firms may behave as though competitors' prices, interest rates, antitrust policy, and other business practices are going to be exactly the same in the future as they have been in the past, even though they may already have enough clues to suggest that this is not so (Cournot, 1897; Cyert and DeGroot, 1970).

Another form of reduction to certainty occurs after a commitment is made. Even though a decision maker may be willing to admit, and even to consider seriously, the uncertainty surrounding a particular event, after choosing an action he may tend to convince himself that events that will favorably affect his decision will occur (Cyert and March, 1963). This particular type of reduction to certainty is closely related to the post-choice dissonance reduction studies by Festinger and his associates (1957, 1964).

Attempting to Reduce Uncertainty in the Environment The responses described above assume that uncertain variables are uncontrollable. If, however, there are still some controllable elements left, then a more active strategy—that of attempted control—may be considered. Since the controllable-uncontrollable dichotomy depends to some extent on resources expended, the expenditure of more resources may lead to further control.

Cyert and March (1963) have emphasized an important form of such control attempts—negotiation with other decision-making units in the environment. In an oligopoly situation, for example, the firm can reduce uncertainty about what prices will be charged by other firms, and consequently the state of the firm's own profits, by explicitly or implicitly colluding with these firms. Managers in some major electric companies adopted this strategy during the 1950's (Fuller, 1962).

Other types of environmental negotiation to reduce uncertainty involve the use of contractual arrangements that may serve as buffers (e.g., inventories) for uncertain variables or transfer the uncertainty to another part of the decision environment (e.g., cost-of-living clauses). Programmed behavior in the form of standard operating procedures and organizational roles also reduce uncertainty (March and Simon, 1958; Cyert and MacCrimmon, 1969).

Although these are useful techniques for reducing uncertainty, even after they have been applied uncertainty will likely remain because of uncontrollable variables in the environment. Hence, techniques for handling uncertainty in general situations, after the uncertainty has been squeezed out of the partially controllable variables, are necessary to aid decision-making.

Uncertainty and Probability

Measurable Uncertainty A long-lived distinction between "measurable uncertainty" and "unmeasurable uncertainty" is attributable to Knight (1920). It is presumed that for "measurable uncertainty"—called "risk"—the probability distribution of the uncertain event is known, whereas for "unmeasurable uncertainty" it is not or cannot be known. The first class comprises gambling situations and mortality tables. The second class is assumed to contain virtually all other uncertain events. Probabilities (based on relative frequencies) would be assigned to the first class but they would be assumed invalid for the second class. Since all managerial decisions fall into the second class, the assumption, if true, would obviate the usefulness of probabilities. The techniques advanced for handling "unmeasurable uncertainty" assume that the decision maker has absolutely no information about the occurrence of such events. This is patently false and the distinction between measurable and unmeasurable uncertainty is untenable on both empirical and logical grounds. It seems to be perpetuated by textbook writers who want to treat cute, but useless, little models that deal with "unmeasurable uncertainty."

On the empirical side, Ellsberg (1961) has suggested that such a "risk"-"uncertainty" distinction exists in decision behavior and has offered examples in which a ball is drawn out of each of two urns. In the first urn, the proportion of red balls to black is 50–50 whereas in the second the distribution of the 100 balls is unknown—that is, there are x red balls and $100 - x$ black balls ($0 \leqq x \leqq 100$). Ellsberg argues that individuals will prefer bets on draws from the first urn rather than the second because the proportions of the first are known. Experiments of this kind with business executives have shown that few executives made this risk-uncertainty distinction at any time, none made the distinction in all the situations presented, and on reflection very few thought that such a distinction was reasonable (MacCrimmon, 1968a).

Quantified Consistent Beliefs: Probability The logical basis for rejecting the measurable-unmeasurable distinction is the view of probabilities as strictly an assignment satisfying some mathematical properties (Kolmogorov, 1950). Relative frequency, the basis for the Knightian "risk," then, is only one interpretation of probabilities and only one method by which probability values may be assigned; there are others that are just as valid (deFinetti, 1968; Kyburg, 1970). The one that is relevant to managers is a personalistic interpretation that is realized by quantifying a set of consistent beliefs.

Not all beliefs will satisfy the probability axioms and it is only those that do that we will call probabilities (deFinetti, 1937). If the initial assignment is not consistent, we would still be interested in finding out if the decision makers would be willing to revise their assignment in order to satisfy the axioms (Savage, 1954).

It may seem desirable to assign two levels of numbers to most events. The first could represent a probability and the second a level of confidence (Ellsberg, Peterson, and Beach, 1967). Savage (1954) has argued that theoretically this is not likely to lead to useful results, and Beach and Wise (1968) have obtained results that suggest that this does not have much empirical usefulness.

Personalistic probability estimates in managerial decisions are becoming more prevalent. In one form they are associated with the time estimates and the project completion time distribution in the PERT technique (Abernathy, 1971). In top-level decisions, Hansberger (1969) has described how probability assessments are made of important uncertain events relevant to major decisions at Boise Cascade.

These procedures are based on the premise that decision makers are better off when they try to anticipate the major sources of uncertainty and to account for them in a manner that will assure that their beliefs will be consistent.

Inconsistent Beliefs A variety of biases become apparent when a probability assignment is attempted. This in itself is a good reason to try to assign and check probabilities. In the urn example, it is easy to show that if the probabilities of red and black in urn I are normalized to add to 1, then under Ellsberg's conjecture the probabilities of red and black in urn II would add to less than 1. This particular implication has been studied in some detail by Fellner (1965), who terms such beliefs "slanted probabilities."

Another bias in probabilities has been suggested by Edwards (1953, 1954a). In a series of experiments his subjects seemed to show a preference for some particular probability numbers (½) and an aversion to others (¾) when confronting bets of the same (positive) expected return; although this may also be interpreted as a bias in preference for payoffs. In some earlier experimental work, Preston and Baratta (1948) found that people tend to overestimate low probabilities and underestimate high probabilities. Raiffa and his associates have found that people assign a much lower subjective probability to extreme values than they should. The 30 per cent in the tails of objective distributions are narrowed to about 2 per cent in subjective distributions.

These results bear some association to the model of uncertainty coping advocated by Shackle (1952, 1969). He has asserted that very improbable events are ignored by decision makers who tend to focus on particular gains and particular losses that would not be too surprising if they occurred. Shackle's theory goes into some detail in developing these concepts based on the unlikelihood of events—that is, surprise at their occurrence. Although there might be some reasonable psychological underpinnings to the theory of potential surprise, it can imply some quite unreasonable behavior. In over 20 years since the theory has been advanced, there still seem to be no applications or empirical tests, and hence it should be classified as only another explanation of biased beliefs rather than as a useful decision method.

Assessments of Probabilities Procedures are available for both the direct and the indirect assessment of probabilities from a set of consistent beliefs. The simplest method is to ask the decision maker directly for the probability value he would assign to a particular event. For example, how likely do you think it is that the Dow Jones average will be higher at the end of this year relative to its current level. When we are dealing with a variable that can take on a number of values, we might ask for the value associated with a particular probability (i.e., fractile of the cumulative probability distribution—see Winkler, 1967a). For example, for what Dow Jones value do you think the chances are 0.20 that the actual year-end average will exceed this value? A slight variant would be to use betting odds rather than probabilities (i.e., 4:1 rather than 0.20) and convert them to probabilities later.

With such a simple, direct method, however, there may be no inducement for the decision maker to tell the truth. There may even be influences in the environment that engender biases (Raiffa, 1969b). For example, if in estimating next period's sales a manager is rewarded when the sales are greater than the estimate and is penalized when the sales are less than the estimate, he will be strongly inclined to make a conservative estimate—that is, to bias the probability estimates downward (Woods, 1966).

In order to elicit the decision maker's true beliefs, various incentive procedures have been considered. These methods involve setting up a mathematical expression that shows the decision maker the penalty attached to making particular assessments depending on the event that occurs. If an event to which he assigned a high probability occurs, he receives a small penalty, but if an event to which he assigned a low probability occurs, he receives a heavy penalty. Mathematical expressions assigning quadratic and logarithmic losses are most commonly used (Toda, 1963; deFinetti, 1962; Winkler, 1967b; Stael von Holstein, 1970). The primary application has been to weather forecasting (Roberts, 1968; Murphy and Winkler, 1971ab).

Instead of asking the decision maker directly for a probability value, it may be more desirable to use indirect procedures in which the probabilities are revealed by the decision maker's choices (Savage, 1954). Suppose, for example, that we need to estimate the decision maker's personal probability that the next U.S. Presidential election would be won by the Republican candidate. Instead of asking for the probability directly, we could form bets, one of which would be on the Republican candidate; others would be based on the outcomes of coin tosses, dice throws, and other events to which we were willing to assign a well-established probability. These latter events, then, would serve as benchmarks that could be used to bound the probability assessment as tightly as desired. Pratt, Raiffa, and Schlaifer (1965) described an associated (canonical lottery) technique in more detail. Winkler (1971) provides some results showing the usefulness of betting procedures.

Combining Probabilities for Multiple Events When the decisions depend on only one uncontrollable variable, the assessment of a single probability distribution provides the desired input in the decision process. In decision situations, however, with a number of uncontrollable variables, the usual decision theory approach would require the assessment of the probability of all possible joint events (Savage, 1954). Luce and Krantz (1971), in their development of conditional expected utility, have provided a formulation in which only the events relating to an alternative, and not all the joint events, need to be considered.

In more complex cases, each alternative involves many uncertain events. A method for dealing with this would be to take a single value (say the mean) for each uncertain variable and to combine these to get a most probable future. It is easy to see, however, that only under special conditions will such a combined mean be equal to the mean of the real joint distribution, and so might lead to quite misleading results. A more elaborate procedure has been set forth by Hertz (1964, 1968) in which the whole distribution of each uncertain variable is used. Monte Carlo simulation procedures are employed to obtain a joint distribution under the assumption that the variables are mutually independent.

An intermediate procedure would use several values of the most prominent variables and combine them to form alternative joint events or scenarios. The alternative scenarios then represent the scope of the uncertainty considered in the decision environment. This method can be used with non-quantitative events and has been used widely in governmental decision-making. See, for example, *The Pentagon Papers* (1971).

Relative Variation If uncertainty can be characterized in terms of values of a random variable, then the variation in the values of the random variable provides a measure of uncertainty. The larger the variation, the more the uncertainty (Raiffa and Schlaifer, 1961). When it is desirable to reflect considerable uncertainty about a random variable, a distribution with a larger dispersion would be used, such as a uniform distribution (DeGroot, 1970). The most common measure of dispersion is the variance. Such procedures are commonly used in buying stocks (Markowitz, 1959), and we shall consider them further in the section on Outcome, Preference, and Risk.

Another stock decision procedure in which uncertainty is reflected in relative variation is the procedure of beta coefficients (Sharpe, 1968). The change in the price of a stock is assumed to be a linear function of the change in the market average. The coefficient of the market average reflects whether the stock price varies more (is more uncertain), varies less (is more certain), or is the same as the market average.

Summary of Uncertainty

In this section we have emphasized the use of personal probabilities for handling uncertainty because they are important parts of almost all general theories of decision-making under uncertainty. Probabilities can be applied in virtually every decision-making situation. Most of the work on probabilities has been done in the field of statistics, as well as in psychology and economics. In addition to assigning probabilities as described herein, there are specialized methods by which a decision maker can deal with uncertainty in particular situations. Despite their lack of emphasis here, they are likely to be very useful in the situations to which they apply.

When the uncertainty is primarily associated with variables that enter period by period, then projective forecasting techniques are often useful.

Exponential smoothing models are simple and popular. When the uncertain variables can be related to others about which more is known, some functional model that sets the variables in some sort of relationship (usually linear) can be determined. Since the coefficients of the expression are usually obtained by multiple regression techniques, they are called regression models. More complex forms with large numbers of variables and equations defining structural relations are called econometric models. Chambers, Mullick, and Smith (1971) provide a good discussion of these various techniques with particular emphasis on their uses to managers.

Less formal but wider-ranging methods are those grouped under the heading of technological forecasting. The methods themselves can employ any of the means already discussed, but they also encompass very informal speculations about the future in the spirit of Jules Verne, H. G. Wells, and others. Recent examples are technological and social forecasts to the year 2000 and beyond; for example, see Kahn and Weiner (1967), Bell (1968), and Jantsch (1968). A good managerial description can be found in Wills (1972).

INFORMATION

Information Acquisition and Transmittal

Throughout the decision process, the decision maker is acquiring information from the environment: information to assess desired and existing states, to make a problem diagnosis, to generate alternatives, to evaluate the likely consequences of alternatives, and so on. The entire decision-making process can be viewed as the acquisition and processing of information.

Information Collection Strategies The efficacy of information collection depends on the categories into which the decision maker can put the information he receives. The categories will influence the particular kind of information he chooses to acquire—or if he receives information automatically, it will influence the way he processes it upon receipt.

The work on concept attainment of Bruner, Goodnow, and Austin (1956) highlights the relationship between information processing strategies and categorization and classification procedures. Their study, and subsequent ones, is too detailed to summarize here, but suffice it to say that two strategies, conservative-focusing and focus-gambling, in which the emphasis is placed on the data instances rather than the alternative solutions (i.e., hypotheses), proved to make reasonable cognitive demands. Conservative-focusing, involving search for "nearby" information, guarantees that some relevant information will be attained. Such a strategy can be very inefficient, however, for a quick decision the more adventurous focus-gambling strategy is preferable. Although no specific applications of these strategies seem to have been made to managerial decisions, a knowledge of the work in the concept attainment area should raise some interesting connections with the information processing involved in managerial roles.

Removal of Uncertainty The intensity of the search for information will depend on the amount of uncertainty that is present. When the uncertainty is high, the search for information is likely to be intensive and is likely to continue until the uncertainty is reduced to a tolerable level (Driscoll and Lanzetta, 1965).

As information is acquired it is passed along to the various decision-making units involved. During this transmittal process, it tends to lose some of its uncertainty and become more precise—that is, a specious precision arises. Units further along the line of transmittal, locations where relevant decisions must be made often do not learn of the high degree of uncertainty that really exists. Woods (1966) describes how this process operates in business firms. March and Simon (1958) have called this behavior "uncertainty absorption."

Information Quantity and Quality

Information Amount Since decision-making requires the collection of information, it would seem desirable to have some measure of the amount of information. Perhaps, then, a basis could be developed for assessing how much information was on hand and how much should be acquired. Consider the information content of a weather forecast (Theil, 1967). Suppose that the forecasting service tells us what percentage of the time the sun will shine tomorrow between sunrise and sunset. How much information is contained in a particular message such as "The sun will shine less than 30 per cent of the day"? First, we need to consider how much information we have before the message. Suppose that at this time of year the chances of less than 30 per cent sunshine in a given day chosen at random are 0.50.

The measure usually used for specifying information amount is the logarithm (to the base 2) of the reciprocal of the probability. That is, the information contained in a (reliable) message about the occurrence of an event with probability P is $h(p) = \text{Log}_2 1/p = -\text{Log}_2 p$. The units of this expression are in bits (*b*inary dig*its*). Hence, before receiving a forecast, we have $\text{Log}_2 1/0.5 = 1$ bit of information. In order to evaluate the information content of the forecast—"The sun will shine less than 30 per cent of the day" —we have to know how frequently the sun does shine less than 30 per cent on days for which a 30 per cent forecast is made. Clearly, such forecasts are never perfect, but we would expect them to be better than 50 per cent. Suppose that the actual conditional probability of such a forecast being followed by the event predicted is 0.68. Then the information content of the message can be calculated as $h(0.5) - h(0.68) = 0.44$ bit, which represents the information gain.

The theory developed around these concepts has been particularly useful in designing communication transmission facilities, coding procedures, and the like (Shannon, 1948). The theory has not been very useful in managerial decision-making because it deals only with probabilities and not with consequences of decisions. Howard (1966) points out that if there is the same probability of your losing all your assets in the stock market and of having a whale steak for dinner, then messages containing both these pieces of information would have the same amount of information. Clearly, a theory of information that is useful in managerial decisions must deal explicitly with values.

Information amount vs. Information capacity: overload Without restrictions on the decision maker's information capacity, more costless information would always be preferable to less since the surplus information could be ignored. In addition, too much information may clog up the system (Ackoff, 1967). With screening or storage costs, more information may lead to higher costs without providing any benefit. Irrelevant information and noise are clearly detrimental, but too much relevant information can be almost as bad (Campbell, 1968).

Miller (1956) has hypothesized a limit of about seven chunks of information in short-term memory and has supported this with various psychophysics studies. More recently, Simon (1969) and others have identified parameters constraining processing activity. When a great deal of information is received, the decision maker may be able to retain more if he organizes it efficiently. By grouping the information into categories (new chunks) and arranging them hierarchically, the decision maker may be able to considerably expand his information processing capacity (Simon, 1969).

For further information on information overload, with particular attention to psychological variables, see Schroder, Driver, and Streufert (1967).

Information partitioning Efficient storage and efficient processing may require a variety of information formats. There is an optimal level of aggregation for any decision at hand. In some cases the information might be too detailed (e.g., store-by-store sales), whereas in other cases it might be too aggregated (e.g., national sales). In general, the more detailed information should be retained because once the information is aggregated it is very difficult to disaggregate for particular purposes (Marschak, 1965).

The form of the information depends on the particular use to which it is being put. For example, suppose that you can buy or sell short a stock that this week may rise or fall by any amount between +$6 and —$6 (Marschak, 1959). You can buy market information of two types: Type *A* information gives you one of two messages (1) the stock price will rise, or (2) the stock price will fall; Type *B* information gives you one of three messages (1) the stock price will rise by $2 or more, (2) the stock price will fall by $2 or more, or (3) the stock price will move by less than $2 in either direction. Which type of market information would you buy? Marschak shows that the information amount is greater in the second case (log 3 to log 2) whereas the average gain from information is greater in the first case ($3 to $2.67). A rational decision maker will clearly pick the information form that provides the greatest gain from information rather than the highest quantity of information. See Marschak (1971) for an excellent discussion interrelating information quantity and quality.

Expected Value of Information In an economic sense, information has value only if it leads to a change in the alternative chosen. In order for a seismographic test to have value to an oil exploration company, there has to be some place in the world for which the information has changed what the company would have done before they received the information (Grayson, 1960). The expected value of the best action before the information is received can be compared with the expected value of the best action after the information is received and utilized in order to establish the expected value of the information (Schlaifer, 1959; Raiffa, 1968).

In the behavioral literature, there is evidence that information is valued even when it does not change the action that the decision maker had previously decided on. Information may be valued because it makes the decision maker more confident about the action he had already decided upon. It also constitutes a basis for power and influence over others (Kelley and Thibaut, 1969).

Information also has a cost. The decision maker is obviously interested in comparing the expected value of the information with its expected cost to determine if it is worth acquiring (Marschak, 1968; Schlaifer, 1969). Sometimes it may be very difficult to make this determination—the expected value part is usually the more difficult to determine—but procedures exist for making the calculations. For an application to coffee marketing, see Newman (1971).

Information Impact on Prior Beliefs and Commitments

Revision of prior beliefs Before acquiring information, the decision maker will have some beliefs—perhaps extremely vague—about conditions he deems relevant to his decision problem. The collection of information will then provide a basis for revising these prior beliefs into a set of posterior beliefs. There is a mathematical expression, called Bayes formula, that shows how prior probabilities should be revised based on information collected (Bayes, 1963; Raiffa, 1968).

Edwards (1968) and others have found that decision makers are conservative revisers of probability in that the revision is less than it should be, given the diagnosticity of the information collected. In other words, the information is perceived as having less content (diagnosticity) than it really contains. So, it may take five or ten pieces of information to change beliefs whereas one observation should have been sufficient (Peterson and Beach, 1967).

One implication drawn from these results is that although decision makers will have to be relied on for a judgment of prior probabilities, the revision process is best taken out of the human decision maker's hands and turned over to a computer. Edwards *et al.* (1968) have described probabilistic information processing (PIP) systems to accomplish this.

Methods have been developed to match up the form of the prior probability distribution with the likelihood distribution in order to facilitate the probability revision process. Distributions that combine readily are conjugate to one another. Raiffa and Schlaifer (1961) provide details for such analyses.

Effect of Prior Commitments After committing himself to a course of action, a decision maker may receive information incongruent with this commitment. This would create a situation of cognitive dissonance (Festinger, 1957). The theory and supporting research suggest that the decision maker will tend to reduce the dissonance by various procedures such as discrediting the post-commitment information. Furthermore, the decision maker may try to arrange his information environment so that he receives only information that confirms his commitment and hence avoids incongruent information (Festinger, 1964). Cyert and March (1963) discuss some observations of post-commitment behavior in business firms that are consistent with a reduction of cognitive dissonance.

Information Flows in Multi-person Decision Situations

Economic Theory of Teams A particularly well-developed normative theory of information flows in multiple person situations is the economic theory of teams provided by Marschak and Radner (1972). The theory focuses on three central problems: (1) how organizational members should acquire information from the uncertain environment, (2) what communication channels and messages should be utilized to communicate this information to other members, and (3) what actions each member should take based on the information he receives. The theory emphasizes that information should be acquired, or communications should be sent, only when the recipient can use the information in his decision, thus yielding a higher payoff to the whole organization.

The term "theory of teams" assumes that there is no conflict of interest among the members—that is, their values and beliefs are completely in accord. This is obviously an unrealistic assumption for real organizations but is used in order to obtain some results that hopefully approximate information processing behavior in real organizations. A team theory problem used in experiments with managers (MacCrimmon, 1972) uncovered many common information processing fallacies also encountered in real information systems (Ackoff, 1967). It would be difficult to apply team theory directly to real organizations but it has provided a solid economic basis to management information system thinking (Emery, 1967).

Communication Networks A descriptive approach to information flows in groups is provided by the communication network studies in psychology. Bavelas (1948) and Leavitt (1950) triggered a large number of studies into the effect of different communication channel patterns on a group's performance. Communication structures such as a wheel (with a single member at the hub), a chain (a linear sequence), a circle (each member connected to two other members), and an all-channel (each member connected to each other member) have been studied in three-, four- and five-person situations. The results indicate that the circle is the most decentralized, active, leaderless, erratic, and satisfying; the wheel is the most centralized, least active, leader-oriented, stable, and unsatisfying. The findings, however, are somewhat contradictory, and despite the plethora of studies it is still somewhat difficult to tell what implications can be drawn for the design of real information systems. For further details on the experimental results see Glanzer and Glaser (1961), Shaw (1964), and Collins and Raven (1969).

Acquiring information from subordinates and experts Of the many possible sources from whom information may be collected, a particularly important one is from other individuals over whom the decision maker has some control. For many managers, the most important information source is his own subordinates. At other times he may have to draw on consultants both within and outside the organization.

If the decision maker has to acquire information from more than one subordinate or consultant (for example, when no one person can provide him with all the information he needs) he must decide how to collect this information. Perhaps the most apparent procedure would be to call the participants together in a meeting and to ask the appropriate questions. Face-to-face interaction, however, can have some dysfunctional consequences in that it can lead to a domination of the meeting by the most forceful member, hence stifling the useful information inputs of the more reticent (Maier, 1963). At the other extreme, the decision maker may separately poll his informants. This procedure has the disadvantage of not utilizing interaction to generate cooperative outputs.

Intermediate procedures exist by which the decision maker may use interactive methods but without running the risk of unbalanced group participation. The DELPHI procedure developed at the Rand Corporation, and used during the 1950's to estimate such things as the Soviet military capability 10 to 15 years in the future, is such a method (Dalkey and Helmer, 1963). In the DELPHI procedure the participants are isolated from one another and are presented with a series of questionnaires in which their opinions and rationale are solicited. After each round of questionnaires, information from the participants is consolidated and circulated anonymously to each member of the group. Different variants of this method may be established, depending on the requirements of the decision situation. Such procedures are widely used in many contexts, such as estimating the quality of life, urban problems, and changes in governmental policies and capabilities (Helmer, Gordon, and Brown, 1966).

The desirability and manner in which information is collected from subordinates and then used in management decisions depends also on such factors as whether the subordinates can be trusted to act in accordance with organizational goals, the quality of the decision necessary, the degree of acceptance necessary, and so on. Vroom (1973) considers a variety of these factors and presents a procedure by which answers to these questions specify a "participation tree" showing the degree to which the manager should consult with his subordinates and the form this interaction should assume.

Information from advocates Another important information source is information advanced by advocates. In most situations the person presenting information has something to gain or lose personally and hence the decision maker may be receiving information that has been biased to reflect a particular point of view (Downs, 1967). For example, asking a project manager for an estimate of the expected duration of a project may be more likely to elicit a figure that the manager would like to see as a standard for evaluating his performance rather than his true estimate of the actual project duration. In other situations there may not be such a strong motivation for biasing information, but the decision maker nevertheless is advised to be on the lookout for even possibly unconscious biases.

In some decision situations, the decision maker may find it useful to set up procedures in which different points of view are explicitly advocated. This is particularly useful in those instances where there is an action that may be quite reasonable but it may be unpopular or disagreeable to advocate it. The main use of advocates has been in the courtroom, but they have also been found useful in other public and business decision contexts (Mason, 1969).

Summary: Information

The study of information value in economics and statistics publications has provided both useful concepts and useful techniques for managerial decision-making. The concepts are relevant to any decision problem, but unfortunately many decision makers still think in terms of information amount rather than information value. The techniques are primarily limited to statistically oriented situations but the range of possibilities is expanding. There are many different approaches to the study of information in the psychology literature. Many of these investigations seem irrelevant for managerial decisions; the contributions of the other studies range from marginally helpful concepts to quite practical techniques.

Managing information flows in a decision process within a group or organization is a difficult managerial problem. Some recent studies are beginning to provide some help. More attention needs to be directed toward making the information strategy responsive to the requirements of the situation and the capabilities of the decision makers involved.

OUTCOMES, PREFERENCE, AND RISK

Evaluating the Alternatives

At various points in the decision-making process a decision maker assesses the outcomes of alternatives. There are two parts to this procedure: (1) an objective description of outcomes, which could be used by other decision makers, and (2) a subjective appraisal of outcomes, which is based on his own preferences. The objective description can be supplied by independent analysts through their analysis of the causal links in the environment. Questions to ask are, "If this action is taken, and if these events occur, then what will the outcome be?" In order to handle the subjective appraisal, the analyst would have to know the personal preferences of the decision maker. A variety of methods have been developed to represent preferences. These methods are useful both for an analyst trying to incorporate a particular decision maker's preferences and for the decision maker himself, since a formal representation allows him to reflect on them and to examine them for consistency. An especially important aspect of preferences of managers is the degree of risk they are willing to take. The interpretation of outcomes, the application of some preference function to these outcomes, and the risk propensity of the decision maker will be the focus of this section.

Outcomes

Outcomes In most decision situations it seems natural to classify outcomes into two categories—the "positive" and the "negative." Positive and negative do not necessarily mean numerical values, but rather reflect the desirability of the change of state to the decision maker. That is, there seems to be a zero point (often the existing state); outcomes that fall above it are called benefits, pleasures, gains, successes, and outcomes that fall below it are called costs, pains, losses, failures. Bentham (1789) even lists pleasures and pains.

Decision makers do not pay the same amount of attention to positive and negative outcomes. McClelland (1961) and Atkinson and Feather (1966), for example, discuss a theory of need achievement that explicitly identifies an individual's propensity to strive for success versus his propensity to avoid failure. Although this theory rests on a weak measurement basis, it has some interesting implication for risk taking. Shackle's theory of potential surprise (1969) also identifies a zero point and is based on the decision maker having a focal gain and a focal loss. Slovic and Lichtenstein (1968) and others have found that in gambling experiments, subjects tend to pay more attention to losses than to gains.

That managers are attentive to gains and losses separately and do not just consider net values is apparent from observations of just about any decision situation—for example, the Cuban missile crisis (Sorensen, 1965) and capital investments in large corporations (Bower, 1970).

In public policy analysis, the major developments in benefit-cost analysis, with its emphasis on how to measure costs and how to measure benefits, have made an important contribution to the specification of outcomes in a decision problem. Space precludes going into these topics here, but every decision maker should be aware of the basic economic notions of marginal analysis, sunk costs, opportunity costs, externalities, and the more sophisticated procedures that benefit-cost analysis encompasses. For further details see Prest and Turvey (1965), Fisher (1971), Hinrichs and Taylor (1969), and Haveman and Margolis (1970).

Outcome Representations The two most useful formats for representing possible outcomes of a decision situation are decision matrices (payoff tables) and decision trees. In a *decision matrix* the rows, say, represent the alternative actions and the columns represent the possible events. A cell in the matrix then represents an outcome resulting from the choice of that particular row (i.e., action) by the decision maker and the occurrence of that particular column (i.e., event). Hence there are as many outcomes possible as there are action-event pairs. See Schlaifer (1959) and Miller and Starr (1967) for more details and many examples.

In a decision tree the branches from the initial (decision) node represent the actions available to the decision maker. The end points of these branches represent an event node in that the new branches emanating from these new nodes represent the events. In simple decision problems, the end points of these event branches will be the possible outcomes of the decision, and so here too an action (branch) and an event (branch) paired together define an outcome. See Magee (1964a, 1964b) for more details and examples.

A decision tree representation is more useful when there are sequential aspects to the decision problem, as for example when sampling or surveys are involved (Raiffa, 1968). Decision matrices are most useful in problems in which it is desirable to make direct comparisons of alternatives for different events that might occur; for example in trying to determine if one alternative dominates another (Savage, 1954; MacCrimmon, 1968a).

Preferences

Aspiration levels and targets Classifying outcomes as successes or failures may be quite easy in mathematical problems and games, but it is much more difficult in management decision situations. For example, is market penetration of 15 per cent a success or a failure? Clearly, the answer will depend very much on the performance of the rest of the product lines, on the performance of competitors, and a host of other factors. Whether this outcome is deemed a success or failure will probably be determined by comparing it with the *a priori* hopes and expectations of the decision maker for the product. These hopes and expectations represent an aspiration level that will separate success from failure, in that outcomes above the aspiration level will be deemed successes and those below it will be deemed failures. Thus, the aspiration level represents a threshold that the decision maker tries to achieve, and there is a noticeable discontinuity in terms of his satisfaction depending on whether outcomes are above or below the aspiration level (Lewin *et al.*, 1944; Siegel, 1957). For some theorists, the aspiration level represents the only way preferences are incorporated into the decision (Simon, 1955).

Aspiration levels that are set too high lead to frustration in that the decision maker continually fails to succeed; aspiration levels that are set too low can be readily achieved but do not serve as an effective motivator of performance. Stedry (1961) provides some empirical results and develops the relationships between high and low aspiration levels and tight and loose budgets. Ansoff (1965) and Hansberger (1969) discuss the uses of aspiration or goal levels (e.g., achieving an increase of 20 percent in earnings per share) in corporate strategy decisions.

Time Preference Outcomes often occur at different times. Decision makers usually have preferences about when outcomes should occur. Some outcomes are preferred as late as possible (e.g., death), others as early as possible (e.g., money yields), and others during particular periods (e.g., extra sales during slack periods).

The main techniques available for handling time preferences deal with money outcomes and assume that the decision maker wants the outcomes to occur as soon as possible. Payback period procedures involve computing the total period of time before the original investment amount is reaccumulated (in current dollars). They are simple to apply but probably misrepresent a decision maker's real time preferences (Weingartner, 1969). Discounting procedures (including net present values, rates of return, etc.) are more sophisticated and also seem to be able to better reflect a decision maker's actual time preference in such contexts. However, the choice of which discount rate to apply to outcomes received in different periods is a thorny issue. For more details see Hitch and McKean (1960), Modigliani and Miller (1958), and Fisher (1971).

Time preferences alone may be a sufficient representation of a decision maker's preferences when the only concern is with cash flows and no uncertainty in outcomes is considered. If other objectives such as distribution effects, management control, and utilization of physical and human resources are of concern to the decision maker, then methods of exhibiting preferences for joint outcomes become relevant. If uncertainty in outcomes is an important element, it is useful to consider techniques that will reflect risk preferences.

Indifference curves and trade-offs A useful way to represent joint preferences for two-dimensional outcomes is through indifference curves. The outcomes that are more preferred are on high indifference curves, and the outcomes that are less preferred are on lower curves. Only judgments of whether one alternative is preferred to another, and not the extent to which it is preferred, are required to set up indifference curves. MacCrimmon and Toda (1969) have devised an efficient technique for obtaining indifference curves for alternatives having two dimensions.

The shape of the curve will reflect the trade-off rate (i.e., the marginal rate of substitution) between the two dimensions at particular levels of the other dimensions (Hitch and McKean, 1960). It seems to be quite natural to most decision makers to think in terms of trade-off ratios, particularly if one of the elements is money—for example, "How much am I willing to pay for a transportation mode that will get me to my destination 30 minutes earlier?"

In order to be able to use indifference curve procedures efficiently when there are more than two dimensions involved, some assumptions are required about the independence of the trade-offs between two dimensions from the levels of the others. As the number of dimensions in a decision problem increases, the indifference curve method—but not the trade-off way of thinking—becomes less useful.

Worth Curves If there are many objectives, to consider in a decision problem and hence many dimensions, worth curves are often used. In order to directly apply the worth curve procedure, the decision maker scales his preferences for each dimension separately in terms of a worth scale (Churchman, Ackoff, and Arnoff, 1956; Miller, 1970). He then scales the relative importance of each dimension to him. Thus, two separate preference judgments are made, one dealing with intra-factor preferences and the other with inter-factor preferences. The importance ratings are used as weights to multiply with the worth ratings, the products of which are then summed.

Rather than querying the decision maker directly about his preferences, linear weighting models can be used in inferring preferences from a set of decisions that already have been made. In such a case, combined weights are inferred using multiple regression techniques. These procedures have been used for medical diagnosis (Hoffman, Slovic and Rorer, 1967), production scheduling (Kunreuther, 1969), judicial cases (Kort, 1968), and graduate student admissions (Dawes, 1971). See Slovic and Lichtenstein (1971) for an excellent review and for references to many more examples.

Such models can be used to help a decision maker improve his future decisions by eliminating the random errors he might make without such an aid. The use of a decision maker's inferred values to improve his subsequent decisions has been called "bootstrapping." Dawes (1970) and Goldberg (1970) have shown how improved decisions and considerable time savings can be realized by using this technique.

Underlying the linear weighting procedure are a number of assumptions. All the attributes should be independent from one another and all the worth values and weights should be comparable. Notice that the worths and the weights must be numerical values (in order to multiply them together). This is more demanding of the decision maker than the simple ordinal judgments required for indifference curves (MacCrimmon, 1968b). Miller (1969) provides practical techniques for helping to make the weight and worth judgments. Fishburn (1965, 1967) and Raiffa (1969a) describe methods for ascertaining independence among attributes. Although the independence assumption seems quite restrictive in most cases (e.g., the trade-off between travel time and travel cost would not be allowed to depend on comfort or safety), in actual practice linear weighting models seem to predict quite well. This is true even in situations in which a high degree of interdependence might be thought to exist (Yntema and Torgerson, 1961; Hoffman, 1968). Green (1968), however, suggests that the linearity may be contributed by the analysis rather than being inherent in the data.

In any case, linear weighting procedures are very popular in management decision-making. For representative applications, see Miller (1969), on job choice, Terry (1966) on new product introduction, and Boggess (1967) on credit risks.

Utility functions If the uncertainties of a decision problem rather than the multiple objectives are predominant, then other kinds of preference representations are needed. Bernoulli (1738) was the first to show the need and usefulness of utility functions for representing preferences in uncertain environments. Ramsey (1931) and von Neumann and Morgenstern (1947) have provided the general mathematical (and behavioral) bases of utility representations. Simple judgments by decision makers of which actions are preferred to others are all that is needed to scale subjective probabilities for the uncertain events, and these in turn can be used to scale the utilities. So information processing demands on the decision-maker are less than with the linear weighting methods. Also, the independence assumptions that are necessary in order to combine utilities and probabilities do not represent a difficulty because the events are mutually exclusive and hence cannot occur simultaneously, as the attributes could (Savage, 1954). The utility function approach, then, has a more solid basis than the linear weighting procedures.

Mosteller and Nogee (1948), Davidson, Suppes and Siegel (1956), and Becker, DeGroot and Marschak (1962) have provided procedures for obtaining utility functions. Such a utility function is unique up to an increasing linear transformation, which means that in drawing a utility function the location of the origin and the distance of a scale unit can be made arbitrarily (Marschak, 1954; DeGroot, 1970; Raiffa, 1968). This does not at all imply that a utility function is linear. The utility function may be convex, in which case the decision maker would be a risk taker; or it may be concave, in which case the decision maker would be a risk averter; or it may be linear, in which case the decision maker would be risk neutral (see Schlaifer, 1959). An actual utility curve obtained from a decision maker may have convex, concave, and linear segments. Friedman and Savage (1948, 1952) and Markowitz (1952) discuss how this reflects a willingness to gamble over particular ranges of outcomes (the convex part), to ensure over other segments (the concave part), and to be indifferent between gambling and ensuring (the linear part).

Grayson (1960) and Swalm (1966) show how utility functions with a variety of different shapes (implying quite different preferences) can exist in the same company. Results derived by Grayson show that utility functions seem to be relatively stable over time. See Hammond (1968) and Brown (1970) for a further discussion of practical applications.

Social preference functions In those decision situations that involve more than one decision maker, it would seem desirable to extend the above analysis to get a utility function for the group. Unfortunately, Arrow (1951) has shown that when some seemingly innocuous conditions are imposed on social choices, it is impossible to have a social utility function.

The major difficulty in attempting to determine social utilities is how to interrelate one person's utility with another's. There seem to be no good methods to make interpersonal comparisons of utility, since people have no inducement to tell the truth; in fact, they probably would be induced to distort their preferences (Rothenberg, 1961; Sen, 1970).

Risk

Risk Propensity A very important aspect of managerial decisions is the risk propensity of the decision maker. A risky decision situation involves some *uncertainty* about the outcomes and some *possibility of loss* (including opportunity loss) of resources. (Notice, then, that this is a meaningful and common use of the term "risk," in contrast to the "risk-uncertainty" fallacy mentioned earlier. A situation that involves either great uncertainty or the possibility of high losses will be perceived as being risky. Slovic and Lichtenstein (1968) present some experimental results from gambling situations that suggest that the probabilities are more important determinants of perceived risk than are the payoffs.

Earlier, it was indicated that the shapes of utility functions can reflect the risk propensity of the decision maker. Arrow (1971) and Pratt (1964) have provided a mathematical measure of risk aversion in terms of the first and second derivatives of a utility function. Although the measure is of considerable theoretical interest, it has limited practical usefulness.

Another characterization of risk propensity that is centered on the distribution of payoffs is the use of the decision maker's preference with regard to the variance of the distribution of outcomes. Pruitt (1962) and Coombs and Huang (1970) suggest that for each possible mean value of payoffs the decision maker has a preferred variance. Decision makers who prefer a smaller variance are more risk averting. Finance studies, on the other hand, suggest that all decision makers will (or should) automatically prefer the investment with the lowest variance for a given mean. The mean-variance criterion (Markowitz, 1959) generated by this assumption has received a great deal of attention, since it is presumably easy to apply. The minimum variance assumption of this criterion is questionable given the results of Coombs and Huang (1970) showing ideal levels of variance that are not at the minimum level. In addition, Tobin (1965) and others have shown that a mean-variance criterion implies either a quadratic utility or a probability distribution of returns that is described with only two location parameters. Both these assumptions seem invalid (Grayson, 1960; Fama and Roll, 1968).

Different measures of risk propensity have been devised by psychologists. Kogan and Wallach (1964) have used choice dilemma problems in which you are asked for the lowest probability of success for which, say, you would advise a middle-aged man to quit his present, secure job to take a position with a new company. Presumably, the lower the minimum acceptable probability you advise, the higher is your propensity to risk. Another measure of risk propensity is derived from classification decisions involving the risks of inclusion and exclusion. Various other measures of risk propensity have been set forth by psychologists. See Kogan and Wallach (1964); Atkinson (1957); and Shure and Meeker (1967).

The measures described here, or the others mentioned in the references, may be used to help a manager and his co-workers obtain a better insight into their own and one another's propensity to take risks. Grayson (1960) gives an example of how two co-owners (brothers) and a geologist in a small oil exploration firm obtained a better understanding of the risks each had been taking in the past and would take in the future when their utility functions were shown to them and the implications were discussed.

Swalm (1966) has shown that most managers in a large company are quite risk averse as indicated in their utility functions. The managers seem to be using their own very risk average utility rather than the more risk prone strategy that would be better for the company as a whole when small amounts of resources (relative to the company's assets) are at stake. This knowledge provides a basis for an organization to change the motivational arrangements designed to encourage managers at lower levels to take more risks.

Slovic, in his own experiments and in summarizing the work of others (1962, 1964), has shown that different measures of risk obtained from a single decision maker can lead to quite different assessments of a decision maker's propensity to take risks. Bassler (1972) has come up with the same results in a study of business executives. These results suggest that risk taking may not be a general personality trait but may be very dependent on the situation the decision maker is in. For a detailed summary of the effects of personal factors and situational influences, see Kogan and Wallach (1967).

Risk Sharing and Diversification When a decision maker confronts a risky situation, he may try to reduce the risk in two main ways. One approach is to try to affect the probabilities either by increasing the probability of gain or by decreasing the probability of loss. The other approach involves an attempt to affect the payoffs, either by increasing the size of the possible gains or decreasing the size of the possible losses.

The primary way to affect the overall probabilities of gains and losses in investment decisions is through diversification. Diversification requires the consolidation of individual components into a portfolio in such a way as to smooth out the extreme probabilities of the aggregate gains and (particularly) losses. In order for diversification to be effective, the components must yield different results under different conditions—that is, they cannot be perfectly correlated. The most significant reduction of risk occurs when alternatives with high negative correlations can be matched (Markowitz, 1959; Borch, 1968).

Another way to reduce risks by changing the probabilities is through bargaining, collusion, or contractual arrangements. These methods were discussed earlier.

The payoffs can be affected through risk sharing agreements. The magnitude of the gains and losses of a particular alternative may be so large that no one decision maker may wish to take it. However, if the gains and (particularly) the losses can be broken up, a group of decision makers (no one of which would have taken the alternative at the original scale) may be put together to share the risk (Raiffa, 1969). This type of risk sharing is particularly prevalent in reinsurance agreements (Borch, 1969).

Risky Shift The preceding two sections have touched on some aspects of risk in multiple person situations, but they did not deal directly with the risk taking propensity of a group. A very practical element in managerial decisions is whether groups take more or less risky decisions than individuals. An unequivocal answer to this question would have important implications, say, for the degree to which committees are set up and used. Early management studies suggested that groups were inclined to take less risk than individuals. Since the early 1960's, however, a number of experiments have been performed, many of them with managers, and the results indicate that groups take riskier decisions (Kogan and Wallach, 1967).

Many of the experiments have used the choice dilemma problems discussed earlier and have the individuals assess their minimum acceptable probability for the situation. Then the individuals are formed into groups that discuss the problem until a consensus is reached. This usually yields a higher probability than the average of the individual recommendations, implying a shift toward risk. Various explanations have been advanced to account for this shift. Three main ones are: (1) there is a diffusion of responsibility throughout the group, (2) there is a social value in being perceived as a risk taker, and (3) the leaders having the most influence over the group discussion are likely to be more risk inclined. No one of these explanations alone seems to account for the risk shift in groups, but each has received some confirmation. Kogan and Wallach (1967) and Clark (1971) give a good summary of the results.

Summary: Outcomes, Preferences, and Risk

A variety of techniques are available to assist the decision maker in assessing the outcomes, ascertaining his preferences, and uncovering his risk propensity. Economics, management science, and psychology have contributed useful methods such as benefit-cost analysis, indifference curves, worth curves, bootstrapping, utility functions, mean-variance, and so on. In addition to practical techniques, these disciplines have provided helpful concepts and insightful ways of evaluating outcomes, preferences, and risk.

The main emphasis in this section has been on methods by which the decision maker can relate his values to the complexity and uncertainty in the alternatives he confronts. When complexity in the form of multiple dimensions predominates, the decision maker can effectively use aspiration levels, indifference curves, or worth curves to represent his preferences in a form that will assist him in making choices. When uncertainty predominates, he can use mean-variance or utility functions to relate his values to his choices. The available techniques for dealing with both uncertainty and multiple-attribute complexity (Raiffa, 1969a) make heavy demands on the decision maker, but this should be an area of important developments in the future.

The direct assessment of a decision maker's risk propensity can allow him to ascertain its appropriateness in different contexts and how his preferences compare to others in his environment. With groups of decision makers, it can provide a basis for recruiting individuals with particular risk propensities or constructing motivational schemes to use with an existing set of individuals in order to get some desired aggregate attitude toward risk.

CRITERIA AND CHOICE

Choice Phase of the Decision Process

The choice phase of the decision process follows directly after outcomes have been specified and preferences ascertained. The decision maker's preferences form criteria that are applied to the possible results of the alternatives. The different forms of criteria and the different comparisons affect the choice. The primary types of choices are: maximizing, satisficing, incrementing, or adapting. These choices are found in both individual and multiple person choice situations, but the variety of different preferences of many persons raises some special problems. These issues will be dealt with in this section.

Criteria

Forms of Criteria The way a problem is formulated can very much determine the criteria that are set up and applied to it. In a multiple-dimension decision, the criteria will relate directly to the dimensions that have been identified. If, for example, you make personal purchase decisions by consulting *Consumer Reports,* the factors listed—puncture resistance, durability, and price, say, for automobile tires—imply some criteria they have in mind and will consequently focus your attention on the same criteria. When *Consumer Reports* groups products into categories such as "acceptable" or "not acceptable," the criteria are being imposed quite directly.

The criteria will usually indicate a desired direction and a desired level. For instance, in choosing transportation, travel times and travel costs are factors for which you (as a user) would prefer lower values to higher ones, whereas for safety and frequency of schedule you would prefer higher values. The level you set may either be a feasible one, in which case it functions as a standard, or it may exist at some idealistic level, in which case you may be attempting to maximize or minimize. The first choice will get you to your destination within 2 hours, whereas the second would involve the minimum travel time. An intermediate type of criteria would be one that tries to maximize the probability of attaining a particular level; for example, the type of transportation that would maximize the probability of a trip time of less than 2 hours.

Different types of comparison processes are implied by the type of level that is specified. If the criteria involve a feasible level (e.g., the 2-hour trip), the alternatives are compared with this level used as a standard. If the criteria involve an idealistic level, then the alternatives are compared with another to determine the relative degree of attainment. Whether the comparisons are alternatives against standards or alternatives against alternatives (or a combination of both) may greatly affect the final choice.

Alternatives versus Standards When standards are set up in a multiple-dimension problem, they are often specified across all the attributes. Hence in a personnel hiring decision we may set as a standard 5 years experience in the industry, a background in accounting, a particular score on a managerial aptitude test, and so on. Notice that the standard can be thought of as a surrogate alternative. It is an alternative that would be acceptable and is used to screen out alternatives that would not be acceptable.

The level at which the criteria are set will obviously affect the chances of finding acceptable alternatives. If the levels are set low and hence are easy to attain, the criteria are likely to be applied *conjunctively*. That is, the alternatives that are compared with the standard will be expected to meet or exceed the standard across *all* the dimensions. If, on the other hand, the levels are set very high and hence are difficult to attain, the criteria are likely to be applied *disjunctively*. With a disjunctive rule, an alternative needs only to meet or exceed the standard of *any one* of the dimensions. Conjunctive rules are much more common, but Dawes (1964) gives an example of a disjunctive rule in which a football team selects a player if his running, passing, *or* kicking ability excels—without expecting anyone to excel in all three. Semi-junctive rules in which the standards need to be met or exceeded on a subset of the dimensions may also be considered (MacCrimmon, 1973b).

When standards are set and used in decision problems, there is no reason why they have to remain fixed throughout the duration of the evaluation. If they are set loosely to begin with, and then gradually are tightened (emphasizing the dimensions that are most important to the decision maker), they can narrow the set of acceptable alternatives as much as desired, so that, for example, only a single alternative is left. Tversky (1971) discusses the efficacy of making decisions by sequential elimination. See also MacCrimmon (1973b) in this regard.

Alternatives versus Alternatives When a maximization criterion is used, alternatives are compared with one another to determine which alternative best attains the maximal value. Special attention has been paid to the maximization criterion when only a single dimension such as money is considered. In these situations, as mentioned earlier, we have benefits and costs for each alternative and we must make a choice. Well-intended, but unsophisticated, decision makers may decide that the criteria they wish to pursue is the maximization of benefits and the minimization of costs. In general, this is impossible to attain. Among a given set of alternatives, there may be one that has the highest benefit and the lowest cost, but it would be very unlikely if we could not find another alternative outside the set that had either a higher benefit or a lower cost.

If we cannot maximize benefits at the same time that we minimize costs, then the question is raised concerning what is an appropriate criterion in such problems. The ratio of benefit to cost is sometimes used; a rate of return criterion is of this form. Unfortunately, applying ratio criteria to alternatives can lead to undesirable results unless alternatives are of about the same scale. The difference between benefits and costs can be a reasonable criterion, when the costs are considered as opportunity costs. McKean (1964) and Bickner (1971) provide a good discussion of these issues and other important considerations such as using the right factors, considering spill-over effects, and so on.

A general alternative-alternative comparison that can be very effective involves the dominance criterion (Wald, 1950). In ascertaining dominance, alternatives are compared with one another in order to see if one alternative is better than another across all dimensions. When we are dealing with a multiple-dimension problem, the alternative has to be better than another for every contingency; when we are dealing with a decision problem involving uncertainty, the alternative has to be better than the other for every possible contingency. Dominance is a well-accepted criterion; the difficulty is that it can seldom be used since an alternative is unlikely even to be considered if it is worse than another across all dimensions.

Compensatory and Non-compensatory Criteria In setting up criteria in a decision situation an important consideration is whether they should be compensatory or not. With compensatory criteria, low values in one dimension can be offset by particularly high values in other dimensions. That is, one dimension can compensate for another. With non-compensatory criteria, particularly high values in one dimension cannot offset low ones in another attribute. Situations wherein each kinds of criteria are appropriate can be found.

The linear weighting approaches, discussed earlier, all imply compensatory criteria. For example, if undergraduate grades are low, a high graduate record exam score can compensate (Dawes, 1971). Furthermore, in such cases, the compensation is constant throughout the range of the factor values. As discussed in MacCrimmon (1968b), the compensations implicit in such weighting models are often not understood by the decision maker.

An interesting, early example of a compensation method is described in a letter from Benjamin Franklin to Joseph Priestly in 1772. After describing how he writes down the reasons *pro* and the reasons *con* on some issue, Frankin continues,

> When I have thus got them all together in one view, I endeavor to estimate their respective weights; and where I find two, one on each side, that seem equal, I strike them both out. If I find a reason *pro* equal to some two reasons *con*, I strike out the three. If I judge some two reasons *con*, equal to some three reasons *pro*, I strike out the five; and thus proceeding I find at length where

the balance lies; and if, after a day or two of further consideration, nothing new that is of importance occurs on either side, I come to a determination accordingly. (Franklin, 1772).

More complex compensatory models have been developed in which some degree of interaction among the dimensions is considered. Keeney (1968b) has incorporated second-order terms into a "quasi-separable" utility and has systematically examined the mathematical and practical implications. Slovic (1969) has used analysis of variance procedures to study the interactions among elements of stock investments as considered by practicing stockbrokers. In these cases, the criteria are compensatory but the compensations are more complex. Einhorn (1970) has considered weighting models represented with hyperbolic and parabolic functions. The effect of this is to make the various dimensions less compensatory.

A primary non-compensatory method that has been considered is the lexicographic approach (Aumann, 1964; MacCrimmon, 1968). In this case, the decision maker orders the attributes in terms of their importance to him. He first focuses on his most important consideration and if one alternative has a better value than any other in terms of this consideration, it is chosen and the decision situation ends. If, however, there are ties, then the tied alternatives are examined in terms of the second most important consideration, and so forth, until only one alternative is left. The term "lexicographic" refers to the similarity in ordering words for a dictionary. Since only one dimension is considered at a time, it is clear that low values in one dimension cannot be directly compensated by high values in another, although the alternative chosen be poor in dimensions that are of secondary importance. Lexicographic procedures have been studied in consumer purchase decisions (Alexis *et al.*, 1968) and in decisions by trust investment officers (Clarkson, 1963).

A variant of this approach recognized that the decision maker may be unable to discriminate perfectly among values, so that if some values are close to the best in the dimension being considered, then those alternatives are carried over to additional dimensions for examination. Such a model has been considered by Luce (1956), Yntema and Torgerson (1961), and Tversky (1969). Russ (1971) has found that this procedure seems to describe the decision behavior of housewives choosing among electric appliances.

Modes of Choice

Maximizing: General In the maximizing mode there is usually a well-established set of alternatives and a clear objective function that specifies an ideal level to attain. The alternative that comes closest to the ideal level is the one to be chosen. Maximizing modes place considerable information processing demands on the decision maker. In the limit, he is expected to generate the complete set of alternatives, to specify all possible outcomes, and then to do the processing and comparisons necessary in applying the criteria to the alternatives. If the decision maker does optimize, he will be better off—by definition. The only reason for not optimizing, then, would be if he is not able to do so.

Another common way of stating the maximizing mode is to say that we are dealing with "economic man." Economic man is presumed to be perfectly informed, perfectly sensitive, and perfectly rational (Edwards, 1954b). In the classical theories of consumer demand and the firm in economics, the consumer maximizes his utility defined over commodity bundles and the firm maximizes its profits (Marshall, 1890).

Maximizing: Expected Utility The most general and well-developed maximizing theory of decision-making involves the maximization of expected utility. The two main components of this theory, personal probabilities and utilities, have been discussed earlier. The theory starts out by specifying the set of alternatives to choose among and identifies the set of payoff-relevant events. Personal probabilities are then assigned to the events and utilities are assigned to the outcomes. The utility of an outcome is then multipled by the probability of the event leading to the outcome, and then these products are summed over all events to get an expected utility for a given action. The expected utilities for all the alternatives are compared and the largest one is chosen (Ramsey, 1931; Savage, 1954; Fishburn, 1969).

The maximization of expected utility is a normative theory—i.e., it specifies what decision makers should do. The "should" can be argued on the ground that since the decision maker's own values and beliefs are reflected in the expected utility, he will be acting contrary to them if he does not maximize expected utility. Perhaps a more convincing case is obtained by noting that formally the theorem prescribing maximization of expected utility is derived from some more simple axioms (or postulates). If on examining these axioms the decision maker wishes to adopt all of them as norms to guide his decision behavior, he should act so as to maximize expected utility. The axioms specify transitivity (i.e., circular judgments should not be made), independence of beliefs from tastes (e.g., no wishful thinking), dominance (as discussed earlier), the irrelevance of identical outcomes (i.e., only outcomes that help to discriminate among alternatives get considered), and a few other structural axioms (Savage, 1954; Marschak, 1964). MacCrimmon (1968) has found that although business executives tend to violate one or more of these axioms in their actual choices, on reflection they would generally accept them as sound norms of behavior and would use them to guide how they should make a decision. That is, they view violations of the axioms as mistakes that they would correct.

The main difficulty with expected utility is in trying to apply it. All possible alternatives can never be completely generated, but this is not a serious practical difficulty as long as the main alternatives are considered. More serious is that the total number of possible relevant events is usually very large. The development of conditional expected utility by Luce and Krantz (1971) helps to modify this situation, but the number of probability judgments is still likely to be prohibitive to do a thorough job of handling the uncertainty in the environment. The sequential procedure using sensitivity analysis described by Howard (1968a, 1968b) is also useful in this regard.

When the outcomes are describable strictly in terms of a single dimension, then the utility function can be obtained without much difficulty. When, however, there are many dimensions to consider, there are no completely general techniques that are useful in helping the decision maker to make these assessments. Recent developments by Raiffa (1969a) and Keeney

(1968b) can help if some independence conditions hold. Keeney discusses some applications to telephone communications, blood banks, and surveying. An interesting expected utility analysis applied to hurricane modification is described by Boyd *et al.* (1971).

Satisficing Given the high information processing demands, and the time and effort entailed in the maximizing methods, the decision maker may be willing to settle for something less than the maximum. He is prepared to *satisfice* (Simon, 1957b). In a satisficing mode the decision maker sets up a feasible aspiration level, then searches for alternatives until he finds one that achieves this level. As soon as he finds a satisfactory alternative, he ends his search and chooses that alternative.

The theory is primarily descriptive, but to the extent that the decision maker cannot maximize, satisficing can be said to have some normative elements too. Correspondences can be made between maximizing and satisficing at least at a formal level by noting that satisficing could be thought of as maximization with a two-valued (i.e., satisfactory and not satisfactory) utility function, or by explicitly taking into account the costs of search and by having an aspiration level that is based on costs and expectations in a direct utility assessment manner (Charnes and Cooper, 1963). Advocates of "satisficing man," however, would claim that the key element is that he cannot in fact make these determinations. Satisficing behavior has been examined in a number of studies; for example, of trust investment officers (Clarkson, 1963) and department store buyers (Cyert and March, 1963).

Incrementing Related quite closely to satisficing is an approach that Lindblom (1959) calls "successive limited comparisons." Under this mode the decision maker will attempt to take only small steps or increments away from the existing state in the desired direction. Few objectives would be considered, and the alternatives would generally be ones that were familiar to the decision maker or that he could generate by local search. Possibly important outcomes, values, and alternatives are neglected. Agreement among the decision makers is sought instead of very high goal attainment. Obviously it is primarily a descriptive model of how decisions are made. Braybrooke and Lindblom (1963) provide a further discussion using the term "incrementalism."

Adapting Although satisficing and incrementalizing require considerably less attention than maximizing, they still require the decision maker to devote resources to explore possible courses of action in order to make choices. "Adapting" involves a different perspective in that the resources are not devoted to search and choice activities but rather to building up a capability to respond quickly when action needs to be taken. For example, in adapting mode you do not attempt to predict what price your competitor is going to set and then choose an action, but rather you build up a flexible system and monitor his price movements in order to be able to respond quickly when action needs to be taken. Ackoff (1970) gives the example of traffic flow in which elaborate calculations are not taken to predict whether it would be better to use a middle lane of a tunnel for inbound or outbound traffic but rather both inbound and outbound traffic is monitored continuously and the direction is changed based on the relative rates of flow in each direction. Ackoff emphasizes a type of adapting planning that contains elements of all four of the choice modes already discussed with heavy emphasis, however, on modifying the motivational incentives used in the system. Adapting is also discussed by Weick (1969).

Multiple-Person Choice Modes

Single- versus Multiple-Person Choice The modes discussed above apply to both single-person and multiple-person choice. In fact, the last three have been primarily applied to organizational decision-making. There is nothing explicit in their description, however, that indicated how individual preferences were to be consolidated into a group choice. Here we shall briefly consider two modes, voting and bargaining, that directly focus on the process of moving from individual preferences to group choice.

Voting The most straightforward means for arriving at multiple-person choice is to have some aggregation rule that will directly transform the set of individual choices into the group choice. A variety of possible voting procedures can be used. As mentioned earlier, Arrow (1951) has shown that no satisfactory social choice can be guaranteed if some reasonable axioms are to apply at all times. One can utilize voting methods, however, that may violate one of the rules at times. The most common voting methods involve either unanimity, plurality, or majority. More generally, Buchanan and Tullock (1962) have made an analytic study of voting processes and consider the degree of conjunctivity of the voting rule, in the sense of how many group members are required to commit the group. They discuss the basis for settling on a rule in terms of the external costs that may be imposed or the external costs that may be prevented depending on the rule chosen.

A voting method that may have some usefulness for committees is the SPAN technique (MacKinnon, 1966). Each individual is given some fixed stock of votes, say 100, which he can allocate among the alternatives or can give to other individuals so they can allocate them. Allowing the individual to split his votes among the alternatives gives him an opportunity to hedge on some alternatives for which his preferences are not strong, and allowing him to give votes to other individuals provides an opportunity to transfer votes to individuals who may have some expertise on a particular issue. Although there are some unexplored gaming aspects, it could be a useful practical technique.

Bargaining Bargaining leads to a joint agreement on the group choice in contrast to the external scheme for aggregating individual preferences with voting methods. Voting is obviously more feasible than bargaining with large groups. Bargaining may lead to a more accepted alternative but the process of getting there is likely to be quite time consuming. Bargaining implies neither a complete agreement nor a complete disagreement in preferences (Thibaut and Kelley, 1959; Kelley and Thibaut, 1969). The process hopefully moves toward mutually preferable points. Lindblom (1965) calls these processes "mutual adjustment" and provides a broad discussion with primary emphasis on governmental decision-making. An excellent discussion of the theory of bargaining is given by Schelling (1960).

Obviously, an important determinant of the choice that emerges from the bargaining process is the choices that each member will have to live with if an agreement is not reached. Bargaining results in coalition formation in which a central concern is deciding on 'each member's shares in the coalition. For more on coalitions and bargaining see Luce and Raiffa (1968) and Rapoport (1970).

Clearly bargaining can, and usually does, precede formal voting methods. An especially interesting combination of bargaining and voting occurs when there is a sequence of votes on different issues. By log-rolling, that is, trading-off votes on unimportant issues to obtain votes on important issues, the strongly felt preferences of a minority can be expressed. For more on log-rolling see Buchanan and Tullock (1962) and Coleman (1966).

Summary: Criteria and Choice

A variety of useful concepts and techniques for setting criteria and making choices are available in publications in economics, psychology, and political science. It should be clear that the criteria set, and the choices made, are very much determined by the earlier phases of the decision process. Hopefully, the relationship of choice to the whole decision process has been clarified.

An important consideration involving choice is when a decision should not be made. The concepts discussed here relate indirectly to this; its importance is suggested by Barnard (1938):

> The fine art of executive decision consists in not deciding questions that are not now pertinent, in not deciding prematurely, in not making decisions that cannot be made effective, and in not making decisions that others should make.

In some decision situations there is discretion whether it is to be handled by a single person or by many persons. A variety of considerations involving such factors as acceptance, trust, and information exchange have been discussed in preceding sections. For a good overview see Kelley and Thibaut (1969) and Maier (1970).

CONCLUDING COMMENTS

Throughout his chaper we have traced the decision process. An attempt has been made to pull together diverse theories, concepts, and techniques and to interrelate them through their role in the decision process. Examples of actual and potential uses have been given. The major areas of theoretical research on decision-making and most of the areas of empirical concern have been discussed. The emphasis employed here, however, does not reflect the emphasis these topics have actually received but is in rough proportion to the potential usefulness for managerial decisions. For readers who wish to (follow up on any particular topic, the pertinent references have been given. A more detailed presentation of the psychological results, organized in the same fashion as this paper, is given in MacCrimmon (1973b).

A major deficiency in the decision-making literature is the lack of analytical studies of actual decision situations. Such studies could serve to indicate the validity of the descriptive models and could serve as a focus for the areas in which normative theories should develop. Allison's study of the U.S. government during the Cuban missile crisis is an excellent example (Allison, 1971).

To the manager or general reader with a concern for improving his decision-making, we would suggest trying some of the methods described in this chapter and over time building up a portfolio of decision procedures that seem useful.

SUGGESTIONS FOR FUTURE READING

ABERNATHY, W. J., "Subjective Estimates and Scheduling Decisions," *Management Science*, Vol. 18, No. 2 (1971), pp. 80–88.

ACKOFF, R. L., "Management Misinformation Systems," *Management Science*, Vol. XIV, No. 4 (1967), pp. B147–B156.

ACKOFF, R. L., *A Concept of Corporate Planning* (New York: John Wiley & Sons, 1970).

ADORNO, T. W., E. FRENKEL-BRUNSWIK, D. J. LEVINSON, AND R. N. SANFORD, *The Authoritarian Personality* (New York: Harper and Bros., 1950).

ALEXIS, M., G. H. HAINES, JR., AND L. SIMON, "Consumer Information Processing: The Case of Women's Clothing," in *Marketing and the New Science of Planning*, R. L. King (Ed.) (Chicago: American Marketing Association, 1968).

ALLISON, G. J., *Essence of Decision* (Boston: Little Brown, 1971).

ANSOFF, H. I., *Corporate Strategy* (New York: McGraw-Hill Book Co., Inc., 1965).

ARROW, K. J., *Social Choice and Individual Values* (New York: John Wiley & Sons, 1951).

ARROW, K. J., *Essays in the Theory of Risk-bearing* (Chicago: Markham Publishing Co., 1971).

ATKINSON, J. W., "Motivational Determinants of Risk-Taking Behavior," *Psychological Review*, Vol. 64 (1957), pp. 359–372.

ATKINSON, J. W., AND N. T. FEATHER (Eds.), *A Theory of Achievement Motivation* (New York: John Wiley & Sons, 1966).

AUMANN, R. J., "Subjective Programming," in M. W. Shelley and G. L. Bryan (Eds.), *Human Judgment and Optimality* (New York: John Wiley & Sons, 1964).

BARNARD, C. I., *The Functions of the Executive* (Cambridge, Massachusetts: Harvard University Press, 1938).

BASSLER, J., The Consistency of Risk Attitudes in Decision Making under Uncertainty. Unpublished Ph.D. Dissertation, Carnegie-Mellon University, 1972.

BAVELAS, A., "A Mathematical Model for Group Structures," *Applied Anthropology*, Vol. 7 (1948), pp. 16–30.

BAYES, T., "Essay Towards Solving a Problem in the Doctrine of Chances," *The Philosophical Transactions*, Vol. 53 (1763), pp. 370–418.

BECKER, G. M., M. DEGROOT, AND J. MARSCHAK, "Measuring Utility By a Simple-Response Sequential Method," *Behavioral Science*, Vol. 9, No. 3 (1964), pp. 226–232.

BELL, D. (Ed.), *Toward the Year 2000* (Boston: Houghton Mifflin, 1968).

Bellman, R. E., and S. E. Dreyfus, *Applied Dynamic Programming* (Santa Monica, California: The Rand Corporation, 1962).

Bentham, J., *An Introduction to the Principles of Morals and Legislation* (London, 1823).

Bernoulli, D., "Speciman Theoriae Novae de Mensura Sortis," *Comentarii Academiae Scientiarum Imperiales Petropolitanae,* Vol. 5 (1738), pp. 175–192. (Translated by L. Sommer in *Econometrica,* Vol. 22 (1954), pp. 23–36).

Bickner, R. E., "Concepts of Economic Cost" in G. H. Fisher (Ed.), *Cost Considerations in Systems Analysis* (New York: American Elsevier Publishing Co., 1971).

Boggess, W. P., "Screen-Test Your Credit Risks," *Harvard Business Review,* Vol. 45, No. 6 (1967), pp. 113–122.

Borch, K. H., *The Economics of Uncertainty* (Princeton, N.J.: Princeton University Press, 1968).

Borch, K. H., and J. Mossin (Eds.), *Risk and Uncertainty* (London: The Macmillan Co., 1968).

Bourne, L. E., B. R. Ekstrand, and R. L. Dominowski, *The Psychology of Thinking* (1970).

Bower, J. L., *Managing the Resource Allocation Process: A Study of Corporate Planning and Investment* (Boston: Harvard University Graduate School of Business Administration, Division of Research, 1970).

Boyd, D. W., R. A. Howard, J. E. Matheson, and D. W. North, *Decision Analysis of Hurricane Modification* (Menlo Park, California: Stanford Research Institute, 1971).

Braybrooke, D., and C. E. Lindblom, *A Strategy of Decision* (New York: The Free Press, 1963).

Brim, O. C., D. S. Glass, D. E. Lavin, and N. Goodman, *Personality and Decision Processes* (Stanford, California: Stanford University Press, 1962).

Brown, R. U., "Do Managers find Decision Theory Useful?," *Harvard Business Review,* Vol. 48 (1970), pp. 78–89.

Bruner, J. S., J. J. Goodnow, and G. A. Austin, *A Study of Thinking* (New York: Science Editions, Inc., 1956).

Buchanan, J. M., and G. Tullock, *The Calculus of Consent* (Ann Arbor: University of Michigan Press, 1962).

Campbell, A. C., "On Introducing Supraminimal Data to Items whose Solution Demands the Use of Indirect Procedures," *British Journal of Psychology,* Vol. 59, No. 3 (1968), pp. 211–217.

Carter, E. E., "The Behavioral Theory of the Firm and Top-Level Corporate Decision," *Administrative Science Review,* Vol. 16, No. 4 (1971), pp. 413–429.

Chambers, J. C., S. K. Mullick, and D. D. Smith, "How to Choose the Right Forecasting Technique," *Harvard Business Review,* Vol. 49, No. 4 (1971), pp. 45–74.

Charnes, A., and W. W. Cooper, "Deterministic Equivalents for Optimizing and Satisficing Under Chance Constraints," *Operations Research,* Vol. 11, No. 1 (1963), pp. 18–39.

Churchman, C. W., R. L. Ackoff, and E. L. Arnoff, *Operations Research* (New York: John Wiley & Sons, 1957).

Clark, R. D., III, "Group Induced Shift Toward Risk: A Critical Appraisal," *Psychological Bulletin,* Vol. 76, No. 4 (1971), pp. 251–270.

Clarkson, G. P. E., *Portfolio Selection: A Simulation of Trust Investment* (Englewood Cliffs, N.J.: Prentice-Hall, Inc., 1962).

COHEN, J., *Behavior in Uncertainty* (London: George Allen and Unwin, 1968).

COLEMAN, J. S., "The Possibility of a Social Welfare Function," *The American Economic Review,* Vol. LVI (1966), pp. 1105–1122.

COLLINS, B. E., AND B. RAVEN, "Group Structure: Attraction, Coalitions, Communication, and Power," in G. Lindzey and E. Aronson (Eds.), *The Handbook of Social Psychology* (Reading, Massachusetts: Addison-Wesley, 1969).

COOMBS, C. H., AND L. C. HUANG, "Tests of a Portfolio Theory of Risk Preference," *Journal of Experimental Psychology,* Vol. 85 (1970), 23–29(a).

COURNOT, A., *Researches into the Mathematical Principles of the Theory of Wealth* translated by N. J. Bacon (New York: The Macmillan Co., 1897).

CROVITZ, H. F., *Galton's Walk* (New York: Harper & Row, 1970).

CYERT, R. M., AND M. H. DEGROOT, "Multiperiod Decisions Models with Alternating Choice as a Solution to the Duopoly Problem," *Quarterly Journal of Economics,* Vol. LXXXIV (1970), pp. 410–429.

CYERT, R. M., AND J. G. MARCH, *A Behavioral Theory of the Firm* (Englewood Cliffs, N.J.: Prentice-Hall, Inc., 1963).

CYERT, R. M., AND K. R. MACCRIMMON, "Organizations," in G. Lindzey and E. Aronson (Eds.), *The Handbook of Social Psychology* (Reading, Massachusetts: Addison-Wesley, 1968).

DALKEY, N., AND O HELMER, "An Experimental Application of the Delphi Method to the Use of Experts," *Management Science,* Vol. 9 (1963), pp. 458–467.

DAVIDSON, D., P. SUPPES, AND S. SIEGEL, *Decision Making: An Experimental Approach* (Stanford, California: Stanford University Press, 1957).

DAVIS, O. A., M. A. H. DEMPSTER, AND A. WILDAVSKY, "On the Process of Budgeting: An Empirical Study of Congressional Appropriation," *Papers on Non-Market Decision Making,* Vol. 2 (1966), pp. 63–132.

DAWES, R., "Social Selection Based on Multidimensional Criteria," *Journal of Abnormal Psychology,* Vol. 23 (1964), pp. 104–109.

DAWES, R., "Graduate Admissions: A Case Study," *The American Psychologist,*

DE FINETTI, B., "Does it Make Sense to Speak of 'Good Probability Appraisers'?", in I. J. Good (Ed.), *The Scientist Speculates—An Anthology of Partly-Baked Ideas* (London: Heinemann, 1962).

DE FINETTI, B., "Foresight: Its Logical Laws, Its Subjective Sources," in H. E. Kyburg and H. E. Smokler (Eds.), *Studies in Subjective Probability* (New York: John Wiley & Sons, 1964).

DE FINETTI, B., "Probability: Philosophy and Interpretation," *International Encyclopedia of the Social Sciences,* Vol. 12 (1968), pp. 496–505.

dEGROOT, A. D., *Thought and Choice in Chess* (The Hague: Mouton, 1965).

dEGROOT, M. H., *Optimal Statistical Decisions* (New York: McGraw-Hill Co., Inc., 1970).

DEWEY, J., *How We Think* (New York: D. C. Heath, 1933).

DOWNS, A., *Inside Bureaucracy* (Santa Monica, California: The Rand Corporation, 1967).

DRISCOLL, J. M., AND J. T. LANZETTA, "Effects of Two Sources of Uncertainty in Decision Making," *Psychological Reports,* Vol. 17, No. 2 (1965), pp. 635–648.

DROR, Y., *Public Policymaking Reexamined* (San Francisco: Chandler Publishing Co., 1968).

DRUCKER, P. F., *The Practice of Management* (New York: Harper & Row, 1954).

DRUCKER, P. F., "Managing for Business Effectiveness," *Harvard Business Review,* Vol. 41, No. 3 (1963), pp. 53–60.

DRUCKER, P. F., *The Effective Executive* (New York: Harper & Row, 1967).

DUNKER, K., "On Problem Solving," *Psychological Monographs,* Vol. 58, No. 270 (1945).

DUNNETTE, M. D., J. P. CAMPBELL, AND K. JAASTAD, "The Effect of Group Participation on Brainstorming Effectiveness for Two Industrial Samples," *Journal of Applied Psychology,* Vol. 47 (1963), pp. 30–37.

EDWARDS, W., "Probability-Preferences in Gambling," *American Journal of Psychology,* Vol. 66 (1953), pp. 349–364.

EDWARDS, W., "The Reliability of Probability Preferences," *American Journal of Psychology,* Vol. 67 (1954a), pp. 68–95.

EDWARDS, W., "The Theory of Decision Making," *Psychological Bulletin,* Vol. 51, (1954b), pp. 380–418.

EDWARDS, W., "Conservatism in Human Information Processing," in B. Kleinmuntz (Ed.), *Formal Representation of Human Judgment* (New York: John Wiley & Sons, 1968).

EDWARDS W., L. D. PHILLIPS, W. L. HAYS, AND B. C. GOODMAN, "Probabilistic Information Processing Systems: Design and Evaluation," *IEEE Transactions on Systems Science and Cybernetics,* Vol. SSc-4 (1968), pp. 248–265.

EINHORN, H. J., "The Use of Nonlinear, Noncompensatory Models in Decision Making," *Psychological Bulletin,* Vol. 73 (1970), pp. 221–230.

ELLSBERG, D., "Risk, Ambiguity and the Savage Axioms," *Quarterly Journal of Economics,* Vol. 75, No. 6 (1961), p. 643.

EMERY, J. C., *Organizational Planning and Control Systems* (New York: The Macmillan Co., 1969).

EMMET, E. R., *The Use of Reason* (London: Longmans, 1960).

FAMA, E. F., "The Behavior of Stock Market Prices," *Journal of Business,* Vol. 38 (1965), pp. 34–105.

FELDMAN, J., and H. E. KANTER, "Organizational Decision Making," in J. G. March (Ed.), *Handbook of Organizations* (Chicago: Rand McNally, 1965).

FELLNER, W., *Probability and Profit* (Homewood, Illinois: Richard D. Irwin, 1965).

FESTINGER, L., *A Theory of Cognitive Dissonance* (Evanston, Illinois: Row, Peterson, 1957).

FESTINGER, L., *Conflict, Decision, and Dissonance* (Stanford, California: Stanford University Press, 1964).

FISHBURN, P. C. *Decision and Value Theory* (New York: John Wiley & Sons, 1964).

FISHBURN, P. C., "Independence in Utility Theory with Whole Product Sets," *Operations Research,* Vol. 13 (1965), pp. 28–45.

FISHBURN, P. C., "Methods of Estimating Additive Utilities," *Management Science,* Vol. 13, No. 7 (1967), pp. 135–153.

FISHBURN, P. C., "Utility Theory," *Management Science,* Vol. 14, No. 5 (1968), pp. 335–378.

FISHBURN, P. C., *Utility Theory for Decision Making* (New York: John Wiley & Sons, 1970).

FISHER, G. H., *Cost Considerations in Systems Analysis* (New York: American Elsevier Publishing Co., 1971).

FRANKLIN, B., "How to Make a Decision" (1772), in N. Goodman (Ed.), *A Benjamin Franklin Reader* (New York: Thomas Y. Crowell, 1945).

FRIEDMAN, M., and L. J. SAVAGE, "The Utility Analysis of Choices Involving Risk," *Journal of Political Economics,* Vol. 56 (1948), pp. 279–304.

FRIEDMAN, M., AND L. J. SAVAGE, "The Expected-Utility Hypothesis and the Measurability of Utility," *Journal of Political Economics,* Vol. 60 (1952), pp. 463–472.

FULLER, J. G., *The Gentlemen Conspirators* (New York: Grove Press, Inc., 1962).

GARDNER, M., "Mathematical Games," *Scientific American,* Vol. 221 (1967).

GLANZER, M., AND R. GLASER, "Techniques for the Study of Group Structure and Behavior: II. Empirical Studies of the Effects of Structure in Small Groups," *Psychological Bulletin,* Vol. 58 (1961), pp. 1–27.

GOLDBERG, W. (Ed.), *Behavioral Approaches to Modern Management* (Gothenburg: B.A.S., 1970).

GORDON, W. J. J., *Synectics* (New York: Harper & Row, 1961).

GORE, W., *Administrative Decision Making* (New York: John Wiley & Sons, 1964).

GRAYSON, C. J., *Decisions Under Uncertainty* (Cambridge: Harvard University Press, 1960).

GREEN, B. F., "Descriptions and Explanations: A Comment on Papers by Hoffman and Edwards," in B. Kleinmuntz (Ed.), *Formal Representation of Human Judgment* (New York: John Wiley & Sons, 1968).

HAMMOND, J. S., "Better Decisions with Preference Theory," *Harvard Business Review,* Vol. 45, No. 6 (1967), pp. 123–141.

HANSBERGER, R. V., as quoted in "Bob Hansberger Shows How to Grow Without Becoming a Conglomerate," J. McDonald, *Fortune* (October, 1969), pp. 134ff.

HAVEMAN, R. H., AND J. MARGOLIS, *Public Expenditures and Policy Analysis* (Chicago: Markham Publishing Co., 1970).

HELMER, O., T. GORDON, AND B. BROWN, *Social Technology* (New York: Basic Books, 1966).

HERTZ, D. W., "Investment Policies That Pay Off," *Harvard Business Review,* Vol. 46, No. 1 (1968), pp. 96–108.

HERTZ, D. W., "Risk Analysis in Capital Investment," *Harvard Business Review,* Vol. 42 (1964), p. 95.

HINRICHS, H. H., AND G. M. TAYLOR, *Program Budgeting and Benefit-Cost Analysis* (Pacific Palisades, California: Goodyear Publishing Co., Inc., 1969).

HITCH, C. J., AND R. N. MCKEAN, *The Economics of Defense in the Nuclear Age* (Santa Monica, California: The Rand Corporation, 1960).

HOFFMAN, P. J., "Cue-Consistency and Configurality in Human Judgment," in B. Kleinmuntz (Ed.), *Formal Representation of Human Judgment* (New York: John Wiley & Sons, 1968).

HOFFMAN, P. J., P. SLOVIC, AND L. G. RORER, "An Analysis-of-Variance Model for the Assessment of Configural Cue Utilization in Clinical Judgment," *Psychological Bulletin,* Vol. 69 (1968), pp. 338–349.

HOWARD, R. A., "Information Value Theory," *IEEE Transactions in Systems Science and Cybernetics,* Vol. SSG-2, No. 1 (1966), pp. 22–34.

HOWARD, R. A., "The Foundations of Decision Analysis," *IEEE Transactions on Systems Science and Cybernetics,* Vol. SSC-4, No. 3 (1968), pp. 211–219.

HOWARD, R. A., "Decision Analysis: Applied Decision Theory," in D. B. Hertz and J. Melese (Eds.), *Proceedings of the Fourth International Conference on Operational Research* (New York: John Wiley & Sons, 1968).

HOWARD, R. A., "Proximal Decision Analysis," *Management Science,* Vol. 17, No. 9 (1971), pp. 507–541.

JANTSCH, E., *Technological Forecasting in Perspective* (Paris: OECD, 1966).

JOHNSEN, E., *Studies in Multiobjective Decision Models* (Lund: Studentlitteratur, 1968).

KAHN, H., and A. J. WEINER, *Toward the Year 2000: A Framework for Speculation* (New York: The Macmillan Co., 1967).

KATES, R. W., *Hazard and Choice Perception in Flood Plain Management* (Chicago: University of Chicago, Department of Geography, 1962).

KAUFMAN, H., *The Forest Ranger* (Baltimore: Johns Hopkins University Press, 1960).

KEENEY, R. L., "Quasi-Separable Utility Functions," *Naval Research Logistics Quarterly,* Vol. 15 (1968), pp. 551–565.

KEENEY, R. L., "Evaluating Multidimensional Situations Using a Quasi-Separable Utility Function," *IEEE Transactions on Man-Machine Systems,* Vol. MMS-9 (1968), pp. 25–28.

KEENEY, R. L., Multidimensional Utility Functions: Theory, Assessment and Application. (Unpublished Ph.D. Thesis, Massachusetts Institute of Technology, 1969).

KELLEY, H. H., AND J. W. THIBAUT, "Group Problem Solving, I," in G. Lindzey and E. Aronson (Eds.), *The Handbook of Social Psychology* (Reading, Massachusetts: Addison-Wesley, 1969).

KEPNER, C. H., AND B. B. TREGOE, *The Rational Manager* (New York: McGraw-Hill Book Co., Inc., 1965).

KLEINMUNTZ, B., "The Processing of Clinical Information By Man and Machine," in B. Kleinmuntz (Ed.), *Formal Representation of Human Judgment* (New York: John Wiley & Sons, 1968).

KNIGHT, F. H., *Risk, Uncertainty and Profit* (New York: Harper and Bros., 1920).

KOESTLER, A., *The Act of Creation* (London: Hutchinson & Co., Ltd., 1964).

KOESTLER, A., *The Ghost in the Machine* (London: Hutchinson Publishing Group, Ltd., 1967).

KOGAN, N., AND M. A. WALLACH, *Risk Taking: A Study in Cognition and Personality* (New York: Holt, Rinehart and Winston, 1964).

KOGAN, N., AND M. A. WALLACH, "Risk Taking as a Function of the Situation, the Person, and the Group," in *New Directions in Psychology, III* (New York: Holt, Rinehart and Winston, 1967).

KOLMOGOROV, A. N., *Foundations of the Theory of Probability,* translated and edited by N. Morrison (New York: Chelsea, 1950).

KORT, F., "A Non Linear Model for the Analysis of Judicial Decisions," *The American Political Science Review,* Vol. 62 (1968), pp. 546–555.

KUEHN, A. A., AND M. J. HAMBURGER, "A Heuristic Program for Locating Warehouses," *Management Science,* Vol. 9, No. 4 (1963), pp. 643–666.

KUNREUTHER, H., "Extensions of Bowman's Theory on Managerial Decision-Making," *Management Science,* Vol. 15 (1969), pp. 415–439.

KYBURG, H. E., JR., *Probability and Inductive Logic* (New York: The Macmillan Co., 1970)

LEAVITT, H. J., "Some Effects of Certain Communication Patterns on Group Performance," *Journal of Abnormal Social Psychology,* Vol. 46 (1951), pp. 38–50.

LEWIN, K., "Behavior and Development as a Function of the Total Situation," Chapter 10 in L. Carmichael (Ed.), *Manual of Child Psychology* (New York: John Wiley & Sons, 1946).

LEWIN, K., J. DEMBO, L. FESTINGER, AND P. SEARS, "Level of Aspiration," in J. M. Hunt (Ed.), *Personality and Behavior Disorders* (New York: Ronald Press, 1944).

LINDBLOM, C. E., "The Science of Muddling Through," *Public Administration Review,* Vol. 19 (1959), pp. 79–88.

LINDBLOM, C. E., *The Intelligence of Democracy: Decision Making through Mutual Adjustment* (New York: The Free Press, 1965).

LUCE, R. D., "Semiorders and a Theory of Utility Discrimination," *Econometrica,* Vol. 24 (1956), pp. 178–191.

LUCE, R. D., AND H. RAIFFA, *Games and Decisions* (New York: John Wiley & Sons, 1957).

LUCE, R. D., AND D. KRANTZ, "Conditional Expected Utility," *Econometrica,* Vol. 39, No. 2 (1971), pp. 253–272.

LUCHINS, A. G., AND E. H. LUCHINS, *Rigidity of Behavior* (Eugene, Oregon: University of Oregon Books, 1959).

MACCRIMMON, K. R., "Descriptive and Normative Implications of the Decision Theory Postulates," in K. Borch and J. Mossin (Eds.), *Risk and Uncertainty* (London: The Macmillan Co., 1968a).

MACCRIMMON, K. R., *Decision Making Among Multiple Attribute Alternatives* (Santa Monica, California: The Rand Corporation, 1968b).

MACCRIMMON, K. R., "Elements of Decision Making," in W. Goldberg (Ed.), *Behavioral Approaches to Modern Management* (Gothenburg: B.A.S., 1970).

MACCRIMMON, K. R., "Descriptive Team Theory," *Management Science,* (1972a), in press.

MACCRIMMON, K. R., "Decision Making and Problem Solving," in M. Dunnette (Ed.), *Handbook of Industrial and Organizational Psychology* (Chicago: Rand McNally, 1973a).

MACCRIMMON, K. R., "The Structure of Multiple Attribute Decisions," *Management Science,* 1973b, in press.

MACCRIMMON, K. R., AND M. TODA, "The Experimental Determination of Indifference Curves," *Review of Economic Studies,* Vol. XXXVI, No. 4 (1969), p. 433.

MACKINNON, W. J., "Elements of the SPAN Technique for Making Group Decisions," *Journal of Social Psychology,* Vol. 70 (1966), pp. 149–164.

MAGEE, J. F., "Decision Trees for Decision Making," *Harvard Business Review,* Vol. 42, No. 4 (1964), pp. 126–138.

MAGEE, J. F., "How to Use Decision Trees in Capital Investment," *Harvard Business Review,* Vol. 42, No. 5 (1964), pp. 79–93.

MAIER, N. R. F., "Reasoning in Humans, II. The Solution of a Problem and Its Appearance in Consciousness," *Journal of Comparative Psychology,* Vol. 12 (1931), pp. 181–194.

MAIER, N. R. F., *Problem Solving and Creativity* (Belmont, California: Brooks/Cole Publishing Co., 1970).

MAIER, N. R. F., *Problem Solving Discussions and Conferences* (New York: McGraw-Hill Book Co., Inc., 1963).

MARCH, J. G., AND H. A. SIMON, *Organizations* (New York: John Wiley & Sons, Inc., 1958).

MARKOWITZ, H., "The Utility of Wealth," *Journal of Political Economics,* Vol. 60 (1952), pp. 151–158.

MARKOWITZ, H. M., *Portfolio Selection* (New York: John Wiley & Sons, 1959).

MARPLES, D. L., "The Decisions of Engineering Design," in *I.R.E. Transactions on Engineering Management* (1961).

MARSCHAK, J., "Remarks on the Economics of Information," in *Contributions to Scientific Research in Management* (Los Angeles: W.D.P.C., 1959).

MARSCHAK, J., "Actual Versus Consistent Decision Behavior," *Behavioral Science,* Vol. 9, No. 2 (1964), pp. 103–110.

MARSCHAK, J., "Decision Making: Economic Aspects," *International Encyclopedia of the Social Sciences,* Vol. 4 (1968), pp. 42–55.

MARSCHAK, J., "Problems in Information Economics," in C. P. Bonni, R. K. Jaedicke, and H. M. Wagner (Eds.), *Management Controls* (New York: McGraw-Hill Book Co., Inc., 1964).

MARSCHAK, J., "Economics of Information Systems," *Journal of the American Statistical Association*, Vol. 66, No. 333 (1971), pp. 192–219.

MARSCHAK, J., AND R. RADNER, *Economic Theory of Teams* (New Haven, Connecticut: Yale University Press, 1972).

MARSCHAK, T., T. K. GLENNAN, JR., AND R. SUMMERS, *Strategy for R and D: Studies in the Microeconomics of Development* (New York: Springer-Verlag, 1967).

MASON, R. O., "A Dialectical Approach to Strategic Planning," *Management Science*, Vol. 15, No. 8 (1969), pp. 403–414.

MCCLELLAND, D. C., J. W. ATKINSON, R. A. CLARK, AND E. L. LOWELL, *The Achievement Motive* (New York: Appleton-Century-Crofts, 1953).

MCDANIEL, H., *An Introduction to Decision Logic Tables* (New York: John Wiley & Sons, 1968).

MCKEAN, R. N., "Criteria," in E. A. Quade (Ed.), *Analysis for Military Decisions* (Santa Monica, California: The Rand Corporation, 1964).

MILLER, D. W., AND M. K. STARR, *The Structure of Human Decisions* (Englewood Cliffs, N.J.: Prentice-Hall, Inc., 1967).

MILLER, G. A., "The Magical Number Seven, Plus or Minus Two: Some Limits on Our Capacity For Processing Information," *Psychological Review*, Vol. 63 (1956), pp. 81–97.

MILLER, G. A., E. GALANTER, AND K. H. PRIBRAM, *Plans and the Structure of Behavior* (New York: Holt, Rinehart and Winston, 1960).

MILLER, J. R., III, *Professional Decision Making* (New York: Frederick A. Praeger, 1970).

MINSKY, M., "Steps Toward Artificial Intelligence," *Proceedings of the I.R.E.*, Vol. 49 (1961), pp. 8–30.

MODIGLIANI, F., AND M. H. MILLER, "The Cost of Capital, Corporation Finance and the Theory of Investment," *American Economic Review*, Vol. 48 (1958), pp. 261–297.

MOSTELLER, F., AND P. NOGEE, "An Experimental Measurement of Utility," *Journal of Political Economics*, Vol. 59 (1951), pp. 371–404.

MURPHY, A. H., AND R. L. WINKLER, "Forecasters and Probability Forecasts: The Responses to a Questionnaire," *Bulletin of the American Meteorological Society*, Vol. 52, No. 3 (1971), pp. 158–165.

MURPHY, A. H., AND R. L. WINKLER, "Forecasters and Probability Forecasts: Some Current Problems," *Bulletin of the American Meteorological Society*, Vol. 52, No. 4 (1971), pp. 239–247.

NEWELL, A., "Heuristic Programming: Ill-Structured Problems," in J. Aronofsky (Ed.), *Progress in Operations Research* (New York: John Wiley & Sons, 1970).

NEWELL, A., J. C. SHAW, AND H. A. SIMON, "Report on a General Problem-Solving Program," *Proceedings of the International Conference on Information Processing* (Paris: UNESCO, 1960).

NEWELL, A., J. C. SHAW, AND H. A. SIMON, "Elements of a Theory of Human Problem Solving," *Psychological Review*, Vol. 65 (1958), pp. 151–166.

NEWELL, A., AND H. A. SIMON, "Computer Simulation of Human Thinking," *Science*, Vol. 134, No. 3495 (1961), p. 2011.

NEWELL, A., AND H. A. SIMON, *Human Problem Solving* (Englewood Cliffs, N.J.: Prentice-Hall, Inc., 1972).

NEWMAN, J. W., *Management Applications of Decision Theory* (New York: Harper & Row, 1971).

NOVICK, D. (Ed.), *Program Budgeting* (New York: Holt, Rinehart and Winston, 1965).

OGDEN, C. K., *The System of Basic English* (New York: Harcourt, Brace and World, 1934).

OSBORN, A. F., *Applied Imagination: Principles and Procedures of Creative Thinking* (New York: Charles Scribner's Sons, 1957).

PETERSON, C. R., AND L. R. BEACH, "Man as an Intuitive Statistician," *Psychological Bulletin*, Vol. 68 (1967), pp. 29–46.

POLYA, G., *How to Solve It* (Princeton, N.J.: Princeton University Press, 1945).

PRATT, J. W., "Risk Aversion in the Small and in the Large," *Econometrica*, Vol. 32, Nos. 1–2 (1964), pp. 122–136.

PRATT, J. W., H. RAIFFA, AND R. SCHLAIFER, *Introduction to Statistical Decision Theory* (New York: McGraw-Hill Book Co., Inc., 1965).

PREST, A. R., AND R. TURVEY, "Cost-Benefit Analysis: A Survey," *Economic Journal*, Vol. LXXV, No. 300 (1965), pp. 683–735.

PRESTON, M. G., AND P. BARATTA, "An Experimental Study of the Auction Value of an Uncertain Outcome," *American Journal of Psychology*, Vol. 61 (1948), pp. 183–193.

PRUITT, D. G., "Pattern and Level of Risk in Gambling Decisions," *Psychological Review*, Vol. 69 (1962), pp. 187–201.

QUADE, E. S. (Ed.), *Analysis for Military Decisions* (Santa Monica, California: The Rand Corporation, 1964).

RAIFFA, H., AND R. SCHLAIFER, *Applied Statistical Decision Theory* (Cambridge, Massachusetts: M.I.T. Press, 1961).

RAIFFA, H., *Decision Analysis* (Reading, Massachusetts: Addison-Wesley, 1968).

RAIFFA, H., *Preferences for Multi-Attributed Alternatives* (Santa Monica, California: The Rand Corporation, 1969a).

RAIFFA, H., "Assessment of Probabilities," Harvard University, mimeographed, 1969b.

RAMSEY, F. P., *The Foundations of Mathematics* (London: Routledge & Kegan Paul Ltd., 1931).

RAPOPORT, A., *N-Person Game Theory* (Ann Arbor: University of Michigan Press, 1970).

REITMAN, W., "Heuristic Decision Procedures, Open Constraints and the Structure of Ill-Defined Problems," in M. Shelley and G. Bryan (Eds.), *Human Judgments and Optimality* (New York: John Wiley & Sons, 1964).

ROBERTS, H. V., "On the Meaning of the Probability of Rain," *Proceedings of the First Conference on Statistical Meteorology* (1968), pp. 133–141.

ROKEACH, M., *The Open and Closed Mind* (New York: Basic Books, 1960).

ROTHENBERG, J., *The Measurement of Social Welfare* (Englewood Cliffs, N.J.: Prentice-Hall, Inc., 1961).

RUSS, F. A., *Consumer Evaluation of Alternative Product Models*, Unpublished Ph.D. Dissertation, Carnegie-Mellon University, 1971.

SAVAGE, L. J., *The Foundations of Statistics* (New York: John Wiley & Sons, 1954).

SCHACKLE, G. L. S., *Expectation in Economics*, 2d ed. (Cambridge: Cambridge University Press, 1952).

SCHACKLE, G. L. S., *Decision, Order, and Time* (Cambridge: Cambridge University Press, 1969).

SCHELLING, J. C., *The Strategy of Conflict* (Cambridge, Massachusetts: Harvard University Press, 1960).

SCHLAIFER, R., *Probability and Statistics for Business Decisions* (New York: McGraw-Hill Book Co., Inc., 1959).

SCHLAIFER, R., *Analysis of Decisions Under Uncertainty* (New York: McGraw-Hill Book Co., Inc., 1969).

SCHRODER, H. M., M. J. DRIVER, AND S. STREUFERT, *Human Information Processing* (New York: Holt, Rinehart and Winston, 1967).

SEN, A., *Collective Choice and Social Welfare* (San Francisco: Holden-Day, 1970).

SHARPE, W. F., "Mutual Fund Performance," *Journal of Business*, Vol. 39, No. 1 (1966), pp. 119–138.

SHAW, M. E., "Communications Networks," in R. Bekowitz (Ed.), *Advances in Experimental Social Psychology*, Vol. 1 (New York: Academic Press, 1964).

SHEEHAN, N., H. SMITH, E. W. KENWORTHY, AND F. BUTTERFIELD, *The Pentagon Papers* (New York: Quadrangle Books, 1971).

SHURE, G. H., AND R. J. MEEKER, "A Personality/Attitude Schedule for Use in Experimental Bargaining Studies," *Journal of Psychology*, Vol. 65 (1967), pp. 233–252.

SIEGEL, S., "Level of Aspiration and Decision Making," *Psychological Review*, Vol. 64 (1957), pp. 253–262.

SIMON, H. A., "A Behavioral Model of Rational Choice," *Quarterly Journal of Economics*, Vol. 69, No. 2 (1955), p. 99.

SIMON, H. A., *Models of Man* (New York: John Wiley & Sons, 1957b).

SIMON, H. A., *Administrative Behavior*, 2d ed. (New York: The Macmillan Co., 1957a).

SIMON, H. A., *The New Science of Management Decision* (New York: New York University Press, 1960).

SIMON, H. A., AND A. ANDO, "Aggregation of Variables in Dynamic Systems," *Econometrica*, Vol. 29 (1961), pp. 111–138.

SIMON, H. A., *The Shape of Automation for Men and Management* (New York: Harper & Row, 1965).

SIMON, H. A., "The Logic of Heuristic Decision Making," in N. Rescher (Ed.), *The Logic of Decision and Action* (Pittsburgh: University of Pittsburgh Press, 1966).

SIMON, H. A., *The Sciences of the Artificial* (Cambridge, Massachusetts: The M.I.T. Press, 1969).

SLOVIC, P., "Convergent Validation of Risk Taking Measures," *Journal of Abnormal and Social Psychology*, Vol. 65 (1962), pp. 68–70.

SLOVIC, P., "Assessment of Risk Taking Behavior," *Psychological Bulletin*, Vol. 61 (1964), pp. 220–233.

SLOVIC, P., "Analyzing the Expert Judge: A Descriptive Study of a Stockbroker's Decision Processes," *Journal of Applied Psychology*, Vol. 53 (1969), pp. 255–263.

SLOVIC, P., AND S. LICHTENSTEIN, "Relative Importance of Probabilities and Payoffs in Risk Taking," *Journal of Experimental Psychology*, Vol. 78, No. 3 (1968), pp. 1–18.

SLOVIC, P., AND S. LICHTENSTEIN, "Comparison of Bayesian and Regression Approaches to the Study of Information Processing in Judgment," *Organizational Behavior and Human Performance*, Vol. 6, No. 6 (1971), pp. 649–749.

SORENSON, T. C., *Kennedy* (New York: Harper & Row, 1965).

STAËL VON HOLSTEIN, C.-A. S., *Assessment and Evaluation of Subjective Probability Distributions* (Stockholm: E.F.I., 1970).

STEDRY, A. C., *Budget Control and Cost Behavior* (Englewood Cliffs, N.J.: Prentice-Hall, Inc., 1960).

SWALM, R. O., "Utility Theory—Insights into Risk Taking," *Harvard Business Review*, Vol. 44, No. 6 (1966), p. 123.

TAYLOR, D. W., "Decision Making and Problem Solving," in J. G. March (Ed.), *Handbook of Organizations* (Chicago: Rand McNally, 1965).

TAYLOR, D. W., P. C. BERRY, AND C. H. BLOCK, "Does Group Participation When Using Brainstorming Facilitate or Inhibit Creative Thinking?," *Administrative Science Quarterly*, Vol. 3 (1958), pp. 23–47.

TERRY, H., "Comparative Evaluation of Performance Using Multiple Criteria," *Management Science*, Vol. 9 (1963), pp. 431–442.

THEIL, H., *Economics and Information Theory* (Chicago: Rand McNally, 1967).

THIBAUT, J. W., AND H. H. KELLEY, *The Social Psychology of Groups* (New York: John Wiley & Sons, 1959).

TOBIN, J., "Liquidity Preference as Behavior Toward Risk," *Review of Economic Studies*, Vol. 25 (1958), pp. 65–86.

TODA, M., "Measurement of Subjective Probability Distribution," Report #3, Division of Mathematical Psychology, Institute for Research, State College, Pennsylvania, 1963.

TVERSKY, A., "Additivity, Utility and Subjective Probability," *Journal of Mathematical Psychology*, Vol. 4 (1967), pp. 175–202.

TVERSKY, A., "Intransitivity of Preferences," *Psychological Review*, Vol. 76 (1969), pp. 31–48.

TVERSKY, A., *Elimination of Aspects: A Probabilistic Theory of Choice* (Jerusalem: The Hebrew University, 1971).

VON NEUMANN, J., and O. MORGENSTERN, *Theory of Games and Economic Behavior* (Princeton, N.J.: Princeton University Press, 1944).

VROOM, V. H., "Leadership," in M. Dunnette (Ed.), *Handbook of Industrial and Organizational Psychology* (Chicago: Rand McNally, 1973).

WALD, A., *Statistical Decision Functions* (New York: John Wiley & Sons, 1950).

WALLAS, G., *The Art of Thought* (New York: Harcourt, Brace, Inc., 1926).

WARTAK, J., "Logic-Structure Tables: Computer Orientated Method of Solving Problems," *Behavioral Science*, Vol. 15, No. 6 (1970), p. 532.

WEICK, K., *The Social Psychology of Organizing* (Reading, Massachusetts: Addison-Wesley, 1969).

WEINGARTNER, M., "Some New Views on the Payback Period and Capital Budgeting," *Management Science*, Vol. 15 (1969), pp. B-594–607.

WHITE, G. F., *Choice of Adjustment to Floods* (Chicago: University of Chicago, Department of Geography, 1964).

WILLS, G., *et al., Technological Forecasting* (Middlesex, England: Penguin Books, 1972).

WINKLER, R. L., "The Assessment of Prior Distributions in Bayesian Analysis," *Journal of the American Statistical Association*, Vol. 62 (1967a), pp. 776–800.

WINKLER, R. L., "The Quantification of Judgment: Some Methodological Suggestions," *Journal of the American Statistical Association*, Vol. 62 (1967b), pp. 1105–1120.

WINKLER, R. L., "Probabilistic Prediction: Some Experimental Results," *Journal of the American Statistical Association*, Vol. 66, No. 336 (1971), pp. 675–685.

WOODS, D. H. "Improving Estimates that Involve Uncertainty," *Harvard Business Review,* Vol. 44, No. 4 (1966), pp. 91–98.

YNTEMA, D. B., and W. S. TORGERSON, "Man-Computer Cooperation in Decisions Requiring Common Sense," *I.R.E. Transactions of the Professional Group on Human Factors in Electronics,* H.F.E., Vol. 2 (1961), pp. 20–26.

ZWICKY, F., *Discovery, Invention, Research through the Morphological Approach* (New York: The Macmillan Co., 1969).

ZWICKY, F. and A. WILSON, *New Methods of Thought and Procedure* (New York: Springer-Verlag, 1965).

Managerial Decision-Making: A Review

Max D. Richards

Professor and Assistant Dean
College of Business Administration
Pennsylvania State University

Since managerial decision making can be influenced by (1) the decision maker's cognitive skills, personality, attitudes, and interpersonal relations; (2) the organization's premises, structure, existing decision rules, and information systems; and (3) the patterns and nature of interactions of the decision maker with others; as well as (4) the existing state of the art of models and decision techniques, it may well be impossible to deal with decision-making in a comprehensive definitive manner in a chapter of a book such as this. An expert in any phase of decision-making may criticize any such paper as overlooking some important concepts and studies.

As the chapter rightly points out, most management science models assume that a problem and an exhaustive list of alternatives for its solution are known. Although this paper improves on this lack by discussing alternative generation and problem definition, it may be useful to backtrack one further step to consider the decision problem that focuses on selecting the *desired state* as a precondition for other decision-making—that is, goal setting and strategic planning.

The necessity for establishing objectives does not automatically become apparent, as do most other decisions of a recurring nature. Organizations may drift along with implicit and inconsistently perceived objectives unless explicit managerial attention is devoted to the goal decision process. Furthermore, because of the environmental uncertainties in factors that impinge on establishing goals, it may appear rational not to establish fixed goals but to muddle through in the Lindblom (1959) sense. Yet, even a "muddling through" response can be an explicit judgment about an organization's goal setting.

Establishing the level of attainment for an objective can be considered a successive process of relating aspiration levels to the possibilities of attainment that the enterprise managers perceive in the environment (Ansoff,

1965). Low aspiration levels tend to be adjusted upward as achievement or possible achievements exceed aspired levels, and vice versa. While the first goal setting attempts of an organization may vary widely from the "possibility level," later approximations tend to be more realistic, usually somewhat slightly above actual achievement levels (Stedry, 1960).

As enterprises engage in formal goal setting, the viability of a single goal may be questioned. Although a single overall goal such as rate of return on investment may be conceptually attractive to a business firm, it is subject to short-term manipulations that have deleterious effects on the enterprise in the long run. Near-term rates of return can be maximized and long-term rates can be suboptimized by failing to maintain equipment or by the managerial abilities of the firm's administrators. As the chapter indicates, a common method for dealing with long-term suboptimization of a single objective is to establish multiple goals, hopefully to generate long-term viability of the organization. This attempt is only partially successful since multiple objectives often are conflicting (e.g. profitability and resource maintenance). Furthermore, it may be extremely difficult to relate a particular level of one of many goals to long-run viability.

Given the establishment of multiple goals, a common suggestion for maximization as indicated in the paper is to weight the relative importance of each goal and to maximize the resultant index. It is doubtful, however, that any single weighting is functionally related to long-run viability at different levels of goal attainment. To illustrate, consider employee morale as one of several goals. If poor morale exists, its improvement can increase productivity; but with extremely high morale levels, productivity will decrease. Simon (1964) has proposed that rather than to consider morale or similar factors as multiple goals, it is more appropriate to consider them as multiple constraints. Maximization in a goal-constraint context would prevent over-attainment of a subgoal although it would not obviate the necessity of establishing prescriptive goal-constraint levels. Furthermore, the level of a constraint might have to be altered as the level of goal achievement changes. Within normal ranges of achievement, however, the goal-constraint context would allow one to deal more rationally with conflicting goals than would a weighted index approach.

In the process of rationally establishing multiple goals, major components contributing to viability or some other long-run goal are identified as subgoals (or constraints) and levels of achievement are specified for them. Descriptive theory and empirical evidence indicate, however, that the rational prescriptive ideal may be illusionary. Only a biased subset tends to appear in an organization's goal statements (Dent, 1959). The nature of the goals that are established are influenced by the relative power and position of the decision makers (Cyert and March, 1963), as well as by managerial value structures (England, 1967). Because these factors influence each decision maker in an organization differently, one will perceive a gap or decision problem between the *environmental possibilities* open to the enterprise and the existing *desired state,* whereas another will not. Furthermore, because of the uncertainty and lack of information associated with future environmental states, conflict resolution from these differing perceptions of whether or not a goal problem exists can be very difficult to achieve.

The prescriptive multiple-goal framework suggested by Drucker (1954) establishes, perhaps, an ideal imperfectly realized in the real world. Because of the unique complexities and uncertainties facing each organization, the goal decision processes and their resultants are, at present, not very predictable. The work of Soelberg (1967) suggests, however, that the possibility of identifying these choice processes and predicting complex decisions does exist. His research on complex, uncertain, unique problems suggests that patterns and order exist for such a decision process. Although not dealing with goal setting or strategy decisions, the prescriptive heuristics for organizational decisions at top levels (Ansoff, 1968, Steiner, 1969 and Warren, 1966) suggest a form similar to Soelberg's problems.

A second area of decision-making that may need consideration involves those of highest frequency in most organizations—the highly structured, repetitive, routine, programmed decisions. Inventory, queuing, and mathematical programming models were early developments in management science and remain today as an important focus. Recent research has shifted to the theoretical and practical limitations of these early models. The linear, certainty, and noninteger assumptions of early mathematical programming models, as an example, have been subject to research in nonlinear, stochastic, and integer programming, respectively.

From a practical standpoint, the costs of calculating some optimizing models often exceed the value of the information received. Thus, substantial research has been undertaken to reduce information costs at the expense, frequently, of achieving optimization. In inventory systems, for example, "over optimizing" approaches are used for high-value items and "under optimizing" techniques are employed for low-value ones. Integer programming models are evaluated on the basis of how quickly they run on a computer as well as whether they can always achieve a solution and how close the solutions are to optimum. These examples show how information costs are implicitly being considered in later research developments in the routine, programmed types of decision models.

The theoretical solutions for some repetitive problems exist, but the computational capacities of current computers are smaller than the problems encountered. Job-shop scheduling is an example of the practical problem being so large that optimal approaches are not regularly attempted. Research for these kinds of problems tends to focus on the development of heuristics and rules appropriate for a decision.

These developments in broadening the ranges of assumptions in decision models and in developing heuristical algorithms to reduce computational costs or provide practical approaches to computation focus on practical application of the theoretical models to real-world problems. Less research attention may be given to new conceptual developments, perhaps, than to modifications of existing approaches. Yet, theoretical and practical problems suggest the need for advancements. Although a great deal is known about optimizing an inventory or a scheduling subsystem, for example, less is known about simultaneous optimization of the two with the supply and distribution subsystems. Their interfaces and interrelatedness are complex problems seeking solutions. As the heuristic and decision rule research becomes extensive on existing models, perhaps we can expect more attention to new theoretical model development.

Finally, it may be useful to give some attention to the variations in management systems suggested by the emerging "conditional theory" of management (Lawrence and Lorsch, 1969). The technological, market, and social environments, together with their changes, impose differing degrees of complexity, uncertainty, and stability on an organization. An enterprise that is affected by a relatively few, stable, and certain variables can enjoy a relatively simple management system. Organizational differentiation tends to be minimized in such a case because the need for research, analysis, and information processing is less than for a firm in a more uncertain, complex, and unstable environment. Similarly, the less complex environment suggests more use of certain, routine decision approaches than might be employed in a research department that must deal with considerable uncertainty and complexity.

The environment within which a firm operates is partly controllable in that the firm can select the products and the markets in which it is going to operate. Furthermore, it may choose from locations with different social or even political environments, thus preselecting to some extent the nature of these external influences. Given these selections, however, the enterprise still must contend with some structure of certainty, complexity and stability. In terms of decision-making, consistency among components of the management system appears important. Decisions concerning organization structure, personnel, information systems, leadership style, and decision approaches are similarly related to the nature of environmental influences. If a highly educated innovative professional is placed in a tightly supervised highly structured management system, for example, he probably will not be very successful because he doesn't fit in with other components in the management system.

The relevance of conditional theory to managerial decision-making lies in its implication for matching decision approaches to the nature of the organization in which it is used. Both descriptive and normative conditional theory suggest tailor-making the decision system in light of the nature of the management system. Thus there is no such thing as "more important" components of decision theory. Each component has an important function to play although its importance varies from system to system as the complexity, uncertainty, and stability of their decision variables vary.

The relative complexity-uncertainty-stability framework provides a perspective within which to view the scope of problems facing different kinds of organizations as well as the types of managerial decision approaches appropriate for dealing with those problems. It is within this framework that additional comments were made in this review concerning complex decisions involving goal setting and about routine highly structured decisions. The paper by Professor MacCrimmon tends to focus intensively on decision problems and approaches between these two extremes of uniqueness and repetitiveness. Since the unique decisions are most important and frequent in typical organizations, their consideration in this review reflects this author's bias as well as Professor MacCrimmon's. Because of space limitations, however, it is not possible to examine these topics in depth here.

SUGGESTIONS FOR FUTURE READING

ANSOFF, IGOR, *Corporate Strategy* (New York: McGraw-Hill Book Co., Inc., 1965).

CYERT, R. M., and J. G. MARCH, *A Behavioral Theory of the Firm* (Englewood Cliffs, N.J.: Prentice-Hall, Inc., 1963).

DENT, J. K., "Organizational Correlates of the Goals of Business Management," *Personnel Psychology*, Vol. XII (1959), pp. 365–393.

DRUCKER, PETER F., *The Practice of Management* (New York: Harper & Row, 1954).

ENGLAND, G. W., "Organizational Goals and Expected Behavior of American Managers," *Academy of Management Journal*, Vol. 10 (1967), pp. 107–118.

LAWRENCE, PAUL R., AND JAY N. LORSCH, *Organization and Environment* (Homewood, Illinois: Richard D. Irwin, 1969).

LINDBLOM, CHARLES E., "The Science of 'Muddling Through,'" *Public Administration Review*, Vol. 19 (1959), pp. 78–88.

SIMON, HERBERT A., "On the Concept of Organizational Goal," *Administrative Science Quarterly*, Vol. 9 (1964), pp. 1–22.

SOELBERG, PEER O., "Unprogrammed Decision Making," *Industrial Management Review*, Vol. 8 (1967).

STEDRY, A. C., *Budget Control and Cost Behavior* (Englewood Cliffs, N.J.: Prentice-Hall, Inc., 1960).

STEINER, GEORGE A., *Top Management Planning* (Toronto: Collier-Macmillan Canada, Ltd., 1969).

WARREN, KIRBY E., *Long Range Planning: The Executive Viewpoint* (Englewood Cliffs, N.J.: Prentice-Hall, Inc., 1966).

Assessing the State of Decision Making

Gerald L. Rose

Assistant Professor
College of Business Administration
University of Iowa

INTRODUCTION

Decision makers will find Professor MacCrimmon's chapter a reasonably comprehensive introduction to descriptive concepts in decision-making.[1] It is also useful in mapping the literature for those interested in a particular concept. But inevitably, given space constraints, it fails to demonstrate the pragmatic value of the concepts that are discussed. That failure cannot be remedied in a short critique. Therefore, this critique will supplement Professor MacCrimmon's work by developing criteria that can be applied to decision-making concepts in order to assess their pragmatic value. This approach, like MacCrimmon's, presumes the reader has, or will seek, a full understanding of each concept from the references provided by the authors rather than relying on the chapter and critiques for adequate descriptions of the concepts.

The state of decision-making can be assessed in three ways: (1) One can examine the pragmatic value of decision theory in real decision situations; (2) one can compare alternative decision-making techniques with evidence from the behavioral sciences on the relative value of the techniques; or (3) one can survey the opinions of experienced decision makers on the comparative merits of alternative techniques. Although MacCrimmon's approach is a mixture of the last two criteria, this critique will focus on the first two. The third, although of value in reflecting the extent of practitioner consensus, and of interest in comparison to the results of the first two criteria, is unlikely to provide new information and is incapable of reflecting a satisfactory criterion of decision quality.

TOWARD A TYPOLOGY OF DECISION-MAKING SITUATIONS

In order to judge the practical value of decision-making concepts, one should consider the dimensions that

[1]The author benefited from the comments of Raymond Dacey, Robert Miller, Bertram Schoner, and John Kennelly of The University of Iowa, on earlier versions of this critique.

might be employed to classify decision situations. Then, by considering the extent to which normative models[2] from decision theory apply to each dimension, one ought to be better able to judge the present state of decision-making.[3] Accordingly, the next section discusses some important dimensions of decision situations: (1) number of objectives, (2) number of decision-making units, (3) preference relationships among decision-making units, (4) degree of uncertainty, and (5) type of decision unit. These dimensions are presented in order of the importance that this author attaches to them and do not reflect the emphasis implied in MacCrimmon's chapter. For simplicity, the extremely important interrelationships among dimensions are not presented.

The *number of objectives,* the criterion problem, is perhaps the single most important dimension to consider in assessing the pragmatic value of normative models. These models tend to assume a single well-defined objective, the most common being utility or profit, which integrates all decision criteria using a single unit of measurement. But in most decision situations a well-defined conceptual, much less measurable, criterion seldom exists in the mind of the decision maker. For example, a marketing executive seeking simultaneously to maximize sales growth, market penetration, and profits cannot specify the logical relationships among these objectives in some form of statement of a means and ends hierarchy, nor can he find a common unit of measurement that would permit him to use a constrained maximization model to reach his decision. If he does use a normative model in such situations, he is nearly certain to make a suboptimal decision (McKean, 1953). Charnes and his associates have proposed a technique that yields "optimal" decisions if the multiple goals can be ranked in terms of their importance to the organization. But the ranking process involves judgments, and their model does not prescribe the optimal method for assigning ranks.

The second dimension, *the number of decision-making units whose decisions interact* to determine an outcome, is omitted in the chapter. But it has been an important dimension in approaches to economic decision-making.[4] Thus, the possible values affecting this dimension range from two to an extremely large finite number. Examples of the former case include bilateral monopoly (one seller with only one customer), duopoly, dyadic interpersonal relationships, and the like. An example with large finite numbers is the economist's perfect market.

Normative models are most completely developed for decision situations involving many decision makers, so that the decision unit takes prices as given and maximizes profits (or utility) by selecting the appropriate level of output. Incomplete normative models exist for cases involving two decision units. In some cases of bilateral monopoly the decision makers should select the price and quantity of output by the usual marginal analysis, treating their separate interests as a single unit. Then they must negotiate the distribution of payoffs between them, a process for which normative models are inadequate. In another two-decision unit case, duopoly, economists have not made substantial progress since the incomplete Cournot "solutions" (Baumol, 1972, 256–357). For the range of situations between three and a very large number of interacting decision makers, normative models are interesting and generate insight but are unable to yield unambiguous optimal decisions. For example, as pointed out in the following paragraphs, a variety of quasi-normative "solutions"

[2]Normative models deduce optimal solutions from a set of assumptions and the requisite information.

[3]This dimensional analysis can also be applied to behavioral science evidence in order to assess the practical value of behavioral research for decision-making. Because of space constraints, that exercise is left to the reader.

[4]Since decisions in which the actions of only one decision unit affect outcomes are extremely rare, they will not be discussed.

have been advanced for three-"person" zero sum games (Luce and Raffia, 1957). Thus, for most variations on the number of interacting decision makers, no satisfactory normative models are available to provide unambiguous optimal decisions.

The *degree of agreement of preferences* among any pair of decision-making units whose decisions interact to determine outcomes is the third important dimension that the chapter omits. When two or more decision units completely agree about the relative ranking of two alternative outcomes for every possible pair of outcomes, they constitute a team and strive for the same objectives. For team members, coordinating member decisions becomes the focus of attention (Marschak, 1955). When any two interacting decision units disagree about the relative ranking of two alternative outcomes for every possible pair of outcomes, they are in a zero, or fixed, sum of payoffs relationship; that is, they are in maximum possible conflict.

Normative analyses provide optimal decision rules in these two extreme cases. In the coordinative relationship, the optimal decision is determined by the information structure available to each decision unit, the costs of communication, and the values of possible outcomes (Marschak, 1955). The practical feasibility of implementing this solution has not been widely tested, but McGuire's study (1961) implies that it deserves more attention.

In the maximum conflict case, each decision-making unit should maximize its minimum payoff by selecting that pure strategy (i.e., decision alternative) that provides the highest payoff under the most adverse possible conditions, conditions that are certain to occur if the other decision-making unit(s) also behave(s) rationally. If the set of strategies selected by the decision-making units does not yield an equilibrium solution—that is, if at least one decision unit could improve its payoff by changing its decision once it knows its payoff—then, by introducing appropriate probability elements, the normatively optimal decision yields the maximin expected payoff for all parties (Rapoport, 1970, pp. 62 ff.).

If the relationship among preference orderings of the interacting decision units is between the extremes—i.e., neither coordinative nor maximally conflicting—normative analyses fail to provide unambiguous optimal decisions. Unfortunately, most actual decisions lie between the extremes. But as a decision situation approaches one of the extremes, an attempt to implement a normative solution may constitute a near optimal decision-making procedure.

The importance of the *degree of uncertainty* as a dimension of decision-making has been frequently stressed (e.g., Shubik, 1954). This dimension is defined as the extent to which a decision unit possesses all the economic information necessary to use a given decision model. Thus, the degree of uncertainty is capable of ranging from complete information to complete lack of information.

Most normative models pertain only to those situations (e.g., certainty, risk, and economic indeterminacy)[5] that Shubik identifies as complete information on economic variables. For example, when complete information on alternative strategies, states of nature, outcomes, payoffs for each outcome, and probability values for each state of nature is at hand, a decision maker should choose the strategy that maximizes the expected value of his objective function (e.g., profit, if it can be assumed that profit is an adequate measure of the worth of outcomes). Even in complete information situations, normative models fail to provide optimal solutions in the case of economic indeterminacy. Normative models have yet to be developed for situations in which economic information is incomplete. But in most decision situations information

[5]Economic indeterminacy exists when the decision situation provides all necessary economic information but the decision model requires both economic and non-economic information.

is incomplete, even after considerable effort has been devoted to formulating the issues and generating alternatives. In cases of incomplete information, even the quasi-normative injunction that information acquisition should be guided by marginal cost and value is of little practical use, because part of the decision maker's ignorance usually involves uncertainty about the appropriate decision criterion (the first dimension): hence, he is unable to evaluate information costs and values.

The type of decision-making unit is a significant situational variable that deserves more than passing mention. When one compares individuals, groups, organizations, and societies on such basic variables as information-processing characteristics and task performance, even casual evidence suggests the danger of ignoring differences among types of decision-making units. Clearly, the amount of storage capacity, number and kind of transformations, redundancy, number of possible channels and structures of channels, and a variety of other information-processing qualities increase as one moves upward in the type of decision unit from individual to societal. Normative models have not completely ignored these types of distinctions. For example, Marschak's (1971) analysis of the costs and value of additional information, information theory's concern with optimal coding (Shannon and Weaver, 1949), and Arrow's social choice axioms (1953) each address parts of the total comparison.

The social choice problem points out how misleading it may be to treat all types of decision units alike. Whenever the decision unit consists of more than one person, some method for combining individual preferences into a single decision unit preference function such as voting, markets, or dictatorship must be generated in order to use normative models. However, as Arrow, Luce and Raiffa, and others have pointed out, a universally accepted optimal combination rule that will maximize each individual's utility as the decision unit's utility is maximized is yet to be discovered for decision situations in which members of a decision unit do not have identical preferences. Since nearly all decisions made by groups, organizations, and societies must thus be made with objective functions that imperfectly reflect the preferences of at least some of the participants involved in making the decision, normative models that yield optimal decisions for any one social unit usually yield suboptimal decisions for some constituents of that unit. The usual practice of assuming an objective function for a firm simply ignores the costs of suboptimal outcomes experienced by individuals and subunits within the firm. Thus, normative models generally fail to generate fully optimal decisions if the decision unit is anything but an individual. If both the ranking and strength of preference for each alternative can be obtained from each decision participant, it may be possible to partially overcome this limitation of normative models (e.g., Minas and Ackoff, 1964).

In summarizing this section, one is forced to conclude that present normative models are not immediately applicable to most decision situations even if a decision maker possesses the ability and will to use them. This conclusion holds even if only a few of the most important dimensions have been examined and even if decision situations jointly defined by two or more dimensions were ignored (see Stigler, 1964 for an example of multi-dimensional normative analysis). Furthermore, as MacCrimmon mentions, even where existing normative models are immediately applicable to decision situations, they may not be feasible because of human or technological constraints. For example, in a game of chess one cannot apply the maximin rule because the number of required calculations exceeds computer capabilities. Consequently, decision makers cannot achieve perfect rationality.

However, the benefits of normative models should not be underestimated. By providing a framework for structuring decisions they often can increase one's insight into the situation (Mason, 1969) and reduce the number of judgments required of a decision maker. For example, sensitivity analyses on alternative linear programming solutions are useful in judging which alternative is most probably optimal. Such judgments may be further improved by considering the comparative empirical method of assessing the state of decision-making. Thus both MacCrimmon's review, by excluding normative issues, and this review, by stressing the limits of normative models, render a disservice if they induce unconcern rather than curiosity about the value of normative models in decision-making.

COMPARATIVE EMPIRICAL ASSESSMENTS OF DECISION-MAKING

Having exploited the full analytical potential of the appropriate normative model, a decision maker can often improve his decisions further by considering evidence from experiments in the behavioral sciences. The advantage of relying on such evidence rather than on historical precedent, managerial lore, and the like, is that the comparative empirical method is primarily concerned with discovering which situational variables "cause" variations in decision quality. Assuming that the research design is adequate (Campbell and Stanley, 1963), the primary barrier to applying comparative empirical results to actual decisions is inadequate knowledge of the generality of experimental findings in complex decision situations.[6]

Even without evidence on the generality of comparative empirical findings, decision makers can use empirical findings to identify factors that they have previously ignored but which may have a significant impact on both decision quality and the implementation of decisions. Unfortunately, many of the methods and variables identified by MacCrimmon, such as the Delphi technique, (Uhl, 1971), advocacy methods of information display (Mason, 1969), and many others, have not received adequate empirical attention. It is beyond the scope of this review to assess the empirical efforts devoted to the variables MacCrimmon has presented. Instead, the remainder of this critique will discuss one example, individual vs. group decision units, and one potential application, the Garbage Can simulator, of the comparative empirical approach.

Contrary to MacCrimmon's implicit assertion, *experiments comparing individual and group decision-making* behavior have reinforced the conclusion, presented above, that different types of decision units cannot be viewed as essentially identical. Experimental results show that, on the average, groups make better decisions than individuals although groups must devote substantial portions of their resources to group maintenance activities. (Collins and Guetzkow, Davis, 1964). But this generalization obscures important considerations. First, group performance is rarely as good as the performance of the best individuals. Second, groups consume more resources than individuals so that their relative efficiency may be less than that of individuals. (However, Hoyt and his associates, 1972 found that groups make better economic decisions than individuals even when the man-hours of time consumed are explicitly considered.) Third, the relative superiority of groups vs. individuals varies according to the nature of the decision task and interpersonal relationships within the group.

Findings on the effects of task content and interpersonal relationships indicate that groups make better decisions than individuals when (1) the decision can be partitioned to achieve a division of labor with different members simultaneously performing different elements of the process; (2) overlap or redundancy among members' tasks permits error checking of individual performance; (3) there are minimal demands for the

[6]Overcoming this barrier is the joint responsibility of managers and behavioral scientists.

generation of new ideas and alternatives; (4) a wide variety of alternative decisions is possible; (5) estimation is a necessary part of the decision, and individual estimates contain random errors; (6) the presence of other individuals stimulates greater effort from each individual without causing distraction; (7) the group is not too large; and (8) group members possess different skills and/or knowledge and accept the contributions of each member according to their relevance to the decision task (Collins and Guetzkow, Davis, 1964). In short, the comparative empirical evidence on the type of decision unit dimension casts serious doubts on the simplistic conventional wisdom that individuals make better decisions than groups.

These conclusions are based on many experiments since the 1920's. In recent years, often stimulated by the risky shift literature,[7] experimental decision tasks have changed from an early focus on simple estimation and insight problems (e.g., missionaries and cannibals) to economically oriented decision situations (e.g., Hoyt *et al.*, 1972). Present research designs investigate the joint effects of several variables at one time on the question of individual vs. group decision quality (e.g., Rose, 1972). Finally, concern has shifted toward explaining why groups differ from individuals. Thus, as the individual vs. group literature has developed, it has provided both clearer insight into (1) the critical variables in decision situations that "cause" groups to be more (or less) likely to outperform individuals; (2) the reasons why this occurs; and (3) the problem of generalizing from controlled studies to real decision situations. The same evolution of systematically generated evidence is occurring in many areas discussed by MacCrimmon (for several examples see Slovic and Lichtenstein, 1971). Consequently, our ability to apply a comparative empirical assessment of decision-making is increasing, probably at a faster rate than our normative capability.

Comparative empirical techniques need not be limited to traditional issues such as individual vs. group decision-making using laboratory experiments. An example of a potentially fruitful comparative empirical approach is *experimentation with computer simulation models* of organizational decision-making. Any mathematical, statistical, or computer simulation model of behavior should be validated[8] to see whether or not it is capable of accurately predicting the values of variables of interest to a decision maker. Once validated, the model can be used "experimentally" by comparing the results of the validated model with modified versions of the validated model. Modified models that yield results superior to the validated model on variables of interest serve as potential models for improving organizational decision-making, as criteria for assessing decision-making, and as research hypotheses. The virtues of "experimenting" with validated vs. modified simulation models include the low cost of research (once the model is validated), the ability to observe the results of the interactions of large numbers of variables in one "experiment," and the feasibility of conducting organizational experiments without disrupting organizations.

Simulation models are particularly apt for organizational experiments because of their reliance on descriptive studies of organizations. Descriptions provide both an indication of the data necessary for validation and suggestions about possible modifications that could be tested. A recent example, the Garbage Can model of organizational decision-making (Cohen *et al.,* 1972) is typical of this approach and is significant because of its differences from normative approaches to decision-making. It begins with the vast wealth of detail in decision situations and attempts to eliminate from consideration variables

[7]MacCrimmon incorrectly infers that groups invariably make riskier decisions than individuals. In some situations individuals are riskier than groups.

[8]Model validation should not be confused with model construction. Validation requires that a model predict organizational behavior in time periods other than those used to contruct the model and/or for similar organizations (Ghiselli, 1964, p. 336 ff).

having minimal impact on the dependent variables of interest. The spirit of the model is captured by the contention that, ". . . [A]n organization is a collection of choices looking for problems, issues and feelings looking for decision situations in which they might be aired, solutions looking for issues to which they might be the answer, and decision makers looking for work" (Cohen *et al.*, 1972, p. 2). This differs obviously from the normative approach, which begins with a limited number of assumptions and attempts to deduce as many propositions as possible that are consistent with reality. Although the Garbage Can model has not been validated, the results generated by the simulation appear to approximate observed organizational behavior and can be viewed as testable hypotheses.

Validated simulation models, such as presented by Cyert and March, have not yet been used for "experimentation" so this source of comparative empirical evidence cannot presently be used to assess the state of decision-making. However, given the integrated and comprehensive nature of simulation models and their advantages, pointed out above, future assessments of decision-making may be improved with evidence generated by the simulation experiment technique.

CONCLUSION

Clearly, any assessment of the state of decision-making that fails to fully explore both the normative and empirical approaches renders an incomplete judgment of the state of knowledge of decision-making techniques By this criterion, both MacCrimmon's chapter and this critique are inadequate. The reader is encouraged to apply the typological and comparative empirical approaches to the issues presented by MacCrimmon in order to develop an adequate understanding of the present state of decision-making.

BIBLIOGRAPHY

ARROW, K. J., *Social Choice and Individual Values* (New Haven: Yale University Press, 1953).

BAUMOL, W. J., *Economic Theory and Operations Analysis*, 3rd ed. (Englewood Cliffs, N.J.: Prentice-Hall, Inc., 1972).

CAMPBELL D. T. AND J. C. STANLEY *Experimental and Quasi-Experimental Designs for Research* (Chicago: Rand McNally, 1963).

CHARNES, A., *et al.*, "A Goal Programming Model for Media Planning," *Management Science*, Vol. 14, No. 8 (April, 1968), pp. 423–430.

COHEN, M. D., J. G. MARCH, AND J. P. OLSON, "A Garbage Can Model of Organizational Choice," *Administrative Science Quarterly*, Vol. 17, No. 1 (March, 1972), pp. 1–25.

COLLINS, B. E., AND H. GUETZKOW, *A Social Psychology of Group Processes for Decision Making* (New York: John Wiley & Sons, 1964).

CYERT, R. M., AND J. G. MARCH, *A Behavioral Theory of the Firm* (Englewood Cliffs, N.J.: Prentice-Hall, Inc., 1963).

DAVIS, J. H., *Group Performance* (Reading, Massachusetts: Addison-Wesley, 1969).

GHISELLI, E. E., *Theory of Psychological Measurement* (New York: McGraw-Hill Book Co., Inc., 1964).

HOYT, G. C., B. SCHONER, AND G. L. ROSE, Quality of Decisions by Individuals and Groups. Unpublished Working Paper, 1972.

LUCE, R. D., AND H. RAIFFA, *Games and Decisions* (New York: John Wiley & Sons, 1957).

MARSCHAK, J., "Economics of Information Systems," *Journal of the American Statistical Association* (March, 1971), p. 192.

MARSCHAK, J., "Elements for a Theory of Teams," *Management Science,* Vol. 1, No. 2 (1955), pp. 127–137.

MASON, R. O., "Dialectics in Decision Making: A Study in the Use of Counterplanning and Structured Debate in Management Information Systems," Internal Working Paper #87, Space Sciences Laboratory, University of California, Berkeley, 1969, pp. 73–74.

MCGUIRE, C. B., "Some Team Models of a Sales Organization," *Management Science,* Vol. 7, No. 2 (January, 1961), pp. 101–130.

MCKEAN, R. N., *Sub-Optimization Criteria and Operations Research* (Santa Monica, California: The Rand Corporation, P-386, 22 April, 1953).

MINAS, J. S., and R. L. ACKOFF, "Individual and Collective Value Judgments," in Shelly, Mynard W., and Glenn L. Bryan (Eds.), *Human Judgment and Optimality* (New York: John Wiley & Sons, 1964), Chapter 17.

RAPOPORT, A., *N-Person Game Theory Concepts and Applications* (Ann Arbor: The University of Michigan Press, 1970).

ROSE, C. L., The Effects of Information Congruency in Individual and Group Decision Making. Unpublished Working Paper, 1972.

SHANNON, C. E., and W. WEAVER, *The Mathematical Theory of Communication* (Urbana: University of Illinois Press, 1949).

SHUBIK, M., "Information, Risk, Ignorance and Indeterminacy," *Quarterly Journal of Economics,* Vol. 68, No. 4 (November, 1954), pp. 629–640.

SIMON, H. A. *Administrative Behavior* (New York: The Macmillan Co., 1961), pp. 61–77.

SLOVIC, P., and S. LICHTENSTEIN, "Comparison of Bayesian and Regression Approaches to the Study of Information Processing in Judgment," *Organizational Behavior and Human Performance,* Vol. 6, No. 6 (November, 1971), pp. 649–744.

STIGLER, G. J., "A Theory of Oligopoly," *Journal of Political Economy,* Vol. 72, No. 1 (January–February, 1964), pp. 44–61.

UHL, N. P., *Identifying Institutional Goals: Encouraging Convergence of Opinion Through the Delphi-Technique.* National Laboratory for Higher Education Research Monograph Number Two, Durham, North Carolina, 1971.

DISCUSSION QUESTIONS

1. What is decision-making? Is there any difference between making decisions and solving problems? What help is all this to management?
2. Define algorithms and heuristics. What is a morphological approach to decisions? And the synectics approach?
3. How might managers deal with uncertainty?
4. How does MacCrimmon differentiate among certainty, risk, and uncertainty? Or does he?
5. What are decision criteria? Are there different types?
6. Differentiate between and discuss: General and utility maximizing, satisficing, incrementing, and adapting.
7. Discuss the ways in which multiple-person choices may be resolved.
8. What are the points of disagreement among MacCrimmon, Rose, and Richards?
9. What are "normative" models of decision-making? Are they of value to management?

16

Managerial Control

Norton M. Bedford

Weldon Powell Professor of Accountancy
and Business Administration
College of Commerce and Business Administration
University of Illinois, Urbana

INTRODUCTION

It seems to be characteristic of man to attempt to control nature and himself so as to adapt the world to his purposes. Through physical science he endeavors to control nature and through social science he seeks to control himself. Although success to date in both areas leaves room for doubt, the development of controls for realizing the benefits of the sciences seems to be the best hope for mankind. Without a means for influencing or controlling the actions or inactions of man and nature, man's fate must rest with the whims of the gods.

Many are the control devices that have been developed over the centuries but increasingly the need for greater control is sensed. In response to this need, there have developed in recent years theoretical and empirical studies of control that have been synthesized in part under the heading of "control theory" and enable rigorous abstract generalized work on the problem. In the context of the foregoing wide scope of the control concept, managerial control represents the application of the concept to the problem of administration. Therefore, to place things in sequential perspective, it seems desirable to seek first an understanding of control concepts and methods and then turn to their application in the area of management.

Definition of Control

In loose terms and restricted to people, control has been defined as the power, the authority, or the influence that one person has to direct the actions of others. In this restricted sense, but in more precise terms, control is any process by which one or more persons direct the behavior of others. Normally, it requires a flow of information and has even been defined as

". . . nothing but the sending of messages which effectively change the behavior of the recipient. . . ."[1]

More broadly, to cover both man and machine, control as a concept may be defined as directing a set of variables toward a preconceived objective. For control to exist there must be something, an activity or a process, to be controlled. But this is not sufficient, for whether the something to be controlled is the actions of a person, a machine, a group of resources, or any process, control cannot be applied unless the way in which the variable components of the process are to be directed has been determined. That is, an objective or goal must be specified for the process, entity, or activity to indicate the way in which it is to be directed. But given a process and specified objectives, a control problem exists.

Control methods involving measurements and information are ways of influencing the variables in the process. If the control methods (also called controls) are capable of influencing the process sufficiently to provide for the achievement of the objective, a controlled structure or system exists. If the control methods are not applied adequately, the system or structure is said to be "out of control."

Normally, there will be a number of ways by which the objective(s) for a process may be attained. The problem of selecting the best way is referred to as the optimal control problem. It requires that some type of performance criterion be established according to which alternative sets of control methods may be ranked. In economic endeavor, cost minimization may be the performance criterion, but conceptually any criterion could be selected.

Control systems, representing different sets of control methods or techniques, may be classified in several ways. They may be deterministic or stochastic depending on the degree of precision with which they control the process. Statistical quality control is a typical stochastic system used in management whereas thermostatic control of building temperature would represent a somewhat deterministic control system. The control systems may be closed (feedback) or open (nonfeedback) depending on the degree to which they are sensitive to the output results. A control system that locks and unlocks a bank vault at specified hours but is insensitive to the varying times that employees need to have access to the vault, so that human interference is needed to adjust the opening and closing times, is an open-loop control system. That is, the control exists independent of the desired opening and closing times. The thermostat that automatically adjusts to changes in the external temperature is the typically cited closed-loop system. Thus an open-loop exists when one or more parts of the operating system are not part of the control system. A closed-loop would exist when all the controls are part of the operating system. A managerial control system might be considered to be of the open-loop variety if policy objectives were subject to change, but closed-loop if policy objectives were not subject to change and the organizational unit operated independent of any non-routine managerial action. Other classifications of control systems are those that distinguish between continuous or discrete signaling with respect to time, be-

[1]Norbert Weiner, *The Human Use of Human Beings* (Boston: Houghton Mifflin Co., 1950), p. 124.

tween process control systems and organizational control systems, and various other distinctions.

In the general sense that control is itself a process that ensures that what "ought" to be done is done, a sense of "oughtness" underlies the control concept. But since "what ought to be done" depends on the situation—the situation ethics notion—control methods may be loose or rigorous, may permit unrestricted objectives to be set or require that objectives be based on human values, and may cover large systems or subsystems.

In the engineering area, the control concept has been defined rather rigorously. Being concerned with feedback control systems, the American Institute of Electrical Engineers defined a feedback control system as a "control which tends to maintain a prescribed relationship of one system variable to another by comparing functions of these variables and using the differences as a means of control."[2] As these control methods, techniques, and principles have been applied to areas outside engineering production processes and machine operations, some of the rigor has been carried forward to systems designed to control social institutions. Evidence of this exists in the use of logical and mathematical tools in dealing with social issues and with the elaborate computer-based information systems now abounding. Included in these tools are linear programming, integer programming, inventory control theory, dynamic programming, statistical measures, and a host of others normally grouped under the heading of management science.

History of Control

Although the modern theory of control that intrigues mathematicians is an invention of the twentieth century, the concept of the closed causal loop had its origin in several regulating mechanisms of the eighteenth century. By the eighteenth century the term "regulator" included regulating devices both with and without feedback; and inventors, not having discovered the closed loop as the principle underlying several control devices, designed feedback mechanisms intuitively.

The closed-loop concept, so important for abstract control theory, is best explained in terms of the four graphic symbols of the block diagram (the arrow, the block, the circle, and the branch point.) In fact, laying out the activities of a system in these graphic symbols is the first step in the mathematical analysis of the system. The *arrow* (Figure 41a) refers to the

[2]A.I.E.E. Committee Report, "Proposed Symbols and Terms for Feedback Control Systems," *Electrical Engineering* (1951), p. 909.

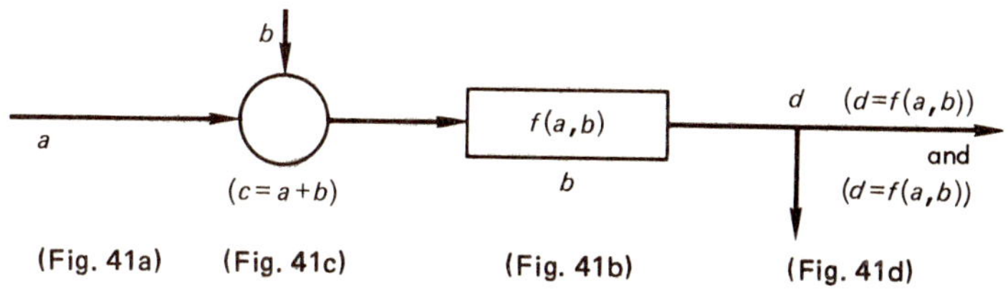

FIGURE 41. The Block Diagram

signal, a quantified physical variable, that indicates a causal relationship, whereas the *block* (Figure 41b) reveals the functional relationship among signals. If the transfer function of a block is known, the output signal from a block is simply the input signal multiplied by the transfer function. When two signals are to be added or subtracted, the *circle* (Figure 41c) is used. The *branch point* (Figure 41d) is used to indicate that one input signal has two output effects.

Arranged in more conventional form and expressed in both words and symbols, the closed loop appears as follows.

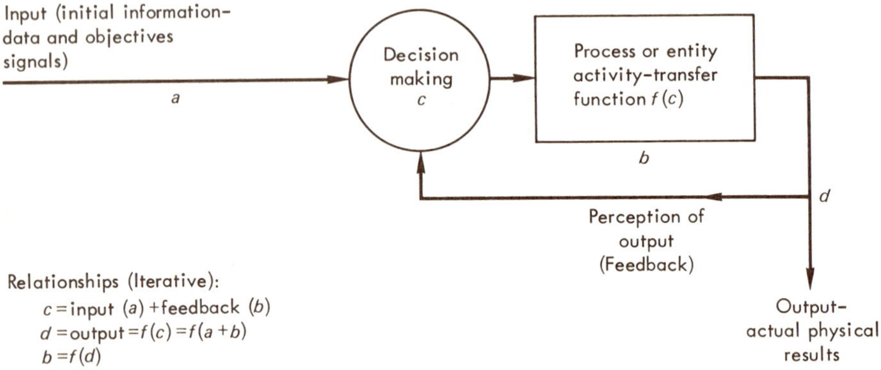

FIGURE 42. Closed-Loop Diagram

Once initiated, the system operates automatically adjusting its decision, c, at each iteration to provide for any variation of perceived output from desired output. The foregoing conventional closed-loop diagram may be generalized by treating the decision-making as a controller and the transformation activity as a plant and including feedback paths as part of the controller. Multiinputs and multioutput may be depicted as vectors of signals. By treating both the controller and the plant as systems, the diagram becomes a functional block diagram similar to Figure 41, subject to expansion and mathematical analysis. The development of the abstract generalized models seems to have taken place gradually.

During the nineteenth century feedback devices of all types were invented but throughout the century the technology of automatic control was part of mechanical engineering. Practice rather than theory dominated the engineering study of control. With the rise of the study of electrical solutions for control problems, particularly communications problems, the important role of the principle of feedback became recognized and Laplace-transform and operational calculus served as the base for the theory of automatic control (1928–1935). During World War II practical control engineering grew rapidly and by 1946 the world had both a theory and a technology for sophisticated automatic control. The war also produced the scientists to educate the world to the new development. The applications of these engineering-based principles were soon extended into the management of organization, exemplified by Forrester's 1961 book on *Industrial Dynamics,* which views an organization as a control system.

In the area of management of organizations, the notion of a hierarchical, authoritative, management structure as the control device used to control an organization is an invention of pre-history. In terms of American society, the development of cost standards and time study programs of the early 1900s, in which a comparison of results with expectations fostered the notion of management by exception, represents the systematic use of information in the control system. This was soon followed by budgetary control systems and today many think of budgetary control when reference is made to managerial control systems. This view is now giving way to elaborate computer-based management information systems as the managerial control system.

Bonini, Jaedicke, and Wagner account for this sequential development in the following way:

> In the formative days of modern business enterprise, management control presented little problem. Typically, the entrepreneur initiated his own plans, directly supervised his employees to execute those plans, and made modifications when necessary....
>
> With the steady growth toward gargantuan organizations, control has become imperative for effective management of such enterprises. Planning, as one facet of control, involves coordinating the efforts of a multitude of individuals in the organization. Execution of these plans must be performed through a hierarchy of managers, supervisors, foremen, and workers, Accurate and timely information is needed to ascertain whether plans are being followed and when they should be modified. The environment for today's firm is not only complex but also subject to rapid change. All of these factors amplify the need for methods to control and regulate the business entity.[3]

The relationship between abstract control theory and managerial controls, although they appear to have distinct histories, can best be explained by distinguishing between an organization, in which managerial controls are applied, and a process, to which control theory applies. Ackoff has called attention to the distinction between an organization and a process (organism) and points out that "Management Scientists are most concerned with the type of system called 'organizations.' Cyberneticians, on the other hand, are more concerned with that type of system called 'organisms,' but they frequently treat organizations as though they were organisms. Although these two types of systems have much in common, there is an important difference between them."[4] The difference referred to is that an organization has elements or entities that have purposes themselves tied together with at least one common purpose, whereas an organism contains no purposeful elements. "In an organism only the whole can display will; none of the parts can."[5]

In an overview sense, the history of constant expansion of engineering controls into new areas and the history of constant improvement in the precision of managerial controls suggests that the two histories are merging

[3]C. P. Bonini, R. K. Jaedicke, and H. M. Wagner (Eds.), *Management Controls* (New York: McGraw-Hill Book Co., Inc., 1964), p. ix.

[4]R. L. Ackoff, "Toward a System of Systems Concepts," *Management Science* (July, 1971), p. 669.

[5]*Ibid.*, p. 671.

into one. Illustrative of this is the use of statistical control and the control chart in maintaining a state of statistical stability. Developed by W. A. Shewhart just before the Second world war, including the 3-sigma control limits as action limits that he justified on an empirical basis, this control technique has expanded in concept and in use until much of managerial control is now based on it.[6]

Relation of Control to Management

Managerial control is the process of directing a set of persons, equipment, and materials according to an established plan of action toward a specified objective. Essentially, managerial control functions by comparing achieved outcomes with desired outcomes and adjusting operations so that the gap between the two is reduced. A part of managerial control involves determining the desired outcomes. To function, managerial control must have a controller (an administrator) who responds to information provided by a feedback procedure. Thus, managerial control includes two functions: The first is motivational in that the system endeavors to prevent variation from desired actions by motivating people to take such actions as to preclude any variation. The second is corrective in that the system seeks to re-establish desired actions if a variation has occurred. The more rapidly corrective feedback information enables the re-establishment of appropriate action, the more the two functions fuse into one. Thus, managerial control encompasses the cycle beginning with an objective on the part of a manager or other person in the organization (*X*), followed by an effort to influence another person or group (*Y*) to so act that the objective of *X* is attained. *X* may use various means to influence *Y*, ranging from assigned or assumed authority to logical reasoning to emotional appeal. But whenever *X* by any means influences *Y's* actions, *X* is said to have exercised managerial control. The degree of managerial control exercised is the probability that *Y* will do that which *X* requests, assuming *Y* would not otherwise have so acted.

The basic instrument of managerial control is an organizational structure. Fundamentally, every organization is a control system that can be represented by the feedback (closed loop) control schema. Each part of every organization can be similarly depicted. Roberts suggests the following diagrammatic view of the organization or any of its parts as a control system.[7]

In this scheme of things, control is a feedback process involving the reiterative performance of the following steps:

1. A decision or policy for action is made in accordance with some decision model that aims to satisfy desired objectives.
2. Subject to various external and internal disturbances, actions are taken to comply with the decision. This action results in some type of accomplishment.

[6]W. A. Shewhart, Statistical Methods from the Viewpoint of Quality Control (Washington, D.C.: The Department of Agriculture, 1939).

[7]E. B. Roberts, "Industrial Dynamics and the Design of Management Control Systems," in C. P. Bonini, R. K. Jaedicke, and H. M. Wagner (Eds.), *Management Controls* (New York: McGraw-Hill Book Co., Inc., 1964), p. 103.

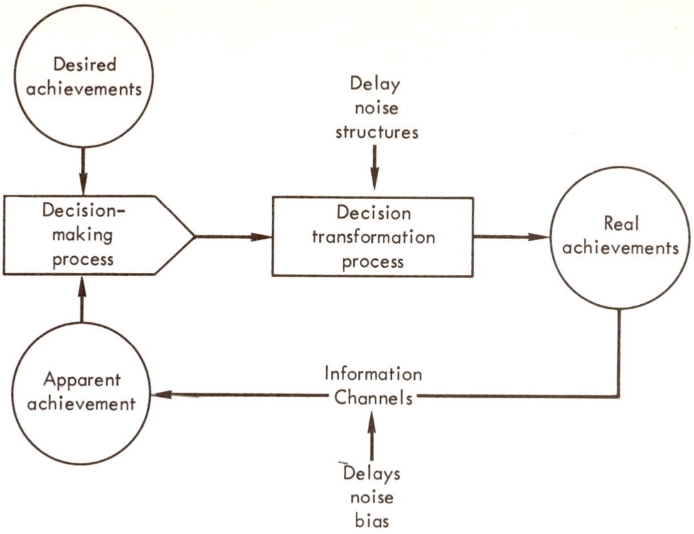

FIGURE 43. Diagrammatic View of the Organization as a Control System

3. The accomplishment success, as perceived by a sensor (observer), and subject to various noise interferences, is reported back to the decision-making apparatus. Typically, the perception is symbolized in terms of measurement and by classification arranged into an effective communication medium for transmission to the decision-making vehicle.
4. The feedback communication, as perceived by the decision maker, is used to evaluate success of past plans and actions.
5. The evaluated comparison and other data are inserted into the decision model and used to develop plans and policies to attain goals.

The foregoing view of the organization as a control system is very similar to engineering control systems, but the distinction between the two needs to be maintained for a time at least. The engineering conception of control, when it is applied in the human area, assumes the prevalance of a rationalistic human behavior norm in the organization that may not be valid. In an organization in which people are directed, one might expect a change in the way leaders exercise control, from the command viewpoint implied by engineering control to a discussion and persuasion viewpoint to motivate individuals. This human feature of control, wherein the effort is to gain willing cooperation, may, of course, ultimately be included in the engineering conception through worker participation in setting goals and objectives. In any event, the emergence of the human aspects of the control process suggest the opportunity for expanding new kinds of controls to supplement those used in the past. A broadening of the control process seems underway.

Upon analysis, the notion that control is "the directing of a set of variables toward a preconceived objective" implies that managerial control is not so much a method of directing as it is a power to direct and motivate variables toward a preconceived objective. In this larger sense, control is not only an efficiency concept directed to determining the technically optimal movement of a set of variables but also is the power to cause the variables to take action. In the sense of power to direct variables, the notion of an amount of control exists that may be quantified in terms of the number and size of variables to be directed. Thus, the amount of control in an organization could be increased by increasing the activities of an organization. Assuming a management motivation toward more and more power, the tendency will ever be for organizations to expand the control element in the organization. The amount of control may be increased by expanding the number of economic resources of the organization or by directing the organization to other activities in society, such as education, crime prevention, pollution control, and other activities. Inevitably, the desire for control will expand the objectives of business entities, move business into social responsibilities, increase the role of business in society, and thus increase the amount of control in the business entity. This effort to increase the total amount of control of the entity will mobilize all management personnel toward a common objective and thus mitigate the competitive struggle among themselves for a greater portion of the total power of the entity. Each management person can increase his power of control by maintaining his fixed proportion of the control in the entity as the amount of control in the entity increases.

Internally, the amount of control in an organization would be increased by improving the efficiency with which human and other resources are directed toward objectives of the organization. Since this view of control as efficiency methods spans both motivational (before the fact) control and corrective (after the fact) control, management control is a broader notion than engineering control, in which emphasis is on corrective control using the theory of feedback information.

Given a set of objectives and a set of means, the amount of internal control would be measured by the smallness of variations from the most efficient pursuit of the objective. It might also be measured as the negative of the amount of entropy (disorder) in the organization. If entropy is conceived as random action, entropy might be measured as the variation between random action in the organization and the actual actions of the organization. A reduction in entropy would reflect an increase in control. In this context statistical control measures, which are based on the assumption that a certain degree of randomness is to be expected in all actions, are devices for eliminating gross entropy elements only. The ultimate pursuit of control is to eliminate all randomness, and as progress is made in reducing the cost of information and the cost of corrective action, more deterministic and less statistical control methods may be expected.

An illustration of the measurement of the amount of control in an organization will best explain the concept. Assume that there are only four possible actions that a decision maker or other individual can take. If he has been given no direction—has been subject to no control—according to the law of equal probability there is an equal chance that each action will be taken. With four options, the probability of each is 0.25, or $\frac{1}{4}$.

Entropy is typically measured as the sum of the products of the logarithm to the base 2 of the reciprocal of the probability of an action times its probability for all possible actions. In the illustration the entropy would be computed as follows:

Possible Action	Probability of Action	Log_2 of Reciprocal of Probability	Product of Probabilities and Log_2 of Reciprocals
A	¼	Log_2 1¼ = Log_2 4 = 2	2⁄4 = ½
B	¼	" 2	= ½
C	¼	" 2	= ½
D	¼	" 2	= ½
		Total entropy	2

Now assume that control is inserted into the situation so that the individual or decision maker is directed away from action *A* and *B* and toward action *D*. Assume the direction is such that the probabilities of his actions are ⅛, ⅛, ¼, and ½, respectively. His new condition of entropy, after having this control inserted, would be

Possible Action	Probability of Action	Log_2 of Reciprocal of Probability	Product of Probabilities and Log_2 of Reciprocals
A	⅛	Log_2 1⅛ = Log_2 8 = 3	⅜
B	⅛	3	⅜
C	¼	2	4⁄8
D	½	1	4⁄8
		Total entropy	14⁄8 = 1¾

The entropy reduction provided by the control is from 2 to 1¾, or ¼. One might say, then, that the amount of control in the situation is 12½ per cent.

Assume more control is inserted into the situation until the decision maker is directed unequivocally to take action *D*. This will reduce entropy to zero and the situation will be 100 per cent under control, as shown here.

Possible Action	Probability of Action	Log_2 of Reciprocal of Probability	Product of Probabilities and Log_2 of Reciprocals
A	0	Log_2 1/1/0 = Log_2 0 = 0	0
B	0	= 0	0
C	0	= 0	0
D	1	= 0	0
		Total entropy	0

Entropy has been reduced to zero and 100 per cent eliminated, and, as negative entropy, the amount of control in the organization is 100 per cent.

In the future, one must anticipate further efforts to quantify the amount of control in an organization or process. This may well bring statistical control techniques under criticism, for complete control requires that all randomness be eliminated, whereas statistical control assumes a certain degree of randomness is normal or that it is too costly to isolate or correct.

Overall measures of the amount of control in an organization are somewhat imprecise. Suggested as indices of control have been:

1. The average span of control of managers
2. The number of levels of management hierarchy in the organization
3. The ratio of the number of managers to total employees, to total value of resources, and to total sales volume.

Broadly, the relationship of control to management appears, from the foregoing, to be the primary means by which management attains its objectives, for managerial control spans organization structure, human relations, information flows, and other aspects of management.

CONTROL CONCEPTS AND METHODS

The gap between the control concept as it is used in engineering feedback systems for machines and the way it is used in directing a people-oriented organization is in part a terminological difference, attributable to the different types of processes to which the concept is applied. In an organization, control is associated with influence, whereas in an engineered process, control is associated with more standardized systems. Tannenbaum's suggestion that control is "the process by which members determine or influence how things get done in an organization"[8] illustrates the human behavior emphasis in managerial control often missing in the engineering concept. Watkins' assertion that "It is desired that control systems operate automatically, and without human intervention"[9] reflects the engineering interest in standardized systems.

Williamson, viewing control as a social issue, distinguishes between the external social controls of competition or its alternative, administrative or regulatory activities, and internal controls processes. From his social control point of view, control methods are devices to influence both "goal formation" by organizations and their internal effectiveness in pursuit of the goal(s).[10]

Broadly, three different, although related, applied control concepts are evident in the literature on the subject:

1. Social control, which is concerned with the goals, ethics, and cooperation of organizations (entities). It is an external control effort applied by the general public through social norms and values and typically takes the form of a public pronouncement of a belief of what should be done by organizations. In more direct form, this social control takes the form of

[8]Arthur S. Tannenbaum, *Control in Organizations* (New York: McGraw-Hill Book Co., Inc., 1968), p. vii.

[9]Bruce O. Watkins, *Introduction to Control Systems* (New York: The Macmillan Co., 1969), p. 6.

[10]Oliver E. Williamson, *Corporate Control and Business Behavior* (Englewood Cliffs, N.J.: Prentice-Hall, Inc., 1970).

government regulatory rulings, court decisions, and other legal actions. At times it is applied by special interest groups such as creditors and shareholders through contractual rights.

The foregoing external control, wherein the feedback mechanism provides very specific directions for changes, may be classified as direct social controls. Indirect social control, arising from the threat of an outside takeover or an inability to raise capital if organization performance is not effective, is a very realistic motivational control applied to top management's action and is therefore a part of social control.

2. Managerial control, which is concerned with the motivations and coordination of people within an organization. This is an internal control system applied by a hierarchy of control levels within the organization. The traditional inverted winter tree representation of an organizational structure reflects the various levels of control centers all tied to the central control of the chief executive office of the organization. But changes in the internal control system may change the organization structure, so managerial controls need not be restricted to the traditional feedback information reports directed to positions in an organization chart. Efficiency, profit, the bounded rationality of members of the organization, and a certain randomness of top management beliefs and actions are the primary motivation for internal control systems. Accountants have defined internal control as follows:

> In the broad sense, internal control includes, therefore, controls which may be characterized as either accounting or administrative, as follows:
>
> a. Accounting controls comprise the plan of organization and all methods and procedures that are concerned mainly with, and relate directly to, safeguarding of assets and the reliability of the financial records. They generally include such controls as the systems of authorization and approval, separation of duties concerned with record keeping and accounting reports from those concerned with operations or asset custody, physical controls over assets, and internal auditing.
>
> b. Administrative controls comprise the plan of organization and all methods and procedures that are concerned mainly with operational efficiency and adherence to managerial policies and usually relate only indirectly to the financial records. They generally include such controls as statistical analyses, time and motion studies, performance reports, employee training programs, and quality controls.[11]

3. Automatic engineering control, which is concerned with the regulation of somewhat standardized operating processes. This concept of control might be labeled "machine control" instead of "managerial control" in that it endeavors to establish automatic feedback and feed forward signals to direct the operation of a process according to a predetermined plan. It requires elaborate sensors and uniform procedures to function and has traditionally been used in controlling the lower-level routine activities of a process.

Supporting all three is the abstract body of knowledge known as con-

[11]Committee on Auditing Procedure, *Statement on Auditing Procedure No. 33* (New York: AICPA), Chapter 5.

trol theory, which explains that the three sets of elements intersect quite broadly. That is, specific control systems may vary in terms of components or methods but underlying them all is a common basic control theory resulting from a synthesis of the specific systems. The existence of this common control field permits a common examination of theory, research, trends, directions, and hypotheses regarding control concepts and methods.

Before examining these common features, certain other aspects of managerial controls must be pointed out. Broadly, the engineering notion of control implies objectives and precise actions whereas the management notion of control implies adaptability and flexibility in a process of constant adjustment to change. Depending upon the amount of change faced by the organization or process, one notion may provide more or less control than the other. The essence of managerial control is interchange and communications among all parties in the organization to encourage the acceptance and fostering of change as a normal condition.

Years ago March and Simon emphasized the need for participative management in managerial control by pointing out that "Where there is participation, alternatives are suggested in a setting that permits the organizational hierarchy to control (at least in part) what is evoked."[12] As psychological studies indicate, the attitude with which an individual carries out directed activities has a great deal to do with the quality of his performance. The control feature of attitude development through participative management, involving sensitivity training and *T* groups, assumes that by participation greater personal involvement will increase communications and eliminate conflicts and effectively coordinate all effort toward the common objective. But the purpose of participative management is to increase control. Should it in fact result in greater conflict among participants and a loss of control, a more authoritarian organizational structure may be necessary. Current evidence is that participative management does normally increase control in the organization. The traditional view of organizations with top-down hierarchical control authority in which the total amount of control in the organization is fixed appears to be a declining concept if a high degree of control is to be required in organizations.

An increase in the amount of control implies greater unified membership action and a greater readiness to support organization goals and objectives, conform to rules and policies, and accept penalties for rule or policy violation. Thus, increased control creates greater conformity.

Tannenbaum's control graph provides an overview of the amount of control in an organization and the distribution of that control among various management levels in the organization.[13]

Under a democratic control system, the distribution of control rises as one moves down the management level (line *a*). The autocratic control system (line *b*) is one wherein the control is distributed largely to top management and decreases as one moves down the management hierarchy. Line *c* indicates a combination of democratic control and autocratic control wherein more control is distributed at all levels, thus indicating a greater amount of control in the organization (area under the line) than that represented by either line *a* or *b*.

[12]J. G. March and H. A. Simon, *Organizations* (New York: John Wiley & Sons, 1958), p. 54.

[13]A. S. Tannenbaum, *Control in Organizations* (New York: McGraw-Hill Book Co., Inc., 1968), p. 13.

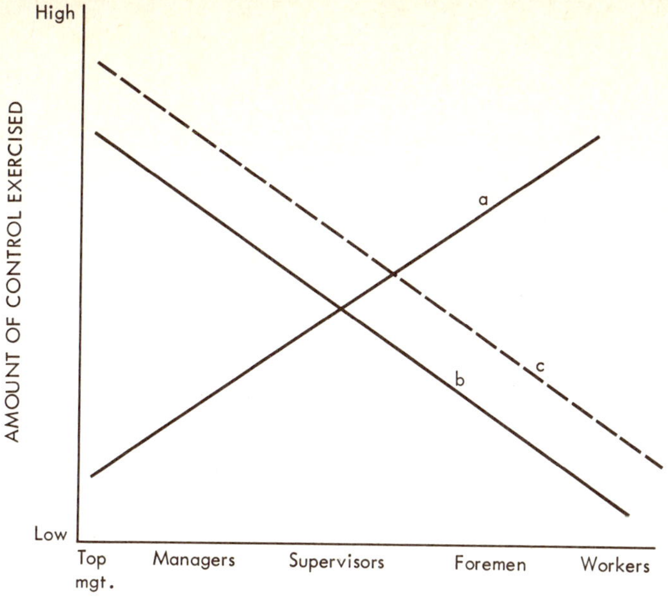

FIGURE 44. Tannenbaum's Control Graph

Control Theory

Since control theory assumes the existence of a process, a motion of some type taking place over time, and controls (methods) for influencing the process, some dynamic structure of the process or rules of change must be developed if the process and controls are to be rigorously analyzed. If one specifies a set of controls to influence the process, the dynamic structure of the process must be such that given the state (Y) of the process (X) at time t, one can predict either deterministically or stochastically the state (Z) at $t + 1$.

By specifying an objective as some desired target state for the process, one can formulate a control structure if controls are available that can influence the transformation of the present state to the target state of the process. In selecting an objective for a control structure, one might well consider the set of all attainable objectives given the set of controls. Selecting the preferred objective (target state) from the set of attainable states may or may not be subject to formal control, although some value considerations are necessarily involved in designating one state as preferred over others.

Normally, there will be a number of ways by which the present state of the process can be moved to the target state, some more preferable than others. Performance criteria may be set up, again reflecting value considerations, to permit the selection of the optimal controls.

Mathematically, the dynamic structure may be in the form of a vector differential equation and the control may be some function in a set of permitted functions valid within some designated control area. By designating the target state as a continuously varying closed set and the control selection criterion as the integral of a real valued function, one may use mathematical analysis to examine ways to move the process from state Y to the target state.[14]

Information is the means of control in that the feedback of measured informance on performance indicates the need to adjust a process and the subsequent feed forward of corrective information serves to motivate the adjustment needed. Theoretically, it should be possible to control any process or situation if the following conditions prevail.

1. It is possible to develop information revealing the performance of a process. Some type of sensor or monitor must be available.
2. A standard of desired performance exists.
3. A means of comparing actual performance with the standard in such a way that information on the extent of the variation is generated.
4. A means of communicating the information is technically feasible.
5. It is possible to make changes that will eliminate the gap or variation between the standard and actual performance.
6. The speed of adjustment of variations can occur fast enough so the corrective activities are relevant. In a continuous operation, if adjustments are slow the gap between actual performance and standard may widen with the result that corrective actions may never be adequate.

Certain theories of control tend to revolve around means for making these conditions prevail for various situations. Because several of the required conditions are aspects of communication and information theory, it is possible to relate the sensing problem to various theories of perception and information transmission that convert a perception to understanding on the part of the receiving apparatus. In the area of managerial control, this relates to the behavioral aspects of management control systems.

One may visualize the communication theory of control systems as consisting of (1) a sensor, observer, or perceiver of events initiated by a decision maker, (2) a symbolizing or measuring of the perceived event, (3) a comparison of the perceived event with expected events, (4) a transmission of the comparison in symbolic terms to the decision makers, (5) a decision by the decision maker, and (6) an action by the performers. Suffice it to note that various theories prevail suggesting what to observe, how to symbolize, how to compare, when and how to transmit, what decision models to use, and how to motivate action.

Arrow's reference to the theory of "barometer control," dealing with the motivation aspect of managers, assuming economic reward is the "carrot," illustrates the various types of theories of control that revolve around the communication theory of managerial control. Distinguishing between control-in-the-large or adaptive or second-order control, which is concerned with the establishment of right goals for control systems, and control-in-the-small, which is concerned with the task of attaining the goals and is largely a behavioral issue of incentives, Arrow reasons as follows:

[14]See Aaron Strauss, *An Introduction to Optimal Control Theory* (New York: Springer-Verlag, 1968) pp. 3–4 which provides, in mathematical terms, a description of a control problem.

> . . . What are the incentives to the individual manager to maximize profits? . . . The usual formulation of the price system requires that an individual be paid his marginal profitability, which means, in effect, that if he manages to save the company money by proper decisions, the whole saving should go to him. It was repeatedly pointed out during the seminar that this doesn't seem to be the way the companies run their business.
>
> . . . barometer control—or, in other words, a profit-sharing arrangement—makes a great deal of sense because what is very important to the company may be exceedingly large by the standards of the individual, so that even a small fraction may be worth a great deal to him, perhaps enough to create adequate incentive.
>
> . . . It is important, though, that the rewards be determined by the amount of gain to the company and nothing else; otherwise there will be incentive for distortion."[15]

In theory, control, when distinguished from planning, should perform the following functions:

1. It should encourage better planning or the development of a better process initially. In part this is an educational function, but it is also motivational in that planners will be sensitive to the need to plan carefully.
2. It should prevent loss of coordination of the total system, which could result if variations from plans by different segments of the organization or process were large.
3. It should provide feedback information to adapt operations to plans or to indicate that a replanning activity is necessary.

RESEARCH ON CONTROL

Research on managerial control is being undertaken in a number of fields, such as accounting, economics, psychology, computer science, and systems engineering. To a significant extent this research is being directed to the problem of determining the proper outcomes to be observed and to the human reaction to various types of controls. In psychology and accounting, empirical field research on feedback in the form of the reactions of individuals to different information, to different transmission formats for the same information, to the same information in different situations, and to excessive information is rapidly expanding. Assumed behavioral responses are being subject to systematic analysis. Ultimately, the hope is that sufficient data will become available to permit the use of more humane control systems. Until this research program was initiated, the motivational consequences of feedback appear to have been largely ignored. The limited evidence now in indicates that a case can be made against the unthinking use of feedback. The evidence is based on the theory of cognitive dissonance,

[15]K. J. Arrow, "Research in Management Controls: A Critical Synthesis" in C. P. Bonini, R. K. Jaedicke, and H. M. Wagner (Eds.), *Management Controls* (New York: McGraw-Hill Book Co., Inc., 1964), pp. 325–326.

which holds that an individual will react unfavorably to feedback controls that prevent him from attaining consistency in his opinions, values, and attitudes. The indications are that each individual strives for this consistency and that feedback should be compatible with this striving.

In economics and sociology, the goals of society and organization, as sub-parts of society, are under critical review. From the control point of view, the extent to which the total society attains its goals depends on the extent to which its sub-parts are under control and if the sub-goals selected foster the attainment of social goals. Thus, total system research is considered the ultimate significant type of control research.

In computer science, accounting, and systems engineering the efforts to improve the software and hardware that permit the introduction of more and more automatic control systems continue. The tendency is to develop automatic or semi-automatic control systems that allot to the machine duties formerly requiring a type of human decision-making process. The hope is that human beings will be able to do human, not machine, work. Systems work designing computer-based control systems are in need of considerable improvement and a large part of control research is directed to that problem. Simulation has proven to be an effective tool in research on control and controls.

Research on the information flow in the control system has encountered the phenomenon of "control loss," which indicates that under serial reproduction of information transfer a significant variation in the message occurs. As applied to management, this phenomenon indicates that as an organization increases its hierarchial levels of management, top management tends to lose control over the activities of the organization because information is distorted as it is passed from one layer of management to the next. To overcome this phenomenon, librarians and accountants have initiated research on information storage and retrieval systems. The research objective is to develop data bases directly accessible to a decision maker where accurate feedback information is available and through which feed forward information can be accurately transmitted.

Much of the more abstract mathematical research in control systems in recent years has involved direct solution of differential equations. Matrix procedures for solving linear equations have been the technique most frequently used to obtain the solution for multiple input and output systems.

Overall control research has the opportunity to aspire to a total society system capable of directing both man and nature to man's purposes and best interests. Although this may be the ultimate objective, much of the current research on control is aimed at far lesser systems. Management information systems that seek to improve the planning aspects of control appear to be the most realistic immediately possible application of basic control theory to managerial control problems.

TRENDS OF CONTROL

The most significant trend in the control area is the increasing generalization of control concepts and the mathematical treatment of the subject. Almost equally significant is the emerging ability to relate applied control systems to basic control theory and to generate new applications from the fundamental theory. Related to this is the expansion in scope of engineering control methods and their application to human problems.

In managerial control, the trend is toward a larger control function, greater utilization of the computer, and the use of management science in planning control, policy control, and operating control. Increasingly it is being recognized that an understanding of managerial control in an organization requires an understanding of the aspirations, reward penalty structure views, personal feelings, and personal goal-setting methods of individuals. Organizationally, the place of controls and control in the management structure seems to move more and more toward an upgraded middle management. Starr traces the place of control from yesterday, through today, and to tomorrow in Table 12.[16]

As the trend toward larger control systems continues, efforts are being directed increasingly toward an improvement in the precision of the feedback signals. Work continues to improve the "sensitivity" of control systems by developing means for determining the degree of variation from the target state or standard necessary to invoke a correcting action. This depends in part on the preciseness of the feedback information, for if the probability dispersion of feedback information is large, a small variation from the target state may be a "normal" error. It also depends on the stability of a process or system in maintaining a designated behavioral pattern. An unstable system with random fluctuation might require less frequent adjustments than would a stable system. The speed with which a system can make adjustments for variations is also involved, as is the cost of an adjustment. If speed is high and cost is low, precise feedback signals may permit more frequent adjustments.

Long-range predictions of the trend of control imply that ultimately most of the functions of organizations and processes of all types will become a part of large control information systems. There are predictions that the human adjustment to the control culture of the future may be somewhat traumatic. But this is a problem of the next generation.

In the even longer run, one may anticipate a cyclical aspect to the trend of controls. As Allport noted in 1955, the natural tendency of all systems is toward disorder, or entropy. He states, "This tending toward entropy (maximum disorganization or disorder) is, so far as we know, a universal law of nature."[17] Thus, even as managerial control in the cybernetic feedback sense expands its role in management, the tendency toward entropy will cause its effectiveness to decline, to resurge, and fluctuate cyclically until it is replaced by another more relevant concept that deals with the then developing entropy. In a secular sense, however, a tendency exists for control to be centralized. This classic conception that control in organizations ultimately becomes oligarchic is supported by studies indicating that the masses of people prefer to be led, that the need for efficient operation of the total systems requires more and more coordination, and that leaders develop a lust for power. All of these suggest increasing controls in

[16]M. K. Starr, *Management: A Modern Approach* (New York: Harcourt Brace Jovanovich, Inc., 1971), p. 461.

[17]F. H. Allport, *Theories of Perception and the Concept of Structure* (New York: John Wiley & Sons, 1955), p. 475.

Yesterday	*Today*	*Tomorrow*
Top management plans and controls the evolution of its plans. It participates in policy formulation and often oversees the implementation and application of its policies.	Top management plans but turns over much of the control of plans to middle management. Policy formulation is also relegated to middle management and control over the policies is seldom considered.	Top management interacts with management science in the planning function. Control of plans is entirely in the hands of computer-oriented middle management. Policy and its control is totally delegated.
Middle management seldom handles policy formulation. It enforces policy, however, subject to the intended constraints of top management.	Middle management exercises judicial control over plans (e.g., PERT) and interacts with management science in the legislative policy-formulation area. Middle management begins to accept the computer as a pervasive force in exercising policy control.	Middle management and management science are merged in the pursuit of planning control, policy formulation, and policy control. Quantitative methods are the overriding features. MBE is the rule—introducing it and supervising it are the new middle-management functions.
Management science has a relatively narrow view of policy formulation and almost no insight or intuition concerning the top-management planning function.	Management science assumes significant responsibility for policy controls, interacts with middle management in policy formulation, and begins to gain a sense of what management means by top-management planning.	

society. Even if leaders are overthrown and human considerations stop the process, ultimately the new leaders and the new concepts turn to increased centralized controls to realize their goals. But this classic trend may be waning as certain control methods move in the direction of "democratic" systems.

Directions of Control

The most evident direction of control in organization is toward the automation of a large amount of clerical work. Inventory control systems, for example, replace stock ledger clerks and assure more automatic reordering of goods as needed. Payroll systems replace payroll clerks. Automatic machine control systems replace assembly-line workers. In a variety of ways repetitive tasks, both clerical and physical, are placed under control systems. But just as the trend is to move the control function to middle management, so the current direction of automatic control is to expand and automate a number of traditional middle-management functions.

The new directions into which control is moving will result in greater reliance on automatic control. In the past, control has depended on a comparison of actual performance with the standard set by a higher level of supervisors. Under the cybernetic concept of control, wherein corrective information is automatically fed back into the process when variations beyond some limit occurs, executives will direct their efforts to the non-routine aspects of control. The human behavior aspects of this new type of control appear to be favorable in that the traditional control methods, based on a boss-employee relationship that carries several disfunctional features, will be replaced by self-guidance control motivations. In research and other innovative work, the cybernetic control model of automatic feedback should allow scientists and professionals more flexibility in their work.

Cybernetic control should involve everyone in the accomplishments of the process or organization by developing horizontal relationships instead of hierarchical authority and control structures. By associating everyone with task and process performance, human activities may be integrated. The result, hopefully, is that workers will internalize their control motivation by relating their own work directly to the accomplishments of the organization or process. Internalized self-motivation has long been recognized as the more desirable control method.

As control moves in the direction of cybernetic controls, it appears to offer an opportunity for more effective decentralization of decision-making. To realize this opportunity, top management will have to provide goals and restrictions to the decentralized decision makers that will provide overall organizational coordination. This will place primary control in central top management. But since cybernetic control will prevent wide variations from all plans and since decentralized managers will not be burdened with routine control problems, it will appear to them that they are able to operate almost autonomously. Real-time computer systems will provide access to information at decentralized locations for decision-making, just as it is now available for top management. Overall, various levels of decision-making could be spread throughout the organization. The result of this development would be to make decisions and actions more rational throughout the organization. This raises an issue for managerial control, expressed by Argyris in the following terms.

> "Management science theorists and practitioners would tend to agree that some day management information systems (MIS) will probably be designed that perform many critical managerial functions. Many also would agree that the realization of this potential is a long way off.
>
> What would happen if an MIS system were developed that could achieve this potential? How would individuals react to increased rationality in their lives? Will they think as many humanists believe, namely that information science rationality can lead to a mechanistic and rigid world that, because of its narrow concept of efficiency, will dominate man and eclipse his humanness? Will individuals believe, as many futurists argue, that the scope of our society has become so broad and the interdependence so pervasive, that without the rationality possible from sophisticated information systems we run the risk of losing control

over our everyday life and our destiny?[18] Hopefully, both humanness and the benefits of control will be the future state. Clearly, there is a need to determine how the incentive aspects of management control can be related more humanly to individual multidimensional needs and wants.

Hypotheses about Control

Speculations regarding the nature, effectiveness, and future of control abound. Some of these are sufficiently well founded, although still undemonstrated or proven, that they qualify as tentative generalizations about the control area.

The Behavioral Emphasis Hypothesis This assertion holds that further improvement in managerial control systems will have to include human wants as necessary constraints. In part this hypothesis is a reflection of some disillusionment with the results of "efficient" control systems. It supports behavioral science study.

The Total Society Hypothesis This view holds that total society is the only entity and that all other organizations and processes are subsystems. Accordingly, general systems theory should be emphasized. In part motivated by ecological and quality of life concern but also fostered by the probable development of supercomputers in the future, this hypothesis emphasizes the study and development of complex control systems.

The Alternative Generalization Hypothesis in the Area of Abstract Control Theory This hypothesis holds that the entire concept of control will be generalized in many different ways.

The Systems Concept Hypothesis This hypothesis is that managerial control will be improved as the systems concept is more rigorously applied. Authority and responsibility for performance will be pinpointed to a degree now not possible because of allocation problems and crude systems. The hypothesis assumes a continued expansion of automatic data processing and techniques of managerial control.

The Common Control Problem Hypothesis Arrow expresses the notion underlying the hypothesis in the following terms:

> In a sense the organizations that we are thinking of here are in fact parts of a larger organization, the whole economy. It is no accident that people who have discussed the theory of socialist economics are concerned with problems which are, as has repeatedly been pointed out, quite similar in form to those in the internal organization of a firm. Presumably, the problems related to co-ordination and transmission of information become more and more predominant relative to other kinds of transactions as we get down to units of the kind we call natural business organizations.[19]

[18]C. Argyris, "Management Information Systems: The Challenge to Rationality and Emotionality," *Management Science* (February, 1971), p. B-275.

[19]Arrow, *op. cit.*, p. 318.

In addition to the foregoing general and somewhat unarticulated hypotheses, a variety of specific hypotheses have been developed. Illustrative are the following.

A. On labor union structure:
   A.1 The union devoted primarily to the enhancement of wages and other specific benefits from management is predicted to develop strong leadership and autocratic control ("the greater the members' interest in narrow and specific ('bread-and-butter') goals, the less democratic the union").
   A.2 The union oriented toward large social goals tends to be associated with internal democratic participative control. ("The greater the members' interest in broad and general social goals, the more democratic the union.")
   A.3 The greater the amount of union-management conflict, the greater the amount of control in the union organization. (It may also result in a greater amount of control in the management organization.)

B. On effectiveness (degree to which an organization fulfills its objectives and preserves its means and resources) of control in voluntary organizations:
   B.1 Organization effectiveness will be related directly to the degree of democratic participation in the organization (the degree of positive slope of the control curve).
   B.2 Organization effectiveness will be related directly to the amount of control in the organization (to the average height of the control curve).

REVIEW OF THE APPLICATION OF CONTROL METHODS IN MANAGEMENT

The notion of managerial control is frequently viewed broadly to encompass both organizational structure arrangements that provide effective supervision of organization activities by foremen, managers, and other "bosses," and information flow arrangements that signal variations from planned operations and permit application of the managerial by exception principle. The latter view presumes that although management control may change the organization structure by increasing the span of control of individual supervisors, it does not include organization structure. In this light, management control is a type of information system. This latter view is closely related to abstract control theory. Also, there are those who believe the man control systems of organization structure are so crude and include so much supervisory irrationality that they will ultimately be largely replaced by management information control systems. These two views may be reviewed in terms of the past, present, and future management controls.

The Evolution of Past Applications

The basic premise of the organizational structure managerial control system is that through specialization of knowledge and assignment of responsibility and authority, the "bosses" know what to do and how to have it done so that each process in the organization attains assigned objectives. In fact, these "bosses" have long been aware that they could not perceive every deficiency in the operation of the process in which they were concerned. They developed crude information systems to provide data on actual activities. Given the profit motive, most of these information systems provided financial data. The managerial control introduced by the accounting information systems was to provide data on actual financial effectiveness that the manager could subjectively compare with what he thought good performance should have been. This managerial control technique merely substituted for direct management perception of performance information developed by others that could serve as a surrogate for the manager's perception. It represented the first application of a control method to management and occurred years ago. Starting shortly before Frederick Taylor, managers came to realize that many of their subjective standards of good performance were not well founded and efforts were directed toward determining proper performance standards. Time and motion studies in the factory emerged as effective ways to determine what performance should be. Thus, responsibility for the establishment of a standard of good performance was transferred to the information system from direct management. In this manner the concept of planning was initiated, although in the form of standards, into the managerial control system. Although each manager was still held responsible for his area of authority and had to evaluate the validity of the management information control system, the operating management function tended to become one of comparing actual results with the standard. This involved the analysis of management control reports and taking action to correct those variations the manager subjectively considered significant.

As managerial control methods were applied in new areas by cost accountants, who began including both financial and non-financial data in management control reports, it became apparent that frequently the variations subjectively considered significant were not or cost more to correct than the loss being sustained. Efforts then were made to develop means for indicating when a variation was significant. The three-sigma (standard deviation) variation was developed as the criterion for a significant variation in precise production processes.

The past indicates that gradually more and more applications of control methods have developed. Three rather distinct stages in the development of control applications in the past may be illustrated by examples from the cost accounting field, where cost reports first disclosed the cost of producing a product or the income from production and sale of products (stage 1) and then turned to including comparative standards to permit an evaluation of performance (stage 2) and finally to the inclusion of analyses of the variations and with an indication of their significance (stage 3).

The Present State of Application

An examination of the present application of control methods to management requires discussion of four areas:

1. The scope of the information included in the control system.
2. The nature and method of developing the standards, target states, or objectives.
3. The nature and implication for action of the variations disclosed by control system and feedback to the controller for action.
4. The nature and method of corrective action information to be provided by the feed forward principle of control.

Although the scope of managerial control systems varies, the following list of performance areas and information indicators suggested by Stokes for a retail supply organization will provide a general idea of the present scope of managerial control.[20] The pertinent key performance areas and indicators for managerial control are:

1. Financial Condition
   Key Indicators
   a. Ratio of gross sales to net margin.
   b. Ratio of operating expense to gross sales.
   c. Ratio of current assets to current liabilities.
   d. Cash position compared with standard.
   e. Capital expenditures compared with budget.
   f. Days credit outstanding compared with budget.
   g. Total book inventory compared with actual count.
   h. Ratio of overtime hours to straight time.
   i. Receipts from routes per day.
   j. Processing costs per unit.
   k. Delivery costs compared with standard.
2. Operations
   Key Indicators: Here there is an advantage in grouping the key indicators as follows:
   Purchasing and Procurement
   a. Cost of sales to total sales.
   b. Percentage of products for resale.
   c. Quantities ordered from mills and processing plants, in dollars.
   d. Number of acres contracted.
   e. Purchases vs. requirements.
   Manufacturing and Processing
   a. Total products processed by classification: feed-seed-fertilizer—petroleum-grain, and so on.
   Sales
   a. Budgeted sales vs. quotes.
   b. Volume figures by product.
   c. Sales targets vs. results.
   d. Dollars allocated to advertising of point-of-sale merchandise/total advertising budget.
   Distribution
   a. Percentage of farm to market.
   b. Percentage of market served.
   c. Customer acceptance of products or services.
3. Employee Relations
   a. Percentage of turnover.
   b. Employee performance compared with job standards.
   c. Ratio of employees available for promotions to total employees.
   d. Ratio of hours spent in training and development to total hours on job.
   e. Accident frequency and severity percentages or days lost.
   f. Employee attitudes toward company compared with atti-

[20] P. M. Stokes, *A Total Systems Approach to Management Control* (New York: American Management Association, 1968), pp. 149–151.

tudes of employees in other companies.

4. Productivity
   a. Ratio of total product purchased to product sold.
   b. Production units compared with man-hours.
   c. Units produced per equipment unit.
   d. Maintenance cost per mile.
   e. Units delivered per mile, per man, per truck, per customer.
   f. Ratio of equipment operating time to down time.
5. Market Position
   a. Percentage of total market served.
   b. Percentage of total market desired compared with market served.
   c. Net increases or decreases compared with total customers or units.
   d. Type of customer desired compared with those available.
   e. Sales, advertising, promotion dollars compared with market increase desired.
   f. Percentage of market penetration.
   g. Discounts compared with regular prices.
6. Public Relations
   a. Attitudes of inspectors and other public servants toward the organization compared with opposition of others.
   b. Respect of key citizens for the organization compared with opposition of others.
   c. Attitudes of civic and public organizations toward company compared with what is desired.
   d. Image of the organization in community compared with image deserved.
   e. Leadership in civic, community, social, religious, educational institutions or other projects compared with nonparticipation.
   f. Degree of legal support when needed (laws, restrictions, ordinances, and so on).
7. Customer Relations
   a. Number and type of communication per customer.
   b. Numbers and types of decisions referred to customers compared with numbers and types of decisions made.
   c. Awareness of customers regarding key operating problems.
   d. Degree of customer identification with business.
   e. Degree of customer support for management decisions.
   f. Teamwork compared with member ownership.
   g. Attitudes of customers compared with attitudes of operating management.
8. Service Leadership
   a. Types and kinds of complaints per customer area, and so on.
   b. Frequency of service per day, per week, or deliveries per customer.
   c. Services offered to customers compared with possible services.
   d. Special deliveries compared with regular deliveries.
   e. Ratio of adjustments to product sold.
   f. Special discounts compared with special groups.

The implication is that a significant part of management's perception of activity responsibility has been assumed by managerial control techniques.

The present state of applications of control in the development of standards and objective for the organization or process is reflected in the literature on planning. Planning represents a control technique in that it uses the assumption that management seeks to minimize or equate the desired future state of affairs (goals) and the otherwise expected future state of affairs (expectations) of the organization. When expected future state and desired future state differ, planning is the control technique used to reduce or eliminate the difference. Planning provides in advance for coordinating the activities of all parts of the organization and for the initial feed forward of information to motivate action. Plans may be in the form of performance programs and assume the status of a standard for repetitive operation or in the form of a project plan for a "one-shot" activity, and assume the status of an outcome objective.

Techniques used in planning include everything from abstract mathematical models, through simulation computer programs, to simple trend extrapolation. All require rational precise analysis, unlike planning in the past wherein the managerial objective was to make a profit, and planning was sort of an opportunistic "adjustment to the immediate situation" judgmental process. The advent of formal planning procedures and techniques not only moved it to the managerial control area but it also provided a means for considerable improvement in the planning process. The extent to which current planning techniques reflect the terminology and concepts of control theory is revealed in the following description of the planning procedures for a business entity.

> The specification of a given quantitative plan consists of placing values on its variables or establishing its functional form. Independence obviously does not exist among all of the variables and relationships that could be used to describe a plan. The choice of the decisions that are treated as independent is essentially arbitrary, and depends to a considerable extent on computational efficiency and how the planner chooses to express his decisions. Those decisions used for this purpose will be called *decision* variables. All other variables used to describe a plan will be termed *outcome* variables. The value of an outcome is implied by the choice of the decision variable.
>
> These notions can be illustrated by an inventory control example. A given inventory plan may be described by such variables as the aggregate inventory investment, the planned stockout probability, and the imputed interest rate on funds invested in inventory. Once an algorithm has been specified for determining inventory decisions (constituting a higher level plan), the stockout probability and imputed interest rate can be treated as decision variables. The resulting aggregate inventory investment represents an outcome variable.[21]

The feedback reports conventionally used to disclose variations from plans vary widely in form. Generalizing the conventional wisdom, there appear to be at least the following five guidelines for feedback management control reports.

1. Feedback reports should reveal both accomplishment and responsibility.
2. Feedback reports should be rendered promptly at the end of regular periods or at any time variation exceeds a specified limit.
3. Feedback reports should reveal trends and relationships to trends of associated variables.
4. Feedback reports should reveal variation from standards (objectives), preferably supported by a probability measure that the variation is or is not normal or due to random fluctuations.

[21] J. C. Emery, *Organization Planning and Control Systems* (London: The Macmillan Co., 1969), pp. 110–111.

5. Feedback reports should be in standardized format whenever possible to facilitate communications.

But the foregoing conventional wisdom merely explains current thinking about the nature of management information control systems. In fact, the cybernetic control systems utilizing computing are expanding rapidly, particularly in production processes, in routine clerical processes, and in the repetitive operating decision process as exemplified by inventory control systems, and considerable research is being directed toward more inclusive management information systems.

As to the nature of corrective action information provided by the feed forward process of control, the present state of application is not well developed. Human analysis and decisions still dominate this process. Continuously the effort is toward including automatic feed forward information in the central system.

The Future Applications

Future applications of controls to management appear to be in the social area. National data bases of information are being established on the social condition of the nation and the ecological systems of the world. Complex and extensive computer-based mathematical models of large segments of society are now underway. These undoubtedly will be used by government and the public to control uncoordinated actions of individual organizations. Pollution elimination of all types, crime reduction, educational improvement, and ecological improvement of the planet Earth are the next areas to be subject to control.

As the applications of control increase, the issue of freedom versus control will face mankind. Whatever may be man's current view of the great value of individual freedom, the emerging problems of society suggest that more control will be required. As Skinner assures us, the science of behavior has developed a substantial technology of control by which we are subject to explicit and implicit "reinforcers" in the form of reward for "good" social conduct and punishment for socially "bad" conduct.[22] But the social control mechanisms applied to date have failed to produce a contented and well-ordered society. With both the need for more control and scientific means of control available, the implication is that man must be induced to prefer controls that will enable him to adjust nature and himself more completely to his purposes.

BIBLIOGRAPHY

ANTHONY, R. N., *Planning and Control Systems: A Framework for Analysis* (Boston: Harvard University, Graduate School of Business, 1965).

BEER, STAFFORD, *Decision and Control* (New York: John Wiley & Sons, 1966).

[22] B. F. Skinner, *Beyond Freedom and Dignity* (New York: Alfred A. Knopf, 1971).

BELLMAN, R. E., *Introduction to the Mathematical Theory of Control Processes* (New York: Academic Press, 1967).

BONINI, C. P., R. K. JAEDICKE, AND H. M. WAGNER (Eds.), *Management Controls* (New York: McGraw-Hill Book Co., Inc., 1964). Proceeding of a seminar of forty eminent scholars on basic research directions in management controls.

CHARNES, A., AND A. C. STEDRY, "Search Theoretical Models of Organization Control by Budgeted Multiple Goals," *Management Science* (January, 1966), pp. 457–482.

CHORAFOS, D. N., *Control Systems Functions and Programming Approaches* (New York: Academic Press, 1966).

DORF, R. C., *Time-domain Analysis and Design of Control Systems* (Reading, Massachusetts: Addison-Wesley, 1965).

EMERY, JAMES C., *Organizational Planning and Control Systems* (London: The Macmillan Co., 1969).

EVANS, C. R., AND A. D. J. ROBERTSON (Eds.), *Cybernetics* (Baltimore: University Park Press, 1968).

FORRESTER, J. W., *Industrial Dynamics* (New York: John Wiley & Sons, 1961). A methodology for designing organizational policy by viewing the organization as a control system.

HODGE, B., AND R. N. HODGSON, *Management and the Computer in Information and Control Systems* (New York: McGraw-Hill Book Co., Inc., 1969).

LEE, E. B., AND L. MARKUS, *Foundations of Optimal Control Theory* (New York: John Wiley & Sons, 1967). A comprehensive mathematical examination of optimal control.

LIKERT, R. L., *The Human Organization: Its Management and Value* (New York: McGraw-Hill Book Co., Inc., 1967).

LITTERER, J. A. (Ed.), *Organizations: Systems, Control, and Adaptation*, Vol. II, 2nd ed. (New York: John Wiley &Sons, 1969).

MUFTI, I. H., *Computational Methods in Optimal Control Problems* (New York: Springer-Verlag, 1970).

NEUSTADT, L. W., "Minimum Effort Control Systems," *SIAM Journal of Control*, Vol. I (1962), pp. 16–31. An examination of highly general cost functionals.

PAIEWONSKY, B., "Optimal Control: A Review of Theory and Practice." *AIAA Journal*, Vol. 3 (1965), pp. 1985–2006. A survey of research efforts to apply optimal control theory to practical problems.

RAMSTRON, D., *The Efficiency of Control Strategies* (Stockholm: Almquist and Wiksell, 1967).

SKINNER, B. F., *Beyond Freedom and Dignity* (New York: Alfred A. Knopf, 1971).

STEDRY, A. C., *Budget Control and Cost Behavior* (Englewood Cliffs, N.J.: Prentice-Hall, Inc., 1960).

STOKES, P. M., *A Total Systems Approach to Management Control* (New York: American Management Association, 1968).

STRAUSS, A., *An Introduction to Optimal Control Theory* (New York: Springer-Verlag, 1968). An introduction to the problems and results of control theory with illustrations of applications.

STRONG, E. P., AND R. D. SMITH, *Management Control Models* (New York: Holt, Rinehart and Winston, 1968).

TANNENBAUM, A. S. (Ed.), *Control in Organizations* (New York: McGraw-Hill Book Co., Inc., 1968).

WATKINS, B. O., *Introduction to Control Systems* (New York: The Macmillan Co., 1969).

WEINER, N., *The Human Use of Human Beings* (Boston: Houghton Mifflin, 1950).

WILLIAMSON, O. E., *Corporate Control and Business Behavior* (Englewood Cliffs, N.J.: Prentice-Hall, Inc., 1970).

ZANNETOS, Z. S., "Some Thoughts on Internal Control Systems of the Firm," *Accounting Review* (October, 1964), pp. 860–868.

Integrating the Hierarchies of Control

J. Leslie Livingstone

Arthur Young Professor of Accounting
College of Administrative Science
Ohio State University

INTRODUCTION

The subject of managerial control is vast, difficult, and multifaceted. Therefore, my strongest reaction to Norton Bedford's paper is one of admiration at so thorough, clear, and comprehensive a piece of work. The targets left exposed for his critics to shoot at appear both small in size and few in number. Under these circumstances, it seems unrewarding for all concerned to quibble on minor points and small details. Instead, my approach will be to attempt to build on his structure and to try to complement rather than to contradict it.

This will be done in two main ways. First, given the complexity of the topic, I will introduce some simplifying frameworks to emphasize a few major concepts that I believe to be of dominant importance. This is not to say that I will put in a great deal that Bedford left out, but rather that I wish to suggest alternative arrangements of the ways in which some things were presented. Second, since Bedford deals slightly more, perhaps, with the engineering-type mathematical control theory approach than with the more exclusively human approach, I will try to complement this orientation by putting my emphasis on the human organizational behavior factors.

LEVELS OF HIERARCHIES OF CONTROL

Bedford lists three descriptive levels of managerial control in his paper. It seems to me convenient, although quite arbitrary, to consider the exercise of managerial control at four different levels, each of a progressively smaller area of scope. These are:

1. *"External" to the organization.* Strictly speaking, few if any organizations are sealed off from their environments. By "external control" we recognize the organization as a coalition of "insiders" and "outsiders." As Cyert and March point out, in a business organization the coalition may include managers, labor, stockholders, creditors, customers, suppliers, government agencies, etc. In a voluntary charitable organiza-

tion, for instance, there may be paid professional workers, volunteers, donors, clients, and so on.[1]

These participants, usually with disparate demands, changing foci of attention, and fluctuating resources, influence the goals of the organization through a series of constraints evolved by means of bargaining, compromises, and environmental pressures. Such arrangements change over time in response to shifts of circumstances, but always they exist in some form or other. The continuous negotiation of coalition members' inducements and contributions set the stage for, and impose bounds on, managerial control in the organization. Therefore, no manager is a free agent—he may exercise a degree of control, but he is in turn subject to the control of others.

2. *Systems Control.* This is the set of internal procedures that are usually the most visible instruments of control within the organization. Most common are budgets, sales quotas, cost standards, time sheets, purchase orders, stores requisitions, and the like.

3. *Social Control.* Often informal in nature, social control may be extremely powerful. Examples are "group norms" for quantity and quality of output, or for helping or sharing in work. Deviation from lesser group norms, or slight or infrequent departures, may evoke nothing more than kidding. However, failure to conform to important norms or significantly large or frequent infractions are likely to result in social ostracism, hostility, and other sanctions that can become unbearable to the transgressor. Rewards for conformity are usually group acceptance, approval, and perhaps a leadership role.

4. *Self-Control.* The above forms of control are all mediated externally to the individual. Self-control differs in being intrinsically motivated, so that individuals act out of personal commitment, rather than extrinsic inducements. The control comes from individual aspirations, expectations, satisfaction, frustration, self-mastery, and so on.

Table 13 shows the three latter kinds of control compared in several respects. Clearly, the various types of control overlap, and also they may act to reinforce or to conflict with one another. For instance, if individual workers are offered an incentive for increased production, but there are strong group norms to restrict output to a "reasonable day's work," then the incentive plan is likely to have a reduced impact. On the other hand, if all the types of control can be lined up congruently, then their combined impetus would be extremely powerful.

THE THERMOSTAT MODEL OF CONTROL

A control system, involving all the preceding types of control, may also be regarded—as Bedford does—as a sequence of steps that are like the operation of the thermostat of a furnace. Bedford refers to a similar communication theory of control that is somewhat broader than the thermostat model. However, I prefer the precision of the thermostat model, because it is more operational. The usefulness of this viewpoint is to expose the constituent elements, or building blocks, of a control system for closer examination and to reveal some of the advantages and disadvantages of using different types of building blocks in putting together a system of control. In describing this approach, we will draw heavily on the work of Lawler.[2]

The thermostat model usually consists of (1) a *sensor* that measures room temperature, (2) an adjustable *standard* for setting the desired room temperature, (3) a *discriminator* to com-

[1]Richard M. Cyert and James G. March. *A Behavioral Theory of the Firm* (Englewood Cliffs, N.J.: Prentice-Hall, Inc., 1963), p. 27.

[2]Edward E. Lawler, III, Control Systems in Organizations. Unpublished manuscript, Yale University, 1971.

TABLE 13. TYPES OF CONTROL IN ORGANIZATIONS

Controls Administered By:	*Direction for Controls Deriving From:*	*Behavioral and Performance Measures:*	*Signal for Corrective Action*	*Reinforcements or Rewards for Compliance:*	*Sanctions or Punishments for Noncompliance*
Organization	Organizational plans, strategies, responses to competitive demands	Budgets, standard costs, sales targets	Variance	Management commendation ↓ Monetary incentives, promotions	Request for explanation ↓ Dismissal
Informal group	Mutual commitments, group ideals	Group norms	Deviance	Peer-approval, membership, leadership	Kidding, ↓ Ostracism, hostility
Individual	Individual goals, aspirations	Self-expectations, intermediate targets	Perceived impending failure, missed targets	Satisfaction of "being in control" ↓ Elation	Sense of disappointment ↓ Feeling of failure

From Gene W. Dalton, "Motivation and Control in Organizations" in Gene W. Dalton, and Paul R. Lawrence (Eds.), *Motivation and Control in Organizations* (Homewood, Illinois: Richard D. Irwin and The Dorsey Press, 1971), p. 15.

pare the sensed temperature with the standard, (4) a *regulator* that responds to the discriminator by increasing or decreasing the heat flow, (5) a *communication* network that wires together components of the system, (6) the *activity* itself, which in this case is the furnace, and (7) *energy* source to power the activity.

Although it is interesting and perhaps instructive to make the thermostat analogy to managerial control systems in organizations, its real value lies in raising questions like the following:

1. What does the *sensor* actually measure? Are many, few, or only one thing measured? Are there clear indicators of performance, or must subjective estimates be used? Are there pressures and opportunities for distorting the data?
2. How are the *standards* set? Are they seen by employers as reasonable? Were they established unilaterally, or through a process of participation?
3. Who acts as the *discriminator*? Is it the person's supervisor, a staff employee, the person himself, or an outsider? What is the nature of the feedback he receives? How prompt is it?
4. Who receives the *information* and how is it used? Is it a basis for rewards and penalties? Is there temptation to want to look good in terms of the measures? Is performance review based mainly on short-run or on longer-term results? Is risk taking encouraged or not?
5. What is the nature of the *activity* being controlled? Is it relatively routine or is it highly variable? Has it been stable over time or is it changing rapidly? Is it independent or is its functioning tied in with that of other activities? Does it require high skill?
6. What are the *people* like? Is there rigid bureaucratic style behavior? Is there alienation and resistance to control? Does there seem to be highly authoritarian or more democratic leadership?

Questions of this type are much easier to pose than to answer. More difficult yet is to use the answers effectively in designing good control systems. Clearly, however, this indicates the way in which we ought to design managerial controls, and if we are not yet fully able to put everything together, at least we know the direction in which to strive for improvement. There needs to be a workable fit between the types of control (systems, social, etc.) on the one hand, and the parts of the control process (sensor, discriminator, etc.) on the other hand. In the next section we offer a modest approach toward an integrative framework for relating the many complex factors involved in constructing and operating effective managerial control systems.

AN INTEGRATIVE FRAMEWORK

Related to Bedford's discussion of applications of control methods to management, one might usefully add the following. A helpful distinction has been made between two broad categories of control. Simon[3] has established the categories of "programmed" vs. "non-programmed" decisions. A similar distinction is that of Anthony's "operational control" vs. "management control."[4] In both cases, the first type of control is applicable to activities in which it is practicable to measure process inputs and outputs and the relationship between them. This requires well-standardized, repetitive, mechanistic operations. Control becomes a matter of specifying and enforcing rules or programmed routines. The second type of control involves less precise activities

[3]Herbert A. Simon, *The New Science of Management Decision*. (New York: Harper and Bros., 1960), p. 49.

[4]Robert N. Anthony, *Planning and Control Systems: A Framework for Analysis*. (Boston, Massachusetts: Harvard University, Division of Research, Graduate School of Business Administration, 1965).

in which input-output relations are difficult to measure, or where there may be no output measures at all: for example, the effectiveness of a basic research group, or a corporate legal department, or a hospital intensive care unit.

Thompson[5] makes the same input-output distinction, but refers to it as "beliefs about cause/effect relations." Usually, these beliefs range from the one extreme of complete knowledge (total certainty) to the other extreme of hardly any knowledge at all (near-complete uncertainty), with most situations occurring in between the extremes.

It is clear that *standards* are also an important aspect of control systems. Standards of performance may involve a single criterion (such as quantity sold) or multiple criteria (such as average sales price per unit, sales expense per order received, new accounts gained, etc.). Where multiple criteria exist, they may not be mutually consistent (e.g., quantity sold may increase, but price per unit may go down at the same time). Or different persons may attach different degrees of importance to different standards. Also, standards may vary from clear cut (who won the World Series this year?) to ambiguous (is Dr. A a better psychiatrist than Dr. B?).

Thompson relates the degree of ambiguity of standards to the level of beliefs about cause/effect relations. For simplicity, each factor is divided into only two categories (obviously, in reality there are many) in a diagram such as this:

		Beliefs About Cause/Effect Relations	
		Complete	*Incomplete*
Standards of Desirability	Crystalized	I	II
	Ambiguous	III	IV

In Cell I, we find Simon's "programmed" rules and Anthony's "operational control." The thermostat model in its most exact form can be applied, and the emphasis would be on accuracy of data, precision of computation, speed and correctness of communication, systems-type control, and authoritarian-style relations.

In Cell II, we are faced with the problem of knowing what we want but not being sure of what actions will achieve these results. In this case, the control system is perforce less mechanistic and rational, and more judgmental. We settle for satisfactory outcomes, not knowing if they are near to optimal or not. There is likely to be more use of staff "expertise" and judgment, and control is generally less close.

In Cell III, in which standards are ambiguous, there is pressure for compromise, especially if outcome preferences differ among persons and social control is likely to be importantly involved. Potential for conflict may be high, especially if multiple yardsticks of performance (often mutually incommensurable) are applied. Emphasis is likely to be placed on scoring well on those criteria that are most visible to those in power.

In Cell IV, in which the most uncertainty exists, attempts to measure outcomes tend to be resisted, and social reference groups are likely to be used for comparison. For instance, public relations or advertising departments may be judged within the organization by the recognition they receive from experts outside it, such as public relations or advertising associations. Also, there

[5]James D. Thompson, *Organizations in Action*. (New York: McGraw-Hill Book Co., Inc., 1967).

is pressure to base measures on activity or input efforts rather than outputs. Research groups may emphasize the number of experiments run, or scientific papers prepared, or the number of doctorates from prestige institutions held by their membership. Self-control may be of relatively great importance in this area.

We may conclude that there are serious errors to be made if, for example, control methods appropriate for Cell III were applied to a Cell I situation, and vice versa. Correspondingly, there is powerful synergy potentially available from perceptive diagnosis and matching of the key variables and control procedures. Successful managerial control appears to depend on effective co-alignment of the types of control, the elements of phases in the control process, the degrees of cause/effect relation and clarity-of-standard knowledge, and the selection of the control techniques appropriate to these many factors.

Managerial Control and Human Systems

T. R. Dyckman

Professor
Graduate School of Business
and Public Administration
Cornell University

INTRODUCTION

We shall begin by examining changes in the environment and what they portend for the area of managerial control. The contributions of engineering control theory are briefly considered next as a prelude to suggesting a more complex model of the managerial control process. The alternate and more complex model highlights the major difficulties in managerial control, particularly those introduced by consideration of the human aspects.

The remaining space is devoted to discussing some of the important issues encountered in implementing a managerial control system. This discussion includes both system construction and monitoring the system once it is operational.

THE NEED FOR CONTROL

There can be little doubt that the pace of technological progress will continue to accelerate in the future. Important factors in this trend include the new insights gained into problem solving through the application of analytical techniques, and the advances in computer technology that permit routine decisions to be resolved rapidly by computer facilities.[1]

One consequence of the increased

[1]For a more detailed development of the trends described here the reader is referred to R. F. Vandell, "Management Evolution in the Quantitative World," *Harvard Business Review* (January–February, 1970, pp. 83–92.

pace of technological progress will be the need for quicker decision-making. The importance of experience and judgment will reassert themselves. Decision makers will find it necessary to recognize patterns in their immediate environment and to react quickly to the subtleties in situations if they are to secure competitive advantages. Furthermore, the advantages attained in this way will be shorter-lived. Tactical and contingency planning will be of great importance in assuring the capability of immediate response to local changes. Managers will have to become experts in how their decisions affect the goals of the organization, and this effect will differ from one market or locality to another.

These trends suggest the necessity of shifting the decision-making responsibility organizationally downward. But the simultaneous erosion of the decision-making hierarchy will require improved managerial control methods if overall organizational goals are to be attained.

The thrust of the above argument is to suggest that decentralized decision-making will increase and with it the necessity to increase and improve on management control methods. The problem is a complex one, and perhaps this explains the attempts of writers to borrow heavily from the theory of control as it has developed in the engineering literature.

ENGINEERING CONTROL THEORY

The engineering control theory literature offers a simplified model of the management control process. Simplification is an essential art in the formulating and solving of problems. A successful simplification will extract a sufficiently rich problem description to permit either a satisfactory (if not optimal) solution or a better understanding of the problem without losing its essence.

If one is careful, useful insights can be obtained from engineering control theory as it relates to control in the managerial arena. Livingstone in his comments does, to my mind, an excellent job of extracting the usefulness contained in the simplistic thermostat model. He uses this model to suggest a series of questions that, when and if answered, will assist in problem understanding. The reader will note that these questions are largely people oriented. This is an essential point since the failure of the engineering model to incorporate the human factors is its major drawback for managerial purposes.[2]

AN ALTERNATIVE CONTROL MODEL

I would like to suggest a model of the decision-making process, and hence also of the control problem that highlights these human problems, since, to my mind, they are the more important, have been less discussed, and are more difficult to resolve. Furthermore, this model will indicate the need to consider the planning-decision-performance-control problem as one system rather than dealing with it in apparently unrelated pieces. Figure 45 suggests the important relationships.

First, notice that there are likely to be several individuals involved in the managerial control process. Among these are the final decision maker, the supplier of the information (also a decision maker in terms of the information processed and the selection of the information process), and one or more performance evaluators. Connecting these individuals are both formal and informal information networks. (The latter may, for simplicity here also be

[2]Livingstone is aware of this, as his introductory remarks indicate. Bedford, too, comments on this point but, in my opinion, gives it secondary importance in his paper.

represented by the connective arrows used to represent the formal flows). Moreover, these networks are subject to noise as the participants attempt to understand and respond to one another's real and perceived needs. The informal feedback networks further complicate an already complex information-transmission situation.

The traditional control model attempts to view the decision process such that the planning and performance-control aspects can be treated separately. Although the primary responsibility for these functions *may* be lodged in separate individuals or departments, the functions are inevitably intertwined in the total decision process. Although this complicates any analysis, it is essential to an understanding of the control function.[3]

Information feeds forward to the decision maker from several sources, including the information processor, the planning activity, and from the performance evaluator. This feed forward includes specifying those aspects of the decision process needed to establish which variables are appropriate for control. The formal and informal feedback networks will lead to evaluation and over time to alterations in the decision process required to respond to environmental changes.

These information flows will result in decisions concerning the important controllable variables to be monitored and their expected variability, estimates of the relevant uncontrollable variables and their values, as well as decisions concerning the form of the appropriate decision model, and the appropriate information to transmit. The process evolves through time and hence is heuristic by nature. Furthermore, the process is also permeated by uncertainty in terms of the state of knowledge of those concerned. The information transfer system both transmits and adds to this uncertainty.

CONTROL THROUGH SYSTEM MONITORING

The result is that simultaneous errors in the control-decision model spec-

[3]For a further discussion see J. S. Demski "Decision-Performance Control," *The Accounting Review* (October, 1969), pp. 669–679. Demski observes that "whether the additional complexities are worthwhile, in a *cost and value sense* (emphasis added), can only be addressed in an empirical setting." (*Op. cit.*, p. 669.)

FIGURE 45. Decision-Control Model[a]

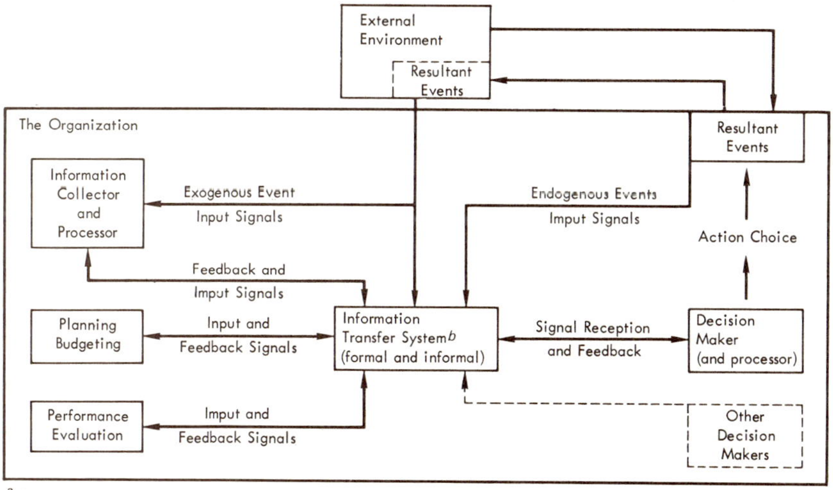

[a]This figure was suggested by Figure 1, page 627 of Feltham, G. A., and Demski, J. S., "The Use of Models in Information Analysis," The Accounting Review, October 1970, pp. 623–40.

[b]Informal feedback outside the established information transfer system will also occur. This informal system is not separated here both for representational simplicity and because it should be considered as part of the total information system.

ified, in the values of the included uncontrollable variables (the model parameters), and in implementing the decision will be the typical situation. As Demski concludes, "In this case variations between actual and expected results may be the result of some combination of output, measurement, performance, and decision error, as well as randomness in the physical process. This further complicates the detection (of the important variances) and significance assessment."[4]

The systems approach, recognizing the existence of several individuals in the total control process, highlights these interactions and suggests that, although complex, they must be understood before meaningful control procedures can be developed, let alone implemented. For example, one question raised is what variables should be monitored? If single variables are chosen, it is necessary to estimate the interaction effects. On the other hand, if more aggregate phenomena are selected, the proper corrective action, if any, may not be clearly indicated.

As an adjunct to this discussion, it is important to get the inevitable uncertainty concerning both the state of the process and the information observed on the process out in the open. It is not economically feasible, even if it were possible, "to eliminate all randomness" in the face of the heuristic and noisy aspects that characterize the control process. Rather, the uncertainty should, subject to cost-benefit considerations, be quantified and explicitly incorporated into any analysis. One could hypothesize that the individuals involved would respond positively to the recognition and explicit inclusion of the important uncertainties.[5] Fortunately, new techniques, particularly in the field of statistical decision theory, are improving our abilities to deal realistically with uncertainty in both new and conventional frameworks.[6]

CONTROL THROUGH IMPLEMENTATION AND EVALUATION

The notion of uncertainty pervades the planning and implementing of control procedures as well as the monitoring process. This severely complicates the task. For example, management offers incentives to employees to assist in motivating behavior. But the attractiveness of an incentive is a function of the perceived probability that the reward (or penalty) will follow the performance attained.

This carries over into setting performance standards. The hope is that such standards will contribute to motivating employee behavior. But whether the standards are successful depends in large part on the individual and the relationships between his job aspirations and those incorporated in the standards (or the payoffs related to his performance as measured by the standards). And even if the appropriate variables to be monitored and standards for an individual can be ascertained, setting the standard's level to attain the desired goal congruence remains a difficult task. The task is made increasingly complex by the fact that, first, similar (if not identical) standards are often necessary (from a practical operational standpoint) for several individuals even if these individuals typically have diverse needs, training, and drives; second, that such standards (including changes therein) must often serve over

[4] *Op. cit.*, p. 675.

[5] See D. H. Wood, "Improving Estimates that Involve Uncertainty," *Harvard Business Review* (July–August, 1966), pp. 91–98.

[6] See A. J. Duncan, "The Economic Design of X-Charts when there is a Multiplicity of Assignable Causes," *Journal of the American Statistical Association* (March, 1971), pp. 107–121; R. S. Kaplan, "Optimal Investigation Strategies with Imperfect Information," *Journal of Accounting Research* (Spring, 1969), pp. 32–43; R. M. Duvall, "Rules for Investigating Cost Variances," *Management Science* (June, 1967), pp. 631–641; and T. Ozan and T. Dyckman, "A Normative Model for Investigation Decisions Involving Multi-Origin Cost Variances," *Journal of Accounting Research* (Spring, 1971), pp. 88–115.

a rather substantial time period,[7] and, third, that the individual may be quite uncertain about how present and future rewards are related to his performance. The latter point is particularly relevant to performance systems incorporating several performance measures. Although it is often necessary to have several measures to properly reflect performance for even relatively simple job descriptions, ambiguity often exists concerning the importance given to the various measures by the evaluator. Hence, if one such measure is perceived to be paramount, it will most likely receive undue emphasis in the behavior of those being evaluated. This has long been one of the problems in using rate-of-return measures in performance evaluation.

Participatory budgeting is one means by which managers hope to secure increased goal congruence and hence better performance and control. The hope is that participation in the planning process to establish goals, necessary sacrifices, and appropriate performance measures will result in an increased acceptance of the goals. But, as Argyris has suggested, meaningful participation may be difficult to achieve in practice. Individuals often feel that the process is a legitimizing one rather than a creative-participatory one.[8]

Use of an evaluation and reward system is still another means by which management hopes to motivate performance. The human element again distinguishes this control technique from those of purely engineering systems. Individuals can and will evaluate themselves, and differences between their evaluation and that of the organization represent potential areas of conflict.

Such differences can occur if changes over which the individual has no control are made but are not considered in measuring his performance. The same is true of deviations occasioned by the actions of others, which affect his own activity. Lack of understanding concerning the measures to be used in evaluation or how they are to be weighed contributes to the problem.

Management should be aware of the way in which performance reports are handled, including the communication of results, since these mechanisms can have serious consequences for the organization. Control procedures that unduly penalize unfavorable events (deviations) and fail to reward favorable ones adequately can lead to undesired behavior patterns.[9] One such pattern is the tendency to just reach stated goals. This tendency often combines with the strategy; if miss, miss big in order to improve the probability of reaching imposed goals in the future.

The tendency to unsymmetrically reward unfavorable (or loss) situations can create unwarranted conservatism in the decision-making behavior of lower-level management. At least one study has shown that managers tend to be more conservative in their decisions than top management would desire.[10] The control function probably contributes importantly to this phenomena.

> Control systems highlight a financial loss but fail to show the potential lost profit on ventures that the manager has avoided. As a result, he plays it safe, avoiding opportunities which have even minutely small probabilities of significant failures. And chances for big successes are usually passed up too, since they are usually

[7]The mere fact that most individuals in viewing their job have a more limited time-reference frame than higher-level management creates difficulties. This partly explains the short-run performance maximization approach taken by many individuals.

[8]C. Argyris, *The Impacts of Budgets on People* (New York: The Controllers Foundation, 1952).

[9]See J. S. Hammond, III, "Better Decisions with Preference Theory," *Harvard Business Review* (November–December, 1969), pp. 123–141.

[10]See R. O. Swalm, "Utility Theory-Insights Into Risk Taking," *Harvard Business Review* (November–December, 1966), pp. 123–138.

accompanied by chances for significant failures.[11]

This problem is compounded by the organization's communication network. Desirable opportunities may be screened out by lower-level management under control systems that highlight failures without proper rewards for outstanding success. Yet these projects may include many that management would wish to elect.[12]

CONCLUSIONS

The difficulties suggested here are not to be taken as fatal to the notion of managerial control by any means, but rather they are presented as a warning against simplistic application. In most applications it is the effect of the multiple and probabilistic interactions coupled with the vagaries of human behavior that create the difficult, the interesting, and the important issues for managerial control.

DISCUSSION QUESTIONS

1. What is the control concept? A control system?
2. Describe and discuss the relation of control to management.
3. Define and discuss the concept of entropy.
4. Differentiate among social control, managerial control, and automatic engineering control. Define each.
5. Describe some of the trends in the control area.
6. Enlarge on the following hypotheses: Behavioral emphasis; Total society; Alternative generalization; Systems concept; Common control problem.
7. What are the elements in a thermostat model of control, and how do these relate? Can this model be generalized to a wider management setting?
8. Describe control through implementation and evaluation.

[11]Hammond, *op. cit.*, p. 140.

[12]We do not claim to consider all means of affecting behavior in these comments. For example, the appeal of an individual's physical working environment can have a direct effect on his performance. Another case is provided by the constraints on internal decisions imposed by external reporting (the emphasis on the earnings per share figure, for example). Such considerations are beyond the main thrust of this discussion.

17

Motivation and Management

Lyman W. Porter

Dean and Professor
Graduate School of Administration
University of California, Irvine

Raymond E. Miles

Professor
School of Business Administration
University of California, Berkeley

Of all the problems that are faced by management, motivation must surely be ranked as one of the most intractable. For years, organizations—both business and non-business types—have attempted to find better ways of motivating employees, or at least better ways of understanding how they are motivated. Likewise, for several decades, social scientists, particularly psychologists, have been proposing theories on the subject and carrying out innumerable research studies relating to it. After all of this time and effort on the part of both scholars and practitioners, we still have at best only a hazy and far from firm grasp of motivation. In our opinion, there is no single theory relating to motivation that can be completely and unqualifiedly accepted as accounting for all the known facts, and there is no definite set of prescriptions that are unequivocally supported by research data.

The main reason that motivation has proven to be so intractable and has eluded the efforts (or, one might say, the motivation) of so many to fathom its arcane mysteries is that it is a complex phenomenon. Since it is, this means that oversimplified explanations of how motivation operates and underqualified prescriptions of how a manager should act with respect to it are almost doomed from the start. However, having said this we should hasten to add that we do think that a considerable amount has been learned about motivation by theorists and researchers, and that there are some rather definite implications for managerial practice that emerge from this knowledge. So, there are a number of important points that can be made about motivation in the work place, but unfortunately these are not always so simple or so clear cut as we all (researchers *and* managers) might wish.

In the remainder of this chapter we will first provide in some detail an overview of motivation theory and research that relates to the organizational situation. Then, in the latter half of the chapter we will consider some of the implications of this theory and research for management thought and action. In the final pages we will provide a few concluding comments that summarize our view of where things presently stand with respect to the topic of "motivation and management."

MOTIVATIONAL THEORY AND RESEARCH

Applications to Work Situations

When we are talking about "motivation" we are talking about what energizes a person's behavior, what directs it, and what maintains and sustains it. As we have already stressed, these constitute an exceedingly intricate set of issues. As with any complex subject, however, one must begin to bring some simplifying structure to it in order to deal with it—without at the same time doing too much damage to its richness and subtleties. Consequently, we find that considering motivation from a "systems" type of approach is helpful—not because it is a currently popular way of analyzing various organizational problems, but because it seems forced on us by the nature of the topic: The topic requires a systems view if one is to gain a basic understanding of it. By "systems approach" in this case, we do not mean some elaborate set of concepts. Instead we mean simply that our analysis will assume (1) that several sets of variables are important determinants of motivation and (2) that these sets of variables operate in interrelated ways in affecting motivation. It is this interrelatedness that we want to stress. Unless this perspective is taken, any analysis of motivation would appear to us to be inadequate.

The three major sets of variables that we regard as most critical for understanding how the motivational process operates in organizational settings are indicated in Table 14. Essentially, these involve: (1) what the individual *brings to* the work situation; namely, the characteristics of the individual: his interests, attitudes and needs. (Note: of course, a person also brings along skills and capabilities, but since this is a chapter on motivation and not on performance *per se,* we will concentrate only on those characteristics that are presumed to affect his motivation and not his ability to perform and stay in a work situation.); (2) what the individual *does* in the work situation: primarily this means what he does on his job—namely, the characteristics of the job; and (3) what *happens to* the individual in the work situation; namely, the characteristics of the immediate work environment—particularly the attitudes and actions of supervisors and peers—and the characteristics of the organization's actions.

Each of the major theoretical or conceptual approaches has focused on one or a combination of these sets of variables, and therefore these approaches and their associated research can be analyzed and reviewed from that standpoint. Thus, in the discussion that follows in this section, we will consider specific theories in relation to the particular class or classes of variables on which they seem to concentrate their attention.

TABLE 14. VARIABLES AFFECTING THE MOTIVATIONAL PROCESS IN ORGANIZATIONAL SETTINGS

I. Individual Characteristics	II. Job Characteristics (Examples):	III. Work Situation Characteristics
1. Interests 2. Attitudes (Examples): — Toward self — Toward job — Toward aspects of the work situation 3. Needs (Examples): — Security — Social — Achievement	— Types of intrinsic rewards — Degree of autonomy — Amount of direct performance feed-back — Degree of variety in tasks	1. Immediate Work Environment a. Peers b. Supervisor(s) 2. Organizational Actions a. Reward practices 1) System-wide rewards 2) Individual rewards b. Organizational climate

Note: These lists are not intended to be exhaustive; they are meant to indicate some of the more important variables influencing employee motivation.

CHARACTERISTICS OF THE INDIVIDUAL

What the Individual Brings to the Work Situation

It is difficult to understand motivation unless we begin by asking ourselves: What does the individual himself contribute to the motivational process? We all know people who give the appearance of being highly motivated (i.e., who expend a high level of well-directed and sustained energy) in almost every situation in which we encounter them. There are others we know who appear to be very unmotivated in almost any situation and who react hardly at all to anything that is done to or for them or that goes on around them in a situation. Clearly, observations and common sense tell us that individual differences account for some proportion of the variance in motivated behavior. The question is: What is the nature of these basic individual differences as they affect motivation?

In Table 14 we indicate that among other things, a person brings to a work situation interests, attitudes, and needs. By interests, we mean the directions of one's attention. It would seem clear that the nature of one's interests would affect the degree of impact of various kinds of incentives and of various actions of others on his motivation. The more one is attending to a particular category of things, presumably the more they can influence his behavior. Although interests have been the subject of a good deal of research by psychologists, most of this research has focused on vocational choice rather than on the role of interests in determining motivation in the work situation. Therefore, we will not elaborate further on this variable.

The basic attitudes or beliefs that a person brings to the work situation also seem clearly likely to affect his motivation. One type of belief that has recently received theoretical attention concerns attitudes toward self. The proposition has been put forth that "individuals will engage in and find satisfying those behavioral roles which will maximize their sense of cognitive balance or consistency" (Korman, 1970, p. 32). More specifically, this is a hypothesis that people in performance-type situations will attempt to behave or perform in a manner that is consistent with their self-image or self-evaluation. Thus, if they have a high regard for their own competence, it would be assumed that they would be motivated to perform in a competent manner. On the other hand, if their self-concept is low, such motivation would be greatly attenuated or reduced. In effect, this is a version of "self-fulfilling prophecies." The point that proponents of this view stress is that it is possible to influence and raise individuals' beliefs in their own competence and that by so doing their motivation to perform well will be enhanced. Some empirical support for this notion appears to exist (Korman, 1970; 1971), but there has not yet been enough substantial research addressed to the role of self-concepts in work motivation to support it strongly. However, this way of viewing motivation seems to have some important implications for managerial practice, and it generally is compatible with some of the other theoretical approaches we will discuss later.

The other current work motivation theory that emphasizes the key role of attitudes and beliefs is "expectancy/valence" (sometimes called "instrumentality/valence") theory. It focuses on beliefs concerning the relationship between behavior and outcomes (rewards), but since it also incorporates other sets of variables we will reserve consideration of it until the end of this section.

It would probably be fair to say that of the characteristics individuals bring to the work situation, those that have received the most attention have been needs or motives—the relatively non-transitory internal states that orient individuals toward certain objects or events in the environment. (Although purists might distinguish between the terms "need" and "motive," the general literature relating to work motivation tends to use them interchangeably and we will do likewise here.) Again, common observation shows us that some people seem particularly concerned about one particular class of objects or situations in the environment (e.g., those that signify security) much more than others. We then assume that a person must have a "need" for them that he is trying to fulfill. The controversies regarding this conceptual approach stem from trying to identify what these needs are and how they operate to motivate a person.

The attention given to needs has been so great in recent years that many people are familiar with the most famous of the theories dealing with them—namely, Maslow's need hierarchy theory (Maslow, 1954). Indeed, there are probably very few managers or diligent students of management in this country today who could not recite in rapid fire and in correct hierarchical order the five Maslow needs if given the magical cue words "Maslow's need hierarchy." The idea of a hierarchy of needs, especially the one proposed by Maslow, has obviously become part of current management lore.

Let us then look for a moment at the essence of the theory as a *motivational* theory. Part of the appealing nature of Maslow's theory is that it proposes a meaningful categorization of possible types of needs: physiological, safety, belongingness and social, esteem, and self-actualization. The list is short enough to remember, and it seems to cover enough ground (i.e., it encompasses most of the more specific needs that one might enumerate). Furthermore, the hierarchical ordering, based on the assumed prepotency of each need for individuals, seems reasonably logical and rational. Out of his clinical experience, Maslow developed the notion that individuals are motivated to try to satisfy the lowest unfulfilled need in the hierarchy. Thus, for example, if an individual seems to be able consistently to obtain physiological and safety fulfillment, but not any of the others, he will behave in a way that concentrates on opportunities to satisfy a need for belongingness. The other two higher-order needs will not motivate him as much because they are less prepotent. If an individual's social or belonging needs eventually are reasonably satisfied, then the theory suggests he will turn to the esteem area. On the other hand, if a lower-order need fulfillment opportunity—such as security—is threatened, he will return (at least temporarily) to that need level. We can see, then, that the heart of the theory rests both in specifying what needs individuals have and in ordering them in a clear-cut hierarchy. To understand a specific person's motivation, one "merely" determines where that person is with respect to needs already fulfilled.

There are many questions that can be raised about the Maslow theory as a theory: Are needs actually arranged in stable hierarchies? Does every individual have the same hierarchy? Can an individual simultaneously be trying to satisfy two needs at once? These are just examples, and the reader can probably think of others. But if we turn to the published research to try to determine the validity or soundness of the theory by answering these kinds of questions, we will be disappointed. Very little research has been carried out directly to *test* the theory (with a few exceptions, such as Hall & Nougaim, 1968). The primary reason for this has not been for lack of interest in testing it. Rather, it is because the theory is not stated in ways that make it easily testable and because the nature of the data that would be required to undertake a comprehensive test are not easily obtained. The validity of the theory, therefore, remains largely a matter of speculation. Nevertheless, the general idea that people have needs and that these needs probably differ in prepotency seems reasonable. It also seems reasonable that individuals will be motivated to engage in behavior that is designed to fulfill the most currently pressing need. It is when one goes beyond these general statements with respect to Maslow's theory that speculation far outruns available evidence.

An interesting recent alternative need theory has been proposed by Alderfer (1969). He collapses Maslow's five needs into three basic categories —existence, relatedness, and growth—but more important, he discards the notion of a strictly ordered hierarchy. Alderfer retains the general concept of a hierarchy but his theory does not assume that satisfaction of lower-level needs is a prerequisite to the emergence of attempts to satisfy higher needs. Likewise, the degree to which higher needs are frustrated is presumed to have an impact on the strength of lower needs. This revision of Maslow's approach is too new to have generated any sufficient amount of research, but it does propose some possibly promising refinements. At the same time, however, it also ends up being somewhat more complicated than Maslow's original theory.

A consideration of need approaches to motivation in work contexts would not be complete without reference to the work of McClelland (1961; 1965; 1971; McClelland and Winter, 1969) on the need for achievement (so called nAch). For McClelland, a motive is a "recurrent concern for a goal state" (1971, p. 13), and hence the "need for achievement" would refer to a recurrent or habitual predisposition to strive for achievement or success. From this perspective, it is a learned rather than an innate tendency and it is activated by appropriate cues in the environment.

There are two important aspects of McClelland's theorizing on nAch in terms of its implications for motivation in organizational settings: (1) the strength of this particular need is presumed to have a strong effect on how hard a person will attempt to do well in *task-type* situations; and (2) the strength of this need (as with others, such as power and affiliation) can be altered by "appropriate" training. McClelland has amassed a wide array of empirical data that bears on both points. He finds that individuals who score high on his measures (primarily obtained through responses to ambiguous stimuli in test situations) of the strength of nAch tend to prefer (a) to work on tasks of intermediate difficulty, (b) to take moderate risks, (c) to take personal responsibility for performance, and (d) to receive concrete feedback on performance. He also claims that such behavior has been influenced by, in effect, teaching people to change their desire for achievement, and that such teaching has had significant effects on actual accomplishment (McClelland, 1965; McClelland and Winter, 1969). Whether such training is really changing basic needs or, rather, an individual's perception of himself and his environment is probably open to question, but in any event it appears to have an impact on behavior. McClelland's work has not generated widespread and rigorous research on motivation (and thus his ideas have not been verified) in everyday work situations, probably because the methods of measuring it (i.e., scoring responses of subjects to Thematic Apperception Tests) are so cumbersome; but it is clearly relevant to management's role in the motivational process.

CHARACTERISTICS OF THE JOB

What the Individual Does in the Work Situation

The second major set of variables that appear to have a strong impact on the motivation of individuals are those having to do with the characteristics of jobs and the tasks that comprise them. Simply put, the question is: How does the nature of what a person does on his job influence his desire to perform well in that job?

The attention given to the role of job characteristics as a factor in employee motivation has greatly increased in the past 10 years or so. Primarily, this greater attention can be attributed to (1) increasing evidence (e.g., Walker & Guest, 1952; Davis, 1957; Blauner, 1964) of the problems caused by overly rationalized job designs that emphasize simple and routine work procedures, and (2) particularly, the appearance of Herzberg's so-called "two-factor theory" of work motivation (Herzberg, Mausner, & Snyderman, 1959; Herzberg, 1966) that emphasizes the distinction between job content and job context. Since this latter approach has been so instrumental in stimulating research on work motivation, it will be necessary to consider it first before commenting on some broader implications of job design.

Herzberg's two-factor theory is probably even better known among practicing managers than Maslow's need hierarchy theory. Perhaps this is because it appears so simple—one need hold in mind only two "factors"—and because it is so intuitively plausible. However, when examined closely it turns out to be neither so simple nor so plausible as one might think at first glance. Even with respect to something so elementary as terminology, for example, complexity starts to arise. As has recently been pointed out, "The two factors themselves are known by many names. One has been called the hygiene factor, the maintenance factor, the extrinsic factor, the dissatisfiers, and the job context factor. . . . The other has been called the motivator factor, the intrinsic factor, the satisfiers, and the job content factor. . . ." (Wolf, 1970).

The most critical issue with respect to the two-factor theory, however, is whether it is merely a theory of satisfaction (i.e., a theory of how people react), or whether it is also a theory of motivation (i.e., a theory about how they will perform in order to obtain satisfaction). Since most of the controversy and most of the research so far seems to have centered on the satisfaction implications, this may be an appropriate point of departure for considering the theory.

The idea of the two-factor theory originated from an empirical study by Herzberg and his colleagues in 1959 and from their earlier review of the research literature (Herzberg *et al.*, 1957). Based on these sources of information, they proposed that the primary causes of job satisfaction are related to intrinsic or content aspects of jobs, specifically: achievement, recognition, the work itself, responsibility, and advancement. Job dissatisfaction, on the other hand, was hypothesized to be caused by an entirely separate group of factors (hence, the term "two-factor" theory) that were associated with the context of the job—e.g., company policy, supervision, working conditions, and the like. As one can see, incidentally, even several of the so-called "content" factors—such as recognition and advancement—could to some degree be regarded as context as well as content (since "others" generally provide most of the recognition and make it possible for the person to be advanced).

Although the notion of two sets of factors, one relating to content and one relating to context, is easy to comprehend, there exists considerable vagueness concerning explicit and precise statements of the theory itself. As a recent article reviewing the theory has pointed out, there are "at least five distinct versions of the two-factor theory [that] have been stated or implied by various researchers" (King, 1970). More specifically, the weakest form of the theory goes something like this (these and other statements of the theory are from King, 1970): "All motivators [job content factors] combined contribute more to job satisfaction than to job dissatisfaction, and all hygienes [job context factors] combined contribute more to job dissatisfaction than to job satisfaction." A stronger version is: "Each motivator contributes more to job satisfaction than to job dissatisfaction, and each hygiene factor contributes more to job dissatisfaction than to job satisfaction." The strongest version, according to King, is "Only motivators determine job satisfaction, and only hygienes determine dissatisfaction."

The apparent imprecision of the two-factor theory obviously leads to disagreements concerning whether the research evidence supports or contradicts it. Several comprehensive reviews cover the studies conducted to date (House and Wigdor, 1967; Whitsett, and Winslow, 1967; King, 1970; Wolf, 1970), and the reader is referred to them for details—both of the individual studies and the disagreements over the interpretation of the evidence. Suffice it to say that the evidence is mixed and that many of the studies that claim to confirm the theory have been attacked on methodological grounds (particularly the use of self-report critical incidents to collect the data). Furthermore, the evidence also seems to point to the conclusion that job *content* factors are especially prominent in subjects' reports of highly satisfying experiences. (This is not to say that context factors are never mentioned as causes of satisfaction, or that content factors are not also fairly prominent as causes of dissatisfaction). To this extent, at least, Herzberg appears to be supported. This leaves us with the question: Do these content factors motivate, and if so, how?

For Herzberg and others, the answer is definite: They do motivate. Just *how* they motivate, however, has never been made completely clear by Herzberg, except to point out that many respondents report that they *feel* highly motivated to perform when they are highly satisfied and that they are highly satisfied when the content factors are definitely present in their jobs. This type of reasoning has led Herzberg in recent years to advocate the implementation of "job enrichment" as a means of increasing the motivation of employees. By job enrichment, Herzberg (1968) means "loading" jobs with the "motivators"—i.e., building into the design of jobs high amounts of responsibility, clear-cut opportunities for advancement, specific recognition for performance, and so forth. The assumption is that if jobs are redesigned in this way, performance will be increased because employees will "want" to do a good job. They will want to do a good job, according to Herzberg, because they have a chance to gain recognition, to experience growth, and so forth.

The evidence pertaining to the effectiveness of enriched or enlarged jobs for influencing satisfaction and performance is somewhat mixed. Certain case-study types of reports (reviewed in Lawler, 1969) indicate that the introduction of job enlargement in specific situations has typically resulted in increased quality of performance but not necessarily better quantity. Furthermore, other types of research data from employees on a wide variety of jobs indicate that certain categories of workers (e.g., those with small-town or rural backgrounds) preferred enriched types of jobs, whereas others had no such preferences (Turner and Lawrence, 1965; Blood and Hulin, 1967; Hulin and Blood, 1968). This latter type of evidence indicates that individual variables as well as job variables must be taken into account in order to predict the motivating effects of particular types of job design.

A recent major study by Hackman and Lawler (1971) tends to substantiate the point just made. They argue that if the content of jobs is to have an effect on employee motivation to perform, the jobs must: "(a) allow workers to feel personally responsible for an identifiable and meaningful portion of the work, (b) provide work outcomes which are intrinsically meaningful or otherwise experienced as worthwhile, and (c) provide feedback about performance effectiveness" (p. 263). They further contend—and here is the key feature of their reasoning—that the effects of such characteristics will occur only if individuals have needs that are appropriately tapped by these characteristics. In general, their data tend to support their conclusion that "individuals with strong desires for higher order need satisfaction respond much more positively to high level jobs [i.e., jobs with high levels of variety, autonomy, etc.] than do individuals who have weaker higher order needs" (p. 280). Or, in other words, enriched or enlarged jobs can be motivating for many, but not necessarily for all, employees.

Let us summarize our conclusions with respect to the function of job characteristics in motivation: The motivating effects of what individuals do on their jobs cannot be ascertained without also taking into account what the individual brings to the work situation in terms of his needs. No single type of job design is most appropriate for all individuals. On thc other hand, an overall evaluation of the evidence to date would appear to support the contention of Herzberg and others that far too often jobs, particularly at lower levels in organizations, are not enriched enough to be able to provide sufficient stimulus for most people to want to work hard at them. In effect, the average person is probably capable of doing much more meaningful work than most jobs allow him to do.

CHARACTERISTICS OF THE WORK SITUATION

What Happens to the Individual in the Work Situation

Characteristics of the Immediate Work Environment The two most important variables in the immediate context of the job appear to be (1) the peer group and (2) the supervisor. Let us look briefly at each of these variables in order.

Even since the time of the Hawthorne studies (Roethlisberger and Dickson, 1939), the peer group in the work situation has been recognized as a potentially powerful influence on an individual's motivation to perform at a certain level. Simultaneously, research in basic social psychology also demonstrated the impact of group norms and attitudes on the behavior of the individual. Thus, there seems little doubt that the immediate work group can affect behavior—and presumably motivation—and the question is one of how, and in what direction, these effects occur. It is not possible to review the detailed evidence here, but in the main it would seem to point to the conclusion that many individuals are motivated to gain the rewards that come from (are given by) peers (e.g., friendship, approval, etc.) and thus will behave in ways they think or perceive as being consistent with the norms or values of their group. Consequently, if the group's norms are positive with regard to high productivity, for example, this will be an added force on the individual in that direction—to the extent that he values the peer reactions. If the group norms are different—e.g., "a high producer is a rate buster"—then this will reduce the overall rewarding value of high production to the individual and will act as a restraining force on his desire to perform at that level. The peer group thus influences an individual's motivation by acting as a source of rewards, but the direction of this influence will depend on a whole host of variables that determine the norms and values of the group (e.g., past experiences of group members with various aspects of the work situation, the attitudes of the most dominant member, the external pressures on the group, and so forth).

The immediate supervisor represents the other major variable in the immediate context of the job that is likely to be a potent influence on the employee. Primarily, of course, this is because the supervisor controls or influences many of the possible desired outcomes—from recognition to bonuses—than an individual might be able to gain from performing well. Besides being a key source of rewards and punishments, the supervisor also plays a major role in structuring the work to be done and setting up the conditions (e.g., specifying performance targets) whereby an individual can obtain rewards in return for specific kinds of behavior. In this latter sense, he determines the nature of the "paths" that the subordinate can take to personal goal attainment.

Considerable theoretical and empirical work on leadership (e.g., Katz *et al.*, 1950; Fleishman *et al.*, 1955; Fiedler, 1967) suggests that the behavior of leaders can be classified into two distinct types: that which is task oriented (also variously referred to as "instrumental," "initiating structure," "production centered," etc.), and that which is person oriented ("expressive," "consideration," "people centered," etc.). There is some dispute over whether these represent the opposite ends of a single dimension or whether they stand for two separate dimensions; however, the weight of the evidence points toward the latter conclusion. This means that a supervisor can be high on both task and person orientations, or low on both, or high on one and low on the other. The major point of all of this for our purposes here, however, is that both types of leader behavior appear to be important in affecting the motivation of subordinates. To the extent that the supervisor is task oriented, he is likely to set goals for subordinate performance and to give attention to making explicit the connections between subordinate behavior and various outcomes (rewards and punishments); to the extent that he is person oriented, he is likely to attempt to provide as many rewarding situations as possible and in a manner that will be seen by subordinates as supportive. This powerful potential influence of the supervisor on employee motivation has always received attention in the literature —even the classic management literature—but several recent articles (Locke, 1970; Evans, 1970; House, 1971) have attempted to specify the nature of it more concretely and to link it directly to current motivational theory (especially expectancy/valence theory).

Characteristics of Organizational Actions In considering the possible kinds of actions that organizations can take that can affect employee motivation, it is important to distinguish between actions that result in "systemwide" rewards and those that provide rewards to individuals on specific groups (Katz, 1964; Katz and Kahn, 1966, Chapter 12). The former kinds of rewards (such as high salary levels, well-funded retirement plans, liberal vacations) are those that influence the individual's "motivation to participate" (March and Simon, 1958). That is, they have an effect on a person's desire to join and stay with an organization, but, because everyone receives the rewards for mere membership in the organization, they are unlikely to have an impact on performance motivation. For this type of impact, the organization will need to reward individuals differentially—i.e., to provide greater amounts of rewards to those that perform significantly better.

As Katz and Kahn (1966) point out, for system rewards to be effective in motivating people to join and stay with an organization, they must be seen as attractive relative to such rewards that could be gained elsewhere, and they must be seen as being fairly administered. If these conditions hold, the rewards will presumably have their desired effect on participation (non-turnover). But, as we mentioned, they cannot be expected to affect performance motivation because their receipt is not contingent on performance. Hence, this is why Herzberg and others regard salary, for example, as ordinarily not being motivating *per se.* Of course, to the extent that the *prospect* of a higher salary is seen by the employee as a possible consequence of good performance, then salary could be regarded as a motivational factor.

For individually administered organizational rewards, such as pay incentives and promotions, to be effective in motivation, they need to meet three primary conditions. They must (according to Katz and Kahn): (1) "be clearly perceived as large enough in amount to justify the additional effort required to obtain them"; (2) "be perceived as directly related to the required performance and follow directly on its accomplishment"; and (3) "be perceived as equitable by the majority of system members, many of whom will not receive them" (1968, p. 353). It is obvious that frequently these conditions are violated, and hence many organizationally administered individual reward plans, such as piece-work pay, often do not have their intended effects (Opsahl and Dunnette, 1966). (See also our further discussion of such plans later in this chapter.)

Particularly crucial in any attempts by organizations to provide individual extrinsic kinds of rewards is the necessity for the organization to measure individual performance differences accurately. Since this is often quite difficult to do on many jobs (e.g., service-type jobs that do not have clear-cut and tangible performance criteria), to say nothing of the remaining jobs, this is an added obstacle to the use of such rewards to motivate. What this means is that organizationally administered individual rewards are theoretically highly motivating, but in practice they are frequently difficult to utilize effectively.

One other aspect of the characteristics of actions of organizations, aside from their reward practices, deserves brief mention. This is the overall "climate" that the organization creates that surrounds the work that is carried out in it. The concept of climate has begun to receive some attention in recent years (Forehand and Gilmer, 1964; Litwin and Stringer, 1968) and has been defined as "the subjective nature or quality of the organizational environment," or in other words, "the perceived or experienced qualities of the total configural environment" (Litwin and Stringer, 1968, pp. 187 and 196). The emphasis here is on the *total* psychological "feel" that the person has about the organization. The concept especially emphasizes the typical or customary *modus operandi* within a given organization—its "personality," as it were. Descriptive dimensions of climate might include an organization's "perceived structure and constraints," "emphasis on rewards vs. punishment," "perceived performance standards," and so forth (Litwin and Stringer, 1968). Climate's importance for motivation is that it is assumed to arouse or stimulate particular motives in the individual. Since climate tends to be created by the steady drip-drip-drip of the myriad daily actions and practices that occur within organizations, it is not a variable that ordinarily can be altered easily and quickly. Yet the evidence seems to point to it's being a real phenomenon—in the sense that people believe that organizations do have climates or personalities—that can influence employee motivation. Hence, it probably deserves more attention than it has so far been accorded.

INTERACTIONS OF VARIABLES: THEORETICAL APPROACHES

In the final part of this section on motivation theory and research, we will consider two theoretical approaches that seem to cut across more than a single major class of variables (i.e., individual characteristics, job characteristics, and situational characteristics) in their analyses of motivation. One of these is equity theory. It will be reviewed only very briefly because most of the research related to it has not been conducted in organizational contexts. The other is expectancy/valence theory, and it will be examined in more detail both because it seems particularly appropriate to attempts to explain work motivation and because it offers a relatively comprehensive view of motivation that incorporates a wide range of variables.

Equity Theory

This is also often referred to as a theory of social comparison, and that appears to us to be its most pertinent feature for the work situation. The major proponent of equity theory has been Adams (1963; 1965), and most of the research on it has been generated by his particular version of it. (Similar ideas have been advanced by others, such as Jaques, 1961, but Adams' work has received the most research attention.) Basically, Adams argues that a person will perceive inequity when the ratio of his outcomes (e.g., pay) to inputs (e.g., effort) and the ratio of the comparison person's outcomes to inputs are unequal. The existence of such a feeling of inequity is assumed to produce tension and consequently behavior by the individual to reduce this tension. This behavior can take many forms, such as leaving the situation, cognitively distorting self or other's inputs or outcomes, changing one's own inputs or outcomes, changing the other's inputs or outcomes, or changing the comparison person. As can be appreciated, the variety of possible means of resolving inequity feelings, plus the difficulty of precisely specifying all the relevant inputs and outcomes and identifying the relevant comparison persons, leads to a number of theoretical complications. Hence, the research methodology that has been designed to test the theory has itself become rather complex. The results of such research have not been clear cut (for details, see reviews by Lawler, 1968; Pritchard, 1969; and Goodman and Friedman, 1971), but there appears to be some support for aspects of the theory.

Equity theory clearly involves consideration of the characteristics of the person—his attitudes towards his inputs and outcomes, his tolerance for feelings of inequity, and the like—and characteristics of organizational actions, especially in terms of reward practices. From a motivational standpoint, some of the major implications of equity have recently been summed up as follows: (1) it "offers a relatively simple model to explain and to predict an individual's feelings about various organizational rewards"; (2) "the delineation of the comparison model an individual uses in evaluating his input-outcome ratio should be relevant for organizational decision-makers involved in determining appropriate levels of rewards"; and (3) it directs attention to the possibility of "the interchangeability of rewards" (Goodman and Friedman, 1971, pp. 285–286). In sum, the theory appears to have relevance for motivation in organizational situations, but more field research will be needed to determine just how far it can go in providing useable guidelines for practice.

Expectancy/Valence Theory

This conceptual orientation to motivation goes under several names—e.g., "expectancy theory," "instrumentality theory," and "path-goal theory." Essentially, these are all labels for the same theory, and we will adopt the "expectancy/valence" terminology here simply to emphasize the key variables involved. As we hope to show, this theoretical approach seems especially useful because it encompasses the several major sets of variables—and their interactions—that we believe are critical for understanding motivation in the work situation.

Current expectancy/valence theory has its roots in the earlier writing of psychologists such as Tolman, Lewin, Peak and Atkinson. Basically, "these theorists focused on the *cognitive* capacities of organisms, their ability to 'think' and to have ideas about the connections between events—even if these events had not yet occurred. That is, emphasis was placed on individuals' capacities to *anticipate* future states of their interactions with their environment" (Porter, 1972).

Applications of an expectancy/valence approach to organizational situations have been proposed by a number of authors in recent years (e.g., Vroom, 1964; Porter and Lawler, 1968). As outlined by them, the basic elements of the theory as it relates to the work situation are three: an expectation of the individual concerning whether more effort will lead to better performance; expectations concerning whether better performance will result in a changing level of outcomes (positive or negative); and the value of, or preference for, various outcomes.

The theory postulates that these variables interact to determine effort or motivational force. The form of such interactions, from a theoretical and empirical standpoint, is a matter of some dispute (Mitchell and Biglan, 1971; Heneman and Schwab, 1973); however, most current versions of expectancy/valence theory hypothesize that the interactions are basically of a multiplicative rather than additive form. That is, if the strength of any of the three variables is near zero, there should be a very low motivation to perform. Or, to phrase this in more practical terms, if an individual is to be motivated to perform well, he must have a fairly strong effort-performance expectancy, have fairly strong performance-reward expectancies, and attach relatively high values to the outcomes available in his work situation. If there is a problem with any one of these variables, there will be a problem with motivation—according to the theory.

It should be stressed that what we have sketched so far is a theory of motivation, not a theory of performance. As a number of theorists have indicated, high levels of effort or motivation do not translate into high levels of performance on a one-to-one basis. Among other important factors that determine the relationship between effort (motivation) and performance are ability and the accuracy of role perceptions. So, although motivation and performance will be positively related in many situations, they are by no means perfectly correlated.

We should also stress that this theory of motivation is not a theory of job satisfaction. Satisfaction is presumably determined by reactions of the individual to various outcomes he receives, whereas motivation refers to what the individual attempts to do to gain positively valued outcomes. An expectancy/valence approach to motivation can, of course, be linked to considerations of the causes and effects of job satisfaction (e.g., as in the Porter and Lawler, 1968, model) but that is beyond the scope of the present chapter.

If an expectancy/valence model is adopted as a useful approach to analyzing work motivation, then we can see how, from a systems point of view, it ties together all the major sets of variables we have been considering in this chapter:

1. Individuals:
   (a) Have needs of varying strength that presumably determine the valence for specific outcomes available from performance.
   (b) Have perceptions of (1) effort-performance probabilities, and (2) performance-outcome probabilities.
2. Jobs:
   Can provide a major source of intrinsically valued rewards.
3. Work Situations (Immediate Job Surroundings, and Organizational Actions):
   (a) Can create performance-outcome relations.
   (b) Can clarify relationships between performance levels and specific outcomes (i.e., clarify path-goal connections).
   (c) Can provide appropriate extrinsic rewards.

Looked at in this manner, the expectancy/valence approach provides a meaningful framework for management to view its role in the motivational process. For example, individuals will bring to the work situation certain expectations about how likely it is that they can convert their effort into performance; such self-confidence is, however, not immutable and *can be* affected by how individuals are dealt with by supervisors and others in the work situation. Jobs *can be* a source of intrinsic rewards if they are designed in such a manner as to provide opportunities for individuals to feel a sense of achievement, accomplishment, and the like. Management has a role to play in this design process, if it chooses to do so. Likewise, strong relationships between performance and the provision of extrinsic rewards do not develop willy-nilly, and management has a number of options available by which it *can* strengthen (or weaken) such ties. It also has wide latitude in how clearly it sets forth such relationships so that they are perceived in the intended manner by lower-echelon employees. Many other examples could be provided, but the point seems clear: This way of conceptualizing the motivational process indicates that there are a *number of points* at which management can influence employee motivation.

Expectancy/valence theory is no panacea. Despite the recent appearance of some supporting evidence (e.g., Lawler and Porter, 1967; Hackman and Porter, 1968; Galbraith and Cummings, 1967; Goodman *et al.*, 1970), many of its details and nuances need to be worked out more precisely and accurately and tested in considerably more detail and with more methodological sophistication (Heneman and Schwab, 1973). Also, it does not explain all aspects of work behavior. In particular, it does not deal directly with either highly emotional behavior or what could be labeled as routine and habitual behavior. Thus, although it seems useful, its applicability should not be overgeneralized to all manner of specific work situations.

Throughout this first part of the chapter, we have been examining some of the more important motivational theories and the evidence related to them. We now turn to considering the larger organizational context and the relationship of this theory and research to the theory and practice of management.

THE ROLES OF MANAGERS IN THE MOTIVATIONAL PROCESS

Managers move quickly into the spotlight in almost any discussion of motivation in modern organizations. They achieve this prominence for at least two reasons. First, managers demand attention in their role as subjects of the motivational processes in their organization. Managers carry heavy responsibilities with regard to the care and allocation of organizational resources, and thus the extent to which they are motivated to perform their own assignments effectively and efficiently is crucial to the accomplishment of the organization's objectives. Second, managers are important in their role as manipulators of many of the factors that may affect the motivation of other members of the organization, particularly their own immediate subordinates. In the following pages of this section we will comment briefly on the motivation of managers, and then will discuss in greater detail the ways in which managerial behavior may affect the motivation of other organization members.

The Motivation of Managers

Only recently have behavioral scientists raised their research attention up from the shop floor and into the managerial hierarchy. Until the 1950's, most efforts to study attitudes and behaviors in organizations were focused on the operative level—the work team and its leader, the first-line supervisor. Increasingly over the past 2 decades, the emphasis has moved toward middle- and upper-level managers and their technical and professional counterparts, such as engineers, research scientists, and so forth. There are at least three reasons for this shift. First, research interest has moved upward simply to fill a rather obvious void—little was known about the needs or attitudes of managers and thus these were attractive targets for scientific curiosity. Second, by the mid-fifties we were increasingly becoming a white-collar society—operatives were decreasing as a percentage of our total labor force and various categories of service, office, and administrative personnel were rapidly growing, a trend that has and will continue. Thus, in purely quantitative terms it made sense to shift research attention from the blue-collar work team to the gray-flanneled desk set. Finally, and most important, it had become increasingly clear that research that focused on lower-level work teams and ignored managers was destined to produce a fragmented and frequently distorted picture of behavior in organizations. Work teams, as suggested earlier, operate within an overall climate that is largely determined by those above them in the hierarchy, and thus any prescriptions for meaningful changes at lower levels would have to take into account the attitudes and behaviors of middle and upper managers.

This upward shift in research attention has been sharp and dramatic —so much so, in fact, that many of the more recent concepts of employee motivation have emerged from studies of office and administrative personnel. This is helpful to the extent that managerial and professional personnel are becoming increasingly important as a proportion of our total work force, but also limiting in that attitudes and behaviors that are found in the executive suite may not be representative of those of lower-level organization members. A quick glance at some of the research results concerning the motivation of managers will illustrate this point.

Research on managers' attitudes suggests that by and large they appear most concerned with the amount of autonomy, challenge, and growth provided by their jobs and much less concerned about opportunities for socializing on the job or about job security (Porter, 1963). Similar results are common for engineers and scientists, many of whom claim that their jobs do not demand or even allow the full utilization of their talents and capabilities (Ritti, 1970). These findings appear to generally support the notion that factors inherent in the job itself can be of great importance to organization members. In general, the research on managers' attitudes related to motivation produces a much more consistent pattern of results in this regard than does research conducted among lower-level personnel. (For example, recall our earlier reference to the studies by Turner and Lawrence and by Blood and Hulin, which appeared to cast doubts on the value of intrinsic rewards for some rank-and-file members.)

This inter-level disparity in research results should not be terribly surprising, however. Managers as a group have a favored position relative to many organizational members, no matter which concepts of motivation one chooses to employ. That is, if attention is focused on monetary rewards, it is clear that opportunities for outstanding returns on effort investments are greater as one moves up the organizational ladder. Similarly, opportunities for recognition, promotion, professional growth and development, and so on, are clearly more abundant at the top of the organization than at the bottom. Moreover, the very fact of having achieved a managerial position is probably enhancing to one's self-concept and perhaps reinforcing to one's needs for further achievement. Finally, even if managers express the view that their jobs do not provide sufficient challenge and responsibility, it seems clear that they provide substantially more of these qualities than do the jobs of most lower-level members.

However, although the empirical evidence is incomplete, it is our view that many lower-level organization mémbers could hold attitudes toward themselves and their jobs that are quite similar to those held by the typical manager. Moreover, it seems unlikely that the differences that may exist between the motivational sets of lower-level members and managers can all be explained in terms of individual differences. Instead, it seems reasonable to assume that some sizable portion of managers' attitudes are the result of their favored circumstances. If these observations are accurate, and if, as it is generally assumed, managers are in fact more highly motivated than lower-level members, organizations would appear to have before them a fairly clear guideline for the enhancement of motivation among rank-and-file employees. *To the extent possible* (and obviously, many barriers exist) the organization should reproduce at the lower levels the job conditions and work situations that managers enjoy.

Whether or not an organization will attempt to follow this general prescription depends on numerous factors, not the least of which is the set of attitudes and beliefs that managers in that organization hold concerning how and why organization members behave and thus how they ought to be managed. These attitudes will help shape the role that managers play as manipulators of motivational forces—the subject to which we now turn.

Managers as Motivators

Over time, various descriptive and prescriptive models of managerial behavior have appeared. Central to each of these models, whether expressed or merely implied, is an approach to motivation. The late Douglas McGregor, in his widely influential description of alternative views of management, Theory *X* and Theory *Y*, clearly acknowledged the crucial role that motivational concepts play in managers' theories of management. Theory *X* managers, according to McGregor, hold the view that the "average human being has an inherent dislike of work and . . . must be coerced, controlled, directed, threatened with punishment . . . to put forth adequate effort toward the achievement of organizational objectives" (1960, pp. 33–34). Such a view obviously ignores the intrinsic rewards that may result from task accomplishment and focuses on extrinsic factors, particularly negative sanctions. McGregor contrasts this view of motivation with the motivational concepts central to Theory *Y*. Managers adhering to Theory *Y* tend to assume that "the expenditure of physical and mental effort in work is as natural as play or rest . . . [and that] commitment to objectives is a function of the rewards associated with their achievement . . . the satisfaction of ego and self-actualization needs can be direct products of effort directed toward organizational objectives." This view fits neatly into an expectancy/valence theory of motivation, with particular emphasis on intrinsic rewards.

Scientific Management and Human Relations Concepts of motivation are made only slightly less explicit in two other models of management —scientific management and human relations—theories that, to some extent at least, can be envisioned as falling somewhere between McGregor's *X* and *Y*. Scientific management, as espoused by Frederick W. Taylor (1911) and his followers, tended to argue that employees would perform effectively if well trained and well paid. That is, Taylor blamed industrial inefficiency on poor methods, poor equipment, and poorly designed reward systems. Scientific methods could be applied, he argued, to determine the "one best way" to perform any job and to construct incentive pay plans appropriate to any task. Taylor acknowledged that workers would have to be convinced of the scientific objectivity underlying both the design of work and the design of pay plans, but felt this would follow if management adhered rigorously to such standards. From a motivational standpoint, scientific management thus anticipated an expectancy-valence model with emphasis on individually apportioned extrinsic rewards, while acknowledging the crucial role of equity.

The human relations model, which emerged in the thirties and forties, focused attention on employees' social and esteem needs. As early as the 1920's (see Bendix, 1956), managers were beginning to argue that organizational policies of impersonality and close and punitive control were producing dysfunctional consequences. These arguments were bolstered by the publication of findings in the famous Hawthorne studies (Roethlisberger and Dickson, 1939), which seemed to indicate employee responsiveness to evidence of managerial concern for their well-being and the opportunity to voice their attitudes and concerns about the conditions of their work. The Hawthorne findings, as indicated earlier, also emphasized the important role played by the employee's peer group in determining his motivation to perform effectively. The motivational concepts implicit in the human relations model thus tended to emphasize situational factors—e.g., the nature of supervision and the overall organizational climate. Moreover, whether intended or not, the human relations model appears to suggest that employees expend effort (cooperate with management) *as the result of* fair and considerate treatment, not in *anticipation of* receiving such rewards. Thus the human relations model does not emphasize expectancy as such. Instead, it argues that cooperation will result from supportive, warm treatment, with resistance and conflict the likely consequence of failing to observe these leadership prescriptions. In effect, the human relations position seemed to be that satisfaction led to performance rather than resulting from the rewards that may follow from (or be inherent in) good performance.

Limited Views of the Motivational Process Reading back across these models of management, it seems clear that Theory *X*, scientific management, and the human relations model each emphasizes a somewhat narrow and probably incomplete view of the process of motivation in organizations. The Theory *X* type of approach is perhaps the most limiting in that it asks us to ignore all but the lowest levels of human needs (e.g., physiological and security) and all intrinsic rewards. Moreover, it implies that extrinsic rewards are granted automatically and have value only through the threat of their removal. On the other hand, this very limited view of the potential of the motivational process is perhaps not inappropriate to this management model in that Theory *X* carries minimal expectations concerning the amount and quality of effort that organization members can and will expend.

Scientific management anticipates high levels of performance as the result of efforts expended in the quest for monetary rewards. Nevertheless, it too is limited in that it considers only a few of the many possible human needs. That is, it appears to minimize all but the physiological and some esteem needs, ignoring the need for fulfillment through self-direction and self-control. With this limited view of human needs, scientific management logically limits the set of rewards available to management—i.e., job designs aimed at enhancing intrinsic satisfaction are sacrificed in the interest of work rationalization, and effort expenditure rests solely on the efficacy of the wage system.

The human relations model takes a different, but similarly limited, view of the motivational process. Physiological, security, social, and esteem needs are recognized, with emphasis on the last two, but reward possibilities are severely constrained. Monetary rewards are downgraded in importance, and support, approval, and the opportunity for involvement in routine decisions are emphasized and granted automatically as part of the organization's effort to humanize the work environment. As with Theory *X*, outstanding performance is not an expected motivational outcome in the human relations model, nor are there rewards designed to induce it. Rather, cooperation—the minimization of conflict and resistance—is the hoped-for consequence of fair and considerate treatment.

A More Complete View of Motivation Models of managerial attitudes and behavior, such as McGregor's Theory *Y*, Likert's System IV (1967), and the human resources model (Miles, 1965; Miles, Porter, and Craft, 1966) all tend to take a more complete view of motivational factors and the motivational process than do their earlier counterparts. As suggested in our previous quotation from McGregor, Theory *Y* managers anticipate that many organization members will gain intrinsic satisfaction from accomplishing organizational objectives that they have had a part in setting. Thus, central to these models is the harnessing of motivational forces through the process of integrating some portion of the individual's goals with those of the organization.

In fact, these models appear to assume that many organizational members are, in a sense, pre-motivated to perform well—that is, they "bring" their motivation with them to the work situation—and that management's prime task is to remove barriers that may divert or constrain their tendencies toward effort and commitment. Thus, enriched jobs, for example, are natural consequences of these models, not as means of inducing motivation, but as means of tapping members' capabilities. Stated more broadly, Theory *Y*, System IV, and human resources managers adopt leadership styles, approaches to job design, systems of communication and control, reward systems, and so forth, all for the primary purpose of utilizing employees' capacities to plan, direct, and evaluate their own behavior as a means of enhancing organizational effectiveness. Satisfaction, in these management approaches (as in expanded expectancy/valence motivational theories), is therefore regarded as a byproduct of performance rather than as simply a goal in itself.

Implicit in the Theory *Y*, System IV, human resources formulations is a recognition of a full set of human needs and the utilization of a *full* set of rewards contingent on high performance. However, although implicitly included, human needs for security and monetary rewards for accomplishments tend to receive relatively little attention in these theories of management. For this reason, these models, too, may present a partially fragmented and incomplete view of motivation.

The Crucial Role of Security In attempting to emphasize the reduced motivational value of threats and coercion, McGregor argued that most members of our society had moved beyond the point at which physiological and security needs dominated their life view. Nevertheless, although many organization members, through welfare legislation and employee organizations, are provided with a modicum of protection from both financial want and arbitrary treatment, a pervasive heritage of employment insecurity still exists in our society. Moreover, this heritage is periodically reinforced by recession layoffs, plant closings, and the general vagaries of a decentralized market system.

Many of the consequences of insecurity are dysfunctional to organization performance—e.g., restrictive work rules, risk avoidance, work stretching, and so on. Nevertheless, organizations, including some with policies advocating modern motivational concepts, frequently either fail to take into account the basic need for security, or perhaps purposely avoid policies or practices that might enhance its fulfillment. When this occurs, conflicting motivational forces may well be set in play. For example, an organization that undertakes a program of job enrichment without providing assurances against job loss may tap only a fraction of the potential motivational forces associated with the improved job design, since some members will likely view such changes as a threat to their jobs.

The interplay between the negative force of insecurity and the desire to achieve personal and/or organizational objectives is most dramatically illustrated in the not infrequent failure of dollar incentive plans. It will be recalled that these plans were central to the motivational schema of scientific management, and a number of apparent initial successes were recorded. Many organizations, however, in an attempt to minimize their total wage bill, installed complicated incentive plans that tended to result in diminishing rates of returns to employees by raising required output standards or lowering piece rates. Moreover, as productivity per employee increased, many organizations were unable or unwilling to increase sales through reduced prices. Their recourse was thus to produce set levels of output and reap the benefits of increased productivity by reducing the work force. The outcome of these tactics was predictable. Employees sought to retain earning levels by forcing management, through bargaining or subterfuge, to set loose standards, and by producing just enough to earn reasonable bonuses without drawing attention to the potential for substantially greater output. Similarly, employees in many organizations began to adhere to a "lump of labor" philosophy, a belief at least partially justified by the behavior of certain organizations. This philosophy held that there was a fixed amount of work to be done, and if employees accomplished this quickly in an effort to earn incentive bonuses, the work force would subsequently be reduced. This, too, led to output restrictions.

It appears crucial, then, that if wage or other specific incentive programs are to operate in ways that do in fact increase employee motivation, they must provide some form of employment security guarantee—as was the case in the widely cited Lincoln Electric Company (1961). Otherwise, the potential increases inherent in such incentive systems will be vitiated by employees' realistic concerns about possible negative consequences. In the terminology of expectancy/valence theory, incentive plans that are not accompanied by security guarantees will result in employees tending to believe that high performance will lead to undesirable outcomes. When this happens, motivation is reduced.

Constraints on Motivational Forces Although the more recent management theories appear to have incorporated more appropriate models of motivation, the process of drawing out and channeling effort remains complex enough to unravel the threads of most blanket prescriptions. Subtle individual and situational differences, combined with difficulties involved in specifying standards of performance (on many jobs) and measuring the effects of individual effort, place constraints on even the most enlightened attempts to tap the full range of motivational forces in modern organizations.

To illustrate this point, consider the case of the perennial "dead-ender" who seems to inhabit many organizations. This is a person who has been with the organization a number of years—and has served it faithfully—but who has "leveled off" in performance and who sees (probably correctly) little likelihood of further advancement. Typically, his performance is minimally adequate but far below the potential that might be demonstrated in the position that he occupies. Also, typically, most of his needs—financial, esteem, self fulfillment—have, from his view, been reasonably well met by this time in his life. Consequently, he is relatively content with his job situation and is not highly motivated toward further significant achievement.

The question for the organization is this: Does it accept this level of motivation and performance from the dead-ender, or does it try to increase it? If the latter, how? Separating the individual from the organization is always a possibility, but when an employee who has spent so long with an organization is precipitously dropped, it can have a devastating impact on the motivation of other employees (quite aside from any ethical considerations that might be involved in such an action). Transferring him to another position is also an option, but there is no guarantee he will perform differently in the new job. If he is kept on in his present job, offering increased incentives for improved performance is unlikely to be effective because the person already has reached an acceptable degree of need satisfaction with his present performance level. Even enriching his job is not likely to change his present self-satisfied amount of effort. This, then, is the kind of case that is understandable from a motivational point of view, but which represents a situation in which it is exceedingly difficult for any management approach—modern or otherwise—to bring about major improvement.

A different kind of motivational problem for organizations occurs with somewhat the opposite situation: individuals (e.g., many newly hired college graduates) who have strong drives toward achievement and accomplishment and hence expect a great deal from the organization in the way of stimulating jobs and work environments. The problem here is that such people may have desires for rewarding work opportunities that far exceed what the organization can reasonably be expected to provide. In other words, they are willing to expend considerable effort and demonstrate intense commitment in return for exciting jobs, rapid advancement, large dollar rewards, and the chance to utilize fully their training and education. But how many organizations can realistically make available these outcomes *even if* performance is exceptionally good? In effect, an organization may know what it needs to do to maintain this initial strong degree of motivation, but it is simply not able to implement a program that meets such extremely high expectations. Presumably, the solution lies somewhere in a combination of attempts to bring about more realistic expectations on the part of these employees and specific efforts by organizations to recognize and respond to the motivational opportunities through providing high levels of desired outcomes contingent on outstanding performance.

The point of these two examples, and others could be cited, is that there exist certain identifiable situations that are not readily amenable to any particular motivational prescription. This does not mean that solutions are not possible, but rather that they do not flow obviously from any current motivational or management theories. Acknowledging the complexity of some of these problems may be the first step toward adequately coping with them.

SOME CONCLUDING COMMENTS

Our discussion to this point would appear to suggest that improved approaches to motivation are contained within recent theories of management—approaches that seem, on the surface at least, capable of releasing sizable levels of energy and commitment within the modern organization. These approaches appear flexible enough to take into account a fairly wide range of individual and situational differences—they acknowledge the value of both intrinsic and extrinsic rewards, particularly intrinsic ones that flow directly from performing the job and extrinsic ones that are keyed to specific levels of individual and group performance. Even with this flexibility, however, certain individuals and circumstances are likely to prove unyielding. Some organizational members, as suggested earlier, bring with them or develop later attitudes of extreme alienation or apathy and thus are unlikely to be aroused by *any* motivational efforts. Moreover, certain types of technologies appear highly resistant to most forms of job enrichment or individually based incentive plans. In our view, however, this set of motivationally resistant individuals and situations is small relative to our total work force and organizational environments.

Nevertheless, although the more forward-looking management theories contain motivational models that are probably adaptable to a large segment of the work force and to a variety of work situations, many of the implications of these models have yet to be widely implemented. Two reasons probably underlie organizational resistance or managerial indifference to these implications: First of all, many managers, research indicates (Miles, Porter, and Craft, 1960), tend to hold attitudes that are closer to those of the human relations model than to those expressed in the Theory *Y*, System IV, or human resources model. They thus seem likely to view the motivation of subordinates primarily in terms of cooperation received in return for concerned and considerate treatment.

The second, and closely related, reason for organizational failure to implement potentially rich motivational models is that many organizations neither desire nor are equipped to handle high levels of motivation. Of course, they would like to have highly cooperative employees, anxious to produce set quantities of goods and services of satisfactory quality. However, with many manufacturing organizations operating below capacity, unlimited output is probably not a widely followed objective. Thus, short of organizational diversification, employees in these circumstances are faced with fixed quantities of work to be done, with increased productivity being achieved only by work force reductions. Service industries and governmental agencies, the rapidly growing segments of our economy, however, do not face the same constraints, and there is some indication of growing implementation of more sophisticated models in these settings. Even here, however, many organizations appear, perhaps appropriately, to bc rather reluctant to introduce new approaches. It may well be that motivation is difficult to achieve in limited amounts. That is, it may be difficult to obtain "just a little bit of increased energy and commitment"—it may be that it is necessary either to seek and be prepared to utilize high levels of effort, or else to accept minimal outputs.

In sum, it seems clear that we know for sure only a fraction of what we need to know about motivation in organizations. At the same time, it also seems likely that we know considerably more about motivation than we are presently using.

BIBLIOGRAPHY

ADAMS, J. S., "Inequity in Social Exchange," in L. Berkowitz (Ed.), *Advances in Experimental Social Psychology*, Vol. 2 (New York: Academic Press, 1965), pp. 267–299.

ADAMS, J. S., "Toward an Understanding of Inequity," *Journal of Abnormal and Social Psychology*, Vol. 67 (1963), pp. 422–436.

ALDERFER, C., "An Empirical Test of a New Theory of Human Needs," *Organizational Behavior and Human Performance*, Vol. 4 (1969), pp. 142–175.

BENDIX, R., *Work and Authority in Industry* (New York: John Wiley & Sons, 1956).

BLAUNER, R., *Alienation and Freedom* (Chicago: University of Chicago Press, 1964).

BLOOD, M. R., AND C. L. HULIN, "Alienation, Environmental Characteristics, and Worker Responses," *Journal of Applied Psychology*, Vol. 51 (1967), pp. 284–290.

DAVIS, L. E., "Job Design and Productivity: A New Approach," *Personnel*, Vol. 33 (1957), pp. 418–430.

EVANS, M. G., "Leadership and Motivation: A Core Concept," *Academy of Management Journal*, Vol. 13 (1970), pp. 91–102.

FIEDLER, F., *A Theory of Leadership Effectiveness* (New York: McGraw-Hill Book Co., Inc., 1967).

FLEISHMAN, E. A., F. F. HARRIS, AND H. E. BURTT, *Leadership and Supervision in Industry* (Columbus, Ohio: Ohio State University, Personnel Research Board, 1955).

FOREHAND, G. A., AND B. GILMER, "Environmental Variation in Studies in Organizational Behavior," *Psychological Bulletin*, Vol. 62 (1964), pp. 361–383.

GALBRAITH, J., AND L. L. CUMMINGS, "An Empirical Investigation of the Motivational Determinants of Task Performance: Interactive Effects between Instrumentality-Valence and Motivation-Ability," *Organizational Behavior and Human Performance*, Vol. 2 (1967), pp. 237–257.

GOODMAN, P. S., AND A. FRIEDMAN, "An Examination of Adams' Theory of Inequity," *Administrative Science Quarterly*, Vol. 16 (1971), pp. 271–288.

GOODMAN, P. S., J. H. ROSE, AND J. E. FURCON, "Comparison of Motivational Antecedents of the Work Performance of Scientists and Engineers," *Journal of Applied Psychology*, Vol. 54 (1970), pp. 491–495.

HACKMAN, J. R., AND E. E. LAWLER, III, "Employee Reactions to Job Characteristics," *Journal of Applied Psychology*, Vol. 55 (1971), pp. 259–286.

HACKMAN, J. R., AND L. W. PORTER, "Expectancy Theory Predictions of Work Effectiveness," *Organizational Behavior and Human Performance*, Vol. 3 (1968), pp. 417–426.

HALL, D. T., AND K. E. NOUGAIM, "An Examination of Maslow's Need Hierarchy in an Organizational Setting," *Organizational Behavior and Human Performance*, Vol. 3 (1968), pp. 12–35.

HENEMAN, H. G., AND D. P. SCHWAB, An Evaluation of Research on Expectancy Theory Predictions of Employee Performance, *Psychological Bulletin*, 1973, in press.

HERZBERG, F., *Work and the Nature of Man* (Cleveland: World Publishing Co., 1966).

HERZBERG, F., "One More Time: How Do You Motivate Employees?", *Harvard Business Review*, Vol. 46 (1968), pp. 53–62.

HERZBERG, F., B. MAUSNER, R. O. PETERSON, AND D. F. CAPWELL, *Job Attitudes: Review of Research and Opinion* (Pittsburgh: Psychological Service of Pittsburgh, 1957).

HERZBERG, F., B. MAUSNER, AND B. SNYDERMAN, *The Motivation to Work* (New York: John Wiley & Sons, 1959).

HOUSE, R. J., "A Path Goal Theory of Leader Effectiveness," *Administrative Science Quarterly*, Vol. 16 (1971), pp. 321–339.

HOUSE, R. J., AND L. A. WIGDOR, "Herzberg's Dual Factor Theory of Job Satisfaction and Motivation," *Personnel Psychology*, Vol. 20 (1967), pp. 369–390.

HULIN, C. L., AND M. R. BLOOD, "Job Enlargement, Individual Differences, and Worker Response," *Psychological Bulletin*, Vol. 69 (1968), pp. 41–55.

JAQUES, E., *Equitable Payment* (New York: John Wiley & Sons, 1961).

KATZ, D., "The Motivational Basis of Organizational Behavior," *Behavioral Science*, Vol. 9 (1964), pp. 131–146.

KATZ, D., AND R. KAHN, *The Social Psychology of Organizations* (New York: John Wiley & Sons, 1966).

KATZ, D., N. MACCOBY, AND N. MORSE, *Productivity, Supervision, and Morale in an Office Situation* (Ann Arbor: University of Michigan Institute of Social Research, 1950).

KING, N., "Clarification and Evaluation of the Two-Factor Theory of Job Satisfaction, *Psychological Bulletin*, Vol. 74 (1970), pp. 18–31.

KORMAN, A. K., Toward an Hypothesis of Work Behavior, *Journal of Applied Psychology*, Vol. 54 (1970), pp. 31–41.

KORMAN, A. K., "Expectancies as Determinants of Performance," *Journal of Applied Psychology*, Vol. 55 (1971), pp. 218–222.

LAWLER, E. E., III, "Equity Theory as a Predictor of Productivity and Work Quality," *Psychological Bulletin*, Vol. 70 (1968), pp. 596–610.

LAWLER, E. E., III, "Job Design and Employee Motivation," *Personnel Psychology*, Vol. 22 (1969), pp. 426–435.

LAWLER, E. E., III, AND L. W. PORTER, "Antecedent Attitudes of Effective Managerial Performance," *Organizational Behavior and Human Performance*, Vol. 2 (1967), pp. 122–142.

LIKERT, R., *The Human Organization* (New York: McGraw-Hill Book Co., Inc., 1967).

LINCOLN, J. F., *A New Approach to Industrial Economics* (New York: Devin-Adair, 1961).

LITWIN, G. H., AND R. A. STRINGER, JR., *Motivation and Organizational Climate* (Boston: Harvard University Graduate School of Business Administration, Division of Research, 1968).

LOCKE, E. A., "The Supervisor as Motivator: His Influence on Goal Setting," in B. M. Bass, R. Cooper, and J. A. Haas (Eds.), *Managing for Accomplishment* (Lexington, Massachusetts: D. C. Heath, 1970).

MARCH, J. G., AND H. A. SIMON, *Organizations* (New York: John Wiley & Sons, 1958).

MASLOW, A. H., *Motivation and Personality* (New York: Harper and Bros., 1954).

MCCLELLAND, D. C., *The Achieving Society* (Princeton: N.J.: D. C. Van Nostrand, 1961).

MCCLELLAND, D. C., "Toward a Theory of Motive Acquisition," *American Psychologist*, Vol. 20 (1965), pp. 321–333.

MCCLELLAND, D. C., *Assessing Human Motivation* (New York: General Learning Press, 1971).

MCCLELLAND, D. C., AND D. G. WINTER, *Motivating Economic Achievement* (New York: The Free Press, 1969).

MCGREGOR, D., *The Human Side of Enterprise* (New York: McGraw-Hill Book Co., Inc., 1960).

MILES, R., "Human Relations or Human Resources?" *Harvard Business Review*, Vol. 43, No. 4 (1965), pp. 148–163.

MILES, R. E., L. W. PORTER, AND J. A. CRAFT, "Leadership Attitudes among Public Health Officials," *American Journal of Public Health*, Vol. 56 (1966), pp. 1990–2005.

MITCHELL, T. R., AND A. BIGLAN, "Instrumentality Theories: Current Uses in Psychology," *Psychological Bulletin*, Vol. 76 (1971), pp. 432–454.

OPSAHL, R. L., AND M. D. DUNNETTE, "The Role of Financial Compensation in Industrial Motivation," *Psychological Bulletin*, Vol. 66 (1966), pp. 94–118.

PORTER, L. W., "Job Attitudes in Management: II. Perceived Importance of Needs as a Function of Job Level," *Journal of Applied Psychology*, Vol. 47 (1963), pp. 141–148.

PORTER, L. W., "Motivation Theory as It Relates to Professional Updating," in R. Piret (Ed.), *Proceedings of the XVII International Congress of Applied Psychology* (Brussels: Editest, 1972).

PORTER, L. W., AND E. E. LAWLER, III, *Managerial Attitudes and Performance* (Homewood, Illinois: Richard D. Irwin, 1968).

PRITCHARD, R. D., "Equity Theory: A Review and Critique," *Organizational Behavior and Human Performance*, Vol. 4 (1969), pp, 176–211.

RITTI, R. R., "Underemployment of Engineers," *Industrial Relations*, Vol. 9 (1970), pp. 437–452.

Roethlisberger, F., and W. J. Dickson, *Management and the Worker* (Cambridge: Harvard University Press, 1939).

Taylor, F. W., *Scientific Management* (New York: Harper and Bros, 1911).

Turner, A. N., and P. R. Lawrence, *Industrial Jobs and the Worker* (Boston: Harvard University Graduate School of Business Administration, Division of Research, 1965).

Vroom, V. H., *Work and Motivation* (New York: John Wiley & Sons, 1964).

Walker, C. R., and R. H. Guest, *The Man on the Assembly Line* (Cambridge: Harvard University Press, 1952).

Whitsett, D. A., and E. K. Winslow, "An Analysis of Studies Critical of the Motivation-Hygiene Theory," *Personnel Psychology*, Vol. 20 (1967), pp. 391–416.

Wolf, M. G., "Need Gratification Theory: A Theoretical Reformulation of Job Satisfaction/Dissatisfaction and Job Motivation," *Journal of Applied Psychology*, Vol. 54 (1970), pp. 87–94.

On the Motivation of Individuals

Harry Levinson

President
The Levinson Institute, Inc.
Cambridge, Massachusetts

Porter and Miles paint a bleak picture indeed of what we know about the relationship of motivation to management, arguing that no theory is completely and unqualifiedly accepted and no definite set of prescriptions is unequivocally supported by the research data. Both the points are valid but they do not support the thesis that we don't know much about motivation related to management.

For example, I presented their thesis to a group of IBM managers and said I was interested in testing it. I suggested that we begin by talking about how they knew where they stood. They in turn began by reporting that their yardstick was an internal one—they had a built-in criterion of what to them was success and good work and the standards by which they wanted to operate. They then talked about feedback on their performance in the form of reactions by superiors, peers, subordinates, members of their family, and members of the community. The responses of these others helped to validate whether they were acting in consonance with that internal criterion.

I asked them how they would feel if they had done well according to their own criteria but had no confirming word from their superiors. They said they were able to tolerate having no approving word for a period of some months but sooncr or later they would expect some favorable word. If they did not get it, they would then begin to be uneasy, fearful, and angry. They would suppress that anger and try to find ways of calling the attention of their bosses to their work to elicit favorable comment from them, or alternatively, they would try to enhance their own sense of competence by somehow inflating themselves.

As we talked about their formulation, it became clear from their reported experience that the same general pattern followed in family relationships as in business relationships.

Out of this discussion there arose a confirmation of the general thesis that the critical element in motivation is a person's ego ideal, that internal image of himself at his future best toward which he is always striving. Each person also has a self-image, a view of himself at any given time, which is usually some distance from his ego ideal. The greater the gap between these two, the lower the self-esteem and the greater the feeling of self-directed criticism and anger and the consequent feeling of inadequacy. Such inadequacy cannot be tolerated for long because people cannot bear the feeling of depression that goes with it. They are therefore motivated to close the gap.

All this is easily derivable from psychoanalytic theory (Levinson, 1964, 1968, 1970). This fundamental conception serves to integrate all the important findings having to do with motivation, occupational stress, and mental health in industry. In turn, this conception relates to all the rest of the comprehensive psychoanalytic theory of personality that gives added meaning to many other aspects of motivation. It further relates motivation at work to contemporary developments in research on a wide variety of issues ranging from sleep and dreams to psychosomatic illness.

The problem arises, as presented by Porter and Miles, because they (and most industrial psychologists and sociologists) approach the problem of motivation by referring to studies and concepts that look on motivation from outside the person. To take an analogy, think of trying to understand what goes on within the bark of a tree. How would one understand the processes that cause the tree to grow, take a certain form, and a certain color? One could measure the tree at various points in time, one could describe the texture of its bark, one could observe what happens to the leaves in season and one could measure which way and how far the tree bends in what kinds of winds. He might then say that the leaves fall in autumn or that the tree grows a foot a year or that it bends more to the North or to the South. All of this would be descriptive but not explanatory.

In order to *understand* and explain what happens within that tree and the manner in which it goes about interacting with its host environment, one has to know something about biological processes and the mode in which the inner invisible activity of that tree is carried on. It is true that one doesn't need to know much about the tree to cut it down and cut it up. On the other hand, if one wants to grow trees, if one wants to select trees that have the promise of greatest growth, one wants to think of placing trees in environments in which they will do best or adapting trees to a given environment, then one has to know their internal processes.

The same is true with respect to individuals. For many years, psychologists have been measuring the outside of people. They have been asking questions, they have been observing work rates, they have changed the environment, they have used different kinds of incentives, and so on. All of these efforts, like efforts to try to understand the tree, have yielded small but not particularly consequential correlations with productivity and job satisfaction. It is to that particular yield and its disappointing results that Porter and Miles speak.

To come back to their point, when we are talking about what energizes a person's behavior, what directs it, what maintains and sustains it, we are talking about what goes on inside the person. Motives will vary significantly among individuals, but there are also certain kinds of collective aspirations and wishes that can be spelled out with considerable clarity (Zaleznik and

Moment, 1964; Zaleznik, 1966; Jaques, 1971).

For example, it is possible to look at the common elements in the aspirations of my IBM managers if one thinks of who these people are. They are managers who want to achieve economic success, who view themselves as active and aggressive, who have high personal standards, who have come by and large from humble origins and who are extremely competitive. Although their individual ego ideals vary considerably, they agreed they shared these elements. They have all come to an organization that as an organization has a collective ideal that complements these characteristics. We can specify and measure significant elements of the ego ideal of these people and that of the organization.

Contrast such a conception with the futility of such conceptions as self-actualization and the general idea of a hierarchy of needs. The hierarchy of needs model is valid, just as it is valid to say that a tree has a thin bark when it is young, a heavier bark when it is older, an even heavier bark in its old age, and that it needs more of certain kind of nutrients at a certain point in its age than at another time. But that makes no differentiation among trees nor does it say whether the same processes occur to the same degree in oak trees, palm trees, or cypress trees. When it comes to the specifics of what one does (either as a manager or a psychologist) to influence motivation, such a conception, since it refers to such a broad class of activity, fails to help us understand enough about people to be able to predict behavior. However, if one thinks in terms of the conception of the ego ideal, he can come much closer to finding out what motivates individual people as well as groups of people, and act accordingly.

Thus we are able to specify what the individual brings to the work situation in much greater detail than Porter and Miles accept. Once we do that, then what the individual does in the work situation and what happens to him in that situation take on meaning in terms of the degree to which they decrease the distance between ego ideal and self-image and thereby affect self-esteem. Money, supervision, time, kinds of work—all these issues have no significance in themselves. They have no significance in any combination. They have significance only as they relate to the ego ideal of the individual or of the group of people who share ego ideals to the extent that they can be treated as a group. In other words, they have significance only as they energize. But energize what?

Porter and Miles refer to Korman's work on self-image, but Korman doesn't carry that self-image work beyond one dimension, to its relationship to the ego ideal. One can hardly conclude that lowered self-image results in lowered motivation. Many people have very low self-images and achieve success specifically because they are trying to overcome them. Many selfmade men are examples.

They refer also to expectancy theory, but what is it a person expects? Out of these conceptions about the ego ideal, my colleagues and I derived a conception of the psychological contract, by which we mean that one can specify what kinds of individual needs (and therefore expectancies) a person brings to an organization and unconsciously assumes the organization will fulfill (Levinson *et al.*, 1962). These have largely to do with the way a person will be enabled to handle the instinctual drives of aggression and sexuality, which in turn lead to feelings of love and hate. Since everyone starts from a state of helpless dependency, each must learn to cope with feelings related to his long period of dependency on others. Finally, as I have indicated, each must deal with his own ego ideal, derived from his identification with his parents and other important figures in his life.

Each of us is always seeking to find those ways that are best suited to handling his dependency feelings and meeting the demands of his ego ideal. These define his expectancies and his needs. The needs may therefore be divided into those having to do with dependency, or what I have called ministration needs; those having to do with growth, or maturation needs; and those having to do with being in charge of oneself and what happens to oneself, or mastery needs. The strength of each of these needs and the degree to which one expects them to be met in a work situation can be tapped by a scale. (I have done so with the Levinson Reciprocation Scale, and others could well devise their own measures.) Such a scale enables a manager to define the intensity of the expectations of his people on each of these dimensions. He can then concentrate on creating an organizational climate that more effectively meets the strength of specific needs of his people and therefore presumably would be highly motivating.

Job enrichment does well in relieving immediate boredom and creating a sense of responsibility, but what after the job is enriched? Even independent professionals with their wide range of opportunity become bored and lose their motivation. Why? I contend because internal ego ideal demands are not being met. The issue, then, is not job enrichment but rather how one adapts to his own internal demands.

The same thing is true with supervision. One can tick off the elements of good supervision, but such lists have yielded precious few results in their elemental form of bits and pieces of traits. How, then, do we understand the psychological significance of supervision? All social institutions in a given culture are recapitulations of the family structure in that culture. As a result, supervisors are psychologically in the same position as the parent in a family and will be regarded as such psychologically by their subordinates. Their supervisory roles and the way in which they are carried out will therefore be related to the psychological contract that people bring to the work situation. Some will require rigid supervisors, having come from an authoritarian family structure; others quite the opposite.

System rewards will have meaning only in terms of internalized values, and the same is true with equity and inequity as they are based on the psychological contract.

Further evidence for this thrust lies in my summary of the literature related to mental health in industry (Levinson and Weinbaum, 1970). The many studies, when consolidated and viewed systematically, all concentrate on the same issue. Executive stress is similarly a matter of vulnerability to lowered self-image and greater inadequacy, with resulting depression and psychosomatic symptoms. Even the problem of adapting unskilled unemployed, high school and college dropouts, and people who have similarly retreated is based on the same issue. People who already feel overwhelmingly inadequate will flee from work situations, or never even enter them, if they feel that they will never be able to attain the goals they hold out for themselves in fantasy or if their small day-by-day errors make them feel even more inadequate. Thus the retreat from competitive effort can be viewed as a way of preserving what little self-esteem such people have, and the modes of orienting them to the business situation require sufficient support for them until they have adequate self-esteem to sustain the inevitable petty difficulties and errors that they will create and make.

Not mentioned by Porter and Miles is the important work of Lawrence and Lorsch, which refers to differentiating the work environment according to kinds of work processes, values, and time constraints (Lawrence and Lorsch, 1967). This is a step in the direction of being able to further refine the view of the work environment to meet the kinds of needs I have postulated. Obviously, if one can differentiate a Sears executive from a Bell Telephone executive from an IBM executive, these differences in personality must be matched by differences in organizational environment if people are to remain in those organizations for extended periods of time.

In sum, my IBM colleagues and I think we know a lot more about motivation in work situations than the psychological and sociological statistical evidence indicates. That evidence is partial and piecemeal because statistical methods and research designs that are geared to measuring external features are simply inadequate to deal with that which is most powerful internally. Although Porter and Miles may well argue that I have biased my audience and my critique, nevertheless I suggest that this bias, based on comprehensive personality theory and verifiable in the everyday experience of blue-collar workers and managers alike, offers us far greater potential for getting at motivational issues than traditional methods.

BIBLIOGRAPHY

JAQUES, E., *Work, Creativity and Social Justice* (New York: International Universities Press, 1971).

LAWRENCE, P. R., AND J. W. LORSCH, *Organization and Environment* (Boston: Harvard University Graduate School of Business, Division of Research, 1967).

LEVINSON, H., *Emotional Health: In the World of Work* (New York: Harper & Row, 1964).

LEVINSON, H., *Executive Stress* (New York: Harper & Row, 1970).

LEVINSON, H., *The Exceptional Executive* (Cambridge: Harvard University Press, 1968).

LEVINSON, H., C. R. PRICE, K. J. MUNDEN, H. J. MANDL, AND C. M. SOLLEY, *Men, Management and Mental Health* (Cambridge: Harvard University Press, 1962).

LEVINSON, H., AND L. WEINBAUM, "The Impact of Organization on Mental Health," in Alan A. McLean (Ed.), *Mental Health and Work Organizations* (Chicago: Rand McNally, 1970).

ZALEZNIK, A., *Human Dilemmas of Leadership* (New York: Harper & Row, 1966).

ZALEZNIK, A., AND D. MOMENT, *Dynamics of Interpersonal Behavior* (New York: John Wiley & Sons, 1964).

The Organization for Motivation

John B. Miner

Professor
College of Business and Public Administration
University of Maryland

The Porter and Miles chapter provides a comprehensive and well-documented review of a subject that probably is as "difficult" as any aspect of the management field. Research in this area is being generated at a very rapid rate and keeping abreast of new developments is a constant challenge. If the authors were to write such a chapter even a year or two hence, they might well come to quite different conclusions.

Given this rapid evolution and continuing change in the field of motivation theory, it appears to the writer that the space allocated to this critique might be utilized most effectively by concentrating primarily on the future rather than on the past. What additions to and variations on the themes of past thinking and research might prove useful in accelerating our understanding of motivation (and performance) in the workplace? What might be added to the approaches Porter and Miles have elaborated so cogently, to make future progress even more pronounced than it has been during the last few years? The ideas that follow are one writer's views on this subject. They represent not so much a prediction of the directions motivation theory will take in the future, as a suggestion of the directions it might benefit from taking.

JOB REQUIREMENTS AS A STARTING POINT

Our concern in the field of management is not with the totality of human motivation, but with the special case of the relationship between motivation and various job requirements. It seems quite possible that an approach that yields a reasonable approximation to a solution of the job or employee motivation problem might be developed long before the total complexity of human motivation comes to be understood.

We might start with various job requirements (role prescriptions), with either those that are formally stated, or perhaps more fruitfully, with those of an informal nature. Then job-specific motivation theories might be developed to indicate what kinds of motivational patterns make a difference in that particular type of job. There would be little concern with specific motives; much more concern with the sum total of motivational inputs that make for satisfying a particular job requirement. These theories might deal with such things as motivation to meet safety rules, motivation to influence superiors, and motivation to impress clients, rather than with security needs, self-actualization motives, and need achievement. It would be assumed that a great variety of different combinations of more basic motives could produce much the same job behaviors in different people. Ideally, we could spell out all of these patterns, but for the moment it may be more fruitful to bypass this problem and look only at the broader question of motivation to meet various role requirements (whatever the specific motives involved).

There is evidence of the potential value of this approach. The research stimulated by McClelland leaves much to be desired insofar as an accepted basic theory of achievement motivation is concerned, but it does appear to have produced a useful theory regarding the motivation to meet certain entrepreneurial role requirements. The writer has utilized the role-motivation approach with managerial jobs of the kind found in large bureaucratic organizations such as corporations, also with some success.

These latter studies indicate that the kinds of motivational patterns that often make for managerial success in the bureaucratic organization are not the same as those that make for success in management consulting, school administration (in the smaller school districts), selling, and research. Yet motivation to meet such job requirements as maintaining favorable relationships with superiors, competition with peers, and exerting power and influence over subordinates has appeared in relation to different indexes of success with sufficient consistency across a variety of managerial positions in large organizations to leave little doubt that an important key to understanding managerial motivation has been identified.

THE DEGREE OF INTEGRATION IN THE ORGANIZATIONAL CLIMATE

In addition to such job-specific, role-motivation theories, greater attention to the matter of the consistency of organizational reinforcements seems needed. In the administration of rewards, such as pay, what really is desired is to motivate employees to learn and do certain things on the job, and thus to exhibit behavior defined as "good performance" on a continuing basis. A variety of theories, and the supporting research, indicate that this desired result is unlikely in the presence of such things as status incongruence, role conflict and ambiguity, unclear behavior models, inconsistent reinforcement, and an uncertain organizational climate.

In the ideal case, to evoke what we call good performance, we need a situation wherein all those who behave in certain pre-established ways are positively evaluated by all their associates at work, and in addition are rewarded with pay, promotion, status symbols, and the like. At the same time, those who behave in other, often opposite, ways are negatively judged and not rewarded. The degree to which job-related behaviors elicit consistency of response within an organization appears to be important not only for the motivation of the particular individual involved, but for the motivation of all others who may be using him as a model to guide their own work behavior.

This matter of the degree of integration within and between value and reward structures has been given little attention in motivation theory to date, although other types of theories have been concerned with it. Yet when we are dealing with motivation at work, not only job requirements but also the organizational context in which the job is performed becomes important. Hopefully, future theories and research will incorporate this type of variable. It seems very likely that tests of existing motivation theories carried out in organizational contexts in which integration is lacking could fail completely, whereas similar tests conducted under conditions of high integration would succeed.

Of course, complete integration of the organizational climate such that total consistency is maintained at all times must remain only an ideal, insofar as ongoing organizations are concerned. However, it is important to know what degrees and types of departures from the ideal have what kinds of effects on motivation. Does it matter as much, for instance, that a manager's subordinates and immediate superior react to his performance differently as that his immediate superior and the manager above him evaluate him differently?

ORGANIZATIONAL CONDITIONS FOR THE MANAGER AS MOTIVATOR

Another consequence of injecting the motivational problem into a real-life organization emerges in the area of leadership styles. The basic consideration here is that the laissez-faire approach is least effective in a motivational sense. Such a manager holds himself completely free from either individual or group decisions. He does not participate in discussions other than to provide information if asked, and he makes no effort to ensure that decisions are made and work performed. Little if anything is done to motivate behavior toward role prescriptions. Under such conditions the manager cannot act as a motivator because he does nothing to motivate.

Now it seems likely that the same type of laissez-faire leadership actually emerges if there is a lack of integration between what the manager does and what the organization values and/or rewards. Say a manager is very democratic and involves his subordinates in all decisions relevant to the group; but the values of the organization as a whole are autocratic, indicating that the "good" manager is one who makes his own decisions and takes the risks involved. Under these circumstances the organizational values as held by superiors and subordinates neutralize any possible positive consequences of the democratic style. The result, for all practical purposes, is laissez faire.

What this suggests is that if one is to study the motivational impacts of variations in leadership approach in real-life organizations, one must incorporate the nature and degree of integration of value and reward climates in the theory. This is not a consideration in laboratory studies normally, but when these studies are carried on in an organizational context, other factors are introduced. The manager may or may not be a motivator not only as a function of whether he tries to motivate or not, but also as a function of the relationship between how he tries to motivate and organizational climate congruencies. Again, aspects of the organizational context appear to be necessary components of a meaningful theory of motivation in the work environment.

THE JOB SATISFACTION-MOTIVATION RELATIONSHIP

There have been many arguments about the relationship between job satisfaction and job performance and/or motivation. As Porter and Miles indicate, early theories saw these relationships as positive; later research provided mixed support at best. Here also the organizational context may provide a meaningful basis for interpretation.

It seems possible that, as in so many other areas of management theory, the satisfaction-motivation quandary is a function of a confusion between normative and descriptive theory. It is likely that, all other factors being equal, high levels of job performance *should* be associated with high levels of job satisfaction if organizational effectiveness is high. In a normative sense, job satisfaction and motivation and/or performance should be integrated to produce an organization that achieves its goals.

But in a descriptive sense, satisfaction and motivation may be negatively related, or perhaps more frequently unrelated. As a result, the organization suffers in its goal attainment, just as it does from satisficing rather than maximizing in its decision-making. However, most organizations are not that effective. Thus, the typical pattern is a mild positive relation between job satisfaction and motivation to meet the role prescriptions of the job.

CONCLUSIONS

The major point made here is that the study of motivation in its occupational and organizational context need not be the same as the study of human motivation generally. The former is a somewhat more limited problem, and we should take advantage of the fact that a theory of employee motivation can be less complex and less general than a total theory of psychological motivation. Past efforts have tended to try to apply drive theory, expectancy theory, and balance or homeostatic theories from general psychology to management problems. Perhaps this is the long way around. Useful results for management may be more likely to emerge from applying shortcuts that apply to the specific problems that management seeks to solve.

DISCUSSION QUESTIONS

1. Why is motivation such a difficult problem for management?
2. Discuss Maslow's theory, giving pros and cons. How does Maslow compare with Alderfer and McClelland?
3. Give examples of two-factor theory and indicate your opinion of it. Why do you hold this opinion?
4. What, in your opinion, seems to happen to the individual in a work situation?
5. Describe and discuss equity theory.
6. Evaluate expectancy/valence theory.
7. Enumerate and discuss some of the motivators of managers.
8. What is the main thrust of Levinson's remarks? Do you agree?
9. Is the study of motivation in its organizational context different from the study of human motivation in general?

18

Management Development

Edward C. Ryterband

E. N. Hay & Associates
Philadelphia

Bernard M. Bass

Professor, and Director
Management Research Center
Graduate School of Management
University of Rochester, New York

Development, growth, and change are continuous. Learning is a life-long affair that can be helped or hindered by the manager himself and the organization to which he belongs.

Managers learn new concepts, ideas, methods, and ways of thinking, deciding, and behaving and discard older ways because: (1) they see some discrepancy between what they do or know or feel and what they would like to do or know or feel; (2) they are told or discover for themselves alternatives to their current ways; (3) they have an opportunity to try alternatives; and (4) they find that some alternative puts them closer to where they believe they should be.

Identifying the discrepancies requires an analysis of current and future needs of the manager and his organization. Information about alternatives or their discovery requires that the manager be in a stimulating environment and that he have wide-angled vision. Opportunities to try alternatives require that the manager be in an environment in which he can make mistakes safely. Receiving feedback about the success or failure of the alternative way depends on whether the environment is structured to provide it and whether the manager is prepared to receive it.

The above are the minimum essentials of management development. They should be found in the most informal of self-study arrangements; they should likewise appear in a formal university executive development program. They apply to training in specific skills as well as in broad educational domains; to present job or future career. They should be understood in the context of the organization in which the manager is located.

GROWTH OF MANAGEMENT DEVELOPMENT

A 1954 survey of American firms indicated that 54 per cent had formal management development programs (Merrill and Marting, 1958). In a similar survey conducted by the Bureau of National Affairs in 1967, "about 3/4 of the 328 firms sampled were found to conduct some type of continuing development training for their present executives" (*Personnel Policies Forum,* 1967).

This growth in management development activities reflects a realization of the many needs that such activities can and do serve. First of all, management development efforts have grown because the number of managerial positions has grown, and has grown faster than the total work force. In fact, the number of white-collar jobs of which managerial jobs are a substantial portion is increasing at many times the rate of blue-collar jobs. In 1967, 300,000 new blue-collar jobs came into being, whereas the same year saw four times as many (1,200,000) white-collar jobs come into existence (Hartman, 1969).

The need for management development has also increased because of rapid growth in managerial knowledge. This is especially evident in the expanded use in management of analytical disciplines such as operations research and linear programming and in the expansion of applications to management of behavioral science and economics fundamentals. The need has emerged for greater knowledge in special areas such as international relations, research and development, or legislation on employment discrimination.

The concern for management development has also grown because we have become increasingly aware of the critical difference managers can make by the way they try (or fail to try) to motivate subordinates, coordinate them in collaborative efforts, and generally aid in providing subordinates with an organizational climate that is conducive to effective performance.

Finally, management development has become more important because the personal development of managers and their effective long-range planning is being given greater emphasis by many firms. In the increasingly complex, changeable, and competitive environments of today's organizations, to keep such managers up to date requires continuous developmental efforts so that they are ready for any of the new demands that may arise. To keep him committed to the firm requires that these efforts be substantially defined and implemented by the manager himself (Bennis, 1966).

All of this growth reflects the increasing importance organizations attribute to management development programs. These programs are judged important because they seem to answer some general needs that organizations have.

FORMAL OR INFORMAL?

Management development can be both formal and informal. It includes whatever may be done to improve current or future managerial performance by imparting knowledge, modifying attitudes, or increasing skills (House, 1967, p. 13). These attempts range from completely formal programs planned and offered by the organization to its manager to informal efforts by the organization to provide an environment for a manager's growth. For formal programs, management development more often is guided by the needs of the organization as its officials and sponsors view those needs. For more informal efforts it is often stimulated by the needs of the individual as he views them.

MANAGEMENT OR ORGANIZATIONAL DEVELOPMENT?

The contrast between the organization's needs and perspectives about training and the needs and perspectives of the individual manager may be a major source of conflict (Argyris, 1964). At one extreme, management development may be seen as the individual adjusting to the demands of the organization. This is how management development has traditionally been conceived. At the other extreme, management development may be seen as the organization of managers and workers changing to make itself a more fruitful environment for the self-development of the individual manager. Concern here is much more with *organizational development* rather than with management development. Increasingly, organizations and those concerned with management development are adopting some aspects of this newer perspective. This view sees the manager as a "critical man," a person who as a generalist can master a number of important jobs. Of prime concern is the continued satisfaction and loyalty of such employees. Self-directed development efforts are a major means of ensuring such satisfaction and loyalty. We feel management development must fit into the larger effort of organizational development. Both the needs of the individual and the needs of the organization must be considered. As one board chairman put it, the success of today's corporations is, in part, dependent on seeing that the right people (well-selected) are able to grow to meet their own needs and those of the organization.

TRAINING OR EDUCATION?

Traditionally, training (management development included) connoted teaching skills for a specific purpose implying a narrow span of content (Bass and Vaughan, 1966). In contrast, education was seen as being designed to fit the whole social, intellectual and physical person, to equip him to take part in the many institutions of society rather than only specific ones. The goals of education were multifaceted and not always specifically defined (Dunnette and Kirchner, 1965).

Today, management development has taken on a broader significance, one approaching the definition of education presented above (Haas, 1969). For example, in recent years, organizations have increasingly relied on university-based Masters in Business Administration programs to provide needed managerial talent (Schein, 1967). These programs, although considered relevant "training" for management positions, are still regarded by universities as the basic educational programs at the graduate and post-graduate level. The broadest forms of education have been provided in some management development programs. Probably most exemplary has been the Institute of Humanistic Studies for Executives at the University of Pennsylvania for Bell Telephone managers (Viteles, 1959; 1971).

ORIENTED TO PRESENT OR FUTURE?

Management development must introduce old and tested skills to new managers. In this sense, management development orients and educates acceptable candidates to the demands of current positions in an organization. Acceptability, of course, is concerned not only with the employee's first managerial position, but with developing acceptable credentials for a series of higher and higher level jobs.

This trend is significant in light of the growing differences that exist between lower-level entry jobs and the top-level position for which these trainees are being groomed. It is becoming increasingly apparent that the EDP revolution is forcing higher-level managers into more creative, innovative positions from which they can make unique contributions apart from those of the computer. In turn, lower-level positions are being involved in more programmed tasks and consequently, in fewer innovative demands (Gibb, 1951). Organizations need to have systematic and thorough definitions of the differential roles and requirements of top, middle, and lower management so that effective development efforts can be evolved that will be sensitive to those differences.

Needs in Future Positions

Increasingly, management development has to be conceived as a process that prepares managers for more than their current positions (AMA, 1968). Instead, it should be a process that looks ahead to the jobs and managers that will be needed in the future. Organizations change. They change because they want to, because their market forces them to, or because the larger society within which they operate changes. Management development is a process that, as a part of organization development, can prepare managers for these changes.

There are critical reasons behind this ever-increasing concern for future as well as present training needs. First, past decades have witnessed unparalleled development in industrial technology. If employees, managers included, are to remain employed, they must upgrade themselves for the most skilled positions and familiarize themselves with new processes and production techniques. New technology has caused many managers to be faced with the problem that their jobs will have to be enlarged and thereby require additional skills and knowledge. In turn, other management jobs are forced by the same technological changes to require a narrower but more detailed range of skills. Of course, it goes without saying that many jobs, management jobs at that, will disappear entirely (Gibb, 1951), sometimes requiring an entire retraining procedure to be initiated by the organization.

In addition to the impact of new technology, updating management development has taken on increased importance because of the growing complexity of organizations. Because of this complexity, these organizations must deal with substantial problems of coordinating and integrating increasing numbers of specialists. For example, information technology is a relatively new development that has led to the creation of a new specialist, the information technologist (Vaughan, Porat, and Haas, 1968). New supervisory and managerial skills are needed when specialists, like the information technologist, are introduced into a firm. Such a specialist may have training, background, and interests that are very different and even alien to those of current managers. The problem is twofold. The original problem is that of a manager familiarizing himself with new skills that arise from new technology. The other problem is that a manager, even if he does not personally have the skills associated with new technology, will probably have to supervise people who do (Bass and Vaughan, 1966).

DESIGNING TRAINING: NEEDS ANALYSIS

The effective implementation of any management development program requires a systematic examination of the question: What are the needs for training? At its most basic level the question should examine whether or not training is needed at all. There are many instances wherein (1) deficiencies may be felt to exist that truly do not exist, (2) some deficiency is felt and is real but can be responded to by some means other than training. In such cases, the introduction of new equipment or entirely new personnel, rather than upgrading the skills of current personnel, might be the answer. If management development is relevant to some organizational problem, the questions that should be pursued from that point include the following:

1. What skills, knowledges, and attitudes should be taught?
2. Who should be trained?
3. How should training be carried out?
4. Where and when should training be done?
5. Why should training be carried out as it is? That is, what evidence is available showing the efficiency of a particular training program (Dunnette and Kirchner, 1965)?

The present section focuses on the first two of these questions: What should be in training and who should be trained? These questions are hopefully answered by a thorough analysis of training needs.

For a number of reasons, the process of analyzing training needs for management development seems to be shifting into a new two-part framework. In this framework, organizational analysis rests on the one side, that analysis focusing on training needs as the firm sees them. On the other side is an analysis of individual managerial needs, that analysis, wholly or in part, being defined, conducted, and implemented by the manager himself. Individual analysis reflects a newer perspective that questions the utility of comprehensive job analyses administered by the organization for management in all of its positions. The tasks of managers are often too complex and covert to analyze. In addition, detailed specifications of objectives and job procedures may be seen as too restricting by managers since it limits the influence they can personally exert in defining orderly procedures for the achievement of job responsibilities. When an organization restricts managers by over-prescribing their job behavior, certain negative implications may arise regarding assumptions the organization is making about those managers. According to Argyris (1964), these implications center on negative and opposing stereotypes managers and their organization may develop about each other. The manager sees the organization's goals and means of achieving them as being in conflict with his own desire for independent and innovative action. On the other hand, the organization supports this view when it is overly prescriptive about its managers. It implies that the manager has limited awareness of the requirements of his job, a too-short time perspective in planning, that he is passive and wants (as well as needs) direction (Halpin, 1957). To avoid the occurrence of these conflicts between individual and organizational needs, less prescriptive job specifications and greater initiative on the part of individual managers is being sought by many firms. These changes emphasize individual orientations in diagnosing training needs, self-development, and self-appraisal. In a recent book, Management by Objectives (1965), George Odiorne elaborated some of the assumptions of this more participative philosophy.

The critical step is to define the overall goals of the organization and its subsystems. The firm's policy makers initiate the process. Subsequently, individual managers in collaboration with their superiors define the goals they are to be responsible for. The behavior of managers is *not* defined. Only expected results are measured against established goals for each manager "rather than in terms of common goals for all managers or common methods of managing." Furthermore, Odiorne indicates that participation is highly desirable in goal setting and decision-making, and is especially useful since the successful manager is a manager of situations about which he will have the most clear picture.

First we will focus on what the organization sees as needed by its management; then on what the managers themselves see as the discrepancies between where they are and where they should be.

ORGANIZATION ANALYSIS

An organization must review its objectives and its resources—human and material—and how the resources are allocated to meet the objectives in the organization's social, economic, and technological environment (March, 1965).

Long-term objectives need to be specified in broad areas (e.g., marketing, production, labor relations) of the entire company. In addition, specific goals need to be stated for the various subsystems within the company. Those subsystems include divisions, smaller departments, or sections, right down to the smallest subgroup.

Specifications are required to describe the company's efforts to meet its objectives through its human resources. Such specifications include manpower inventories that determine who is in the company, where they come from, who they are, and what and how well they are doing. Pending retirements, promotions, transfers, and potential deaths call for a replacement schedule. Several possible replacements may be desired for each higher-level position currently occupied.

Sources of Managerial Manpower

Candidates for management positions are often sought from sources outside the organization, as shown in Table 15. Among the forty-seven companies surveyed, six of the seven sources of recruits came from outside the company (Foreman, 1967). Of course, firms vary in their dependence on outside recruiting, either turning to experienced executives in other firms or fresh recruits from business schools to furnish their manpower needs. There are both rewards and costs in such practices.

"Pirating" experienced managers away from other firms can help an organization obtain more mature, seasoned personnel. The problem with "pirating" is that such managers are experienced, but in settings that are not identical to those of their new home. Organizations can thus run the risk of underestimating the adjustments that will be required of these transplanted executives. Moreover, transplanted managers have already proven a somewhat limited loyalty to their former firm, and in so doing, may indicate a greater than average turnover risk to their current firm. In fact, general turnover of capable managers is becoming an increasingly serious concern. Over fifty-seven per cent of firms in one study revealed managerial turnover was on the increase in the late 1960's (Albrook, 1968). Management mobility will become even greater if vested rights to managerial pension plans are obtained so that managers' equity is maintained despite the move from one company to another.

TABLE 15. SOURCES OF RECRUITMENT CONSIDERED MOST PRODUCTIVE IN SELECTING MANAGEMENT TRAINEES

Sources of Recruitment	*Corporations Using*	*Percentage*
College Placement Bureaus	42	89
Voluntary Applications	40	85
Employees From Within Company	33	70
Advertising Appeals	25	53
Employment Agencies	21	45
Personal Contacts	21	45
Recommendations From Others	18	38
Professional and Trade Associations	8	17
Trade Schools	2	4
High Schools	1	2
Other	1	2
Total Companies, 47.		

From Foreman, 1967.

Taking on fresh graduates from MBA programs provides another selection-oriented alternative to promotion and training from within the company. It has been a popular alternative in recent years. In 1968, MBA graduates received an average of 4.7 job offers per man (Rukeyser, 1969). As products of advanced schooling, MBA's are usually of superior intellectual capacities and are "up to date" on the latest techniques. They can transfer some of what they have learned to non-MBA colleagues already in the firm. But they usually are young, inexperienced, and likely to be transient. At least they expect to move on. Most students say they expect to stay with their first employer only about three years. They seek in their entry jobs opportunities for learning and sufficiently challenging tasks to maintain the level of intellectual stimulation they have become accustomed to in school. Companies often cannot provide such opportunities and disillusionment sets in quickly. Conflicts in values also are likely between the rookies and their new organization.

MBA programs act as an influential source of values for their students (Schein, 1966). Schein appraised student values before and after they completed their course of study. At both times, those values were compared to those of (1) the business college faculty, and (2) actual managers. At the beginning of their program, student values were oriented toward business interests but resided somewhere in between the more idealistic-scientific values of faculty and the more pragmatic values of managers. At the end of their studies, however, the student values were far more similar to those of faculty than of managers. In time, however, the graduates began moving back in values more toward those common in the firms they had joined.

An organization that sees disagreement and incipient conflict as bad may have a hard time accepting an influx of bright, young, educated Turks. But an organization that can tolerate some degree of confrontation may see the young Turks providing a constant source of renewal and inputs of creative, new ideas of importance.

SPECIFYING WHAT IS DONE

It is often difficult to specify the levels of skill, knowledge, and performance required for management jobs for they involve many complex skills whose importance will vary over time. At a monthly or seasonal peak, coordinating and supervising skills may be more important than planning skills. On the other hand, ability to plan may be more important at other times when season schedules or future activities are being considered. One thing we can be reasonably certain about—managers get work done in collaboration with others. They must have some way of effectively working with people. Interpersonal competence is a "must."

Measuring Job Effectiveness

The extent to which each manager is meeting the requirements of his job effectively needs to be appraised. A variety of efficiency indices may be used. They include direct and indirect costs of performing his job, the quality of the goods or services he is responsible for producing, and the effectiveness with which he utilizes machines, equipment, and people in producing his goods or services. These indices may be provided by objective criteria, such as the profitability of operations under his charge, turnover, absenteeism and lateness in his staff, scrap, or waste. Such indices, however, have certain disadvantages. Although they are objective, they may reflect conditions outside the manager's control and thus have little bearing on his own competence. For example, out-of-date equipment may yield unfavorable scores on such indices for even the best of managers. Other "subjective" indices such as ratings of his effectiveness by peers, subordinates, superiors and/or outside consultants, although not so reliable, may allow for some estimation of his effectiveness, considering all the constraints within which he must work.

Describing the Organization's Environment

Most organizations have little, if any, control over the social, economic, and political environment in which they must operate (although they try to increase such control wherever possible through lobbying for favorable legislation, pushing for monopolistic power in the marketplace, or spending large sums to improve their public image). Knowing the environment will allow the firm to be aware of the constraining realities that it cannot change within which training needs will be defined. In addition to the external environment, the organization should also know something about its internal environment. As a social-technical system, the firm is made up of employees who belong to a mixture of separate groups, which nonetheless are forced by work demands to be dependent on one another (Trist *et al.*, 1963). In this internal environment, interdependent individuals and groups will learn about their jobs, one another, and the company. As a result of their interaction, an organizational climate will evolve. That organizational climate will be a reflection of its members' attitudes toward various aspects of work, supervision, company procedures, goals, and membership in the organization.

This climate needs to be known. For example, training that seeks to improve managers' attitudes toward participative supervision will create a conflicting state of affairs in an organization whose climate is essentially authoritarian. In fact, there is a good chance that those managers trained to do things, no matter how good they are in an absolute sense, which are contrary to current practice and beliefs in an organization, will be worse off than before the training (Fleishman, 1953; Fleishman, Harris, and Burtt, 1955).

Problems

Specifying the current objectives, resources, and environment of the organization is an elaborate and time-consuming process. It is elaborate because both current and future conditions are important to know. By looking into the future, a firm can refine current management development programs. In addition, plans can be made for subsequent programs that will consider the changes occurring now and the changes that are likely to occur in the future. Its time-consuming nature derives from the many and complex variables that need to be considered. Organization-wide (and subunit) goals, strategies for their achievement, and environmental constraints all have to be defined. Moreover, goals, strategies, and constraints are each multifaceted issues that do not readily lend themselves to easily applicable definitions.

INDIVIDUAL ANALYSIS

Assessing needs as the individual sees them gives rise to many problem issues that complicate the effective realization of that task. These problems include:

1. The clear definition of the complexities and subtleties of managerial jobs so that managers may have a useful framework to guide their self-analysis.
2. The choice of methods to accomplish self-diagnosis and planning of developmental action.
3. Integration of the individual's analyses with the goals, plans, and constraining parameters of the firm.

Management Development is Self Development

The role of the manager in his own development is crucial. It is not enough simply to have training programs available nor is it enough to send or force managers through various kinds of development programs. The managers must want to undergo training. But many tend to be motivated more by today's challenges than by tomorrow's, more by current than by future performance. In his own self-interest, however, a manager cannot afford to let today's pressures preclude his thinking about tomorrow's world of work and his role in it. Thus a large part of a successful development effort is to increase the manager's own desire to learn. "A man who wants to develop himself does—a man who wants to be developed rarely is." (Hull, 1964, p. 39.) "Ideally, . . . each . . . should go through a careful process of self-examination, and if necessary, indoctrination." (Berkwit, 1966, p. 107.) The ultimate goal of the organization should be, as Gardner (1963) suggests, "to shift to the individual the burden of pursuing his own education." (Barrett, Bass, and Miller, 1970, p. 12.) By involving the manager himself in the process of defining needs, the organization increases the probability of his greater commitment to the total development process (Chowdry, 1963).

Self-analyses and direction of development involve establishing a learning agenda. Dill, Crowston and Elton (1965) point out that well-stated learning agendas are rare.

Included in the learning agenda must be:

1. Statements of *aims*—changes that they would like to make in their knowledge, skills, attitudes, values, or relationships with other men and organizations.

2. Definitions of areas for *study, search, reflection,* or *testing*—lists of activities, experiences, or questions that can help them accomplish their aims.
3. Ideas about *priorities*—feelings of preference or urgency about what should be learned first.

We now look at several ways individual managers, with assistance, can construct their own learning agendas as part of other activities in which they are engaged.

Laboratory Groups

Here, in a sensitivity training encounter, or similar self-analysis group, the individual's own insights can become the basis for defining and implementing the need for change (Schein and Bennis, 1965). The laboratory group participant can examine his own actions and the way he relates to and affects others, and on this basis, define the areas of personal and interpersonal behavior that require change. Feedback from others can help him to discover, confirm, or refute what he feels are his important needs. In addition, laboratory training can provide a place where he can test out these new insights and work toward the development of greater interpersonal skills (Argyris, 1962).

Structured Exercises

The pure T-group experience, with its lack of structure, focuses heavily on socio-emotional issues and neglects task-related issues (Bass, 1967). A more structured self-examination is provided by Exercise Self-Appraisal (Bass, Vaughan, and Schein, 1968) Exercise Self-Appraisal gives participants in various kind of training groups a structured framework in which to appraise themselves and contrast this self-appraisal with the way they would prefer to be. The areas covered include style of learning (speed, persistence, breadth, focus, etc.) and style of managing (risk taking, delegation, time perspective, concern for rules, etc.). Trainees can complete the forms twice, early and late in training. The second administration gives participants a chance to reappraise themselves and examine changes in their self-appraisals that may have occurred during training. In addition, the post-assessment can be contrasted with an appraisal of the trainee offered by other participants to confirm or refute self-appraisals.

Much more task-relevant is Exercise Future, which consists of a questionnaire concerning an individual's preferences and expectations about his job in the next 5 years. Figure 46 shows the set of items dealing with need for educational upgrading. Other of the forty-six items deal with the reward structure—what he sees required by his organization and the outside environment. After completing the questionnaire, the participant is directed to locate those trends on which there are large discrepancies (column *C*) among expectations (Column *B*) and preferences (column *A*), important trends to the participant (column *D*), and under his control (column *E*). The participant then has an opportunity to consider specific steps he might take. These he is able to test for feasibility in discussions with two other fellow participants.

ITEM	A PREFER (Ideally would like)	B EXPECT	C DIFFERENCE (Col. A–B Col. B)	D IMPORTANT TO ME	E CONTROL
	5 = great increase 1 = great decrease				X = much O = little
EDUCATIONAL UPGRADING					
1. Importance of my knowing analytical techniques of decision-making	____	____	____	____	____
2. Need for additional knowledge in my field of specialization	____	____	____	____	____
3. My skill in attending to many and diverse kinds of information	____	____	____	____	____
4. Time spent by me in my own development and training	____	____	____	____	____
5. Importance of reading fast and effectively	____	____	____	____	____
6. Importance of writing effectively	____	____	____	____	____
7. Importance of speaking effectively	____	____	____	____	____

For Column A:

I ideally would prefer the condition to:

For Column B:

I actually expect the condition to:

5 - Increase greatly over the next five years
4 - Increase to some extent
3 - Stay the same
2 - Decrease to some extent
1 - Decrease greatly

For Column C:

Subtract Column B from Column A, without regard to sign. Many of these entries will be 0; the maximum difference is, of course, 5–1 or 1–5=4.

For Column D:

The importance of this condition to me, or the amount of effect this has on me is:

For Column E:

The amount of control or influence I have over this condition is:

X - Very much
O - Comparatively little

FIGURE 46. Excerpts from future world of work questionnaire, part of exercise future. (From Miller *et al.*, 1970, pp. 2, 3).

Management-by-Objectives

Another task-oriented approach to self analysis occurs when management-by-objectives is practiced (Odiorne, 1965). Management-by-objectives requires defining organizational and subsystem goals. Then each individual defines his own best way of meeting these goals and is judged on how well goals are met. Management-by-objectives thrusts responsibility for substantial self-examination and self-planning on the individual manager. He must look ahead to his own performance review and decide how to develop himself and his subordinates as well in order to fare well when review time comes around.

The Assessment Center

Although the main purpose of an assessment center may be to assess the management potential of candidates, some emphasis can be placed on diagnosis and self-definition of needs. The individual and group tests and observations information may be fed back to the manager to point up current strengths and deficiencies and aid the manager in defining a plan for self-development. Most illustrative is the Talent Development Program offered by General Electric (Storey and Baker, 1969). In the program, young, qualified (high growth potential) managers are selected by their supervisors, and after being screened by corporate management development staff, are sent to an off-premise facility. There, small groups of twenty or so managers are put through a week of testing, group exercises, and interviews. Results from these experiences as well as peer ratings are digested and partially fed back to the participants while they are still in attendance. Most of the feedback occurs after a final report is written and approved by the TDP staff. After returning to his home location, the manager receives a review of his performance and self-developmental suggestions based on that review. In addition, his manager receives that same information plus the complete final report with all data gathered at the center included. In that data, guides for the participant's manager are also included, which suggest how he may help the participant in developing the potential observed at the center. In collaboration with a corporate staff member, the three meet at the participant's job location to review his performance at the center, integrate that with his on-the-job behavior, and set up plans for development. The participant and his manager are then on their own to establish methods, benchmarks, and schedules to enhance the assets and overcome the agreed-on deficiencies.

Clinical Diagnosis

Professionally administered diagnosis and counseling provides diagnoses of strengths and weakness of the individual manager. Often, these diagnostic techniques include non-objectively scoreable projective tests such as the Rorschach (Ink Blot) tests, which provide an in-depth picture of the individual's personality; interviews; and objective testing. The useful application of projective tests and other such diagnostic techniques is still somewhat in question (Kurtz, 1948), but occasions are evident wherein they have been found to be empirically valued in assessing higher level personnel (Campbell, 1962; Campbell *et al.*, 1962). In one study, the combination of techniques described above correlated quite highly with promotability ratings done on supervisors by their managers and by managers two levels above them (Huse, 1962). The application of these techniques of individual diagnosis is found in the work of such consulting firms as Rohrer, Hibler, and Replogle. In their approach to define development needs, they are called in as psychological consultants by firms and work with individuals, diagnosing and counseling them on their personal qualities and needs. Their focus is on the manager's self concept and the motives within him that are helping or will help him to perform in an executive role. Attention is paid not only to the man but also to the managing process (effective communications and decision making), the responsibilities of managing (the imperatives of authority, self and other's development), and the purposes of managing. The counseling is often an extended process that puts a premium on the manager's self-awareness and self-generated insights about how to integrate his personal concerns into the role of an effective executive (Flory, 1967).

INTEGRATING INDIVIDUAL AND ORGANIZATIONAL DEFINITIONS OF DEVELOPMENTAL NEEDS

Individual and organizational aims in training must mesh. At some point, the *T*-group must deal with "back-home" implications of insights. Structured exercises must allow time for considering organizational constraints on individual plans. Management-by-objectives must involve an examination of the connections between organizational and individual goals. Diagnoses of individual managers in assessment centers or in individual psychological testing and counseling must be in terms of the organization's climate, tasks, and expectations.

What will help in this integration is for an organization to pursue a policy that rewards managers for developing themselves and their subordinates. Among the usual criteria for judging the worth of a manager, such as his and his subordinates' contributions to profits, cost reduction, morale, and efficiency of operations, should be added the extent to which he increases his potential worth, his capabilities, and the capabilities of his subordinates through developmental efforts.

DESIGNING OPPORTUNITIES FOR DEVELOPMENT

Most managers and professionals have some awareness of the basic principles of learning. Unfortunately, they are not applied to management training programs as often as they should be. Merely providing a set of problems to solve or assignments to complete will be insufficient for learning. Trainees must receive feedback on the success or failure of their solutions and efforts to complete training assignments. And the more meaningful and relevant to the real job these problems and assignments, the greater will be the learning and the transfer of what is learned to the job following training.

However, there are other issues of consequence in the design of training and developmental experiences. These include the extent to which the training design is self-controlled and whether it is in-house or outside the company.

Who Decides

Increasingly, efforts are being made to involve the manager in the design for his own development. This follows the same reasoning as the effort to involve the manager in the analysis of his own training needs. The aim is to maximize commitment through participation. There are obvious limits to such participation. There may be substantial changes occurring in technology that require new information to be disseminated to all managers whose jobs will be affected by the new technology. It is unrealistic to suggest that managers choose whether or not they receive this information. Many times, organizations feel that a manager "ought to" go through some kind of training program. For example, a manager's superior may feel that the manager is experiencing some difficulty in successfully relating to his own subordinates, or that a manager being geared for promotion needs certain new kinds of learning that he has not had to deal with in the past. In the first case, the superior may want to consider having the manager undergo some form of human relations training. In the second case, the manager's superior is looking to broaden the basic knowledge the manager will need at higher positions in the organization. The superior, thus, may have to decide whether or not to send the promotable manager into a special course of studies provided for up-and-coming executives at a management institute or business school. Obviously, the superior will want to consult fully with the manager in question before the final decisions are made concerning the training to be taken.

In-House or Out-House?

Program planners must decide whether to go outside for training opportunities or to try to organize efforts inside the firm. Some elements in favor of each are listed below:

Stay Inside	*Go Outside*
1. Transfer of learning more likely; applications more relevant.	1. Less overhead costs.
2. Less chance for managers to be "pirated" while away.	2. More cross-firm and cross-industry sharing of ideas and cross-fertilization possible.
3. More control over training contents and staff.	3. Greater feeling of freedom to experiment with new learnings.
4. Staff understands local problems better.	4. Staff less likely to "fossilize."

Naturally, a large firm can better afford to stay inside. It can bring in outside trainers to reduce inside stultification.

SELECTING THE APPROPRIATE TECHNIQUE

Recently, forty-nine of the country's largest organizations in terms of sales responded to a survey of the training techniques they used in their management development efforts (Foreman, 1967). The techniques included on-the-job training (96%); conference and discussion (93%); job rotation (76%); special projects (71%); case studies (49%); problem solving (49%); management games (18%); role playing (18%); programmed instruction (16%); and sensitivity training (9%).

Guidelines are difficult to establish to determine which one or combination of these techniques ought to be used in a particular management development program. Specific evaluations of the effectiveness of a particular approach are about as available as the evaluation of the utility of a particular college course. The designer needs to know whether the technique is feasible and fits with what he knows about effective learning.

Selection also depends on the purpose of a program. For example, if the purpose is to disseminate new information, a straightforward lecture presentation in a conference with time for questions may be more appropriate than any other technique.

The financial, time, and space constraints existing within an organization also have to be considered. Will the expected benefits of training exceed the costs? With these points in mind, let us review development procedures for managers.

JOB ROTATION

Managers commonly rotate in a planned way through positions of increasing responsibility and complexity transferring across departmental boundaries in an upward spiral until stopped for lack of further openings or lack of confidence above them that further promotions are warranted. They may rotate as "assistants-to" or as interns or as heads of the units to which they are assigned. Feedback about performance and coaching should come from the immediate supervisor in each different job assignment and from other executives who are responsible for the trainee's overall development.

Job rotation provides trainees with a perspective of the overall interrelationships of various functions within the organization. In addition, it exposes managers to greater knowledge about the problems and processes occurring within various departments. It may also serve to enhance a manager's identification with the company as a whole. While providing him with experience in several departments, the company is indicating its enduring interest in his affiliation with the firm (Bass and Vaughan, 1966; Haas, 1969).

To be effective, job rotation should be purposeful and flexible, tailored to the particular needs and capabilities of the individual manager. Canned rotation programs can result in considerable waste of time and talent. Some men will not need all the exposures that are provided in a canned program, at least not to the extent that they are provided. Thus, the aims and contents of a particular job rotation program ought to be established by a particular manager working with his supervisor toward setting mutual goals while reviewing progress toward those goals at regular intervals. Such reviews can also take place with other trainees or with the organization's training staff.

The disadvantages of job rotation lie in its costs in time and resources. Mistakes by trainees can have serious consequences for the organization. In addition, there is no guarantee that the manager being rotated will be welcome in a new department or that its personnel will provide him with information and guidance. They may see him as "just passing through," or as a competitor for a desirable position in the organization (Tosi and House, 1967).

Coaching

Trainees may be coached by superiors and other managers on performance, problem solving, handling of human relations, and so on. The effectiveness of coaching depends on whether the coach sees the trainee as a rival. Moreover, the coach is less effective if he rejects out of hand the independent needs of the trainee, if he is intolerant of mistakes, or if he does not allow sufficient time for coaching. The coaching should also strive for openness on the part of both the trainee and the coach.

Effective coaching, in general, requires that the coach be a model with whom the trainee identifies. For such identification to occur, the trainee must see the coach as skilled in coaching and in other aspects of his and the trainee's job. The acceptance of the superior as a qualified coach will largely depend on the extent to which the coach accepts his responsibilities both as a superior and as a coach, and if he provides the trainee with immediate feedback, recognizing both achievements and needed improvements (Levinson, 1962).

The skills attendant to effective coaching may be developed as part of a particular manager's own training. It has even been suggested that coaching should be regarded as a formal activity for training new subordinates and as a regular, day-to-day activity for all managers (Mahler, 1967). Thus, new management trainees might include a course in coaching as part of their own developmental efforts. In fact, managers themselves should see such training in coaching skills as necessary for their own self-development. Coaching skills in line with management-by-objectives practices are more frequently being advocated. In such a framework, mutual goal setting and performance appraisal interviews become the basis of coaching. The emphasis in the superior-subordinate coaching relationship is on the sharing of work structuring and performance evaluation. A formal guide may be used to aid in setting goals and in reviewing and analyzing performance (Banaka, 1967).

SPECIAL ASSIGNMENTS

The developing manager may be given special problems to solve, reports to prepare, or tasks to complete that are not part of his regular job. His performance can be evaluated and his success or failure with tasks of increasing complexity can be reviewed with his coach. Assignments may involve joining special committees, task forces, or brands of inquiry.

LECTURES AND LIVE TELEVISION

These techniques remain popular, particularly abroad. The dynamic lecturer still has a role as a stimulator but probably is not so effective in imparting general information to be retained as the printed word. Some value seems to accrue from meeting or seeing in person the source of ideas. However, the learning value of the presentation often will depend on the advance preparation of the listener and his subsequent opportunities for discussion.

FILMS, AUDIO, AND VIDEOTAPES AND CASSETTES

The field seems flooded with these devices. Yet, in general, they do not seem to have been used imaginatively or creatively or flexibly. Rather, they tend to remain "talk shows" similar to lectures. Again, the context in which they are used will determine their learning value. Trainees require opportunities to discuss, test, and review what they have seen or heard.

VIDEO TAPE REPLAY

With video tape replay (VTR) systems, self-confrontation becomes possible. One may see oneself as others do and, thus, apply different and hopefully more useful standards of perceiving oneself and others. Sandia Corporation, for example, has already used VTR systems in its sensitivity training programs. One purported benefit of such application is the "authentic confrontation of oneself and of others on a realistic and undeniable level" (Dehon, 1967). Despite its obvious strengths, however, VTR's recent state of development and frequent misuse have contributed little empirical evidence so far of positive behavior change that can be uniquely achieved through its use (Stroh, 1969).

SPECIAL STUDY

As part of their development, managers can read an article or book, attend a conference, enroll in a university course or curriculum leading to a degree, or attend a special management development program of 2 days to 2 years at an institute, business school, or university. Study can range from capital budgeting to organizational psychology and from applied mathematics to community affairs. A number of evaluations of these kinds of activities (which were more than merely asking trainees how they felt about their education experience) have reported favorable results (Gruenfeld, 1966). For instance, a most unusual 10-months university program in the humanities for Bell Telephone of Pennsylvania executives found participants to be more flexible and innovative in problem solving than a control group that was still solving problems in older, more conservative ways (Viteles, 1959).

CASE DISCUSSIONS AND CONFERENCES

Case examinations by a group of participants of an organizational problem and its background history is a profitable learning experience to the extent that participants can identify principles involved in the situation. Learning may accrue from tackling a problem for which there is no necessarily right answer through a review of the adequacy of each person's attempted diagnosis. On occasion, trainees may also receive information on what actually happened to the real organization that was the subject of the discussion (Pigors and Pigors, 1961). The effective discussion leader is the most important person in a conference, just as he is in a case study. He becomes effective to the extent that he poses questions and creates conditions that enable and encourage trainees to discover answers for themselves, and then to evaluate them. The ability of a conference leader to provide those conditions is not a simple skill. It is quite easy for a less than well-trained discussion leader to turn a discussion into a lecture or an exhibition of his own biases. Moreover, if the discussion leader does not have a fairly good idea of the course he expects the discussion to take, it can easily degenerate into nothing more than a series of irrelevant or incorrect contributions by the individual trainees (Lerda, 1967).

ROLE PLAYING

Rather than discussing problems, trainees assume roles of the various people involved in the problem. They spontaneously act as they think the person might whose role they are playing. Participants can become aware of another person's feelings in this way and become more susceptible to real behavior change (Brehm and Cohen, 1962; Janis and King, 1954). A manager placed in the role of a shop steward is forced to verbalize opinions that the steward but not the manager holds. In doing so, there is some tendency to begin to accept what the real steward might say.

Unfortunately, trainees may resist role playing as childish or to avoid embarrassing exposure. Also, acting ability and wit may be emphasized instead of useful insights.

GAMES AND SIMULATION

Here, some critical feature of an organization is abstracted and presented to a trainee. He is not to study or analyze it as such, but rather he is supposed to experience it as a realistic lifelike circumstance. Such simulation of business organizations had its beginnings in 1956 when the American Management Association introduced its first computer-based model (Ricciardi *et al.*, 1957). At about the same time, the Andlinger or McKinsey game, a non-computerized game, was developed with computations done by hand calculation (Andlinger, 1958). Since then, hundreds of both types have appeared ranging from running oil refineries to managing research and development programs (Denault, 1967). To increase complexity and fidelity to real life, many options may be open, like purchasing market research information or dissolving or expanding current facilities. Special incidents may be built into the game such as depressed markets, changes in government policy, and accidents.

Winning or losing is characteristic of games. Teams compete in a common market—or they perceive themselves in competition but may be actually playing against a standard market model. Ordinarily, teams receive information, make decisions, and receive information on the effects of their decisions. The cycle can be repeated. Learning is expected to occur as a consequence of observing the effects of one's performance. Often, however, players put too much emphasis on winning or beating the computer and not enough on critiques of the decisions. The highly involving business game usually forces the trainee to analyze information, to experiment with new solutions, to cooperate with other people with whom he is supposed to represent an organization, and to generally be flexible and attentive. Unfortunately, often, because of time compression when four quarters of a real year may be four half-hours of a game, more attention is given to immediate crises and less on long-range planning. Results of the training effectiveness of games have been mixed. Game and non-game training were compared in developing accounting skills. The game group learned more and received higher grades at the completion of training than a comparable group of managers who were trained without using a game (Steinmetz and Patten, 1967). On the other hand, trainees obtained a greater "mastery of the facts" in production management from a case discussion than from a game (Moore, 1967).

In both studies, authors attributed their opposing results to motivation. Gamesters were involved and therefore more interested in accounting, but they also tried to beat the system and therefore did not learn as much about production management. At this point, we can only say that a game may increase motivation to learn, which may or may not be helpful depending on what else accompanies it.

In the *in-basket* simulation, an individual exercise, each trainee assumes the role of an executive who has just found, on returning from a trip, a collection of memos, letters, messages, and notes left in his in-basket by his secretary. Each item is a problem. The role player tries to draft appropriate instruction to his secretary on how each is to be dealt with. Again, the critique that follows the trainee's attempt may be the most important part of the learning experience. Trainees can see how they differ from others in such managerial behavior as making quick decisions rather than reserving judgment (Belman and Hull, 1967; Gagne, 1962, p. 457).

PROGRAMMED TEXTS AND STRUCTURED EXERCISES

Applications of programmed instruction in management training have mostly been restricted to factual information transmission. Thus far, programmed instruction has been successfully used with newly hired managers at Union Electric Co. of St. Louis to orient them to company policies and practices (McClintock, Vanderplas, and Zick, 1967). When compared to conventional techniques, the programmed orientation took less time and participants retained more information. Programmed instruction has also been used at Lockheed Corporation to familiarize managers with PERT (Programmed Evaluation and Review Technique) as an approach to problem and system analysis (Sugden, 1967). Programmed texts appear most relevant for factual instruction rather than for dealing with the interpersonal and socio-emotional issues of management. For this, programs of structured group exercises become more relevant. These incorporate elements of case studies, small group experiments, role playing, and laboratory training. Sets of these programs have been developed for management (Bass, 1965). The fifteen exercises for managers deal with budgeting, compensation, supervision, negotiating, communications, risk preferences, investment strategies, and so on. For a given exercise, each manager first records his own responses to the problem posed in a booklet. Subsequently, the small groups meet to discuss overall results and implications. "Here-and-now" behavior associated with the individual and small-group decisions are also reviewed.

The advantages of standardized programs of exercises as opposed to similar cases and role plays is that normative results are collected and provided trainers on a large sample of trainees. (Although in existence only for 5 years, norms on 11,000 managers were distributed in 1971 for the Program of Exercises in Management and Organizational Development (Bass, Alexander, and Krusell, 1971.) Individual trainees can immediately compare their own performance with relevant management groups. Research is currently in progress in developing norms for effective and ineffective managers so that trainers may be in a position ultimately to answer the common question of exercise participants: "What is a good response? What does a good manager do?"

Laboratory Training

The essence of such training is its focus on the "here-and-now" behavior of small groups of participants. The participants tackle some problem together. Then they share their opinions and feelings about what happened. Ostensibly, each can learn how he affects others and how they affect him on matters that often lie submerged in everyday life but interfere with the effectiveness of individuals and teams at work.

The problem may be extremely unstructured, as in sensitivity training, to develop a group with shared norms, mutual trust, acceptable decision-making processes and clear goals. Or the problem may be structured initially to focus on one's own managerial style, as in Grid Training (Blake and Mouton, 1964). Or the problem may be structured initially so that participants can focus as members of a team on a budget, compensation plan, or investment portfolio, as in the case of standardized small-group exercises (Bass, 1965) discussed earlier. A trainer may be present to help the group in its review of its processes. Trainers are most necessary if no structured problems are provided. Proponents argue that effective managerial action must be based on emotional as well as intellectual understanding (Argyris, 1964; Bennis, 1962), as well as greater skill in relating to other people (Tannenbaum *et al.*, 1961). These objectives are met by increasing the accuracy with which the individual manager perceives himself and others (Argyris, 1964; Bennis *et al.*, 1961). A knowledge of group processes can be derived. Moreover, the trainee can learn how to learn from others (Schein and Bennis, 1965). More authentic relationships with others are sought; relationships that are open and above board. With such authentic relationships, both collaboration and conflict may be more effectively considered (Reed, 1966).

Subject to close scrutiny, the empirical data supporting the effectiveness of laboratory training approaches are still quite equivocal (Campbell and Dunnette, 1968; Harrison, 1967). Studies have shown its impact on reported critical incidents 6 months after training (Morton and Bass, 1964). Judged or observed behavior changes in the trainees sometime after training have been found (Miles, 1965; Bunker, 1965). On the other hand, other controlled studies have failed to obtain such results (Gassner, Gold, and Snadowsky, 1964; Underwood, 1965). Moreover, some instances are recorded in which *T*-groups did induce change but not in entirely desirable directions (Buchanan and Brunstetter, 1959).

Laboratory training needs to be considered in terms of the organizational climate to which a manager-participant will return after training. The experience may be counter-productive and frustrating, for example, if he returns to a highly authoritarian boss and politically oriented subordinates, all of whom value power rather than power-equalization. For this and other reasons, the opportunity for pre- and post-training consultations by the trainer with relevant organization officials and training participants may prove an effective design feature (Friedlander, 1968). The goals of the laboratory training need to be defined by the goals of the organization. Most generally, laboratory training must be seen as part of a larger organizational development effort.

ILLUSTRATIVE INTEGRATED PROGRAMS

Integrated management development involves a continuing affair that begins with recruiting strategies and ends with retirement planning. Its main features include assessment and diagnosis at various stages of a manager's career, counseling, self-improvement to avoid obsolescence, reading, attending special lectures, conferences, workshops, and regular enrollment in longer courses and curricula of training and education at universities and institutes or at company-sponsored centers. These longer enrollments at centers are often highlights in the management development process.

A typical company-sponsored center is Western Electric's Corporate Training Center in New York City (Keough, 1967). Each session of the program takes 22 weeks of full-time training for fourteen of the company's most promising second- and third-level supervisors. The program begins with 2 weeks of laboratory training, which focuses on building better interpersonal relations. The laboratory training is supplemented by the use of programmed exercises, video tape, and lectures. Next comes a section on labor relations utilizing mostly lecture material. Subsequently, the program turns its attention to administrative policies and practices in which case studies of Western Electric are utilized. Next, business in the American economy is covered, including such issues as economic history, theories of economics, and the role of the Federal Reserve Board. This is followed by an examination of managerial control, accounting, and financial analysis. Later on, newer developments in management science are covered. Finally, the program winds up with discussions and lectures on the role of the organization in public affairs and community relations. Following the conclusion of the program, the managers who are selected are sent to new job locations in areas other than the one they occupied before training began.

The *Health Services Administrator's Development Program* is in marked contrast to the Western Electric program. The first and last 2 weeks are in a rural setting away from home positions. In between, participants correspond with faculty of the University of Alabama Medical School. Simulation of a real hospital setting is featured during the first 2 weeks. During the correspondence phase, the participants receive selected readings, case studies, and essay questions from the Medical Center Faculty at the University of Alabama in the form of lessons in sequence. Each lesson is completed, returned to the Medical Center, graded, and returned to participants. After it has been graded, the lesson is returned to the student's preceptor who discusses the outcomes and directions for future improvement with the student.

Public Programs

Numerous associations and organizations specialize in training programs for managers from a variety of organizations—so-called public workshops. They include the American Society for Training and Development, the American Management Association, the National Conference Board, the Society for the Advancement of Management, and many others. There are, in addition, other associations concerned with management training related to specific fields. For example, there is the American Accounting Association, the Life Office Management Association, and the National Society of Sales Training Executives. The combined efforts of these various associations produce an almost overwhelming number of different training activities. For example, in the general training area, the American Management Association schedules approximately 1,850 meetings a year with a total attendance of over 112,000 participating managers (Gardiner, 1967). The majority of the programs last from 1 to 5 days and some are broken down into fifteen sessions of 1½ hours twice weekly, seventeen sessions of 3 hours based on intervals of two weeks, and so on. Meetings are held in hotels, college campuses, resort clubs, local facilities such as the YMCA, and special training facilities such as the Hamilton, New York, facility of the American Management Association. Each of these institutions usually provides a variety of training programs covering technical as well as human relations issues for managers. More specialized training programs in specific areas range from the Gellerman Film Series, which focuses on a variety of topics and uses a mixture of film presentations and lecture discussions, to the well-known Blake and Mouton Managerial Grid, which focus each manager's attention on his own interpersonal style and its implications for his performance in his own department, in relating to other departments and to the organization. In another area is the Kepner-Tregoe program, which focuses on management problem solving and decision-making. In the Kepner-Tregoe program, an analytical framework for approaching decisions and problem analysis is provided and applied to various job situations. Small team effort is featured, with each member having a different function, such as quality control or product manager. Each case presented to a team attempts to provide a clear picture of the key ideas of problem analysis. Diversity of actions in the various teams are compared. Comparisons of team outcome include problem definition, analysis, and outcomes. The course focuses first on recognizing problems prior to decision-making, specifying these problems, testing out various possible causes, and verifying actual causes. In the workshop, a distinction is made between problem and decision analysis in that a different analysis is required to determine the cause of the problem from that which is required to select a best alternative action (Tregoe, 1966).

EVALUATION

We now return full circle to where we began. Training should be based on an organization's objectives and a manager's needs. Evaluation should deal with how well training efforts help managers and organizations to meet needs and objectives.

At least five "publics" may be interested in finding out about the success of such training efforts: (1) the trainees; (2) the trainer; (3) the supervisor; (4) the organization's policy makers: the training program's sponsors; and (5) the training technologists and scientists (Bass, Thiagarajan, and Ryterband, 1968). These five groups may, in fact, do the evaluating as well. Which means that one can concur (as was done by Hesseling, 1966) in at least 25 possible types of evaluations! These are displayed in Table 16. Thus, for example, if trainees are evaluating training for their own purpose, they will be interested in clarifying their own learning processes. In contrast, their supervisors may be assessing trainees for the sake of improving trainee job performance. In such a case, the contents of evaluation ought to focus on a formal appraisal, based on job performance.

TABLE 16. A TYPOLOGY OF EVALUATIONS

Assessment by Whom	Assessment for Whom: *Trainees*	*Trainers*	*Supervisors*	*Policy makers*	*Scientists*
Trainees	1 gradual clarification of learning process; looking glass for each other's behaviour	2 feed-back from learner-teacher relation; process control	3 reporting personal impressions	4 reporting personal impressions (usually via superiors)	5 data for further analysis; direct observation, interviews, tests
Trainers	6 feed-back from teacher-learner relation; steering evaluation	7 exchange of experiences e.g. trainers' conferences	8 formal reporting on activities	9 reporting suggestions for follow-up (usually via superiors)	10 data for further analysis; first step evaluation
Supervisors	11 formal appraisal based upon job performance and training appraisal	12 depending on position of trainer; appraisal or indication for support	13 exchange of experience; preparation for policy	14 major indication for success or failure, suggestions for policy	15 data for further analysis; organizational variables
Policy makers	16 sometimes formal introduction or conclusion of training programme	17 depending on position; determination of training objectives and general standards of performance	18 formal appraisal of training activities	19 general appraisal of training objectives and means; long-term policy	20 organizational variables and starting point for evaluation research
Scientists	21 in adapted form material for reading and lecturing	22 guidelines for improved training; standards of training	23 support for appraisal; standards of performance	24 preparation for decision making; practical prognoses	25 understanding dynamics of change; methodology and theory of change

THE DESIGN OF AN EVALUATION

The most basic element in an evaluation of training design is the comparison of a trainee's behavior, attitudes and/or opinions both before and after training. The basic assumption is that if the training had some viability, behavior will have changed as a result of training. The critical question is not whether a change in behavior occurs, but whether it is because managers were trained. To locate the cause of any changes that occur in training itself rather than any extraneous factors is the most difficult achievement in the training design. It requires, among other things, the use of control groups. That is, trainees must be assessed before and after training and *compared* to similar managers at identical times whose only difference from the trainee is that they did not have training. In addition, when to evaluate is an important question. A before-after comparison is essential. But at what times? Often, the desired behavior change is expected to reveal itself as soon as participants leave training. For example, supervisors who are given new information on how to improve budgets should immediately make fewer and less serious errors in budgets that they submit to their superiors. In contrast, participants may be involved in a business game that focuses on making better policy decisions. The outcomes of such an experience may not be expected to reveal themselves for some time. In either case, the duration and number of observations made in evaluating training should be sufficient to allow effects of training to show and to prevent chance fluctuations in day-to-day or week-to-week performance from contaminating the reliability of observations made (Hesseling, 1966).

Many more subtle factors need to be considered here but space limitations prohibit protracted considerations. Rather, we can only suggest strongly that evaluation of training (1) be planned at the same time as the training is being planned rather than introduced as an afterthought; (2) that the most vigorous rather than the most inexpedient experimental design be followed; and (3) that multiple, repeated measurements be employed rather than relying on a single measurement to confirm or refute the benefits of the training effort.

SUMMARY

If an organization is to successfully accomplish its goals, it must have on hand a continuous and sufficient supply of competent management personnel. To provide for this ongoing supply of management personnel, an organization must realize through its management development program (1) that new positions will be created as it grows; (2) old positions will become vacant due to voluntary and involuntary retirement; (3) new managers will have to acquire old skills; and (4) new skills will need to be introduced into the repertoire of present managers.

Management development is one activity of the organization of mutual concern to the individual manager and the organization.

An organization provides formal and informal management development programs. These aim to improve current and future managerial performance by imparting appropriate knowledge, attitudes, and increasing skills. To conduct effective management programs, organizations initially need to involve themselves in a systematic analysis of management development needs. This requires an analysis of the needs of the organization as a whole, the jobs for which training will be needed, and the men who will receive the training. Thereafter, the organization must provide the conditions in which the desired learning can occur.

There are many methods by which an organization can involve itself in management development. There are techniques that communicate a variety of behaviors, both on-the-job and off-the-job, and techniques that focus on individuals or on groups. These techniques, including lectures, case studies, simulations, and sensitivity training cover a continuum ranging from intellectual methods involving essentially teach-and-tell paradigms to experiential and exploratory techniques.

Finally, in conducting management development programs, the organization should continuously evaluate its efforts. The purpose of these evaluations should be to enhance experiences that are increasing effectiveness on the job and alter, reduce, or do away with those that are having no such positive effect.

SUGGESTIONS FOR FUTURE READING

ALBROOK, R. C., "Why It's Harder to Keep Good Executives," *Fortune,* Vol. 78, No. 6 (1968), pp. 136–140.

American Management Association, *Management 2000* (Hamilton, New York: American Foundation for Management Research, 1968).

ANDLINGER, G. R., "Business Games—Play One," *Harvard Business Review,* Vol. 36, No. 2 (1958).

ARGYRIS, C., *Interpersonal Competence and Organizational Effectiveness* (Homewood, Illinois: Richard D. Irwin and The Dorsey Press, 1962).

ARGYRIS, C., *Integrating the Individual and the Organization* (New York: John Wiley & Sons, 1964).

ARGYRIS, C., "T-groups for Organizational Effectiveness," *Harvard Business Review,* Vol. 42, No. 2 (1964), pp. 60–74.

BANAKA, W. H., "Invention: A Key to Effective Coaching," *Training and Development Journal,* Vol. 21, No. 4 (1967), pp. 44–52.

BARRETT, G. V., B. M. BASS, AND J. A. MILLER, "Combatting Obsolescence Using Perceived Discrepancies in Job Expectations of Research Managers and Scientists—A Preliminary Report. Technical Report 37, ONR Contract N00014-67-A-0398-0006, NR 151-314 (Rochester, New York: The University of Rochester, July 1, 1970).

BASS, B. M., *A Program of Exercises in Management and Organizational Psychology* (Pittsburgh: Management Development Associates, 1965).

BASS, B. M., "The Anarchist Movement and the T-group," *Journal of Applied Behavioral Science,* Vol. 3 (1967), pp. 211–226.

BASS, B. M., R. A. ALEXANDER, AND J. KRUSELL, Selected Manager Norms (as of

September, 1970) for *A Program of Exercises for Management and Organizational Psychology.* Technical Report 41, ONR Contract N00014-67-A-0398-0002, NR 171-029 (Rochester, New York: The University of Rochester, April 1, 1971).

BASS, B. M., K. M. THIAGARAJAN, AND E. C. RYTERBAND, On the Assessment of the Training Value of Small Group Exercises for Managers. Technical Report 22, ONR Contract NONR N00014-67(A) (Rochester, New York: The University of Rochester, August 15, 1968).

BASS, B. M., AND J. A. VAUGHAN, *Training in Industry: The Management of Learning* (Belmont, California: Wadsworth Publishing Co., 1966).

BASS, B. M., J. A. VAUGHAN, AND E. H. SCHEIN, *Exercise Self-Appraisal* (Rochester, New York: INSTAD, Ltd., 1968).

BELMAN, H. S., AND T. F. HULL, "Supervisor Development," in R. L. Craig and L. R. Bittel (Eds.), *Handbook of Training and Development* (New York: McGraw-Hill Book Co., Inc., 1967), pp. 338–362.

BENNIS, W. G., "Goals and Meta-goals of Laboratory Training," *Human Relations Training News,* Vol. 6, No. 3 (1962), pp. 1–4.

BENNIS, W. G., "Organizational Developments and the Fate of Bureaucracy," *Industrial Relations Review,* Vol. 2 (1966), pp. 41–55 (a).

BENNIS, W. G., K. BENNE, AND R. CHIN (Eds.), *The Planning of Change* (New York: Holt, Rinehart and Winston, 1961).

BERKWIT, G. J., "Middle Management vs. the Computer," *Dun's Review* (November, 1966), pp. 40–42 ff.

BLAKE, P. R., AND J. S. MOUTON, *The Managerial Grid* (Houston, Texas: Gulf Publishing Co., 1964).

BREHM, J. W., AND A. R. COHEN, *Explorations in Cognitive Dissonance* (New York: John Wiley & Sons, 1962).

BUCHANAN, P. E., AND P. H. BRUNSTETTER, "A Research Approach to Management Development," Part II, *Journal of American Society of Training Directors,* Vol. 15 (1959), pp. 18–27.

BUNKER, D. R., "The Effect of Laboratory Education upon Individual Behavior," in E. H. Schein and W. G. Bennis (Eds.), *Personal and Organizational Change through Group Methods* (New York: John Wiley & Sons, 1965).

CAMPBELL, J., "Assessments of Higher Level Personnel, I: Background and Scope of the Research," *Personnel Psychology,* Vol. 15 (1962).

CAMPBELL, J., J. OTIS, R. E. LISKE, AND E. P. PRIEN, "Assessments of Higher Level Personnel, II: Validity of the Over-all Assessment Process," *Personnel Psychology,* Vol. 15 (1962).

CAMPBELL, J. P., AND M. D. DUNNETTE, "The Effectiveness of T-group Experience in Managerial Training and Development," *Psychological Bulletin,* Vol. 70, No. 2 (1968), pp. 73–104.

CHOWDRY, K., "Management Development Programs: Executive Needs," *Industrial Management Review,* Vol. 4, No. 2 (1963), pp. 31–40.

DEHON, W. H., "Self Confrontation via TV: Video Taped Feedback for Training at Sandia Laboratory," *Training and Development Journal,* Vol. 21, No. 10 (1967), p. 43.

DENAULT, M. F., "Developing the Engineer as a Manager Using Computerized Simulation," *Training and Development Journal,* Vol. 21, No. 9 (1967), pp. 83–87.

DILL, W. R., W. B. S. CROWSTON, AND E. J. ELTON, "Strategies for Self-education," *Harvard Business Review* (November–December, 1965), pp. 119–130.

DUNNETTE, M. D., AND W. K. KIRCHNER, *Psychology Applied to Industry* (New York: Appleton-Century-Crofts, 1965).

FLEISHMAN, E. A., "Leadership Climate, Human Relations Training and Supervisory Behavior," *Personnel Psychology*, Vol. 6 (1953), pp. 205–222.

FLEISHMAN, E. A., E. F. HARRIS, AND J. BURTT, *Leadership and Supervision in Industry* (Columbus, Ohio: Ohio State University Bureau of Educational Monographs, No. 33, 1955).

FLORY, C. D. (Ed.), *Managers for Tomorrow* (New York: New American, Library, 1965).

FOREMAN, W. J., "Management Training in Large Organizations," *Training and Development Journal*, Vol. 21, No. 5 (1967), pp. 11–18.

FRIEDLANDER, F. A., "Comparative Study of Consulting Processes and Group Development," *Journal of Applied Behavioral Science*, Vol. 4, No. 4 (1968), pp. 377–401.

GAGNE, R. M., *Psychological Principles in System Design* (New York: Holt, Rinehart and Winston, 1962).

GARDINER, G. L., "Special Programs," in R. L. Craig and L. R. Bittel (Eds.), *Handbook of Training and Development* (New York: McGraw-Hill Book Co., Inc., 1967), pp. 459–473.

GARDNER, J. W., *Self-Renewal* (New York: Harper & Row, 1963).

GASSNER, S. M., J. GOLD, AND A. M. SNADOWSKY, "Changes in the Phenomenal Field as a Result of Human Relations Training," *Journal of Psychology*, Vol. 58 (1964), pp. 33–41.

GIBB, C. A. "An Experimental Approach to the Study of Leadership," *Occupational Psychology*, Vol. 25 (1951), pp. 233–248.

GRUENFELD, L. W., "Management Development Effect on Changes in Values," *Training and Development Journal*, Vol. 20, No. 6 (1966), pp. 18–26.

HAAS, J. A., Middle Manager's Expectations of the Future World of Work: Implications for Management Development. Unpublished Doctoral Dissertation, University of Pittsburgh, 1969.

HAAS, J. A., B. M. BASS, AND E. C. RYTERBAND, *Exercise Future* (Rochester, New York: INSTAD, Ltd., 1969).

HALPIN, A. W., "The Leader Behavior and Effectiveness of the Aircraft Commanders," in R. M. Stogdill and A. E. Coons (Eds.), *Leader Behavior: Its Description and Measurement* (Columbus, Ohio: Ohio State University Bureau of Business Research, Monograph 88, 1957).

HARRISON, R., "Problems in the Design and Interpretation of Research in Human Relations Training," *Explorations: Human Relations Training and Research* (Washington, D.C.: NTL Institute for Applied Behavioral Science, 1967).

HARTMAN, R. I., "Some Managerial Implications of the Cybernation Revolution," *Personnel Journal*, Vol. 48, No. 1 (1969), pp. 42–48.

HESSELING, P., *Strategy of Evaluation Research* (Assen, Netherlands: VanGorcum & Co., 1966).

HOUSE, R. J., *Management Development* (Ann Arbor: University of Michigan Graduate School of Business Administration, Bureau of Industrial Relations, 1967).

HULL, J. W., "Management's Responsibilities for Tomorrow's Managers," in S. Ramo, M. W. Gross, J. W. Hull, and L. A. Appley (Eds.), *Meeting Today's Responsibilities for Tomorrow's Managers* (Pasadena: California Institute of Technology Industrial Relations Center, 1964).

HUSE, E., "Assessments of Higher Level Personnel, IV: Validity of Assessment Techniques Based on Systematically Varied Information," *Personnel Psychology,* Vol. 15 (1962), pp. 195–205.

JANIS, I. L., AND B. T. KING, "The Influence of Role Playing on Opinion Change," *Journal of Abnormal and Social Psychology,* Vol. 49 (1954), pp. 211–218.

KEOUGH, E. T., "An Evolving Management Training Program," *Training and Development Journal,* Vol. 21, No. 9 (1967), pp. 64–70.

KURTZ, A. K., "A Research Test on the Rorschach Test," *Personnel Psychology,* Vol. 1 (1948), pp. 41–51.

LERDA, L. W., "Conference Methods," in R. L. Craig and L. R. Bittel (Eds.), *Training and Development Handbook* (New York: McGraw-Hill Book Co., Inc., 1967), pp. 154–174.

LEVINSON, H. A., "A Psychologist Looks at Executive Development," *Harvard Business Review,* Vol. 40, No. 5 (1962), pp. 69–75.

MAHLER, W. R., "Coaching," in R. L. Craig and L. R. Bittel (Eds.), *Training and Development Handbook* (New York: McGraw-Hill Book Co., Inc., 1967), pp. 129–140.

MARCH, J. G. (Ed.), *Handbook of Organizations* (Chicago: Rand McNally, 1965).

MCCLINTOCK, M., J. VANDERPLAS, AND D. C. ZICK, "Orientating the New Employee with Programmed Instruction," *Training and Development Journal,* Vol. 21, No. 5 (1967), pp. 18–20.

MERRILL, H. F., AND E. MARTING (Eds.), *Developing Executive Skills* (New York: American Management Association, 1958).

MILES, M. B., "Learning Processes and Outcomes in Human Relations Training: A Clinical-Experimental Study," in E. Schein and W. Bennis (Eds.), *Personal and Organization Change through Group Methods* (New York: John Wiley & Sons, 1965), pp. 244–254.

MILLER, J. A., J. A. HAAS, B. M. BASS, AND E. C. RYTERBAND, *Exercise Future* (Pittsburgh: INSTAD, Ltd., 1970).

MOORE, L. F., "Business Games vs. Cases as Tools of Learning," *Training and Development Journal,* Vol. 21, No. 10 (1967), pp. 13–23.

MORTON, R. B., AND B. M. BASS, "The Organizational Training Laboratory," *Training Directors Journal,* Vol. 18, No. 10 (1964), pp. 2–18.

ODIORNE, G. S., *Management by Objectives: A System of Managerial Leadership* (New York: Pitman Publishing Co., 1965).

Personnel Policies Forum, *Executive Development* (Washington, D.C.: Bureau of National Affairs, 1967).

PIGORS, P., AND F. PIGORS, *Case Method in Human Relations: The Incident Process* (New York: McGraw-Hill Book Co., Inc., 1961).

REED, J. H., "Two Weeks of Managed Conflict at Bethel," *Training and Development Journal,* Vol. 20, No. 2 (1966), pp. 6–16.

RICCIARDI, F. M. *et al., Top Management Decision Simulation* (New York: American Management Association, 1957).

RUKEYSER, W. S., "How Youth is Reforming the Business World," *Fortune,* Vol. 79, No. 1 (1969), pp. 76.

SCHEIN, E. H., "Attitude Change during Management Education," *Administrative Science Quarterly,* Vol. 11 (June–March, 1966–67), pp. 601–607, 614–628.

SCHEIN, E. H., AND W. G. BENNIS (Eds.), *Personal and Organizational Change through Group Methods* (New York: John Wiley & Sons, 1965).

STEINMETZ, L. L., AND R. J. PATTEN, "Enthusiasm, Interest and Learning: The

Results of Game Training," *Training and Development Journal*, Vol. 21, No. 4 (1967), pp. 26–37.

STOREY, W. D., AND B. L. BAKER, *Talent Development Program* (Ossining, New York: General Electric Company, Management Development Institute, 1969).

STROH, T. F., *The Uses of Video-tape in Training and Development* (New York: American Management Association, 1969).

SUGDEN, V. M. (Ed.), "Management Development Programs in Selected Industries On Long Island," *Hofstra University Yearbook of Business*, Vol. 3, Series 4 (1967), p. 329.

TANNENBAUM, R., I. R. WESCHLER, AND F. MASSARIK, *Leadership and Organization: A Behavioral Science Approach* (New York: McGraw-Hill Book Co., Inc., 1961).

TOSI, H. L., AND R. J. HOUSE, "Policies and Management Practices Specifically Related to Management Development," in R. J. House (Ed.), *Management Development* (Ann Arbor: University of Michigan Press, 1967), pp. 31–45.

TREGOE, B. B., "Management Problem Solving and Decision Making," *Training and Development Journal*, Vol. 20, No. 8 (1966), pp. 20–22.

TRIST, E. L., G. W. HIGGIN, H. MURRAY, AND A. B. POLLOCK, *Organizational Choice, Capabilities of Groups at the Coal Face under Changing Technologies: The Loss, Rediscovery and Transformation of a Work Tradition* (London: Tavistock, 1963).

UNDERWOOD, B. J., "Evaluation of Laboratory Method Training," *Training Directors Journal*, Vol. 19, No. 5 (1965), pp. 34–40.

VAUGHAN, J. A., A. M. PORAT, AND J. A. HAAS, *FDIC Study of the Impact of Computers on Managerial and Organizational Behavior in Small to Medium Sized Banks* (Pittsburgh: University of Pittsburgh Management Research Center, 1968).

VITELES, M. S., "Human Relations and the Humanities in the Education of Business Leaders: Evaluation of a Program of Humanistic Studies for Executives," *Personnel Psychology*, Vol. 12 (1959), pp. 1–28.

VITELES, M. S., "The Long-range Impact of a Program of Humanistic Studies for Business Executives on Managerial Attitudes and Behavior," *International Review of Applied Psychology*, Vol. 20 (1971), pp. 5–23.

Comments on "Management Development"

Robert J. House

Professor
Bernard M. Baruch College
City University of New York

If I were writing a chapter on management development, I would assume it would necessarily be an overview of present-day theories, research, and practices. Accordingly, I believe the following topics should be addressed:

1. Definition of Management Development.
2. Objectives of Management Development.
3. Distinguishing characteristics—i.e., what makes a managerial action eligible for inclusion under the topic.
4. Kinds of management development efforts that serve as inputs to achieve the desired objectives.
5. Conditions under which the various inputs are likely to have desired, neutral, or undesired effects.
6. A listing of methods or strategies that historically have been shown to be effective together with those currently in common use today.
7. An evaluation of the methods listed in (6) above in terms of their objectives, advantages, and disadvantages, and a brief summary of the empirical research that has been conducted on each.
8. An overall assessment of the scientific state of the art.
9. Prescriptive implications of above.
10. Implications of above for future research.

Lest the reader or the authors of this chapter accuse me of hypothetical wishful thinking, I refer them to Appendix I of House (1967) in which I indeed attempted to write such a piece. In any event, I will use the above outline as a guide to my comments.

First, the chapter addresses most of the topics I have listed, to a greater or lesser extent. As such it provides the reader with an overview of the field, some illustrations of management development methods and strategies, some caveats concerning their appropriate use, and some discussion of the conditions required for effective development to occur.

My criticisms of the chapter are for the most part concerned with the general and somewhat loose and incomplete manner in which it was written. Although I believe that some relatively important topics were omitted, I do not see these omissions as fair game for criticism.

My criticism of the manner of writing requires further elaboration. There appears to be no overall conceptual framework or integrated outline from which the authors were working. Consequently, a large number of topics and subtopics are covered. Some were given more space (and this implies to me more weight) than others, but the reason for this uneven treatment is not explained.

At times the authors are descriptive rather than evaluative or prescriptive. At other times they are evaluative and/or prescriptive. Some topics are well documented and others are not. Consequently, I found it hard to determine what the major points were and what the message was intended to be.

Referring now to my hypothetical outline, I think the chapter adequately handles topics (1), (2), and (3). I found the authors' discussions of laboratory groups, structured exercises, management-by-objectives, assessment centers, clinical diagnosis, and their discussion of various techniques (job rotation, coaching, special assignments, etc.) to be relevant to topics (4) and (6). However, I would like to have seen a more even treatment of these topics, and more recognition of the empirical research relevant to each. The reader is entitled to know not only the opinion of the writers but also the evidence on which this opinion is based. For many of these topics I found the authors' failure to cite, and/or describe, relevant research to be a serious omission. For example, the work of Carroll and Tosi (1970) and Tosi and Carroll (1968) and Meyer and Walker (1961) clearly is relevant to the developmental effects of management-by-objectives. Campbell and Dunnette's (1968) rather exhaustive and critical review of laboratory training was not mentioned, nor were some of the alleged dysfunctions of laboratory training. Nor was the extensive work of Maier (1963) on role playing. Thus, the reader is left with the impression that the validity of the various methods listed is approximately equal and the major differences are only in their content and objective.

The authors place a great deal of emphasis on climate and needs analysis, which I believe is warranted. I would like them to have (1) recognized the difficulties in carrying out such analyses, (2) informed the reader that the allotted space for these topics can only introduce them, (3) pointed out the major considerations involved, and (4) provided the reader with references for more intensive reading. I felt they implied (1) and accomplished (3) admirably. I would have preferred an explicit treatment of the difficulties and some guides to the reader for extended study.

I found topic (9) of my hypothetical outline running throughout and somewhat unfocused because of the uneven style. A lesser criticism, and perhaps attributable to my own bias and taste, concerns the almost complete lack of attention to topics (8) and (10). I personally believe these topics are important to the student, academician, and practitioner.

SUGGESTIONS FOR FUTURE READING

CAMPBELL, J. P., AND M. D. DUNNETTE, "Effectiveness of T-Group Experiences in Managerial Training and Development," *Psychological Bulletin*, Vol. 70 (1968), pp. 73–104.

CARROLL, S. J., Jr., AND H. L. TOSI, "Goal Characteristics and Personality Factors in a Management-by-Objectives Program," *Administrative Science Quarterly*, Vol. 15 (1970), pp. 295–305.

HOUSE, R. J., "Leadership Training: Some Dysfunctional Consequences of Leadership Training," *Administrative Science Quarterly*, Vol. 12 (1968), pp. 556–571.

HOUSE, R. J., *Management Development: Design, Evaluation and Implementation* (Ann Arbor: University of Michigan, Bureau of Industrial Relations, 1967).

MAIER, N. R. F., *Problem Solving Discussions and Conferences* (New York: McGraw-Hill Book Co., Inc., 1963).

MEYER, H. H., AND H. B. WALKER, "A Study of Factors Relating to the Effectiveness of a Performance Appraisal Program," *Personnel Psychology*, Vol. 3 (1961), pp. 291–298.

TOSI, H. L., AND S. J. CARROLL, JR., "Managerial Reactions to Management by Objectives," *Academy of Management Journal*, Vol. 11 (1968), pp. 415–426.

Goal Definition and Development

George S. Odiorne

Dean and Professor
College of Business
University of Utah

Few could find mistakes of omission in the splendid summary of the state of the art in management development by Professor Bass and Mr. Ryterband. One might express a small caveat, however, that some of the alternative approaches to management development are not fully treated. To the extent that pointing up such new trends is critique, this commentary might be considered as such. Several brief sentences might summarize the possible additions needed to round out the current picture of management development.

1. Management development should change behavior that produces a good result on a job, which is to say that *goal setting and objectives definitions is a necessary first step* to defining manager development needs.
2. The purpose of development should be to change behavior, and the desired behavior may be more significantly affected by *the job itself* than any planned training effort.
3. Once objectives have been defined and designed to affect the environment in such a way that desired behavior is more probable than under prior environmental conditions, *the need* for much formal training may have been eliminated.

GOAL DEFINITION COMES FIRST

Managerial behavior can only be judged as successful or unsuccessful if it relates to organization goal attainment. The evidence is reasonably clear that two unfavorable conditions exist that comprise a most prevalent explanation of wrong behavior. (1) In all human organizations there is a normal and perhaps natural tendency to start out for what was a once visible or clear objective only to find that the act of getting there has become more important than the objective. This "activity trap" produces a built-in diminishing of effectiveness, for the behavior thus becomes low yield rather than high yield. (2) In most organizations the average manager and his superior will not agree about what is expected in terms of results or outputs, even if the boss is quite diligent in demanding certain levels, forms, and styles of activity.

These two prevalent conditions point up the necessary first step in all management development. At the beginning of every time period (such as a quarter or a year) every manager and subordinate manager must sit down and talk about the results expected and the conditions that will exist if these results are well achieved or inadequately produced. These agreements should conform to good administration practices and transaction theory; they should be confirmed in writing. Thus, when the curtain rises on the play all actors have the same script, which improves the quality of the play.

How does this provide for future performance requirements? A second category of objectives is needed for the higher levels of management, often called strategic goals, in contrast with short-run or operational goals.

What comprises a fair statement of strategic objectives?

1. The top management will know where it now is in terms of statistical and qualitative elements.
2. It will be sufficiently alert to what is going on around it in the world to determine approximately where the organization would be if it did not do anything differently in 1, 2, 5, or 10 years.
3. It will have determined whether such projections look satisfactory. (Do we like the answer to question (2)?)
4. If it thus has defined possible areas of dissatisfaction in the future, it will present optional courses for the future and will have made directional choices among them. These choices are then converted into operational objectives for responsible people who will be committed to attainment of the first year of the multi-year plan.

The strategic goals and operational goals developed in the form of objectives statements that are strategic for higher-level management and staff positions and are operational for the managers and workers who must accept responsibility for delivering result are the fountainhead of behavior requirements. That is, the entire organization must be prepared, capable, and willing to behave in such a way as to achieve the results required and agreed on.

The first step in management development is goal setting, not for training and development goals, but organizational goals. The behavior of managers is derived from the needs of the organization.

DEVELOPMENT SHOULD CHANGE BEHAVIOR

Once it is understood that the objectives should produce relevant behavior, the steps in management development flow from the job results and outputs needed. If the person can produce the results, then no training is needed, and in fact might be damaging. If he can produce, and this is known because he has produced in the past, or is producing now, with good results, then no development need exists. If, however, his results are bad, a series of managerial actions of a developmental nature may be required.

1. *Informational steps.* One of the first requirements is that we assure ourselves that the man really is crystal clear about the specific character of the results sought. The assumption that he should be able to measure the results of his own efforts while he is doing his work is a sound one, too. This requires that goals be set periodically, but more, that he obtain information from the job itself indicating whether he is succeeding or failing, and to what degree, in attaining his objectives.

2. *Interference steps.* Many managers fail to achieve their goals because they live in a work environment in which systematic and unintended interference has been permitted to enter the work situation. The salesman with high goals who finds himself hampered by inadequate demonstration materials, broken promises from the plant, or lengthy and time-consuming paperwork is receiving negative stimuli that cause him to downgrade the importance of the goals.

3. *Payoff equations.* All too often there is a failure to provide payoff information for the right behavior. This involves more than simply pay, benefits, praise, and bonuses. It is more complex than Herzberg's KITA, or the traditional carrot-and-stick mixture. Often people adopt their behavior to the feedback they receive from their environment in a fashion as follows: (1) They behave wrongly because there are too many unfavorable payoffs from the system for doing the productive thing, and too many favorable consequences for the wrong or unproductive thing. The police official who condones graft, the sales manager who does not push new products, are behaving in response to favorable influences that accrue to them for that behavior, matched by few if any favorable consequences for honesty and hard selling. (2) They behave well and grow because there are numerous

affirmative signals for such behavior and because there are unfavorable signals from the organizational system for failing to achieve.

The management of these work systems, the social structure, the policies, the peer-group relations, are perhaps the new frontier for management development. They are often left untreated by those who would leap immediately into the more difficult domain of personality, attitude, and motivational change.

Thus, when a behavioral gap—the difference between the actual and the desired—is observed, it would probably be more productive for managers to check information, interferences, and payoffs before launching into more complex measures.

USE TRAINING AS A LAST RESORT

The trouble with training isn't that it doesn't work. It is that after the training is concluded, the people trained must return to a job where they will *continue to learn.* They will learn from their boss, from their peers, from the social environment, from the information coming to them, from interferences with work, from payoffs both favorable and unfavorable. Thus, the first step in training is to check the environment and determine if it will support the proposed behavior change objective for the course. If not, it would be advisable either to abandon training until conditions will support it or change the job conditions.

Once this environmental condition has been made consistent with the training, or the training has been adapted to provide behavior that can be supported, then the many excellent training prescriptions in Chapter 18 will fit well.

DISCUSSION QUESTIONS

1. Distinguish between organizational development and management development.
2. Discuss the sources from which managers are recruited and the advantages and disadvantages of recruiting from each source.
3. Elaborate on the statement: "Management development is self-development."
4. Compare laboratory groups, structured exercises, and management-by-objectives as methods of management development.
5. How can opportunities for management development be designed in an organization? What are some of the techniques used?
6. Discuss the use of games or simulation in management development.
7. What does Odiorne mean when he says: "The behavior of managers is derived from the needs of the organization."
8. Do you really believe that management development programs should change behavior? Why?

19

The Social Attitudes of Management

R. Joseph Monsen, Jr.

Professor
Graduate School of Business Administration
University of Washington

PUBLIC EXPECTATION, SOCIAL RESPONSIBILITY, AND PROFIT MAXIMIZATION

Why is there so much concern about the corporation's social responsibility in our contemporary society?[1] Why have public pressures for business to become active in solving social and ecological problems become a major phenomena in recent years? The plaintive question of corporative executives to these demands—"why us?"—and the corollaries—"What is social responsibility?" and "What corporate behavior does the public really expect of the corporation?" are seldom answered. The very term "social responsibility" is so vague and indeterminate that many economists and businessmen alike are reluctant to use it for fear of having to define it. Yet by pretending it does not exist does not make the demands for socially responsible business behavior go away. What kind of behavior, indeed, does the term imply?

A recent survey—made at the Stanford Business School—reported that of the 150 (out of 500) firms replying to the question, "Should business take an aggressive role in solving social problems?" 20 per cent of these firms directly committed their resources to social action projects. Another 50 per cent agreed in theory that business should become more heavily involved in solving social problems (but had themselves no specific programs). Twenty-five per cent believed that business carried out its social obligation by being profitable, paying taxes, and supplying jobs. The remaining 5 per cent felt that the proper role of business is not to become involved in social problems. Furthermore, the estimate was that "very few of the non-respondents would fit in the 'direct commitment' category." If the persistence of current demands continues, however, we may expect that the small proportion involved in "direct commitments" will increase.

A brief résumé of some of the major arguments *for* and *against* social responsibility by business may be useful as an overview.

A. Major arguments *for* social responsibility:

1. It is in the *long run self-interest* of the firm to promote and improve the communities where it does business.
2. It improves the *public image* of the firm.
3. It increases the *viability of the business system.* Business exists because it gives society benefits. Society can amend or take away its charter. This is the "iron law of responsibility."
4. It is necessary to *avoid government regulation.*
5. *Socio-cultural norms require it.*
6. Laws cannot be passed for all circumstances. Thus, business must assume responsibility to maintain an *orderly legal society.*
7. It is in the *stockholder's best interest.* It will improve the price of stock in the long run (as John Narver argues in the March 1971 *Academy of Management Journal*) because the stock market will view the company as less risky and open to public attack and, therefore, award it a higher price-earnings ratio.
8. Society should *give business a chance* to solve social problems that government has failed to solve.
9. *Business,* by some groups, *is* considered to be *the institution with the financial and human resources* to solve social problems.
10. *Problems can become profitable* if firms become involved.
11. *Prevention of problems is better than cures*—so let business solve problems before they become too great.

B. Major arguments *against* social responsibility:

1. *Violates profit maximization.*
2. *Cost* of social responsibility too great and would increase prices too much.
3. *Business lacks social skills* to solve societal problems.
4. *It would dilute business's primary purposes.*
5. *It would weaken U.S. balance of payments* because price of goods will have to go up to pay for social programs.
6. *Business already has too much power.* Such involvement would make business too powerful.
7. *Business lacks accountability to the public.* Thus the public would have no control over its social involvement.
8. *Such business involvement lacks broad public support.*

I am indebted to Keith Davis for the presentation of these arguments.

All of this does not say why there is pressure from various sources for direct corporate commitment to solve social problems. The most persuasive answer, to me, lies in a combination of the following facts: (1) Numerous social and ecological problems in our society exist and have grown worse with both action and inaction of government. These problems have been receiving wide publicity in the past decade—indeed, many such problems (such as industrial pollution) exist because of business. (2) Business represents one of the two most powerful institutions in our society. Only the government itself can be considered more powerful—and many, such as Ralph Nader, argue that government responds largely to business interests and thus business is the dominant institution in our nation.

These reasons, therefore, argue that since business is a major power in our society, it has an obligation (some would say a responsibility) toward solving those problems of public concern. If business demurs, then society's only recourse—usually through legislative action—is to withdraw some of the power business enjoys and bestow it on those institutions most able to fulfill public expectations. This would mean that in the majority of instances there will be increased government involvement—despite its uneven performance record in solving public needs.

For the businessman, this line of reasoning has introduced the new independent variable of *public expectation.* Corporations, of course, have had long experience in gauging consumer expectations. The successful business survives only if on balance it reads future demands correctly. In the case of public expectations regarding business behavior, the reading can be taken in similar fashion. Just as the White House seems to keep a weather eye on the various polls of public opinion (regardless of the question of accuracy), the corporation suite that follows this line of reasoning must do likewise.

In essence then, *the "social responsibility" of business is defined most simply,* in this approach, by *public expectations.* As long as business executives are reading these polls correctly (i.e., in accord with majority opinion) and pursuing business policies accordingly, they are being "socially responsible." In this form, however, this definition of social responsibility says nothing about corporations exerting leadership to change or "lead" public opinion.

No definition of social responsibility has gained much general acceptance. Indeed, the criterion for any definition depends on its use. Thus the various definitions of social responsibility imply certain levels of "activism" and should be examined in that light.

Apart from those definitions that say profit maximization is business's only social responsibility (which can justify any level of corporate "activism"), it appears that there is a *hierarchy of levels of business "activism"* depending on the particular definition of *social responsibility* used. At the bottom level, the meeting of legal requirements is *the* only necessary and sufficient socially responsible course *for the firm;* the second step suggests that *public expectations determine the minimal level of social responsibility,* which is usually beyond what the law requires; the third step *requires* business to take actions that *"anticipate" future public expectations and demands;* the fourth step actually involves the *creating of public expectations* by setting standards at the highest level of moral and social responsibility. Thus there are a number of different floors regarding what actions might be called socially responsible—depending on which definition of social responsibility is used and for what purpose. Ultimately, one's own values will determine what level of social responsibility one prefers.

Although some may criticize the "public expectations" level of business responsibility as too conservative, it can be argued that realistically that level is about as far as present-day management may go on their own without major legislation being enacted. Depending on the rate of change desired, or felt possible in our society without causing too much social friction, one may wish to accept more innovative proposals, which will be discussed presently.

On the surface, the definition using public opinion polls to determine "public expectations" seems operationally simple enough. But what of the usual cases in which public values conflict? in which the profitability of the corporation (and its ability to create goods and jobs) is threatened by its involvement in social and ecological costs also demanded by the public? How then is the corporation to behave and fulfill its social responsibility charge?

One may retort that those kinds of decisions are why top management is the highest paid section of our labor force. True. But the inherent problem in using the above definition of social responsibility operationally is that the course of action the corporation may take to maintain its viability (given marginal profitability conditions) may eliminate or even contradict those ecological or social involvement actions that the public demands. Hence, a dilemma.

The conundrum, of course, may apply only to marginal firms whose demise (à la Gilbert and Sullivan) would "never be missed." Even this assumption, however, only places us on the horns of another dilemma; namely, that of uneven and inequitable wealth redistribution among the stockholders of those firms that cannot pass on the added costs of socially responsible actions. Why, in fairness, should only stockholders of firms in such competitive markets where they cannot pass on added costs be made to pay the brunt of social responsibility? Why should not those costs be borne by all of society? Or, why one group of stockholders over another? Indeed, should it be stockholders, at all, who are selected by society to pay the costs of solving certain general social problems?

To say that these added expenditures are merely additional costs of doing business or that they are charges rectifying past windfall gains made by some corporations (i.e., by being able to freely pollute) is not, in all fairness, placing the costs on those individuals who originally may have received the dividends and profits.

Obviously, some firms see that socially responsible actions—such as the attempts to improve and save downtown Chicago by those banks, for instance, that by law are unable to move—are only economically justifiable long-run behavior. Most corporate behavior of a socially responsible kind today often turns out to be of this type. Even in these cases, however, could one equitably charge only those businesses that are unable to move from a city with the full costs of preventing urban deterioration because of a white exodus and a black population expansion? Maintaining our cities is a national cultural benefit, just as migration of population from one area of the country to another to find work is a problem of national, not just local, scope. Hence, government action or taxation on a federal level seems logically more just in solving such public concerns.

But where does this leave us regarding socially responsible business behavior? Are there any guidelines during the past half century to this riddle in business thought?

BUSINESS THOUGHT ON SOCIAL RESPONSIBILITY DURING THE PAST HALF CENTURY

The ebb and flow of business opinion regarding social responsibility has been documented by Herman Krooss.[2] In looking at what business

[2]H. Krooss, *Executive Opinion, What Business Leaders Said and Thought on Economic Issues 1920's–1960's* (Garden City, New York: Doubleday, Inc., 1970).

leaders said about economic issues since the 1920's, he found that "By the late twenties, the idea of service and its allied concepts had come to be known as the 'New Capitalism'." What "service" meant, however, remained far from unanimous throughout the decade. It carried with it the connotations of social responsibility—but remained undefined. To Owen D. Young, Chairman of General Electric, service meant trusteeship or stewardship. He wrote: "to get capital at the lowest rate, to have workers think the institution was a good place to work and that wages were as good or better than anywhere else . . . products so good and prices so reasonable that buyers would prefer it to other products." To Henry Ford, it meant "low cost production of high grade goods, made by well-paid labor, and distributed at a profit." However, such talk changed abruptly in the 1930's.

The rhetoric of idealism of the prosperous 1920's was but one of the victims of the depression of the 1930's. Although businessmen may have been just as convinced that the robber barons of the turn of the century were crass, badly motivated, and in error, profits became too scarce to take this stance, so popular a decade earlier. Profits were indeed too scarce to be treated so cavalierly. As Eugene Grace of Bethlehem Steel pointed out, "Nothing has ever been invented in wartime or peacetime that would make men work as hard as the lure of money and profits."

Krooss argues that it took the heady profits of the post-World War II era to bring back comments about professionalization of management and the doctrine of "social responsibility" that sounded so reminiscent of the twenties. However, as he puts it, "The opinions that business leaders expressed in the years after World War II about business motives and objectives combined the main themes of the prosperous twenties and the depressed thirties—the doctrine of 'service' from the former and the respectability of profits from the latter." Thus the term "social responsibility" appears to be just another substitute for the word "service," according to this argument. Like the confusion over the meaning of "service" in the 1920's, so "social responsibility' today seems equally vague and difficult to unanimously define. Krooss can be interpreted as suggesting that "social responsibility" in historical perspective is a product of a search for business respectability during profitable and prosperous times.

A BROADER CONCEPT OF SOCIAL RESPONSIBILITY

If we look farther back into history, it is possible to trace distinctly different philosophical and ideological attitudes about business responsibilities over several centuries. Certainly most of Adam Smith's followers took a far different view than that followed by Robert Owens at New Larnack in the early 1800's. The existence of the businessman as a social instigator or innovator, although not the norm, appears in every generation. Henry Kaiser's Group Health Plan is an example of successful innovation in health care in our own post-World War II era. Kaiser is only one example of a businessman taking a very broad view of his social responsibilities. The Robert Owen tradition lives, therefore, even if vastly outnumbered by Adam Smith's followers.

Yet the Classical Ideology (as Smith's theories are now called) has been on the defensive for a good deal of this century. Certainly since the great depression and the New Deal, the traditional business approach has been under concerted attack from other groups. The passage of the Wagner Act in 1935 was a new high-water mark in labor power. It is awareness of these pressures and the fact that the National Association of Manufacturers (NAM) was being unsuccessful in meeting them by remaining tied to a pre-Keynesian ideology that gave the impetus to the establishment of The Committee for Economic Development (CED) in the early 1940's. The CED has attempted to represent a newer, more professional managerial ideology.

Among major business groups the CED has taken the lead in advocating a broader interpretation of business's responsibilities. In 1971, for example, its fifty-man research and policy committee adopted some principles and guidelines for corporate social action that listed, among them, the following:

1. The "constituency" of a large firm includes not only its stockholders and workers—but consumers and community neighbors, people living near its plants who are inevitably affected by its activities. All these groups have claims on the corporation.
2. Firms should adopt specific social goals, such as pollution control and the hiring of minorities, as part of their business objectives. Indeed, they should develop quantitative means of measuring their success in these areas as well.
3. Younger executives should be encouraged to contribute time to community projects in the areas of health, education, and recreation—as an "essential ingredient for managers aiming to equip themselves for broader corporate responsibility."
4. Large firms should look for potentially profitable activities in such fields as rebuilding ghettos and designing efficient transportation systems. To implement aggressively this search into "social market" areas, top executives with a staff should be specifically appointed for this purpose.
5. Government should attempt to work more closely with business by development contracts, loans, and subsidies to spur social programs—as well as penalties for socially or environmentally harmful activity. Business itself has a moral obligation to lobby for tough federal pollution standards to see that all firms, rather than only a few, are contributing to solving the problems.

These guidelines suggest a broader social role for business than any ever proposed by a major business group. As one would expect, they draw some sharp dissents from among some of the CED's own members—particularly from those who hold that business best serves society by most efficiently pursuing its own operations.

As an indication of the temper of public opinion, however, *Time*, in reporting the CED discussion, commented, "Many businesses need to do a much better job of fulfilling their basic economic functions. That, however, does not excuse them from pursuing broader social goals."[3] Thus it is apparent that much of the public, as well as some within business' own

[3] *Time*, July 12, 1971.

ranks, have raised considerably the level of expectation regarding business' social obligations.

ALTERNATIVE COURSES OF ACTION FOR FIRMS PURSUING SOCIALLY RESPONSIBLE BEHAVIOR

What are the alternative courses of action, then, for firms regarding socially responsible behavior? Let us look at what appears to be some of the major possibilities.

1. The traditional alternative simply argues (as Milton Friedman puts it) that the social responsibility of the business firm is solely to maximize profits. Following classical economic theory and ideology, the firm by maximizing profits would be producing at its most efficient point. And, assuming competitive markets, the firms would then be producing the maximum number of goods at the lowest possible price to the consumer. Thus you have the best of all possible worlds. As firms maximize their profits, they wind up maximizing the welfare of society in the process.[4] The catch is, of course, that the perfectly competitive markets that this all depends on seldom exist in our society. In most oligopolistic markets it seems that increased efficiency is seldom passed on to the consumer in lower prices, but rather passed on to the workers in higher wages and to the firm in higher profits. One can think of exceptions—but they really do seem to be exceptions in our contemporary economy.

Nonetheless, the classical ideology is so strong that Barry Goldwater made it his political basis for campaigning against Lyndon Johnson for the Presidency. The Nixon administration's economic policies were influenced by this philosophy until it became no longer politically expedient to follow it. Thus the classical approach to business responsibility is not dead, but it is under strong attack—primarily because its basic approach to ignore any but profit concerns by the firm and to refuse to concern itself with social and ecological problems runs counter to the majority of public opinion in our society today.[5]

2. A second alternative course for business regarding what is socially responsible behavior is as follows: Business should merely adhere to the law regarding minority hiring, pollution standards, consumer safety, and the like, *but the firm should also involve itself in social concerns if it is profitable to do so, particularly through government contracts.* That is, *government must provide the guidelines for social action through laws* or by deciding in what areas to let *government contracts.* Government, therefore, must make it profitable for firms to pursue those social goals that the government selects by awarding grants and contracts at competitive levels with other business investments. The ability, of course, of the government

[4]Interestingly enough, both Milton Friedman and Michael Harrington agree that social responsibility is anti-capitalist behavior.

[5]Chauncey Medberry, III, Chairman of the Bank of America, argues that this alternative is already academic. It is no longer a question of *if* firms should be socially responsible—but *how*.

to choose "correct" priorities and to take consistent actions to fulfill them can be argued, too.

This alternative is nevertheless logical and consistent with our traditional capitalist democratic value system. It eliminates confusions about what is socially responsible action for the firm since it confines it largely to obeying the law and to following the cues (in the form of economic incentives) concerning what is profitable. Furthermore, priorities (including social priorities) are determined merely by following what is the most profitable business. It is not necessary to attempt to gauge public opinion or to wonder what issues the firm should be involved in—the traditional quest for maximizing profits should determine such rankings.

If there is a flaw in this argument, it is that it may not meet much of the current public expectation regarding business responsibility. If we look across the country at various cities to see what some of the finest recent achievements have been—Lincoln Center in New York, the cultural centers in Seattle, Los Angeles, or Atlanta, to name only a few—it is apparent that none of these would have been built if business leaders in these communities had restricted themselves to the role that this alternative suggests. In each case it was business initiative and leadership in the community that created them. Most Americans recognize this. The highest level of initiative and administrative ability seems to reside more among our business executives than in any other sector of our society.

Under these circumstances, the increasing and impatient demands for solutions (particularly heard on college campuses) points the finger at the most dynamic sector of our society—business—for action. Thus, I am dubious that this second alternative (well-reasoned and logical as it is—at least based on past values) is now fully in keeping with the value shifts that may be occurring in our society. Such a course relies on the profitability of business ventures in the social needs sector. Yet with a "satisfactory" profit level requirement, even professional managers will be reluctant to commit firm resources that have demonstrated potential yields of return considerably lower than the firm's normal investments. Indeed, as Eli Goldston found when Eastern Gas and Fuel developed ghetto housing in Roxbury, outside Boston, a profit could be made in such enterprise but it was too low to justify putting much of the firm's resources into such projects. Furthermore, it is unlikely that Congress would ever allow sufficiently large economic returns in such social needs areas to make them competitive with most business alternatives. Thus to even be able to justify putting "some" corporate resources into such public needs type projects, under this alternative, requires profit levels from such projects generally higher than would be available.

Moreover, to even consider such a proposal would require that firms be profitable enough in normal business activities that they could "afford" such socially responsible projects. This makes firm involvement in social issues a less than continuous commitment.

One might argue, of course, that if the general level of profitability in the economy goes down, the lower yield "public needs" investment projects would then become more attractive. This argument, I suspect, is in error—not only because firms would feel they could afford such projects even less than in boom times, but also because the risk factors involved in public investment projects might appear too high.

Business often feels that public areas are relatively risky—because of interference from resident interest groups, government bureaucracy, coupled with the government and public reaction if the firm were, accidentally, to make large profits; for example, in new housing in ghetto areas. All these facts will tend to keep firm investment down in such public needs areas. In strictly economic terms *the risk seems high in relation to the return* compared with the usual business investment. Therefore, under this alternative, activistic as it may seem to many, investment would remain highly constrained because of the general expected level of return. To invest many assets, personnel, or total effort in such projects could not be justified by most firms.

Indeed, some industry profit pictures in the short term will be adversely affected because of pollution control costs, minority hiring programs and the like already required by law. Even in those industries in which most such costs can be passed on to the consumer, the very increase in the basic cost structure of the firm is apt to exert a cautioning influence on firm policy regarding new areas of high risk and low expected returns. Public needs areas for such investment could be defined by legislation either broadly or narrowly. If the public concern was particularly directed toward housing, for example, firms could be allowed to invest only in providing additional housing stock within a certain price range.

3. *Allocating corporate resources directly to public needs—either by inducement or by requirement.*

This alternative suggests the activistic approach of direct corporate involvement in public needs areas. This could be regarded as a more *dynamic* form of contemporary capitalism—since the corporation's sphere of action in society would be enlarged.

The general rationale for increasing the corporation's involvement in society. The rationale for bringing firms into much more active participation in societal problems is twofold. One, to attempt to meet what appears to be a rising level of public expectation regarding corporate behavior and involvement; and two, to prevent the demise of pluralistic capitalism.

These two points are so interwoven that it is best to discuss them together. Those who suggest direct corporate involvement see a desire and need for more rapid social solutions in the public needs areas. Among the younger generation, the desire for greater social change may indeed be common. Thus, greater societal involvement by one of the two major institutions in our society—business—is more consistent with the assumptions of traditional capitalism than having government continually expand its role in the society. For as government's influence and power increase, the role of business in the society accordingly is diminished. Hence, the private sphere of society dwindles in influence—and our pluralistic system becomes more monistic.

The fact that government has been expanding its functions rapidly in our society for the past 40 years or more makes it difficult for us to envision any other institution in the society becoming a major public problem solver—or for any other institution to increase its functions in competition with government. Yet the public at large regards business as more efficient and dynamic than government bureaucracy (whether right or wrong).

Perhaps after decades of turning to government to solve problems—and now finding the quality of life deteriorating in both cities and rural areas—public reliance on government as a universal problem solver is waning. Therefore, it is appropriate in a pluralistic system for the public to expect such an institution to undertake the solution of problems that the government has failed to handle or handle well. The higher level of public expectations regarding business's social responsibilities can be read in this manner.

Indeed, from the broader perspective of economic systems, our own version of capitalism has been on the defensive more or less continually since the great depression of the 1930's, yet a more aggressive form of capitalism can be visualized. A new evolution of capitalism within our society—which would reverse what critics have long decried as a movement toward increasing socialization—would result if business aggressively took a leadership role in society's problems.

Modes of Implementation. 1. Tax incentives. The use of tax incentives to induce firms to allocate a portion of their resources (both in dollars and personnel) to public needs areas has been tried but not with great success because in the past the incentives were either too small or the methods too complicated. If, however, a firm could *deduct investment in public needs* areas from their federal income tax bill *on a dollar-for-dollar basis,* the incentive should be too attractive to resist. Some such arrangement could provide an incentive for firms to enter new public project areas without fear of not making a "satisfactory" rate of return. Public needs areas for such investment could be defined by Congress as it desired. If the public concern was particularly directed toward housing, for example, firms could be allowed to invest only in providing additional housing stock within a certain price range. An upper limit of say 10 per cent of a firm's total tax bill would be possible to invest directly in public needs investments—any return on these investments would represent a profit—and would indeed provide a strong incentive to enter such projects and to run them efficiently.

Politically, this alternative (of diverting federal tax dollars to public needs via the private sector) might be easier to win congressional approval than the proposal to allow equally high rates of return to be made totally from direct social needs areas. Furthermore, it could provide a much more flexible policy for different investment projects and programs than most public programs by obviating the repeated necessity of going through Congress to introduce new programs. Instead, private firms could continually search out investment opportunities as they saw fit (within the overall policy framework originally provided by Congress). One might call this, factitiously, private revenue sharing, for it could provide local communities with unusual opportunities for corporate aid within specific public need areas.

The relatively small amount of the nation's total tax bill diverted in the above manner *on a private basis* would be worth experimenting with because of the increased local and state flexibility in handling problems and providing newer and possibly more efficient ways of solving social needs. Since business seems more attuned to consumer's demands (and thus the public) than does the government, experimentation using institutions other than the federal government may have merit. Government institutions tend to search for ease of administrating programs and stress a uniform product or type of service to conform with the principle of equalitarianism and ease of administration. The difference between privately designed and governmentally designed housing is an example of the difference in concern for consumer reactions between business and government bureaucracies. Business, might, therefore, be able to satisfy public needs on a higher level than is presently done by government administration using similar amounts of resources.

2. Investment by requirement. Another version of the above alternative is to rely on regulation rather than incentive to create private investment in the public needs area. Firms over a certain size (either by sales or assets) could be required to invest a specific percentage of their resources (defined either as profits or cash flow) in designated public needs areas. This would force business to find profitable ventures, if possible, in such public needs areas. The result would, hopefully, be more innovative and competitive with government institutions—examples such as education and health care come to mind most readily. Various tax incentives could, of course, be adopted to make such a course more palatable to business. This type of simple legislative fiat is, of course, considerably more controversial than the use of incentives. It has been used recently regarding foundations, however, which are now required to disburse a given percentage of their assets every year or else lose their favorable tax status as foundations. This approach is not, however, inconsistent with a more dynamic form of capitalism. Indeed, a tax of this type on the corporation might improve their popular image considerably and make them less the targets of unfavorable legislation in the long run.

3. Loaning corporate personnel to the government. By providing executive leadership at city, state, and even federal levels so that social problems could be approached on a more pragmatic basis—preferably on a city-by-city approach—business might be able to develop a variety of different solutions to public problems. Current criticism of New York City's bureaucracy centers in part on the incompetence of higher-level bureaucrats in the system.

The city-by-city approach could make possible the actual testing of alternatives to similar social problems. Business, by focusing first on the local problems, would have the advantage over uniform federal solutions in being able to tailor programs directly to specific local conditions. In this nation, business contains the most experienced body of administrators of any segment of our society.

Thus, if business loaned executives to administer, for example, the welfare department, or the sanitation department, in a city on a rotating basis, considerable reorganization might be effected that could vastly increase the operating efficiency of local government. It must be added quickly, however, that the type of business executive who has succeeded in government (vs. those who have failed) has been the type who was not necessarily an industry specialist but rather was an administrative specialist—à la McNamara. Although McNamara, like all executives, may be questioned about some of his decisions, it still appears that he was the only Secretary of Defense in modern times who ever clearly gained control of the defense bureaucracy. What is suggested here is that the "newer" type of professionally trained administrator (with some experience in public relations or politics) is the ideal type that would be most effective in "loans" to government service from the business sector.

4. Government contracts to business for public needs projects. If government lets contracts directly to business to undertake to administer and run certain programs handled by government, the results could produce both innovation and greater efficiency (although, of course, they could result in the opposite as well). However, on the basis of hope and desperation, such experimentation should be useful. The current changes in the Post Office system suggest that even Congress may be prepared for more innovation in government administration. Also, the Comsat case is an illustration of joint business and government ownership that might have some useful applications in other areas.

5. Increasing corporate philanthropy. Corporations should be stimulated to make larger tax deductible contributions in their local communities (in the form of both parks and public overhead investment, as well as support for those cultural, education, and welfare organizations that in this country are still supported primarily by private contributions). Up to now, corporation contributions have been all too negligible in a society such as ours, which is still dependent on the private sector to sustain almost all of its cultural organizations and a major share of its private education. Individual giving has consistently been vastly greater than corporate giving in our society. A higher level of participation from corporations needs to be developed—even if it requires greater incentives (both positive and negative). Indeed, as mentioned under point (2) above, the new ruling on foundations may be suggestive here (i.e., where a specific percentage of foundation assets must be given away each year to qualify for preferred tax treatment).

CONCLUSION

If our society is to remain basically a pluralistic one, other institutions besides the government must begin to play larger roles within the system. Business—more than unions, educational institutions, or even foundations—is central to any such development because of its very size and scope within our society. If the government continues to be the only institution that will attempt to satisfy public needs, then inevitably our society will cease to be a pluralistic one. The result would be not only the failure and inefficiency to meet many public needs, but the danger of increasing power in a single institution with more and more voters beholden to it. Competition among institutions in the public sector can only be stimulating and innovative—just as it has been in the private sector.

The three major alternatives for corporate social responsibility, described earlier in this paper, have vastly different effects on capitalism. The pursuit of the first two alternatives, which are most likely, leads to an increasingly less pluralistic system and one that is less amenable to capitalism in the long run. What appears certain is that given the continuing value shift in the society and the increasing awareness of unfilled public needs, the traditional response of business that its only responsibility is to maximize profits can only hasten the rapid demise of what still passes for capitalism in this country. On the other hand, although the chances for an aggressive new variation of capitalism developing are not high, it is possible—if business leadership actually pursued the CED guidelines to their logical conclusions and the above prescriptions for the savings of capitalism were followed in some form. Hence, a new form of "Dynamic Capitalism" is still possible, requiring only the activating of business leadership. Most other courses of action, unfortunately, will likely make the term "capitalism" as applied to our society seem anachronistic by the time this century is played out.

Serious concerns have been voiced, of course, about a larger role for the business corporation in our society. Hazel Henderson argues that there is considerable danger in such business expansion.[6] She visualized the danger of well-meaning corporate chiefs becoming paternalistic, if benevolent, rulers as the possible outcome of social responsibility that took firms further into the public needs field. "If we, through our government, abdicate areas of public concern, then we abdicate all rights to criticize performance, and we may find it increasingly difficult to regain control of the situation."

Neither of these two arguments seems to me effective. As a major institution in society, business will always remain susceptible to criticism—just as the government is. Also, since government is the ultimate power in our society—and in our society voters on a mass basis determine who controls government—business is subject to constraints and controls far more than is government. This has been increasingly evident in the flood of legislation regulating business activity passed in this century. It follows, therefore, that a greater role for business in our society would not endanger capitalist democracy, only strengthen it. Particularly is this so since the rapid growth of government bureaucracy threatens to swamp all other countervailing forces in our society.

There appears to be a growing trend for large consumer-oriented firms to include representatives of consumer organizations and minority groups on their boards of directors. This could have some beneficial effect on firm behavior (even on its concept of social responsibility). Indeed, since the CED has argued for a broader interpretation of the corporation's constituency, this would appear to be a logical development. Perhaps a better policy would be for Congress to require such representation. However, such a course is presently remote.

Despite such recognition by some business leaders of social responsibility extending to a broader range of areas than business has previously acknowledged, the most potent effect on business behavior is still likely to come through the channels presently in use—government legislation and administrative demands, public suits, and exposure brought by such groups as those of Ralph Nader, and occasionally some industry groups. The strengthening of private watch-dog organizations, although basically critical of most presently administered institutions, has had a major effect in changing both public and business's expectations regarding corporate social responsibility. Interestingly enough, it seems to be *non-governmental groups* that are attempting to make both government agencies and business take a conscientious stance toward the consumer. Thus, the idea of developing either new channels or revamping old ones to become more effective in

[6]Hazel Henderson, "Should Business Tackle Society's Problems?" *Harvard Business Review*, Vol. 46, No. 4 (July–August, 1968), pp. 77–85.

protecting the public suggests strongly that the usual liberal approach of relying on government to solve social problems needs rethinking. Indeed, all this is an argument for a "Dynamic Capitalism" in which the business sector becomes more aggressively involved in public needs.

Even those critics of a more involved and aggressive concept of social responsibility appear to recognize the value shift that seems to be occurring in our society. "Increasingly, private enterprise is finding itself caught in a bind because society, which laid down the traditional ground rules for private enterprise, has now decided to change them in midstream. No wonder, then, that business leaders are left with a philosophy gap."[7] In essence, this is the crux of the problem in which business finds itself. Accustomed to playing the business game with more traditional rules, the shift in values that is changing those ground rules is creating a business policy crisis. Businessmen find their traditional ideology increasingly less acceptable to the public at large. Thus there is an ideological as well as a resulting policy lacuna for most business firms today.

The recent CED attempts to correct this hiatus in ideology and policy are significant. As their recent guidelines suggest, they are moving into new ground. The CED, of course, represents only the advanced edge of business ideology. The median business position is obviously some distance behind a socially activistic program of social responsibility. But with public expectations and values changing, the large corporation in particular must change its policies and ideology or reap a whirlwind of regulative legislation and public disapproval. Unless such changes do occur on the part of our leading business corporations, capitalism may well become even more unfashionable within its own heartland during the life of the present generation.

Thus, the hope for saving contemporary capitalism involves, at a beginning level, the meeting of public expectations. This, however, is unlikely to be adequate in the long run for it is essentially a defensive role rather than a dynamic or aggressive one. For our pluralistic capitalism to continue to exist will require that business attempt to "anticipate" public expectations and, finally, have a broader philosophy about what the "good life" is than our society has had during the past century and a half of industrialization. The post-industrial society and its emerging value emphasis on other than materialism alone suggests that business can remain a major institution only if it plays a leading role in providing means for individuals with an already high level of abundance to find greater personal satisfaction and feel that they are part of an equitable, just, and humane society. Those institutions that fail to meet these newer and much more difficult standards are likely to be found wanting and their names erased from the ledger of our society.

This suggests that many, if not most, businesses will need to re-think their product, organization, employee, and social relationships if capitalism is to survive into a full-blown post-industrial state in the next century. Company chairmen up to now have seldom been philosophers, yet this will be the great need in business ranks during the last quarter of this century. The gap between the outlook, values, and expectations of the chairmen of most of our largest corporations that I have met are light-years away from even those of my own business administration students. With the right training and luck, the long run may be more promising than the short term.

[7] *Ibid.*, p. 82.

The new generation, labeled the "impatient generation," may change the economic and political guidelines in our society even more effectively than they have attempted to change college campuses. The presently forecasted high rates of unemployment during much of the decade of the seventies may not necessarily act as a social tranquilizer in the voting booth. Furthermore, the crisis for business and American capitalism may well be greatest during the next quarter century—before the present generation is able to assume the leadership of which it is presently so critical. If so, the bombshell of demand for change that has hit college campuses in the past decade may not augur well for those corporations that prefer the quiet life.

Indeed, the quiet life appears to have "gone with the wind" on college campuses and in more and more corporate boardrooms. Soul searching is neither easy nor pleasant, but the business executives will inevitably be doing a good deal more of this unusual business activity before long. Their own individual answers will determine not only the future of their corporations, but inevitably as well, the whole future of American capitalism.

The Meaning and Scope of Social Responsibility

Keith Davis

Professor
College of Business Administration
Arizona State University

THE MEANING OF SOCIAL RESPONSIBILITY

It is true that social responsibility is a vague and indeterminate term that analysts are reluctant to use for fear of having to define it. On the other hand, in a discussion of this type it seems appropriate to offer some type of definition. One definition arises from the fact that business is part of a complex and interdependent social system in which business actions influence other parts of the system. It follows that a responsible businessman, and indeed a responsible member of any other type of organization, must act with due concern for the effects of his decisions on the system.

Social responsibility, therefore, refers to a person's obligation to evaluate in the decision-making process the effects of both his personal and institutional decisions and actions on the whole social system. The substance of social responsibility arises from concern for the ethical consequences of one's acts as they might affect the interests of others. This idea exists in most religions and philosophies of the world. Quite frequently, however, a tendency exists to limit its application to person-to-person contacts. Social responsibility moves one large step farther by including institutional actions and their effect on the whole social system. Without this additional step, personal and institutional acts tend to be divorced. History has shown that a businessman can lead a model personal life, but continue to rationalize his organization's pollution of a river because no direct personal consequence is involved. He can consider that river pollution results from the operation of an impersonal market and that it is a public problem to be solved by public action. The idea of social responsibility, however, requires him to consider his acts in terms of a whole social system and holds him responsible for the effects of his acts anywhere in the system. When this system relationship is known and accepted by a businessman, it becomes a cultural value that affects his decisions, along with technical, economic, and other values that he must weigh.

A socially responsible decision does not necessarily guarantee results in the public interest. The decision may, because of poor judgment or unforeseen events, actually work against the public interest, but society expects most decisions to affect the public interest favorably. Actually, many business decisions start a series of developments, some of which serve the public interest and some of which, considered by themselves, are against it. The only realistic approach is to consider the net effect on the public interest expected from the whole decision, adding positive and negative effects.

Actions for the benefit of an organization may still be socially responsible. To require that institutional acts be only in the public interest, without regard for the private interest, is to deny the pluralistic organization of society in which many private centers of initiative together achieve a high quality of life. To maintain these centers of initiative, their goals must be served, as well as the general welfare. But the price that society exacts for these pluralistic freedoms is that private organizational acts will be taken with due concern for public responsibility. This is the meaning of the term "social responsibility."

Defined in this way, social responsibility is something more than mere compliance with the law, because not all system effects of business decisions are covered by law, and it is unlikely that they ever can be. In fact, a profit-maximizing firm under the rules of classical economics would comply with the law, and it makes no claim that it is being socially responsible. Social responsibility goes one step further. It is a firm's recognition of social obligations beyond the requirements of law, along with the obligations represented by law.

Social responsibility may also be considered as something more than a passive response to public expectations. Expectations vary among groups, and there is no automatic guideline concerning which expectation to follow. Furthermore, public expectations do not necessarily represent all the areas in which business influence is felt. Certainly, public expectations need to be considered, but business is not automatically responsible to respond to every desire of the public. This may, in fact, be a rather irresponsible mode of business action, because it bends to whims and emotions and contradictory goals.

Social responsibility is also something more than an intelligent anticipation of future public expectations, because this kind of approach is still tied only to public expectations. The more complete meaning of social responsibility is that the businessman offers *leadership* in social areas instead of merely responding to public expectations. He interacts with society and helps it reach social decisions, contributing his own special talent and expertise. He is an active participant, rather than a passive respondent. He analyzes system effects and initiates the remedial actions before serious problems develop. By helping to keep society from getting sick, he practices a preventive leadership that is similar to preventive medicine. The other less effective approach, which is called up when the preventive approach fails, is to treat social ills after they develop. This is curative leadership.

The Iron Law of Responsibility

Professor Monsen is correct when he explains that if business demurs in accepting its social responsibility, then society's only recourse is to withdraw some of the power business enjoys. I refer to this idea as the Iron Law of Responsibility, which states that in the long run those who do not use power in a manner that society considers responsible will tend to lose it. The law's application to man's institutions certainly stands confirmed by history. Although the "long run" may require decades and even centuries in some instances, society ultimately acts to reduce power when it is not used responsibly.

History supports the mutuality of power and responsibility in business. Take safe working conditions as an example. Under the protection of common law, employers during the nineteenth century gave minor attention to worker safety. Early in the twentieth century, in the face of pressure from safety and workmen's compensation laws, employers changed their attitudes to accept responsibility for job safety. Since then, very few restrictions have been imposed on business power in this area because business in general has been acting responsibly. Accident rates have been reduced dramatically until most work places are safer than most areas away from work.

For an opposite example, consider unemployment. Business in the first quarter of this century remained callous about technological and market layoff. As a result, business lost some of its power to government, which administers unemployment compensation, and to unions, which restrict business by means of tight seniority clauses, supplementary unemployment benefits, and other means. Now business finds itself in the position of paying unemployment costs that it originally denied responsibility for, but having less control than when it did not pay! Perhaps unemployment *should* be a governmental problem rather than a business one, but this development is nevertheless an example of how business power has drained away to bring the power-responsibility equation back into balance.

In line with the foregoing analysis, proposals for a strictly economic function of business with no social responsibility lose some of their glamour because they mean substantial loss of business power. It is unlikely that businessmen will concede their social power so easily, because they are men of action who will not sit quietly on the sidelines. They want to be in the midst of progress, offering their innovations in all areas. It is even unlikely that society would permit businessmen to concede their power, because it is coming to recognize its need for them. The probable outcome is that society will persuade businessmen to accept more social responsibility in order to balance the power-responsibility equation.

AREAS OF SOCIAL RESPONSIBILITY

It is appropriate to ask: In what areas will business social responsibility develop? In a general way, social responsibility will apply wherever business has the power to influence the social system. And the amount of responsibility will approximate the amount of social power. Consider the situation of two companies in the same city. Company "A" is a substantial metal foundry whose processes threaten to pollute the air. Company "B" is a retail store that employs just as many persons as Company "A" but whose only pollutant is a small incinerator. Other things being equal, it appears that company "A" has greater responsibility in the area of air pollution than Company "B" because of the greater effect its processes have on air pollution.

Even accepting the greater responsibility of Company "A," there is no present measure of exactly how much more responsibility it has or how it should adjust to its greater responsibility. Thus, the equation of balanced social power and responsibility serves only as a rough guide, albeit a real one. For example, do businessmen by their industrial engineering decisions have the power to affect workers' feelings of accomplishment and self-fulfillment on the job? If so, there is a balancing need for social responsibility. Do businessmen have the power to mislead with advertising? To the degree that they do, does not social responsibility also arise?

Although social responsibility is an obligation of business, it is not solely a business matter. Many of our social problems are national in scope, and the responsibilities *and costs* for them will be borne by many segments in society. The stockholders will bear some costs, particularly in marginal firms that cannot pass their costs on to consumers. Stockholders are major economic risk takers in society. When extra costs come along, stockholders bear some of them through reduced profits; and, likewise, when extra gains arise, they share these. Consumers will bear other costs through increased prices, and labor will share costs through reduced wages. Each group benefits from improvements in the quality of life, so each can share the cost. However, as Professor Monsen indicates, much of the cost of social improvement will be borne by the taxpayer because many social problems are national in scope. Business obligations in this area will be to respond to tax rebates, direct contracts, and other government incentives for social improvements.

The Public Visibility of Business

One additional reason for a rising demand that business show social responsibility is the public visibility of business compared with other institutions. Public visibility refers to the extent to which an organization's activities are known to persons outside the organization. The activities may be directly observed, such as polluting smoke seen coming from a smokestack. Activities also may be indirectly communicated by news media, neighbors, and other sources. The importance of public visibility is that it makes business subject to public examination, discussion, and judgment. If acts are not known, they cannot be discussed and judged.

Since business is an advertiser, a major employer, and a supplier of customers—to name just a few of its activities—its acts are widely visible most of the time. It is an open system. It lives in a glass house.

Public visibility is different from the idea of public image often mentioned in public relations. Public image refers to what people think about an organization's acts, whereas public visibility refers to the extent to which its acts are known. A business may have high visibility and either high or low image. Similarly, it may have low visibility and either high or low image.

EXECUTIVE TIME IN COMMUNITY ACTIVITIES

One of the CED recommendations that Professor Monsen mentions is that younger executives should be encouraged to contribute time to community projects. My research in one community indicates that this is already an accomplished fact, although certainly there is room for improvement. The executives surveyed in a community of about 1 million persons were mostly middle managers and younger men. The executives reported that they spent an average of 19 hours a month in community service work. An important point was that, even when company policy did not support this kind of activity by executives, they still went ahead and spent nearly as much time in community service as their counterparts who had support from company policy. This suggested that the executives themselves had basic drives for community service work regardless of company policy; however, these drives were more easily satisfied with company support, because then the executives could use more job time for service activities.

All respondents reported involvement in community service work both during their regular working day and after work hours. The most involvement was in civic groups (such as Rotary Clubs), service groups (such as Boy Scouts of America), and charitable groups (both religious and non-religious). Moderate involvement was in cultural activities, and minimum involvement was in political-governmental activities.[1]

THE SOCIALLY PROFITABLE BUSINESS AND SOCIAL CAPITALISM

Few people in society would deny that business should be "profitable," provided the term is interpreted to mean net outputs of all types in relation to inputs of all types. Obviously, business or any other institution will waste social resources unless it can provide outputs greater than inputs; and the greater the net gain, the better it is for society. The principal issue in modern industrial society, and the key to the evolving role of business, is differing expectations of what kinds of outputs should be emphasized and what groups should receive them. People want the outputs, but they want them in the form of broad social benefits along with economic benefits.

These new conditions mean that business will have to think about how to produce social values efficiently, as well as economic values. Society is not rejecting the idea of profit, but it is extending that idea to include social profits (outputs greater than inputs) as well as economic profits. For these conditions I prefer the terms "socially profitable business" and "social capitalism." It will be the businessman's responsibility to adapt to these new conditions and to manage them effectively.

[1]Keith Davis and Frank H. Besnette, "Management's Obligation to Public Service Activities," *Advanced Management Journal* (April, 1969), pp. 33–39.

Enlightened Self-interest and Enlightened Public Interest

Clarence C. Walton

President
The Catholic University of America

Prompt recognition of those delicious ambiguities that, lurking within the term "business social responsibility," allow proponents of different views to sit together in rather comfortable alliance has resulted in Professor Monsen's seeking, rather successfully, to settle the matter of defining terms quickly. The chore is necessary. Indeed, the genius of the businessman's philosophical pragmatism is probably no more visible than in current efforts by corporate managers to redefine their "social" role in ways that assure continuation of present benefits and present securities while not foreclosing future advantages. One may to ensure this happy result is to celebrate regularly the marriage vows solemnized centuries ago by Adam Smith between the two concepts of self-interest and public interest, respectively.

To those who sense an ill-concealed cynicism in such an approach, let it be noted that living with ill-defined definitions is not alien to the American experience. The concepts of competition in the Sherman Antitrust Act, of happiness in the Declaration of Independence, or of due process in the judicial system carry a ring of definitional finality, although hard experience often demonstrates the contrary.

Awareness of the semantic thicket is, obviously, one motive prompting Monsen to lift his analysis quickly from an historical review to a conceptual level embodied in "alternative courses" of action that he sees available to the socially conscious firm.

But limitations of space may have been as equally important as requirements of logic. Whatever the motives, the result is an argument advanced with great economy in both style and reasoning. There are some omissions. If, therefore, praise is notable for its absence in this critique, it is largely because of agreement with Monsen's basic approach and major conclusions and, furthermore, an inclination to identify, for those who do not share our views, areas in which an additional commentary or two could bring greater overall balance to the exposition. To avoid repetition, let me identify five areas that relate to the following:

1. The social utility of the invisible hand;
2. The assumptions underlying "dynamic capitalism";
3. The concept of the corporation;
4. The major forms of management's motives in pursuing social responsibilities; and
5. The relevance of organization theory to an understanding of corporate social responsibility.

THE "INVISIBLE" HAND

Monsen's distillation of the meaning of the classical or traditional approach to societal obligations is admirable. But there are three omissions or understatements in dealing with the contemporary articulations of the Smithian philosophy. In the first place, whether one thinks of Milton Friedman,[1] Henry Manne,[2] or Paul Heyne[3] as exemplars of the classical model, they all stress that market prices should take into account *all* costs, including the social ones, for doing business. These costs include those directly imposed by government through taxation and others indirectly induced by the public's greater expectations. There is, therefore, greater recognition of J. M. Clark's theory of social overhead cost than was ever present in the original formulations of the classical ideology.[4]

On this basis, General Motors justifies its extensive and expanding program in the many areas of pollution control. Expenditures in the United States in 1971 were approximately $124 million for automotive emissions and over $64 million for capital facilities in connection with industrial air and water pollution control. Dr. William Agnew of the General Motors Laboratory stated the rationale quite succinctly when he wrote:

[1]Milton Friedman, *Capitalism and Freedom* (Chicago: University of Chicago Press, 1962).

[2]Henry Manne, "The Myth of Corporate Responsibility—or Will the Real Ralph Nader Please Stand Up?" *The Business Lawyer* (November, 1970), pp. 533–539.

[3]Paul Heyne, *Private Keepers of the Public Interest* (New York: McGraw-Hill Book Co., Inc., 1968), see Chapters 2, 3, and 9, especially.

[4]J. M. Clark, *Economic Institutions and Human Welfare* (New York: Alfred A. Knopf, Inc., 1957).

> One of the most pressing challenges on the American scene today is the need to preserve a quality environment. The automotive transportation system—through the products we build and the facilities which manufacture them—has a lot to do with our environment. *It is natural, therefore that General Motors is sincerely concerned and deeply involved in the environmental issue.*[5]

This stricture places sharper limitations on the profit-maximizing possibilities than flow from the earlier interpretations of the model—a stricture that, in fairness to the proponents of the austere model, needs to be constantly stressed because it forces business to be responsive to industry-related social problems.

There is a second point. The austere or classical model embodies another advantage in that it lends precision to the definition of social responsibilities by proposing an equation between public good and the optimal allocation of resources, which, in turn, maximizes the value of the total output. And, it must be stressed, rational profit-maximizing efforts under pure competition are viewed mainly as a decision-making rule and not a philosophy of life. The manager, as citizen, is called on to behave like other good citizens by undertaking a broad range of social activities often unrelated to the profits of his enterprise.

And finally, the advantages of "social role" specialization, which places the two most powerful instruments in society—business and government—in positions of countervailing forces, has singular benefits for the overall good of a free society.

In short, stress on (1) the *total* cost of doing business, (2) sharp and lean definitions, and (3) the maintenance of a government-business equipoise are things that have served Western societies for nearly 2 centuries. Advocates of a new role for business through new definitions of expanded business responsibilities often tend to underplay these features.

THE ASSUMPTIONS OF "DYNAMIC CAPITALISM"

Monsen's preferred model, which allocates a specific percentage of corporate resources to public needs, is stated as having great potential for "Dynamic Capitalism." The pejorative terminology suggests that the other two models are somehow less "dynamic"—which is something critics of a more commodious theory of management stoutly resist. On the contrary, they claim that when managers move beyond strictly business concerns to public or social affairs, business and government suffer because capitalism becomes less dynamic as the goal of profit-maximizing becomes more diluted.

The practical effects of dynamic capitalism bear qualifications. Monsen's stress on a "city-by-city" approach to allow local adaptations to different local needs carries great plausibility. One is aware, for example, of the significant roles played by local corporations in San Francisco in the completion of a totally new high-speed electric transportation system at a cost of $1.4 billion. One of business' unconventional but successful decisions was to secure bids for the transit vehicle from aircraft manufacturers. And the employment of the systems approach resulted in a highly innovative, socially-engineered system. One also thinks of the success of businessmen in modernizing local government in Indianapolis—the only case in the country since 1915 in which a metropolitan area has consolidated suburbs and inner city into one.

But dangers also lurk. One is the assumption that government officials are necessarily less effective in politically tinged matters than are businessmen. Penn Central, Lockheed, and some steel

[5]General Motors Corporation, *Programs in Areas of Public Concern,* Melford, Michigan, 1972, p. 5, italics mine.

industries provide grim testimony to nightmarish performances by business executives themselves. Will "loaned executives" do a better job in sanitation or welfare departments if their participation is on a temporary basis? Or is the real answer to be found in better trained public and civil servants?

Monsen further assumes that a "city-by-city" approach will prove more effective than a centralized approach dominated by government. In some cases it will. But suppose Prudential in Newark and Monsanto in St. Louis undertook such efforts in their respective cities? Would release from a percentage of income taxes provide incentives for significant penetration into problems in cities burdened with monumental illnesses?

What is being suggested here is that even urban problems cannot be localized because they are part of a vast permeative network. Every major social problem has spill-over effects requiring coordinated efforts within the business community itself and often in partnerships with government. The point at issue is not the stress on government incentives through tax credits, and the like, but the author's feeling that localized efforts will meet the problem and satisfy public expectations. On both counts doubts can be registered. On the other hand, if these suggestions are intended only to *illustrate* how a corporation might begin to look at its social responsibilities, then this criticism is ill-directed.

THE CONCEPT OF THE CORPORATION

It is a bit surprising that, in his treatment, Monsen never adverts to the classic "Berle-Means" hypothesis and its role in the theory of social responsibility.[6] Postulated was the view that the modern corporation is the result of a historic rupture between owners and managers. Is the modern corporation a "private-property" organization? Or a private enterprise operation? The practical consequences of accepting one or the other viewpoint are substantial. Acceptance of the second viewpoint seems common among today's managers, and Donald MacNaughton, Chairman and Chief Executive Officer of Prudential Insurance Company, drew the logical conclusion of this acceptance when he said:

> And what is a private enterprise institution as contrasted with a private property one? In essence, it can best be described as a business organization whose managers act as trustees for *all* who have an interest in the enterprise—the stockholders, employees, suppliers, consumers, and public. And if this is the case, then the private enterprise institution is truly a social force with all the duties and responsibilities of a social organization . . . .
>
> The franchise under which business functions is granted for the benefit of the people. Now let's ask ourselves: what are the duties a business franchise entails? . . . For a long time, the contract between the public and business good called for nothing but economic performance on the corporation. . . . Today, however, . . . it is now accepted that business goals are not limited to making or selling more things, improving production and increasing consumption. . . .
>
> The time has come, it seems to me, for us to recognize that the future role of business must be *social* as well as economic.[7]

That this distinction is vital to the theory of corporate social responsibilities is not lost on protagonists of the for example, began one recent attack on "old" or narrower view. Henry Manne, "corporate responsibility" by declaring that Berle's theory of private property

[6]A. A. Berle, Jr., and Gardiner Means, *The Modern Corporation and Private Property* (New York: The Macmillan Co., 1932).

[7]Donald MacNaughton, "A Responsible Business," October 10, 1971 address, *passim*.

was such "an uninformed strawman that nothing in the modern world could fit it; nevertheless, that has not in the least interfered with its being mouthed and elaborated through academic generations."[8]

Over time, Berle's view has tended to reinforce J. M. Keynes' dictum, advanced in 1926, that "big business tends to socialize itself" and that this trend is part of a steadily evolving process leading to assumptions of greater responsibilities.[9] Inclusion of this aspect of intellectual history would have been helpful.

MANAGEMENT MOTIVES

Why does—or why should—a corporation manager lead his enterprise into the thicket of social responsibilities? Generally speaking, for two reasons. The first asserts that assumption of corporate responsibilities assures greater possibilities for long-term success in the firm's pursuit of *enlightened self-interest*. The second advances the proposition that such efforts are the necessary responses of companies committed to *enlightened public-interest*. Bethlehem Steel, for example, seems to favor the former position when it says that it supports private institutions of higher education in direct proportion to the value the company receives from that institution in men who have potential leadership, and technical and administrative ability. Bethlehem addresses its efforts in terms of enlightened self-interest.

Burlington Industries in North Carolina, on the other hand, leans to the latter view when it says that support of higher education—as one area of its responsibilities—is not an option but a necessity because our entire civilization rests on educated men.[10]

Is the distinction real and important? I rather think so. The way the language of policy is articulated reflects not only a substantive difference in approaching responsibilities theoretically but one that has highly pragmatic effects. The young, especially college youth, want broad-scale responsible businesses. One philosophical stance could induce a measure of skepticism among youth; the other could elicit short-lived idealism. How may they be reconciled? Perhaps a paradox is in the making by suggesting that "what is good for the country is good for General Motors."

ORGANIZATION THEORY AND SOCIAL RESPONSIBILITY

One of the thorniest problems will deal with ways of (1) meshing into corporate decision-making the idea of corporate responsibilities as a goal equally important as the objective of profit-making, and (2) monitor and audit the results of that philosophy.[11] Consciously integrating the values of those not in control of the enterprise and not necessarily shared by those in control represents a "first step" for the socially responsible enterprise. Can steps in the right direction be identified? Illustrations come to mind. If the board's agenda never includes matters related to the firm's social responsibilities, then it is clear that the corporation's overall philosophy is either deficient or that its recognition is honored in the breach. Is the company library up to date on the literature of social responsibility? Are in-house training programs devoted to the topic? Is a senior officer entrusted with the task of keeping the company genuinely responsible? Or is the effort overwhelmingly concerned with public relations? Is the decision-making process so structured that production and mar-

[8]Manne, *loc. cit.*, p. 533.

[9]See Morrell Heald, *The Social Responsibilities of Business: Company and Community 1900–1960*. (Cleveland: Case-Western Reserve University Press, 1970).

[10]Richard Eells, *Corporation Growing in a Free Society* (New York: Harper & Row, 1956), pp. 81–104.

[11]Kenneth G. Patrick and Richard Eells, *Education and the Business Dollar* (New York: The Macmillan Co., 1969).

keting goals (invariably oriented toward traditional economic objectives of productivity and profitability) are set with due attention to social goals? In short, how is success to be measured in the future?

Frederick Andrews, writing on "the arithmetic of quality" in the *Wall Street Journal,* said that the firm's first step must be to inventory its own social impact through a "social audit" and then consciously to elicit a wide diversity of viewpoints, so that it accepts accountability of the widest type."[12]

Meaningful corporate responsibilities, therefore, necessarily involve creation of an organization structure in which corporate decision-making occurs with full awareness of the primacy of secondary consequences—the good of society!

DISCUSSION QUESTIONS

1. Why is there pressure for direct corporate commitment to solve social problems? Where does this pressure come from? Discuss.
2. How can social responsibility be dependent on "public expectations"? Define "public expectations." Discuss.
3. What is *your* definition of "social responsibility"? What is Monsen's? And Davis'?
4. List and discuss the CED guidelines for corporate social action.
5. What are the alternatives for a company that wants to behave "responsibly"?
6. How might tax incentives be used to implement a new "social responsibility"?
7. What are some of the other ways that "social responsibility" might be implemented? What do you think of these?
8. What are the arguments for and against social responsibility?
9. Discuss the "Iron Law of Responsibility."

[12] *Wall Street Journal,* October 10, 1971. Relevant also is William C. Stolk, "Business Involvement in Social Problems: Tokenism or Leadership," in Clarence C. Walton (ed.), *Business and Social Progress* (New York: Frederick A. Praeger, 1970), Chapter 7.

20

Management in the Future

Joseph W. McGuire

Vice President—Planning
University of California

A management consultant once confided to me that he liked to make long-range predictions, because when the distant future finally arrived his forecasts would probably have long since been misplaced or forgotten. If, by some chance, his projections were recalled, and if he was subsequently chided for his errors, he at least could take a great deal of satisfaction from the fact that he had been paid in the present.

The role of this chapter is not to make forecasts similar to those of the gentleman described above, nor is our attitude toward the future the same. To be sure, the world is changing rapidly, and it is difficult in many ways to predict the future of management. Yet, as the preceding chapters have so graphically illustrated, we can perceive some of the trends, some of the changes, some of the demands, and some of the recent developments that are likely to be important during the next decade or two, and point to some of the areas that are likely to undergo significant changes in the future within the field of management.

It is most convenient to undertake this examination of the future by conducting our search within the context of the major divisions of this book. Thus, we shall look, in turn, at the future of management education, the basic disciplines underlying the field, the environment of management, and the managerial core. Through the use of this broad framework we can relate this final chapter to earlier chapters.

Two points of caution should be raised before we launch into our exploration of the future of management: (1) Each reader is free to assign his own probability distributions to the future outcomes discussed in this chapter. Obviously, some of the changes described are more probable than others. (2) At times we shall be discussing *normative* futures—what we hope will happen, rather than more *positive* futures—what we expect will happen. Rather deliberately, the distinction between hopes and expectations is sometimes vague.

MANAGEMENT EDUCATION IN THE FUTURE

A former colleague once claimed that the popularity of academic fields moves in cycles, and that young Ph.D. aspirants should select the least popular disciplines for their studies, since these would be in demand by the time they obtained their degrees. Whether the approaches to, and objectives of, management education also move in cyclical patterns is more difficult to determine. Nevertheless, it is obvious that management education in the 1960's had changed radically from its earlier forms. These dramatic changes were in part hastened by the prestigious Gordon and Howell report on collegiate business schools, financed by the Ford Foundation.[1]

In the 1950's, and before, management education at most schools was largely vocational. Economics formed the sole underlying discipline of importance. Most management texts were descriptive, and most professors considered themselves to be experts in specific—often minute—areas. The functional approach to management almost completely dominated the field.

In the 1960's the behavioral sciences and quantitative methods found their way into most management curricula, and many professors became deeply involved with methodology rather than content. At most good management schools, vocationalism was disdained. At many schools, professionalism was passed over completely as the pendulum of faculty values moved toward more traditional, academic, scholarly approaches to human (as opposed to merely managerial) behavior, and toward the rigor of the scientific method. Many modern professors, oriented toward mathematics, computers, and the behavioral sciences, abandoned the study of management *per se*, and many of them came to believe that their mission, even indirectly, had little to do with the preparation of students for a managerial career. It became, among a certain class of schools and a certain type of faculty, fashionable to write articles for scholarly but non-management journals, and often the faculty member of distinction, pointed to with pride by his dean, was the one who had published most in the *Review of Economics and Statistics*, the *Psychological Bulletin*, the *Quarterly Journal of Economics*, the *American Journal of Sociology*—in short, in any or every learned journal with only remote ties to management. (Dr. Starbuck comments on this "prestige syndrome" somewhat in Chapter 6.) In a letter, Professor Israel Unterman mentions one experience with these attitudes as follows:

> In 1968 as part of a study I did for Harvard, I visited a number of people in management education. . . . The subject dealt with the means of recruiting minority students. One of my set questions was "Have you had any pressure from any businesses or business advisory council to enroll additional minority students?" One official of ——— school answered: "What do we care what the business world wants? We are teachers."[2]

[1]R. A. Gordon and J. E. Howell, *Higher Education for Business* (New York: Columbia University Press, 1959).

[2]Israel Unterman, Professor of Management, Roth Graduate School of Business Administration, C. W. Post Center, Long Island University, Letter to J. W. McGuire, April 4, 1972.

We are surprised only that the official said "teachers" rather than "scholars" or "professors."

During the 1970's, and well into the 1980's, we expect that the fashion cycle will swing slowly back toward professionalism in management education. Hopefully there will not be an over-reaction, for it would be most unfortunate to return to the vocational objectives that prevailed in the pre-1960 era. In the light of the developments of the 1960's, however, such an over-reaction is most unlikely. In fact, it is more likely that the movement toward professionalism will be relatively slow and gradual, for there are too many faculty members in management schools who have been educated, employed, and promoted to tenure positions solely because of their knowledge of psychology, sociology, economics, computers, and mathematics rather than because of their knowledge *and* their interest in managerial problems. Certainly, as the chapters of this book have in general indicated, the blend of sophisticated tools and disciplines, reinforced by a concentration on the decision-making, problem-solving, managerial core, and with considerable attention to the organizational and external environment, can and should prepare students for managerial careers more satisfactorily than ever before—but only if there also is enlightened dedication to the goal of professional education for management. We perceive this shift toward professionalism moving slowly but inexorably in the next decade. If it does not occur, there is some doubt that management education will remain viable, and, indeed, it might well be swallowed up completely by the social sciences.

Second, we do believe that the changes, now evident throughout the nation toward broader schools of management, will continue in the future. This broadening process appears to be appropriate, and may become increasingly fruitful. There are, as this book illustrates, many useful statements that can be made, many generalizations drawn, and many approaches initiated, to, for, and about management without *a priori* limiting the exploration to the managerial role in only one type of organization. Indeed, in our opinion managers, whether they be in education, in government, in business, or in other types of organizations, share much in common. We would expect, therefore, that the number of schools of management (administration) would increase during the coming decade.

Third, some of the greatest advances in the next few decades will probably occur in several of the "soft" behavioral areas, and in the impact of these areas on managerial practices. There will also be considerable progress in organizational design, and in defining the role of the organization in its environment. Advances appear probable in these areas largely because it seems that the vacuum existing in such fields as leadership, authority, motivation, development, and organizational design are too important to remain relatively neglected, and too prominent to withstand the onrush of academic curiosity. Thus, in coming years it is probable that more and more scholars will focus on problems such as the following: Is one general type of organization better suited to a certain class of problems, or to a certain environment, than another? Is it possible to scan the social environment and to predict important societal changes? And can the organization benefit from such predictions? Are some types of leadership and authority relationships better suited to specific organizations than other types? Or to certain levels and positions in organizations? Or to certain external and internal conditions? How can managers best be trained and developed? How are employees motivated? All of these, and similar questions, will require continuing research. We predict that a mounting tide of research on these questions will flow from management scholars in the near future. Some of this flood, of course, will be worthless, but much of it will advance knowledge and produce more rigorous approaches and results useful both to students of management and to practicing managers.

Fourth, the quantification and computerization of the management curricula will continue in the future, but hopefully the faculty will become more discriminating in these areas than they have been in the past. If, indeed, management education is to become more professional in the next 20 years, it is evident that mathematical models and techniques and computer technology will have increasingly important roles to play in this process. Quantitative applications to management in the 1960's (perhaps more than any other single factor) have been most instrumental in producing more rigorous thought processes and innovative managerial methodologies. The computer, likewise, has proved to be a most effective managerial tool. Yet, the flight of many management scientists and operations researchers away from managerial problems and toward the esoteria of pseudo "pure" mathematics has been one of the great disappointments of the last 20 years. Likewise, the great initial promise of the computer has not yet been *fully* attained, either in organizations or in management education, and there has been some disenchantment with the computer and its potential in recent years. As we continue to work with quantitative models and techniques, and with computer technology, however, it seems evident that their greatest potential remains to be realized, and that they will be increasingly useful in management education, and to management, in coming decades.

Fifth, and finally, it is likely that there will be a considerable increase in both the quality and quantity of research in management itself. As has been pointed out elsewhere:

> The repetition of the word POSDCORB—planning, organizing staffing, directing, and the rest—over and over again is not likely to produce rapid and thoughtful progress. We desperately need more and better scholars working on these central problems. Unless we can determine the nature of management, and then begin to probe into it deeply and sensibly, we shall never satisfactorily create a discipline of administration.[3]

The attack on the central managerial problem is well underway, and research on management will undoubtedly mount in coming decades.

THE DISCIPLINARY FOUNDATIONS OF MANAGEMENT

In the early chapters of this book Professors Preston, Schein, Starr, and Brandenburg, together with their reviewers, reported on their impressions of the disciplinary and historical foundations underlying modern management. In these chapters three features stand out: (1) the large

[3]Joseph W. McGuire, "The Collegiate Business School Today: Whatever Happened to the World We Knew?" *Collegiate News and Views*, Vol. XXV, No. 3 (Spring, 1972), p. 5.

number of theories explaining behavior—many of which conflict; (2) the difficulty of "proving" that one or more theories are superior to others; and (3) the problems involved in transforming social science concepts into managerial practice.

Social science hypotheses are most difficult to substantiate. Unlike most laboratory experiments in the physical sciences, the "other variables" are difficult to keep constant when one is dealing with individuals, groups, organizations, and cultures. The managerial ploys that produce success in one situation may end in disastrous failure in another, although in each case they may stem from the same economic or social theoretical base. Nevertheless, some experts have argued that, in the social sciences, there are useful theories and practical concepts, and that the true test of any social theory is its predictive power. Milton Friedman, for example, has argued that the economic theory of the firm (i.e., that companies behave as if they were attempting to maximize profits) (1) has withstood the test of time, (2) is parsimonious and simple, and, (3) is substantiated by the evidence. He also has claimed that (4) a theory cannot be tested by comparing its assumptions directly with reality.

> Indeed, there is no meaningful way in which this can be done. Complete "realism" is clearly unattainable, and the question whether a theory is realistic "enough" can be settled only by seeing whether it yields predictions that are good enough for the purpose in hand or that are better than predictions from alternative theories. Yet the belief that a theory can be tested by the realism of its assumptions independently of the accuracy of its predictions is widespread and the source of much of the perennial criticism of economic theory as unrealistic. Such criticism is largely irrelevant, and, in consequence, most attempts to reform economic theory that it has stimulated have been unsuccessful.[4]

Needless to add, this is a debatable position, and indeed has been debated at length over the past decades without being firmly resolved.[5] Nevertheless, it is evident that we can agree with George Katona, who has written:

> At a higher level the goal is the establishment of a theory of social behavior rather than economic behavior. Integrated principles of motivation, group membership, learning, and decision making must be developed in several areas of human activity. We need not only more field study of [organizational] behavior but also more and better theory.[6]

And, indeed, there are so many problems confronting organizations and managers today that have their roots in social science disciplines that it is evident that more and better theory about social behavior is desperately needed. As our society grows increasingly complex, furthermore, managers will increasingly require insights based on solid research and sound and sophisticated theory. As Alan C. Filley and Robert J. House have written:

[4]Milton Friedman, *Essays in Positive Economics* (Chicago: University of Chicago Press, 1953), p. 41.

[5]See, Joseph W. McGuire, *Theories of Business Behavior* (Englewood Cliffs, N.J.: Prentice-Hall, Inc., 1964), Chapter 1, for a more complete recounting of this debate.

[6]George Katona, "Appendix A," in Howard R. Bowen, *The Business Enterprise as a Subject of Research* (New York: Social Science Research Council Pamphlet 11, 1955), p. 43.

Several social science theories hold great promise of application to the practice of management. For example, theories of leadership, motivation, intergroup conflict and cooperation, and control have been advanced and are now being systematically tested by social scientists. Once tested and demonstrated to be valid, these theories will still have to be made operational through the development of technology.[7]

Perhaps in the next decade or two, as the amount of information in the social sciences, quantitative methods, and computers continues to mount cumulatively, it will become common in large organizations to staff an office with "transformation" agents. These individuals would be specialists whose role would be to transform information from various disciplines into the pragmatic framework of the organization, and to conduct research on specific developments that appear to offer benefits to the organization. The questions to be answered by such an office might range from such generalizations as "Is the pursuit of this organization's private interests compatible with the public interest?," to specific social-environmental forecasts, to "What type of leadership style should we search for in a particular branch office?" Some of the functions of transformation agents are already performed in some enterprises by economists, engineers, and computer scientists. For years many large corporations have encouraged the growth of research and developmental efforts in the physical sciences. However, to our knowledge there have been relatively few similarly balanced transformation endeavors in the social sciences. Yet, if we are to make maximum utilization of the disciplines underlying management, it is urgent that organizations make every effort to ease and encourage the flow of information from these disciplines. One way to do this, certainly, is through the use of transformation agents whose mission would be to search for social science theories and concepts useful to the organization, to experiment, and to conduct research on significant disciplinary issues in order to assist management. Needless to add, in most organizations the benefits from this work would have to exceed its costs.

THE ENVIRONMENT OF MANAGEMENT IN THE FUTURE—ORGANIZATIONAL AND EXTERNAL

In many ways the organizational world since the end of World War II appears to be growing less harsh, less cold, and less austere than in earlier years. Perhaps this apparent softening of the environment is caused by the almost uninterrupted affluency of the post-war years, by the growth of an educated and sophisticated population, by the resurgence of a seemingly new sort of humanistic spirit, by the increasing number of protective institutions, or because of a multitude of other forces. Certainly, inside the organization, there has been a movement toward recognition of the fact that work (even when menial) can have dignity, a substitute of technology for onerous or dehumanizing tasks wherever possible, a freeing of bureau-

[7]Alan C. Filley and Robert J. House, "Management and the Future," *Business Horizons*, Vol. XIII, No. 2 (April, 1970), p. 12.

cratic rigidities, and an emphasis on job security and affirmative action. External to the organization there has been concern about the compatability between the missions of giant corporations and the public interest, the issue of consumerism, the protection of the physical environment, and the welfare of the old, the young, the poor, and those in minority groups. Both in and external to organizations there seems to be more tolerance than before; the demands for more freedom (and, at the same time, for more security) have mounted; aspirations for upward mobility appear to be less blatant, and perhaps less universal; and the social ethic that rose in the 1950's to confront the Protestant ethic of long-standing has perhaps been tempered by a certain ennui induced by leisure, television, the Vietnam war, campus conflicts, and other changes.

Given the organizational and social state of affairs today, it appears that we are, indeed, a society in transition, uncertain whether we are headed toward the fate that beset the Roman Empire or toward some sort of golden age. Whichever it is, management will face some unusual and unique organizational and environmental problems in the coming years.

One feature that has troubled many organizations in recent years has been the emergence of participatory democracy as a form of managerial governing. To some extent this movement flows from a political model, but in part it comes from educational circles wherein the faculty and administration (and to an increasing extent, students) have participated in some types of decisions about the educational process, and in part it may be attributable to the role of government and labor in decision-making in business. In any event, the organizational form that comes forth from participatory democracy is a far cry from that fashioned by the traditional executive who decides what is best for his organization. Participatory democracy requires group interaction in the decision-making process at all levels. As a consequence, the "acceptability" of a decision becomes at least as important—and probably more important—than the propriety of its outcomes. Any organization that stresses participatory democracy will contain committees by the score, will find that decisions are based on consensus, and that the process of decision-making is slow, convoluted, and laborious. Yet, the participatory democracy form of organization will probably become more widespread in the future, especially if affluence continues, and especially in those environments wherein competition is not intense.

The organizational world is constantly changing and shifting. It is likely, too, that the members of this world are growing in number, and are interacting across wider distances and in strange arenas. There is no organization today that is "an island unto itself." Each organization is continually coming into contact with (colliding with, passing by, cooperating with, in conflict with) other organizations. The congestion in organizational traffic patterns is mounting and broadening. A large corporation, for example, in a single day, may find that it has related to local, state, federal, and foreign governmental agencies, to organized consumer groups, to other corporations, to agricultural organizations, to labor unions, and to a host of other organizations. At the same time environmental experts—lawyers, public relations personnel, collective bargaining professionals, individuals with language skills and a knowledge of foreign affairs—are being added to organizational staffs. In the future, organizational relationships will be increasingly frequent, and most large organizations will have to be better organized to deal with these interactions. In addition to the transformation agents described above, therefore, there will probably be a growing need for individuals and segments within organizations that can play an important "boundary" role, at the edge of the organization, to buffer it and to deal with the institutions within which the organization comes into contact.

Not only the environment will call for new alignments in the future, however. There will also be significant changes *within* the organization that will require organizational adaptations. One such change, for example, will be the continued growth of an educated work force. This development will probably lead to some of the following organizational changes:[8]

1. *The ratio of salaried to wage employees in an industrialized society may be expected to increase steadily.* Payments to employees are both a reward for work done and the motivation for future efforts. In a world dependent on human energy, wages are appropriate payments and may be made to vary with productivity. A worker may be rewarded for his efforts through piecework systems, or may be exhorted to produce more through similar incentive payments. If knowledge rather than energy is the crucial factor, however, it is not likely that this will vary greatly from hour to hour, although it may considerably over a person's lifetime. Employee payments are made to stimulate the learning process when knowledge is essential. Salary plans, therefore, will become ever more significant to encourage learning by employees. Salaries and status will have to become increasingly differentiated to represent (supposedly) the knowledge level of the employer. Such salary and status levels will change yearly, or at least over long periods of time, rather than hourly or monthly, to reflect the cumulative acquisition of knowledge and the long-term effects of learning on employee productivity.

2. *Personnel, educational, and developmental departments within the organization are going to expand and play a more important and somewhat different role.* In recent decades, especially among rapidly expanding industrial consumers of knowledge, the function of the personnel department and its allied branch of education and training has changed dramatically. A growing number of corporations are now skillfully recruiting knowledgeable college graduates. As the success of the organization depends more and more on knowledge, the personnel department will of necessity grow in stature, sophistication, and prestige. An organization's success will be, more than now, a function of its recruiting endeavors. Also, educational efforts within the organization and its links with the universities will have to be expanded steadily.

3. *The tendency toward "professionalism" in organizations will become more important.* The emphasis on knowledge and education in organizational life will bring with it a rise of professionalism, with all the advantages and disadvantages associated with this "cult." Professionals employ their own codes of conduct, and generally adhere to service-oriented, non-materialistic, "ethical" standards. Already, the major goals of the modern corporation are vague and non-operational. The increasing emphasis on knowledge and the growth of an educated labor force can be expected to make business goals even more ambiguous and unclear to

[8]The following points are drawn from: Joseph W. McGuire, "Knowledge: The Basic Business Commodity," *Business Horizons* (June, 1969), pp. 31–38.

organization members. The simple motivation of profits has never been sufficiently attractive to motivate professionals; they typically seek goals of a higher order.

4. *Increased demands for independence and competence will be associated with professionalism.* The organization is finding increasingly that the old rules and structures for the supervision of work are rapidly changing. The educated professional employee demands greater independence than his uneducated predecessor. He simply will not tolerate the close supervision of the traditional worker, and consequently the old-fashioned time and motion expert is disappearing from the industrial scene. Furthermore, the emphasis on knowledge is creating a group of cosmopolitans rather than locals. The former owe their first allegiance to their professions and to the competent performance of their tasks rather than to their corporation. These persons are much more mobile than unskilled, or even skilled wage workers—for example, the engineers who continually shift throughout the space industry.

5. *In order to attract and hold educated workers, it will be necessary for organizations to create task forces to work on interesting and stimulating projects that tend to optimize specific subgoals.* This phenomenon can already be observed in some corporations. In the space-oriented industries, for example, teams are established to get a missile into space or to design a jet airplane. The workers involved in these projects tend to identify with their work, as television showed us so dramatically when the U.S. moon shot was successful. These men are not concerned about overall company goals or profit levels. Self-involvement and the resulting productivity of knowledge applications result from the challenges of the work and from the non-wage incentives. Companies will probably find that the use of sabbaticals and leaves for formal education will become increasingly important as a means of reducing self-imposed pressures on technical workers, and in providing them with needed respites between tasks.

6. *Old concepts of line organization will be increasingly revised to take advantage of knowledge most efficiently.* The concepts of line-and-staff will become more and more outmoded as the real work of the enterprise is increasingly performed by professionals and experts, as research and development becomes ever more important, and as the storage and maintenance of knowledge within the organization becomes vital to its success and perhaps even its very existence. In a task force organization the staff member is an integral part of the team. No one sits on the sidelines; everyone is involved. The effort must be truly interdisciplinary. In such an organization, the lines of authority and responsibility should be quite short. Perhaps the task forces of educated persons will be under project heads who will report directly to the president, the executive committee, or to one of the senior vice-presidents. Possibly there will be, at most, only three levels of line executives above the lowliest technical worker.

7. *Organizational communications will become a problem of growing significance.* Experts tend to cluster and discuss problems in their own unique jargon and symbols. Often they are unable to express their ideas to experts in other fields, much less to management. A knowledge organization, therefore, runs the real risk of becoming a Tower of Babel, unable to move forward because of semantic and conceptual difficulties.

8. *Adaptability lags within the organization will have to be shortened.* It used to be possible to delay much needed reorganization in a company;

for example, General Wood delayed the reorganization of Sears Roebuck from 1932 to 1948. The luxury once enjoyed by management of waiting for crises to develop before adapting to change will not be possible for an organization located in an industrial environment in which knowledge is of vital importance. An orientation toward knowledge automatically implies an orientation toward change and unlimited growth, and organizations that remain static rather than dynamic will not survive.

9. *Finally, as a corollary to the preceding points, the work environment will have to be conducive to innovation.* The heart of education lies in the advancement of knowledge through research. As more and more employees become educated, the whole atmosphere will become permeated with progress and change. Unless the organization itself encourages and rewards innovative behavior, it will not be able to survive. Flexible organizational forms that will support and stimulate innovation are going to have to be established.

In order to deal with change, with information, with new aspirations on the part of society, and with the complex organizational environment, it is evident that organizations in the future are going to have to be more dynamic and more flexible than ever before . . . to become what Max Ways has called the "free form" organization.[9] Warren Bennis has summarized some of the attributes of "free form" organizations in the future in the following passage:

1. Organizations will be operating in a turbulent environment which requires continual change and adjustment.
2. Organizations will continue to expand their boundaries and domain. They will increase in size and complexity.
3. Organizations will continue to differentiate their activities, causing increased problems of integration and coordination.
4. Organizations will continue to have major problems in the accumulation and utilization of knowledge. Intellectual activities will be stressed.
5. Greater emphasis will be placed upon suggestion and persuasion rather than upon coercion based upon authoritarian power as the means for coordinating the activities of the participants and functions within the organization.
6. Participants at all levels in organizations will have a greater influence. Organizations of the future will adopt a power-differentiation model.
7. Problems of interface between organizations will be greater. New means for effective interorganizational coordination will be developed.
8. Computerized information-decision systems will have an increasing impact upon organizations.
9. The number of professionals and scientists and their influence within organizations will increase. There will also be a decline in the proportion of independent professionals with many more salaried professionals.
10. Goals of complex organizations will expand. Emphasis will be upon satisficing a number of goals rather than maximizing any one.
11. Evaluation of organizational performance will be difficult. Many new

[9]Max Ways, "Tomorrow's Management: A More Adventurous Life in a Free-Form Corporation," *Fortune* (July 1, 1966), pp. 84ff.

administrative techniques will be developed for evaluation of performance in all spheres of activity."[10]

Bennis' eleven points include several on which we have already commented. Although we do not agree with all of his perceptions of the organizational future, he does list other changes that we believe are likely to occur during the next decade or two. In the remaining paragraphs of this section we shall discuss two of these points—the future role of information systems and the evaluation processes for organizational performance, and conclude with the external environment.

In 1960 the output of computer hardware in the United States was valued at $975 million. By 1970 the value of this output was $15 billion. Some experts believe that the computer industry will be the largest in the world by 1980 (it is now number three), and perhaps bigger than automobiles and petroleum combined. Frankly, we believe this projection is too optimistic, but it is indicative of the potential magnitude of growth of the computer industry. Furthermore, the statistics on the recent past and the estimates of future expansion convey the significant idea that the impact of the computer on organizational life has already been substantial, and that organizations can expect to be increasingly affected by the growth of information technology in the future.

The computer is already used to solve many well-structured, and some ill-structured, problems in organizations. For the most part, it has changed organizations by performing the repetitive, time-consuming tasks once conducted by clerical workers, by production workers, and by middle management. Thus, the computer today can, and does, perform such jobs as ordering, billing, payroll, replenishing stocks, inventory, and even the operation of certain types of production processes. The computer has also proved immensely useful in assisting in the solution of complex mathematical models, and in simulation exercises. The electronic computer is used in library systems, in hospitals (for diagnostic as well as other purposes), and in education and government. It has not yet replaced managerial judgement in most ill-structured situations and, despite the optimistic predictions of its advocates in the late 1950's and early 1960's, it is doubtful that it will do so in the near future. It has, on the other hand, radically changed the work habits of thousands of organizations, and it is likely to permeate thousands more in the coming years.

Organizational evaluations in business have always been relatively simple matters. The more profitable the company, the "better" it was. Even in business, such easy answers may not always be the correct ones. Thus, the time period over which profits are made may be of great significance, for great returns in excess of costs in a particular year may sometimes portend disaster in the long run. In other instances, management may desire to retain market position rather than profits, or may prefer rapid growth even though profits may not be so great.

It is not simple, therefore, even in business, to evaluate organizational performance. In non-profit organizations—universities and governmental agencies, for example—the task is still more complex, for there is no objec-

[10]Warren G. Bennis, "Organizations of the Future," *Personnel Administration* (September–October, 1967), p. 6.

tive criterion against which to measure success and progress. In a university, for example, we are not currently certain of the definition of output, and finding a precise definition is most elusive. For a decade in the late 1950's and early 1960's, program-planning-budgeting-systems (PPBS) were all the rage in government as efforts were made to evaluate the effectiveness of governmental agencies. Unfortunately, PPBS was most difficult to implement, and appears to have diminished in popularity. Nevertheless, there is considerable work going on in performance evaluation, and it is evident that this area is going to become increasingly important in future years.

And, finally, returning to the opening paragraphs of this section, it is apparent that organizations are going to have to devote increasing attention to their relationships with the physical and social environment. Examples of the necessity for such involvement abound as the decade of the 1970's begins: The California Division of Highways, a barony in itself, is forced to reconsider several of the freeway projects that were so happily announced a decade ago. Recreational development efforts by Disney and others, awaited with anticipation just a few years ago, are coming under increasingly severe attacks. The story of GM vs. Nader is well known, and the complaints of the public against the "simplified" tax forms of the Internal Revenue Service will soon produce further reforms. It simply is not possible in most organizational activities today to move with reckless disregard for the social or physical environment. As the years pass, it is likely that all organizations will have to exercise care in their relationships with the public. The future, then, will probably bring forth more considerate organizations—considerate of their employees, of the environment, and of the public.

THE MANAGERIAL "CORE"

Max Ways once argued that the United States needed an ever expanding number of managers because change was so central to American society. He suggested that the number of managers would rise because "... management creates change and change creates the need for management. As the 'inventory' of management people in a society rises (in quantity and quality) the demand for still more management rises with it; or, to put it another way, the rate of innovation and the managerial function are interdependent . . .[11]

If, indeed, there are going to be more managers in the future, simply because the pace of change will accelerate and because innovation will become even more important than at present, what characteristics will the general manager have to possess? In a prize-winning article, Deans H. Igor Ansoff and R.G. Brandenburg claim that the archetype requirements for general management will necessitate that he be: a leader, an administrative planner, an extrapolative planner, an entrepreneur, a statesman, and a systems architect.[12] An extrapolative planner, by the way, is one who perceives and establishes complex relationships, extrapolating the past into

[11]Ways, *op. cit.*, p. 87.

[12]H. Igor Ansoff and R. G. Brandenburg, "The General Manager of the Future," *California Management Review*, Vol. XI, No. 3 (Spring, 1969), p. 69.

the future. More importantly, Ansoff and Brandenburg predict that the manager of the future will have to be a leader, an administrator, and a planner. They believe that these qualities will probably only rarely be found in one man, and that the large organization will contain several chief executive officers.

It is possible, of course, that giant organizations will commonly be staffed by a chief executive office rather than a chief executive. Perhaps the demands on, work load, and talents required of, a top manager will be too great for one man. We do believe that some organizations will be managed by a troika, a quartet, or even an octet. However, we also believe that many organizations will continue to have but one top executive. But there is no question that the work load of top executives will be heavy, and that their managerial functions will become increasingly complex.

One factor adding to the complexity of management, certainly, will be the need for control over experts, specialists, and professionals. The difficulties confronting such managers can already be perceived in some large universities with their multitudes of departments, medical schools, and organized research units. In large part, managerial difficulties with such individuals stem from the divergence in values. Experts, specialists, and (especially) professionals frequently operate according to their own codes, which may or not be the same as, or in accord with, the aspirations of the management or the goals of the organization. Managers often do learn to deal with such people, and to guide their actions so that the objectives of the organization are forwarded. This is not, however, an easy or simple managerial problem, as every department head, dean, chancellor, and president in a large university knows. As Laurence Gould, President of Carleton College in Minnesota, once said:

> The college or university president must have the innocence of a lamb, the wisdom of an owl, the cheerfulness of a cricket, the complacency of a camel, the adaptability of a chameleon, the diligence of a beaver, the vision of an eagle, the patience of an ox, the strength of a lion, the nerves of a cow, the stomach of a boa constrictor, the skin of a rhinoceros, the brass of a monkey, and the charm of a domesticated deer.[13]

Peter Drucker once described the manager of the future as a "tool user." We agree that the future executive is going to have to possess a greater breadth and intensity of knowledge than did managers past and present. The complexity of future organizations, and the confusion of society, will require that managers have a considerable knowledge of the techniques of economics and the behavioral sciences, perhaps some grasp of engineering and the physical sciences, and certainly a good conception of quantitative methodology and computer technology. More than being a mere "tool user," however, the future manager is going to have to be a humanist as well as a technocrat. He will have to have the ability to understand people and to appraise situations and to make judicious decisions that will be followed. Even in today's complicated environment management becomes a delicate "feeling" process in a large number of organizational circum-

[13]As quoted in Vernon R. Alden, "The Responsibilities of a University President," *Comparative Administration: Proceedings of the Academy of Management"* (December 27–29, 1965), p. 77.

stances. In some giant organizations, for example, knowing what is "right" to produce effectiveness may be less important than the manner in which the organization is moved toward the correct posture. In certain cases dramatic and abrupt changes may be called for, perhaps by "lopping-off" a department or two, or discharging or transferring personnel. In other circumstances it might be more satisfactory to make changes slowly, increment by increment, so that in the long run the results are the same, but the methods of carrying out such changes differ substantially. These types of choices will have to be made more frequently in the future as the pace of change mounts, and in many instances all the "tools," by themselves, will not produce solutions to such problems. This is one important reason why the future manager is going to have to be a humanist as well as a technocrat.

One of the great developments of the decade of the 1960's was the increasing involvement by business, government, and other organizations in social affairs. The documentation of this social activity has been, at best, sporadic and episodic, but anyone who has tried to trace its course cannot but be impressed by its growth. The total price of this commitment is impossible to calculate, but all the evidence indicates that it is substantial, and that it has mounted year by year. Thousands of executives, gathered in national and civic organizations or acting alone, have contributed to projects ranging from the rehabilitation of high school dropouts to the furthering of black capitalism. Individual managers have embarked on countless schemes designed to provide employment training, housing, and other social, economic, and educational opportunities for the impoverished. More and more executives are engaged in ventures to upgrade the physical environment.

There is little doubt that the spirit of social action in business and other organizations received a mighty impetus from the affluent nature of the 1960's. This decade brought with it organizational "slack" that permitted executives both the time and the funds to develop their interests in social activities. Furthermore (as Professor Monsen observed earlier), the societal attitudes pressured executives into social postures that were increasingly "responsible."

In our opinion it is likely that executives—especially in business—will become more and more socially responsible. There are several reasons why this would seem to be the case, in addition to the corporate "slack" argument.

1. *The broadened concept of profits.* In recent years executives have argued that, through their efforts to improve the community, they are returning to their shareholders a new type of dividend in the form of cleaner cities, safer streets, and reduced welfare and crime costs. Or that modern management is "investing" in society in the same manner that its traditional forerunners invested in plant and equipment. Or that the corporate "do-good" endeavors will reduce poverty and raise aspiration levels, thus creating new markets for company profits.
2. *The vagueness of the profit concept permits other goals to assume greater importance.* The cynic may scoff at such objectives as tranquility, the preservation of the free enterprise system, public service, altruism, and the rest, but the fact is that, in the 1970's, it is difficult to explain a growing number of social actions by business unless one is willing to

twist and turn with sophistry every such act in order to make it conform with the traditional view of profit-oriented business behavior.

3. *The changing age composition of the American people and the changing attitudes of youth will probably reinforce and strengthen the social role of management during the next decade.* More than one-half of our population is currently under 30 years of age. This generation appears to be interested in making its "contribution" and to have less interest than earlier generations in merely making money. It appears very probable that, as this generation matures and assumes managerial roles, the trend toward social involvement in and by organizations will be accelerated.[14]

DISCUSSION QUESTIONS

1. Give your interpretation of management education that is "professional" but not "vocational." Why is the former acceptable and the latter not?
2. What are some of the modern trends in management education? Why are these desirable? Or are they?
3. Indicate several ways in which behavioral science concepts, and other theories and methods and models, might be "transformed" into management practice. Which way do you believe is best? Why?
4. Argue pro or con: "In many ways the organizational world since the end of World War II appears to be growing less harsh, less cold, and less austere than in earlier years."
5. Define and discuss "participatory democracy." Is this MacGregor's "Theory *Y*" in action? Why?
6. What will be the impact of knowledge on management? Discuss.
7. Create your own model for interorganizational interaction. Give examples of conflict and cooperation.
8. What are some of the reasons why social attitudes of executives have changed in the 1960's, and why they will probably continue to change in the future?

[14]This section on social responsibility is largely based on Joseph W. McGuire, "The Future Social Role of the Business Organization," *Review of Social Economy*, Vol. XXVIII, No. 1 (March, 1970), pp. 9–14.

INDEX